Register Now for Online / Your Book!

SPRINGER PUBLISHING COMPANY
C☐NNECT.™

Your print purchase of *EMDR Therapy Scripted Protocols and Summary Sheets: Treating Eating Disorders, Chronic Pain, and Maladaptive Self-Care Behaviors,* **includes online access to the contents of your book**—increasing accessibility, portability, and searchability!

Access today at:

**http://connect.springerpub.com/content/book/978-0-8261-9472-5
or scan the QR code at the right with your smartphone
and enter the access code below.**

9W30YJ5U

*Scan here for
quick access.*

SPC

SPRINGER / PUBLISHING COMPANY
View all our products at springerpub.com

Marilyn Luber, PhD, is a licensed clinical psychologist and has a general private practice in Center City, Philadelphia, Pennsylvania. In 1992, Dr. Francine Shapiro trained her in eye movement desensitization and reprocessing (EMDR). She has coordinated trainings in EMDR-related fields in the greater Philadelphia area since 1997. She teaches facilitator and supervisory trainings and other EMDR-related subjects both nationally and internationally and was on the EMDR Task Force for Dissociative Disorders. She was on the Founding Board of Directors of the EMDR International Association (EMDRIA) and served as the chairman of the International Committee until June 1999.

In 1997, Dr. Luber was given a Humanitarian Services Award by the EMDR Humanitarian Association. Later, in 2003, she was presented with the EMDR International Association's award "For Outstanding Contribution and Service to EMDRIA," and in 2005, she was awarded "The Francine Shapiro Award for Outstanding Contribution and Service to EMDR."

In 2001, through EMDR HAP (humanitarian assistance programs), she published the *Handbook for EMDR Clients*, which has been translated into eight languages; the proceeds from sales of the handbook go to EMDR HAP organizations worldwide. Four times a year, she writes the "Around the World" and "In the Spotlight" articles for the EMDRIA Newsletter, and has done so since 1997. In 2009, she edited *Eye Movement Desensitization and Reprocessing (EMDR) Scripted Protocols: Basics and Special Situations* and *Eye Movement Desensitization and Reprocessing (EMDR) Scripted Protocols: Special Populations*.

She interviewed Francine Shapiro and coauthored the interview with Dr. Shapiro for the *Journal of EMDR Practice and Research* and later wrote the entry about Dr. Shapiro for E. S. Neukrug's *The SAGE Encyclopedia of Theory in Counseling and Psychotherapy*.

Several years later, in 2012, she edited Springer Publishing Company's first CD-ROM books: *Eye Movement Desensitization and Reprocessing (EMDR) Scripted Protocols With Summary Sheets CD-ROM Version: Basics and Special Situations* and *Eye Movement Desensitization and Reprocessing (EMDR) Scripted Protocols With Summary Sheets CD-ROM Version: Special Populations*.

In 2014, she edited *Implementing EMDR Early Mental Health Interventions for Man-Made and Natural Disasters: Models, Scripted Protocols and Summary Sheets* (print and CD-ROM versions) and in 2016 *Eye Movement Desensitization and Reprocessing (EMDR) Therapy Scripted Protocols With Summary Sheets: Treating Anxiety, Obsessive-Compulsive, and Mood-Related Conditions* (print and CD-ROM versions) and *Eye Movement Desensitization and Reprocessing (EMDR) Therapy Scripted Protocols With Summary Sheets Version: Treating Trauma and Stressor-Related Conditions* (print and CD-ROM versions).

Currently, there are two new volumes to the EMDR Scripted Protocol Series: *Eye Movement Desensitization and Reprocessing (EMDR) Therapy Scripted Protocols and Summary Sheets: Treating Trauma in Somatic and Medical-Related Conditions* and *Eye Movement Desensitization and Reprocessing (EMDR) Therapy Scripted Protocols and Summary Sheets: Treating Eating Disorders, Chronic Pain, and Maladaptive Self-Care Behaviors*.

In 2014, she was part of the Scientific Committee for the EMDR Europe Edinburgh Conference. Currently, Dr. Luber is a co-facilitator for the EMDR Global Alliance to support upholding the standard of EMDR worldwide. She has worked as a primary consultant for the FBI field division in Philadelphia. She has a general psychology practice, working with adolescents, adults, and couples, especially with complex posttraumatic stress disorder (C-PTSD), trauma and related issues, and dissociative disorders. She runs consultation groups for EMDR practitioners.

Eye Movement Desensitization and Reprocessing

EMDR Therapy

Scripted Protocols and Summary Sheets

TREATING EATING DISORDERS, CHRONIC PAIN, AND MALADAPTIVE SELF-CARE BEHAVIORS

Edited by

Marilyn Luber, PhD

SPRINGER PUBLISHING COMPANY

Springer Publishing Company, LLC
11 West 42nd Street
New York, NY 10036
www.springerpub.com

Acquisitions Editor: Sheri W. Sussman
Compositor: S4Carlisle Publishing Services

ISBN: 978-0-8261-9471-8
ebook ISBN: 978-0-8261-9472-5

18 19 20 21 22/5 4 3 2 1

The author and the publisher of this Work have made every effort to use sources believed to be reliable to provide information that is accurate and compatible with the standards generally accepted at the time of publication. The author and publisher shall not be liable for any special, consequential, or exemplary damages resulting, in whole or in part, from the readers' use of, or reliance on, the information contained in this book. The publisher has no responsibility for the persistence or accuracy of URLs for external or third-party Internet websites referred to in this publication and does not guarantee that any content on such websites is, or will remain, accurate or appropriate.

Library of Congress Cataloging-in-Publication Data
Names: Luber, Marilyn, author, editor.
Title: Eye movement desensitization and reprocessing (EMDR) therapy scripted
    protocols and summary sheets. treating eating disorders, chronic pain and
    maladaptive self-care behaviors / Marilyn Luber.
Other titles: Eating disorders, chronic pain and maladaptive self-care
    behaviors
Description: New York : Springer Publishing Company, [2018] | Includes
    bibliographical references.
Identifiers: LCCN 2018037013| ISBN 9780826194718 | ISBN 9780826194725 (eISBN)
Subjects: | MESH: Eye Movement Desensitization Reprocessing |
    Desensitization, Psychologic—methods | Feeding and Eating
    Disorders—therapy | Chronic Pain—therapy | Stress Disorders,
    Post-Traumatic—therapy | Interview, Psychological—methods | Handbooks |
    Practice Guideline
Classification: LCC RC552.E18 | NLM WM 34 | DDC 616.85/260651—dc23 LC record available at
https://lccn.loc.gov/2018037013

Contact us to receive discount rates on bulk purchases.
We can also customize our books to meet your needs.
For more information please contact: sales@springerpub.com

Publisher's Note: **New and used products purchased from third-party sellers are not guaranteed for quality, authenticity, or access to any included digital components.**

Printed in the United States of America.

To Bob Raymar
my friend, my husband, my supporter,
for your love for me, your community, your country,
and the world we live in

Trauma is hell on earth. Trauma resolved is a gift from the gods.
—Peter A. Levine

Contents

Contributors

Sirin Haciomeroglu Atceken, MFT, is a marriage and family therapist. She received her bachelor's degree from the Middle East Technical University (METU) Psychology Department and her master's degree from Drexel University's Marriage and Family Therapy Program. After graduation, she worked with families and individuals at Thomas Jefferson Hospital's Methadone Clinic and Family Therapy Treatment Program–PHMC in Philadelphia. She is currently cofounder of the Salt Psychology Institute in Antalya, Turkey. Apart from using eye movement desensitization and reprocessing (EMDR) as a frequent therapy approach, she has been working in research and projects about EMDR's usage in various cases and problem areas and integration into other psychotherapy approaches. Her areas of expertise include chronic headache, performance improvement, addictions, attachment disorders, early trauma intervention, and anxiety disorders. She is a board member of EMDR Turkey Association and an EMDR Europe–approved consultant and supervisor. She has also worked as a member of the EMDR Humanitarian Assistance Program (HAP) in different trauma-related situations in Turkey and Holland.

Paula Baldomir Gago, MS, MC, CP, is a psychologist and psychotherapist. Since 2008, she has worked as an expert in personality disorders, trauma, and dissociation at the Institute for the Research and Treatment of Trauma and Personality Disorders (INTRA-TP). Paula is an expert in childhood and adolescent psychopathology as well as psychosomatic medicine. She is an accredited EMDR practitioner for adults, children, and adolescents. Paula collaborates with the Gender Violence Program in her community, serving both female victims and their children. She has offered different training courses for professionals in the network of educational and youth centers in her community, as well as talks and presentations in different cities on working with children and adolescents with complex trauma.

Renée Beer, MSc, is a clinical psychologist and cognitive behavioral therapist. She is an EMDR Europe–accredited trainer for EMDR with children and adolescents, and has been involved in trainings in the Netherlands since 2000. She participated in the Child & Adolescent Committee of EMDR Europe from the start until 2017. Abroad, she delivered trainings on "EMDR With Children and Adolescents" in Suriname and Australia. She specialized in the treatment of eating disorders at the Department of Child Psychiatry of the University Medical Center in Utrecht from 2000 to 2005. She and Karin Tobias developed a protocol for cognitive behavioral therapy for adolescents, based on the theoretical model of Fairburn (2003), which they published in 2011. She was coordinator of the Center for Trauma and Family in Amsterdam from 2005 to 2013. Together with Carlijn de Roos, she edited the *Handbook of EMDR With Children and Adolescents* in 2017. Besides her EMDR activities, she is accredited as a trainer in trauma-focused cognitive behavioral therapy (TFCBT). Her major concerns are to establish both EMDR and TFCBT in the Netherlands as the major therapy approaches for the treatment of trauma-related psychopathology in children and adolescents and to promote the implementation of cognitive behavioral therapy (CBT) and EMDR in the treatment of patients (adults and adolescents) with an eating disorder.

Wolfgang Eich, MD, is specialized in internal medicine and rheumatology as well as in psychotherapeutic medicine and psychoanalysis. After studying medicine in Tübingen and Freiburg, Germany, he published his medical dissertation in 1980 on the topic "Medical Semiotics Between 1750 and 1850" (*summa cum laude*). He continued his studies of internal and psychotherapeutic medicine in Hanover and Heidelberg. In 1994, he completed his postdoctoral qualification at the Medical Faculty of Heidelberg University on "Subjective Illness and Self-Regulatory Control in Ankylosing Spondylitis (M. Bechterew)." In 2002, he was appointed to be medical director of the Acura-Clinic for Psychosomatic Medicine Baden-Baden within the framework of a cooperation agreement between the Medical Faculty, the Medical University Hospital, and the Center of Rheumatology in Baden-Baden. Since 2004, he is a full professor of integrated psychosomatics and head of the Section of Integrated Medicine at the Medical University of Heidelberg. He is the head of numerous research projects on shared decision making and on chronic pain (most recently, he was the coordinator of the LOGIN (Localized and Generalized Musculoskeletal Pain: Psychobiological Mechanisms and Implications for Treatment) consortium and the principal investigator of LOGIN's subproject 6: Subgroups characterized by psychological trauma, mental comorbidity, and psychobiological patterns and their specialized treatment funded by the German Ministry of Research and Education. Within this framework, numerous publications on EMDR and chronic pain followed.

Ana Cris Eiriz, MS, MC, LSW, CP, is a psychologist and psychotherapist specializing in trauma, personality disorders, mood disorders, and dissociation. She is an accredited systemic family therapist and an accredited EMDR practitioner. She has been working in the INTRA-TP team since 2004. She is an expert in personality disorders, trauma, and affective disorders. She collaborates with two gender violence programs in her community, one for women who are victims of violence and one for men with anger issues. Ana Cris has published two books on bipolar disorder and several articles on personality disorders and trauma. Ana has presented many psychoeducational workshops on personality disorders at different associations directed at patients and their families. She teaches about personality disorders, trauma, and family interventions to clinicians and regularly supervises the work of other professionals.

Hejan Epözdemir, PhD, is a clinical psychologist and psychotherapist working and living in Istanbul. She studied psychology and later graduated in clinical psychology, receiving her doctoral degree from Hacettepe University Department of Clinical Psychology. Dr. Epözdemir has her own private clinical practice working with adults, couples, and families and also works part-time as faculty and clinical supervisor in both Istanbul Bilgi University and Bahcesehir University. She was a founding member of the Board for EMDR Turkey and is an accredited EMDR consultant and supervisor and an editor of *EMDR Turkey Bulletin.* She is also interested in research and has had several academic studies, including academic texts, articles, and presentations in both national and international publications, journals, and conferences.

Raquel Fernández Domínguez, LSW, is a social care worker and licensed pedagogue. She has worked as an expert in personality disorders, trauma, and dissociation at the INTRA-TP since 2008. Raquel has specific training in attachment, trauma, and dissociation. She has more than 8 years of experience working with families of severely traumatized children as well as families of people with personality disorders. She has offered different training courses for professionals in the network of educational and youth centers in her community, as well as talks and presentations in different cities on working with children and adolescents with complex trauma. She has also been a speaker at workshops for professionals on the treatment of borderline personality disorder, as well as doing talks and workshops for relatives of people with personality disorders in different cities in Spain.

Carol Forgash, LCSW, BCD, was a president of and on the board of the EMDR HAPs. She has a clinical and consulting practice in Smithtown, New York. She is a facilitator and an EMDR International Association (EMDRIA)-approved consultant. She is a lecturer and consultant on the treatment of dissociation, complex posttraumatic stress disorders, the complex health issues of sexual abuse survivors, and the integration of EMDR with ego state therapy and psychodynamic treatment. She has coauthored and edited *Healing the Heart of Trauma and Dissociation With EMDR and Ego State Therapy* (Springer Publishing, 2007), the first book to offer an integrative approach to successfully treating clients with the most severe trauma-related disorders.

Önder Kavakçı, MD, is a psychiatrist and psychotherapist specializing in the areas of trauma, anxiety disorders, and pregnancy-related disorders. He is an associate professor at the Medical School of Cumhuriyet University. He is a member of EMDR-Turkey (EMDR-TR). He is president of the Research and Publishing Committees of EMDR Turkey and has been actively working with the Turkish Psychiatry Association Trauma and Disaster Committees. He is the author of the first Turkish EMDR book, *EMDR for Psychological Trauma (Ruhsal Travma Tedavisi İçin EMDR).*

Jim Knipe, PhD, has been using EMDR since 1992. He is an EMDR HAP trainer and an EMDRIA-approved consultant and instructor, and was designated a "Master Clinician" by EMDRIA in 2007. He has been an invited speaker at national EMDR conferences in 14 countries in the United States, Canada, Europe, and Asia, and he has been involved since 1995 with the Trauma Recovery/EMDR Humanitarian Assistance organization, coordinating EMDR training programs in developing countries where significant trauma has occurred. He is a coauthor of a published outcome research documenting the effects of EMDR with survivors of the New York 9/11 terrorist attack and with those traumatized by the 1999 Marmara earthquake in Turkey. Dr. Knipe has contributed chapters to *EMDR Casebook* (2002); *EMDR Solutions, Volumes I and II* (2005, 2009); *Healing the Heart of Trauma and Dissociation* (2007); *EMDR Scripted Protocols: Special Populations* (2009); and *EMDR and Dissociation* (2012). His book *EMDR Toolbox: Theory and Treatment for Complex PTSD and Dissociation* was published in August 2014, and he is a coauthor (with Dolores Mosquera) of two recent articles in the *Journal of EMDR Practice and Research*, entitled "Understanding and Treating Narcissism With EMDR Therapy" (Winter, 2015) and "Idealization and Maladaptive Positive Responses: EMDR Therapy for Women Who Are Ambivalent About Leaving an Abusive Partner" (Winter, 2017). An online streaming video of his two-day training—*EMDR-related methods of treating complex PTSD and dissociation*—is available through Trauma Recovery/HAP (www.emdrhap.org).

Emre Konuk, MA, is a clinical psychologist. He received his undergraduate degree at Istanbul University, followed by a graduate degree in clinical psychology at Bogazici University. He received his family therapy training at the Mental Research Institute, Brief Therapy Center, Palo Alto. He became a pioneer in Turkey establishing psychotherapy as a profession by founding the Institute for Behavioral Studies (DBE, Davranış Bilimleri Enstitüsü) in 1985, with the vision of providing psychological services to individuals, couples, and families. In 1998, he established the Organizational Development Center in order to contribute to the improvement and growth of organizations and human resources. He is an EMDR Institute and EMDR Europe trainer, president of the Institute for Behavioral Studies–Istanbul, president of EMDR Association and EMDR HAP–Turkey, and general secretary of Couples and Family Therapy Association–Turkey. He was a board member for the Turkish Psychologists Association, Istanbul Branch, between 1990 and 2002, and president and projects coordinator between 1998 and 2002. At present, he is a member of the Ethics Committee for the Turkish Psychologists Association. Since the 1999 Marmara earthquake, he has been responsible for EMDR HAP and EMDR basic trainings in Turkey. More than 600 professionals have been trained during EMDR and several HAP projects. He has participated in EMDR HAP projects in Thailand, Palestine, Kenya, Lebanon, and Iraq. His major concern is to establish EMDR as a major therapy approach in Turkey.

Dolores Mosquera, MS, MC, CP, is a psychologist and psychotherapist specializing in severe and complex trauma, personality disorders, and dissociation. She is an accredited EMDR Europe trainer and supervisor. Dolores is the director of the INTRA-TP in A Coruña, Spain—a three-clinic private institution initially founded in 2000 as LOGPSIC. She collaborates with two different domestic violence (DV) programs, one focused on women victims of DV and another one on males with violent behavior. She belongs to the Spanish National Network for the Assistance of Victims of Terrorism and also collaborates with an organization aiding victims of emergencies, accidents, violent attacks, kidnapping, and other traumatic incidents. Dolores has extensive teaching experience, leading seminars, workshops, and lectures internationally. She has participated as a guest speaker in numerous conferences and workshops throughout Europe, Asia, Australia, and North, Central, and South America. She has published 15 books and numerous articles on personality disorders, complex trauma, and dissociation, and is a recognized expert in this field. She also teaches in several universities and collaborates supervising clinical psychologists in postgraduate training programs in Spain. She is coauthor of the books *EMDR and Dissociation, The Progressive Approach*, and *EMDR Therapy and Borderline Personality Disorder*. Dolores received the David Servan-Schreiber award for outstanding contribution to EMDR in 2017 from the EMDR Europe Association.

Marco Pagani, MD, PhD, received his MD in 1985 and his PhD in Brain Neurophysiology and Nuclear Medicine Methodology in 2000 from the Karolinska Institute of Stockholm. He is a Senior Researcher at the Institute of Cognitive Sciences and Technologies of the Italian National Research Council. His work focuses on the pathophysiology of neurological and psychiatric disorders as investigated by neuroimaging methodologies. In these fields, he has published more than 130 full papers, more than 30 of which are on PTSD and EDMR. In 2011, he was awarded the Francine Shapiro Award from EMDR-Europe for the best 2010 scientific contribution in EMDR for the paper, *Grey Matter Changes in Posterior Cingulate and lLmbic Cortex in PTSD Are Associated with Trauma Load and EMDR Outcome*. He was presented with an Italian award for his work on PTSD and EMDR.

Livia Sani, MS, is a clinical psychologist. She graduated from La Sapienza University in Rome, specializing in psychotraumatology and emergency psychology at Lumsa University, Rome. She conducted research on PTSD as a research assistant at Vrije University in Amsterdam and collaborated with the Institute of Cognitive Sciences and Technologies in Rome. She is currently finishing her PhD in clinical psychology at the University of Strasbourg, France. Her work is focused on perinatal death and the long-term psychological consequences of parents.

Günter H. Seidler, MD, was head of the Department of Psychotraumatology at the Center for Psychosocial Medicine of the Heidelberg University Hospital from 2002 until his retirement in summer 2015. He began his career as a neurosurgeon and is now working on a freelance basis as an author, coach, consultant, training therapist, and supervisor. He is a medical specialist in neurology and psychiatry as well as in psychosomatic medicine and psychotherapy. Moreover, he is a training analyst, a group training analyst, and a certified EMDR supervisor. The preliminary draft of his first book (*In Others' Eyes: An Analysis of Shame*; Madison: International Universities Press, 2000) was given the sponsorship award of the German Psychoanalytic Society in 1989. The empirical examination of this construct, which he developed and explored in his postdoctoral qualification thesis ("Inpatient Psychotherapy on the Test Bench: Inter-subjectivity and Health Improvement," 1999), was awarded the "Research Prize for Psychotherapy in Medicine." His findings led him to a paradigm shift, and he turned to psychotraumatology. He is founder and chief editor of the journal *Trauma & Violence* and of the *Handbook of Psychotraumatology*. He has carried out numerous scientific projects on the consequences of individual violence and large-scale disasters as well as on the development of novel psychotherapeutical approaches. He is internationally regarded as one of the leading psychiatric therapists. In his practical work, he combines a scientific orientation with his own therapeutic approaches based on extensive competence in numerous established therapeutic procedures.

Natalia Seijo, PhD, is a psychologist and psychotherapist who specializes in eating disorders, dissociation, and complex trauma. She is the director of an outpatient clinic, which she founded 20 years ago in A Coruña, Spain. She is an EMDR Europe consultant and facilitator for the EMDR Institute. She developed her expertise on eating disorders in one of the most important eating disorders units in Spain. She is currently developing her doctoral thesis on the "Prevalence of Dissociation in Outpatients in Spain" and is also researching eating disorders with several different projects. She teaches EMDR and eating disorders workshops for the Spanish EMDR Association and is a presenter at various international conferences, and also gives workshops on eating disorders. Her publications in the eating disorders field link trauma, attachment, and dissociation. She collaborates with several universities in Spain with programs to train students on the clinical aspects of therapy and is a teacher for the EMDR Master's Program at UNED University in Spain on eating disorders.

Jonas Tesarz, MD, is a specialist in internal medicine and is working as a medical doctor and clinical researcher at the Heidelberg University Hospital, Department of General Internal Medicine and Psychosomatics. After completing his doctor's degree at the Heidelberg University on the neurobiology of pain processing, he focused his scientific work on the investigation of the role of myofascial tissue in the development and maintenance of low-back pain, before he started working as a medical assistant at the Department of General Internal Medicine and Psychosomatics (Section for Musculoskeletal Pain) at the University of Heidelberg. There, he worked on the relationship between biopsychosocial factors and low-back pain. Since that time, he has focused on the modulation of pain perception by psychosocial factors. In addition to researching the influence of traumatizing life events on pain processing, his particular scientific interest lies in the development and scientific evaluation of EMDR in the treatment of chronic pain syndromes. Tesarz has been researching and publishing internationally in the field of pain research for many years. He is the principal investigator of the first randomized controlled trial on EMDR in chronic back pain patients, writer of the German reference book *Pain*

Treatment With EMDR, and author of numerous scientific publications on EMDR in pain therapy. In 2015, he received the "German Award for Pain Research" for his work on the influence of psychological trauma on pain.

Asena Yurtsever, MA, clinical psychologist and psychodramatist, graduated and completed her master's degree from İstanbul University. She specializes in EMDR, family therapy, expressive arts therapy, and psychodrama and works with adults and adolescents. Ms. Yurtsever is an EMDR Europe–accredited trainer, consultant, and supervisor. She gives EMDR trainings in Turkey. She supports EMDR Trauma Aid locally and internationally. She worked with Syrian refugees, and at the Atatürk airport explosion, the Beşiktaş explosion, and the Soma mine disaster in Turkey. She is also a part of establishing EMDR basic trainings in Northern Iraq with EMDR Trauma Aid Europe. She gas trained participants in Lebanon (2015) and Germany (2016) with EMDR R-TEP and EMDR G-TEP trainings.

Maria Zaccagnino, PhD, is a clinical psychologist and psychotherapist with a cognitive evolutionary approach. She is co-director of the Center of EMDR Therapy for Eating Disorders in Milan with Dr. Isabel Fernandez. She is an EMDR Europe–approved supervisor and facilitator and she works in the field of attachment theory and eating disorders, where she has achieved remarkable results in both clinical and research contexts. She coordinates much research concerning these areas of EMDR application for the Italian EMDR Association, and she has also presented workshops in Italy and Europe. She has published articles regarding the application of EMDR treatment in the context of parenting problems, attachment dynamics, and eating disorders.

Zeynep Zat, MSc, is a psychologist and psychotherapist specializing in the areas of trauma and anxiety disorders. She had been working for the National Health Service at the Psychodynamic Psychotrauma Institute in London. She is an EMDR practitioner and a member of EMDR-TR. She has been actively working on the Research, Clinical Applications, and Protocol Committees. Her roles in these committees include writing an EMDR-TR newsletter and translating an EMDR book into Turkish. She also gives workshops on using EMDR with different populations. She has recently developed a protocol on the "Treatment of Panic Disorder With EMDR." A version of the protocol, which is integrated with Strategic Family Therapy, was presented at the last International Family Therapy Association Conference. Currently, she works at the Institute for Behavioral Studies in Istanbul.

Foreword

Eye movement desensitization and reprocessing (EMDR) came about because of the fortuitous combination of unusual events and an extraordinary person. The discovery of the effects of spontaneous rapid eye movements during the waking state was an unusual event; the extraordinary person was Francine Shapiro. Her books and presentations on EMDR recount that discovery and need not be repeated here. Her extraordinary qualities—an intelligence largely unfettered by preexisting bias and guided by a willingness to explore a largely ignored phenomenon, the quiet grace of an excellent teacher, and a true humanitarian's willingness to endure rebuffs during the development of a powerful tool for psychological healing—made her exactly the right person at the right place and at the right time.

From the very beginning, Dr. Shapiro believed the psychotherapy of EMDR would be useful to a wide range of conditions and disorders. In the years following EMDR's introduction in 1989, researchers focused almost entirely on EMDR as a therapy for the treatment of posttraumatic stress disorder (PTSD); so did Dr. Shapiro's first publication. Her reasoning was straightforward—if PTSD and its symptoms were the result of an experience in life and EMDR successfully treated PTSD, then EMDR might be useful in the treatment of other negatively impacting life experiences.

Conservative in terms of client safety, Dr. Shapiro encouraged clinicians to explore EMDR's potential usefulness in treating conditions other than PTSD but to do so in an organized fashion allowing research and replication. Her concern was with the problem of clinician enthusiasm for the new without accepting the necessary discipline and organization needed for examination and research of their variations of EMDR's well-researched protocol for trauma treatment. She felt this so strongly, her first trainings required attendees to promise to not teach EMDR until corroborating research occurred.

Initially, the challenge for EMDR was acceptance. Potential researchers were slow to respond to its steady growth of clinicians. The classic division between academic researchers and therapists in the field seemed to play a role. After a few years the situation gradually changed. Research remained a trickle, but it seemed that a critical mass of therapists was reached. As was the history of other psychotherapies, newly trained individuals started offering their own variations of the EMDR protocol. Some said their changes were needed to serve new populations, while others claimed their changes made EMDR even more effective. To be honest, most of the variations I heard of—they were seldom presented in a juried journal—struck me as ad-libbed procedures whose variations from the original EMDR protocol had little to do with clinical experience and a great deal to do with the ego or financial needs of the presenters.

In counterpoint, individuals and small groups of clinicians treating client populations affected by conditions other than PTSD worked to discover alternative procedures utilizing EMDR for those populations. Probably, the first of these groups were clinicians, led by Gerry Puk, PhD, who were treating dissociative disordered clients. The development of an EMDR approach to dissociative disorders made use of experts in the field of dissociative disorders as well as experts in EMDR (and, as in the case of Dr. Puk, several clinicians who were both). Understanding both the condition and the treatment led to procedural modifications emphasizing client safety as well as therapeutic efficiency.

Now, more than 20 years after the development of an EMDR procedure for the treatment of dissociative disorders, we are at a point where clinicians have taken EMDR into a wide variety of conditions. Dr. Marilyn Luber watched the development of these new approaches over the years and began to build a library of the most promising of them. These variations in the original EMDR protocol have several things in common:

- First, these variations on the original protocol have built on that protocol—any EMDR clinician would recognize the source of the variants. What we are seeing is not so much a change in the original protocol of Francine Shapiro but an addition to that protocol.
- Second, the additions allow a clinician to adapt EMDR to the particular needs and presentations of client populations defined by their condition.

- Third, they identify the steps needed to assist the client in selecting the most efficient target for EMDR's bilateral stimulation.
- Fourth, they note the information and client history particulars needed not only to determine the potential targets for processing but to make the more basic decisions about a client's readiness and appropriateness for treatment.
- Fifth, the developers have expertise from experience and training with the problem areas as well as EMDR.

Not all of the "variation protocols" in this and the other *Scripted Protocol* books Dr. Luber has edited are supported by published research. On the other hand, in providing step-by-step instructions for the use of the variation protocol, they clearly establish their procedure. This enables research and replication. I might also add that all of the variation protocols have a clinical case history evidence demonstrating EMDR's positive effects with the particular treated population.

I first met Dr. Marilyn Luber in the early 1990s. Though we worked in different venues, we both found EMDR fascinating in its efficient effects. I led an inpatient PTSD treatment program open to male and female veterans of wars from Korea to the present. Dr. Luber has a private practice in Center City, Philadelphia, and works with clients, offering a broad range of conditions, including complex PTSD and dissociative disorders. Together, we ran a small group consultation for EMDR clinicians. She began a long effort to network with other EMDR clinicians in the Pennsylvania–New Jersey–Delaware–Maryland area. We continued to work together when I, as an EMDR Institute Senior Trainer, presented workshops that Dr. Luber organized in Philadelphia. I have read almost all of her previous books, particularly those on emergency service workers, clinician self-care, man-made and natural disasters, and treating trauma and stressor-related conditions, and have more than once wished this information had been available earlier in my career.

An examination of the topics covered in her most recent book of *Scripted Protocols* demonstrates by the details of the subject matter the fifth commonality I noted when describing the most promising of the variation protocols, the expertise of the developers.

Within the broad area of eating disorders, several different protocols are presented. Readers are invited to note similarities and differences where they occur. This area of application is young; it may take a research "horse race" to determine which version is the best or best for which subpopulation. Clinicians with a specialty in eating disorders will find much here for careful consideration.

In other areas, variation protocols appear to have less in the way of competition. Body image distortion, intimate partner violence, and personal health and self-care open new areas for EMDR. A section on chronic pain, one I am particularly interested in, offers three variation protocols for broad-ranging chromic pain as well as the particular forms of migraine and fibromyalgia.

With growing attention on the body–mind connection, it is not surprising to find a discussion on the use of EMDR with complex PTSD and attachment conditions impacting health as well as on the use of EMDR with maladaptive self-care.

Food for thought? Of course. You have in your hands an image, a picture of a psychotherapy still young enough to be in development as clinicians expand its treatment envelope. Nothing here is carved in stone, not yet, but this book, along with its earlier volumes, offers a solid base for taking EMDR to the people who need it. Read, understand, treat, and provide the community with feedback and be a part of the development. And thank Dr. Luber for its organization.

Steven M. Silver, PhD
Certified Clinician, Approved Consultant, EMDR International Association
Facilitator and Senior Trainer, EMDR Institute
First Programs Chairperson, EMDR Humanitarian Assistance Programs

Preface

One of the important themes of this volume is based on the early adverse life experiences and traumas that Felitti et al. (1998) spoke about in their historic adverse childhood experiences (ACE) study that allowed us to begin to understand with real numbers the impact that trauma and stressful experiences have on child development. They include the following:

- Childhood abuse (emotional, physical, and sexual)
- Neglect (emotional and physical)
- Growing up in a seriously dysfunctional household (battered spouse, substance abuse or mental illness in the house, parental separation or divorce, family member in prison)

They found that as the categories of childhood exposures increase, each of the adult health risk behaviors and diseases increased. Participants who had *four* or more types of childhood exposure, compared to those with *none*, had 4 to 12 times increased health risks for alcoholism, drug abuse, depression, and suicide attempt; a two to four times increase in smoking; poor self-rated health; or more sexual partners and sexually transmitted disease; and a 1.4 to 1.6 times increase in physical inactivity and severe obesity. They also reported that the number of types of ACEs showed a ranked relationship to the presence of adult diseases, which included ischemic heart disease, cancer, chronic lung disease, skeletal fractures, and liver disease. More than *seven* categories were interrelated with persons with multiple health risk factors later in life. They also found that both the number and the severity of ACEs are found to have poor health outcomes across many physical and mental health domains (Anda et al., 2006).

Guillaume et al. (2016) studied the types of associations between ACEs and clinical characteristics of eating disorders. They assessed four clinical characteristics—restraint, eating, shape, and weight concerns—on the Eating Disorder Examination Questionnaire and daily functioning and childhood trauma by the Childhood Traumatism Questionnaire. Their results showed that "emotional abuse independently predicted higher eating, shape and weight concerns and lower daily function whereas sexual and physical abuse independently predicted just higher eating concerns."

In the *Physician's Guide to Intimate Partner Violence and Abuse*, Anda et al. (2006) wrote about their "Insights Into Intimate Partner Violence From the Adverse Childhood Experiences (ACE) Study." They studied what the relationship of childhood physical/sexual abuse/growing up with a battered mother was to the danger of intimate partner violence and abuse (IPVA) as an adult. They found that each of these *three* ACEs was connected to the real possibility of IPVA. The more violent ACEs a person has, the increased risk of IPVA. It is in this way that exposure to abuse and domestic violence may turn into revictimization and the perpetuation of a cycle of violence rise.

Concerning pain-related medical conditions, Sachs-Ericsson, Sheffler, Stanlye, Piazza, and Preacher (2017) did an interesting study looking at 10-year longitudinal data from the National Comorbidity Surveys (NCS-1 and NCS-2). Through NCS-1, they had reports about ACEs, current health issues, current pain severity, and mood and anxiety disorders, while NCS-2 looked for painful medical conditions such as arthritis/rheumatism, chronic back/neck problems, severe headaches, and other chronic pain. In conclusion, it showed that the retrospective reports of ACEs and lifetime mood and anxiety disorders independently contribute to the occurrence of painful medical conditions. Also, ACEs intensified the chance of mood and anxiety disorders, and these disorders seem to effect the development of painful medical conditions. Even though ACEs added to more painful conditions irrespective of the level of mood and anxiety disorders, interestingly lower levels of mood and anxiety disorders showed a stronger result than those with higher levels. If these results are looked at together, they show that

ACEs have potent effects on the growth of pain-related medical conditions, and mood and anxiety disorders may, in part, explain this connection.

A large number of patients present with eating disorders, chronic pain, intimate personal violence and abuse, and/or maladaptive self-care habits, so there was never a more important time for the EMDR practitioner to learn to address these ubiquitous problems.

Shapiro highlights the importance of this study in the third edition of her text *Eye Movement Desensitization and Reprocessing (EMDR) Therapy: Basic Principles, Protocols, and Procedures*. It supports the Adaptive Information Processing (AIP) model that underlies EMDR therapy. The AIP model hypothesizes that inadequately processed dysfunctionally stored memories establish the basis for psychopathology and that these memories can impact our psychological and physical well-being throughout our lives. The ACE study enlarges our understanding to include not only trauma but also the adverse life experiences of everyday life, and illuminates working with medical and somatic issues in our patients.

Following this line of thinking, Hase et al. (2015) and Hase, Balmaceda, Ostacoli, Liebermann, and Hofmann (2017) discuss the idea of "pathogenic memory" (Centonze, Siracusane, Calabresi, & Bernardi, 2005). It broadens the "origin of many mental disorders to the formation and consolidation of implicit dysfunctional memory that leads to the formation of the theory of pathogenic memories (Hase et al., 2017, "Abstract"). They connect this to EMDR and the AIP model:

> Research proposes to extend the range of disorders that are linked with pathogenic memories beyond PTSD and other trauma-based disorders. This is in line with the EMDR literature, where the AIP model of EMDR has predicted that PTSD is not the only memory-based disorder and has linked many other disorders to "dysfunctionally stored memories." (Hase et al., 2017, "Discussion")

This is an important expansion of the use of EMDR therapy to include working with adverse life experiences. Many clinicians have already expanded this concept into their work with patients and research is beginning to confirm this as well in the areas of *affective disorders* (Hase et al. 2015; Hofmann et al., 2014; Landin-Romero et al., 2013; Novo et al., 2014), *chronic pain* (de Roos et al., 2010; Gerhardt et al., 2016; Schneider, Hofmann, Rost, & Shapiro, 2008; Wilensky, 2006), *addiction* (Abel & O'Brien, 2010; Hase, Schallmayer, & Sack, 2008), and *obsessive compulsive disorders* (Marsden, Lovell, Blore, Ali, & Delgadillo, 2018).

This volume is the seventh in a series of books that support the principles, protocols, and procedures of EMDR therapy. In the very first book, *Eye Movement Desensitization and Reprocessing (EMDR) Scripted Protocols: Basics and Special Situations* (Luber, 2009a), the purpose was to build on the foundation of Francine Shapiro (1995, 2001, 2018), the originator of EMDR therapy, by scripting her basic six protocols and including other EMDR-related work to basic knowledge for an EMDR practitioner. The second book, *Eye Movement Desensitization and Reprocessing (EMDR) Scripted Protocols: Special Populations* (Luber, 2009b), broadened the base of the original book to include special populations that included children and adolescents, couples, dissociative disorders and complex posttraumatic stress disorder, addictive behaviors, pain, specific fears, and clinician self-care. Some changes occurred with the order of the books as there seemed to be a need for *Implementing EMDR Early Mental Health Interventions for Man-Made and Natural Disasters* (2014), in book, CD, and ebook formats, before publishing *Eye Movement Desensitization and Reprocessing (EMDR) Therapy Scripted Protocols and Summary Sheets: Treating Anxiety, Depression and Medical-Related Issues*. In 2011, there were more than 300 man-made and natural disasters, including the Japanese earthquake and tsunami, tropical storm Washi in the Philippines, flooding in Thailand and Brazil, the earthquake in Turkey, and severe drought and famine in the Horn of Africa (Swissre, 2012). In discussion with Springer Publishing and colleagues in EMDR-related humanitarian work around the globe, we decided to move up the publication of the disaster-focused book. It was published in 2014 and included the most up-to-date information of the collected wisdom of the EMDR community concerning early EMDR intervention for individuals, groups, first responders, law enforcement, the military, mineworkers, self-care, and resources for patients as well as practitioners. There was a large section on how to respond with early mental interventions in Israel, Turkey, Spain, Mexico, the United States, and India.

By the time this author was ready to start working on *Eye Movement Desensitization and Reprocessing (EMDR) Therapy Scripted Protocols and Summary Sheets: Treating Anxiety, Depression and Medical-Related Issues,* the American Psychiatric Association had released the fifth edition of the *Diagnostic and Statistical Manual of Mental Disorders (DSM-5)*, which resulted in a need to update some of the chapters. In fact, the reorganization resulted in four books so the material was more easily accessed. *Eye Movement Desensitization and Reprocessing (EMDR) Therapy Scripted Protocols and Summary Sheets: Treating Anxiety, Obsessive-Compulsive, and Mood-Related Conditions* and *Eye Movement Desensitization and Reprocessing (EMDR) Therapy Scripted Protocols and Summary Sheets: Treating Trauma and Stressor-Related Conditions*, with the choice of print, CD, and/or ebook formats for both volumes, were the first two books. They were published in 2016. The next book should have been *Eye Movement Desensitization and Reprocessing (EMDR) Scripted Protocols and Summary Sheets: Medical-Related Issues*; however, the wealth of material resulted in *Eye Movement Desensitization and Reprocessing (EMDR) Therapy Scripted Protocols and Summary Sheets: Treating Trauma in Somatic and Medical-Related Conditions* and this book, *Eye Movement Desensitization and Reprocessing (EMDR) Therapy Scripted Protocols and Summary Sheets: Treating Eating Disorders, Chronic Pain, and Maladaptive Self-Care Behaviors*, to be released at nearly the same time.

These volumes hold a unique place and use a distinctive design for the EMDR library of books. The following description from *Eye Movement Desensitization and Reprocessing (EMDR) Scripted Protocols: Basics and Special Situations* gives a clear understanding of the evolution and importance of this format:

> *Eye Movement Desensitization and Reprocessing (EMDR) Scripted Protocols: Basics and Special Situations* grew out of a perceived need that trained mental health practitioners could be served by a place to access both traditional and newly developed protocols in a way that adheres to best clinical practices incorporating the Standard EMDR Protocol that includes working on the past, present, and future issues (the 3-Pronged Protocol) related to the problem and the 11-Step Standard Procedure that includes attention to the following steps: image, negative cognition (NC), positive cognition (PC), validity of cognition (VoC), emotion, subjective units of disturbance (SUD), and location of body sensation, desensitization, installation, body scan, and closure. Often, EMDR texts embed the protocols in a great deal of explanatory material that is essential in the process of learning EMDR. However, sometimes, as a result, practitioners move away from the basic importance of maintaining the integrity of the Standard EMDR Protocol and keeping AIP in mind when conceptualizing the course of treatment for a patient. It is in this way that the efficacy of this powerful methodology is lost.
>
> "Scripting" becomes a way not only to inform and remind the EMDR practitioner of the component parts, sequence, and language used to create an effective outcome, but it also creates a template for practitioners and researchers to use for reliability and/or a common denominator so that the form of working with EMDR is consistent. The concept that has motivated this work was conceived within the context of assisting EMDR clinicians in accessing the scripts of the full protocols in one place and to profit from the creativity of other EMDR clinicians who have kept the spirit of EMDR but have also taken into consideration the needs of the population with whom they work or the situations that they encounter. Reading a script is by no means a substitute for adequate training, competence, clinical acumen, and integrity; if you are not a trained EMDR therapist and/or you are not knowledgeable in the field for which you wish to use the script, these scripts are not for you.
>
> As EMDR is a fairly complicated process and, indeed, has intimidated some from integrating it into their daily approach to therapy, this book provides step-by-step scripts that will enable beginning practitioners to enhance their expertise more quickly. It will also appeal to seasoned EMDR clinicians, trainers and consultants because it brings together the many facets of the eight phases of EMDR and how clinicians are using this framework to work with a variety of therapeutic difficulties and modalities, while maintaining the integrity of the AIP model. Although there are a large number of resources, procedures and protocols in this book, they do not constitute the universe of protocols that are potentially useful and worthy of further study and use.
>
> These scripted protocols are intended for clinicians who have read Shapiro's text (2001) and received EMDR training from an EMDR-accredited trainer. An EMDR trainer is a licensed mental health practitioner who has been approved by the association active in the clinician's country of practice. (Luber, 2009a, p. xxi)

In 2012, the CD-ROM versions of the original 2009 books were published in a different format. Included in the CD-ROM were just the protocols and summary sheets (the notes were not included and are in the 2009 texts in book form). As explained in the Preface of *Eye Movement Desensitization and Reprocessing (EMDR) Scripted Protocols With Summary Sheets CD-ROM Version: Basics and Special Situations* (Luber, 2012a):

> The idea for *Eye Movement Desensitization and Reprocessing (EMDR) Scripted Protocols: Basics and Special Situations* grew out of the day-to-day work with the protocols that allowed for a deeper understanding of case conceptualization from an EMDR perspective. While using the scripted protocols and acquiring a greater familiarity with the use of the content, the idea of placing the information in a summarized format grew. This book

of scripted protocols and summary sheets was undertaken so that clinicians could easily use the material in *Eye Movement Desensitization and Reprocessing (EMDR) Scripted Protocols: Basics and Special Situations*. While working on the summary sheets, the interest in brevity collided with the thought that clinicians could also use these summary sheets to remind themselves of the steps in the process clarified in the scripted protocols. The original goal to be a summary of the necessary data gathered from the protocol was transformed into this new creation of data summary and memory tickler for the protocol itself! Alas, the summary sheets have become a bit longer than originally anticipated. Nonetheless, they are shorter–for the most part–than the protocols themselves and do summarize the data in an easily readable format.

The format for this book is also innovative. The scripts and summary sheets are available in an expandable, downloadable format for easy digital access. Because EMDR is a fairly complicated process, and often intimidating, these scripted protocols with their accompanying summary sheets can be helpful in a number of ways. To begin with, by facilitating the gathering of important data from the protocol about the client, the scripted protocol and/or summary sheet then can be inserted into the client's chart as documentation. The summary sheet can assist the clinician in formulating a concise and clear treatment plan with clients and can be used to support quick retrieval of the essential issues and experiences during the course of treatment. Practitioners can enhance their expertise more quickly by having a place that instructs and reminds them of the essential parts of EMDR practice. By having these fill-in PDF forms, clinicians can easily tailor the scripted protocols and summary sheets to the needs of their clients, their consultees/supervisees and themselves by editing and saving the protocol scripts and summary sheets. The script and summary sheet forms are available as a digital download or on a CD-ROM, and will work with any computer or device that supports a PDF format.

Consultants/Supervisors will find these scripted protocols and summary sheets useful while working with consultees/supervisees in their consultation/supervision groups. These works bring together many ways of handling current, important issues in psychotherapy and EMDR treatment. They also include a helpful way to organize the data collected that is key to case consultation and the incorporation of EMDR into newly-trained practitioners' practices. (Luber, 2012a, p. iv)

This book is divided into four parts with 10 chapters, including material on eating disorders and body image dysregulation from different perspectives, transforming relationship distortion such as physical violence injury, shifting chronic pain experience, and treating maladaptive self-care behaviors. The editor asked each author to write the chapter from an EMDR therapist's viewpoint that includes the principles, protocols, and procedures that form EMDR therapy and the AIP model. The authors shaped their eight-phase protocol to tailor their history-taking phase to their specific population's requirements and a clear treatment plan. They included the resources that they often adapted to their patients' needs and added the types of cognitions and interweaves through the next phases. They were all asked to include pertinent research that is relevant for their work.

After the Preface, there is a short commentary by Marco Pagani and Livia Sani on "Neurobiological Foundations of EMDR Therapy." Pagani holds posts at the Institute of Cognitive Sciences and Technologies in Rome and the Department of Nuclear Medicine in Karolinska Hospital in Stockholm. Sani is his trainee from the institute. They discuss how traumatic events affect us and how neuroimaging techniques such as positron emission tomography, single photon emission tomography, electroencephalography, and functional and structural magnetic resonance imaging have helped us to identify what is happening concerning the pathophysiology of PTSD and how EMDR therapy affects it.

In Part I, the focus is on "Treating Eating and Body Image Dysregulation With EMDR Therapy." This section begins with Renée Beer's work "Protocol for EMDR Therapy in the Treatment of Eating Disorders." Beer is an EMDR Europe–accredited trainer for EMDR with Children and Adolescents from the Netherlands. Recently, she and Beer and de Roos (2017) edited the *Handbook of EMDR With Children and Youth*. She specialized in the treatment of eating disorders at the Department of Child Psychiatry of the University Medical Center in Utrecht from 2000 to 2005 and brings her updated Dutch perspective to treating patients with eating disorders. Maria Zaccagnino represents her Italian perspective in her chapter, "EMDR Therapy Protocol for the Management of Dysfunctional Eating Behaviors in Anorexia Nervosa." Zaccagnino is a co-director with Isabel Fernandez of the Center of EMDR Therapy for Eating Disorders in Milan, where she coordinates research as well. Natalia Seijo contributes two chapters to this section: "EMDR Therapy Protocol for Eating Disorders" and "The Rejected Self EMDR Therapy Protocol for Body Image Distortion." Seijo brings a Spanish viewpoint to the treatment of eating disorders. She developed her expertise in one of the most influential eating disorders units in Spain, and she is involved in teaching and clinical work in a number of different places nationally and internationally.

There is one chapter in the section on "Transforming Relationship Distortion With EMDR Therapy." Dolores Mosquera and Jim Knipe integrate their expertise to write about "EMDR Therapy and Physical Violence Injury: 'Best Moments' Protocol." Mosquera has a wide range of interests, and among them she collaborates with the Women Victims and Domestic Violence Program and the Males and Violent Behavior Program. Knipe has been presenting on dysfunctional positive affect for many years and has written about this extensively.

The third section addresses "Shifting Chronic Pain Experiences Using EMDR Therapy." Chronic pain is ubiquitous, and these chapters contribute to provide us with some answers to use with our patients. "EMDR Therapy and Chronic Pain Conditions" features work by Tesarz, Seidler, and Eich. These three medical doctors are connected to the Medical University of Heidelberg. Each of these men has dedicated himself to research and clinical work on chronic pain and has been recognized by his peers. They write about three different protocols to use with chronic pain. The second chapter is "EMDR Therapy Treatment for Migraine" by Emre Konuk, Hejan Epözdemir, Zeynep Zat, Sirin Haciomeroglu Atceken, and Asena Yurtsever. This team from Davranış Bilimleri Enstitüsü (DBE; Institute for Behavioral Studies) has focused their interest on headaches over a number of years. "Fibromyalgia Syndrome Treatment With EMDR Therapy" is the eighth chapter, written by Konuk, Zat, and Kavakçı. Emre Konuk brings his wealth of experience as a pioneer in Turkey who established psychotherapy as a profession by founding DBE. Zeynap Zat is an active member of the Research, Clinical Applications, and Protocol Committees for EMDR-Turkey, and Önder Kavakçı is an associate professor at the Medical School of Cumhuriyet University and involved with research and publishing for EMDR-Turkey.

The last section is focused on "Treating Maladaptive Self-Care Behaviors Using EMDR Therapy" and features two important chapters devoted to teaching patients better self-care behaviors. Carol Forgash's chapter on "The Impact of Complex PTSD and Attachment Issues on Personal Health: An EMDR Therapy Approach" is an important subject for all therapists dealing with patients suffering with dissociative disorders and complex PTSD. She has been writing and presenting on the subject and has been particularly devoted to helping abuse survivors deal with their complex health issues. Dolores Mosquera, Paula Baldomir Gago, Ana Cris Eiriz, and Raquel Fernández Domínguez write about the "EMDR Therapy Self-Care Protocol." They work at the Institute for the Study of Trauma and Personality Disorders (INTRA-TP). Together, they have developed seven self-care protocols: understanding self-care, learning how to take care of ourselves, preventing relapse, developing resources, learning about and managing self-harm and self-destructive behaviors, developing and installing positive alternative behaviors, and working with the inner child.

Each chapter is accompanied by summary sheets that serve as checklists and memory support to highlight the distinctive parts in each of these protocols.

There are updated versions of Appendix A's Worksheets for the Past Memory Worksheet Script, the Present Trigger Worksheet Script, and the Future Template Worksheet. These were updated to include material from Shapiro's updated text, *Eye Movement Desensitization and Reprocessing—Basic Principles, Protocols, and Procedures*, third edition (2018). To ensure fidelity to the model, the past, present, and future worksheets in Appendix A show the important elements of the Standard EMDR Protocol. These worksheets can be copied and put into patients' charts. In Appendix B, there are updated versions of Luber "EMDR Summary Sheet" (2009a, 2009b, 20016b) and the EMDR Session Form (2016a, 2016b) as a way to summarize and quickly see important patient information. In Appendix C, there is a list of EMDR Worldwide Regional Associations who support EMDR therapy standards around the world and their contact information.

Eye Movement Desensitization and Reprocessing (EMDR) Therapy Scripted Protocols and Summary Sheets: Treating Eating Disorders, Chronic Pain, and Maladaptive Self-Care Behaviors is accessible in print and electronic formats. This book follows the structure of the previous six books in this series. Experts in their fields show how they work with their patients with EMDR therapy. Again, this book is not a comprehensive look at eating disorders and body dysregulation, physical violence injury, chronic pain conditions, and maladaptive self-care behaviors. However, the goal is to assist us to use what we have observed and gathered data on to enrich our effectiveness as EMDR therapy practitioners.

REFERENCES

Abel, N. J., & O'Brien, J. M. (2010). EMDR treatment of comorbid PTSD and alcohol dependence: A case example. *Journal of EMDR Practice and Research, 4,* 50–59. doi:10.1891/1933-3196.4.2.50

Anda, R. F., Felitti, V. J., Brown, D., Chapman, D., Dong, M., Dube, S. R., . . . Giles, W. (2006). Insights into intimate partner violence from the Adverse Childhood Experiences (ACE) study. In P. R. Salber &

E. Taliaferro (Eds.), *The physician's guide to intimate partner violence and abuse: A reference for all health care professionals* (2nd ed., pp. 77–88). Volcano, CA: Volcano Press.

Beer, R., & de Roos, C. (Ed.). (2017). *Handboek: EMDR bij kinderen en jongeren (Handbook: EMDR for children and youth)*. The Netherlands: Uitgeverij LannooCampus.

Centonze, D., Siracusane, A., Calabresi, P., & Bernardi, G. (2005). Removing pathogenic memories. *Molecular Neurobiology, 32*, 123–132. doi:10.1385/MN:32:2:123

de Roos, C., Veenstra, A. C., de Jongh, A., den Hollander-Gijsman, M., van der Wee, N., Zitman, F. G., & van Rood, Y. R. (2010). Treatment of chronic phantom limb pain using a trauma-focused psychological approach. *Pain Research and Management, 15*, 65–71. doi:10.1155/2010/981634

Felitti, V. J., Anda, R. F., Nordenberg, D., Williamson, D. F., Spitz, A. M., Edwards, V., ... Marks, J. S. (1998). Relationship of childhood abuse and household dysfunction in many of the leading causes of death in adults: The adverse childhood experiences (ACE) study. *American Journal of Preventive Medicine, 14*(4), 245–258. doi:10.1016/s0749-3797(98)00017-8

Gerhardt, A., Leisner, S., Hartmann, M., Janke, S., Seidler, G. H., Eich, W., & Tesarz, J. (2016). Eye movement desensitization and reprocessing vs. treatment-as usual for non-specific chronic back pain patients with psychological trauma: A randomized controlled pilot study. *Frontiers in Psychiatry, 7*, 201. doi:10.3389/fpsyt.2016.00201

Guillaume, S., Jaussent, I., Maimoun, L., Ryst, A., Seneque, M., Villain, L., ... Courtet, P. (2016). Associations between adverse childhood experiences and clinical characteristics of eating disorders. *Scientific Reports, 6*, 35761. doi:10.1038/srep35761

Hase, M., Balmaceda, U. M., Hase, A., Lehnung, M., Tumani, V., Huchzermeier, C., & Hofmann, A. (2015). EMDR AIP model and pathogenic memories in the treatment of depression—A matched pairs study in an in-patient setting. *Brain and Behavior, 5*, e00342. doi:10.1002/brb3.342

Hase, M., Balmaceda, U. M., Ostacoli, L., Liebermann, P., & Hofmann, A. (2017). The AIP model of EMDR therapy and pathogenic memories. *Frontiers in Psychiatry, 8*, 1578. doi:10.3389/fpsyg.2017.01578

Hase, M., Schallmayer, S., & Sack, M. (2008). EMDR reprocessing of the addiction memory: Pretreatment, posttreatment, and 1-month follow-up. *Journal of EMDR Practice and Research, 2*(3), 170–179. doi:10.1891/1933-3196.2.3.170

Hofmann, A., Hilgers, A., Lehnung, M., Liebermann, P., Ostacoli, L., Schneider, W., & Hase, M. (2014). Eye movement desensitization and reprocessing (EMDR) as an adjunctive treatment in depression—A controlled study. *Journal of EMDR Practice and Research, 8*, 103–112. doi:10.1007/s10899-013-9422-5

Landin-Romero, R., Novo, P., Vicens, V., McKenna, P. J., Santed, A., Pomarol-Clotet, E., . . . Amann, M. (2013). EMDR therapy modulates the default mode network in a subsyndromal, traumatized bipolar patient. *Journal of Neuropsychobiology, 67*, 181–184. doi:10.1159/000346654

Luber, M. (Ed.). (2009a). *Eye movement desensitization and reprocessing (EMDR) scripted protocols: Basics and special situations*. New York, NY: Springer Publishing.

Luber, M. (Ed.). (2009b). *Eye movement desensitization and reprocessing (EMDR) scripted protocols: Special populations*. New York, NY: Springer Publishing.

Luber, M. (Ed.). (2012a). *Eye movement desensitization and reprocessing (EMDR) scripted protocols with summary sheets (CD-ROM Version): Basics and special situations*. New York, NY: Springer Publishing.

Luber, M. (Ed.). (2012b). *Eye movement desensitization and reprocessing (EMDR) scripted protocols with summary sheets (CD-ROM Version): Special populations*. New York, NY: Springer Publishing.

Luber, M. (Ed.). (2014). *Implementing EMDR early mental health interventions for man-made and natural disasters: Models, scripted protocols and summary sheets*. New York, NY: Springer Publishing.

Luber, M. (Ed.). (2016a). *Eye movement desensitization and reprocessing (EMDR) therapy scripted protocols and summary sheets: Treating trauma and stressor-related conditions*. New York, NY: Springer Publishing.

Luber, M. (Ed.). (2016b). *Eye movement desensitization and reprocessing (EMDR) therapy scripted protocols and summary sheets: Treating anxiety, obsessive-compulsive, and mood-related conditions*. New York, NY: Springer Publishing.

Marsden, Z., Lovell, K., Blore, D., Ali, S., & Delgadillo, J. (2018). A randomized controlled trial comparing EMDR and CBT for obsessive-compulsive disorder. *Clinical Psychology and Psychotherapy, 25*(1), e10–e18. doi:10.1002/cpp.2120

Novo, P., Landin-Romero, R., Radua, J., Vicens, V., Fernandez, I., Garcia, F., ... Amann, B. L. (2014). Eye movement desensitization and reprocessing therapy in subsyndromal bipolar patients with a history of traumatic events: A randomized, controlled pilot-study. *Psychiatry Research, 219*, 122–128. doi:10.1016/j.psychres.2014.05.012

Sachs-Ericsson, N. J., Sheffler, J. L., Stanlye, I. H., Piazza, J. R., & Preacher, K. J. (2017). When emotional pain becomes physical: Adverse childhood experiences, pain and the role of mood and anxiety disorders. *Journal of Clinical Psychology, 73*(10), 1403–1428. doi:10.1002/jclp.22444

Schneider, J., Hofmann, A., Rost, C., & Shapiro, F. (2008). EMDR in the treatment of chronic phantom limb pain. *Pain Med, 9*(1), 76–82. doi:10.1111/j.1526-4637.2007.00299.x

Shapiro, F. (1995). *Eye movement desensitization and reprocessing—Basic principles, protocols, and procedures.* New York, NY: Guilford Press.

Shapiro, F. (2001). *Eye movement desensitization and reprocessing—Basic principles, protocols, and procedures* (2nd ed.). New York, NY: Guilford Press.

Shapiro, F. (2018). *Eye movement desensitization and reprocessing—Basic principles, protocols, and procedures* (3rd ed.). New York, NY: Guilford Press.

Swissre. (2012). Natural catastrophes and man-made disasters in 2011: Historic losses surface from record earthquakes and floods. Retrieved from http://www.swissre.com/library/archive/22012_Natural_catastrophes_and_manmade_disasters_in_2011_historic_losses_surface_from_record_earthquakes_and_floods.html

Wilensky, M. (2006). Eye movement desensitization and reprocessing (EMDR) as a treatment for phantom limb pain. *Journal of Brief Therapy, 5*, 31–44.

Neurobiological Foundations of EMDR Therapy

Marco Pagani and Livia Sani

Traumatic events damage the mental and emotional processes and affect brain physiology. According to the *Diagnostic and Statistical Manual of Mental Disorders* (5th ed.; *DSM-5;* American Psychiatric Association [APA], 2013), people with posttraumatic stress disorder (PTSD) may present with the following:

- Negative alterations in cognitions and mood
- Symptoms of irritability and outbursts of anger
- Reexperiencing of the traumatic event
- Self-destructive behavior
- Hypervigilance
- Alarm response exaggerated
- Trouble concentrating
- Trouble falling asleep or staying awake

In recent years, many researchers have focused on trauma and its symptoms, obtaining important results concerning the understanding of traumatic memory and how it affects the brain and human behavior.

Through neuroimaging techniques such as positron emission tomography, single photon emission tomography, electroencephalography (EEG), and functional and structural magnetic resonance imaging, it has been possible to identify the brain circuits involved in the pathophysiology of PTSD. Changes in metabolism, brain morphology, and networking have been found in the amygdala, the medial prefrontal cortex (mPFC), and the hippocampus (Martin, Ressler, Binder, & Nemeroff, 2009; Shin, Rauch, & Pitman, 2006; Wager, Lindquist, & Kaplan, 2007; Yehuda & LeDoux, 2007), which together form the so-called neural model of PTSD (Shin et al., 2006).

These are the types of changes that occur in the different areas of the brain in PTSD patients:

- *Amygdala:* At the amygdala level, psychological traumas give rise to excessive arousal, resulting in a reaction of exaggerated alarm in response to external stimuli (Herry et al., 2007; Sander, Grafman, & Zalla, 2003).
- *Dorsolateral frontal cortex (DLFC):* In PTSD, DLFC does not exert its inhibitory effect on the amygdala, resulting in hyper-activation of the latter following traumatic stimuli.
- *Medial prefrontal cortex (mPFC):* The increased responsiveness of the amygdala interferes with the functioning of the mPFC regions, which include the rostral anterior cingulate cortex, the ventral medial frontal gyrus, and the orbitofrontal cortex (Etkin & Wager, 2007). This region is pivotal in executive functions and in mediating the transfer of traumatic memories from subcortical structures.
- *Hippocampus:* A reduction in the volume of the hippocampus has been repeatedly found in PTSD patients. In patients, this would cause a functional inhibition of the ability to cognitively evaluate their experiences, resulting in explicit memory disorders and unelaborated memories (Liberzon & Sripada, 2008).

xxv

- *Limbic and paralimbic cortical regions*: Differences in the density of gray matter were also recorded in the limbic and paralimbic cortical regions (Bremner et al., 1997; Chen et al., 2006), eliciting emotional distress and parasympathetic symptoms.
- *Broca's area*: Broca's area is partially disabled, and this could explain the difficulty that patients with PTSD have in describing, verbalizing, and cognitively restructuring their traumatic experience (Hull, 2002).

A few functional studies on traumatized patients have disclosed the impact of various psychotherapies, such as cognitive behavioral therapy (CBT), brief eclectic therapy, and mindfulness, on the neurobiology of PTSD as investigated before and after therapy. In this respect, research on the efficacy of EMDR therapy in psychological trauma has identified that postintervention, there is a significant normalization of blood flow, mainly in the limbic and in the frontal cortex areas, thus determining a higher control over the amygdala. In turn, this normalization decreases the pathological cortical hyper-activation, resulting in the disappearance of PTSD symptoms, including a reduction in anxiety, somatosensory symptoms, flashbacks, intrusive memories, and the feeling of reliving the trauma with persistent sensations even at somatic level (Lansing, Amen, Hanks, & Rudy, 2005; Oh & Choi, 2007; Pagani et al., 2007).

In a study where traumatized subjects suffering with PTSD were compared to traumatized subjects not developing PTSD, Nardo et al. (2010) found a decrease in gray matter density in several limbic regions, such as the posterior cingulate, para-hippocampal, and insular cortex in those subjects with PTSD. These regions are implicated in processes such as integration, encoding, and retrieval of autobiographical and episodic memories, self-referential conscious experience, emotional processing (i.e., classical conditioning, cognitive appraisal, experience of feeling states), and interoceptive awareness (Pagani, Högberg, Fernandez, & Siracusano, 2013), and are the typical target regions of EMDR therapy. The same investigation highlighted that the subjects *not* responding to EMDR therapy showed significantly lower neuronal density in the same areas, suggesting that the therapeutic failure might be due to a previous atrophic state not allowing for any neurobiological effect of EMDR therapy.

Most recently, EEG investigations, performed during the bilateral stimulation phase of EMDR sessions, have deepened the knowledge about the neurobiological processes occurring during the therapy. The comparison between the prevalent cortical activation during the first and last EMDR therapy sessions showed a significant deactivation of the orbitofrontal and subcortical limbic structures and an increased activation of the temporo-occipital cortex, mainly on the left side (see Figure 1).

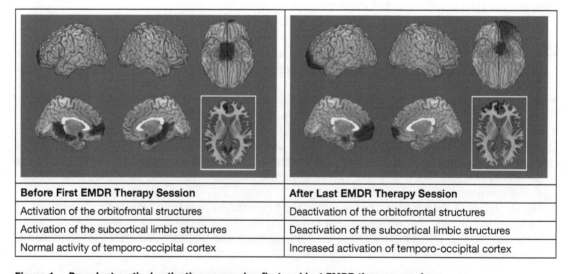

Before First EMDR Therapy Session	After Last EMDR Therapy Session
Activation of the orbitofrontal structures	Deactivation of the orbitofrontal structures
Activation of the subcortical limbic structures	Deactivation of the subcortical limbic structures
Normal activity of temporo-occipital cortex	Increased activation of temporo-occipital cortex

Figure 1.   Prevalent cortical activation comparing first and last EMDR therapy sessions.
Source: Images from Pagani, M., Di Lorenzo, G., Verardo, A. R., Nicolais, G., Monaco, L., Lauretti, G., & Fernandez, I. (2012). Neurobiology of EMDR—EEG imaging of treatment efficacy. *PloS One, 7(*9), e45753. doi:10.1371/journal .pone.0045753

As a result, traumatic experiences and memories move from an implicit subcortical state to an explicit cortical state and are properly processed, reelaborated, and adapted into patients' semantic memory (Pagani et al., 2011, 2012, 2015; Trentini et al., 2015).

The following are some of the models to explain the mechanisms of action used to elucidate EMDR therapy:

- *Psychological* (e.g., orienting and working memory account)
- *Psychophysiological* (e.g., REM sleep model)
- *Neurobiological* (e.g., changes in inter-hemispheric connectivity, neural integration and thalamic binding model, structural and functional brain changes associated with EMDR therapy)

The neurobiological model provides solid foundations in how to unravel the functional and structural correlates of effective treatments. Taking also into account the rapid eye movement (REM) sleep model, a further possible mechanism has been hypothesized (Carletto, Borsato, & Pagani, 2017; Pagani, Amann, Landin-Romero, & Carletto, 2017). During bilateral stimulation in EMDR therapy, the cortical activity as recorded by EEG resembles that of slow wave sleep (SWS), in which fragmented episodic and traumatic memories move from the amygdalar–hippocampus complex to the neocortex, in which they will be further integrated and encoded during REM sleep. Since during EMDR therapy the frequency of bilateral stimulation matches that of SWS (0.5–4 cycles per second, delta waves), the repetition of such stimulation during several sessions might be its "added value," mimicking the natural physiological memory processes and favoring the traumatic traces to be contextualized in the neocortex. This would make EMDR faster and more effective in treating PTSD than other psychotherapies.

In conclusion, all changes found in EMDR therapy research confirm at various levels a solid neurobiological basis for the psychotherapy, resulting in improved symptoms and quality of life in patients with a PTSD diagnosis.

REFERENCES

American Psychiatric Association. (2013). *Diagnostic and statistical manual of mental disorders* (5th ed.). Arlington, VA: American Psychiatric Publishing.

Bremner, J. D., Randall, P., Vermetten, E., Staib, L., Bronen, R. A., Mazure, C., ... Charney D. S. (1997). Magnetic resonance imaging-based measurement of hippocampal volume in posttraumatic stress disorder related to childhood physical and sexual abuse—A preliminary report. *Biological Psychiatry, 41*(1), 23–32. doi:10.1016/S0006-3223(96)00162-X

Carletto, S., Borsato, T., & Pagani, M. (2017). The role of slow wave sleep in memory pathophysiology: Focus on post-traumatic stress disorder and eye movement desensitization and reprocessing. *Frontiers in Psychology, 8*, 2050. doi: 10.3389/fpsyg.2017.02050

Chen, S., Xia, W., Li, L., Liu, J., He, Z., Zhang, Z., ... Hu, D. (2006). Gray matter density reduction in the insula in fire survivors with posttraumatic stress disorder: A voxel-based morphometric study. *Psychiatry Research, 146*(1), 65–72. doi:10.1016/j.pscychresns.2005.09.006

Etkin, A., & Wager, T. D. (2007). Functional neuroimaging of anxiety: A meta-analysis of emotional processing in PTSD, social anxiety disorder, and specific phobia. *The American Journal of Psychiatry, 164*(10), 1476–1488. doi:10.1176/appi.ajp.2007.07030504

Herry, C., Bach, D. R., Esposito, F., Di Salle, F., Perrig, W. J., Scheffler, K., ... Seifritz E. (2007). Processing of temporal unpredictability in human and animal amygdale. *Journal of Neuroscience, 27*(22), 5958–5966. doi:10.1523/JNEUROSCI.5218-06.2007

Hull, A. M. (2002). Neuroimaging findings in post-traumatic stress disorder. *British Journal of Psychiatry, 181*(2), 102–110. doi:10.1192/bjp.181.2.102

Lansing, K., Amen, D. G., Hanks, C., & Rudy, L. (2005). High-resolution brain SPECT imaging and eye movement desensitization and reprocessing in police officers with PTSD. *Journal of Neuropsychiatry and Clinical Neurosciences, 17*(4), 526–532. doi:10.1176/jnp.17.4.526

Liberzon, I., & Sripada, C. S. (2008). The functional neuroanatomy of PTSD: A critical review. *Progress in Brain Research, 167*, 151–169. doi:10.1016/S0079-6123(07)67011-3

Martin, E. I., Ressler, K. J., Binder, E., & Nemeroff, C. B. (2009). The neurobiology of anxiety disorders: Brain imaging, genetics, and psychoneuroendocrinology. *Psychiatric Clinics of North America, 32*(3), 549–575. doi:10.1016/j.psc.2009.05.004

Nardo, D., Högberg, G., Looi, J., Larsson, S. A., Hällström, T., & Pagani, M. (2010). Grey matter changes in posterior cingulate and limbic cortex in PTSD are associated with trauma load and EMDR outcome. *Journal of Psychiatry Research, 44*(7), 477–485. doi:10.1016/j.jpsychires.2009.10.014

Oh, D. H., & Choi, J. (2007). Changes in the cerebral perfusion after EMDR. *Journal of EMDR Practice and Research, 1*(1), 24–30. doi:10.1891/1933-3196.1.1.24

Pagani, M., Amann, B. L., Landin-Romero, R., & Carletto, S. (2017). EMDR and slow wave sleep: A putative mechanism of action. *Frontiers in Psychology, 8*, 1935. doi:10.3389/fpsyg.2017.01935

Pagani, M., Di Lorenzo, G., Monaco, L., Daverio, A., Giannoudas, I., La Porta, P., ... Siracusano, A. (2015). Neurobiological response to EMDR therapy in clients with different psychological traumas. *Frontiers in Psychology, 6*, 1614. doi:10.3389/fpsyg.2015.01614

Pagani, M., Di Lorenzo, G., Verardo, A. R., Nicolais, G., Monaco, L., Lauretti, G., & Fernandez, I. (2011). Preintra- and post-treatment EEG imaging of EMDR—Methodology and preliminary results from a single case. *Journal of EMDR Practice and Research, 5*(2), 42–56. doi:10.1891/1933-3196.5.2.42

Pagani, M., Di Lorenzo, G., Verardo, A. R., Nicolais, G., Monaco, L., Lauretti, G., & Fernandez, I. (2012). Neurobiology of EMDR—EEG imaging of treatment efficacy. *PloS One, 7*(9), e45753. doi:10.1371/journal.pone.0045753

Pagani, M., Högberg, G., Fernandez, I., & Siracusano, A. (2013). Correlates of EMDR therapy in functional and structural neuroimaging: A critical summary of recent findings. *Journal of EMDR Practice and Research, 7*(1), 28–38. doi:10.1891/1933-3196.7.1.29

Pagani, M., Högberg, G., Salmaso, D., Nardo, D., Tärnell, B., Jonsson, C., & Sundin, Ö. (2007). Effects of EMDR psychotherapy on 99mTc-HMPAO distribution in occupation-related post-traumatic stress disorder. *Nuclear Medicine Communications, 28*(10), 757–765. doi:10.1097/MNM.0b013e3282742035

Sander, D., Grafman, J., & Zalla, T. (2003). The human amygdala: An evolved system for relevance detection. *Reviews in the Neurosciences, 14*(4), 303–316. doi:10.1515/REVNEURO.2003.14.4.303

Shin, L. M., Rauch, S. L., & Pitman, R. K. (2006). Amygdala, medial prefrontal cortex, and hippocampal function in PTSD. *Annals of the New York Academy of Sciences, 1071*(1), 67–79. doi:10.1196/annals.1364.007

Trentini, C., Pagani, M., Fania, P., Speranza, A. M., Nicolais, G., Sibilia, A., ... Ammaniti, M. (2015). Neural processing of emotions in traumatized children treated with eye movement desensitization and reprocessing therapy: A hdEEG study. *Frontiers in Psychology, 6*, 1662. doi:10.3389/fpsyg.2015.01662

Wager, T. D., Lindquist, M., & Kaplan, L. (2007). Meta-analysis of functional neuroimaging data: Current and future directions. *Social Cognitive and Affective Neuroscience, 2*(2), 150–158. doi:10.1093/scan/nsm015

Yehuda, R., & LeDoux, J. (2007). Response variation following trauma: A translational neuroscience approach to understanding PTSD. *Neuron, 56*(1), 19–32. doi:10.1016/j.neuron.2007.09.006

Acknowledgments

The idea for the EMDR Scripted Protocols series originally grew out of supervisory/consultant trainings that I was doing for EMDR practitioners in Germany and Israel in the late 1990s. At the time, clinicians at that level did not have a firm grasp of the EMDR protocols and procedures, so, after consulting with Arne Hofmann, I created a manual that incorporated Shapiro's six basic protocols from her text (Shapiro, 1995) and others that I thought would be helpful. In 2007, Bob Gelbach, the director of the EMDR HAP (now Trauma Aid) at that time, and I were at the EMDR International Association's annual conference in Dallas, Texas, and we were talking about doing something with the manual I had put together for HAP. He suggested that I go speak to the representative at the Springer Publishing booth. With some prodding, I went over and spoke to Sheri Sussman. She took a copy of my manual from my thumb drive on the spot and 5 days later offered me a contract. I was very surprised and excited and asked my very talented colleagues if they were interested in contributing to this project, and they did. Their additions became *Eye Movement Desensitization and Reprocessing (EMDR) Scripted Protocols: Basics and Special Situations (2009a)* and *Eye Movement Desensitization and Reprocessing (EMDR) Scripted Protocols: Special Populations* (2009b), which basically followed the structure of Shapiro's 1995 text. I found interacting with my colleagues exhilarating as we worked together to put their chapters into the scripted protocol format to help fellow clinicians learn EMDR therapy.

I found the work so compelling that I started to formulate a book that would address major issues in the psychotherapeutic world: anxiety, depression, and medical-related issues. However, before I got too far with this idea, I felt that it would be more important to address the increase in man-made and natural disasters that were occurring worldwide in 2011, such as the Tohoku earthquake and tsunami in Japan; the East African drought; Tropical Storm Washi in the Philippines; the April 27th tornado in the U.S. southeast; the Joplin, Missouri, Tornado; and many wildfires, snowstorms, and wind storms. I discussed the idea with my colleagues who were actively involved in responding to many of these disasters—such as Elan Shapiro, Brurit Laub, Nacho Jarero, Sushma Mehrotra, Derek Farrell (director of HAP Europe), and Carol Martin (director of EMDR HAP/Trauma Aid)—using the work that they had crafted or the organizations with which they responded. *Implementing EMDR Early Mental Health Interventions for Man-Made and Natural Disasters: Models, Scripted Protocols and Summary Sheets* (2014) was born.

I had already begun the book mentioned earlier on anxiety, depression, and medical issues before I started *Implementing,* so when it was done I was ready to move forward with this project that I had been thinking about for a while. The one book became four books because of the wealth of material I had collected from EMDR experts in these areas. Two were published in 2016: *Eye Movement Desensitization and Reprocessing (EMDR) Therapy Scripted Protocols and Summary Sheets: Treating Trauma- and Stressor-Related Conditions* (Luber, 2016a) and *Eye Movement Desensitization and Reprocessing (EMDR) Therapy Scripted Protocols and Summary Sheets: Treating Anxiety, Obsessive-Compulsive, and Mood-Related Conditions* (Luber, 2016b).

Recently, the medical-related book turned into *Eye Movement Desensitization and Reprocessing (EMDR) Therapy Scripted Protocols and Summary Sheets: Treating Trauma in Somatic and Medical-Related Conditions,* and into this volume, *Eye Movement Desensitization and Reprocessing (EMDR) Therapy Scripted Protocols and Summary Sheets: Treating Eating Disorders, Chronic Pain, and Maladaptive Self-Care Behaviors.*

The EMDR Scripted Protocol books are now a series of seven volumes with 143 chapters (11 are updated chapters), 145 authors coming from 15 different countries (Australia, Brazil, Canada, Germany, Greece, India, Israel, Italy, Lebanon, Mexico, The Netherlands, Spain, Turkey, the United Kingdom and Scotland, and the United States).

I would like to thank all of my contributors to this book. It is through the joint efforts of all 18 of them that *Eye Movement Desensitization and Reprocessing (EMDR) Therapy Scripted Protocols and*

Summary Sheets: Treating Eating Disorders, Chronic Pain, and Maladaptive Self-Care Behaviors (Luber, 2019) is in your hands. I want them to know how much I appreciated their patience as different personal issues and another book got in the way of the timely publishing of this volume. The authors are my colleagues and, for this volume, they come from Germany, Italy, the Netherlands, Spain, Turkey, and the United States. It has been an honor and a privilege to work with them and to learn from their expertise and passion for their work. I have grown more sensitive in so many ways from working on these chapters and rediscovered working with the body as a focus of attention. I hope that the clinicians who read and use this book will be inspired to think of their patients within the context and structure of EMDR therapy.

I am indebted to Springer Publishing for the support and the faith they have put in me, and the work of experts in the field of EMDR therapy, in these sixth and seventh books in the EMDR Scripted Protocols series. The past year was the first time I visited the physical space of Springer Publishing in the Salmon Tower Building in New York City across the street from Bryant Park. It was a great treat to meet professionals such as Mindy Chen and Joanne Jay, with whom I had only shared emails over the past 11 years. I cannot thank Sheri Sussman enough for the amount of encouragement, work, and patience she has demonstrated over these past years. She has been dedicated to this series and has always supported me through difficulties with deadlines and the wealth of great material!

Whenever you write seriously, especially when it is not your regular job, it is hard to do it without friends and colleagues who are supportive and caring. Thank you Elaine Alvarez, Renee Beer, Michael Broder, Valentina Chiorino, Herb Diamond, Robbie Dunton, Elisa Faretta, Isabel Fernandez, Catherine Fine, Carol Forgash, Irene Geissl, Richard Goldberg, Arlene Goldman, Barbara Grinnell, Barbara Hensley, Phyllis Klaus, Brurit Laub, Tali Perlman, Zona Scheiner, Bonnie Simon, Cynthia Thompson, Howard Wainer, Stuart Wolfe, and Bennet Wolper.

I would like to thank Andrew Leeds for faithfully writing about EMDR-related research in the EMDR International Association's newsletter over many years.

I would like to mention my appreciation to Barbara J. Hensley. Through her focus and tenacity, she built the Francine Shapiro Library—a gift to all of us who are interested in EMDR therapy.

Thank you to Francine Shapiro for always upholding the standard of EMDR and her gift of EMDR therapy to me personally and the world in general.

I would like to acknowledge the death of my friend and mentor Donald Nathanson. After a long illness, he left us. The world is a lot dimmer without his wit and his enormous intelligence.

My appreciation as always goes to the people involved in my daily life and how they help me in so many ways, allowing me to work as a clinician, an editor, and an author. They are Harry Cook, Jorge Alicea, Dennis Wright, and Rose Turner. Without Lew Rossi, my chosen way of writing would not happen. Thank you for keeping my computers up-to-date and always going out of your way—even at inconvenient times—to assist me in the latest catastrophe.

The pets in our lives are our hearts. My dear Emmy, who kept me company during the writing of all my previous books, left us 2 years ago, but she remains with us in spirit. We have a new 1-year-old schnauzer, Henry, who has sometimes made writing a challenge, but he is always a joy and ready to play when I take a break.

Thank you to my mother, Shirley Luber, who continues to give me support, friendship, and love even as she goes through the trial of her own chronic disease.

This book I am dedicating to Bob Raymar. Bob came back into my life after we originally met on July 4, 1968, at the Fourth of July Celebration in Geneva, Switzerland, where I was living and Bob was at an internship for the summer. We got to know each other there and when I returned to attend college in the United States later that year. Then, we lost touch for 45 years. About 4 years ago, LinkedIn reached out and we reconnected. In January 2018, Bob asked me to marry him when we were at the extraordinary Mamounia Hotel in Marrakech, where his parents were married. I said yes.

Since we reconnected, Bob, you have been my friend, my confidante, and my love. Throughout the writing of these last four volumes, you have been there every step of the way supporting me as a second reader and catching my missed commas, helping me pick the right phrase, and being a sounding board to help me think through all of the difficult issues that come up while writing a book. You have also been gracious about the missed concerts, movies, family and friend get-togethers, and taking care of Henry. You are a kind, wise, and knowledgeable man who has enriched my life in so many ways. This book is in honor of you, Bob.

REFERENCES

Luber, M. (Ed.). (2009a). *Eye movement desensitization and reprocessing (EMDR) scripted protocols: Basics and special situations.* New York, NY: Springer Publishing.

Luber, M. (Ed.). (2009b). *Eye movement desensitization and reprocessing (EMDR) scripted protocols: Special populations.* New York, NY: Springer Publishing.

Luber, M. (Ed.). (2014). *Implementing EMDR early mental health interventions for man-made and natural disasters: Models, scripted protocols and summary sheets.* New York, NY: Springer Publishing.

Luber, M. (Ed.). (2016a). *Eye movement desensitization and reprocessing (EMDR) therapy scripted protocols and summary sheets: Treating trauma- and stressor-related conditions.* New York, NY: Springer Publishing.

Luber, M. (Ed.). (2016b). *Eye movement desensitization and reprocessing (EMDR) therapy scripted protocols and summary sheets: Treating anxiety, obsessive-compulsive, and mood-related conditions.* New York, NY: Springer Publishing.

Luber, M. (Ed.). (2019). *Eye movement desensitization and reprocessing (EMDR) therapy scripted protocols and summary sheets: Eating disorders, chronic pain, and maladaptive self-care behaviors.* New York, NY: Springer Publishing.

Shapiro, F. (1995). *Eye movement desensitization and reprocessing—Basic principles, protocols, and procedures.* New York, NY: Guilford Press.

TREATING EATING AND BODY IMAGE DYSREGULATION WITH EMDR THERAPY

1

Eating disorders (EDs) are on the rise around the world. Even as early as 2003, The Renfrew Center for Eating Disorders reported that EDs affected up to 24 million Americans and 70 million individuals worldwide. The documentation of EDs began in 1873 when Sir William Gull in England and Charles Laseque in France first described anorexia nervosa (AN) as a "morbid mental state." This marked the beginning of the modern study of EDs (Gull, 1874; Vandereycken & van Deth, 1990). The 20th century extended the investigation mainly into Western cultures with people of European descent. During the mid-to-late 1960s, EDs rose in the aftermath of the counterculture movement (Gordon, 2001). At first, it was considered to be "afflictions primarily affecting wealthy, white, educated, young women in industrialized Western nations" (Bruch, 1973). The epitome of female beauty was to be the high fashion models at the time, Twiggy, who resembled her name and had the body dimensions of a 12-year-old boy. This was the goal that Western women wanted to achieve.

With the dawning of the new millennium, EDs in non-Western cultures have increased. Pike and Dunne (2015) note that many Asian countries are observing an increase in EDs as these countries have become more industrialized and globalized (Gordon, 2001; Lee & Lock, 2007; S. Lee, Ng, Kwok, & Fung, 2010; Mond, Chen, & Kumar, 2010; Pike, Yamamiya, & Konishi, 2011; Wan, Faber, & Fung, 2003). In fact, even in those parts of Asia where it was believed that EDs were not prevalent, comparative studies demonstrate that eating approaches and body dissatisfaction levels are similar or worse than those in the West (Jung & Forbes, 2006; Jung, Forbes, & Lee, 2009; Jung, Forbes, & Chan, 2010; Kayano et al., 2008; Tsai, 2000).

From the National Association of Anorexia Nervosa and Associate Disorders website (2018), here are some of the statistics on EDs in the United States:

- At least 30 million people of all ages and genders suffer from an eating disorder in the United States (Hudson, Hiripi, Pope, & Kessler, 2007; Le Grange, Swanson, Crow, & Merikangas, 2012).
- Every 62 minutes at least one person dies as a direct result of an eating disorder (Eating Disorders Coalition, 2016).
- Eating disorders have the highest mortality rate of any mental illness (Smink, van Hoeken, & Hoek, 2012).
- As many as 13% of women over age 50 engage in eating disorder behaviors (Gagne et al., 2012).
- In a large national study of college students, 3.5% of sexual minority women and 2.1% of sexual minority men reported having an eating disorder (Diemer, Grant, Munn-Chernoff, Patterson, & Duncan, 2015).
- As many as 16% of transgender college students reported having an eating disorder (Diemer et al., 2015).
- In a study following active duty military personnel over time, 5.5% of women and 4% of men had an eating disorder at the beginning of the study, and within just a few years of continued service, 3.3% more women and 2.6% more men developed an eating disorder (Jacobson et al., 2009).
- Eating disorders affect all races and ethnic groups (Marques et al., 2011).
- Genetics, environmental factors, and personality traits all combine to create risk for an eating disorder (Culbert, Racine, & Klump, 2015).

These statistics are chilling. As a result, many different groups have joined together to make a difference. The Academy for Eating Disorders is one of these organizations and the members used #WorldEDHealthcareRights to call for a World Eating Disorder Action Day. The idea came from parents and affected activists in a virtual advocacy group for the International Eating Disorders Action in November 2015 who raised awareness and interest across the globe. The first and second World Eating Disorders Action Day took place on June 2, 2016, and then on June 2, 2017, with the idea to continue them annually. The Steering Committee is made up of leaders from diverse people and communities.

In support of understanding EDs more fully, the members of The Academy for Eating Disorders partnered with Cynthia Bulik, PhD, FAED, distinguished professor of eating disorders in the School of Medicine at the University of North Carolina at Chapel Hill. The nine truths about EDs are based on her 2014 "9 Eating Disorders Myths Busted" talk at the National Institute of Mental Health:

Truth 1: Many people with eating disorders look healthy, yet may be extremely ill.

Truth 2: Families are not to blame and can be the patients' and providers' best allies in treatment.

Truth 3: An eating disorder diagnosis is a health crisis that disrupts personal and family functioning.

Truth 4: Eating disorders are not choices but serious, biologically influenced illnesses.

Truth 5: Eating disorders affect people of all genders, ages, races, ethnicities, body shapes and weights, sexual orientations, and socioeconomic statuses.

Truth 6: Eating disorders carry an increased risk for both suicide and medical complications.

Truth 7: Genes and environment play important roles in the development of eating disorders.

Truth 8: Genes alone do not predict who will develop eating disorders.

Truth 9: Full recovery from an eating disorder is possible. Early detection and intervention are important.

Their NINE goals are a proposed manifesto to present to policy makers and governments to take action against the growing epidemic of EDs worldwide. Patients with an ED have a higher incidence of death compared to any other mental illness. They ask that the policy makers and organizations involved in the implementation of services systematically review their policies to achieve these NINE goals:

1. We call for all frontline providers (including pediatricians, primary care doctors, dentists, emergency rooms, and school health providers) to be educated in the identification, diagnosis, and referral to appropriate services of EDs.
2. We call for accessible and affordable evidence-based treatment, with early diagnosis and intervention a priority.
3. We call for public education about EDs to be accurate, research based, readily available, and geared to end stigma about EDs.
4. We call for an end to mandatory weighing and body mass index (BMI) screening in schools and development of evidence-based health programs.
5. We call for increased awareness of diversity in EDs, as EDs affect a wide cross-section of the world's population, including people of all ages, sizes, weights, genders, sexual orientations, ethnicities, nationalities, and documentation status.
6. We call for community and family ED treatment support programs to be available for all.
7. We call for research-based interventions to be delivered in schools and universities on the facts about EDs, and how peers and staff can best support patients and families during treatment.
8. We call for government agencies to include ED services as part of health systems, public education campaigns, and regulatory bodies.
9. We call for the World Health Assembly and the World Health Organization to formally recognize June 2 as World Eating Disorders Action Day.

The groups in support of the International Eating Disorders Action have an active presence on social media and use Facebook, Twitter, and Instagram to spread their message (taken from www .worldeatingdisordersday.org).

Members of the EMDR therapy community began speaking about EDs at one of the earliest EMDR Network Conferences (Bitter, 1992). Since then, EDs have been an important conversation in our community. Based on information from the Francine Shapiro Library when the tag "Eating Disorders" was entered, there are *two books* with a third on the way (Plassmann, 2009; Seubert & Virdi, 2018; Shapiro, R. 2009—26 chapters), *five dissertations* (Cameron, 2013; Carpenter, 1999; Fiol, 1997; Gamba, 2005; Miceli, 2009), *16 book chapters* (Beer & Hornsveld, 2008; Gross & Ratner, 2002; Schulherr, 2005; Shapiro, 1998; Van Trier, 2009; Shapiro, R. 2009—8 chapters; Plassman, 2009—2 chapters; Zaccagnino , Cussino, Callerame, Civilotti, & Fernandez, 2017a), *17 journal articles* (dating from 1998 to 2017, such as Balbo, Zaccagnino, Cussino, & Civilotti, 2017; Beer & Hornsveld, 2008; Bloomgarden & Calogero, 2008; de Jongh & de Roos, 2013; Dziegielewski & Wolfe, 2000; Janssen, 2012; Seijo, 2012; Yasar, Usta, Abamor, Taycan, & Kaya, 2017; Zaccagnino, Cussino, Callerame, Civilotti, & Fernandez, 2017b), *one reported magazine article* (Brewerton, 2008), and *67 conference presentations* for regional and national associations for the EMDR International Association, EMDR Canada, EMDR Europe, EMDR Iberoamerica, and EMDR Asia.

Hudson, Chase, and Pope's work (1998) cautioned against premature acceptance of EMDR therapy in the treatment of EDs because they were unable to find any methodologically sound studies showing its efficacy with EDs. They did mention that there was no sound theoretical basis to expect EMDR to be successful with this population; however, the understanding of the Adaptive Information Processing (AIP) Model in conjunction with the research on adverse child experiences and their proven contribution becomes relevant here. In fact, Guillaume et al. in their *Scientific Reports* article, "Associations Between Adverse Childhood Experiences and Clinical Characteristics of Eating Disorders," conclude:

> Our results contribute to research on the effects of early life trauma on eating disorders by demonstrating that childhood abuse increases the severity of EDs symptoms. These exacerbations are partially independent of comorbid psychiatric disorders. The subtypes of abuse do not all have the same impact, but they act additively to exacerbate the severity of a wide range of EDs features, including clinical and neuropsychological dimensions and daily functioning. (2016, "Discussion")

They implied that EMDR is a "recovered memory" therapy. This has never been a claim of Francine Shapiro in her texts or in her teachings. In fact, she clearly states in her 1995 text:

> There is often no way of knowing whether a memory that emerges is true or not. Indeed, the very attempt at memory retrieval as a therapeutic goal may establish the belief in the client that a memory of abuse exists, that it should be revealed, and that there was indeed a perpetrator. Thus, this scenario could provide the perfect conditions for eliciting "false" or mistaken memories. When a memory is reported during EMDR, there is a possibility that (1) the image is a symbolic representation, (2) the event in question was only vicariously experienced (e.g., through identification with a character in a story), (3) the image is the result of trickery (such as a perpetrator in disguise), or (4) that it is valid. *(Shapiro, 1995, p. 293)*

Their second concern is that using EMDR "may prevent or delay other therapies of established efficacy for eating disorders." Most EMDR practitioners see EMDR as part of a biopsychosocial model and use different modalities as well as EMDR to advance treatment efficacy. In 2018, EMDR therapy offers important contributions to the treatment of EDs.

Dziegielewski and Wolfe's (2000) single-subject case study design examined body image disturbance and self-esteem of the client. They used the Self-Esteem Rating Scale, the Body Image Avoidance Questionnaire (pre- and post-tests), and a self-developed Daily Body Satisfaction Log over 43 days. The scores showed improvement after EMDR, and they concluded EMDR merits further research. Bloomgarden and Calogero (2008) published the article titled "A Randomized Experimental Test of the Efficacy of EMDR Treatment on Negative Body Image in Eating Disorder Inpatients." They studied the short- and long-term effects of EMDR in a residential ED population. They used a randomized, experimental design and compared 43 women receiving standard residential eating disorders treatment (SRT) to 43 women receiving SRT and EMDR therapy, looking at measures of negative body image and other clinical outcomes. At the end of treatment, the SRT+EMDR group had less distress about negative body image memories and lower body dissatisfaction, and this improvement remained consistent in 3-month and 12-month follow-ups compared to the SRT group. The positive trend of the research suggested that EMDR might be helpful when working with specific aspects of negative body image while using SRT. More research was suggested.

Beer and Hornsveld (2008) wrote about EMDR and EDs. Although cognitive behavioral therapy (CBT) has a prominent place in the Multidisciplinary Guideline for Eating Disorders (Trimbos Institute, 2006), they noted that there were few controlled studies and they showed mixed results with significant relapses. Therefore, researchers and practitioners were looking for new perspectives on treatment. They decided to work with their adolescent ED patients with AN, and adults with binge EDs. They also shared clinical experiences in their working group of "EMDR with EDs." EMDR was part of a multidisciplinary outpatient treatment, so it is hard to determine what intervention did what. However, they noted that EMDR was able to create improvement where it would have been difficult or impossible to achieve with other methods.

Katrine Halvgaard (2015) reported a single case study with Emotional Eating (EE) using an adjusted version of the desensitization of triggers and urge reprocessing (DeTUR) protocol (Popky, 2009), including resource installation, affect management, ego state work, and the Standard EMDR Protocol. A 55-year-old woman had six weekly meetings of 1.5 hours and follow-ups at 3 and 6 months. The patient experienced an overall change after EMDR treatment in her eating behavior shown by self-report measures, including affect regulation, specific eating behaviors before and after, decrease of her urge to EE in triggering situations and EE over the week, and a more positive body image. Halvgaard concluded that this treatment could help reduce weight and stabilize weight after weight loss.

Zaccagnino, Cussino et al. (2017b) reported on a clinical case of a 17-year-old female inpatient with AN. At pretreatment, she weighed 62 pounds and had a BMI of 14. She had a dismissing attachment style. EMDR therapy was used for 6 months in twice-weekly sessions using the standard procedures and focusing on her relational traumas with psychoeducational talk therapy and ego state therapy. Post-treatment, she weighed 121 pounds and had a BMI of 21.5. She did not meet the diagnostic criteria for AN, and her attachment style changed to autonomous. She had an increase in her self-confidence, and she was more able to manage different social challenges. She maintained these gains at 12- and 24-month follow-ups. They viewed this as a promising finding for working with AN patients using EMDR. Yasar et al. (2017) reported using EMDR therapy on trauma-based restrictive eating cases. Two patients (one aged 18 years and another aged 20 years) presented with similar complaints of the sense of food sticking in their throat, breathing difficulties, increased heart rate, difficulty swallowing, and a fear of choking. Both noted that they had past traumatic events about being out of breath while swallowing that led them to restricting their food intake and choice of foods to eat. This resulted in their losing weight, health problems, changes in their daily routines, and social isolation. They were treated with EMDR therapy and, after five sessions, were able to return to their normal, healthy eating habits and lead a happier daily life. Yasar et al. concluded that EMDR can be used to treat EDs with trauma-related experiences.

There is a great need to find ways to resolve the turmoil and difficulties that patients with EDs face. As can be seen with the studies discussed previously, EMDR is showing a great deal of promise in working with EDs. There is a need for randomized controlled trials with the different types of EDs to see what EMDR can offer in the treatment of this complex and difficult-to-treat population.

The first section of *Eye Movement Desensitization and Reprocessing (EMDR) Therapy Scripted Protocols and Summary Sheets: Treating Eating Disorders, Chronic Pain, and Maladaptive Self-Care Behaviors* is called "Treating Eating and Body Image Dysregulation With EMDR Therapy" and includes four chapters on these issues. The authors demonstrate three different ways to conceptualize the treatment of eating and body image dysregulation.

The first chapter is by Renée Beer from the Netherlands, who is an EMDR Europe–accredited trainer for EMDR with children and adolescents. She emphasizes the importance in treating these disorders, as they have the possibility of developing into a chronic condition that creates a whole range of other problems such as medical complications, psychosocial problems, and other disorders. She discusses the Fairburn et al. (2013) "transdiagnostic model" as her framework for treatment. It is a model applicable to patients with AN, bulimia nervosa (BN), and binge eating disorder (BED) and consists of 11 modules: EMDR therapy is helpful in six of them (suffering from distressing memories, ED-related fears, ED-related urge-driven behaviors, low self-esteem, clinical perfectionism, and negative body image). She does not suggest that EMDR is a standalone therapy for ED and focuses on where EMDR adds value to the method. Her rationale is that symptoms such as fear of weight gain, negative body image, and low self-esteem seem to be sustained by intrusive and distressing negative images of either past or anticipated future experiences. Signs like binges and other compensatory behaviors create a compelling internal impulse to complete the behaviors; often they are triggered by intrusive positive images of anticipated effects of these behaviors.

She uses six procedures/paths for target selection representing five additional procedures/paths developed by Dutch trainers: *intrusion* (i.e., the most disturbing image; F. Shapiro, 2001), *timeline* (or first method, looking at symptoms or symptom clusters fixed on a timeline choosing the strongest connected to the onset; de Jongh, ten Broeke, & Meijer, 2010), *dysfunctional belief* (second method, includes identifying the memories that serve as the foundation for the dysfunctional core beliefs and discrediting them through processing; de Jongh et al., 2010), *flash-forward* (third method, the worst image of the disaster scenario that addresses irrational fears and anticipatory anxiety responses that continue after the past memories are processed; van der Vleugel, van den Berg, de Bont, Staring, & de Jongh, 2016), *dysfunctional positive targets* (positive memories of past-, present-, or future-oriented fantasies that activate the urge to perform the dysfunctional behaviors; Hornsveld & Markus, 2018; Markus & Hornsveld, 2015), and *emotion* (addresses common difficult emotions; F. Shapiro, 2001). When the outcome of a module is reached and the appropriate memories are deactivated, the next module is chosen until all are completed.

Maria Zaccagnino is the co-director of the Center of EMDR Therapy for Eating Disorders in Milan with Isabel Fernandez. She writes about the very serious disease of AN in her chapter, "EMDR Therapy Protocol for the Management of Dysfunctional Eating Behaviors in Anorexia Nervosa." AN is due to many biopsychosocial and cultural components and is one of the psychiatric disorders with the highest mortality rates (Arcelus, Mitchell, Wales, & Nielsen, 2011; Harris & Barraclough, 1997). According to the *Diagnostic and Statistical Manual of Mental Disorders* (5th ed.; *DSM-5;* American Psychiatric Association, 2013), the criteria for diagnosing AN are the following: a terror of gaining weight and looking fat, restriction of food intake, disturbed body image and weight experiences, as well as a denial that anything is wrong. AN patients also demonstrate more depression, attention deficit disorder, loss of libido, obsessive symptoms, and social isolation. She noted a number of traits and behaviors that can be risk factors for AN: body image distortion for self and attributed to others, need for control, perfectionism, sense of inadequacy/social insecurity/low self-esteem, and alexithymia. She reported that AN patients often have a life that has many traumatic experiences that can include physical and/or psychological maltreatment and sexual abuse in childhood, as well as neglect (Johnson, Cohen, Kasen, & Brook, 2006; Speranza & Alberigi, 2006; Steiger & Zankor, 1990; Vize & Cooper, 1995; Welch & Fairburn, 1994). They have difficulty with emotional regulation and often have dysfunctional attachment relationships resulting in internal working models (IWMs) of attachment that form the framework for future relationships (Siegel, 1999). Zaccagnino et al. (2016, submitted) reported on a research study to see if processing of traumatic memories related to patients' ED with EMDR will allow them to separate past and present, eventually leading to a decrease in their ED. They compared EMDR with CBT and found that with the CBT group there was noticeable improvement with symptoms of EDs. On the other hand, EMDR therapy resulted in a resolution of unresolved psychological issues, a change in the internal representations of caregivers, an increase in the positive neural networks related to their distressing memories, and an amelioration of their negative beliefs about their self-worth and vulnerability, resulting in a greater sense of well-being and health.

In working with target identification, Zaccagnino addressed the following important targets: the triggering/precipitating event, big "T" traumas, food-related relational history using parts to address bingeing and purging behaviors or restrictive behaviors, food issues with family, and targets connected to symptomatology. When working with this population, working with parts—especially the control part—is helpful, and Zaccagnino explains how to go about it, including the script for the use of the Dissociative Table Exercise with both acute and nonacute situations. However, her main protocol is for work with AN patients during the nonacute phase. She includes a helpful case conceptualization worksheet that incorporates past memories, present triggers/flash-forwards, future templates, resource identification, and a resource installation script.

Natalia Seijo is the author of Chapters 3 and 4, "EMDR Therapy Protocol for Eating Disorders," and its companion, "The Rejected Self EMDR: Therapy Protocol for Body Image Distortion." Her publications in this field link trauma attachment and dissociation, as do her chapters. She believes in going to the heart of the trauma to work with what created the disorder, and she believes that EMDR is successful in doing just that and repairing it. Her main focus is on identifying the structure of the client's inner world, defusing the defenses, and working through the big "T" and small "t" traumas. Her other suggestion is to remember that when you are working with a patient with an ED, there is a hurt little boy or girl who needs assistance. In the preparation phase, it is crucial to work to identify the patient's inner world and soothe and process the defenses. When doing this, it is important to validate the client, demonstrate empathy and understanding, and help with organizing the client's inner world and its parts. She names the inner girls/boys and assists patients in understanding the protective function that each one has: The Little Girl/Boy Who Never Was (working with control), the Little Girl/ Boy Who Could Not Grow Up (working with guilt), the Pathological Critic/the Piranha (working with perfectionism), the Hidden Self (working with shame and fear), the Rejected Self (working with body image distortion and the subject of Chapter 4), and the Fatty Self (working with rejection and submission). She promotes working from the outside layer by starting with the Part (i.e., the Little Girl/Boy

Who Never Was, etc.), then moving to the next layer—the Defense—and the next layer—the Trauma. When the defenses are neutralized, the traumas can be processed. She suggests different sub-protocols to reprocess the main defenses. The defenses that she works with are the following: lack of illness awareness, somatic, alexithymia, hunger, and fear of improvement. Also, she points out that during the desensitization phase, patients do somatic processing and if therapists pay attention to the body, it is possible to identify changes.

"EMDR Therapy Protocol for Body Image Distortion" is a more in-depth view of "The Rejected Self" that was discussed in Chapter 3. The idea behind this chapter is to deactivate the three emotional defenses—rejection, shame, and worry—as well as the body image distortion defense that prevents patients from having a complete awareness of their bodies and creates a barrier between the true body image and the rejected self. Ultimately, patients need to develop awareness of their bodies and reach a time of acceptance. It is important to assess how real the patient's self-image is and—if it is not—how it came to be this way. The body image distortion can be in the past or in the present. The rejected self of the past often is related to attachment traumas, whereas the rejected self of the present is connected to a traumatic incident. To support patients dealing with the rejected self, she suggests building resources such as "Positive Comments/Affect," using "Loving Eyes," and/or accessing an "Ideal Figure" that makes them feel good. She helps patients learn about healthy self-care for basic day-to-day functions. Often, it is the mother figure who comes out as the main relationship that needs to be repaired. This is because the maternal figure's acknowledgment and validation provides the building blocks for the concept of self, and when it is lacking, patients' self-concepts are built on a weak foundation. The actual rejected self is a dissociated part and the body image distortion is how the rejected self defends itself from the pain it would feel if facing reality.

After the rejected self is accessed, the defenses of rejection, shame, and worry are explored individually, and then together, as work with the standard EMDR protocol occurs. This is processed until it is clear and positive associations occur. The installation includes Knipe's (2015) "Loving Eyes" protocols to support the integration of the part. The Future Template and Video Check are also used.

To support the use of these protocols, summary sheets accompany chapters to produce a reminder of the most important themes in the chapter and to give a space to enter information about patients.

REFERENCES

American Psychiatric Association. (2013). *Diagnostic and statistical manual of mental disorders* (5th ed.). Arlington, VA: American Psychiatric Publishing.

Arcelus, J., Mitchell, A. J., Wales, J., & Nielsen, S. (2011). Mortality rates in patients with anorexia nervosa and other eating disorders: A meta-analysis of 36 studies. *Archives of General Psychiatry, 68*(7), 724–731. doi:10.1001/archgenpsychiatry.2011.74

Balbo, M., Zaccagnino, M., Cussino, M., & Civilotti, C. (2017, October). Eye movement desensitization and reprocessing (EMDR) and eating disorders: A systematic review. *Clinical Neuropsychiatry, 14*(5), 321–329.

Beer, R., & Hornsveld, H. (2008). [EMDR in the treatment of eating disorders]. In E. ten Broeke, A. de Jongh, & H. Oppenheim (Eds.), *Praktijkboek EMDR: Casusconceptualisatie en specifieke patientengroepen* (pp. 201–243). Amsterdam, The Netherlands: Harcourt Press. [Dutch]

Bitter, J. (1992, April). *Eating disorders*. Presentation at the EMDR Network Conference, Sunnyvale, CA.

Bloomgarden, A., & Calogero, R. M. (2008, October-December). A randomized experimental test of the efficacy of EMDR treatment on negative body image in eating disorder inpatients. *Eating Disorders, 16*(5), 418–427. doi:10.1080/10640260802370598

Brewerton, T. D. (2008, May 1). The links between PTSD and eating disorders. *Psychiatric Times, 25*(6), 1–7.

Bruch, H. (1973). *Eating disorders: Obesity, anorexia nervosa, and the person within* (Vol. 5052). New York, NY: Basic Books.

Cameron, V. L. (2013, May). *EMDR: Promising treatment for co-occurring eating disorders and childhood sexual abuse* (Master's thesis, St. Catherine University). Retrieved from http://sophia.stkate.edu/msw_papers/160

Carpenter, M. N. (1999). *Eye movement desensitization and reprocessing in battered women: Alleviation of post-traumatic stress disorder*. Retrieved from Proquest Dissertations and Theses database (UMI. No. 1394355).

Culbert, K. M., Racine, S. E., & Klump, K. L. (2015). Research review: What we have learned about the causes of eating disorders—A synthesis of sociocultural, psychological, and biological research. *Journal of Child Psychology and Psychiatry, 56*(11), 1141–1164. doi:10.1111/jcpp.12441

de Jongh, A., ten Broeke, E., & Meijer, S. (2010). Two method questioning approach: A case conceptualization model in the context of EMDR. *Journal of EMDR Practice and Research, 4*(1), 12–21. doi:10.1891/1933-3196.4.1.12

de Jongh, A., & de Roos, C. (2013). [If memories are in the way]. *Modern Medicine, 3*, 85–88. [Dutch]. Retrieved from https://www.hgpdesign.nl/news/138/210/Modern-Medicine

Diemer, E. W., Grant, J. D., Munn-Chernoff, M. A., Patterson, D., & Duncan, A. E. (2015). Gender identity, sexual orientation, and eating-related pathology in a national sample of college students. *Journal of Adolescent Health, 57*(2), 144–149. doi:10.1016/j.jadohealth.2015.03.003

Dziegielewski, S., & Wolfe, P. (2000, September). Eye movement desensitization and reprocessing (EMDR) as a time-limited treatment intervention for body image disturbance and self-esteem: A single subject case study design. *Journal of Psychotherapy in Independent Practice, 1*(3), 1–16. doi:10.1300/J288v01n03_01

Eating Disorders Coalition. (2016). Facts about eating disorders: What the research shows. Retrieved from http://eatingdisorderscoalition.org.s208556.gridserver.com/couch/uploads/file/fact-sheet_2016.pdf

Fairburn, C. G., Cooper, Z., Doll, H. A., O'Connor, M. E., Palmer, R. L., & Dalle Grave, R. (2013). Enhanced cognitive behavior therapy for adults with anorexia nervosa: A UK–Italy study. *Behavior Research and Therapy, 51*, R2–R8. doi:10.1016/j.brat.2012.09.010

Fiol, I. T. (1997). *Emotional overeating and EMDR: A case study* (Doctoral dissertation). Argosy University, Chicago, IL.

Gagne, D. A., Von Holle, A., Brownley, K. A., Runfola, C. D., Hofmeier, S., Branch, K. E., & Bulik, C. M. (2012). Eating disorder symptoms and weight and shape concerns in a large web-based convenience sample of women ages 50 and above: Results of the gender and body image (GABI) study. *International Journal of Eating Disorders, 45*(7), 832–844. doi:10.1002/eat.22030

Gamba, M. (2005). EMDR integration into the psychotherapy of eating disorders. University of Padova. Retrieved from http://www.emdritalia.it/ita/tesi_di_laurea-M_Gamba_-__Emdr_e_disturbi_del_comportamento.pdf [Italian]

Gordon, R. A. (2001). Eating disorders East and West: A culture-bound syndrome unbound. In M. Nasser, M. Katzman, & R. Gordon (Eds.), *Eating disorders and cultures in transition* (pp. 1–16). New York, NY: Brunner-Routledge.

Gross, L., & Ratner, H. (2002). The use of hypnosis and EMDR combined with energy therapies in the treatment of phobias and dissociative, posttraumatic stress, and eating disorders. In F. P. Gallo (Ed.), *Energy psychology in psychotherapy: A comprehensive sourcebook* (1st ed., pp. 219–231). New York, NY: W. W. Norton.

Guillaume, S., Jaussent, I., Maimoun, L., Ryst, A., Seneque, M., Villain, L., ... Courtet, P. (2016). Associations between adverse childhood experiences and clinical characteristics of eating disorders. *Scientific Reports, 6*, 35761. doi:10.1038/srep35761

Gull, W. W. (1874). Anorexia nervosa (apepsia hysterica, anorexia hysteria). *Transactions of the Clinical Society of London, 7*, 22–28.

Halvgaard, K. (2015). Single case study: Does EMDR psychotherapy work on emotional eating? *Journal of EMDR Practice and Research, 9*(4), 188–197. doi:10.1891/1933-3196.9.4.188

Harris, E. C., & Barraclough, B. (1997). Suicide as an outcome for mental disorders. A meta-analysis. *British Journal of Psychiatry, 170*, 205–228. doi:10.1192/bjp.170.3.205

Hornsveld, H., & Markus, W. (2014). *EMDR bij verslaving.* [Protocol for alcohol dependency]. Retrieved from https://hornsveldpsychologenpraktijk.files.wordpress.com/2018/06/peia_en-final-june-20181.pdf

Hudson, J. I., Chase, E. A., & Pope, H. G. (1998, January). Eye movement desensitization and reprocessing in eating disorders: Caution against premature acceptance. *International Journal of Eating Disorders, 23*(1), 1–5. doi: 10.1002/(SICI)1098-108X(199801)23:1<1::AID-EAT1>3.3.CO;2-P

Hudson, J. I., Hiripi, E., Pope, H. G., & Kessler, R. C. (2007). The prevalence and correlates of eating disorders in the national comorbidity survey replication. *Biological Psychiatry, 61*(3), 348–358. doi:10.1016/j.biopsych.2006.03.040

Jacobson, I. G., Smith, T. C., Smith, B., Keel, P. K., Amoroso, P. J., Wells, T. S., . . . Ryan, M. A. (2009). Disordered eating and weight changes after deployment: Longitudinal assessment of a large US military cohort. *American Journal of Epidemiology, 169*(4), 415–427. doi:10.1093/aje/kwn366

Janssen, J. (2012, February). A special case (series): EMDR treatment of early childhood trauma in a client with an eating disorder. *Tijdschrift voor Psychotherapie, 38*(1), 21–37. doi:10.1007/s12485-012-0003-3 [Dutch]

Johnson, J. G., Cohen, P., Kasen, S., & Brook, J. S. (2006). Dissociative disorders among adults in the community, impaired functioning, and axis I and II comorbidity. *Journal of Psychiatric Research, 40,* 131–140. doi:10.1016/j.jpsychires.2005.03.003

Jung, J. H., & Forbes, G. B. (2006). Multidimensional assessment of body dissatisfaction and disordered eating in Korean and US college women: A comparative study. *Sex Roles, 55*(1–2), 39–50. doi:10.1007/s11199-006-9058-3

Jung, J. H., Forbes, G. B., & Chan, P. (2010). Global body and muscle satisfaction among college men in the United States and Hong Kong-China. *Sex Roles, 63*(1–2), 104–117. doi:10.1007/s11199-010-9760-z

Jung, J. H., Forbes, G. V., & Lee, Y. J. (2009). Body dissatisfaction and disordered eating among early adolescents from Korea and the US. *Sex Roles, 61*(1–2), 42–54. doi:10.1007/s11199-009-9609-5

Kayano, M., Yoshiuchi, K., Al-Adawi, S., Viernes, N., Dorvlo, A. S., Kumano, H., ... Akabayashi, A. (2008). Eating attitudes and body dissatisfaction in adolescents: Cross-cultural study. *Psychiatry and Clinical Neurosciences, 62*(1), 17–25. doi:10.1111/j.1440-1819.2007.01772.x

Knipe, J. (2015). Loving eyes: "Looking" from one part to another. In J. Knipe, *EMDR Toolbox: Theory and treatment of complex PTSD and dissociation* (pp. 173–182). New York, NY: Springer Publishing.

Lee, H. Y., & Lock, J. (2007). Anorexia nervosa in Asian-American adolescents: Do they differ from their non-Asian peers. *International Journal of Eating Disorders, 40*(3), 227–31. doi:10.1002/eat.20364

Lee, S., Ng, K. L., Kwok, K., & Fung, C. (2010). The changing profile of eating disorders at a tertiary psychiatric clinic in Hong Kong (1987–2007). *International Journal of Eating Disorders, 43*(4), 307–314. doi:10.1002/eat.20686

Le Grange, D., Swanson, S. A., Crow, S. J., & Merikangas, K. R. (2012). Eating disorder not otherwise specified presentation in the US population. *International Journal of Eating Disorders, 45*(5), 711–718. doi:10.1002/eat.22006

Markus, W., & Hornsveld, H. K. (2015). EMDR en verslaving [EMDR and addiction]. In H-J. Oppenheim, H. K. Hornsveld, E. ten Broeke, & A. de Jongh (Eds.), *Praktijkboek EMDR II* (pp. 437–491). Amsterdam, the Netherlands: Pearson.

Marques, L., Alegria, M., Becker, A. E., Chen, C.-N., Fang, A., Chosak, A., & Diniz, J. B. (2011). Comparative prevalence, correlates of impairment, and service utilization for eating disorders across US ethnic groups: Implications for reducing ethnic disparities in health care access for eating disorders. *International Journal of Eating Disorders, 44*(5), 412–420. doi:10.1002/eat.20787

Miceli, E. (2009). *Eye movement desensitization and reprocessing (EMDR) in the treatment of eating disorders, with quantitative evaluations using electroencephalograms (QEEG) and self-reports as subjective evaluations* (Dissertation). Argosy University, Atlanta, GA.

Mond, J. M., Chen, A., & Kumar, R. (2010). Eating-disordered behavior in Australian and Singaporean women: A comparative study. *International Journal of Eating Disorders, 43*(8), 717–723. doi:10.1002/eat.20771

National Association of Anorexia Nervosa and Associated Disorders. (2018). Eating disorder statistics. Retrieved from http://www.anad.org/get-information/about-eating-disorders/eating-disorders-statistics

Pike, K. M., & Dunne, P. E. (2015). The rise of eating disorders in Asia: A review. *Journal of Eating Disorders, 3,* 33. doi:10.1186/s40337-015-0070-2

Pike, K. M., Yamamiya, Y., & Konishi, H. (2011). Eating disorders in Japan: Cultural context, clinical features, and future directions. In R. H. Streigel-Moore, S. A. Wonderlich, B. T. Walsh, & J. Mitchell (Eds.), *Developing an evidence-based classification of eating disorders: Scientific findings for* DSM-V. Arlington, VA: American Psychiatric Association.

Plassmann, R. (Ed.). (2009). [*In our own rhythm, the connection allergy disorders EMDR treatment of eating disorders, pain, anxiety disorders, tinnitus and addictions*]. Giessen, Germany: Psychosozial-Verlag.

Popky, A. J. (2009). The desensitization of triggers and urge reprocessing (DeTUR) protocol. In M. Luber (Ed.), *Eye movement desensitization and reprocessing (EMDR) scripted protocols:* Special populations (pp. 489–511). New York, NY: Springer Publishing.

Schulherr, S. (2005). Exiting the binge-diet cycle. In R. Shapiro (Ed.), *EMDR solutions: Pathways to healing* (pp. 241–262). New York, NY: W. W. Norton.

Seijo, N. (2012). EMDR and eating disorders. *Revista Iberoamericana de Psicotraumatologa y Disociacin, 4*(2). Retrieved from http://revibapst.com/data/documents/YORECHAZADO.pdf

Seubert, A., & Virdi, P. (Eds.). (2018). *Trauma-informed approaches to eating disorders.* New York, NY: Springer Publishing.

Shapiro, F. (1995). *Eye movement desensitization and reprocessing (EMDR): Basic principles, protocols, and procedures.* New York, NY: Guilford Press.

Shapiro, F. (1998). Eye movement desensitization and reprocessing (EMDR): Historical context, recent research, and future directions. In L. Vandecreek, S. Knapp, & T. L. Jackson (Eds.), *Innovations in clinical practice: A source book* (pp. 143–162). Sarasosta, FL: Professional Resource Press.

Shapiro, F. (2001). *Eye movement desensitization and reprocessing (EMDR): Basic principles, protocols, and procedures* (2nd ed.). New York, NY: Guilford Press.

Shapiro, R. (2009). *EMDR Solutions II: For depression, eating disorders, performance, and more.* New York, NY: W. W. Norton.

Siegel, D. J. (1999). *The developing mind: Toward a neurobiology of interpersonal experience.* New York, NY: Guilford Press.

Smink, F. E., van Hoeken, D., & Hoek, H. W. (2012). Epidemiology of eating disorders: Incidence, prevalence and mortality rates. *Current Psychiatry Reports, 14*(4), 406–414. doi:10.1007/s11920-012-0282-y

Speranza, A. M., & Alberigi, E. (2006). La relazione tra abuso e disturbi alimentari: il ruolo della dissociazione. *Maltrattamento e Abuso all'Infanzia, 8*(1), 23–47.

Steiger, H., & Zankor, M. (1990). Sexual traumata among eating-disordered, psychiatric, and normal female groups: Comparison of prevalences and defense styles. *Journal of Interpersonal Violence, 5,* 74–86. doi:10.1177/088626090005001006

The Renfrew Center Foundation for Eating Disorders. (2003). *Eating disorders 101 guide: A summary of issues, statistics and resources.* Philadelphia, PA: The Renfrew Center.

Trimbos Institute. (2006). *Multidisciplinaire Richtlijn Eetstoornissen [Multidisciplinary Guideline for Eating Disorders]. Diagnostiek en behandeling van eetstoornissen.* Houten, the Netherlands: Trimbos-Instituut.

Tsai, G. (2000). Eating disorders in the Far East. *Eating and Weight Disorders—Studies on Anorexia, Bulimia and Obesity, 5*(4), 183–197. doi:10.1007/bf03354445

Vandereycken, W., & van Deth, R. (1990). A tribute to Lasegue's description of anorexia nervosa (1873), with completion of its English translation. *British Journal of Psychiatry, 157,* 902–908. doi:10.1192/bjp.157.6.902

van der Vleugel, B., van den Berg, D., de Bont, P., Staring, T., & de Jongh, A. (2016). EMDR for traumatized patients with psychosis. In M. Luber (Ed.), *Eye movement desensitization and reprocessing (EMDR) therapy: Scripted protocols and summary sheets: Treating trauma- and stressor-related conditions* (pp. 97–148). New York, NY: Springer Publishing.

Van Trier, J. (2009). Case 3—Plaything of my emotions . . . : An eating disorder after a rape at lbiza: An unexpected turn in the treatment. In H. K. Hornsveld & S. Berendsen (Eds.), *Casusboek EMDR, 25 voorbeelden uit de praktij* (pp. 75–84.) Houten, the Netherlands: Bohn Stafleu Van Loghum.

Vize, C. M., & Cooper, P. J. (1995). Sexual abuse in patients with eating disorder, patients with depression and normal controls: A comparative study. *British Journal of Psychiatry, 167,* 80–85. doi:10.1192/bjp.167.1.80

Wan, F., Faber, R. J., & Fung, A. (2003). Perceived impact of thin female models in advertising: aAcross-cultural examination of third person perception and its impact on behaviors. *Asia Pacific Journal of Marketing and Logistics, 5*(1/2), 51–73. doi:10.1108/13555850310765079

Welch, S., & Fairburn, C. G. (1994). Sexual abuse and bulimia nervosa: Three integrated case control comparisons. *American Journal of Psychiatry, 151,* 402–407. doi:10.1176/ajp.151.3.402

Yasar, A. B., Usta, F. D., Abamor, A. E., Taycan, S. E., & Kaya, B. (2017). EMDR therapy on trauma-based restrictive eating cases. *European Psychiatry, 41,* S560–S561. doi:10.1016.j.eurpsy.2017.01.81

Zaccagnino, M., Cussino, M., Callerame, C., Civilotti, C., & Fernandez, I. (Submitted 2016). *EMDR and CBT for anorexic patients: A clinical comparative study, eating and weight disorders—Studies on anorexia, bulimia and obesity.*

Zaccagnino, M., Cussino, M., Callerame, C., Civilotti, C., & Fernandez, I. (2017a, February). EMDR in anorexia nervosa: From a theoretical framework to the treatment guidelines. In I. Jauregui-Lobera (Ed.), *Eating disorders—A paradigm of the biopsychosocial model of illness* (pp. 195–213). Rijeka, Croatia: InTech.

Zaccagnino, M., Cussino, M., Callerame, C., Civilotti, C., & Fernandez, I. (2017b). Anorexia nervosa and EMDR: A clinical case. *Journal of EMDR Practice and Research, 11*(1), 43–53. doi:10.1891/1933-3196.11.1.43

PROTOCOL FOR EMDR THERAPY IN THE TREATMENT OF EATING DISORDERS

1

Renée Beer

INTRODUCTION

Eating disorders (ED)—anorexia nervosa (AN), bulimia nervosa (BN), and binge eating disorder (BED)—are persistent and complex disorders and, therefore, a challenge for therapists with any theoretical orientation. Regularly, eating disorders develop into chronic disorders supplemented by medical complications, psychosocial problems, (ED) and comorbid psychopathology. International guidelines advise treatment by an interdisciplinary team of specialists with a common view, offering a broad-spectrum approach (Multidisciplinary Guidelines for Eating Disorders, 2006; National Institute for Health and Clinical Excellence, 2004, 2017).

A prominent place is reserved for cognitive behavioral therapy (CBT). However, empirical data of treatment outcome studies show mixed results with significant relapse rates for all eating disorders (American Psychiatric Association, 2013; Steinglass et al., 2011). BN and BED patients show relatively positive results after treatment with CBT (Agras & Apple, 1997; Dingemans, Bruna, & van Furth, 2001; Wilson & Fairburn, 2007). Nonetheless, for AN no treatment of choice is available yet, based on empirical grounds, and for other eating disorders current treatments are inadequate for relapse prevention (Steinglass et al., 2011). This implies that treatment of patients with an eating disorder—especially AN—is expensive because generally patients are "in treatment" for many years. Existing treatments are insufficient, and new effective and efficient treatment approaches are needed.

Patients with different eating disorders not only have distinct features but also share common ones. Besides, patients can switch over time from one disorder to another. For this reason, Fairburn, Cooper, and Shafran (2003) introduced the "transdiagnostic perspective": a theoretical cognitive behavioral model applicable to different eating disorders explaining how the disorder is maintained by mechanisms that perpetuate vicious circles. This transdiagnostic model (Fairburn et al., 2003) assumes that eating disorders share *core psychopathology* (i.e., overvaluation of eating, weight, and shape and their control) and several *additional factors* that are present in different degrees in affected individuals and can interact with both these core symptoms and with each other (i.e., clinical perfectionism, low self-esteem, trouble with intense mood states, and interpersonal problems).

This model is applicable to AN, BN, and BED and has been translated into therapeutic programs that have been tested empirically (Dalle Grave, Calugi, Doll, & Fairbirn, 2013; Fairburn et al., 2009, 2013). Binge eating and purging stop completely in 30% to 50% of the patients, another group shows some improvement, and the rest drop out of treatment or do not respond (Wilson & Fairburn, 2007).

Based on Fairburn's transdiagnostic model, a treatment program has been developed for adolescent patients with AN, BN, and atypical eating disorders, consisting of 11 potential modules, each focusing on different aspects of eating disorders that are treated with cognitive behavioral interventions (Beer & Tobias, 2011). Clinical experience has demonstrated that EMDR therapy can be implemented efficiently in several of these modules and that a combination of CBT interventions and EMDR enhances the effectiveness of both. Moreover, therapists who do not work with CBT interventions can work with these modules and apply EMDR, when there is an indication for EMDR. This is the case whenever intrusive images are motivating the psychopathology. EMDR therapy can play a significant role in the following modules:

- Suffering from distressing memories
- Eating disorder–related fears
- Eating disorder–related urge-driven behaviors
- Low self-esteem
- Clinical perfectionism
- Negative body image

In this chapter, an EMDR eating disorders (EMDR-ED) protocol, as integrated in the eight phases of the Standard EMDR Protocols, will be described. It is geared to treat the unique issues that arise when using EMDR therapy to treat either the potential focuses of concern or parts of the disorder translated into modules.

In line with the guidelines, EMDR therapy is considered a valuable supplement, but not sufficient as a standalone therapy for the treatment of an eating disorder. Neither is the case with CBT or family therapy because eating disorders demand a broad-spectrum treatment. The aim of this chapter is to clarify when and how EMDR therapy can be a part of the broad-spectrum treatment of patients with an eating disorder.

Because the EMDR-ED protocol involves six modules, covering relevant mechanisms mentioned by Fairburn et al. (2003), and six potential procedures for target selection, both the potential modules and procedures will be explained. Five of these procedures for target selection to be described have been developed in the Netherlands.

The application of the EMDR-ED protocol, as described here, has not yet been validated empirically. An earlier version, focusing on binges, self-esteem, and body image, has been used in the Netherlands since its publication (Beer & Hornsveld, 2012), but no data are available related to its effectiveness.

Members of the Special Interest Group for EMDR and Eating Disorders of the Dutch EMDR Association have been exchanging clinical experiences with this "protocol-in-progress" since 2010.

In 2014, a pilot study was published that tested the efficacy of the standard EMDR protocol on change in the body image while distressing memories of adverse experiences were reprocessed by the participants. After 5.4 sessions on average, a positive change was found in the body image of all 13 women included (Pepers & Swart, 2014). Whether this change had an impact on their eating disorder or on treatment progress is not clear. This was not measured.

Roedelof (2016) started a study exploring whether empirical validation can be established for the efficacy of this EMDR-ED protocol on the change of distorted negative body image.

FEATURES IN EATING DISORDERS

The most prominent psychological features of distinct eating disorders according to the *ICD-10* (www .eatingdisorders.org.au) are listed. Pica, rumination, and avoidant/restrictive food intake disorders are left out.

Anorexia Nervosa (AN)

- Body weight is maintained at least 15% below that expected (either lost or never achieved), or Quetelet body mass index is 17.5 or less. Prepubertal patients may show failure in making the expected weight gain during the period of growth.
- Weight loss is self-induced by avoidance of food intake and possibly one or more compensatory behaviors: self-induced purging (vomiting, using laxatives and/or diuretics), excessive exercise, and/or use of appetite suppressants.
- Distorted body image; a dread of fatness persists as an intrusive, overvalued idea, and the patient imposes a low weight threshold on him/herself.
- In prepubertal patients, the pubertal development may be delayed or arrested.

Bulimia Nervosa (BN)

- Persistent preoccupation with eating, irresistible craving for food, and episodes of overeating where large amounts of food are consumed in short periods of time (binges).

- Attempts to counteract the "fattening" effects of food by one or more compensatory behaviors: self-induced purging (vomiting, using laxatives and/or diuretics), excessive exercise, and/or use of appetite suppressants.
- A morbid dread of (disgust for) fatness, leading to setting a sharply defined threshold for him/herself, well below a normal, healthy weight.

Binge Eating Disorder (BED)

- Recurrent episodes of binge eating, characterized by frequently eating excessive amounts of food, often when not hungry.
- Binges represent a distraction that allows a person to avoid thinking about the real root of the problems.
- Feelings of guilt, disgust, and depression often follow a bingeing episode.
- Binge eating disorder is not the same as overeating, as it is recurrent and more serious.
- The binges are not associated with recurrent inappropriate compensatory behavior (self-induced purging: vomiting, using laxatives and/or diuretics).

MEASURES

Different validated instruments are available in different countries/languages. The following instruments are recommended:

- *Eating Disorder Inventory—3* (EDI-3; Garner, 2004). The EDI assesses psychological domains that have conceptual relevance in understanding and treating eating disorders.
- *Eating Disorder Examination* (EDE; Fairburn & Cooper, 1993). The EDE is a semistructured interview directed at general ED symptomatology, not specifically at distorted body perception.
- *Eating Disorder Examination Questionnaire* (EDEQ; Fairburn & Beglin, 1994). The EDEQ is a self-report questionnaire derived from the EDE, which contains its three main subscales (restraint, weight concern, and shape concern).
- *Body Shape Questionnaire* (BSQ; Cooper, Taylor, Cooper, & Fairburn, 1987). The BSQ is a self-report questionnaire that measures body dissatisfaction, the fear of becoming fat, self-devaluation due to physical appearance, the desire to lose weight, and avoidance of situations where physical appearance might draw others' attention.

PREVALENCE AND PROGNOSIS

The prevalence of eating disorders is relatively high among adolescents, taking the third position in the top five of psychiatric disorders (Vandereycken & Noorderbos, 2008). Eating disorders have been identified as one of the most common and serious forms of adolescent disorders in developed societies (Slade, 1995). However, in the general population this is different: Prevalence of AN is about 0.3% and BN 1%. AN is manifested mainly among women. The peak of onset for AN is between 14 and 18 years of age and for BN it is between 16 and 20 years. Over the past years, the onset of AN at even younger ages has been rising. If the onset is during puberty/adolescence after the menarche, the prognosis is better than with an earlier start before the menarche or an onset later in life. In about 50% of AN patients there is complete recovery, 30% show progress, and 20% remain chronically ill (van Elburg & Danner, 2015).

BED though is not primarily a female disorder; the prevalence is comparable to BN, around 1%, and the rate of prevalence is equal for men and women (Hoek & Van Hoeken, 2003).

Eating disorders have the highest mortality rate of all psychiatric disorders. As many as 15% of AN patients die of the consequences (complications) of the disorder, two-thirds by starvation, and one-third by suicide (van Elburg & Danner, 2015).

EATING DISORDERS AND TRAUMA

Specific risk factors for either onset or maintenance of eating disorders have not been identified yet. Adverse or traumatic experiences—like having been bullied or excluded or having been sexually assaulted—often precede the onset of the disorder, but they are not specific factors. They happen more often than in healthy controls, but not in the same degree in comparison to other psychiatric patients (Multidisciplinary Guidelines for Eating Disorders, 2006). It has been observed that sexual trauma plays a role in 20% to 40% of all adult patients with an eating disorder (Vandereycken & Noorderbos, 2008). Fairburn et al. (2003) discuss the vital importance of negative self-esteem as a risk factor, but the potential significant role of traumatic or adverse experiences in this respect is not mentioned.

Group therapy is "core business" in most specialized institutions for eating disorders, focused on the change of eating patterns and the general themes, as described by Fairburn and colleagues. In most cases, there is neither room nor expertise for individual treatment of trauma. Eating disorders and trauma are considered two separate issues. In clinical practice and in published case studies, nevertheless, adverse or traumatic experiences are reported to be "present" in many patients with an eating disorder.

A full-blown PTSD is diagnosed rarely because, often, the patient develops the eating disorder more as a kind of self-medication or coping against trauma symptoms. Minor "t" traumas, like being assaulted or neglected, result regularly in the presence of negative self-esteem, negative beliefs about body appearance, and dieting issues in this population (Ferreira, Pinto-Gouveia, & Duarte, 2013; Pepers & Swart, 2014).

A negative body image is a persistent and invalidating aspect of an eating disorder, difficult to treat, and a significant predictor of relapse, if it has not disappeared by the end of treatment (Stice & Shaw, 2002). Anorexia nervosa patients have an internal model of their body size that is bigger than reality (Keizer et al., 2015), which can manifest as a delusional symptom. This internal model can result from adverse (traumatic) experiences. In patients where this is the case EMDR therapy could have a significant effect on this delusional symptom.

EATING DISORDERS AND EMDR THERAPY

The rationale for the implementation of EMDR therapy in the treatment of an eating disorder is that several symptoms, such as fear of weight gain (or other fears), negative body image, and low self-esteem, seem to be motivated and maintained by *intrusive and distressing negative images of either past or anticipated future experiences*. Other symptoms—like binges and compensatory behaviors (vomiting, using laxatives, or hyperactivity)—seem to be motivated by a compelling urge to perform these behaviors, where this urge is activated by *intrusive positive images of anticipated effects of these specific behaviors*. These anticipated effects are positive because either a required state is achieved or a feared state is avoided. Some examples of these required states are the following: an emotional state (relief, consolation) or a physical sensation (liberation of satiation or bloating). Distressing for the patient is the fact that he/she knows that the behavior leads to negative consequences ultimately, but he/she is short of alternative responses.

Whenever any (eating disorder) behavior serves to cope with problems that result from *intrusive and distressing images*, EMDR therapy is to be considered an option.

In addition to this rationale, there is a collateral attraction to use EMDR therapy because it is a pleasant therapy approach for patients with an eating disorder for several reasons:

- *Experiential orientation*: In EMDR therapy, cognitive, physical, and emotional changes happen instantly and simultaneously. Changes are not the result of explicit self-control and motivation-based efforts, but they simply arise and the patient needs to only notice them.
- *Respect*: EMDR therapy relies on the AIP model (F. Shapiro, 2001) and the self-healing power of the individual. Whatever the patient experiences during the process is regarded as valuable. This is often a relief for these patients, who have been confronted with irritation, frustration, and incomprehension by people in their environment and by themselves during many years of futile attempts at improving self-control.

EMDR PROTOCOL FOR EATING DISORDERS SCRIPT NOTES

The Standard EMDR Protocol has eight phases, and the EMDR protocol for eating disorders (EMDR-ED) protocol covers these phases. The EMDR-ED protocol indicates how six potential modules can fit into the structure of the eight phases of the standard protocol.

Part of the history-taking phase (the target selection) is repeated several times for the identification of targets to be reprocessed within a module. Reevaluation is expanded by the selection of the next module with which to continue intervention. Figure 1.1 shows an overview of the similarities and differences.

Standard EMDR Protocol	Protocol for Eating Disorders: EMDR-ED Protocol
1. History-taking and case conceptualization	1. History-taking and case conceptualization: - *Identify relevant modules for EMDR* - *Select relevant targets within the module with appropriate procedures for target selection*
2. Preparation	2. Preparation: - *Introduce EMDR; explain when it is possible and useful.* - *Assist in regulation of eating pattern* - *If useful: RDI* - *Choose first module when ready to start EMDR*
3. Assessment	3-8. Assessment—reevaluation: *Reprocess/neutralize every relevant target within one module successively until module is treated sufficiently.*
4. Desensitization	
5. Installation	8+ Reevaluation+: - *When module is treated sufficiently, select relevant next module* *Then repeat:* *Selection of targets (=1)*
6. Body scan	
7. Closure	*Assessment–reevaluation (3 to 8) on every single relevant target.*
8. Reevaluation	*Continue until all modules are treated sufficiently.*

Figure 1.1   Standard EMDR Protocol and EMDR-ED protocol.
RDI, resource development and installation.

All phases will be described in detail after clarification of the following: therapist criteria, potential procedures for target selection, and the content of the six modules.

EMDR Therapist Criteria

For efficient implementation of EMDR therapy with the EMDR-ED protocol discussed here, we recommend some prerequisites for therapists:

- *Experience in treatment of patients with eating disorders*
  Practitioners should be experienced in working with this difficult population to be able to recognize and cope with the characteristic dynamics in the therapeutic process and in the relationship between therapist and patient.
- *Understanding motivating through case conceptualization*
  For optimizing full cooperation, therapists should be able to develop an accurate case conceptualization and explain clearly their analysis and treatment plan, including the rationale for using EMDR. This is discussed with the patient, depending on the age of the patient (younger than 16 years) and the circumstances the patient is currently living in, as well as the patient's parents/family. Keeping the patient motivated to continue treatment is a fragile variable in this population and merits careful attention.
- *Understanding procedures for target selection*
  In this EMDR-ED protocol five additional procedures for target selection are included besides the regular one (F. Shapiro, 2001). These additional procedures have been developed by Dutch trainers, some of which are published in this series (de Jongh, 2016; Horst & de Jongh, 2016; Logie & de Jongh, 2016; van der Vleugel, van den Berg, de Bont, Staring, & de Jongh, 2016) and others elsewhere (de Jongh, ten Broeke, & Meijer, 2010; Logie & de Jongh, 2014; Markus & Hornsveld, 2015, 2017).
  Because these procedures have been published before in the English language under the name "First and Second" in the "Two Methods Questioning Approach" (de Jongh et al., 2010) and "Third" (Logie & de Jongh, 2016; van der Vleugel et al., 2016), it would be consequent to call the next ones the "Fourth," the "Fifth," and the "Sixth." However, because these names are neither meaningful nor instructive, the procedures are renamed and will be indicated in this chapter by more meaningful names. The procedures will be described briefly, including situations where they are applicable. For further information, reading of relevant publications of the developers of these procedures mentioned previously is recommended. Understanding them and being able to apply them properly is essential for working with this EMDR-ED protocol.

Procedures for Target Selection

In search of ways to optimize the efficiency of EMDR therapy with different kinds of psychopathology, distinctive procedures for target selection have been developed. These procedures mark different paths the therapist can follow in looking for the most relevant targets. Therefore, these procedures are referred to as paths. The exact questions to be asked during these structured procedures are scripted in the scripted protocol that follows. In this section, the procedures/paths will be clarified roughly so the therapist can understand in general when and how to use them. They will be described more specifically later, in the script part. Figure 1.2 shows an overview of the potential paths.

All of these paths can be relevant for the selection of targets when working with patients with EDs.

I. Intrusion Path

This path is relevant in case of intrusive and distressing memories of specific events, when a direct connection between memories and symptoms is obvious. Relevant targets are identified by asking the patient which memory or which image of the memory is the most disturbing (F. Shapiro, 2001).

Targets are ranked by subjective units of disturbance (SUD)'s level.

Key questions: Which memory is bothering you the most?

What is the worst image of that memory?

II. Timeline Path

This path, called "the First Method" in earlier publications (de Jongh et al., 2010), is used for conceptualizing EMDR therapy in the treatment of symptoms or *symptom clusters*, which have developed over time gradually after several events. The path starts with the selection of the specific target symptom that the patient wants to get rid of primarily, because of the disturbance the symptom is causing. Subsequently, events are sought after that the selected symptom started and aggravated later. These events are positioned on a timeline and then the patient indicates which of these events contributed strongest to onset and aggravation of the symptom (in this population this is frequently "fear of being excluded or rejected").

Targets (memories of the selected events) are reprocessed chronologically to eliminate the symptom (de Jongh et al., 2010; Logie & de Jongh, 2014).

Key questions: After what experience did . . . (the symptom) start?

After what experiences did it increase?

When all relevant memories have been reprocessed, the therapist checks if there are any related anticipatory fears (flash-forwards) to be reprocessed. The next step is preparing the patient for the future with a future template or a mental video check. With a mental video check, the patient is asked, with eyes closed, in his or her imagination, to go through a future (formerly anxiety-provoking) situation from beginning to end, and check whether there are aspects ("cues") that provoke any tension and, therefore, might prevent the person from confronting the formerly frightening situation. The patient is asked to open his/her eyes when discomfort or tension is sensed and to concentrate on the anxiety-provoking or disturbing cue. Then one set of eye movements is performed and the patient continues this movie until he/she experiences his/her next tension. Another set follows. This procedure is continued until the end.

I. Intrusion path	From intrusive and distressing memories to targets
II. Timeline path	From symptoms that developed gradually over time to targets
III. Dysfunctional belief path	From symptoms that are driven by core beliefs to targets
IV. Flash-forward path	From symptoms that are driven by negative future-oriented fantasies to targets
V. Dysfunctional positive targets path	From urge-driven symptoms to urge-evoking targets: Positive memories (1) Present trigger situations (2) Positive future-oriented fantasies (3)
VI. Emotion path	From (problematic) emotions to targets

Figure 1.2 Overview of procedures (paths) for target selection.

III. Dysfunctional Belief Path

This path, called "The Second Method" in an earlier publication (de Jongh et al., 2010), is devised for the identification of memories of events that underlie dysfunctional core beliefs or associated assumptions that elicit dysfunctional behavioral patterns and/or persistent psychopathology. Core beliefs are not just thoughts connected to specific situations but enduring beliefs that are generalized, absolute, and deeply rooted and, therefore, rigid and hard to modify. In these situations, there is a great stock of potentially relevant events in the past, mostly starting early in life, which have resulted in the formation of negative dysfunctional beliefs about the self and others (Beck, 1995). These *core beliefs* will elicit, through *intermediate beliefs* (precepts resulting from the core beliefs), behavioral and emotional reactions that cause negative emotional and/or interactional experiences. These experiences in turn are stored in the memory as "confirmation" of the cognitive bias and increase its credibility. Core beliefs are regarded here as the primary symptom or "the driving force," leading to secondary symptoms: behavioral, emotional, and interactional problems. For the modification of core beliefs, we need another search strategy to find constituting memories because an abundance of events could be placed on a timeline, whereas it is unclear on what criteria to select relevant ones from these. For these cases the "Google-search strategy" (de Jongh et al., 2010; E. Shapiro & Laub, 2009, 2014) is proposed because here a selection seems relevant of events that "prove" for the patient—in the strongest way—the credibility of the belief. The aim is to "discredit" the "evidence" for the belief. In computer terminology, therefore, the selected core belief or assumption is the *keyword* and all potential relevant past events are in the World Wide Web. As with Google search, the therapist and the patient search for the most relevant "hits." Memories of the events appearing at the top of the list seem to be the most crucial ones, and these "proofs" are "discredited" one after another by reprocessing these memories with EMDR (de Jongh et al., 2010; ten Broeke, de Jongh, & Oppenheim, 2012). Sometimes a patient provides evidence that doesn't concern a single experience, but a bunch of experiences, repeated over and over during a certain period. This is referred to as an "archive." Then, the next step is selection of one experience per archive to symbolize the experience. The criterion for selection of a memory as target is how much it is experienced in the present as a "piece of evidence" for the validity of core belief.

Targets are ranked by degree of sustaining credibility to the belief instead of SUD's level or chronology.

Key questions: Which past experiences still prove for you, at this moment, that you are _____ (state the dysfunctional belief)?

How do you know that you are ____ (state the dysfunctional belief)?

IV. Flash-Forward Path

The flash-forward path—called the Third Method in "EMDR for Traumatized Patients With Psychosis" (van der Vleugel et al., 2016)—is devised for the treatment of irrational fears, provoked by intrusive fantasies of catastrophic events that might happen to the patient in the future. With the fear-related behaviors, the patient intends to prevent from happening what he or she sees in imagination. The target image is the worst image of this nightmare or scenario, the so-called flash-forward. Common flash-forwards in this population include the following: being rejected, despised, or ridiculed because of their appearance. Although the patient's focus is on the future, the fears are experienced in the present, triggered by negative, irrational thoughts and images associated with a catastrophic content. The flash-forward path addresses patients' irrational fears and anticipatory anxiety responses that persist after the memories of past events have been fully processed. However, if no relevant past events can be identified, then the flash-forward should be processed straight away. The flash-forward path has proven to be an effective application of EMDR to deal with the second prong ("present") of the three-pronged approach, if the first one ("past") is either dealt with or does not seem relevant. This path is based on experimental findings, showing that vividness and emotional intensity of recurrent intrusive images can be reduced by taxing working memory using eye movements—not only of past events but also of potential future catastrophes (Engelhard, van Uijen, & van den Hout, 2010; Logie & de Jongh, 2014).

Targets are ranked by SUD's level.

Key question: What is the worst scenario of what might happen to you in the future in your imagination?

What would be the worst thing about that?

What is the worst image in your head about that?

V. Dysfunctional Positive Targets Path

This path is used for the treatment of specific eating disorder–related behaviors, like dieting, binge eating, or vomiting. These behaviors are urge-driven and can be motivated by either *positive memories of past experiences* or *images of present situations* (present triggers) activating the urge to perform the dysfunctional behavior or *positive future-oriented fantasies* (also present triggers) of what might happen to the patient in the future resulting from this behavior.

The aim of the behavior is to achieve a positive affect or sensation. The targets are intrusive and compelling images of these anticipated effects: dysfunctional positive flash-forwards. The use of EMDR therapy on dysfunctional positive targets (Hornsveld & Markus, 2014; Markus & Hornsveld, 2015) is based on research that has shown repeatedly that eye movements make negative images less negative, but dysfunctional positive ones less positive (Engelhard et al., 2010). Neutralization can move in two directions. Similarly, Knipe (2010) observed this phenomenon and developed a procedure for reprocessing "dysfunctional positive affect." Popky (2009) used this phenomenon in the treatment of addiction disorders to desensitize memory representations of triggers that elicit an urge to take the substance to which the patient is addicted.

Three kinds of dysfunctional positive targets can be distinguished:

V1. MEMORIES OF POSITIVE EXPERIENCES

Activation of the memory evokes an urge to relive the desired state and, thus, to perform the specific behavior to achieve this state. The target must be identified that evokes the strongest *level of urge* to perform the behavior (LOU) and/or the strongest *level of positive affect* (LOPA).

Targets are ranked by LOU or LOPA, whichever evokes the strongest urge.

For the negative cognition, words must be identified that intensify the urge maximally (e.g., "I always want to feel like this") and the positive cognition is the standard "I am strong" or "I can deal with the image, resisting the urge" or "I can resist the image."

Key questions: What is your most positive memory of having performed _____ (state the specific behavior: dieting/binge eating/excessive exercising/vomiting/using laxatives)?

Which positive memory now evokes the urge to _____ (state the specific behavior) the strongest?

V2. IMAGES OF PRESENT TRIGGERS (POSITIVE OR NEGATIVE)

A variety of situations can activate the urge to perform these specific ED behaviors. The choice for desensitization of these triggers is based on the work of Popky (2005, 2009, 2010), Hase (2009), and Markus and Hornsveld (2015), who use their procedures in patients with different kinds of addictions. Daily recurring trigger situations can evoke the urge to perform the ED behavior. In these situations, the patient expects a reward from the ED behavior of positive emotions/sensations or relief by escape from negative ones. The outcome of the ED behavior is positive either way.

The target is an image of the situation that evokes the strongest level of urge to perform the behavior (LOU).

Targets are ranked by LOU.

For negative cognition, words are identified that intensify the urge the most or are the most disturbing. The positive cognition is the standard "I am strong" or "I can deal with this image, resisting the urge" or "I can resist the image."

In the assessment phase the therapist asks for both LOU and SUD.

Key question: Which situations are difficult for you because they evoke the urge to perform _____ (state the specific ED behavior)?

V3. POSITIVE FLASH-FORWARDS

Patients often have clear fantasies of what might happen to them if they succeed in achieving their goal with this specific behavior. These future-oriented fantasies are present triggers.

The target is identified that gives the strongest level of urge to perform the behavior (LOU) and/or the strongest level of positive affect (LOPA).

Targets are ranked by LOU or LOPA, whichever is the strongest.

Instead of a negative cognition those words are identified that strengthen the urge the most or are the most disturbing. The positive cognition is the standard "I am strong" or "I can deal with this image, resisting the urge" or "I can resist the image."

I. Intrusion path	Images of intrusive and distressing memories
	- Ranked by SUD's level
II. Timeline path	Memories of crucial experiences for development of symptom
	- Ranked chronologically
III. Dysfunctional belief path	Intrusive memories sustaining credibility to dysfunctional core/intermediate belief
	- Ranked by degree of sustaining credibility
IV. Flash-forward path	Images of anticipated frightening future experiences (catastrophes)
	- Ranked by SUD's level.
V. Dysfunctional positive targets path	Images evoking a compelling urge to perform unhealthy behavior
	1. Memories of positive affect of the specific behavior (symptom)
	- Ranked by LOU, LOPA (whichever is the strongest).
	• Instead of NC: words that evoke maximally the urge or the positive affect • Standard PC: "I can resist the image" or "I am strong"
	Not mentioned in assessment, but installed after LOU or LOPA is reduced significantly
	• Back to target/process measures: LOU/LOPA instead of SUD
	2. Images of present trigger situations
	- Ranked by LOU to perform the specific behavior
	• Instead of NC: words that evoke maximally the urge • Standard PC: "I can resist the image" or "I am strong"
	Not mentioned in assessment, but installed after LOU is reduced significantly and SUD = 0
	• Back to target/process measures: LOU besides SUD
	3. Positive images of required future experiences (fantasies)
	- Ranked by LOU or LOPA (whichever is the strongest)
	• Instead of NC: words that evoke maximally the urge or the positive affect • Standard PC: "I can resist the image" or "I am strong."
	Not mentioned in assessment, but installed after LOU or LOPA is reduced significantly
	• Back to target/process measures: LOU/LOPA instead of SUD
VI. Emotion path	Memories that evoke the problematic emotion
	- Ranked by SUD's level

Figure 1.3 Characteristics of paths for target selection: Type of targets, (-) sequence of targets, (o) deviations from standard protocol.
LOPA, level of positive affect; LOU, level of urge; NC, negative cognition; PC, positive cognition; SUD, subjective units of disturbance.

Figure 1.3 provides an overview of characteristics of paths for target selection.

Key questions: What is the most desired outcome of performing _____ (state the specific ED behavior)? Or What are you most looking forward to when you _____ (state ED behavior)?

VI. Emotion Path

The emotion path is appropriate for the treatment of symptoms that result from problematic emotions. The procedure, though it seems similar to the floatback technique (Shapiro, 2001), is different. In the floatback technique, the therapist asks the patient to look for memories of the first time he/she remembers feeling this way, whereas in this procedure the patients look for memories that evoke the emotion the most. Common problematic emotions in this population are disgust, anger, guilt, shame, and sadness.

Key question: As you bring up your _____ (state the problematic emotion), which memory evokes this emotion the strongest?

This section offers an overview of the potential modules for EMDR therapy with their indication criteria, relevant targets, associated procedures for target selection, and goals.

All in all there are six modules and six paths for target selection.

Module 1: Distressing Memories

This module is relevant when intrusive memories of specific experiences are causing distress or are obstructing progress in the treatment of the eating disorder. The distress does not induce additional symptoms necessarily. There is a direct link between memories and distress. The targets are the most intrusive and disturbing memories, and the therapist finds the targets with the intrusion path.

Goal: Distressing memories are neutralized so much that they no longer obstruct progress in the treatment of the eating disorder and no longer cause suffering.

Module 2: Eating Disorder–Related Fears

This module is applied when irrational fears—related to eating, weight, or appearance—start and exacerbate later on after specific experiences. In these cases, there is no suffering from memories of experiences, but from symptoms (fears), which resulted from or were aggravated after these negative experiences. The targets are memories of relevant experiences, and two procedures for target selection can be considered here:

1. If specific experiences can be identified as a clear "starting point" or as the "cause" of exacerbation of already existing symptoms, targets are identified with the timeline path.
   Goal: Memories maintaining the fears are neutralized, so the fears will disappear or diminish so much that they no longer obstruct progress in the treatment of the eating disorder.
2. If there are irrational fears for anticipated future negative experiences (e.g., "If I will continue treatment, I will end up like an elephant and everybody will ridicule me"), and relevant past experiences either have been reprocessed or cannot be identified, then the therapist asks for the worst scenario in the patient's head about the specific anticipated future experience and its potential consequence. The target is the worst image of this scenario. For target selection, the "Flash-Forward Path" is to be used.
   Goal: Future-oriented fantasies maintaining the fears are neutralized, so that fears disappear or diminish so much that they no longer obstruct progress in the treatment of the eating disorder.

Module 3: Urge-Driven ED Behaviors

Behavioral eating disorder (ED) symptoms like having binges, dieting, or performing compensatory behaviors (moving excessively/purging) are urge-driven behaviors. They are performed either to avoid or to escape from negative outcomes (emotional states or sensations) or to achieve positive outcomes (required emotional states), whereas the patient realizes that these behaviors have unhealthy consequences in the long run. The patient seems incapable of resisting the urge or impulse; the resulting behavior looks like voluntary behavior, but it is not.

The targets that reflect a "dysfunctional" positive outcome of this behavior should be neutralized.

Three kinds of dysfunctional positive targets can be relevant: memories of past experiences, images of daily recurrent situations that trigger the urge, and fantasies about future experiences.

1. *Memories of positive experiences*: Examples are positive feelings of autonomy after having exercised excessively, comfort after a binge episode, relief after having vomited, and pride after dieting. Memories of experiences of this "dysfunctional" positive affect are positive targets to be reprocessed.
2. *Present trigger situations*: Daily recurring present situations can activate the urge to perform the ED behavior. This does not concern specific events stored in the episodic memory, but global images or memories evoking the urge in daily life (Hornsveld & Markus, 2014); for example, the sensation of a full stomach, or seeing an empty plate after eating. Neutralization of memory representations of these situations should promote the patient's ability to resist the urge that is evoked.
3. *Positive flash-forwards*: If the patient has intrusive fantasies, evoking required anticipated positive affect, the target can be the image of the fantasy that evokes the positive affect the strongest. Examples are "After having vomited, I will feel free"; "After a binge, I will feel relaxed"; "If I keep on moving my body/take these laxatives, my weight will remain below 40 kg"; "If I can keep my weight below 40 kg, I am fully in control of myself, which will make me feel happy."

However, if the urge seems to be activated primarily by a predominant negative emotion like anger, disgust, or shame, then it can be helpful to look for those memories that evoke this problematic emotion the strongest. Then the emotion path might be helpful for finding relevant memories.

Goal: The relevant memories, trigger situation, and/or fantasies no longer elicit the urge to perform the dysfunctional behaviors, or the patient is better able to resist the urge that is evoked, and/or the dysfunctional behaviors disappear or diminish so much that they no longer obstruct progress in the treatment of the eating disorder.

Module 4: Low Self-Esteem

Predominant hypothesis in many case conceptualizations is that the eating disorder is maintained by negative dysfunctional belief(s) about the self, a so-called low or damaged self-esteem (Fairburn et al., 2003). Negative dysfunctional beliefs about the person usually have resulted from a multitude of negative experiences, starting early in life. It is obvious that the negative self-image is still "activated" and sustained in a clinically sub-threshold way. Therefore, it is important to identify those targets that will "deactivate" the dysfunctional beliefs. In other words, the dysfunctional belief should no longer feel as valid, when those targets (memories) will have been reprocessed. The selected targets are supposed to contribute substantially to loss of credibility of the belief. The dysfunctional beliefs path is appropriate here for target selection.

Goal: Reduction of credibility of the core belief to such a degree that behaviors and moods resulting from this core belief stop or are diminished so much that they no longer obstruct progress in the treatment of the eating disorder. Reduction of the credibility of the core belief is achieved by neutralizing relevant memories.

Module 5: Clinical Perfectionism

Clinical perfectionism (setting unhealthy and unrelenting standards for oneself) is closely associated with low self-esteem and can be regarded as an avoidance strategy for being confronted with feelings of weakness, failure, and worthlessness. People with clinical perfectionism consider making an error as a proof for being imperfect, not good enough, or even a bad person. Clinical perfectionism can be a focus for EMDR therapy when dysfunctional core beliefs and intermediate beliefs can be identified that motivate the behavior, for example, "I must do everything that helps me look perfect"; "If I do not look perfect, everybody will reject me"; "If I do not look perfect, this means I am a weakling." Intermediate beliefs are precepts, expectations, and assumptions—derived from core beliefs—that govern and guide our behavior (Beck, 1995). The targets are memories of negative experiences that still "prove" that the person is, for example, "worthless." The recommended path for target selection is the dysfunctional belief path, for the same reasons as described in Module 4. If the patient has clear fantasies of what might happen to him/her in the future when he/she would appear to be imperfect, according to his/her intermediate belief(s), then the flash-forward path or the dysfunctional positive targets path can be relevant to find relevant targets for reprocessing: negative or positive flash-forwards.

Goal: Reduction of the credibility of the core belief and associated intermediate beliefs (if x, then y) by neutralizing relevant memories or fantasies so much that behaviors and moods resulting from this core (intermediate) belief stop or at least diminish so much that they no longer obstruct progress in the treatment of the eating disorder.

Module 6: Negative Body Image

Characteristic for eating disorder patients is the overrating of their body shape as a determining element for their self-image and specific for AN patients is the rigid, distorted perceptions of their body shape, that is, body shape being not congruent with reality. This phenomenon of AN patients, called "(delusional) body image disturbance" by some, has features of both an obsession and a delusion (Steinglass, Eisen, Attia, Mayer, & Walsh, 2007). A body image that is negative—distorted or even delusional—ultimately may have developed gradually after several experiences. In that case, relevant memories must be identified, clarifying how the body image got damaged. Often, specific experiences can be traced that are relevant for the start and exacerbation of the body image. However, if this is not the case, then experiences can be looked for that "prove" the validity of the dysfunctional core belief such as "My body is fat/ugly/despicable, therefore I am worthless." If relevant memories for the development of the negative body image cannot be found with the timeline path or the dysfunctional belief path, then the emotion path can be an option to look for relevant memories. The negative body image

MODULES	TARGETS	PROCEDURES	GOALS
1. Distressing memories	Distressing memories of past experiences	Intrusion path (I)	Reduction of (di)stress, caused by intrusive images of past experiences; elimination of any psychopathology, caused by this distress
2. Fears	Memories of experiences relevant for development of symptom, if traceable	Timeline path (II)	Reduction of fear by reprocessing relevant images of past experiences
	Fantasies about anticipated negative future experiences, if relevant past experiences are not traceable or have been reprocessed	Flash-forward path (IV)	Reduction of fear by reprocessing relevant images of anticipated future experiences
3. Urge-driven ED behaviors: binges, fasting, and compensatory behavior (purging or hyperactivity)	Memories of positive affect/effect caused by the ED behavior	Dysfunctional positive target path (V.1)	Stop the dysfunctional behaviors by neutralization of relevant images of past, present, or future (feared or required) experiences that activate the urge to perform the behavior
	Present trigger situations: images of situations that elicit the urge to perform the behavior	Dysfunctional positive target path (V.2)	
	Images of anticipated positive future experiences (fantasies)	Dysfunctional positive target path (V.3)	
	Images of memories evoking the emotion, which activate the urge to perform the behavior	Emotion path (VI)	
4. Low self-esteem	Memories of experiences that "prove" the current validity of the negative core belief	Dysfunctional belief path (III)	Stop the behavioral and/or mood problems resulting from dysfunctional core beliefs. Weaken the dysfunctional core beliefs
5. Clinical perfectionism controlled by dysfunctional (intermediate) beliefs	Memories of experiences that "prove" the actual validity of the dysfunctional belief(s)	Dysfunctional belief path (III)	Stop setting irrational standards for oneself, resulting from dysfunctional core/intermediate beliefs
	Fantasies of anticipated negative consequences of not realizing the set standards	Flash-forward path (IV)	Stop setting irrational standards for oneself, resulting from negative images of anticipated feared experiences
	Fantasies of anticipated positive consequences of realizing the set standards	Dysfunctional positive target path (V.3)	Stop setting irrational standards for oneself, resulting from positive images of anticipated desired experiences
6. Negative body image	Memories of experiences relevant for the development of negative body image	Timeline path (II)	Improve the body image and restore damage to the body image caused by maladaptively stored memories
	Memories of experiences that "prove" the current validity of the dysfunctional core belief about the body	Dysfunctional belief path (III)	
	Memories of experiences that evoke the negative emotion accompanying the negative body image	Emotion path (VI)	

Figure 1.4   Overview of modules: Type of targets, procedures for target selection, and goals.
ED, eating disorder

is accompanied usually by strong emotions like disgust, anger, and sadness. With this procedure, the memories are looked for that evoke the specific emotion the strongest, triggering the delusional body image as it is stored in the long-term memory.

When no more relevant memories are left to be neutralized, then the focus can move to present triggers. The next group of targets to focus on can be distressful images of current or anticipated future body shape, activating their delusional negative body image as it is stored in the long-term memory.

Procedures for target selection in this module in the preferred order (minding the three-pronged approach) are as follows:

- *Timeline* path: To be used when past experiences can be identified that contributed to the development of a negative body image.
- *Dysfunctional belief* path: To be used when the learning history is diffuse and past experiences can be identified that prove the validity of dysfunctional beliefs about their body shape.
- *Emotion path*: To be used when relevant past experiences for the development of the negative body image cannot be identified and problematic negative emotions accompanying the negative body image are predominant.

Goal: Change of the distorted, or even delusional, body image, by neutralizing relevant memories so much that the body image no longer obstructs progress in the treatment of the eating disorder.

See Figure 1.4 for a summarizing overview of potential modules for EMDR based on the transdiagnostic features with their associated targets and procedures for target selection and goals as mentioned by Fairburn et al. (2003).

INTEGRATION OF THE EATING DISORDERS PROTOCOL WITH THE EIGHT PHASES OF THE STANDARD PROTOCOL

Phase 1: History-taking and case conceptualization

In this phase the therapist collects sufficient relevant information in order to be able to formulate hypotheses regarding factors eliciting and maintaining the symptoms. Both personal and interpersonal factors are explored. Wherever possible, the therapist uses validated questionnaires.

The therapist formulates in consultation with the patient a hypothesis concerning the supposed function of the eating disorder: What is achieved or avoided by having and keeping the disorder? Potential functions for an eating disorder are as follows:

- Avoidance of maturation
- Escape from taking responsibilities
- Punishment of oneself
- Supply oneself with an identity, becoming "someone special"
- Get the feeling of having control
- Avoidance of negative memories
- Disconnection from negative feelings
- Adaptation to the family as a way of life

In the case of comorbidity, the therapist formulates hypotheses concerning the relationship between the eating disorder and additional psychopathology.

See Figure 1.5 for relevant issues to explore on behalf of the case conceptualization.

Based on the case conceptualization (gathered information, analyses, and hypotheses) an overall treatment plan is composed, making explicit which interventions are supposed to be relevant—including EMDR therapy—for the treatment of which symptoms. Also, the potential modules for EMDR are mentioned. The case conceptualization is explained and discussed with the patient and the parents (if the patient is younger than 18 years of age or still living in his/her parental home).

Phase 2: Preparation

Priority in this phase is to ascertain if the patients' illness has brought them into mortal danger. Survival is the highest priority. Quality of life becomes an issue for therapy only when there is no (more) mortal danger. In this phase, patients start with normalizing their eating patterns and restoration of a

CLINICAL SYMPTOMS AND SUSTAINING FACTORS	DESCRIPTION
Symptoms related to eating, appearance, weight: behavioral, cognitive, emotional, physical, interactional	
Distressing memories or future-oriented fantasies related to eating, appearance, weight, interfering with daily life	
Present triggers for these memories or fantasies	
(Lack of) skills • Social skills • Affect regulation	
(In)adequate functioning in: • Family • School/work • Peers	
Aspiration level	
Mood problems	
Comorbidity	
• Developmental history: Adverse-traumatic experiences • Psychological diagnostics: (neuro)psychological vulnerabilities	
Supposed function of ED	
Diagnosis *ICD-10*	
Hypotheses	

Figure 1.5   Worksheet for case conceptualization.
ED, eating disorder; ICD-10, *International Statistical Classification of Diseases and Related Health Problems*

healthy body weight, assisted by therapeutic interventions (not per se EMDR), including behavioral interventions, consultation with a dietician, and physical checkups by a pediatrician or internist. If outpatient care is not effective enough, day clinical or more extensive clinical treatment is considered.

In general, EMDR therapy becomes possible and useful when patients can keep their attention focused, feel emotions or sensations, tolerate high SUDs, and concentrate on cognitions. These are requirements for reprocessing.

Generally, these requirements are met when the body mass index (BMI) is greater than 17 or standard deviation (SD) is greater than –1x (for children and adolescence).[1] There are exceptions, of course, but in the case of patients who are severely underweight, attempts to reprocess traumatic material can be a very disappointing endeavor for both therapists and patients. It is essential to support them in regulating their eating patterns for the restoration of a healthy body weight, if useful. If necessary, monitoring this process can be continued during the next phases. Either the EMDR therapist or a colleague within the interdisciplinary team can do this.

If there is an indication that there is insufficient internal support for the patient during the process of identification and selection/reprocessing of memories, the protocol for resource development and installation (RDI; Korn & Leeds, 2002) can be applied here. This protocol is not described in this chapter.

If the patient has agreed to the treatment plan (Phase 1), EMDR therapy is introduced as soon as the eating pattern is regulated enough for EMDR to be viable and useful. The order of modules to be applied can be determined more accurately in this phase. Potential modules for EMDR have been explained in Phase 1.

---

[1]*Body mass index* or *Quetelet index* is a value derived from the weight and height of an individual. It is calculated by dividing the body mass (weight in kilograms) through the square of the body height (length in meters). *Standard deviation* (*SD*) is used in children and adolescents because BMI must be corrected for age. Degree of underweight is expressed by comparison of length and weight with the growth curve of the patient. With 0.5 to 1 SD, there is 10% to 20% weight loss, meaning severe underweight.

Phases 3 to 8: Assessment—Reevaluation

When a specific target memory to be processed is identified with the appropriate path for target selection in Phase 1, the therapist continues with Phases 3 to 8 (assessment, desensitization, installation, body scan, closure, reevaluation) and repeats these for all relevant targets, until all the targets within one specific module have been reprocessed one by one (SUD = 0, VoC = 7). Then, a check takes place to ascertain whether the stated goal for that module has been reached and whether additional interventions are needed.

Phases 3 to 8 follow the standard EMDR protocol, except for a few exceptions. Therefore, description of all phases will not be repeated for all modules. Deviations from the standard procedure will be mentioned and described.

Reevaluation +

When the goal of a module is reached and relevant memories are neutralized, the next module is selected to continue. Subsequently, relevant targets must be identified again and selected with appropriate paths for target selection (Phase 1).

During treatment it may be necessary to adjust the previously determined order of modules, depending on the progress of the patient. Based on theoretical grounds and clinical experience, the order of modules, as described here, is recommended; however, this is not yet validated empirically. The case conceptualization of the individual patient is guiding in this respect.

EMDR PROTOCOL FOR EATING DISORDERS SCRIPT

Phase 1: History-Taking and Case Conceptualization

Presenting Problem

Say, *"What is the problem that is bringing you into therapy?"*

_____

_____

Say, *"Which are the behaviors related to this that are bothering you the most?"*

_____

_____

Say, *"What thoughts or beliefs do you have connected with your problem?"*

_____

_____

Say, *"What firm beliefs do you have about yourself and/or others that you regard as guiding you in life?"*

_____

_____

Say, *"What are the emotions that you are having connected with your problem?"*

_____

_____

Say, *"What are the physical symptoms that you are having connected with your problem?"*

_____

_____

Say, *"What are the relational problems that you are having connected with your problem?"*

_____

_____

Say, *"Do you have disturbing memories of events that happened to you in the past or intrusive fantasies about events that might happen to you in the future?"*

_____

_____

Say, *"Do you know in what situations these disturbing memories or intrusive fantasies happen to appear?"*

_____

_____

Etiology

Say, *"Do you have any ideas about circumstances or factors that may have caused your problems?"*

_____

_____

Maintenance

Say, *"Do you have any ideas about what might keep your problems going?"*

_____

_____

Say, *"Are you satisfied with your relations with peers? Any problems there?"*

_____

_____

Say, *"Do you have problems with your emotions, either to be aware of them or to express them?"*

_____

_____

Say, *"How are you getting along with your family members? Any problems there?"*

_____

_____

Say, *"How are you dealing with school/work? Any problems there?"*

_____

_____

Say, *"Do you have an explanation for the problems you are having* (if there are any) *with other people?"*

_____

_____

Say, *"Could you be demanding too much of yourself by setting high standards for yourself?"*

_____

_____

Say, *"How is your mood predominantly?"*

_____

_____

Comorbidity

Say, *"Do you have any other emotional or behavioral problems or diagnoses besides your problems with eating?"*

_____

_____

Developmental History

Say, *"During intake, your developmental history has been explored. Did you experience adverse, or maybe even traumatic, experiences in your past that you have not mentioned then and that might be relevant?"*

_____

_____

Say, *"You took some psychological tests. If details were found that I consider relevant for our work here, we will incorporate these in our treatment plan. Do you have any questions about this?"*

_____

_____

Measures

Say, *"To understand your problems as fully as possible, I would like you to fill in these paper-and-pencil tests, if you have not done this already. The results of these measures combined with what we discussed so far will give us enough information for a good analysis and understanding of your situation. We will devise a treatment plan based on this information and I will explain that to you. Are you willing to cooperate?"*

_____

_____

Scores

Say, *"Thank you for filling in these tests. We read what you filled in and our conclusions are _____ (state the conclusions). What do you think about this? Please comment on what you heard."*

_____

_____

Function

Say, *"Did your behaviors related to eating, like dieting or having binges, start because you chose for them to start or did they just seem to happen to you?"*

_____

_____

Say, *"What, in your opinion, has having an eating disorder added to your life since it started?"*

_____

_____

Say, *"By having your eating disorder, what do you think you have achieved?"*

_____

_____

Say, *"By having your eating disorder, what do you think you were able to avoid?"*

_____

_____

Say, *"Have you ever thought about what you should learn (to do) to be able to give up your eating disorder?"*

_____

_____

Say, *"It seems that the meaning of the eating disorder for you is* ____ *(state your understanding of the meaning of the ED for the patient). What do you think about that?"*

_____

_____

Case Conceptualization

Say, *"I have figured out through our work that you have* _____ *(state the diagnosis). I know this because you are troubled by the following symptoms* _____ *(state the patient's behaviors, emotions, cognitions, physical symptoms, and relational problems). Does this make sense to you?"*

_____

_____

Say, *"We have also discussed what circumstances or factors may have caused your problems and what keeps your problems going. It may seem as if your behavior started not because you chose it, but as if it just happened to you. So, I will help you address the distressing behaviors and emotions that are troubling you. I have discussed the factors that may explain why you arrived where you are now. It is my job to proceed from here. Do you want to add anything to this?"*

_____

_____

Say, *"We also discussed what function the eating disorder seems to have for you. By maintaining the disorder, you achieve* _____ *and/or you avoid* _____ *(state what is achieved and/or avoided). So, in order to be able to give up the eating disorder, you will have to learn to* _____ *(state the goal/s of treatment). And therefore you will work on* _____ *(state issues for interventions) by* _____ *(state type of interventions). Part of your treatment will incorporate EMDR therapy that can be used for several purposes. To give you an idea of how this works, I will show you the themes we can work on with EMDR therapy."*

Introduction to Modules

Say, *"Here is a list of possible issues for our EMDR work. We call them 'modules':*

Module 1. Distressing memories of negative experiences.

Module 2. Fears related to the eating disorder.

Module 3. Eating disorder (ED) behaviors that you feel compelled to do, like binges, fasting, or compensatory behaviors, like excessive moving or purging: vomiting and using laxatives, or diuretics.

Module 4. Low self-esteem resulting in dysfunctional behavior patterns and/or negative moods.

Module 5. Clinical perfectionism.

Module 6. Negative body image.

These issues appear to occur frequently with patients who have an eating disorder. It seems that for you _____ *(state modules) could be useful. In a while, when we will start with EMDR, we will decide what modules we will use specifically and in what order. So, this is your treatment plan* _____ *(show concept treatment plan).* _____ *(I/the team) consider(s) these interventions essential to give you good treatment."*

Discuss the treatment plan. Show Figure 1.4 and explain which modules will be chosen.

> Say, *"Do you agree with this plan? Please let me know if you have any doubts or questions, so we can discuss them!"*

Phase 2: Preparation

Introduction to EMDR

> Say, *"Your problems seem partly related to memories of experiences from your past or images in your head about potential future experiences that might happen to you. These memories or images get activated in the present in certain situations and they are causing you problems. For dealing with these problems, I will introduce EMDR therapy to you. The treatment plan has been discussed with you before. To begin with, your eating pattern must improve so much that we can start working on these other related issues with EMDR therapy. When we start with EMDR therapy we will run through your treatment plan once more and then we will concentrate on our goals with EMDR. For now, it is important that you realize that we can release you from the problems these images and memories are giving you. Is that clear for you?"*

> Say, *"Although we are not starting with EMDR right away, I will explain to you what EMDR is now, so you know what you can expect."*

Give the regular introduction to EMDR.

> Say, *"When a person gets traumatized, the memory of the experience seems to get locked in the nervous system with frozen pictures, sounds, thoughts, and feelings. With EMDR we facilitate the unlocking of the nervous system to allow the brain to process the experience. It is important to note that it is your own brain that will be doing the healing and that you are the one in control."*

Regulation of Eating Pattern

> Say, *"Our first goal is to help you restore a more regular eating pattern and a healthy weight, so that you will not be in mortal danger any longer. We can start working on other issues only when you are out of the 'danger zone.' We will start working with EMDR therapy, when you will be able to keep your concentration focused and when you can feel emotions and physical sensations again. Do you understand this? And, do you agree to this?"*

Resource Installation

Introduce other planned interventions; these do not have to be guided by an EMDR practitioner necessarily. If resource work seems relevant for the patient, the therapist can work with the protocol for resource installation here.

Selection of First Module

Say, *"We have discussed before which modules could be relevant for you potentially, when we discussed the treatment plan. Let us look now to see if that idea is still correct or if there are better choices in the meantime. Based on our view of your problems my guess is that we should start with _____ (state the module). Do you agree, or would you suggest another module to start with?"*

_____

_____

Say, *"Okay, then we agree that we can start with _____ (state the module for EMDR therapy processing). When we have finished this one, we can continue with other modules for EMDR processing, based on what you need. We will start working on a new module after we are satisfied with our results achieved with this one. We will know that we accomplished our goal when the issue of the module seems no longer to interfere with making progress in recovering from your eating disorder. That will be our criterion. Okay, so now we have a plan, a reason, and a purpose for EMDR within your treatment plan."*

Directions for therapist:

1. Choose one of the modules listed in Figure 1.6.
2. Identify the most appropriate path for target selection.
3. Follow the designated path script (see Note 1).
4. Work with any target until completion.
5. After having completed all relevant targets within one module, choose the next module until all necessary modules are completed.

Note 1: The scripts for each path are listed in the following order for easy access and use:

- I. Intrusion path
- II. Timeline path
- III. Dysfunctional belief path
- IV. Flash-forward path
- V. Dysfunctional positive targets paths 1, 2, 3
- VI. Emotion path

Note 2: In all the paths, skip asking for the positive cognition during assessment if the negative cognition is, "I am powerless/I cannot deal with the image," because the positive cognition can only be, "I can deal with the image." However, install the standard positive cognition, "I can deal with the image," after SUD has become 0.

Phase 3 to 8: Assessment—Reevaluation

On the next pages, the full scripts are described for all paths for target selection/modules, including Phases 1 and 3 to 8.

MODULES	POTENTIAL PATHS
1. **Distressing memories**	• Intrusion path (I)
2. **Fears**	• Timeline path (II)
	• Flash-forward path (IV)
3. **Urge-driven ED behaviors**	• Dysfunctional positive targets path (V)
	• Emotion path (VI)
4. **Negative self-image**	• Dysfunctional belief path (III)
5. **Clinical perfectionism**	• Dysfunctional belief path (III)
	• Flash-forward path (IV)
	• Dysfunctional positive targets path (V)
6. **Negative body image**	• Timeline path (II)
	• Dysfunctional belief path (III)
	• Emotion path (VI)

Figure 1.6   Modules with potential paths.[a]
[a]Preliminary suggestions based on theoretical/pragmatic grounds and clinical experience.
Empirical validation may prove other paths to be more efficient/effective.

I. INTRUSION PATH SCRIPT

Modules: Applicable in Module 1 (distressing memories) and Module 6 (negative body image).

Reference: F. Shapiro (2001).

Core: "Classical" procedure for target selection. The most disturbing memories are ranked by SUD's level and then reprocessed until related symptoms are gone.

Use the Standard EMDR Protocol on each relevant memory/target until the patient is no longer suffering from the memories.

> Say, *"We discovered that you are bothered by distressing memories of past negative experiences. We will work on these until they no longer bother you. What are the experiences whose memories trouble you the most?"*

> *List of Distressing Memories of Past Negative Experiences*

> _____

> _____

> Say, *"What memory is bothering you the most? Tell me how this experience is stored in your head as a picture."*

> _____

> _____

Phase 3: Assessment

Image

> Say, *"What image of this picture is the most distressing to look at?"*

> _____

> _____

Negative Cognition (NC)

Say, *"What words go best with the picture that express why the picture is still distressing to you now?"* Or *"What words go with the picture that express what you believe about yourself now?"*

_____

_____

Positive Cognition (PC)

Note: Skip asking for the positive cognition during assessment if the negative cognition is, "I am powerless/I cannot deal with the image," because the positive cognition can only be, "I can deal with the image." However, install the standard positive cognition, "I can deal with the image," after SUD has become 0.

Say, *"When you bring up that picture or* _____ (state the issue), *what would you rather like to believe about yourself now?"*

_____

_____

Validity of Cognition (VOC)

Say, *"When you think of the incident* (or picture) *how true do those words* _____ (clinician repeats the positive cognition) *feel to you now on a scale of 1 to 7, where 1 feels completely false and 7 feels completely true?"*

1	2	3	4	5	6	7

(completely false)   (completely true)

This question is skipped if the NC is, "I cannot deal with the image," and no PC is asked.

Emotions

Say, *"When you bring up the picture or* _____ (state the issue) *and those words* _____ (clinician states the negative cognition), *what emotion do you feel now?"*

_____

_____

Subjective Units of Disturbance (SUD)

Say, *"On a scale of 0 to 10, where 0 is no disturbance or neutral and 10 is the highest disturbance you can imagine, how disturbing does it feel now?"*

0	1	2	3	4	5	6	7	8	9	10

(no disturbance)   (highest disturbance)

Location of Body Sensation

Say, *"Where do you feel it* (the disturbance) *in your body?"*

_____

_____

Phase 4: Desensitization

To begin, say the following:

> Say, *"Now, remember, it is your own brain that is doing the healing and you are the one in control. Please focus mentally on the target and follow my fingers* (or any other bilateral stimulation [BLS] you are using). *Just let whatever happens, happen. After a set, just tell me what comes up, and don't discard anything as unimportant. Any new information that comes to mind is connected in some way. Anything that comes up is good and valuable. If you want to stop, just raise your hand."*

_____

> Then say, *"Bring up the picture and the words* _____ (clinician repeats the negative cognition [NC]) *and notice where you feel the distress in your body. Now follow my fingers with your eyes* (or other BLS).*"*

_____

_____

Continue until SUD = 0.

Phase 5: Installation of PC

> Say, *"How does* _____ (repeat the PC, or introduce here *"I can deal with the image,"* if the NC was, *"I cannot deal with the image"*) *sound?"*

_____

_____

> Say, *"Do the words* _____ (repeat the PC) *still fit or is there another positive statement that feels better?"*

_____

_____

If the patient accepts the original positive cognition (PC), the clinician should ask for a VOC rating to see if it has improved.

> Say, *"As you think of the incident, how do the words feel, from 1 being completely false to 7 being completely true?"*

1	2	3	4	5	6	7

(completely false)   (completely true)

> Say, *"Think of the event and hold it together with the words* _____ (repeat the PC).*"*

_____

_____

Do a set of bilateral stimulation (BLS).

Say, *"And now as you think of the incident, how do the words feel, from 1 being completely false to 7 being completely true?"*

  1   2   3   4   5   6   7

(completely false)   (completely true)

Say, *"Think of the event and hold it together with the words _____ (repeat the PC)."*

_____

_____

Repeat until VOC = 7.

Phase 6: Body Scan

Say, *"Close your eyes and keep in mind the original memory and the positive cognition. Then bring your attention to the different parts of your body, starting with your head and working downward. Any place you find any tension, tightness, or unusual sensation coming up?"*

_____

_____

Phase 7: Closure

Say, *"Things may come up or they may not. If they do, great. Write it down and it can be a target for next time. You can use a log to write down triggers, images, thoughts, cognitions, emotions, and sensations; you can rate them on our 0-to-10 scale where 0 is no disturbance or neutral and 10 is the worst disturbance. Please write down the positive experiences, too."*

"If you get any new memories, dreams, or situations that disturb you, just take a good snapshot. It isn't necessary to give a lot of detail. Just put down enough to remind you so we can target it next time. The same thing goes for any positive dreams or situations. If negative feelings do come up, try not to make them significant. Remember, it's still just the old stuff. Just write it down for next time. Then use the tape or the safe-place exercise to let as much of the disturbance go as possible. Even if nothing comes up, make sure to use the tape every day and give me a call if you need to."

_____

_____

Phase 8: Reevaluation

It is important to pay attention to the following questions when the patient returns after doing EMDR work.

Say, *"When you think of whatever is left of the problem that we worked on last time, how disturbing is it now on a scale of 0 to 10, where 0 is no disturbance or neutral and 10 is the highest disturbance you can imagine, how disturbing does it feel now?"*

  0   1   2   3   4   5   6   7   8   9   10

(no disturbance)   (highest disturbance)

Say, *"Have you noticed any other material associated with the original memory since the last session?"*

_____

_____

Say, *"Have all the necessary targets been reprocessed so that you can feel at peace with the past, empowered in the present, and able to make choices for the future?"*

_____

_____

Say, *"Has the work that we have done with EMDR helped you be more adaptive in your day-to-day life?"*

_____

_____

Say, *"Okay, then we can move on and start with the next module."*

II. TIMELINE PATH

Modules: Applicable in Module 2 (fears) and Module 6 (negative body image).

References: de Jongh (2012); de Jongh, ten Broeke, and Meijer (2010); Hofmann and Luber (2009); Logie and de Jongh (2014).

Core: For treatment of symptoms that have developed over time gradually after several events. Relevant memories are reprocessed chronologically.

The scripted questions are concentrated on fears here. If used for other symptoms, then replace "fear" by whatever is the alternative symptom.

Rationale

Say, *"For better understanding of your fear we must figure out which memories are crucial. You were not born with this fear, right? So, it started after one specific event or a series of events and then subsequently got worse after another series of events. Due to these events, you have learned to fear and avoid certain objects and situations (e.g., having a meal with others).*

Memories of these past events are still active. This means that your memories of these events can be triggered and reactivated, consciously or unconsciously, every time you are exposed to a situation that reminds you of these former 'distressing' events, like being criticized about your figure by a relative, or being excluded by a friend.

With EMDR, I will help you resolve/integrate these memories so they become neutral and will no longer disturb you and keep you from participation in these situations. Your fear will disappear and you can re-experience a sense of safety and confidence and do things you couldn't do before. To find the crucial memories for the development of this fear, I'll ask you, as if in a time machine, to search your mind through time to determine which events on your timeline started, or aggravated, your fear. Is this clear to you?"

_____

_____

Say, *"We discovered that distressing memories of past negative experiences have gradually made you afraid of* _____ (state the specific fear). *In this module, we will work on these memories until your fear has gone."*

_____

_____

Timeline

Say, *"When, after which event, did this* _____ (fear) *start?"*

_____

_____

Say, *"Are you sure that you did not suffer from this* _____ (fear) *before this event already?"*

_____

_____

Say, *"What other events came later that increased your* _____ (fear)*?"*

_____

_____

Options Only for Fears

Say, *"What in this situation specifically frightens you?"*

_____

_____

Say, *"When, after which event, did this specific fear start?"*

_____

_____

Say, *"What other events came later that increased your fear?"*

_____

_____

Say, *"What do you expect that might happen to you when you are exposed to the object/ situation you fear?"*

_____

_____

Say, *"When and what event started this fear?"*

_____

_____

Say, *"When and what event aggravated this fear?"*

_____

_____

Say, *"Now, we have collected the events that seem related to your fear. Let's put them on a timeline."*

_____

_____

Use pencil and paper to create the timeline with your patient.

Progression of the Symptom in Time

Say, *"Let us now look at how your specific fear was affected by these events over time. Please indicate which of the events had the biggest impact on the increase of your fear. Not all of them will have contributed in the same degree. Which of them contributed the most? You can indicate this in different ways, like drawing a line that shows how your fear developed over time, marking with an angle upward how strong the fear increased after specific events. Another way to indicate this is highlighting those events that gave a strong increase in fear. Please choose a way and indicate it, so we see which events seem to be the most crucial ones."*

Sequence of the Targets

A reason for deviation from chronology might be if a specific, more recent event seems to have contributed more than an earlier one on the timeline and is now still strongly distressing (i.e., high SUD). In case of doubt, the therapist can ask the following question, to identify relevant memories:

Say, *"Which of these memories raises your fear most, right now?"*

_____

_____

Determine which memory to start with, based on the patient's answer.

Phase 3: Assessment

Say, *"Okay, so we start with the memory of ___ (state the selected memory). What is the worst image of that memory?"*

_____

_____

Negative Cognition (NC)

Say, *"What words best go with the image that express your negative belief about yourself, or the image now?"*

_____

_____

Positive Cognition (PC)

Note: Skip asking for the positive cognition during assessment if the negative cognition is, "I am powerless/I cannot deal with the image," because the positive cognition can only be, "I can deal with the image." It is not useful to ask for the PC during assessment. However, install the standard positive cognition, "I can deal with the image," after SUD has become 0.

Say, *"When you bring up that picture or _____ (state the issue), what would you like to believe about yourself now?"*

_____

_____

Validity of Cognition (VOC)

Say, *"When you think of the incident* (or picture) *how true do those words _____* (clinician repeats the positive cognition) *feel to you now on a scale of 1 to 7, where 1 feels completely false and 7 feels completely true?"*

1   2   3   4   5   6   7

(completely false)   (completely true)

Emotions

Say, *"When you bring up the picture or _____ (state the issue) and those words _____* (clinician states the negative cognition), *what emotion do you feel now?"*

_____

_____

Subjective Units of Disturbance (SUD)

Say, *"On a scale of 0 to 10, where 0 is no disturbance or neutral and 10 is the highest disturbance you can imagine, how disturbing does it feel now?"*

0   1   2   3   4   5   6   7   8   9   10

(no disturbance)   (highest disturbance)

Location of Body Sensation

Say, *"Where do you feel it* (the disturbance) *in your body?"*

_____

_____

Continue with the rest of the Standard EMDR Protocol.

Phase 4: Desensitization

To begin, say the following:

Say, *"Now, remember, it is your own brain that is doing the healing and you are the one in control. I will ask you to mentally focus on the target and to follow my fingers (or any other bilateral stimulation [BLS] you are using). Just let whatever happens, happen, and we will talk at the end of the set. Just tell me what comes up, and don't discard anything as unimportant. Any new information that comes to mind is connected in some way. If you want to stop, just raise your hand."*

_____

Then say, *"Bring up the picture and the words* _____ (clinician repeats the negative cognition [NC]) *and notice where you feel it in your body. Now follow my fingers with your eyes* (or other BLS).*"*

_____

_____

Phase 5: Installation

Say, *"How does* _____ (repeat the PC) *sound?"*

_____

_____

Say, *"Do the words* _____ (repeat the PC) *still fit or is there another positive statement that feels better?"*

_____

_____

If the patient accepts the original positive cognition (PC), the clinician should ask for a VOC rating to see if it has improved.

Say, *"As you think of the incident, how do the words feel, from 1 being completely false to 7 being completely true?"*

1	2	3	4	5	6	7

(completely false)   (completely true)

Say, *"Think of the event and hold it together with the words* _____ (repeat the PC).*"*

_____

_____

Do a long set of bilateral stimulation (BLS) to see if there is more processing to be done.

Phase 6: Body Scan

Say, *"Close your eyes and keep in mind the original memory and the positive cognition. Then bring your attention to the different parts of your body, starting with your head and working downward. Any place you find any tension, tightness, or unusual sensation, tell me."*

_____

_____

Phase 7: Closure

Say, *"Things may come up or they may not. If they do, great. Write it down, and it can be a target for next time. You can use a log to write down triggers, images, thoughts, cognitions, emotions, and sensations; you can rate them on our 0-to-10 scale where 0 is no disturbance or neutral and 10 is the worst disturbance. Please write down the positive experiences, too."*

"If you get any new memories, dreams, or situations that disturb you, just take a good snapshot. It isn't necessary to give a lot of detail. Just put down enough to remind you so we can target it next time. The same thing goes for any positive dreams or situations. If negative feelings do come up, try not to make them significant. Remember, it's still just the old stuff. Just write it down for next time. Then use the tape or the safe-place exercise to let as much of the disturbance go as possible. Even if nothing comes up, make sure to use the tape every day and give me a call if you need to."

_____

_____

Phase 8: Reevaluation

It is important to pay attention to the following questions when the patient returns after doing EMDR work.

Say, *"When you think of whatever is left of the problem that we worked on last time, how disturbing is it now on a scale of 0 to 10, where 0 is no disturbance or neutral and 10 is the highest disturbance you can imagine?"*

    0   1   2   3   4   5   6   7   8   9   10

(no disturbance)   (highest disturbance)

Say, *"Have you noticed any other material associated with the original memory since the last session?"*

_____

_____

Say, *"Have all the necessary targets been reprocessed so that you can feel at peace with the past, empowered in the present, and able to make choices for the future?"*

_____

_____

Say, *"Has the work that we have done with EMDR helped you be more adaptive in your day-to-day life?"*

_____

_____

Other Targets: Flash-Forward

After having neutralized all relevant memories that currently fuel the fear, check as part of the timeline path whether the patient has an explicit imagination about a future event, a so-called flash-forward.

Say, *"We have to figure out now what you fear will happen when you are confronted with _____ (object or situation that is avoided). Basically, what catastrophe do you expect to happen, that prevents you from doing what you want or need to do? What's the 'worst nightmare' that's in your head? And what is the worst image of it?"*

_____

_____

The standard NC is, "I cannot deal with the image."

And the standard PC is, "I can deal with the image."

Continue with the assessment and desensitization phases until SUD = 0. Do installation until VOC = 7.

Preparation for the Future

Prepare the patient for the future with either the mental video check or future template. The mental video check seems to be an effective alternative for the future template. Application of both, however, may be redundant. However, because this is not yet validated empirically, consider using both, if an extra boost seems useful for this patient.

Mental Video Check

Say, *"And now I'd like you to imagine yourself stepping into the scene of a future confrontation with the object or the situation. Close your eyes and play a movie of this happening, from the beginning until the end. Imagine yourself coping with any challenges that come your way. Notice what you are seeing, thinking, feeling, and experiencing in your body. And tell me about that. While playing this movie, let me know if you hit any blocks of tension. If you do, just open your eyes, concentrate on what you see or otherwise experience, and I will do one set of eye movements. Then continue playing the mental video until you feel any tension again. Open your eyes, concentrate on what you experience, and I will do another set. Resume the movie, and run the movie until the end."*

If the patient is at the end of his or her mental video, he or she is asked to play the movie once more, from the beginning until the end; eye movements are introduced if the patient encounters any new tension.

Say, *"Okay, play the movie one more time from beginning to end and open your eyes when you experience tension. Concentrate on what you see or experience otherwise. When you open your eyes, this is a sign for me to perform another set of eye movements."*

_____

_____

Repeat this procedure until the movie can be played without any tension or significant disturbance during the movie.

Future Template

Say, *"What is the image of the situation that you want to be capable of dealing with again, now that you have come so far?"*

_____

_____

Say, *"To what extent do you feel capable of dealing with this situation, on a scale of 1 to 7?"*

_____

_____

Continue installing the PC until the VOC does not increase any further.

Homework Assignment

Say, *"Let us make an agreement now about your homework for the coming week to profit from the wonderful work you have done. I suggest that you _____ (give assignments with behavioral experiments, building up confrontation with the phobic objects or situations)."*

III. DYSFUNCTIONAL BELIEF PATH

Modules: Applicable in Module 4 (low self-esteem) and Module 5 (clinical perfectionism).
References: de Jongh, ten Broeke, and Meijer (2010); de Jongh, ten Broeke, and Hornsveld (2014); ten Broeke, de Jongh, Oppenheim (2012).
Core: When dysfunctional beliefs have resulted in persistent symptom clusters, memories of events are reprocessed that are "pieces of evidence" for the patient currently for the validity of these dysfunctional beliefs. The aim is to discredit these core beliefs.

Rationale

Say, *"We discovered that some of your problems, like _____ (state specific symptoms), are related to one or more several deeply rooted beliefs you have about yourself, like _____ (state core belief: I am ____)."*

If the core beliefs are not clear yet, say the following:

Say, *"Some of your problems, like _____ (state specific symptoms), seem related to one or more deeply rooted beliefs about yourself. First, we are going to find out what specific beliefs you have about yourself that causes these problems. We are looking for beliefs that have resulted from big or minor experiences, mostly with other people, which you may have had early in your life, like being bullied, violated, neglected, or sexually abused. Also, other kinds of experiences may have played a role, like having failed in school or sports, having done or left things that you regret deeply.*

Because a lot of experiences in your past and current life confirmed and strengthened this belief continuously and still do, this belief became firm like a conviction. Beliefs like these become like the glasses through which you look at the world.

One of the characteristics for these kinds of beliefs is that you know that they are not true, but they feel true. Do you recognize this?"

_____

_____

Goal of EMDR Therapy

Say, *"With EMDR we are going to change these deeply rooted beliefs that are causing you problems. We do this by working with your memories of early experiences that 'prove' to you still today that your belief is true. To this end, we will first look for memories of your most key experiences upholding this belief about yourself. When we have found these, we will make this belief lose its credibility by reprocessing your memories of these experiences. Does this make sense?"*

_____

_____

Identification of Core Belief

Say, *"Negative beliefs about oneself can result in various psychological symptoms, like depressive moods and persistent behavioral patterns, or _____ (state the* symptoms of the patient). *What negative belief about yourself is related to these problems? What is the conviction you have about yourself that drives you to do or feel like this?"*

_____

_____

Say, *"When you think of this belief, how true does it feel now on a scale of 0 to 100, where 0 is not true at all and 100 means that the belief is completely true?"*

0   10   20   30   40   50   60   70   80   90   100

(not true)   (completely true)

Identification of "Pieces of Evidence"

Say, *"At this moment, which past experiences still prove to you that you are _____ (state core belief)?"*   .

_____

_____

Or ask alternative questions:

Say, *"What have you experienced in your life that makes you believe _____ (state core belief) so constantly and persistently?"*

_____

_____

Say, *"What made you start believing that you are _____ (state core belief)?"*

_____

_____

Say, *"What or who 'taught' you that you are _____ (state core belief)?"*

_____

_____

Say, *"Which early experience/s 'prove' to you still that you are _____ (state core belief)?"*

_____

_____

Say, *"Think of a more recent situation that makes it clear to you that you are _____ (state core belief)."*

_____

_____

Say, *"Convince me that you are* _____ *(state core belief)?"*

_____

_____

Say, *"Let's give a brief title to each memory or situation that you just mentioned."*

_____

_____

Say, *"Please write down now between three and five of the 'strongest proofs for the belief' that feel like 'pieces of evidence' for this belief. Use a maximum of 10 lines to describe each memory."*

_____

_____

If a patient mentions a number of experiences instead of a single experience, you can propose an *archive*:

Say, *"It seems that this evidence concerns not just a single experience, but a bunch of experiences that fit together, like in an archive. Which one is the most relevant memory of this archive, proving most convincingly that your belief is true? We are going to target that one with EMDR. If needed, we can target more than one memory within this archive. Just let me know, if you think several ones of this archive must be selected. We will start with one. And, when this one is 'ready', we will see how we continue from there."*

Ranking of the Memories as "Pieces of Evidence"

Say, *"We selected* _____ *(state a number between three and five) 'pieces of evidence'. Now we must decide which memory to start with. Tell me, which experience proves to you most strongly that* _____ *(mention core belief) is true?"*

_____

_____

Continue from here with the Standard EMDR Protocol until the end of Phase 4: SUD = 0.

Start with the strongest "piece of evidence" and go on with the next one until all memories ("pieces of evidence") have been reprocessed.

Postpone installation of the PC (if in the domain of self-esteem) until all pieces of evidence have been neutralized, so that the positive cognition can become VOC = 7.

The first targets (pieces of evidence) usually take quite some time before they get neutralized, SUD = 0.

Say, *"We will keep on working on each of the memories, pieces of evidence, that we have selected, successively, until you can think of them without believing any longer that you are a* _____ *(state core belief).*

_____

_____

Phase 4: Desensitization

Desensitize all relevant memories ("pieces of evidence") from the archive for one belief.

Phase 5: Installation

Say, *"Now we are going to finish all targets we have been working with so far. I will mention per target* (memory/image that we worked on) *the positive words that you have chosen before, and I am going to ask you to think of the image together with these words. We will finish them one by one."*

"As you think of the first image ___ (state the title of the event), *how do the words ___* (state PC) *feel, from 1 being completely false to 7 being completely true?"*

1	2	3	4	5	6	7

(completely false)   (completely true)

Say, *"Think of the image and hold it together with the words _____* (repeat the PC)."

_____

_____

Repeat this for all images until PC for all images has become VOC = 7.

Continue until Phase 8.

The Standard EMDR Protocol is repeated for all "pieces of evidence."
For each piece of evidence, select the image that the patient experiences/sees as the strongest proof (until there is no convincing evidence left).

COMPLEMENTARY INTERVENTIONS

Future Template

Say, *"What could be a good alternative to believe about yourself?"*

_____

_____

Say, *"Slowly but surely you will start to believe in your new positive belief about yourself or at least you will lose your firm conviction that your negative belief is true. Imagine that you no longer believe in your* (negative) *core belief _____* (state belief) *but instead you're starting to believe your new, positive assumption more and more strongly. What would your life look like? Take a moment for this and make it as specific and detailed as possible."*

_____

_____

Say, *"What would you do that you are now* not *doing* (e.g., "I would dare to speak up, if I would want to")?"

_____

_____

Say, *"What current behavior would you stop* (e.g., "I would stop apologizing all the time")?"

_____

_____

Say, *"Start practicing this new behavior and for now, just pretend,
it, 'til you make it.' Once you practice, you'll get better and bette*
you are it!'"

IV. FLASH-FORWARD PATH

Modules: Applicable in Module 2 (fears) and Module 5 (clinical perfectionis.
References: Logie and de Jongh (2014, 2016).
Core: For symptoms of anticipatory anxiety caused by images of distressing a
a potential feared future experience (catastrophe). The most distressing image

Rationale

Say, *"Fears or worries can be aroused in people by images in their head of pas*
and also by images of future experiences. People can have fantasies of
happen to them in the future, and these fantasies can guide their present be   . and
emotions. These fantasies can be positive and negative. Both can cause problems. Now
we are going to work on your negative images of possible future events. Our aim is to
help you realize that this image is only an image in your head, and that also your body
is going to realize that, so that you will be able to tolerate looking at these images and
they will no longer disturb you."

Identify the Catastrophic Event

Say, *"We need to figure out what kind of image is in your head making you scared about*
a future confrontation with what you fear. What is the worst thing you could imagine
happening? Basically, we look for your ultimate doom scenario."

_____

_____

If necessary, ask additional questions:

Say, *"What do you imagine might go wrong if you* _____ (state the concern, like, 'Eat
everything that is on your plate', 'Will have gained weight according to your sched-
ule', or 'Stop vomiting after eating', etc.)?"

_____

_____

Say, *"If you had a terrible nightmare about* _____ (state the concern), *what would the*
most disturbing picture look like?"

_____

_____

Follow the Event to Its Ultimate Conclusion

Say, *"Why would this be so terrible for you?"*

_____

_____

at would be the worst thing about that?"

_____

_____

Repeat as necessary until the patient cannot identify anything worse.

Phase 3: Assessment

Make a Detailed Picture of Flash-Forward

Image

Say, *"What would the worst image of this nightmare* _____ (the flash-forward identified previously) *look like exactly?"*

_____

_____

Or say, *"What do you see?"*

_____

_____

If more than one picture:

Say, *"If you were forced to choose, what would be most disturbing for you now: the picture of* _____ (state the most disturbing) *or the picture that represents* _____ (state the picture)*?"*

_____

_____

Negative Cognition (NC)

Say, *"The words coming with that picture must be 'I cannot deal with the image,' right?"*

_____

_____

Positive Cognition (PC)

Assessment of positive cognition is skipped because it has no added value to ask for it. There is only one option: "I can deal with the image." It will be installed, however, when SUD = 0.

From here continue with the Standard EMDR Protocol until SUD = 0.

Emotions

Say, *"When you bring up* _____ (state the flash-forward) *and those words* _____ (clinician states the negative cognition), *what emotion do you feel now?"*

_____

_____

Subjective Units of Disturbance (SUD)

Say, *"On a scale of 0 to 10, where 0 is no disturbance or neutral and 10 is the highest disturbance you can imagine, how disturbing does it feel now?"*

0	1	2	3	4	5	6	7	8	9	10

(no disturbance)   (highest disturbance)

Location of Body Sensation

Say, *"Where do you feel it* (the disturbance) *in your body?"*

_____

_____

Phase 4: Desensitization

Apply the Standard EMDR Protocol in the usual way. During the reprocessing, the therapist should ask the patient to do the following:

Say, *"Go with that."*

Or say, *"Notice that,"* for subsequent sets of BLS.

To begin, say the following:

Say, *"Now, remember, it is your own brain that is doing the healing and you are the one in control. I will ask you to mentally focus on the target and to follow my fingers (or any other bilateral stimulation [BLS] you are using). Just let whatever happens, happen, and we will talk at the end of the set. Just tell me what comes up, and don't discard anything as unimportant. Any new information that comes to mind is connected in some way. If you want to stop, just raise your hand."*

_____

Then say, *"Bring up the picture and the words* _____ (clinician repeats the negative cognition [NC]) *and notice where you feel it in your body. Now follow my fingers with your eyes* (or other BLS).*"*

_____

Even though the target is a future catastrophe, the patient may spontaneously bring up the original trauma even though it had previously, apparently, been fully processed. If this occurs, the therapist should continue to allow the patient to go with the past event because the flash-forward may have elicited other channels connected to the trauma that had not previously been processed.

As appropriate, the therapist should use cognitive interweaves if these become necessary.

Note: EMDR focused on flash-forwards usually goes smoothly and therapists rarely need to use cognitive interweaves.

Phase 5: Installation

Install the PC.

Say, *"As you think of the* _____ (state the flash-forward), *how true do the words, 'I can deal with the picture,' feel from 1 being completely false to 7 being completely true?"*

1	2	3	4	5	6	7

(completely false)   (completely true)

Say, *"Think of the* _____ (state the flash-forward) *and hold it together with the words* _____ (repeat the PC). *Go with that."*

_____

_____

Continue this procedure until the VOC is 7. Then continue with body scan.

Prepare for the Future

As in the timeline path, the mental video check can be used as an alternative for the future template.

Mental Video Check

Say, *"This time, I'd like you to imagine yourself stepping into the scene of a future confrontation with the object or a situation that we just worked on. Close your eyes and play a movie of this happening, from the beginning until the end. Imagine yourself coping with any challenges that come your way. Notice what you are seeing, thinking, feeling, and experiencing in your body and tell me about that. While playing this movie, let me know if you hit any blocks. If you do, just open your eyes and let me know. If you don't hit any blocks, let me know when you have viewed the whole movie."*

_____

_____

If the patient encounters a block and opens his/her eyes, it is a sign for the therapist to instruct the patient further and do one more set of bilateral stimulation. Then let the patient continue going through the scene. Repeat this until the movie can be played without any blocks or significant disturbances.

Future Template

Say, *"What is the image of the situation that you want to be capable of dealing with again, now that you have come so far?"*

_____

_____

Say, *"To what extent do you feel capable of dealing with this situation, on a scale of 1 to 7?"*

_____

_____

Continue installing the PC until the VOC does not increase any further.

Homework Assignment

Say, *"Let us make an agreement now about your homework for the coming week to profit from the wonderful work you have done. I suggest that you* _____ (give assignments with behavioral experiments, building up confrontation with the phobic objects or situations)."*

Phase 7: Closure

Say, *"Things may come up or they may not. If they do, great. Write it down and it can be a target for next time. You can use a log to write down triggers, images, thoughts, cognitions, emotions, and sensations; you can rate them on our 0-to-10 scale where 0 is no disturbance or neutral and 10 is the worst disturbance. Please write down the positive experiences, too.*

If you get any new fantasies, memories, dreams, or situations that disturb you, just take a good snapshot. It isn't necessary to give a lot of detail. Just put down enough to remind you so we can target it next time. The same thing goes for any positive dreams or situations. If negative feelings do come up, try not to make them significant. Remember, it's still just the old stuff. Just write it down for next time."

Phase 8: Reevaluation

After the application of the flash-forward procedure, there may still be a need for additional targeting and other strategies necessary to ensure that the treatment goals are met. An evaluation of what still remains to be done should be made at the beginning of the next session. The patient is asked about his/her current symptoms and about his/her progress. It is advisable to always evaluate in terms of a patient's SUD level on the already processed material.

Say, *"As you think back on the target that we were working on last time* (mention the flash-forward the patient had), *on a scale of 0 to 10, where 0 is no disturbance or neutral and 10 is the highest disturbance you can imagine, how disturbing does it feel now?"*

0	1	2	3	4	5	6	7	8	9	10

(no disturbance)   (highest disturbance)

If the disturbance level has increased above 0, these reverberations need to be targeted or otherwise addressed. The therapist should assess the necessity of teaching the patient additional self-control techniques or other relevant exercises that could further enhance his/her ability to confront the former anxiety-provoking situation in real life.

Say, *"So what other resources do you think might be helpful in assisting you to deal with this situation?"*

_____

_____

V. DYSFUNCTIONAL POSITIVE TARGET PATH

Modules: Applicable in Module 3 (urge-driven ED behaviors) and Module 5 (clinical perfectionism).
References: Hornsveld and Markus (2014) and Markus and Hornsveld (2015).
Core: For reduction of specific urge-driven ED behaviors: having binges (uncontrolled eating), fasting, or compensatory behaviors (excessive motor activity or purging, vomiting, taking laxatives or diuretics); also for behaviors related to clinical perfectionism. Aim is neutralization of images (of past, present, or future situations) that activate the urge to perform these behaviors. There are three potential steps.

V.1. Positive Memories

Rationale

Say, *"Now we are going to work on behaviors that you keep on doing, though you know that they are not good for you. We will focus specifically on _____* (state the symptom such as binges, fasting, vomiting, using laxatives, diuretics, excessive moving; optionally also: setting extremely high standards for yourself). *These behaviors are so persistent, because the urge to perform them is triggered by images of either positive past experiences* (like seeing yourself feeling content with yourself) *or images of possible future experiences* (like seeing yourself being admired by others). *Our aim is to* *make sure that these images will no longer elicit your _____ (state the symptom). Therefore, we will look for the images that elicit in you the strongest urge to perform them and then we will neutralize these memories/fantasies. Okay?"*

_____

Say, *"We discussed that your _____ (state particular behavior) is difficult to stop because of the positive consequences of it. The positive consequences that we discussed are _____ (state the positive consequences). We will work in three steps; first, we will focus on past memories, then on the present triggers for your _____ (state particular behavior), and finally on your expectations of the future."*

Positive Memories of the Past

Say, *"What is your most positive memory related to having performed your _____ (state specific behavior)?"*

_____

_____

Say, *"What positive memory has contributed the most to your _____ (state specific behavior)?"*

_____

_____

Say, *"What positive memory evokes the strongest urge to perform this _____ (symptom) right here and now?"*

_____

_____

Phase 3: Assessment

Say, *"So we can conclude that probably your most positive memory evoking the urge currently to perform ___ (state behavior) is _____ (have patient choose the strongest memory of those just mentioned)."*

_____

_____

Say, *"Which image of this picture evokes the urge the strongest?"*

_____

_____

Say, *"What words about yourself go with this image that evoke the strongest urge in you to _____ (state the symptom)? So this time we are not looking for words that cause the distress of the image, but words that maximize the effect of the image on your urge."*

_____

_____

Say, *"When you look at the image, and you say to yourself* _____ (state the positive
words), *what emotion do you feel right now?"*

_____

_____

The SUD is not measured. Instead, measure the level of urge (LOU) and the level of positive affect (LOPA) that the image is evoking.

Say, *"When you look at the image, and you say to yourself* ___ (the chosen words), *how
strong is the urge to* _____ (mention the symptom) *that you are experiencing right now,
on a scale from 0 to 10, where 0 is no urge or neutral and 10 is the highest urge you
can imagine?"*

| 0 | 1 | 2 | 3 | 4 | 5 | 6 | 7 | 8 | 9 | 10 |

(no disturbance)   (highest disturbance)

Level of Urge _____/10

_____

_____

Say, *"When you look at the image and say to yourself* ___ (the chosen words), *how positive or attractive is it right now on a scale from 0 to 10, where 0 is neutral and 10 is the
most positive or attractive you can imagine?"*

| 0 | 1 | 2 | 3 | 4 | 5 | 6 | 7 | 8 | 9 | 10 |

(no disturbance)   (highest disturbance)

Level of Positive Affect ___/10

_____

_____

Say, *"So the strongest of these two is* ___ (mention either LOU or LOPA). *Where in your
body do you feel this urge/positive affect the strongest?"*

_____

_____

From here continue with desensitization with the Standard EMDR Protocol.

Phase 4: Desensitization

Back to target deviates from the regular procedure: either LOPA or LOU is monitored instead of SUD.

Say, *"Bring up the image that we started with, as it is now. How much* ___ (LOU or LOPA)
goes with it now?"

_____

_____

Say, *"What in the image is causing this?"*

_____

_____

Say, *"Focus on that and go on."*

_____

_____

Continue desensitization until there is a significant decrease of LOPA or LOU—not necessarily until 0, but a significant decrease.

Then continue with installation.

Phase 5: Installation

Say, *"Bring up the image that we started with, as it is now, and say to yourself, 'I can deal with the picture' (meaning 'I can resist the image'), or 'I am strong.' Which of these do you prefer?"*

Say, *"On a scale from 1 to 7, how true do the words feel from 1 being completely false to 7 being completely true?"*

1	2	3	4	5	6	7

(completely false)   (completely true)

Continue until VOC = 7 and the last part of the Standard EMDR Protocol.

After having reprocessed relevant memories, the focus can move to present trigger situations that evoke the urge.

V.2. Present Trigger Situations

Images of Present Trigger Situations

Say, *"As I told you at the start of this module, the first step for reducing your ___ (state the symptom) was to work with relevant memories, so that they would no longer evoke the urge to perform this behavior. Now we are ready for the next step, that is, to work with current situations. We know that a lot of situations can trigger an urge to perform your _____ (state symptom). Our next goal is that you will get more control over yourself in these situations and not be seduced any longer to perform this behavior. Does this make sense to you? Are you ready for it?"*

_____

_____

Say, *"What situations are difficult for you, because they evoke the urge to do this? I will give you some suggestions and let me know please if they fit for you."*

- *When you are depressed, nervous, lonely, bored, sad, or angry?*   ☐ Yes ☐ No
- *When you are relaxed and happy?*   ☐ Yes ☐ No
- *When you are alone?*   ☐ Yes ☐ No
- *When you are dissatisfied with your body?*   ☐ Yes ☐ No
- *When you are dissatisfied with yourself?*   ☐ Yes ☐ No
- *Other situations* _____

Say, *"Let us make a list of the five most difficult situations for you."*

Trigger Situation 1: _____

Trigger Situation 2: _____

Trigger Situation 3: _____

Trigger Situation 4: _____

Trigger Situation 5: _____

Phase 3: Assessment

Say, *"With respect to the first trigger situation* _____ (state Trigger Situation 1), *which image gives you the strongest urge to perform* _____ (state symptom). *Look at the picture of this situation and pause it at the image where you feel the strongest urge."*

Image: _____

Then identify the NC by asking for the words that go with the picture, strengthening maximally the urge to perform the behavior.

Say, *"What words do you say to yourself that maximize the urge to perform* _____ (state symptom)*? For example: 'I need this'; 'This food is my best friend'; and/or 'I have earned it.'"*

Or say, *"Vomiting gives me the relief that I need,"* or *"Performing excellently shows the world that I count."*

_____

_____

Say, *"When you look at the image of the trigger situation and say those words* _____ (state the words), *what emotion do you feel now?"*

_____

_____

Say, *"When you look at the image of the trigger situation and say those words* _____ (state the words), *what is the intensity of your urge to perform the behavior on a scale of 0 to 10, where 0 is no urge or neutral and 10 is strongest urge you can imagine. How strong is your urge right now?"*

0	1	2	3	4	5	6	7	8	9	10

(lowest urge)   (highest urge)

LOU _____

Say, *"When you look at the image and you say to yourself the words* ___ (state the words), *how much disturbance do you feel right now on a scale from 0 to 10, where 0 is no disturbance or neutral and 10 is the most distress you can imagine."*

0	1	2	3	4	5	6	7	8	9	10

(no disturbance)   (highest disturbance)

SUD: _____

Say, *"Where do you feel this in your body?"*

_____

_____

Say, *"Go with that."*
From here continue with the Standard EMDR Protocol from Phase 4 until Phase 8.
Process the image of this first trigger situation until the LOU no longer decreases. Repeat the procedure for all relevant trigger situations.

Phase 4: Desensitization

Note: Back to target is again deviating from the regular procedure: Both LOU and SUD are monitored.

Say, *"Bring up the image that we started with, as it is now. How much ___ (state the measure of LOU/SUD you are using) is it now?"*

____/10

Say, *"What in the image is causing this urge/disturbance?"*

_____

_____

Say, *"Focus on that and go on."*

_____

_____

Continue desensitization until there is a significant decrease of LOU/SUD—not necessarily until 0, but a significant decrease.

Phase 5: Installation

Say, *"Bring up the image that we started with, as it is now, and say to yourself, 'I can deal with the picture' (meaning 'I can resist the image'), or 'I am strong.' Which of these do you prefer?"*

_____

_____

Say, *"On a scale from 1 (completely false) to 7 (completely true), how true do the words feel?"*

1	2	3	4	5	6	7

(completely false)   (completely true)

Continue until VOC = 7.

Preparation for the Future

Use the mental video check as an alternative to the future template.

Mental Video Check

Say, *"Now close your eyes and imagine yourself going through this trigger situation that we have been working on. Imagine yourself going there and see how you manage from beginning until the end. Check if there are any cues or aspects in this situation that are still difficult for you to deal with because they evoke so much disturbance or urge that they could keep you from dealing with this situation adequately. Open your eyes when you experience any disturbance or urge. Notice what you are seeing, thinking, feeling, and experiencing in your body and tell me about it. While going through this scene, let me know if you hit any blocks. If you do, just open your eyes. Then we will do another set of _____ (state BLS). If you do not hit any blocks, let me know when you have gone through the whole scene of the situation."*

If the patient encounters a block and opens his/her eyes, this is a sign for the therapist to do one more set ____ (state BLS). Then let the patient continue going through the scene. Repeat this until the movie can be played without any blocks or significant disturbances.

Then prepare homework assignments and behavior experiments for the coming week.

After having reprocessed relevant memories and images of present trigger situations, activating the urge, the focus can move to dysfunctional images of desired future experiences (fantasies), positive flash-forwards.

V.3. Positive Flash-Forwards

Positive Images of Future Situation

Say, *"What is the most desired outcome you see in your head of performing ____ (the specific behavior)?*

_____

_____

Say, *"Please make an image of that, representing the most desirable outcome that you have in your head and tell me what you see."*
Give an example if your patient does not understand the question.

Say, *"For example, some people say that they vomit because they expect to feel free afterwards, so an image of yourself feeling free after vomiting could be what we are looking for. Other people may say that they expect to feel relaxed after eating a lot of food, or that they expect to feel in control when they are below a certain weight level. What is the outcome that you desire of the behavior we are now focusing on?"*

_____

_____

Phase 3: Assessment

Say, *"What is the image that you have in your head?"*

_____

_____

Note: The NC is not asked, but instead words that go with the picture and strengthen the urge and the positive affect.

Say, *"What words about yourself go with this image that evoke the strongest urge in you to _____ (state the symptom)? So, we are not looking for words that cause distress of the image, but words that maximize the effect that the image has on your urge."*

_____

_____

Say, *"When you look at the image, and you say to yourself _____ what emotion do you feel right now?"*

_____

_____

Instead of SUD, ask for level of positive affect (LOPA) and level of urge (LOU) that the image is evoking.

Say, *"When you look at the image, and you say to yourself ___ (the chosen words), how strong is the urge to _____ (mention the symptom) that you are experiencing right now, on a scale from 0 to 10, where 0 is no urge or neutral and 10 is the highest urge you can imagine, how much urge do you experience right now?"*

0	1	2	3	4	5	6	7	8	9	10

(no urge)   (highest urge)

Level of Urge _____

Say, *"When you look at the image and say to yourself ___ (the chosen words), how positive or attractive is it right now on a scale from 0 to 10, where 0 is neutral and 10 is the most positive or attractive you can imagine?"*

0	1	2	3	4	5	6	7	8	9	10

(not attractive)   (highest attraction)

Level of Positive Affect ___

Say, *"So the strongest of these two is ___ (mention either LOU or LOPA). Where in your body do you feel this urge/positive affect the strongest?"*

_____

_____

From here continue with the desensitization phase in the regular way.

Phase 4: Desensitization

Note: Back to target is deviating from the regular procedure: Either LOPA or LOU is monitored instead of SUD. The strongest sensation of the two is chosen in the assessment phase and that one is monitored.

Say, *"Bring up the image that we started with, as it is now. How much ___ (LOU or LOPA) goes with it now?"*

___/10

"What in the image is causing this?"

_____

_____

Say, *"Focus on that and go on."*

_____

_____

Continue desensitization until there is a significant decrease of LOPA or LOU—not necessarily until 0, but a significant decrease. Then continue with installation.

Phase 5: Installation

Say, *"Bring up the image that we started with again as it is now and say to yourself: 'I can deal with the picture' (meaning 'I can resist the image'), or 'I am strong.' Which of these do you prefer?"*

_____

_____

Say, *"On a scale from 1 (completely false) to 7 (completely true), how true
    feel?"*

| 1 | 2 | 3 | 4 | 5 | 6 | 7 |

(completely false)   (completely true)

Continue until VOC = 7 and then proceed to the last phases of the Standa
    Protocol.

VI. EMOTION PATH

Modules: Applicable in Module 3 (urge-driven ED behaviors) and Module 6 (negative be
Reference: de Jongh and ten Broeke (2012).
Core: For predominant emotions, behaviors in Module 3 can be motivated by either anticipated positive emotions/sensations or by currently experienced negative emotions. The emotion path is appropriate when negative emotions are problematic intrinsically or if they are the driving force for
symptomatic behavior.

Rationale

Say, *"Now we are going to work on behaviors that you keep on doing, though you know
    that they are not good for you. We will focus specifically on _____ (state the
    symptom such as binges, fasting, vomiting, using laxatives, diuretics, excessive mov-
    ing; optionally also: setting extremely high standards for yourself). These behaviors
    are so persistent because the urge to perform them is triggered by a powerful negative
    emotion. What emotion could that be do you think?"*

_____

_____

If the patient cannot tell, say the following:

Say, *"My impression is that you feel a lot of ____ (state emotions, like anger, shame, guilt,
    disgust) that motivates you to perform this behavior. Does that make sense, and do you
    recognize this?"*

_____

_____

Or say, *"Maybe you are troubled by the predominant presence of _____ (state emotions,
    like anger, shame, guilt, disgust)."*

_____

_____

Say, *"What we are going to do now is look for memories that instantly evoke the strongest
    ___ (state the identified emotion) in you. By reprocessing the most important memory
    or memories that evoke this ___ (state emotion) in you, you will regain more control
    over this emotion and eventually, ultimately, also over this behavior. Okay?"*

_____

_____

Say, *"Which memory evokes the strongest feeling of ___ (state emotion) now?"*

_____

_____

Say, *"What is the image of that memory the makes you the most ___ (state emotion)?"*

_____

_____

From here continue with the Standard EMDR Protocol.

After having completed this target, continue with the next target: the memory that is acutely evoking the most emotion by then. Continue until the patient has more control over this problematic emotion and potentially resulting behavioral symptoms.

REEVALUATION+

Each module uses the reevaluation + script as follows.

To check if the module has been worked on sufficiently, the next questions are asked:

Say, *"Do you think that all relevant memories/images concerning this issue/module that kept your problems going are neutral now? Are any of these images still disturbing you?"*

_____

_____

Say, *"Shall I tell you which module I think is appropriate to continue with and why? Or, do you want to tell your suggestion first? We will discuss this, so we come to an agreement for our next step. I am encouraged by your progress. What do you think?"*

_____

_____

SUMMARY

Existing treatments for eating disorders are not sufficiently effective and efficient. This chapter describes how and for what symptoms EMDR therapy can be implemented in a multidisciplinary broad-spectrum treatment of patients with an eating disorder. An experimental protocol is introduced, consisting of six potential modules and six procedures of target selection. The protocol is based on the transdiagnostic theoretical model of Fairburn et al. (2003) and has shown positive results in clinical practice. Empirical validation is needed, and empirical results may necessitate adaptations in this protocol.

ACKNOWLEDGMENT

I acknowledge Hellen Hornsveld, who contributed to this manuscript by her valuable comments on earlier versions and who described a procedure for target selection with Wybren Markus (Markus & Hornsveld, 2015, 2017), part of which is included here (dysfunctional positive targets). Also, I am grateful to Ankie Roedelof for her thoughtful questions and comments, which were helpful for clarification of the protocol that is described in this chapter.

REFERENCES

Agras, W. S., & Apple, R. F. (1997). *Overcoming eating disorders: A cognitive-behavioral treatment for bulimia nervosa & binge-eating.* Oxford, UK: University Press.

American Psychiatric Association. (2013). *Diagnostic and statistical manual of mental disorders* (5th ed.). Arlington, VA: American Psychiatric Publishing.

Beck, J. S. (1995). *Cognitive therapy. Basics and beyond.* New York, NY: Guilford Press.

Beer, R., & Hornsveld, H. (2012). EMDR in de behandeling van eetstoornissen [EMDR in the treatment of eating disorders]. In E. ten Broeke, A. de Jongh, & H. J. Oppenheim (Eds.), *Praktijkboek EMDR* [Book for Clinical Practice] (pp. 225–265).. Amsterdam, the Netherlands: Harcourt.

Beer, R., & Tobias, K. (2011). *Protocol voor cognitieve gedragstherapie bij jongeren met een Eetstoornis [Protocol of cognitive behavior therapy for adolescents with an eating disorder].* Houten, the Netherlands: Bohn Stafleu Van Loghum

Cooper, P. J., Taylor, M. J., Cooper, Z., & Fairburn, C. G. (1987). The development and validation of the body shape questionnaire. *International Journal of Eating Disorders, 6*(4), 485–494. doi:10.1002/1098-108X(198707)6:4<485::AID-EAT2260060405>3.0.CO;2-O

Dalle Grave, R., Calugi, S., Doll, H. A., & Fairburn, C. (2013) Enhanced cognitive behavior therapy for adolescents with anorexia nervosa: An alternative to family therapy? *Behavior Research and Therapy, 51*(1), 9–12. doi:10.1016/j.brat.2012.09.008

de Jongh, A. (2016). EMDR therapy for specific fears and phobias: The phobia protocol. In M. Luber (Ed.), *Eye movement desensitization and reprocessing (EMDR) scripted protocols and summary sheets: Treating trauma, anxiety and mood-related conditions* (pp. 9–40). New York, NY: Springer Publishing.

de Jongh, A., & ten Broeke, E. (2012). *Handboek EMDR.* Amsterdam, the Netherland: Pearson Assessment and Information.

de Jongh, A., ten Broeke, E., & Hornsveld, H. (2014). The second method protocol: Procedure for changing (core) beliefs with EMDR. Retrieved from https://hornsveldpsychologenpraktijk.files.wordpress .com/2016/01/p-2014-emdrfor-core-beliefs-preparationform.pdf and https://hornsveldpsychologen-praktijk.files.wordpress.com/2016/01/p-2014-emdr-for-core-beliefs-therapist-form.pdf

de Jongh, A., ten Broeke, E., & Meijer, S. (2010). Two method questioning approach: A case conceptualization model in the context of EMDR. *Journal of EMDR Practice and Research, 4*(1), 12–21. doi:10.1891/1933-3196.4.1.12

Dingemans, A. E., Bruna, M. J., & van Furth, E. F. (2001). Vreetbuien-stoornis: een overzicht. *Tijdschrift voor Psychiatrie, 43*, 321–330.

Engelhard, I. M., van Uijen, S. L., & van den Hout, M. A. (2010). The impact of taxing working memory on negative and positive memories. *European Journal of Psychotraumatology, 1*(1), 5623. doi:10.3402/ejpt.v1i0.5623

Fairburn, C. G., & Beglin, S. J. (1994). Assessment of eating disorder psychopathology: Interview or self-report questionnaire? *International Journal of Eating Disorders, 16*, 363–370.

Fairburn, C. G., & Cooper, Z. (1993). The eating disorder examination. In C. G. Fairburn & G. T. Wilson (Eds.), *Binge eating. Nature, assessment, and treatment* (12th ed., pp. 317–360). New York, NY: Guilford Press.

Fairburn, C. G., Cooper, Z., Doll, H. A., O´Connor, M. E., Bohn, K., Hawker, D. M., . . . Palmer, R. L. (2009). Transdiagnostic cognitive-behavioral therapy for patients with eating disorders: A two-site trial with 60 weeks follow–up. *American Journal of Psychiatry, 166*, 311–319. doi:10.1176/appi .ajp.2008.08040608

Fairburn, C. G., Cooper, Z., Doll, H. A., O'Connor, M. E., Palmer, R. L., & Dalle Grave, R. (2013). Enhanced cognitive behavior therapy for adults with anorexia nervosa: A UK–Italy study. *Behavior Research and Therapy, 51*, R2–R8. doi:10.1016/j.brat.2012.09.010

Fairburn, C. G., Cooper, Z., & Shafran, R. (2003). Cognitive behavior therapy for eating disorders: A transdiagnostic theory and treatment. *Behavior Research and Therapy, 41*, 509–528. doi:10.1016/ S0005-7967(02)00088-8

Ferreira, C., Pinto-Gouveia, J., & Duarte, C. (2013). Self-compassion in the face of shame and body-image dissatisfaction: Implications for eating disorders. *Eating Behaviors, 14,* 207–210. doi:10.1016/j.eatbeh.2013.01.005

Garner, D. M. (2004). *Professional manual.* Odessa, FL: Psychological Assessment Resources.

Hase, M. (2009). CravEx: An EMDR approach to treat substance abuse and addiction. In M. Luber (Ed.), *EMDR scripted protocols: Special populations* (pp. 467–488). New York, NY: Springer Publishing.

Hoek, H. W., & Van Hoeken, D. (2003). Review of the prevalence and incidence of eating disorders. *International Journal of Eating Disorders, 34,* 383–396. doi:10.1002/eat.10222

Hofmann, A., & Luber, M. (2009). History taking: The time line. In M. Luber (Ed.), *EMDR: Scripted protocols: Basics and Special Situations* (pp. 5–10). New York, NY: Springer Publishing.

Hornsveld, H. K. (2014). EMDR with positive targets. Keynote presented at Conference of Dutch EMDR Association, Nijmegen, the Netherlands.

Hornsveld, H. K., & Markus, W. (2015). EMDR bij verslaving [Protocol for alcohol dependency] (pp. 437–498). Retrieved from http://hornsveldpsychologenpraktijk.com/downloadpagina-voor cursisten/protocollen

Horst, F., & de Jongh, A. (2016). EMDR therapy protocol for panic disorders with and without agoraphobia. In M. Luber (Ed.), *Eye movement desensitization and reprocessing (EMDR) scripted protocols and summary sheets: Treating trauma, anxiety and mood-related conditions* (pp. 51–70). New York, NY: Springer Publishing.

Keizer, K. A., Smeets, M. A., Dijkman, H. C., Urumbajahan, S. A., Elburg, A. van, & Postma, A. (2015). Too fat to fit through the door. *Tijdschrift voor psychiatrie, 57,* 923–927. doi:10.1371/journal.pone.0064602

Knipe, J. (2010). Dysfunctional positive affect: To clear the pain of unrequited love. In M. Luber (Ed.), *EMDR scripted protocols* (pp. 459–462). New York, NY: Springer Publishing.

Korn, D. L., & Leeds, A. M. (2002). Preliminary evidence of efficacy for EMDR resource development and installation in the stabilization phase of treatment of complex post-traumatic stress disorder. *Journal of Clinical Psychology, 58,* 1465–1487. doi:10.1002/jclp.10099

Logie, R., & de Jongh, A. (2014). The "Flashforward Procedure': Confronting the catastrophe. *Journal of EMDR Practice and Research, 8,* 25–32. doi:10.1891/1933-3196.8.1.25

Logie, R., & de Jongh, A. (2016). The flashforward procedure. In M. Luber (Ed.), *Eye movement desensitization and reprocessing (EMDR) scripted protocols and summary sheets: Treating trauma, anxiety and mood-related conditions* (pp. 81–90). New York, NY: Springer Publishing.

Markus, W., & Hornsveld, H. K. (2015). EMDR en verslaving [EMDR and addiction]. In H.-J. Oppenheim, H. K. Hornsveld, E. ten Broeke, & A. de Jongh (Eds.), *Praktijkboek EMDR II* (pp. 437–498). Amsterdam, the Netherlands: Pearson.

Markus, W., & Hornsveld, H. K. (2017). EMDR interventions in addiction. *Journal of EMDR Practice and Research, 11*(1), 4–29. doi:10.1891/1933-3196.11.1.3

Multidisciplinary guidelines for eating disorders. (2006). Houten, the Netherlands: Trimbos Instituut.

National Institute for Health and Clinical Excellence. (2004). *Eating disorders. Core interventions in the treatment and management of anorexia nervosa, bulimia nervosa and related eating disorders. Clinical guideline.* London, UK: National Health Service. Retrieved from https://www.ncbi.nlm.nih.gov/pubmed/23346610

National Institute for Health and Clinical Excellence. (2017). Eating disorders: Recognition and treatment. Retrieved from http://nice.org.uk/guidance/ng69

Pepers, A., & Swart, M. (2014). Welke bijdrage kan EMDR leveren aan de behandeling van eetstoornissen. *GGzet wetenschappelijk, 18*(2), 79–91.

Popky, A. J. (2005). Detur, an urge reduction protocol for addictions and dysfunctional behaviors. In R. Shapiro (Ed.), *EMDR solutions: Pathways to healing*(pp. 167–188). New York, NY: W. W. Norton.

Popky, A. J. (2009). The desensitization of triggers and urge reprocessing (DeTUR) protocol. In M. Luber (Ed.), *EMDR scripted protocols: Special populations* (pp. 489–511). New York, NY: Springer Publishing.

Roedelof, A. (2016). *EMDR in the treatment of patients with an eating disorder.* Workshop at conference of EMDR-Europe. The Hague: Netherlands.

Shapiro, E., & Laub, B. (2009). The New Recent Traumatic Episode Protocol (R-TEP). In M. Luber (Ed.), *Eye movement desensitization and reprocessing (EMDR) scripted protocols: Basics and special situations* (pp. 251–270). New York, NY: Springer Publishing.

Shapiro, E., & Laub, B. (2014). The New Recent Traumatic Episode Protocol (R-TEP). In M. Luber (Ed.), *Implementing EMDR early mental health interventions for man-made and natural disasters: Models, scripted protocols and summary sheets* (pp. 193–207). New York, NY: Springer Publishing.

Shapiro, F. (2001). *Eye movement desensitization and reprocessing (EMDR). Basic principles, protocols, and procedures.* New York, NY: Guilford Press.

Slade, P. (1995). Prospects for prevention. In G. Szmukler, C. Dare, & J. Treasure (Eds.), *Handbook of eating disorders. Theory, treatments and research* (pp. 385–398). Chichester, UK: Wiley.

Steinglass, J. E., Eisen, J. L., Attia, E., Mayer, L., & Walsh, B. T. (2007). Is anorexia nervosa a delusional disorder? An assessment of eating beliefs in anorexia nervosa. *Journal of Psychiatric Practice, 13*(2), 65–71. doi:10.1097/01.pra.0000265762.79753.88

Steinglass, J. E., Sysko, R., Glasofer, D., Albano, A. M., Blair Simpson, H., & Timothy Walsh, B. (2011). Rationale for the application of exposure and response prevention to the treatment of anorexia nervosa. *International Journal of Eating Disorders, 44*(2), 134–141. doi:10.1002/eat.20784

Stice, E., & Shaw, H. (2002). Role of body dissatisfaction in the onset and maintenance of eating pathology: A synthesis of research findings. *Journal of Psychosomatic Research, 53*, 985–993. doi:10.1016/S0022-3999(02)00488-9

ten Broeke, E., de Jongh, A., & Oppenheim, H.-J. (2012). *Praktijkboek EMDR.* Amsterdam, the Netherlands: Harcourt.

Vandereycken, W., & Noorderbos, G. (2008). *Handboek eetstoornissen* [Handbook Eating Disorders]. Utrecht, the Netherlands: de Tijdstroom.

van der Vleugel, B., van den Berg, D., de Bont, P., Staring, T., & de Jongh, A. (2016). EMDR for traumatized patients with psychosis. In M. Luber (Ed.), *Eye movement desensitization and reprocessing (EMDR) scripted protocols and summary sheets: Treating trauma, anxiety and mood-related conditions* (pp. 97–148). New York, NY: Springer Publishing.

van Elburg, A., & Danner, U. (2015). Anorexia nervosa en adolescenten. *Tijdschrift voor psychiatrie, 57*, 923–927.

Wilson, G. T., & Fairburn, C. G. (2007). Treatments for eating disorders. In P. E. Nathan & J. M. Gorman (Eds.), *A guide to treatments that work* (3rd ed., pp. 579–609). New York, NY: Oxford University Press.

SUMMARY SHEET
Protocol for EMDR Therapy in the Treatment of Eating Disorders

Renée Beer
SUMMARY SHEET BY MARILYN LUBER

Name: _____ Diagnosis: _____

☑ Check when task is completed, response has changed, or to indicate symptoms or diagnosis.

Note: Please keep in mind that it is only a reminder of different tasks that may or may not apply to your client. The exact scripts are in the chapter.

EATING DISORDERS CLINICAL FEATURES

ICD-10: Criteria Anorexia Nervosa (AN)

- ☐ Body weight is maintained at least 15% below that expected.
- ☐ Weight loss is self-induced by avoidance of food—intake and one or more compensatory behaviors: self-induced purging, excessive exercise, use of appetite suppressants.
- ☐ Distorted body image, dread of fatness as intrusive, overvalued idea. Patient imposes low weight on self as an intrusive, overvalued idea, and the patient imposes a low weight threshold on him/herself.
- ☐ Pubertal development may be delayed or arrested.

ICD-10: Criteria for Bulimia Nervosa (BN)

- ☐ Preoccupation with eating, irresistible craving for food, episodes of overeating where large amounts of food are consumed in short periods of time (binges).
- ☐ Attempts to counteract the "fattening" effects of food by one or more compensatory behaviors: self-induced purging (vomiting, using laxatives and/or diuretics), excessive exercise, use of appetite suppressants.
- ☐ Morbid dread of (disgust for) fatness, leading to setting a sharply defined threshold for self, well below a normal, healthy weight.

ICD-10: Criteria for Binge Eating Disorder (BED)

- ☐ Recurrent episodes of binge eating, characterized by frequently eating excessive amounts of food, often when not hungry.
- ☐ Binges represent a distraction to avoid thinking about the real root of the problems.
- ☐ Feelings of guilt, disgust, and depression often follow a bingeing episode.
- ☐ Binge eating disorder is not the same as overeating, as it is recurrent and more serious.
- ☐ Binges are not associated with recurrent inappropriate compensatory behavior (self-induced purging: vomiting, using laxatives and/or diuretics).

MEASURES

- ☐ *Eating Disorder Inventory-3 (EDI-3)*
- ☐ *Eating Disorder Examination (EDE)*
- ☐ *Eating Disorder Examination Questionnaire (EDEQ)*
- ☐ *Body Shape Questionnaire (BSQ)*

INDICATIONS FOR EMDR

- ☐ Intrusive negative images of past or anticipated future experiences, causing/maintaining:
  - ○ Distress
  - ○ Fear of weight gain/other fears
  - ○ Low self-esteem
  - ○ Perfectionism
  - ○ Negative (distorted, delusional) body image
- ☐ Intrusive positive images of past or anticipated effects of specific behaviors causing/maintaining:
  - ○ Binges/dieting
  - ○ Compensatory behaviors (purging/hyperactivity)

EMDR PROTOCOL FOR EATING DISORDERS SCRIPT

Phase 1: History Taking and Case Conceptualization

- ☐ Relevant information is gathered
  - ○ *Presenting problem*

Problem: _____

_____

Behaviors bothering you most: _____

_____

Thoughts and beliefs connected with problem: _____

_____

Firm (core) beliefs that guide you in life: _____

_____

Emotions connected to problem: _____

_____

Physical symptoms connected to problem: _____

_____

Relational problems connected to problem: _____

_____

Disturbing memories of event that happened to you in past, intrusive fantasies about events that might happen in future: _____

_____

_____

_____

In what situations do these memories of fantasies appear: _____

_____

☐ *Etiology*

Circumstances/factors that may have caused problems: _____

_____

☐ *Potential Maintaining Factors*

What keeps your problems going: _____

_____

Problems in relationships with peers: _____

_____

Problems with being aware or expressing emotions: _____

_____

Problems with relationships with family members: _____

_____

Problems with school/work: _____

_____

Explanation for problems with other people: _____

_____

Demanding too much for yourself by setting high standards: _____

_____

Predominant mood: _____

_____

☐ *Comorbidity*

Other emotional/behavioral problems or diagnoses besides your eating problems: _____

_____

☐ *Developmental History*

Any adverse or traumatic experiences: _____

_____

☐ *Scores*

Comments on scores on testing: _____

_____

☐ *Function*

Change of eating behaviors started because you chose them intentionally or they just happened:

_____

_____

What ED added to your life since started: _____

_____

What was achieved by having ED: _____

_____

What was avoided by having ED: _____

_____

Any thoughts about what you should learn prior to giving up ED: _____

_____

Any thoughts about what you can achieve by giving up ED: _____

_____

The meaning of ED for you seems to be _____ (state your understanding). _____

_____

_____

Case Conceptualization

☐ Diagnosis: _____

☐ Hypotheses concerning what the patient needs to learn/achieve with therapy to be able to let go of the ED. Fill in what interventions you think are needed: _____

_____

☐ Relevant modules for this patient based on case conceptualization:

- *Module 1. Distressing memories of negative experiences*
- *Module 2. Specific fears*
- *Module 3. Impulsive behavior:* binges, compensatory behavior (hyperactivity or purging)
- *Module 4. Low self-esteem*
- *Module 5. Clinical perfectionism*
- *Module 6. Negative body image*

☐ Goals for EMDR therapy in treatment: _____

_____

_____

☐ Potential modules are introduced to patient: ☐ Yes ☐ No

☐ Directions for therapist to follow as soon as the patient is ready to start EMDR:

1. Choose one of the modules from those listed earlier.
2. Identify the most appropriate path for target selection.
3. Go to the designated path script. The scripts for each path are listed for easy access as follows. Target selection occurs in Phase 1 (return to Phase 1 when necessary). When a specific target is selected, continue with Phases 3 to 8.
4. After completion of targets within one module (remember, there can be more than one path for target selection), choose the next module until all the necessary modules and their targets are completed.

Note: Flash-forward is described twice: as a target within the timeline path and as a path for target selection.

Phase 2: Preparation

☐ Introduction to EMDR ☐ Yes ☐ No

"Your problems seem partly related to memories of experiences from your past or images in your head about potential future experiences that might happen to you. These memories or images get activated in the present by certain situations, and they are causing you problems. For dealing with these problems, I will introduce EMDR therapy to you. The treatment plan has been discussed with you before. To begin with, your eating pattern must improve so much that we can start working on these other related issues with EMDR therapy. When we start with EMDR therapy we will run through your treatment plan once more and then we will concentrate on our goals with EMDR. For now, it is important that you realize that we can release you from the problems these images and memories are giving you. Is that clear for you?"

☐ Assistance in regulation of eating pattern ☐ Yes ☐ No

"Our first goal is to help you restore a more regular eating pattern and a healthy weight, so that you will not be in mortal danger any longer. We can start working on other issues only when you are out of the "danger zone." We will start working with EMDR therapy when you will be able to keep your concentration focused and when you can feel emotions and physical sensations again. Do you understand this? And, do you agree to this?"

☐ Resource development and installation ☐ Yes ☐ No

Phase 3 to Phase 8: Assessment—Reevaluation

Assessment with the Standard EMDR Protocol starts after the selection of an individual memory to work on. The preceding steps for identification and selection of relevant (target) memories are listed as follows for easy access. There are six different paths and six modules.

In all paths, do not ask for the PC during the assessment if the NC is, "I am powerless/I cannot deal with the image," because the PC is always, "I can deal with the image." It is not useful to ask for this PC during the assessment. However, install the PC after the SUD = 0.

PATHS FOR TARGET SELECTION

I. INTRUSION PATH (FOR MODULES 1 AND 6)

List of distressing memories of past negative experiences:

_____

_____

_____

Target (memory/image): _____

_____

_____

NC: _____

PC (if applicable): _____
VOC: ____/7

Emotions: _____
SUD: ___/10

Location of body sensation: _____

Do the standard EMDR protocol to completion.

Finish list of targets (distressing memories of past negative experiences) with the Standard EMDR Protocol.

Move on to the next path in this module (Module 6), if appropriate, or choose the next module and the appropriate path or complete the ED protocol.

II. TIMELINE PATH (FOR MODULES 2 AND 6)

Memories of the events that are relevant for the development of a specific symptom are indicated on a timeline.

Symptom: Fear of _____ (state what you are afraid of) (or other symptoms).

Start of symptom (after which event): _____
_____

Events increasing symptom: _____
_____
_____

Any specific aspect of the situation is frightening?   ☐ Yes ☐ No

Comment: _____

Events that aggravated this fear: _____
_____

If yes, when, and after what event, the fear started: _____
_____

What might happen to you if exposed to object/situation of your fear: _____
_____
_____

When and the event that started the fear: _____
_____
_____

Event that aggravated this fear: _____
_____
_____

Create a timeline and plot events. Indicate those with the biggest impact on the timeline.

Memory that influences fear most: _____
_____

Memory to start with; first one on the timeline or most influential: _____
_____

Regular assessment on selected memory:

Target (memory/image)

NC: _____

PC (if applicable): _____

VOC: ____/7

Emotions: _____

SUD: ___/10

Location of body sensation: _____

Continue the Standard EMDR Protocol to completion.

Finish list of targets related to the symptom along the timeline with the Standard EMDR P.

Flash-Forward

Identify the feared catastrophic event: We need to figure out what image is in your head that s_
you about a confrontation with the situation that you avoid. What is the worst thing you could
happening? What is the worst nightmare that is in your head?

Follow the event to its ultimate conclusion. Worst thing about it: _____

_____

_____

Repeat as necessary until client cannot identify anything worse.

Identify a detailed picture of flash-forward.

Use this as a target for processing with the Standard EMDR Protocol (SUD = 0, VOC = 7).

Target (memory/image): _____

_____

NC is always: I am powerless/I cannot deal with the image.

During assessment, do not ask for the PC or VOC. PC: "I can deal with it (the image)."

VOC: ____/7

Emotions: _____

SUD: ___/10

Location of body sensation: _____

Continue with the Standard EMDR Protocol to completion. When SUD = 0, install PC: "I can deal with
the image." Finish the list of distressing images of fantasy/fantasies.

Mental Video Check or Future Template

*"This time, I'd like you to imagine yourself stepping into the scene of a future confrontation with the
object or the situation. Close your eyes and play a movie of this happening, from the beginning until
the end. Imagine yourself coping with any challenges that come your way. Notice what you are seeing,
thinking, feeling, and experiencing in your body. And tell me about that. While playing this movie, let
me know if you hit any blocks of tension. If you do, just open your eyes, concentrate on what you see or
otherwise experience, and I will do one set of eye movements. Then continue playing the mental video
until you feel any tension again. Open your eyes, concentrate on what you experience, and I will do
another set. Resume the movie, and run the movie until the end."*

Repeat until no tension. Use BLS if any tension:

*"Okay, play the movie one more time from beginning to end and open your eyes when you experience
tension. Concentrate on what you see or experience otherwise. When you open your eyes, this is a sign
for me to perform another set of eye movements."*

Future Template

(Mental video check seems to be an effective alternative to future template.)

Image of situation you want to deal with: _____

_____

Capable of dealing with situation (1 to 7): ____/7

Move on to the next path in this module, if appropriate, or choose the next module, or complete the ED protocol.

III. DYSFUNCTIONAL BELIEF PATH (FOR MODULES 4, 5, 6)

Give rationale for the dysfunctional belief path.

State the identified core belief: _____

Validity of core belief 0% = not true to 100% = totally true: ____/100

Identification of pieces of evidence:

Life experiences can be single events or series of events that belong together and are called archives:

_____

_____

Write down three to five of the "strongest proofs for the belief" that feel like "pieces of evidence" for this belief. Use a maximum of 10 lines to describe each memory.

1. _____

_____

_____

2. _____

_____

_____

3. _____

_____

_____

4. _____

_____

_____

5. _____

_____

_____

Then, choose the memory of either a single event or an event being representative of the archive that proves to you most strongly that the negative core belief is true.

Negative Core Belief Proof

Target is memory/image that is strongest evidence for the belief: _____

_____

Memory/Image: _____

NC: _____

PC: _____

VOC: ____/7

Emotions: _____

SUD: ___/10

Location of body sensation: _____

Do the Standard EMDR Protocol to completion. Finish the list of "pieces of emotional" evidence for negative core belief with the Standard EMDR Protocol.

If appropriate, repeat the same for other dysfunctional core beliefs.

Future Template

Image of a good alternative to believe about yourself: _____

_____

"Slowly but surely you will start to believe in your new positive conviction about yourself or at least you will lose your firm conviction that your negative belief is true. Imagine that you are no longer convinced of your negative core belief _____ (state belief) but instead you're starting to believe your new, positive creed. What would your life look like?"

What you would do that you are not doing now: _____

_____

What current behavior you would stop: _____

_____

"Take a moment for this and make it as specific and detailed as possible in your mind. How much do you feel capable of dealing with in this situation?" ____/7

Homework: Practice this new behavior.

IV. FLASH FORWARD PATH (FOR MODULES 2 AND 5)

Rationale: *"Fears and worries can be aroused in people by images in their head of past experiences and also by images of future experiences. People can have fantasies of what might happen to them in the future, and these fantasies can guide their present behavior and emotions. These fantasies can be positive and negative. Both can cause problems. Now we are going to work on your negative images of possible future events. Our aim is to help you realize that this image is only an image in your head, and that also your body is going to realize that, so that you will be able to tolerate looking at these images and they will no longer disturb you."*

Identify the catastrophic event: *"We need to figure out what image is in your head that makes you scared or makes you worry. What is the worst thing you could imagine happening? What is the worst nightmare that is in your head?"*

_____

_____

Make a list of catastrophic events:

_____

_____

_____

Rank the targets by SUD's level:

_____

_____

_____

Follow the event to its ultimate conclusion.

Worst thing about it: _____

_____

Repeat as necessary until client cannot identify anything worse.

Identify a detailed picture of flash-forward.

Use this as a target for processing with the Standard EMDR Protocol (SUD = 0, VOC = 7).

Target (memory/image): _____

_____

NC ("I cannot deal with the image"): _____

Emotions: _____
SUD: ___/10

Location of body sensation: _____

Do the Standard EMDR Protocol to completion. Install PC: "I can deal with this image," when SUD = 0.

Finish list of flash-forwards with the Standard EMDR Protocol.

Mental Video Check or Future Template

"This time, I'd like you to imagine yourself stepping into the scene of a future confrontation with the object or the situation. Close your eyes and play a movie of this happening, from the beginning until the end. Imagine yourself coping with any challenges that come your way. Notice what you are seeing, thinking, feeling, and experiencing in your body. And tell me about that. While playing this movie, let me know if you hit any blocks of tension. If you do, just open your eyes, concentrate on what you see or otherwise experience, and I will do one set of eye movements. Then continue playing the mental video until you feel any tension again. Open your eyes, concentrate on what you experience, and I will do another set. Resume the movie, and run the movie until the end."

Repeat until no tension. Use BLS if any tension:

"Okay, play the movie one more time from beginning to end and open your eyes when you experience tension. Concentrate on what you see or experience otherwise. When you open your eyes, this is a sign for me to perform another set of eye movements."

Future Template

Image of neutral, but until now avoided, situation patient wants to deal with: _____

_____

Feeling capable of dealing with situation (1 to 7): ___/7

Move on to the next path in this module, if appropriate, or choose the next module, or complete the ED protocol.

V. DYSFUNCTIONAL POSITIVE TARGET PATH (FOR MODULES 3 AND 5)

V.1: Positive Memories

Rationale: *"Now we are going to work on behaviors that you keep on doing, though you know that they are not good for you. We will focus specifically on _____ (state the symptom such as binges, fasting, vomiting, using laxatives, diuretics, excessive moving; optionally also: setting extremely high standards for yourself). These behaviors are so persistent because the urge to perform them is triggered by images of either positive past experiences (like seeing yourself feeling content with yourself) or images of possible future experiences (like seeing yourself being admired by others). Our aim is to make sure that these images will no longer elicit your _____ (state the symptom). Therefore, we will look for the images that elicit in you the strongest urge to perform them and then we will neutralize these memories/fantasies. Okay?*

*We discussed that your _____ (state particular behavior) is difficult to stop because of the positive consequences of it. The positive consequences that we discussed are _____ (state the positive conse-*quences). *We will work in three steps; first, we will focus on past memories, then on the present triggers for your _____ (state particular behavior), and finally on your expectations of the future."*

Positive memories related to binges/fasting, vomiting, using laxatives, diuretics, excessive moving, and/or setting extremely high standards for self should be recalled.

List memories that elicit the strongest urge to perform the behavior.

_____

_____

_____

Positive memory related to performing the behavior: _____

Positive memory contributing most to the behavior: _____

Positive memory evoking strongest urge to perform the behavior right now: _____

Choose strongest memory of the previously noted items to evoke the behavior: _____

Continue with the Standard EMDR Protocol.

Image evoking the urge the strongest: _____

_____

Words that evoke the strongest urge: _____

Emotions: _____

Level of urge (LOU)

"When you look at the image, and you say to yourself ___ (the chosen words), how strong is the urge to _____ (mention the symptom) that you are experiencing right now, on a scale from 0 to 10, where 0 is no urge or neutral and 10 is the highest urge you can imagine?" LOU=___/10

Level of positive affect (LOPA)

"When you look at the image and say to yourself ___ (the chosen words), how positive or attractive is it right now on a scale from 0 to 10, where 0 is neutral and 10 is the most positive or attractive you can imagine?"

Choose strongest of the LOU or LOPA: _____

Location of body sensation: _____

Process this target with the standard EMDR protocol, monitoring LOU or LOPA instead of SUD.

Desensitization until a significant decrease, then install with either "I can deal with the picture" or "I am strong."

VOC: ____/7

Questions to ask when you go back to target: "How strong do you feel the urge?" instead of "How much distress do you feel?"

Process all relevant memories.

V.2: Present Trigger Situations

Images of triggers in the present: Check which situations are relevant to evoking the urge.

☐ *"When you are depressed, nervous, lonely, bored, sad, angry?"*   ☐ Yes ☐ No

☐ *"When you are relaxed and happy?"*   ☐ Yes ☐ No

☐ *"When you are alone?"*   ☐ Yes ☐ No

☐ *"When you are dissatisfied with your body?"*   ☐ Yes ☐ No

☐ *"When you are dissatisfied with yourself?"*   ☐ Yes ☐ No

List of five most difficult trigger situations for you:

Trigger Situation 1: _____

Trigger Situation 2: _____

Trigger Situation 3: _____

Trigger Situation 4: _____

Trigger Situation 5: _____

Image giving strongest urge: _____

_____

Statement increasing the urge (instead of NC): _____

Emotions: _____

Level of urge: ___/10

Sensation: _____

Do the Standard EMDR Protocol until the LOU no longer decreases.

Repeat the procedure for all relevant trigger situations.

Desensitization until there is a significant decrease. Then install either "I can deal with the picture" or "I am strong." VOC: _____/7

Repeat until patient can go through the imaginary situation without tension or urge.

Questions to ask when you go back to target: "How strong do you feel the urge?" instead of "How much distress do you feel?"

Mental video check:

"Now close your eyes and imagine yourself going through this trigger situation that we have been work-ing on. Imagine yourself going there and see how you manage from the beginning until the end. Check if there are any cues or aspects in this situation that are still difficult for you to deal with, because they evoke so much disturbance or urge that they could keep you from dealing with this situation adequately. Open your eyes when you experience any disturbance or urge and tell me what you are experiencing."

Reprocess all present triggers that activate the urge using the Standard EMDR Protocol.

V.3: Positive Flash-Forwards

Positive images of the future situation

"Some people say that they vomit because they expect to feel free afterwards, so an image of yourself feeling free after vomiting could be what we are looking for. Other people may say that they expect to feel relaxed after eating a lot of food, or that they expect to feel in control when they are below a certain

weight level. What is the outcome that you desire of the behavior we are now focusing on?" Desired outcome of performing the specific ED behavior: _____

_____

_____

Image evoking the strongest urge: _____

_____

Words that evoke the strongest urge: _____

Emotions: _____

Level of urge (LOU):

"When you look at the image, and you say to yourself ___ (the chosen words), how strong is the urge to _____ (mention the symptom) that you are experiencing right now, on a scale from 0 to 10, where 0 is no urge or neutral and 10 is the highest urge you can imagine?"

LOU=____/10

Or, level of positive affect (LOPA)

"When you look at the image and say to yourself ___ (the chosen words), how positive or attractive is it right now on a scale from 0 to 10, where 0 is neutral and 10 is the most positive or attractive you can imagined, how attractive does it feel now?"

Choose the strongest of the LOU or LOPA: _____

Location of body sensation: _____

Process this target with the Standard EMDR Protocol, monitoring LOU or LOPA instead of SUD. Desensitize until a significant decrease, then install with either "I can deal with the picture" or "I am strong."

VOC: _____/7

Questions to ask when you go back to target: "How strong do you feel the urge?" instead of "How much distress do you feel?"

Process all relevant fantasy images.

VI. EMOTION PATH (FOR MODULES 3 AND 6)

"Now we are going to work on behaviors that you keep on doing, though you know that they are not good for you. We will focus specifically on _____ (state the symptom such as binges, fasting, vomiting, using laxatives, diuretics, excessive moving; optionally also: setting extremely high standards for yourself). These behaviors are so persistent because the urge to perform them is triggered by a powerful negative emotion. This emotion seems to be ____ (state the problem emotion)."

Emotion-triggering behavior: _____

_____

List memories that evoke the strongest feeling of the emotion:

_____

_____

_____

_____

Choose memory that evokes the strongest feeling of the emotion: _____

_____

Continue with the Standard EMDR Protocol. Go through the list of collected memories until the patient has control over the problematic emotion.

Phase 8: Reevaluation+

Are all targets (memories/images) neutralized now concerning this module that kept the problem going?

☐ Yes ☐ No

Next module (if necessary): Module ____

Completed: ☐ Module 1   ☐ Module 2   ☐ Module 3
                  ☐ Module 4   ☐ Module 5   ☐ Module 6

Go through each module until all relevant modules for the patient are completed.

☐ EMDR-ED protocol completed

EMDR THERAPY PROTOCOL FOR THE MANAGEMENT OF DYSFUNCTIONAL EATING BEHAVIORS IN ANOREXIA NERVOSA

Maria Zaccagnino

INTRODUCTION

Eating disorders are a pervasive sociocultural phenomenon today, almost exclusively affecting the population of the Western world, in particular adolescents and young women. International epidemiological studies have revealed an increased incidence of eating disorders in women between 12 and 25 years of age. Estimates in Western countries, including Italy, have indicated the prevalence of anorexia nervosa (AN) at 0.2% to 0.8%, of bulimia nervosa (BN) at 3%, and eating disorder not otherwise specified (EDNOS) between 3.7% and 6.4% (Ministry of Health, Italy, 2014). Furthermore, the incidence of AN is four to eight new cases per year per 100,000 people, and for BN is 9 to 12 new cases. The age of onset is between 10 and 30 years, with a mean age of onset at age 17 (Abbate Daga et al., 2011).

Over the past few years, however, a progressive increase has been registered in the percentage of youths and young male adults afflicted by this disorder (Smink, van Hoeken, Oldehinkel, & Hoek, 2014). In this chapter, the female patient is referred to exclusively for simplicity of exposition.

In the context of psychopathological disorders, eating behavior disorders are considered to be those with the highest mortality rate. This finding is supported by the National Center for Epidemiology, Surveillance, and Health Promotion and by a number of scientific studies that have analyzed the issue in great depth (Fichter & Quadflieg, 2016; Suokas et al., 2014). They confirm that individuals with eating disorders have significantly elevated mortality rates, with the highest rates occurring in those with AN (Arcelus, Mitchell, Wales, & Nielsen, 2011).

In recent decades, in light of such findings, the scientific community has approached the study of these phenomena with increasing interest, in order to clarify risk and precipitating factors, placing special emphasis on all those factors that contribute to maintaining the symptomatology. Such findings clearly indicate that the treatment of this condition is very complex. It thus becomes important to rely on an evidence-based approach widely recognized by the scientific community, such as the eye movement desensitization and reprocessing (EMDR) therapy, which can actively address the characteristics underlying this condition (Bisson, Roberts, Andrew, Cooper, & Lewis, 2013; Bradley, Greene, Russ, Dutra, & Westen, 2005; Lee & Cuijpers, 2013; Omaha, 2000; Seidler & Wagner, 2006; F. Shapiro, 2001).

The purpose of the protocol for the management of dysfunctional eating behaviors, therefore, is to define a specific treatment with EMDR therapy for one of the possible expressions of eating disorders, that is, AN. To this end, the main theoretical contributions concerning the risk factors involved in its onset and/or maintenance will be reviewed, with special emphasis on those connected with traumatic life events, so as to define basic guidelines for an effective treatment and the importance of EMDR therapy to this resolution.

DIAGNOSTIC CRITERIA ACCORDING TO *DSM-5* AND RISK FACTORS

The term "eating disorder" is used to define a set of persistent weight-controlling behaviors that damage physical health or psychological function and that are not secondary to any known medical or psychiatric condition (American Psychiatric Association [APA], 2013).

According to the *Diagnostic and Statistical Manual of Mental Disorders* (5th ed.; *DSM-5*; APA, 2013), following are the main diagnostic categories of feeding and eating disorders:

- *AN*: An eating behavior that induces a significant low body weight (at or below 15% of the normal value) and an intense fear related to the possibility of gaining weight.
- *BN*: Recurring binge eating characterized by the consumption of a high quantity of food followed by unsuitable compensatory strategies (e.g., vomiting)
- *Binge eating disorder*: Cyclic episodes of eating a large quantity of food in a relative short period of time without a real sensation of hunger and with a feeling of lack of control.
- *Pica*: Persistent appetite for substances that are nonnutritive.
- *Rumination disorder*: Cyclic vomiting of food that could be re-masticated, re-ingested, or spat out.
- *Avoidant/restrictive food intake disorder*: The impossibility to reach a suitable nutritional level because of specific disorders in eating behavior (e.g., apparently no interest in food).

Indeed, the recently published *DSM-5* (APA, 2013) clearly reconsiders the diagnostic criteria that define such disorders and is open to considering new forms of the condition, which were previously erroneously grouped into the EDNOS category, without taking into account the specificity of each disorder. The explicit intent is to attribute the proper diagnostic and clinical importance to the categories of patients whose disorder does not meet the main diagnostic categories, but that can still cause significant distress and interfere with the daily life of affected patients (Brown, Keel, & Weissman, 2012). The acronym EDNOS was thus replaced with feeding and eating condition not elsewhere classified (FECNEC). This new diagnostic category includes the following:

- *Atypical AN*: Fulfills some of the features of AN, but the overall clinical picture does not justify that diagnosis.
- *Subclinical BN*: Fulfills some of the features of BN, but the overall clinical picture does not justify that diagnosis.
- *Subclinical binge eating disorder*: Fulfills some of the features of binge eating disorder, but the overall clinical picture does not justify that diagnosis.
- *Purging disorder* (*PD*): Purging to control shape or weight, in the absence of binge eating episodes.
- *Night eating syndrome* (*NES*): Intake of most calories at night or during evening meals.

An in-depth understanding of the nature of eating behavior disorders requires a comprehensive assessment and knowledge of the trends that may be risk factors and/or may contribute to maintaining the symptoms reported by the patient (Stice, Rohde, Shaw, & Gau, 2011). Moreover, for preventive purposes, the possibility of providing for a better identification of such risk factors would help to develop prevention programs and define the most effective strategy to address such disorders.

According to Jacobi's review (Jacobi, Abascal, & Taylor, 2004; Stice, Ng, & Shaw, 2010), the risk factors that need to be addressed are as follows:

- *General and social factors*: Age and gender, the ethnic group to which the individual belongs, the cultural level and economic status, as well as the psychosexual orientation
- *Family-related factors*: Interactions within and function of the dynamics within patient's family, with particular focus on attachment styles and on the presence of a family history of psychiatric disorders
- *Development-related factors*: Body mass index and other weight-correlated variables, possible eating problems in childhood, and so on
- *Psychological and behavioral factors*: All risk factors of a traumatic nature, such as physical and/or sexual abuse, neglect, and psychiatric disorders; this category also includes all the factors related to low self-esteem, perfectionism, and so on
- *Biological factors*: Genetic predisposition

The most recent investigations have produced a body of scientific evidence proving that each of these factors may in some way be correlated with a particular form of eating behavior disorder.

ANOREXIA NERVOSA

AN is a serious psychiatric illness characterized by an inability to maintain an adequate, healthy body weight. AN is prevalent among adolescents and young women in the Western world (although its incidence in the male population should not be underestimated). According to Treasure, Claudino, and Zucker's study (2010), in Western societies the prevalence rate of this disorder has reached 5%. Its onset may be mostly traced back to adolescence; however, some research has shown a possible correlation between eating disorders in childhood and AN (Stice et al., 2011). While the overall incidence rate has remained stable over the past decades, there has been an increase in the high-risk group of 15- to 19-year-old girls. It is unclear whether this reflects earlier detection of AN cases or an earlier age at onset (Arcelus et al., 2011).

Among all psychiatric disorders, AN was also found to have one of the highest mortality rates (Arcelus et al., 2011; Harris & Barraclough, 1997). In their 2014 meta-analysis, Keshaviah, Edkins, Hastings, and Krishna re-estimated the risk of premature mortality and concluded that participants with AN were 5.2 (3.7–7.5) times more likely to die prematurely from any cause and 18.1 (11.5–28.7) times more likely to die by suicide than 15- to 34-year-old females in the general population. Although it has now spread to alarming levels, to date its etiopathogenesis is largely unknown. Moreover, as far as treatment is concerned, the guidelines issued by the National Institute of Clinical Excellence do not provide any specific indications (Bulik et al., 2006; National Institute for Health and Care Excellence, 2004; Treasure et al., 2010). Thus, this disorder cannot be considered as having only one variable involved in its etiology, but rather is due to multiple biopsychosocial and cultural components, as reported by the scientific literature on this issue.

According to the *DSM-5* (APA, 2013), the criteria used to diagnose this form of eating behavior disorder include reaching a significantly low body weight compared to others. The patient feels horror about gaining weight and looking fat. This causes dysfunctional behaviors concerning food consumption, especially restriction of food intake. All this revulsion works against weight gain, even if it is low. As body image and weight experiences are disturbed in the AN patient, it leads her to her own self-evaluation to deny the presence of problems related to low body weight.

The changes introduced in the previous edition, the *DSM IV-TR*, especially concern the criteria that measure the fear of gaining weight and regarding bodily image. Moreover, the criterion concerning the absence of menstruation was eliminated, as it excluded from the possible diagnosis women in menopause or young girls who had not yet reached puberty. Unfortunately, it was reported that about 10% to 20% of individuals affected by AN develop a chronic condition that lasts for their entire lifetime (APA, 2013).

Two diagnostic subtypes have been identified by the *DSM-5*:

- *Restricting type*: In the previous 3 months, the subject has not experienced any binge eating episodes or purging behaviors like self-induced vomiting or use of laxatives or diuretics.
- *Binge-eating/purging type*: In the previous 3 months, the subject experienced recurrent binge eating episodes or purging behaviors. The subjects affected by this disorder generally tend to show severe weight loss, to the extent that *DSM-5* specifies the degree of severity of the disorder. The minimum level for adults is based on the current body mass index (BMI), while for children and adolescents, it is based on the percentiles of the BMI. The BMI could be mild, moderate, severe, or extreme.

In addition to the prevailing symptom of significant weight loss, the diagnosis of AN involves a series of symptoms and disorders that may be frequently found to be comorbid with this condition. In particular, it was observed that patients with AN show greater levels of depression and attentive deficit disorder, as well as presenting problems related to loss of libido, obsessive symptoms, and social isolation (Hudson, Hiripi, Pope, & Kessler, 2007; Swanson, Crow, Le Grange, Swendsen, & Merikangas, 2011).

Individual Risk Factors

The current scientific literature has identified specific categories that would seem to be more involved in the onset and/or maintenance of AN. Specifically, the risk factors that studies have focused on more include those related to the family, economic, and sociocultural environment in which the subject lives (e.g., eating disorders, depression, alcoholism, obesity within the family). Individual risk factors include, for example, certain personality traits (such as obsessive and perfectionistic traits) as well as excessive control and concern about weight and body shape.

Negative Cognitive Beliefs and Behavioral Risk

A number of traits and behaviors can be risk factors for AN.

- *Body image distortion for self and attributed to others*: In regard to body weight, these patients are deeply dissatisfied with their own body, due, in particular, to their body image distortion. They tend to feel and perceive themselves as fat, in spite of their evident state of malnutrition; they may perceive certain specific parts of their body (like the abdomen and thighs) as disproportionate (Nicholls, Lynn, & Viner, 2011). They may believe that others share their distorted perception, and this erroneous belief elicits in them feelings of inadequacy, insecurity, and low self-esteem, which only serve to foster weight loss in a dysfunctional cycle for AN patients. In fact, they believe that others see their body as unpleasant or deformed, even in the absence of objective indicators (Ruffolo, Philips, Menard, Fay, & Weisberg, 2006; Russo, d'Angerio, Carcione, & Di Maggio, 2009).

- *Need for control*: This is fundamental to the etiology and maintenance of AN (Surgenor, Horn, Plumridge, & Hudson, 2002), especially concerning food intake and all aspects of the patient's daily life. Dysfunctional eating behaviors could be seen as an attempt to manage/cope with overwhelming emotions, memories, and stressors experienced during a stressful, difficult, or traumatic event. It is a sort of coping strategy in which the subject tries in every way to control all unpredictable events and threats coming from the surrounding environment (D. Shapiro & Astin, 1998).
- *Perfectionism*: For AN patients, perfectionism is a dysfunctional self-evaluation system where individuals judge themselves exclusively on their ability to pursue and achieve demanding, self-imposed standards, regardless of adverse consequences.
- *Sense of inadequacy/social insecurity/low self-esteem*: Lack of self-esteem is due to a negative belief of not being able to cope with the feared situation, materially and/or emotionally. It may affect not only the individual's ability to establish intimate relations, but also the possibility of effectively conveying his or her emotional state. Bruch (1973) reported how in female patients with anorexia, the use of food or body shape could be considered as a means to avoid interpersonal or intrapersonal situations that they would usually fear.
- *Alexythymia*: Female patients with anorexia are unable to identify and describe emotions; this is a deficit of emotional self-awareness such as a difficulty in labeling and expressing emotions, accompanied by a conflict between the way in which one should feel and the way in which one actually feels (Garner & Dalle Grave, 1999).

Attachment Wounds and Traumatic Experiences

Traumatic Experiences

In the past 30 years, research on eating disorders has significantly contributed to understanding the relationship between a *life history characterized by traumatic events* (especially during infancy) and the development of an eating behavior disorder; according to Putnam (2001), the percentage is 30% to 50%. In recent years, studies investigating the risk factors and/or factors responsible for maintaining AN have especially focused on traumatic life events, in particular on histories of physical and/or psychological maltreatment and physical and/or sexual abuse in childhood. Many researchers observe that sexual abuse or neglect holds significant roles for risk factors that can lead people to develop eating disorders (Johnson, Cohen, Kasen, & Brook, 2006; Speranza & Alberigi, 2006; Steiger & Zankor, 1990; Vize & Cooper, 1995; Welch & Fairburn, 1994). These results are in line with the adverse child experiences (ACEs) study funded by Kaiser Permanente (Dube, Felitti, & Rishi, 2013; Felitti et al., 1998; Murphy et al., 2013), which found that exposure to ACEs, including abuse, neglect, and household dysfunction, is associated with multiple long-term physical and mental health problems (Murphy et al., 2013). In fact, these adverse experiences may remain unresolved and unprocessed over time; in this way, the perceptions, bodily sensations, emotions, and expectations related to the memories of traumatic events tend to be crystallized in a memory network that is not metabolized in the brain. The remaining un-metabolized memories within neural networks are associated with maladaptive sensations, emotions, beliefs, and images. Furthermore, any present reminder can activate them, leading to dysfunctional emotional regulation and behavioral responses.

Dysfunctional Emotional Regulation

An eating disorder is characterized by self-destructive behaviors by these patients in order to cope with the overwhelming emotions related to traumatic memories (Hund & Espelage, 2005). Cole and Putnam (1992) stressed how a traumatic event could lead to deficits in the management of overwhelming emotions and other internal experiences in these patients. The prolonged stress experienced could cause the interruption of the development of self-regulatory processes and finally the onset of the deficits mentioned previously (Messman-Moore & Garrigus, 2007). These patients who are experiencing difficulty in coping with strong, negative affects might use eating disorder behaviors such as self-starvation, overeating, and vomiting as a means of coping with these emotions (Schwartz & Gay, 1996). Regarding the impact on emotional regulation, some researchers have stressed that there is a strong positive association between the experience of a traumatic event and alexithymia (Bandura, 2003; Monson, Price, Rodriguez, Ripley, & Warner, 2004).

Attachment Wounds

Relational traumas, experienced in childhood, could be a risk factor for the development of an eating disorder as a dysfunctional attachment relationship has a negative impact on the long-term well-being of the child. According to Bowlby's theory (1969, 1982), the attachment behavior is an inborn system that motivates an infant to seek proximity to an adult caregiver (George & Solomon, 1996). These initial proximity-seeking attachment behaviors result in repeated interactions with a caregiver that become encoded in *internal working models* (IWMs) *of attachment* that act as schemata for future relationships (Siegel, 1999). These IWMs are the cognitive script that guides the interactions with other persons and forms the basis for the emotional regulation style of the subject.

- *Secure attachment*: The possibility to experience a good and secure relationship in the parent–child interaction may develop a self-representation of being worthy of care; therefore, the secure child will develop effective coping strategies and will become aware of the possibility to count on others in the case of need.
- *Insecure attachment*:
  - *Avoidant*: Early relationships characterized by difficulties in dyadic regulation or poor maternal responsiveness will instead lead to the construction of IWMs that may be *avoidant* (child learns to "switch off" attachment behaviors due to the inaccessibility of the parental figure).
  - *Ambivalent* (the child activates attachment behaviors in an exaggerated way due to the unpredictability of the caregiver): Attachment insecurity may, therefore, contribute to the development of maladaptive affect regulation strategies, which in turn may be a risk factor for the development of future psychopathology.
  - *Disorganized*: When the relationship between the child and the caregiver is characterized by frightening, maltreating, and/or abusive attitudes, dysfunctional dynamics may set in, to the point of eliciting a *disorganized* IWM, which in turn may be considered as a risk factor for the onset of psychological disorders (Bowlby, 1969, 1973, 1980; Liotti & Farina, 2011; Main & Hesse, 1990; Main & Solomon, 1986). The attachment classification of disorganization is considered a risk factor associated with the development of externalizing problems (such as aggressive behaviors) and posttraumatic stress disorder in middle childhood (Carlson, 1998; Fearon, Bakermans-Kranenburg, van IJzendoorn, Lapsley, & Roisman, 2010) and psychiatric disorders in adulthood (Lyons-Ruth & Jacobvitz, 2008). Parents of disorganized infants were observed to demonstrate behaviors that were frightening and damaging to their children who experience a state of unresolved fright without solution. In this condition, children experience a growing sense of fear and despair, because they are in a paradoxical situation where they are frightened by their "haven of safety" (Liotti, 2004; Schore, 2002). These early dysfunctional interactions are defined as "early relational traumas" (Liotti, 2004; Schore, 2001, 2002). The simultaneous and paradoxical activation of defense and attack systems can lead to a deficit of the integrative functions of consciousness, which, in turn, can lead to an increased vulnerability to dissociative reactions in response to traumatic stressors later in life (Liotti, 2004; Schore, 2001, 2002). Unresolved and disturbing affects resulting from early traumatic experiences may also be fragmented into parts of the self, forming different ego states.

COGNITIVE BEHAVIORAL THERAPY AND EYE MOVEMENT DESENSITIZATION AND REPROCESSING (EMDR) THERAPY

Cognitive Behavioral Therapy

The treatment of AN and other eating disorders is complex; even the NICE guideline does not provide the criteria for treatment. Within the scientific literature, there are some positive results for *cognitive behavioral therapy* (CBT) and family-based treatment (Dalle Grave, Calugi, Sartirana, & Fairburn, 2015; Fairburn, Cooper, Doll, Palmer, & Dalle Grave, 2013; Hildebrandt, Bacow, Greif, & Flores, 2014; Hoste,

Lebow, & Le Grange, 2015). The most effective approach is CBT, which focuses on reducing the behavioral symptoms of the disorder (e.g., dieting, binge eating, purging) and addressing the distorted cognitions about body weight and shape (Glasofer et al., 2013; Grilo, Masheb, Wilson, Gueorguieva, & White, 2011). However, although this approach has proved to be effective, it does not take into account the importance of traumatic events and experiences to the onset of eating disorders. For this reason, integrating EMDR therapy to target traumatic memories and adverse life experiences (Omaha, 2000) should be considered. In 2013, EMDR therapy was recommended by the World Health Organization (WHO) in their guidelines for the treatment of posttraumatic stress disorder, acute stress, and bereavement (WHO, 2013).

EMDR therapy is an *eight-phase* psychotherapy designed to address past negative experiences that contribute to the development of disorders as well as the current triggers of the symptoms developed from those experiences and any future blocks to effective functioning. Francine Shapiro describes EMDR therapy as guided by the *Adaptive Information Processing (AIP) model*, which posits that psychological disorders without an organic cause are caused by non-metabolized memories stored in the brain (F. Shapiro, 2001).

The goal of EMDR procedures is to reactivate the client's own neurologically based information processing through bilateral stimulation (BLS), which ultimately integrates the memory into the larger memory networks and allows it to reach adaptive resolution. AIP sees this process as a normal function of most life experiences; for instance, a problem arises when normal information processing becomes "blocked" or is otherwise unable to gain a resolution for an experience. Using this "innate, physiological, healing mechanism" (F. Shapiro & Forrest, 1998), EMDR makes it possible to retrieve and reprocess all the memories connected with the traumatic event that were not adequately processed before and thus remained "frozen" in the patient's neural nets, thus becoming the basis and/or a risk factor for the disorder. The efficacy of EMDR for the treatment of trauma has been well demonstrated in several meta-analyses (Bisson et al., 2007; Bradley et al., 2005; Davidson & Parker, 2001; Seidler & Wagner, 2006). In particular, a recent meta-analysis conducted by Watts et al. (2013) recommends EMDR as the most effective treatment for PTSD. EMDR's efficacy as an evidence-based treatment for trauma is also supported by the recent study by Pagani et al. (2012) regarding the EMDR's mechanism of action and its neurobiological substrate; findings suggest that, after bilateral ocular stimulation, traumatic events are processed at a cognitive level with a significant activation shift from limbic regions with high emotional valence to cortical regions. So far, EMDR therapy has been chiefly employed for work on the body image rather than in the processing of traumatic events associated with the disorder (Beer & van der Meijden, 2013; Bloomgarden & Calogero, 2008; Seijo, 2014). Few studies have considered using EMDR therapy in connection with possible traumatic experiences characterizing the onset of eating behavior disorders (Forester, 2014).

RESEARCH STUDY

Based on the lack of processing traumatic events with AN patients, Zaccagnino, Cussino, Callerame, Civilotti, and Fernandez (2016, submitted) created a research project to address processing traumatic memories related to the eating disorder. The study is a pilot clinical comparative study of two active interventions: EMDR therapy and CBT. The authors applied a specific EMDR Protocol for Anorexia Nervosa on 20 adolescents and young adult subjects diagnosed with AN to treat their eating disorder and improve their mental and physical well-being. The study's hypothesis was that processing traumatic memories related to their eating disorders with EMDR will result in the patient gradually becoming able to separate them from their past and to start an effective reprocessing of such memories, leading to an improvement in eating disorder conditions (Zaccagnino et al., in preparation), and that this approach will be more effective than CBT.

Measures

The following measures were used:

- *BMI calculation*: The BMI is a measure of body fat based on height and weight that applies to adult men and women.
- *Adult attachment interview* (AAI; George, Kaplan, & Main, 1985): AAI is a semi-structured interview whose purpose is to assess the representations of parents in relation to their own earliest attachment experiences (Hesse, 1999). Questions are asked about infant–parent relationship; moments

of vulnerability like illness, physical hurts, or emotional upsets; possible major separation; experiences of rejection; significant loss; and possible episodes of abuse.

- *Eating disorders inventory-3* (EDI-3; Garner, 2004): EDI-3 is a standardized and easily administered measure yielding objective scores and profiles that are useful in case conceptualization and treatment planning for individuals with a confirmed or suspected eating disorder. In EDI-3, the 91 items from EDI-2 scored using a six-choice format (always, usually, often, sometimes, rarely, or never) have been systematized into 12 subscales: three eating-disorder-specific subscales (drive for thinness, bulimia, and body dissatisfaction) and nine wide-ranging psychological subscales (low self-esteem, personal alienation, interpersonal insecurity, interpersonal alienation, interoceptive deficits, emotional dysregulation, perfectionism, asceticism, and maturity fears), which are pertinent to eating disorders but not strictly specific to these kinds of clinical conditions.
- *ACE questionnaire* (Dube, Anda, Felitti, Chapman, & Giles, 2003; Felitti et al., 1998): The ACE questionnaire attributes one point for each category of exposure to child abuse and/or neglect included in the study. Scores range from 0 to 10. The higher the score, the greater the exposure to adverse experiences during childhood and therefore the greater the risk of negative consequences.
- *Symptom checklist-revised* (SCL-90-R; Derogatis, 1990): This test contains 90 items and helps to measure nine primary symptom dimensions: somatization, obsessive compulsion, interpersonal sensitivity, depression, anxiety, hostility, phobic anxiety, paranoid ideation, and psychoticism. The GSI can be used as a summary of the test.
- *Difficulties in Emotion Regulation Scale* (DERS; Gratz & Roemer, 2004): The DERS is a 36-item self-report instrument that assesses six factor-analytically-derived facets of emotion regulation: nonacceptance of emotional responses (6 items), difficulties engaging in goal-directed behavior (5 items), impulse control difficulties (6 items), lack of emotional awareness (6 items), limited access to emotion regulation strategies (8 items), and lack of emotional clarity (5 items). Nonacceptance of emotional responses refers to the tendency to have negative secondary reactions to negative emotions (e.g., feeling angry about being sad). Difficulties engaging in goal-directed behavior refer to problems concentrating and completing tasks when experiencing distress. Impulse-control problems refer to difficulties remaining in control of behavior when upset. Lack of emotional awareness refers to problems attending to and acknowledging emotions. Limited access to emotion regulation strategies refers to the belief that little can be done to effectively change emotions once upset. Finally, lack of emotional clarity refers to the ability to clearly identify the emotions one is experiencing.

Results

In the study, it was evaluated whether the different psychotherapy treatments (EMDR or CBT) administered to the patients during the clinical work of this research project had a different impact on the BMI and on the psychological subscales studied.

The following are the results obtained:

- In our sample, during the specific assessment phase with the administration of ACE score, the majority of patients reported a high number of adverse events during the first years of life.
- Consistent with our hypothesis, and in line with the previous scientific literature, both EMDR and CBT intervention led to significant results as regards emotion regulation, psychopathological indicators, and increase in body weight.
- In line with previous studies, the use of EMDR methodology in the treatment of traumatic memories related to the onset and maintenance of the ED seems to achieve a greater improvement than those in the CBT group (Bloomgarden & Calogero, 2008). This led to a general improvement more related to emotional components of the ED psychopathology, rather than on a behavioral level.
- Significant differences from pre- and post-EMDR therapy on drive for thinness and bulimia scales underline a reduced concern and thoughts about weight and body shape in the whole sample.
- Reduction in interpersonal distrust, impulse regulation, and social isolation scales suggest a more balanced and enhanced quality of life of these patients. The weaker improvement observed in the CBT group, instead, may indicate an improvement in the aspects of the disorder related to the management of control, but limited efficacy in the management of the thoughts and concerns about the thinness and the ideal of thinness.
- The improvement in the emotion and impulse regulation is supported by a reduction in the DERS scores for both treatments: Significant results were found also in the CBT group, but still significantly

lower than those obtained by the EMDR group. In the EMDR group, the improvement in the lack of emotional clarity subscale underlines how individuals, after this treatment, experienced less confusion or apprehension in recognizing and accurately responding to emotional states.

- With regard to SCL-90, we found an improvement in both samples and psychopathological symptoms were significantly reduced upon completion of the treatment in both groups. However, the largest effects could be found on the obsessive compulsive, interpersonal sensitivity, and hostility subscales for the EMDR group.
- With regard to attachment categories, it is important to note that in the CBT group, the two patients classified as primary unresolved continued to show the same U classification after 1 year of treatment. EMDR, due to its capacity to intervene in an active way on traumatic memories related also to family dynamics, is able to lead to a resolution of the unresolved material and to a real change in the representations of early attachment relationships with caregivers (Verardo, Zaccagnino, & Lauretti, 2014; Wesselmann & Potter 2009; Zaccagnino & Cussino, 2013).

In conclusion, in agreement with the scientific literature in this field, we can highlight that in the CBT group, there was noticeable improvement regarding the presence of symptomatology associated with eating disorders. This outcome is probably linked more on a behavioral and cognitive level linked to AN symptomatology (drive for thinness and perfectionism; Calugi, Dalle Grave, Sartirana, & Fairburn, 2015; Glasofer et al., 2013; Grilo et al., 2011). Given its capacity to intervene in an active way on these early traumatic memories, the EMDR treatment seems to be able to lead to a resolution of the unresolved psychological material, to a real change in the representations of early attachment relationships with caregivers, to an increased access to adaptive information related to distressing memories, and to a decrease in negative beliefs related to self-worth and vulnerability with a greater impact on the AN symptomatology and emotion regulation, and on the general well-being and mental health.

THE EMDR ANOREXIA NERVOSA PROTOCOL SCRIPT NOTES

Phase 1: History Taking

Patient History

In Phase 1, the main goal is to collect information on patient history and present functioning such as living, working, social, and health conditions, in order to understand specifically how the eating problem(s) is adversely affecting life in general, including tracing back possible traumatic events that may have contributed to the onset of the disorder. In particular, it is important to glean in-depth information on the patient's present significant relationships and any problem areas or distress connected with such relationships, and pay special attention to the collection of specific information on the family of origin.

There are many important types of questions to inquire about, such as the following:

- *Attachment history (including deaths and traumatic experiences)*: Use questions from the adult attachment interview (AAI; George, Kaplan, & Main, 1985) to assess multidimensional information about patients' histories. Other questions are asked to help patients reflect on the following: How early infancy experiences might have influenced their adult personality; which experiences may have constituted obstacles to growth; and what they thought caused their parents to behave in the way they did. Also, it includes a detailed account of the losses and episodes of traumatic events. It is extremely important to ask the patient to provide a narrative on this issue, because only in this way will the clinician be able to identify possible nonresolution indices such as loss of coherence, which may lead to an unresolved classification with respect to loss or trauma in the AAI (for a complete illustration of this issue, please see Verardo & Zaccagnino, 2016.)
- *AN history*: It is helpful to have an overview of the disorder. The elements of this questioning are divided into specific areas of investigation.
  - *Eating disorder history*: It is important to investigate the onset and course of the disease, in order to gain a deeper understanding of the life-events that characterized the patient's life before the onset of the eating disorder. This way, it may be possible to obtain as clear a picture of the triggering event that led to the onset of AN. Moreover, it would be useful to ascertain whether in the

course of her history the patient engaged in different dysfunctional eating behaviors. In this section, bingeing and purging behaviors and the restriction history will be investigated. A number of questions are also posed concerning the history of the treatment of the disorder.

- *Eating history*: This section relates to the patient's eating history within her family.
- *Risk and maintenance factors*: This section investigates all of the aspects that are more directly related to food in the relational environment in which the patient grew up, and that may be considered as risk or maintenance factors for the dysfunctional behavior. It is important to understand the meaning that the patient's parents attribute to food, and try to determine the modes of food intake that allowed the parents to regulate their emotions and their relationship with their children.

Resource Identification

The main goal is to help the patient review her life history and identify times or actions when she felt well and full of life, but that she can no longer experience because of her illness. This way, the therapist will work on the patient's sense of self-effectiveness, while fostering her sense of security and motivation for treatment. The patient may be asked to focus on recalling a positive moment that she would like to experience again once she is well.

Therapeutic Relationship

Establish a client–clinician alliance based on trust by creating a climate of security within the therapeutic relationship. This allows the client to feel safe and strong enough to explore her memories, while maintaining that double focus of one foot in the past and one foot in the present. In particular, the therapist's ability to accept the different parts of the patient's self, understand them, and let the history of each one of them speak out is absolutely crucial to the effectiveness of the subsequent phases of this protocol.

Target Identification and Work Plan

In accordance with the Standard EMDR Protocol, targets will be identified in keeping with the Three-Pronged Protocol (past–present–future sequence). In order to identify the targets in the client's past history, the clinician can use the floatback or affect bridge technique to find the earlier precursors to her present difficulties; this underlines the connection between her current problems and earlier experiences. The therapist may ask, "When was the first time you remember feeling this way? When was the first time you learned ____?" Once the targets in the patient's history and the history of the eating disorder are identified, it may be useful to structure the therapeutic plan by grouping together the data collected in the history taking in the following order:

- *Triggering or precipitating event*: Address the triggering event (if any) that elicited the onset of the disorder. Use the floatback to trace back all the episodes connected with the triggering event in the patient's life history.
- *Big "T" traumas*: Process major traumas.
- *Food-related relational history*: Identify directly connected targets using "parts work," in particular through work with the *control* part of the anorexic patient (see Phase 2 for a more comprehensive description), in particular the profound meaning related to food, which can be traced in the patient's relational history. Identify other targets to help the patient cope with the difficult moment at mealtime, especially concerning the following:
  - *Bingeing and purging behaviors*: Use targets concerning the times preceding and following the bingeing and purging behaviors and then use the floatback to find related/connected episodes.
  - *Restrictive behaviors*: Find targets that represent the most difficult moment the patient has to face when sitting down to a meal and is asked to eat, and use the floatback to trace back connected episodes; ask, "How do you feel when you eat? If you think about these moments, what is the negative belief about yourself?" Also, check for when the patient does not eat and adopts restrictive behaviors, for example, "If you think about these moments, what can you say positive about yourself?" Proceed with the floatback to trace back all targets connected with this area.

   It is important to bear in mind that if no triggering event seems to have caused the onset of the disorder (or the patient does not recall such an event having happened), the *food-related relational history* will become a priority and must be addressed first.

- *Food issues*: Investigate life and disorder history to find the targets directly connected with food. Identify the targets explaining why the patient chose food (rather than something else) to manifest her difficulties. Process them in a chronological order.
- *Targets connected to symptomatology*: Work on symptoms and memories connected to symptomatology in accordance with the Standard EMDR Protocol.

Phase 2: Preparation

Eating Disorders

Using eating as a way of coping can result in specific consequences to physical and mental health. In fact, trauma can be pivotal to developing an eating disorder. It is important to assist patients in becoming more aware of the ways in which they function and leading them toward the exploration and implementation of new and more adequate coping strategies in the management of disturbing events.

EMDR Therapy

Explain EMDR therapy, including how the EMDR session works. Explore their expectations and assist them to become familiar through demonstration with how the method works (concerning distance, BLS methods, etc.). It is useful to reassure patients about the possible emotional intensity by including the train metaphor and the stop signal. Investigating patients' motivation to change is helpful so that it can be used during the more difficult parts of treatment.

Working Protocol With Eating Disorders in the Nonacute Phase (Hospitalization) Guidelines

WORK ON MOTIVATION

To obtain this information, it is useful to ask: "Which part of you wants to eat? Which part of you wants to feel better?" In case patients have difficulty in finding the necessary motivation to face the therapeutic treatment, it is important to ask questions such as: "How difficult is it for you to work on that target on a scale of 0 to 100 where 0% = no difficulty and 100% = the most difficulty?" If the response of the patient is over 50%, it is necessary to ask the patient to focus on physical sensations and emotions linked to poor motivation and proceed with sets of BLS. Continue with BLS until the patient does feel adequate motivation to change. It is important to proceed with the specific work on motivation every time the patient feels he cannot deal with difficult moments of the therapeutic process.

PARTS WORK

The work with parts should be considered applicable at different stages of the treatment. The following are some general guidelines that can help the clinician to orientate in the treatment. However, it is important to remember that the use of the *parts work* must be calibrated with respect to the specific needs and problems of each patient. The following are important elements in parts work:

- *Construction of the therapeutic alliance*: Through the identification and validation of different parts of the personality that play a fundamental role in the disorder, it is possible to establish a relationship of trust between patient and clinician, which could encourage the patient's motivation. The patient may experience a feeling of security that will help her to deal with possible difficult phases of treatment. In order for a climate of trust to be established between the therapist and the patient, the therapist must co-construct together with the patient shared knowledge about a specific aspect of her personality that plays a crucial role in maintaining the symptom: the control part. By acknowledging and making the patient aware of the existence of this control part in a welcoming, nonjudgmental, and collaborative manner, she feels more accepted as she learns about the part's mechanism of action.
- *Knowledge of parts*: Explain the meaning of parts of the personality to patients and that the parts play a fundamental role in their histories and their eating disorder histories. Only after working in a spirit of co-awareness, acceptance, and recognition will it be possible to ask specific questions of this part, to understand its history such as where it comes from; where the patient has learned to use this specific defense strategy; and whether anyone within her family uses this strategy, and to investigate whether the food control aspect, in particular, has involved her parents or other significant persons with whom the patient has had relations. By asking specific questions on when this control part was born, the therapist may gain a clearer and more complete picture of the triggering

factors underlying the disorder. Through the narration of the history of this fragile part that needs to be protected from the control part, it may be possible to trace back the associative processes most directly connected with the disorder. They may be identified as targets and consequently be treated according to the Standard EMDR Protocol.

Note: In order for the control part to be legitimatized and feel accepted, it may be important to address it directly and ask the control part (through the patient's adult part) to tell its personal history and the history of the disorder from her point of view. The therapist may thus gain access to information that may not emerge otherwise. For more in-depth information about parts work, refer to the studies conducted by Gonzalez and Mosquera (2012, 2015); van der Hart, Groenendijk, Gonzalez, Mosquera, and Solomon (2013); and Steele, van der Hart, and Nijenhuis (2005). The parts work is useful for the following:

- *Target identification*: The parts work could be used as a way to access the past relational history of the patient and to trace back the associative processes most directly connected with the disorder. They may be identified as targets and consequently be treated according to the Standard EMDR Protocol.
- *Blocks/defenses*: Specific work with different parts of the personality may be used in case of blocking or looping during the reprocessing of specific memories. Through the identification and understanding of the different parts present during the EMDR process, it is possible to establish a cooperative atmosphere, validating all the emotions connected to different parts involved, in order to complete the EMDR work.
- *Specific work on symptoms*: Explain that every person has different parts and that these parts must interact with one another to help the patient cope with the difficult task being asked of her. (See dissociative table at mealtime later in text.)
- *Worsening of symptoms*: Parts work is also important every time the patient experiences a moment of difficulty, in which the symptomatology tends to worsen. In such situations, it is important to understand, through the different parts of the patient, what are the dynamics that play a fundamental role in this condition. It is only through this work that it is possible to access the real feelings and reasons related to the worsening and plan a specific treatment.
- *Dissociative table*: The dissociative table exercise may be used to help patients with anorexia to face mealtime, with the help of parts work.

In Phases 3 to 8: assessment, desensitization, installation, body scan, closure, and reevaluation, use the Standard EMDR Protocol.

Working Protocol With Eating Disorders in the Acute Phase (Hospitalization)

GUIDELINES

There are guidelines for the treatment of patients with severe eating disorders in the acute phase:

- *Use resources*: With patients in this acute situation, work on resources (see Part 2: Preparation previously) to actively work on the patient's motivation for treatment. Work on resources in *every EMDR session*.
- *Work with control part*: In order to ensure the patient's cooperation with the control part, it is important to accept, validate, and support the control part *at every EMDR session*.

Given the emergency nature of this condition, it is necessary to focus the treatment on the aspects that will help the patient to handle difficult moments linked, for example, to hospitalization. For this reason, it is useful to focus on a target related to the disorder (including positive cognition [PC] related to restriction and bodily sensations).

It is helpful to structure the case conceptualization for the patient according to the following priorities:

- Triggering event (see protocol script later in text)
- Dissociative table at mealtime (see the following section)
- Desensitization of the positive affect when the patient does not eat. Ask the following, "What is the most positive thing about your not eating?" Desensitization of positive feedback when not eating and the consequent weight loss are both targets to be treated using the desensitization of triggers

and urge reprocessing (DeTUR) protocol. By working on these two aspects, the goal is to help the patient become aware of the dysfunctional nature of her behavior and to help her find more effective coping strategies.

- Work on the patient's body image and the possible unpleasant physical sensation related to the time when she eats.

Note: The following script refers to working with patients in the *nonacute* phase.

THE ANOREXIA NERVOSA PROTOCOL SCRIPT

Phase 1: Collection of Patient History Data

Attachment History (including deaths and traumatic experiences):

> Say, *"I'd like to ask you to choose five adjectives or words that reflect your relationship with your mother/father starting from as far back as you can remember in early childhood."*

> _____

> _____

> Say, *"Can you think of a memory or an incident that would illustrate why you choose to describe your relationship as _____ (insert an adjective or a word chosen by client)?"*

> _____

> _____

> Say, *"When you were upset or worried, and/or in emotional difficulty as a child, what would you do? And how did your parents react?"*

> _____

> _____

> Say, *"Can you tell me about some specific incident?"*

> _____

> _____

> Say, *"When you got hurt physically, what would happen? Can you think of any particular incident?"*

> _____

> _____

> Say, *"Do you remember the first time you were separated from your parents?"*

> _____

> _____

Say, *"How did you react?"*

_____

_____

Say, *"And how did they react?"*

_____

_____

Say, *"Can you think of other significant separations?"*

_____

_____

Say, *"Did you ever feel rejected as a child?"*

_____

_____

Say, *"How old were you when you experienced this and what did you do then?"*

_____

_____

Say, *"Why do you think your parents behaved this way? Do you think they realized how you felt?"*

_____

_____

Trauma History

Other questions are asked, including those relating to losses and traumatic events during childhood and later life.

Say, *"Did you experience the loss of a parent or other close loved one while you were a young child?"*

LIST LOSSES

_____

_____

_____

Ask the following questions about each memory on the list:

Say, *"Could you tell me about the circumstances?"*

_____

_____

_____

Say, *"How old were you at the time?"*

_____

_____

_____

Say, *"How did you react at the time? And your parents?"*

_____

_____

_____

Say, *"Was this death sudden or was it expected?"*

_____

_____

_____

Say, *"Can you remember your feelings at the time? Have they changed since then?"*

_____

_____

_____

Say, *"Are there any other experiences that you consider might have been traumatic?"*

_____

_____

_____

Anorexia Nervosa History

Say, *"When was the first time you started to restrict food intake? How old were you?"*

_____

_____

Say, *"In which moments of your life have you restricted more? Or less?"*

_____

_____

Say, *"Did you notice any change in your restrictive/bingeing and purging behaviors during your life?"*

_____

_____

Say, *"Do you remember whether in the period leading up to the onset of restricting food an especially distressing event occurred? What was going on in your life at that time?"*

_____

_____

If yes, say, *"Were there other times in your life that you felt or experienced distress like that?"*

_____

_____

Say, *"What was happening with your parents at that time?"*

_____

_____

Say, *"When was the first time you were underweight? How old were you?"*

_____

_____

Say, *"Were there times in your history in which you both vomited and engaged in restriction?"*

_____

_____

Say, *"Were you ever hospitalized?"*

_____

_____

Say, *"How many times? For how long?"*

_____

_____

Say, *"Did your disorder improve?"*

_____

_____

Say, *"Did you ever undergo specific treatment for the disorder?"*

_____

_____

Say, *"For how long?"*

_____

_____

Say, *"Why did you decide to abandon treatment? What went wrong?"*

_____

_____

Say, *"Instead, what worked in your opinion? Did you notice an improvement?"*

_____

_____

Eating History

The questions in this section refer to the patient's eating history within her family.

Say, *"Were you breastfed?"*

_____

_____

Say, *"How did the breastfeeding take place?"*

_____

_____

Say, *"Up to what age were you breastfed?"*

_____

_____

Say, *"What happened when your mother breastfed your sister or brother?"*

_____

_____

In order to obtain more accurate information and help the patient with the narrative of these memories, it may be useful to ask her to bring pictures to the session depicting the specific breastfeeding moment. If the patient does not have any pictures showing the moment of breastfeeding, it may be important to ask her to imagine it.

Say, *"What do you think your mother must have been like with you while she was breastfeeding you? Try to describe the scene."*

_____

_____

In order to obtain more accurate information about the role of food in the history of the patient's family, specific questions may also be asked about her parents' eating habits.

Say, *"Do you know anything about your parents' eating habits?"*

_____

_____

Say, *"What was your parents' approach to food?"*

_____

_____

Say, *"Do you remember what happened at meal times?"*

_____

_____

Say, *"Can you describe a typical scene?"*

_____

_____

Risk and/or Maintenance Factors

This section investigates all of the aspects that are more directly related to food in the relational environment in which the patient grew up and that may be considered as risk or maintenance factors for the dysfunctional behavior. It will be important to understand the meaning that the patient's parents attribute to food, and try to determine how food intake allowed the parents to regulate their emotions and their relationship with their children.

Specific questions such as the following may be asked:

Say, *"Did you ever happen to eat on your own? What would happen?"*

_____

_____

Say, *"Try to think back to when you were sitting down to a meal and your mother was with you. Can you try to describe how she looked at you?"*

_____

_____

Say, *"What did your mother do at those times?"*

_____

_____

Say, *"And how did you react?"*

_____

_____

Say, *"Now try to concentrate on a time in which you were sitting at the table but did not eat. How did your mother look at you?"*

_____

_____

Say, *"What did she do?"*

_____

_____

Say, *"What did she say?"*

_____

_____

Say, *"And how did you react?"*

_____

_____

Say, *"Do you remember any specific times in which your mother would calm down/feel better when you started to eat?"*

_____

_____

Say, *"Can you think of other ways in which your mother was able to regulate her emotions?"*

_____

_____

It is helpful to ask the same questions about the father at the table.

Say, *"Try to think back to when you were sitting down to a meal and your father was with you. Can you try to describe how he looked at you?"*

_____

_____

Say, *"What did your father do at those times?"*

_____

_____

Say, *"And how did you react?"*

_____

_____

Say, *"Now try to concentrate on a time in which you were sitting at the table but did not eat. How did your father look at you?"*

_____

_____

Say, *"What did he do?"*

_____

_____

Say, *"What did he say?"*

_____

_____

Say, *"And how did you react?"*

_____

_____

Say, *"Do you remember any specific times in which your father would calm down/feel better when you started to eat?"*

_____

_____

Say, *"Can you think of other ways in which your father was able to regulate his emotions?"*

_____

_____

It is also important to find out how the parent approached her daughter's disorder to understand the attachment dynamics and modes of regulating underlying emotions.

Say, *"How did your parents react when you were distressed or disturbed?"*

_____

_____

Questions may also be posed about the patient's relationship with her body and her parents' relationship with her body.

Say, *"How do you see your body?"*

_____

_____

Say, *"What is your relationship with your body?"*

_____

_____

Say, *"What were your parents' relationships with your body?"*

_____

_____

Say, *"What was your mother's relationship with her own body?"*

_____

_____

Say, *"What was your father's relationship with his own body?"*

_____

_____

Questions may also be asked about the times in which the patient received positive reinforcement about her initial weight loss, which may thus have contributed to the maintenance of the dysfunctional behavior.

Say, *"How do you feel when you eat?"*

_____

_____

Say, *"If you think about the moments, what is the negative belief about you that you tell yourself?"*

_____

_____

Say, *"Now, please bring up that picture of _____ (repeat the disturbing experience) and those negative words ____ (state the negative cognition [NC]). Now notice what feelings are coming up for you and where you are feeling them in your body, and just let your mind float back to an earlier time in your life—don't search for anything; just let your mind float back and tell me the earliest scene that comes to mind where you had similar thoughts of ___ (repeat NC) and feelings of ___ (repeat emotions) and where you feel it in your body."*

_____

_____

Say, *"If you think about these moments* (when you eat), *what can you say positive about yourself?"*

_____

_____

Once the PC is identified, continue by asking for the floatback to identify all the times in which the patient felt that she *lacked* this PC in her life history.

Say, *"Where, in your life, have you felt the lack of _____ (state the PC)?"*

_____

_____

Say, *"Do you remember what your parents said when you started to lose weight and were normal weight?"*

_____

_____

Say, *"What did your friends/acquaintances tell you?"*

_____

_____

Resource Identification

Say, *"Imagine you are healed. What would be the positive aspects?"*

_____

_____

Say, *"In particular, what would be the most important aspect to you?"*

_____

_____

If unable to recall any positive memories, say the following:

"Think about what you would like to do once you are healed and tell me what you are thinking."

_____

_____

Case Conceptualization: Target Identification and Work Plan

In order to identify a triggering or precipitating event, say the following:

"Do you remember in the period leading up to the onset of the disorder if an especially distressing event occurred?"

_____

_____

Say, *"What was going on in your life at that time?"*

_____

_____

Say, *"What was going on in the life of your parents?"*

_____

_____

Once the event is identified, use the floatback to trace back all the episodes connected with the triggering event.

Say, *"Now, please bring up that picture of _____ (repeat the disturbing experience) and those negative words ____ (state the NC). Now notice what feelings are coming up for you and where you are feeling them in your body, and just let your mind float back to an earlier time in your life—don't search for anything; just let your mind float back and tell me the earliest scene that comes to mind where you had similar thoughts of ___ (repeat the NC) and feelings of ___ (repeat emotions) and where you feel it in your body?"*

_____

_____

Once the work with triggering or precipitating events is completed, say the following:

"Are there other experiences that you consider might have been traumatic in your life?"

List of Traumatic Experiences

_____

_____

_____

_____

_____

_____

_____

_____

Again, process the triggering experience for the eating disorder. Then, before starting with all the questions investigating the meaning related to food, it is useful to process all the targets related to traumatic experiences. As in the Standard EMDR Protocol, clinicians must reprocess the list of traumatic experiences following their chronological order.

Bingeing Behaviors

In order to investigate the profound meaning related to food, say the following:

"How do you feel the moment before you start to binge?"

_____

_____

Say, *"If you think about the moment before you start to binge, what words best go with the picture that express your negative belief about yourself now?"*

_____

_____

Say, *"Now, please bring up that picture of _____ (repeat the disturbing experience) and those negative words ____ (state the NC). Now notice what feelings are coming up for you and where you are feeling them in your body, and just let your mind float back to an earlier time in your life—don't search for anything; just let your mind float back and tell me the earliest scene that comes to mind where you had similar thoughts of ___ (re-peat the NC) and feelings of ___ (repeat emotions) and where you feel it in your body."*

_____

_____

Say, *"If you think about these moments* (when you eat), *what can you say positive about yourself?"*

_____

_____

Once the PC is identified, continue by asking for the floatback to identify all the times in which the patient felt that she *lacked* this PC in her life history.

Say, *"Where, in your life, have you felt the lack of _____ (state the PC)?"*

_____

_____

Say, *"Are there any other times that you felt the lack of ____ (state the PC)?"*

_____

_____

Purging Behaviors

In order to investigate the profound meaning related to food, say the following:

"How do you feel the moment before you start to purge?"

_____

_____

Say, *"If you think about the moment before you start to purge, what words best go with the picture that express your negative belief about yourself now?"*

_____

_____

Say, *"Now, please bring up that picture of _____ (repeat the disturbing experience) and those negative words ____ (state the NC). Now notice what feelings are coming up for you and where you are feeling them in your body, and just let your mind float back to an earlier time in your life—don't search for anything; just let your mind float back and tell me the earliest scene that comes to mind where you had similar thoughts of ___ (re-peat the NC) and feelings of ___ (repeat emotions) and where you feel it in your body."*

_____

_____

Say, *"If you think about these moments* (when you purge), *what can you say positive about yourself?"*

_____

_____

Once the PC is identified, continue by asking for the floatback to identify all the times in which the patient felt that she *lacked* this PC in her life history.

Say, *"Where, in your life, have you felt the lack of _____ (state the PC)?"*

_____

_____

Restrictive Behaviors

In order to investigate the profound meaning related to food, say the following:

"How do you feel the moment before you start to restrict?"

_____

_____

Say, *"If you think about the moment before you start to restrict, what words best go with the picture that express your negative belief about yourself now?"*

_____

_____

Say, *"Now, please bring up that picture of _____ (repeat the disturbing experience) and those negative words ____ (state the NC). Now notice what feelings are coming up for you and where you are feeling them in your body, and just let your mind float back to an earlier time in your life—don't search for anything; just let your mind float back and tell me the earliest scene that comes to mind where you had similar thoughts of _____ (repeat the NC) and feelings of _____ (repeat emotions) and where you feel it in your body?"*

_____

_____

Say, *"If you think about these moments* (when you restrict), *what can you say positive about yourself?"*

_____

_____

Once the PC is identified, continue by asking for the floatback to identify all the times in which the patient felt that she *lacked* this PC in her life history.

Say, *"Where, in your life, have you felt the lack of _____ (state the PC)?"*

_____

_____

Family Behaviors

It is important to bear in mind that if no triggering event seems to have caused the onset of the disorder, these questions will become a priority and must be addressed first.

In order to identify food-related issues, say the following:

"What were your parents' relationship with your body?"

_____

_____

Say, *"What was your mother's relationship with her own body?"*

_____

_____

Say, *"What was your father's relationship with his own body?"*

_____

_____

Say, *"Did someone in your family suffer from an eating disorder?"*

_____

_____

Targets Related to Symptomatology

In order to work on targets connected to symptomatology, say the following:

"Do you remember the first time you started to binge/purge/restrict?"

_____

_____

Say, *"Do you remember the worst time that you had bingeing/purging/restrictive behaviors?"*

_____

_____

Say, *"And the last time?"*

_____

_____

Case Conceptualization Worksheet

PAST

Target Identification

ATTACHMENT ISSUES

First Time: _____

Floatback/Other Times: _____

_____

_____

TRAUMATIC EXPERIENCES

First Time: _____

Floatback/Other Times: _____

_____

_____

LOSSES

First Time: _____

Floatback/Other Times: _____

_____

_____

FOOD RELATIONAL HISTORY TARGETS (PARTS)

Part Problem: _____

Floatback/Other Times: _____

_____

_____

BINGEING BEHAVIORS

First Time: _____

Floatback/Other Times: _____

_____

_____

PURGING BEHAVIORS

First Time: _____

Floatback/Other Times: _____

_____

_____

RESTRICTIVE BEHAVIORS

_____

_____

_____

(*continued*)

(continued)

EATING/FOOD ISSUES

First Time: _____

Floatback/Other Times: _____

_____

_____

SYMPTOMATOLOGY

First Time: _____

Floatback/Other Times: _____

_____

_____

TRIGGERING EVENT

First Time: _____

Floatback/Other Times: _____

_____

_____

RELATIONSHIP WITH YOUR BODY

Identified Parts

_____

_____

_____

PRESENT TRIGGERS/FLASH-FORWARDS

Current Symptoms and Experience Triggers

_____

_____

_____

FUTURE TEMPLATES

Future Issues

_____

_____

_____

RESOURCE IDENTIFICATION

Resources

_____

_____

_____

Phase 2: Preparation

Explain Eating Disorders and Consequences

Explain eating disorders and the type of consequences that occur relevant to the patient's physical and mental health. It is also important to clarify the role of traumatic events in developing difficulties in eating behaviors to assist clients in the exploration and implementation of new and more adequate coping strategies in the management of disturbing events.

> Say, "Eating disorders are persistent weight-controlling behaviors that damage physical health and psychological function. There are many risk factors implied in the onset and maintenance of eating disorders, but one of the most important is the impact of traumatic or difficult events that have occurred during life. These events, in fact, can contribute to the development of maladaptive affect regulation strategies, which in turn may represent other risk factors for the development of this psychopathology."

_____

_____

Explaining EMDR Therapy: Psychoeducation

It is important that clients have a clear understanding of what is involved in an EMDR session, and expectations are clarified. By helping clients to become familiar with the mechanics of BLS, the clinician helps them feel more at ease with the method.

> Say, "When a trauma occurs, it seems to be locked in the nervous system with the original picture, sounds, thoughts, and feelings. The eye movements we use in EMDR seem to unlock the nervous system and allow the brain to process the experience. That may be what is happening in REM or dream sleep—the eye movements may help to process the unconscious material. It is important to remember that it is your own brain that will be doing the healing and you are the one in control. With your permission, I'm going to _____ (state the type of BLS used)."

> Say, "Now I'll show you the procedure in order to decide which is the best distance for you and whether you feel comfortable with both eye stimulation and tapping. Feel free to tell me if you don't feel comfortable and try to relax and be calm."

_____

_____

It has proven useful to reassure the client about the emotional intensity that the reprocessing can generate, using the train metaphor and specifying that, at any point in the course of reprocessing, should the client feel the need to stop the process, all she has to do is make a _stop_ signal with her hand.

> Say, "In order to help you just notice the experience and handle the intensity of the emotions, you can imagine riding on a train and the feelings and thoughts are just the scenery going by. If during the processing you have a problem or you feel you have to stop, please raise your hand and we will stop."

Work on Motivation

Investigate the patient's motivation to change.

> Say, "Which part of you wants to eat?"

_____

_____

Say, *"Which part of you wants to feel better?"*

_____

_____

In the case of difficulty in finding the necessary motivation to face the therapeutic treatment, ask questions such as the following:

Say, *"On a scale of 0% to 100%, where 0% is no difficulty and 100% is the most difficulty, how difficult is it for you to work on that target?"*

_____%

If the response is over 50%, say the following:

"Focus on the physical sensations and emotions linked to _____ (state what the poor motivation is) and go with that."

Do a set of BLS.

Continue with the BLS until there is a decrease in the patient's lack of motivation.

Note: Work on motivation every time patients feel they cannot deal with difficult moments in the therapeutic process.

Parts Work: The Control History

The control history is part of Phase 2 because all of the questions are a portion of parts work. Parts work can be seen as a way to stabilize the client; therefore, it is useful in Phase 2.

Say, *"Everyone has different parts of the personality, and these parts play a fundamental role in your history and in the history of your disorder. You can have an adult part who is present oriented and that handles your daily life. Then, you can have, for example, a very fragile part that needs to be protected and another part that has always acted to protect you. What part/s do you have?"*

_____

_____

Say, *"Is this part visible?"*

_____

_____

Say, *"How old is _____ (she/he)?"*

_____

_____

Say, *"What happened to _____ (her/him)?"*

_____

_____

Say, *"Was that the first time that happened?"*

_____

_____

Say, *"Where or from whom did ____ (she/he) learn to control?"*

_____

_____

Say, *"Did anyone in your family use this way of controlling?"*

_____

_____

Say, *"Has the food control aspect involved your parents or other significant persons with whom you have had a relationship?"*

_____

_____

Say, *"What is the task assigned to this part?"*

_____

_____

Say, *"Is ____ (she/he) protecting someone?"*

_____

_____

Say, *"If the control part was no longer there, what would happen?"*

_____

_____

Say, *"Are you able to see the part that ____ (she/he) is protecting?"*

_____

_____

Say, *"Can you describe it?"*

_____

_____

Say, *"What is ____ (her/his) history?"*

_____

_____

DISSOCIATIVE TABLE AT MEALTIME EXERCISE SCRIPT

After the parts of the patient are identified, they need to be understood and validated concerning their needs, objectives, and functions. It is useful to work together with parts and support co-knowledge and co-awareness. Parts work may be useful to help the patient understand the profound meaning of her or his suffering and to deal with difficult moments or blocks. During the EMDR work with the Anorexia Protocol, the clinician moves on to the dissociative table at mealtime exercise. This exercise may be used to help anorectic patients face the time they sit down to a meal. It should be part of every treatment plan (even in the acute phase) and is crucial to the achievement of the shared therapeutic goals.

Note: This is an example of what you may need to say to your client. Make sure to adapt it to the person sitting in front of you.

> Say, *"Together, we must look for a way to allow your different parts to communicate. We all have parts or aspects of the self that, at certain times, compete to emerge, and this conflict contributes to the distress you may feel. We all have different parts that feel different emotions and have different longings. To be able to solve the difficult task connected with mealtime, it is helpful to identify and come into contact with the different parts of the self, so that they may help you in this endeavor."*

_____

_____

The patient is then asked to think of a safe meeting place, like a room with a large table.

> Say, *"Please think of a safe meeting place, like a room with a large table or anywhere else that works for you."*

_____

_____

Ask the patient's adult part to make itself comfortable.

> Say, *"Please ask your adult self to make ___* (himself/herself) *comfortable in this safe place."*

_____

_____

Calmly call on all the parts that represent the different aspects of the patient's self.

> Say, *"Now let's ask all the parts that represent the different aspects of yourself to come forth and* _____ (make themselves comfortable, take a seat, etc.)."

_____

_____

Before continuing, with the help of the patient's adult part, the therapist must become acquainted with all the parts that are present. The therapist may want to ask questions about the age, sex, physical description, and function of each part, and try to capture as much information as possible from the description provided by the patient. The adult part will play a crucial role in mediating between various parts and the therapist; alongside that, the control part will be equally important.

> Say, *"If the adult part could facilitate, I would like to meet each one of you; would that be okay?"*

_____

_____

Ask the adult part of the patient to interact directly with the other part.

Say, *"Could your _____ (name the adult part) interact directly with the part?"*

_____

_____

Always ask questions through the adult when wanting to know more information about other parts.

Say, *"Okay, I would like to ask the adult part about _____ (state the part). Could the adult ask ___ (state the part) the following":*

How old are you?

_____

_____

What is your gender?

_____

_____

What do you look like?

_____

_____

What is your role and function for this person?

_____

_____

Thanks to the specific work carried out previously, this part will be able to more easily accept being of assistance in this delicate process.

Say, *"I would like to thank the adult and all of you for letting me get to know you and for you to get to know each other more. Your working together will help what we are doing together."*

In this context, it is especially important to make the control part understand that she or he is welcome, that we need her or his help, and that it will have to find the ways and means to let us know if we are going too fast or are asking her or him to do things she or he does not want to do or cannot do.

Say, *"I am glad that the _____ (control, in charge, etc.) part has come and I want the adult part to let ___ (her/him) know that _____ (she/he) is very welcome. Please let us know if we are going too fast or we are asking you to do things you do not want or cannot do. Okay?"*

_____

_____

The goal shared by the control part, the adult part, and the therapist is the patient's well-being.

Say, *"The goal that we share is this person's well-being."*

_____

_____

To this end, the control part will have to be encouraged to soften up; it will have to be made to understand the importance of taking in additional calories in order for the patient to survive.

> Say, *"We will have to work on some difficult areas such as the importance of taking in additional calories so that you can survive. I know that this will be difficult. I am hoping that by working together, we can be successful."*

_____

_____

Once the history of each part is fully understood and after a meaning is attributed to each one of the parts, the therapist may wish to ask the following:

> Say, *"Do we all agree that we need to discuss what happens at mealtimes and that we have to do something to increase food intake so that this situation is as positive as possible?"*

_____

_____

> Say, *"Which part/s of you do/does not want to eat?"*

_____

_____

> Say, *"Which part/s of you want/wants to eat?"*

_____

_____

> Say, *"Which part/s of you want/wants to feel better?"*

_____

_____

It is useful to make all the parts understand that saying "no" would involve further weight loss, which would have extremely adverse consequences on the patient's life and would jeopardize it.

> Say, *"I would like to help you understand with* ___ (the adult part or whatever you name this part) *that saying no would involve further weight loss, which would have very adverse consequences on your life and could jeopardize it."*

_____

_____

It is also useful to ask specific questions related to motivation to change, in order to plan a specific work on this area.

> Say, *"How motivated do you think that you are to change so that we can figure out what to do next?"*

_____

_____

Address the control part and ask it how it is feeling, whether what it is feeling now it has already felt in other circumstances in the past, and whether it is willing to help find other ways to manage the situation if it believes the ways being proposed are not functional.

Say to the control part, *"Please ask the adult to ask _____ (name of control part) how are you feeling?"*

_____

_____

Say, *"Have you felt this feeling in the past?"*

_____

_____

Say, *"Are you willing to help find other ways to manage the situation if you believe that what we are proposing won't work?"*

_____

_____

The therapist will have to accept the distress felt by the control part and point out that it must have had a good reason to act as it did in the past.

Say, *"I understand how ___ (state the feeling such as distressed, anger) you are feeling. I am sure that you have had a good reason to act as you did in the past."*

_____

_____

However, the control part will have to be encouraged to take a leap in time by being told that the situation now is different and that no one will ask it to do anything it does not wish to do.

Say, *"You are hearing things you have been told before, and you have every right to be skeptical; however, we are here now, and we want to help. What can we do to help you?"*

_____

_____

Say, *"Do you think there is a way we could get along? You will always be with us; actually, we need you."*

_____

_____

Say, *"Would you consider giving us a sign to tell us when you feel it's too much for you and that you are not being respected?"*

_____

_____

It may also be useful to ask the control part whether it is afraid that other parts of self may gain the upper hand.

Say, *"Are you afraid that some other part might step in and acquire too much power? Or is there some part that you do not trust?"*

_____

_____

Ascertain whether it is external intervention that the control part fears, which may exert pressure on the control part and in so doing may somehow jeopardize a particularly fragile and weak part.

Say, *"Are you* _____ (state the control part's name) *concerned that if we intervene, it will jeopardize something or someone in your system?"*

_____

_____

Say, *"If so, how can the other parts help you? What strategies might they adopt?"*

_____

_____

RESOURCE INSTALLATION SCRIPT

Identify the resource/s such as a skill or strength patients reported in Phase 1 concerning the moments in which the patient felt well by engaging in a given behavior (that she can no longer do because of her illness), and then install it/them.

Say, *"Think about a skill, strength, or resource that you feel you will need to help you with your issue."*

_____

_____

Emotions and Sensations

Have the client focus on the image, feelings, and sensations associated with the corresponding skill, strength, or resource.

Say, *"Focus on the image, feeling, and sensations associated with your* _____ (state skill, strength, or resource). *What do you notice and feel?"*

Enhancement

Verbally enhance with soothing guided imagery stressing positive feelings and sensations associated with the client's skill, strength, or resource.

Say, *"Focus on your* _____ (state skill, strength, or resource), *its sights, sounds, smells, and body sensations. Tell me more about what you are noticing."*

_____

_____

Bilateral Stimulation

Once enhanced, add several brief sets of BLS (four to six passes or taps). Repeat several times if the process has enhanced the client's positive feelings and sensations.

Say, *"As you think of _____ (state skill, strength, or resource), concentrate on where you feel the pleasant sensations in your body and allow yourself to enjoy them. Now concentrate on those sensations and follow my fingers (or whatever BLS you use)."*

Use four to six sets.

Say, *"How do you feel now?"*

_____

_____

Cue Word

Have clients identify a single word that represents their skill, strength, or resource. Repeat several times, adding BLS with each experience.

Say, *"What word or phrase best represents your _____ (state skill, strength, or resource)? Now concentrate on that word or phrase and the positive thoughts or sensations associated with it and follow _____ (state BLS)."*

Use short sets (four to six eye movements/tactile) of BLS with any positive response.

Repeat several times.

Say, *"How do you feel now?"*

_____

_____

Phase 3: Assessment

Incident

Say, *"The memory that we will start with today is _____ (select the incident from the treatment plan)?"*

_____

_____

Picture

Say, *"What picture represents the most disturbing part of this incident now?"*

_____

_____

_____

Negative Cognition

Say, *"What words best go with the picture that express your negative belief about yourself now?"*

_____

_____

Positive Cognition

Say, *"When you bring up that picture or* _____ (state the issue), *what would you like to believe about yourself now?"*

_____

_____

Validity of Cognition (VOC)

Say, *"When you think of the incident* (or picture) *how true do those words* _____ (clinician repeats the PC) *feel to you now on a scale of 1 to 7, where 1 feels completely false and 7 feels completely true?"*

1	2	3	4	5	6	7

(completely false)   (completely true)

Emotions

Say, *"When you bring up the picture or* _____ (state the issue) *and those words* _____ (clinician states the NC), *what emotion do you feel now?"*

_____

_____

_____

Subjective Units of Disturbance (SUD)

Say, *"On a scale of 0 to 10, where 0 is no disturbance or neutral and 10 is the highest disturbance you can imagine, how disturbing does it feel now?"*

0	1	2	3	4	5	6	7	8	9	10

(no disturbance)   (highest disturbance)

Location of Body Sensation

Say, *"Where do you feel it* (the disturbance) *in your body?"*

_____

_____

Continue with the rest of the Standard EMDR Protocol.

Phase 4: Desensitization

The work in Phase 4 follows the Standard EMDR Protocol.

To begin, say the following:

"Now, remember, it is your own brain that is doing the healing and you are the one in control. I will ask you to mentally focus on the target and to _____ (state the BLS you are using). *Just let whatever happens, happen, and we will talk at the end of the set. Just tell me what comes up, and don't discard anything as unimportant. Any new information that comes to mind is connected in some way. If you want to stop, just raise your hand."*

The client is asked to focus on the image, the NC, and the bodily sensation of each of the target events, after which the clinician must proceed with the BLS (eye movements or other).

Say, *"Bring up the picture and the words* _____ (clinician repeats the NC) *and notice where you feel it in your body. Now follow* _____ (state the BLS)."

It is important to reprocess all of the associative channels involved in the network.

After each set of BLS, say the following:

Say, *"What do you notice?"*

_____

_____

Then, on the basis of the client's reply, say, *"Good. Go with that."*

Proceed with another set of BLS.

If the material that emerges from each set is neutral, or no other material emerges, it is necessary to ask the client to return to the target and check the SUD.

Say, *"On a scale of 0 to 10, where 0 is no disturbance or neutral and 10 is the highest disturbance you can imagine, how disturbing does it feel now?"*

0	1	2	3	4	5	6	7	8	9	10

(no disturbance)   (highest disturbance)

Repeat the procedure until the SUDs = 0. Next, install the PC. Each traumatic event associated with the problem that is not reprocessed during the normal course of the first target needs to be processed using this protocol until the SUDs reach 0 and the PC is installed. In this way, the memory will no longer appear isolated, but will be integrated into the broader network and thus assimilated in a more adaptive and functional manner.

Phase 5: Installation

The client is asked to concentrate on the original memory and to pay attention to all parts of her body, to see if there are any residual tensions, rigidity, or strange sensations. If there are, proceed with eye movements until the discomfort completely disappears. If there are any pleasant sensations, proceed with brief sets of BLS in order to reinforce them.

The work in Phase 5 follows the Standard EMDR Protocol.

Say, *"How does* _____ (repeat the PC) *sound?"*

_____

_____

Say, *"Do the words* _____ (repeat the PC) *still fit, or is there another positive statement that feels better?"*

_____

_____

If the client accepts the original PC, the clinician should ask for a VOC rating to see if it has improved:

Say, *"As you think of the incident, how do the words feel, from 1* (completely false) *to 7* (completely true)?"

1	2	3	4	5	6	7

(completely false)   (completely true)

Say, *"Think of the event and hold it together with the words _____ (repeat the PC)."*

Do a long set of BLS to see if there is more processing to be done.

_____

_____

Phase 6: Body Scan

The work in Phase 6 follows the Standard EMDR Protocol.

Say, *"Close your eyes and keep in mind the original memory and the positive cognition. Then bring your attention to the different parts of your body, starting with your head and working downward. Any place you find any tension, tightness, or unusual sensation, tell me."*

_____

_____

If any tension, tightness, or unusual sensation, say the following:

"Go with that."

Do several sets of BLS.

If pleasant sensations are perceived, say the following:

"Go with that."

Do several sets of BLS.

Phase 7: Closing

At the end of each session, it is important to support the patient's accessing a more neutral and positive memory network. Ask the patient to recall the exercise on resources, and reinforcement may be provided by means of a short set of BLS.

Say, *"Think back to ____ (state the resource or safe base exercise). Go with that."*

_____

_____

Do a short set of BLS.

The client is also reminded that processing can continue even after the session is over and that she may find new insights, thoughts, memories, physical sensations, or dreams. In these cases, it is useful for the client to write down whatever emerges and to talk about it with the therapist in the next session or, in case she needs to touch base, to call her.

Say, *"Things may come up or they may not. If they do, great. Write them down and it can be a target for the next time. You can use a log to write down your triggers, images, thoughts, cognitions, emotions, and sensations; you can rate them on our 0-to-10 scale, where 0 is no disturbance or neutral and 10 is the worst disturbance. Please write down the positive experiences, too."*

Say, *"If you get any new memories, dreams, or situations that disturb you, just take a good snapshot. It isn't necessary to give a lot of detail. Just put down enough to remind you so we can target it the next time. The same thing goes for any positive dreams or situations. If negative feelings do come up, try not to make them significant. Remember, it's still just the old stuff. Just write it down for the next time. Then use the tape or the safe base exercise to let as much of the disturbance go as possible. Even if nothing comes up, make sure to use the tape every day and give me a call if you need to."*

_____

_____

Phase 8: Reevaluation

At the beginning of every subsequent session, the patient should once again access the target worked on at the previous session and monitor possible residual distress, making sure that the previously reached SUD and VOC levels are maintained. Possible new elements that emerged and were noted by the patient will also be assessed, as well as the progress observed. The work in Phase 8 follows the Standard EMDR Protocol.

Say, *"On a scale of 0 to 10, where 0 is no disturbance or neutral and 10 is the highest disturbance you can imagine, how disturbing does it feel now?"*

0   1   2   3   4   5   6   7   8   9   10

(no disturbance)   (highest disturbance)

Say, *"When you think of* _____ (state the issue or picture), *how true do those words* _____ (clinician repeats the PC) *feel to you now on a scale of 1 to 7, where 1 feels completely false and 7 feels completely true?"*

1   2   3   4   5   6   7

(completely false)   (completely true)

PRESENT TRIGGERS

It is necessary to identify the dysfunctional behavior and triggers related to every part of the work plan. Typical triggers could be problems related to attachment issues, dysfunctional eating behaviors, problems related to food, and so on. While investigating the present conditions and the people or situations that evoke the problem, help the client recognize each of the factors that will be necessary to reprocess.

Say, *"What are the situations, events, and/or stimuli triggers that still bring up the hoarding behaviors?"*

SITUATIONS, EVENTS, OR STIMULI TRIGGER LIST

_____

_____

_____

_____

_____

_____

Incident

Say, *"What situation, event, or stimulus would you like to use as a target today?"*

_____

_____

Picture

Say, *"What picture represents the most disturbing part of this incident now?"*

_____

_____

Negative Cognition

Say, *"What words best go with the picture that express your negative belief about yourself now?"*

_____

_____

Positive Cognition

Say, *"When you bring up the picture of the incident, what would you like to believe about yourself now?"*

_____

_____

Validity of Cognition

Say, *"When you bring up the picture of the incident, how true do those words _____ (clinician repeats the PC) feel to you now on a scale of 1 to 7, where 1 feels completely false and 7 feels completely true?"*

_____

_____

1	2	3	4	5	6	7

(completely false)   (completely true)

Emotions

Say, *"When you bring up the picture* (or incident) *and those words* _____ (clinician states the NC), *what emotion do you feel now?"*

_____

_____

Subjective Units of Disturbance

Say, *"On a scale of 0 to 10, where 0 is no disturbance or neutral and 10 is the highest disturbance you can imagine, how disturbing does it feel now?"*

0	1	2	3	4	5	6	7	8	9	10

(no disturbance)   (highest disturbance)

Location of Body Sensations

Say, "Where do you feel it (the disturbance) in your body?"

_____

_____

FUTURE TEMPLATE

Inquire about the client's concerns regarding the future and hoped-for behavior. The clinician talks about that behavior and the abilities the client would like to achieve and the new goals to aim for. More specifically, ask the client to focus on the abilities required to achieve these objectives.

Install the Future Template

Say, "Okay, we have reprocessed all of the targets that we needed to do that were on your list. Now, let's anticipate what will happen when you are faced with _____ (state the concern). What picture do you have in mind?"

_____

_____

Say, "I would like you to imagine yourself coping effectively with _____ (state the trigger) in the future. Bring up this picture and say to yourself: 'I can handle it,' and feel the sensations. Okay, have you got it? Follow my fingers (or any other forms of BLS)."

_____

_____

Say, "Bring up the picture again, on a scale of 1 to 7, where 1 feels completely false and 7 feels completely true. To what extent do you think you can manage to really do it?"

1	2	3	4	5	6	7

(completely false)   (completely true)

Install with sets of eye movements until a maximum level of VOC has been achieved.

If there is a block, meaning that even after 10 or more installations, the VOC is still below 7, there are more targets that need to be identified and addressed. The therapist should use the Standard EMDR Protocol to address these targets before proceeding with the template (see worksheets in Appendix A). Also, evaluate whether the client needs any new information, resources, or skills to be able to comfortably visualize the future coping scene. Introduce this needed information or skill.

Say, "What would you need to feel confident in handling the situation?"

_____

_____

Or say, "What is missing from your handling of this situation?"

_____

_____

Use BLS, if blocks are not resolved; identify unprocessed material; and process with the Standard EMDR Protocol.

Video Check (Future Template as a Movie)

Say, *"This time, I'd like you to imagine yourself stepping into the scene of a future confrontation with the object or the situation for which the future template was meant. For example, close your eyes and play a movie of this happening, from the beginning until the end. Imagine yourself coping with any challenges that come your way. Notice what you are seeing, thinking, feeling, and experiencing in your body. While playing this movie, let me know if you hit any blocks. If you do, just open your eyes and let me know. If you don't hit any blocks, let me know when you have viewed the whole movie."*

_____

_____

If the client encounters a block and opens her eyes, this is a sign for the therapist to instruct the client to say the following:

"Say to yourself 'I can handle it' and follow my fingers (introduce a set of eye movements).*"

To provide the clinician with an indication regarding the client's self-efficacy, ask her to rate her response on a VOC scale from 1 to 7. This procedural step may give the clinician feedback on the extent to which the goals are met.

Say, *"As you think of the incident, how do the words feel from 1 being completely false to 7 being completely true?"*

1   2   3   4   5   6   7

(completely false)   (completely true)

If the client is able to play the movie from start to finish with a sense of confidence and satisfaction, the client is asked to play the movie once more from the beginning to the end, BLS is introduced, and the PC, "I can handle it," is installed. In a sense, this movie is installed as a future template.

Say, *"Okay, play the movie one more time from beginning to end and say to yourself, 'I can handle it.' Go with that."*

_____

_____

SUMMARY

The Anorexia Nervosa Protocol is based on the main theoretical contributions concerning the dynamics of eating disorders with particular focus on the risk factors involved in its onset and/or maintenance and a special emphasis on those connected with traumatic life events. The most relevant concepts related to the dynamics of AN explained in the protocol are the following: individual risk factors, attachment wounds and traumatic experiences, dissociative table at mealtime, and parts work.

REFERENCES

Abbate Daga, G., Quaranta, M., Notaro, G., Urani, C., Amianto, F., & Fassino, S. (2011). Family therapy and eating disorders in young female patients: State of the art. *Journal of Psychopatology, 17*(1), 40–47.
American Psychiatric Association. (2013). *Diagnostic and statistical manual of mental disorders* (5th ed.). Arlington, VA: American Psychiatric Publishing.
Arcelus, J., Mitchell, A. J., Wales, J., & Nielsen, S. (2011). Mortality rates in patients with anorexia nervosa and other eating disorders. A meta-analysis of 36 studies. *Archives of General Psychiatry, 68*(7), 724–731. doi:10.1001/archgenpsychiatry.2011.74
Bandura, A. (2003). Observational learning. In J. H. Byrne (Ed.), *Encyclopedia of learning and memory* (2nd ed., pp. 482–484). New York, NY: Macmillan.

Beer, R., & van der Meijden, H. (2013, April). *Why EMDR in the treatment of an eating disorder? How? So...: Ideas, hypotheses and findings with respect to EMDR aimed at influencing a negative body image.* Presentation at the 7th Vereniging EMDR Nederland Conference, Nijmegen, the Netherlands.

Bisson, J. I., Ehlers, A., Matthews, R., Pilling, S., Richards, D., & Turner, S. (2007). Psychological treatments for chronic post-traumatic stress disorder: Systematic review and meta-analysis. *British Journal of Psychiatry, 190,* 97–104. doi:10.1192/bjp.bp.106.021402

Bisson, J. I., Roberts, N. P., Andrew, M., Cooper, R., & Lewis, C. (2013). Psychological therapies for chronic post-traumatic stress disorder (PTSD) in adults. *Cochrane Database of Systematic Reviews, 12,* CD003388. doi:10.1002/14651858.CD003388.pub4

Bloomgarden, A., & Calogero, R. M. (2008). A randomized experimental test of the efficacy of EMDR treatment on negative body image in eating disorder inpatients. *Eating Disorders: The Journal of Treatment & Prevention, 16*(5), 418–427. doi:10.1080/10640260802370598

Bowlby, J. (1969). *Attachment and loss: Vol. 1. Attachment.* New York, NY: Basic Books.

Bowlby, J. (1973). *Attachment and loss, Vol. 2: Separation: Anxiety and anger.* New York, NY: Basic Books.

Bowlby, J. (1980). *Attachment and loss, Vol. 3: Loss, sadness and depression.* New York, NY: Basic Books.

Bowlby, J. (1982). *Costruzione e rottura dei legami affettivi.* Milan, Italy: Raffaello Cortina Editore.

Bradley, R., Greene, J., Russ, E., Dutra, L., & Westen, D. (2005). A multidimensional meta-analysis of psychotherapy for PTSD. *American Journal of Psychiatry, 162,* 214–227. doi:10.1176/app i.ajp.162.2.214

Brown, T. A., Keel, P. K., & Weissman, R. S. (2012). Feeding and eating conditions not elsewhere classified (NEC). *DSM-5 Psychiatric Annals, 42,* 421–425. doi:10.3928/00485713-20121105-08

Bruch, H. (1973). *Eating disorders: Obesity, anorexia nervosa and the person within.* New York, NY: Basic Books.

Bulik, C. M., Sullivan, P. F., Tozzi, F., Furberg, H., Lichtenstein, P., & Pedersen, N. L. (2006). Prevalance, heritability, and prospective risk factors for anorexia nervosa. *Archives of General Psychiatry, 63,* 305–312. doi:10.1001/archpsyc.63.3.305

Calugi, S., Dalle Grave, R., Sartirana, M., & Fairburn, C. G. (2015). Time to restore body weight in adults and adolescents receiving cognitive behaviour therapy for anorexia nervosa. *Journal of Eating Disorders, 3*(1), 21. doi:10.1186/s40337-015-0057-z

Carlson, E. A. (1998). A prospective longitudinal study of attachment disorganization/disorientation. *Child Development, 69*(4), 1107–1128. doi:10.1111/j.1467-8624.1998.tb06163.x

Cole, P. M., & Putnam, F. W. (1992). Effect of incest on self and social functioning: A developmental psychopathology perspective. *Journal of Consulting and Clinical Psychology, 60,* 174–184. doi:10.1037/0022-006X.60.2.174

Dalle Grave, R., Calugi, S., Sartirana, M., & Fairburn, C. G. (2015). Transdiagnostic cognitive behavior therapy for adolescents with an eating disorder who are not underweight. *Behavior Research and Therapy, 73,* 79–82. doi:10.1016/j.brat.2015.07.014

Davidson, P. R., & Parker, K. C. H. (2001). Eye movement desensitization and reprocessing (EMDR): A meta-analysis. *Journal of Consulting and Clinical Psychology, 69,* 305–316. doi:10.1037/0022-006X.69.2.305

Derogatis, L. R. (1990). *SCL-90-R. A bibliography of research reports 1975-1990.* Baltimore, MD: Clinical Psychometric Research.

Dube, S. R., Anda, R. F., Felitti, V. J., Chapman, D. P., & Giles, W. H. (2003). Childhood abuse, neglect and household dysfunction and the risk of illicit drug use: The adverse childhood experiences study. *Pediatrics, 111,* 564–572. doi:10.1542/peds.111.3.564

Dube, S. R., Felitti, V. J., & Rishi, S. (2013). Moving beyond childhood adversity: Associations between salutogenic factors and subjective well-being among adult survivors of trauma. In M. Linden & K. Rutkowski (Eds.), *Hurting memories and beneficial forgetting: Posttraumatic stress disorders, biographical developments and social conflicts* (pp. 139–152). Waltham, MA: Elsevier.

Fairburn, C. G., Cooper, Z., Doll, H. A., Palmer, R. L., & Dalle Grave, R. (2013). Enhanced cognitive behavior therapy for adults with anorexia nervosa: A UK-Italy study. *Behavior Research and Therapy, 51,* R2–R8. doi:10.1016/j.brat.2012.09.010

Fearon, R. M. P., Bakermans-Kranenburg, M. J., Van IJzendoorn, M. H., Lapsley, A., & Roisman, G. I. (2010). The significance of insecure attachment and disorganization in the development of children's externalizing behavior: A meta-analytic study. *Child Development, 81,* 435–456. doi:10.1111/j.1467-8624.2009.01405.x

Felitti, V. J., Anda, R. F., Nordenberg, D., Williamson, D. F., Spitz, A. M., Edwards, V. . . . Marks, J. S. (1998, May). Relationship of childhood abuse and household dysfunction to many of the leading causes of death in adults. The adverse childhood experiences (ACE) study. *American Journal of Preventive Medicine, 14*(4), 245–258. doi:10.1016/S0749-3797(98)00017-8

Fichter, M. M., & Quadflieg, N. (2016). Mortality in eating disorders—Results of a large prospective clinical longitudinal study. *International Journal of Eating Disorders, 49,* 391–401. doi:10.1002/eat.22501

Forester, D. (2014). *EMDR with eating disorders.* Presentation at the 20th EMDR International Association Conference, Denver, CO.

Garner, D. M. (2004). *Eating disorder inventory-3 professional manual.* Odessa, FL: Psychological Assessment Resources.

Garner, D. M., & Dalle Grave, R. (1999). *Terapia cognitivo comportamentale dei disturbi dell'alimentazione.* Verona, Italy: Positive Press.

George, C., Kaplan, N., & Main, M. (1985). *Adult attachment interview.* Unpublished manuscript, Department of Psychology, University of California, Berkeley, CA.

George, C., & Solomon, J. (1996). Representational models of relationships: Links between caregiving and attachment. *Infant Mental Health Journal, 17,* 198–216. doi:10.1002/(SICI)1097-0355(199623)17:3<198::AID-IMHJ2>3.0.CO;2-L

Glasofer, D. R., Haaga, D. A. F., Hannallah, L., Field, S. A., Kozlosky, M., Reynolds, J., . . . Tanofsky-Kraff, M. (2013). Self-efficacy beliefs and eating behavior in adolescent girls at-risk for excess weight gain and binge eating disorder. *International Journal of Eating Disorders, 46,* 663–668. doi:10.1002/eat.22160

Gonzalez, A., & Mosquera, D. (Eds.). (2012). *EMDR and dissociation: The progressive approach.* Charleston, SC: Amazon Imprint.

Gonzalez, A., & Mosquera, D. (Eds.). (2015). *EMDR e dissociazione: l'approccio progressivo.* Rome, Italy: Giovanni Fioriti Editore.

Gratz, K. L., & Roemer, L. (2004). Multidimensional assessment of emotion regulation and dysregulation: Development, factor structure, and initial validation of the Difficulties in Emotion Regulation Scale. *Journal of Psychopathology and Behavioral Assessment, 26,* 41–54. doi:10.1023/B:JOBA.0000007455.08539.94

Grilo, C. M., Masheb, R. M., Wilson, G. T., Gueorguieva, R., & White, M. A. (2011). Cognitive-behavioral therapy, behavioral weight loss, and sequential treatment for obese patients with binge-eating disorder: A randomized controlled trial. *Journal of Consulting and Clinical Psychology, 79*(5), 675. doi:10.1037/a0025049

Harris, E. C., & Barraclough, B. (1997). Suicide as an outcome for mental disorders. A meta-analysis. *British Journal of Psychiatry, 170,* 205–228. doi:10.1192/bjp.170.3.205

Hesse, E. (1999). The adult attachment interview: Historical and current perspectives. In J. Cassidy & P. R. Shaver (Eds.), *Handbook of attachment: Theory, research, and clinical applications* (pp. 395–433). New York, NY: Guilford Press.

Hildebrandt, T., Bacow, T., Greif, R., & Flores, A. (2014). Exposure-based family therapy (FBT-E): An open case series of a new treatment for anorexia nervosa. *Cognitive and Behavioral Practice, 21*(4), 470–484. doi:10.1016/j.cbpra.2013.10.006

Hoste, R. R., Lebow, J., & Le Grange, D. (2015). A bidirectional examination of expressed emotion among families of adolescents with bulimia nervosa. *International Journal of Eating Disorders, 48,* 249–252. doi:10.1002/eat.22306

Hudson, J. I., Hiripi, E., Pope, H. G., & Kessler, R. C. (2007). The prevalence and correlates of eating disorders in the National Comorbidity Survey Replication. *Biological Psychiatry, 61*(3), 348–358. doi:10.1016/j.biopsych.2006.03.040

Hund, A. R., & Espelage, D. L. (2005). Childhood sexual abuse, disordered eating, alexithymia, and general distress: A mediation model. *Journal of Counseling Psychology, 52,* 559–573. doi:10.1037/0022-0167.52.4.559

Jacobi, C., Abascal, L., & Taylor, C. B. (2004). Screening for eating disorders and high-risk behavior: Caution. *International Journal of Eating Disorders, 36,* 280–295. doi:10.1002/eat.20048

Johnson, J. G., Cohen, P., Kasen, S., & Brook, J. S. (2006). Dissociative disorders among adults in the community, impaired functioning, and axis I and II comorbidity. *Journal of Psychiatric Research, 40,* 131–140. doi:10.1016/j.jpsychires.2005.03.003

Keshaviah, A., Edkins, K., Hastings, E. R., & Krishna, M. (2014). Re-examining premature mortality in anorexia nervosa: A meta-analysis redux. *Comprehensive Psychiatry, 55*(8), 1773–1784. doi:10.1016/j.comppsych.2014.07.017

Lee, C. W., & Cuijpers, P. (2013). A meta-analysis of the contribution of the eye movements in processing emotional memories. *Journal of Behavior Therapy and Experimental Psychiatry, 44*, 231–239. doi:10.1016/j.jbtep.2012.11.001

Liotti, G. (2004). Trauma, dissociation and disorganized attachment: Three strands of a single braid. *Psychotherapy: Theory, Research, Practice, Training, 41*, 472–486. doi:10.1037/0033-3204.41.4.472

Liotti, G., & Farina, B. (2011). *Sviluppi traumatici. Eziopatogenesi, clinica e terapia della dimensione dissociativa.* Milan, Italy: Raffaello Cortina.

Lyons-Ruth, K., & Jacobvitz, D. (2008). Attachment disorganization: Genetic factors, parenting contexts, and developmental transformation from infancy to adulthood. In J. Cassidy & P. R. Shaver (Eds.), *Handbook of attachment: Theory, research and clinical applications* (2nd ed., pp. 666–697). New York, NY: Guilford Press.

Main, M., & Hesse, E. (1990). Parents' unresolved traumatic experiences are related to infant disorganized attachment status: Is frightened and/or frightening parental behavior the linking mechanism? In M. Greenberg, D. Cicchetti, & E. M. Cummings (Eds.), *Attachment in the preschool years: Theory, research and intervention* (pp. 161–184). Chicago, IL: University of Chicago Press.

Main, M., & Solomon, J. (1986). Discovery of an insecure-disorganized/disoriented attachment pattern. In T. B. Brazelton & M. W. Yogman (Eds.), *Affective development in infancy* (pp. 95–124). Westport, CT: Ablex Publishing.

Messman-Moore, T. L., & Garrigus, A. S. (2007). The Association of Child Abuse and Eating Disorder Symptomatology: The importance of multiple forms of abuse and revictimization. *Journal of Aggression Maltreatment and Trauma, 14*(3), 51–72. doi:10.1300/J146v14n03_04

Ministry of Health, Italy. (2014). Disturbi del comportamento alimentare [Eating behavior disorders]. Retrieved from http://www.salute.gov.it/portale/temi/p2_6.jsp?lingua=italiano&id=1930&area=saluteBambino&menu=alimentazione

Monson, C. M., Price, J. A., Rodriguez, B. F., Ripley, M. P., & Warner, R. A. (2004). Emotional deficits in military-related PTSD: An investigation of content and process disturbances. *Journal of Traumatic Stress, 17*, 275–279. doi:10.1023/B:JOTS.0000029271.58494.05

Murphy, J. G., Yurasek, A. M., Dennhardt, A. A., Skidmore, J. R., McDevitt-Murphy, M. E., MacKillop, J., & Martens, M. P. (2013). Symptoms of depression and PTSD are associated with elevated alcohol demand. *Drug and Alcohol Dependence, 127*, 129–136. doi:10.1016/j.drugalcdep.2012.06.022

National Institute for Health and Care Excellence. (2004). *Eating disorders: Core interventions in the treatment and management of anorexia nervosa, bulimia nervosa and related eating disorders.* NICE Clinical Guidelines 9. Leicester, UK: British Psychological Society.

Nicholls, D. E., Lynn, R., & Viner, R. M. (2011). Childhood eating disorders: British national surveillance study. *The British Journal of Psychiatry, 198*(4), 295–301. doi:10.1192/bjp.bp.110.081356

Omaha, J. (2000, September). *Treatment of bulimia and binge eating disorder using the Chemotion/EMDR protocol.* Presentation at the 5th EMDR International Association Conference, Toronto, ON.

Pagani, M., Di Lorenzo, G., Verardo, A. R., Nicolais, G., Monaco, L., Lauretti, G., . . . Fernandez, I. (2012). Neurobiological correlates of EMDR monitoring—An EEG Study. *PLoS One, 7*(9), e45753. doi:10.1371/journal.pone.0045753

Putnam, R. D. (2001). Social capital: Measurement and consequences. *Canadian Journal of Policy, 2*, 41–51.

Ruffolo, J. S., Philips, K. A., Menard, W., Fay, C., & Weisberg, R. B. (2006). Comorbidity of body dysmorphic disorder and eating disorders: Severity of psychopathology and body image disturbance. *International Journal of Eating Disorders, 30*, 11–19. doi:10.1002/eat.20219

Russo, M., d'Angerio, S., Carcione, A., & Di Maggio, G. (2009). Disfunzioni meta cognitive nel disturbo del comportamento alimentare: uno studio su caso singolo. *Cognitivismo Clinico, 6*(2), 178–195.

Schore, A. (2001). The effects of a secure attachment relationship on right brain development, affect regulation, and infant mental health. *Infant Mental Health Journal, 2*, 27–66. doi:10.1002/1097-0355 (200101/04)22:1<7::AID-IMHJ2>3.0.CO;2-N

Schore, A. (2002). Dysregulation of the right brain: A fundamental mechanism of traumatic attachment and the psychopathogenesis of posttraumatic stress disorder. *Australian and New Zealand Journal of Psychiatry, 36*, 9–30. doi:10.1046/j.1440-1614.2002.00996.x

Schwartz, M., & Gay, P. (1996). Physical and sexual abuse, neglect and early disorder symptoms. In M. F. Schwartz & L. Cohn (Eds.), *Sexual abuse and eating disorders* (pp. 15–30). New York, NY: Brunner/Mazel.

Seidler, G. H., & Wagner, F. E. (2006). Comparing the efficacy of EMDR and trauma focused cognitive-behavioral therapy in the treatment of PTSD: A meta-analytic study. *Psychological Medicine, 36*(11), 1515–1522. doi:10.1017/S0033291706007963

Seijo, N. (2014). *Advanced EMDR strategies for the body image distortion treatment in eating disorders, in EMDR in the treatment of the fears and phobias/eating disorders/borderline disorder* (Derek, Farrell, Chair). Presentation at the 2nd EMDR Asia International Conference, Manila, The Philippines.

Shapiro, D., & Astin, J. (1998). *Control therapy*. New York, NY: John Wiley & Sons.

Shapiro, F. (2001). Eye movement desensitization and reprocessing (EMDR) and the anxiety disorders: Clinical and research implications of an integrated psychotherapy treatment. *Psicoterapia Cognitiva e Comportamentale, 7*(1), 43–75.

Shapiro, F., & Forrest, S. (1998). *EMDR. Una terapia innovativa per il superamento dell'ansia, dello stress e dei disturbi di origine traumatica*. Rome, Italy: Astrolabio Ubaldini.

Siegel, D. J. (1999). *The developing mind: Toward a neurobiology of interpersonal experience*. New York, NY: Guilford Press.

Smink, F. E., van Hoeken, D., Oldehinkel, A. J., & Hoek, H. W. (2014). Prevalence and severity of *DSM-5* eating disorders in a community cohort of adolescents. *International Journal of Eating Disorders, 47*(6), 610–619. doi:10.1002/eat.22316

Speranza, A. M., & Alberigi, E. (2006). La relazione tra abuso e disturbi alimentari: il ruolo della dissociazione. *Maltrattamento e Abuso all'Infanzia, 8*(1), 23–47.

Steele, K., van der Hart, O., & Nijenhuis, E. R. S. (2005). Phase-oriented treatment of structural dissociation in complex traumatization: Overcoming trauma-related phobias. *Journal of Trauma and Dissociation, 6*(3), 11–53. doi:10.1300/J229v06n03_02

Steiger, H., & Zankor, M. (1990). Sexual traumata among eating-disordered, psychiatric, and normal female groups: Comparison of prevalences and defense styles. *Journal of Interpersonal Violence, 5*, 74–86. doi:10.1177/088626090005001006

Stice, E., Ng, J., & Shaw, H. (2010). Risk factors and prodromal eating pathology. *Journal of Child Psychology and Psychiatry, 51*(4), 518–525. doi:10.1111/j.1469-7610.2010.02212.x

Stice, E., Rohde, P., Shaw, H., & Gau, J. (2011). An effectiveness trial of a selected dissonance-based eating disorders prevention program for female high school students: Long-term effects. *Journal of Consulting and Clinical Psychology, 79*, 500–508. doi:10.1037/a0024351

Suokas, J. T., Suvisaari, J. M., Grainger, M., Raevuori, A., Gissler, M., & Haukka, J. (2014). Suicide attempts and mortality in eating disorders: A follow-up study of eating disorder patients. *General Hospital Psychiatry, 36*(3), 355–357. doi:10.1016/j.genhosppsych.2014.01.002

Surgenor, L. J., Horn, J., Plumridge, E. W., & Hudson, S. M. (2002). Anorexia nervosa and psychological control: A reexamination of selected theoretical accounts. *European Eating Disorders Review, 10*, 85–101. doi:10.1002/erv.457

Swanson, S. A., Crow, S. J., Le Grange, D., Swendsen, J., & Merikangas, K. R. (2011, July). Prevalence and correlates of eating disorders in adolescents. Results from the national comorbidity survey replication adolescent supplement. *Archives of General Psychiatry, 68*(7), 714–723. doi:10.1001/archgenpsychiatry.2011.22

Treasure, J., Claudino, A. M., & Zucker, N. (2010). Eating disorders. *The Lancet, 375*, 583–593. doi:10.1016/S0140-6736(09)61748-7

van der Hart, O., Groenendijk, M., Gonzalez, A., Mosquera, D., & Solomon, R. (2013). Dissociation of the personality and EMDR therapy in complex trauma-related disorders: Applications in the stabilization phase. *Journal of EMDR Practice and Research, 7*, 81–94. doi:10.1891/1933-3196.7.2.81

Verardo, A. R., & Zaccagnino, M. (2016). Working on attachment issues with EMDR therapy: The attachment protocol. In M. Luber (Ed.), *Eye movement desensitization and reprocessing EMDR therapy scripted protocols and summary sheets: Treating trauma- and stressor-related conditions* (pp. 45–96). New York, NY: Springer Publishing.

Verardo, A. R., Zaccagnino, M., & Lauretti, G. (2014). Applicazioni cliniche nel contesto delle dinamiche di attaccamento: Il ruolo dell'EMDR. = Clinical applications in the context of attachment: The role of EMDR. *Infanzia e Adolescenza, 13*(3), 172–184.

Vize, C. M., & Cooper, P. J. (1995). Sexual abuse in patients with eating disorder, patients with depression and normal controls: A comparative study. *British Journal of Psychiatry, 167*, 80–85. doi:10.1192/bjp.167.1.80

Watts, B. V., Schnurr, P. P., Mayo, L., Young-Xu, Y., Weeks, W. B., & Friedman, M. J. (2013). Meta-analysis of the efficacy of treatments for posttraumatic stress disorder. *Journal of Clinical Psychiatry, 74*, 541–550. doi:10.4088/JCP.12r08225

Welch, S., & Fairburn, C. G. (1994). Sexual abuse and bulimia nervosa: Three integrated case control comparisons. *American Journal of Psychiatry, 151*, 402–407. doi:10.1176/ajp.151.3.402

Wesselmann, D., & Potter, A. E. (2009). Change in adult attachment status following treatment with EMDR: Three case studies. *Journal of EMDR Practice and Research, 3*(3), 178–191. doi:10.1891/1933-3196.3.3.178

World Health Organization. (2013). Guidelines for the management of conditions specifically related to stress. Retrieved from http://apps.who.int/iris/bitstream/10665/85119/1/9789241505406_eng.pdf

Zaccagnino, M., & Cussino, M. (2013). EMDR and parenting: A clinical case. *Journal of EMDR Practice and Research, 7*(3), 154–166. doi:10.1891/1933-3196.7.3.154

Zaccagnino, M., Cussino, M., Callerame, C., Civilotti, C., & Fernandez, I. (Submitted October 2016). *EMDR and CBT for Anorexic Patients: A Clinical Comparative Study, Eating and Weight Disorders—Studies on Anorexia, Bulimia and Obesity.*

Maria Zaccagnino
SUMMARY SHEET BY MARILYN LUBER

Name: _____ Diagnosis: _____

Medications: _____

Test Results: _____

☑ Check when task is completed, response has changed, or to indicate symptoms.

Note: This material is meant as a checklist for your response. Please keep in mind that it is only a reminder of different tasks that may or may not apply to your incident.

DIAGNOSES

According to the *Diagnostic and Statistical Manual of Mental Disorders* (5th ed.; *DSM–5*; American Psychiatric Association, 2013), these are the main diagnostic categories of feeding and eating disorders:

☐ *Anorexia nervosa (AN)*: An eating behavior that induces a significant low body weight (at or below 15% of the normal value) and an intense fear related to the possibility of gaining weight.

☐ *Bulimia nervosa (BN):* Recurring binge eating characterized by the consumption of a high quantity of food followed by unsuitable compensatory strategies (e.g., vomiting).

☐ *Binge eating disorder*: Cyclic episodes of eating a large quantity of food in a relatively short period of time without a real sensation of hunger and with a feeling of lack of control.

☐ *Pica*: Persistent appetite for substances that are nonnutritive.

☐ *Rumination disorder*: Cyclic vomiting of food that could be re-masticated, re-ingested, or spat out.

☐ *Avoidant/restrictive food intake disorder*: Impossible to reach a suitable nutritional level because of specific disorders in the eating behavior (e.g., apparently no interest in food).

The acronym EDNOS was thus replaced with feeding and eating condition not elsewhere classified (FECNEC). This new diagnostic category includes:

☐ *Atypical AN*: Fulfills some of the features of AN, but the overall clinical picture does not justify that diagnosis.

☐ *Subclinical BN:* Fulfills some of the features of BN, but the overall clinical picture does not justify that diagnosis.

☐ *Subclinical binge eating disorder:* Fulfills some of the features of binge eating disorder, but the overall clinical picture does not justify that diagnosis.

☐ *Purging disorder (PD)*: Purging to control shape or weight, in the absence of binge eating episodes.

☐ *Night eating syndrome (NES) disorder*: Intake of most calories at night or during evening meals.

The diagnostic subtypes identified by *DSM-5* are of two types:

☐ *Restricting type*: In the previous 3 months, the subject has not experienced any binge eating episodes or purging behaviors like self-induced vomiting or the use of laxatives or diuretics.
☐ *Binge eating/purging type*: In the previous 3 months, the subject has experienced recurrent binge eating episodes or purging behaviors. The subjects affected by this disorder generally tend to show severe weight loss, to the extent that *DSM-5* specifies the degree of severity of the disorder. The minimum level for adults is based on the current body mass index (BMI), while for children and adolescents, it is based on the percentiles of the BMI. The BMI could be mild, moderate, severe, or extreme.

MEASURES

☐ *BMI calc*ulation
☐ Adult attachment interview (AAI)
☐ Eating disorders inventory-3 (EDI-3; Garner, 2004)
☐ Adverse childhood experiences (ACEs) questionnaire
☐ Symptom checklist-revised (SCL-90-R; Derogatis, 1990)
☐ Difficulties in Emotion Regulation Scale (DERS; Gratz & Roemer, 2004)

THE EMDR ANOREXIA NERVOSA SCRIPTED PROTOCOL NOTES

Target Identification and Work Plan (Use the Three-Pronged Protocol)

☐ *Triggering or precipitating event*: Address the triggering event (if any) that elicited the onset of the disorder. Use the floatback technique.
☐ *Big "T" traumas*: Process major traumas.
☐ *Food-related relational history*: Identify directly connected targets using "parts work," in particular through work with the *control* part of the anorexic patient (see Phase 2 for a more comprehensive description), in particular the profound meaning related to food that can be traced in the patient's relational history. Identify other targets to help the patient cope with the difficult moments at mealtime, especially concerning the following:

  o *Bingeing and purging behaviors*: Use targets concerning the times preceding and following the bingeing and purging behavior and then use the floatback.
  o *Restrictive behaviors*: Find targets that represent the most difficult moment the patient has to face when sitting down to a meal and is asked to eat, and use the floatback.

Note: If no triggering event seems to have caused the onset of the disorder (or the patient does not recall such an event having happened), use the food-related relational history first.

  o *Food issues*: Investigate life and disorder history, to find the targets directly connected with food. Identify the targets explaining why the patient chose food (rather than something else) to manifest her difficulties. Process them in a chronological order.

Targets connected to symptomatology: Work on symptoms and memories connected to symptomatology in accordance with the Standard EMDR Protocol.

Working Protocol With Eating Disorders in the Nonacute Phase (Hospitalization) Guidelines

WORK ON MOTIVATION

"Which part of you wants to eat? Which part of you wants to feel better?" _____

_____

*"How difficult is it for you to work on that target on a scale of 0% to 100% where 0% = no difficulty and 100% = the most difficulty?"*____/100

For over 50%: Focus on physical sensations + emotions linked to poor motivation + BLS

Note: Continue until the patient feels adequate motivation to change. Do this every time a patient feels unable to deal with the therapeutic process.

PARTS WORK (can be used throughout treatment)

Construction of the Therapeutic Alliance—welcome parts, especially the "control" part

Knowledge of Parts: Explain the meaning of parts of personality to patients. When there is a spirit of acceptance and recognition, the therapist can ask questions about the part to understand more of the picture of what is going on. As targets are identified, they can later be used in the Standard EMDR Protocol.

Note: Ask through the adult part for the control part to tell its history.

Parts work is helpful for:

☐ *Target identification*: access past relational history to trace associative processes directly connected with the disorder
☐ *Blocks/defenses*: work with parts can be used as interweaves and/or targets
☐ *Specific work on symptoms*: every person has parts and they must interact with each other to help the patient cope with the task at hand
☐ *Worsening of symptoms:* through the parts, find out about the dynamics that are fundamental to this condition and access the real feelings and reasons related to the worsening to plan a specific treatment
☐ *Dissociative table:* to help patients with anorexia face sitting down to a meal

   In Phases 3 to 8: assessment, desensitization, installation, body scan, closure, and reevaluation, use the Standard EMDR Protocol.

Working Protocol With Eating Disorders in the Acute Phase (Hospitalization)

GUIDELINES FOR EVERY EMDR SESSION

☐ Use resources
☐ Work with control part

Structure case conceptualization according to the following:

☐ Triggering event
☐ Dissociative table at mealtime
☐ Desensitization of the positive affect when the patient does not eat.

   What is the most positive thing about your not eating: _____

   _____

   Target: Positive feedback when not eating and the consequent weight loss using DeTUR protocol. This is to help the patient become aware of the dysfunctional nature of her behavior and to help her find more effective coping strategies.

☐ Work on the patient's body image and the possible unpleasant physical sensation related to the time when she eats.

THE EMDR ANOREXIA NERVOSA SCRIPTED PROTOCOL

Phase 1: History Taking

Attachment History (including deaths and traumatic experiences) Five adjectives reflecting relationship in early childhood with mother/father: _____

_____

_____

Memory illustrating why you chose the previous examples to describe relationship: ☐ Yes ☐ No

Comment: _____

If yes:

When upset as child, what you did: _____

_____

Reaction of parents: _____

_____

Example of specific event: _____

_____

What happened when you got hurt physically (specific incident): _____

_____

First time separated from parents: _____

_____

Your reaction: _____

_____

Their reaction: _____

_____

Other significant separations: _____

_____

Felt rejected as a child: □ Yes □ No

Comment: _____

You were how old and what you did: _____

_____

Your reason for parents behaving this way: _____

_____

Do you think they realized how you felt: □ Yes □ No

Comment: _____

Trauma History

LIST LOSSES

_____

_____

_____

Your age: _____

_____

Your reaction: _____

_____

Their reaction: _____

_____

Death sudden or expected: _____

_____

Your feelings at the time: _____

_____

Have they changed since then: ☐ Yes ☐ No

Comment: _____

Other traumatic experiences: ☐ Yes ☐ No

Comment: _____

Anorexia Nervosa History

First time restricted food: _____

_____

How old: _____

_____

When in life restricted more: _____

_____

When in life restricted less: _____

_____

Changes in restrictive/bingeing/purging behaviors in your life: ☐ Yes ☐ No

Comment: _____

Leading up to onset of restricting food was there a distressing event: ☐ Yes ☐ No

Comment: _____

What was happening with parents at the time: _____

_____

First time you were underweight: _____

_____

What was going on in your life: _____

_____

How old: _____

_____

Times you both vomited and restricted: ☐ Yes ☐ No

Comment: _____

Hospitalized: ☐ Yes ☐ No

Comment: _____

How many times: _____

_____

How long: _____

_____

Did your disorder improve: ☐ Yes ☐ No

Comment: _____

Did you undergo specific treatment for the disorder: ☐ Yes ☐ No

Comment: _____

How long: _____

_____

What happened with treatment: _____

_____

What worked: _____

_____

Eating History—Patient's Eating History Within her Family

Breastfed (patient):   ☐ Yes ☐ No

Comment: _____

How did breastfeeding take place: _____

_____

Up to what age breastfed: _____

_____

Can ask for pictures depicting the moment.

What you think mother was like when breastfeeding you: _____

_____

_____

Do you know anything about your parents' eating habits: ☐ Yes ☐ No

Comment: _____

Parents' approach to food: _____

_____

Do you remember what happened at meal times: ☐ Yes ☐ No

Comment: _____

Describe a typical scene: _____

_____

Risk and/or Maintenance Factors

Did you even eat on your own: ☐ Yes ☐ No

Comment: _____

When sitting down to a meal with mother can you describe how she looked: ☐ Yes ☐ No

Comment: _____

What your mother did: _____

_____

How you reacted: _____

_____

Concentrate on a time sitting at the table but you didn't eat. How did mother look at you: _____

_____

_____

What mother did or said: _____

_____

How you reacted: _____

_____

Remember times would calm down/feel better when you started to eat: ☐ Yes ☐ No

Comment: _____

Other times mother regulated her emotions: ☐ Yes ☐ No

Comment: _____

When sitting down to a meal with father can you describe how he looked: ☐ Yes ☐ No

Comment: _____

What father did: _____

_____

How you reacted: _____

_____

Concentrate on a time sitting at the table but you didn't eat. How did father look at you: _____

_____

_____

What did father do and say: _____

_____

How you reacted: _____

_____

Remember times would calm down/feel better when you started to eat: ☐ Yes ☐ No

Comment: _____

Other times father regulated his emotions: ☐ Yes ☐ No

Comment: _____

How parents reacted to you when feeling disturbed: _____

_____

How you see your body: _____

_____

Your relationship with your body: _____

_____

Your parents' relationship with your body: _____

_____

Your mother's relationship to her own body: _____

_____

Your father's relationship to her own body: _____

_____

How you feel when you eat: _____

_____

What are the negative beliefs you tell yourself: _____

_____

Floatback: *"Now, please bring up that picture of _____ (repeat disturbing experience) and those negative words _____ (state the NC). Now notice what feelings are coming up for you and where you are feeling them in your body, and just let your mind float back to an earlier time in your life–don't search for anything–just let your mind float back and tell me the earliest scene that comes to mind where you had similar thoughts of ___ (repeat NC) and feelings of ___ (repeat emotions) and where you feel it in your body."*

_____

_____

When you eat what can you say positive about yourself: _____

_____

Where in your life have you felt the lack of ___ (state the PC): _____

_____

Do you remember what your parents said when you started to lose weight and were
a normal weight: ☐ Yes ☐ No

Comment: _____

Do you remember what friends told you: ☐ Yes ☐ No

Comment: _____

Resource Identification

Imagine yourself healed; what would be the positive aspects: _____

_____

What would be the most important aspect to you: _____

_____

If can't remember positive memories:

Think about what you would do once you are healed and tell me: _____

_____

Case Conceptualization: Target Identification and Work Plan

Do you remember leading up to the onset of the disorder if an especially
distressing event occurred: ☐ Yes ☐ No

Comment: _____

What was going on in your life at that time: _____

_____

What was going on in parents' lives at that time: _____

_____

Floatback: *"Now, please bring up that picture of _____ (repeat disturbing experience) and those negative words _____ (state the NC). Now notice what feelings are coming up for you and where you are feeling them in your body, and just let your mind float back to an earlier time in your life—don't search for anything—just let your mind float back and tell me the earliest scene that comes to mind where you had similar thoughts of ___ (repeat NC) and feelings of ___ (repeat emotions) and where you feel it in your body."*

_____

_____

List of Traumatic Experiences

_____

_____

_____

_____

Bingeing Behaviors

Feeling moment before you binge: _____

_____

Words that best go with the picture that express your negative belief about yourself now: _____

_____

Floatback: *"Now, please bring up that picture of _____ (repeat disturbing experience) and those negative words ____ (state the NC). Now notice what feelings are coming up for you and where you are feeling them in your body, and just let your mind float back to an earlier time in your life—don't search for anything—just let your mind float back and tell me the earliest scene that comes to mind where you had similar thoughts of ___ (repeat NC) and feelings of ___ (repeat emotions) and where you feel it in your body."*

_____

_____

When you think about when you eat, what can you say that is positive about yourself: _____

_____

Where in your life, have you felt the lack of ___ (state the PC): _____

_____

Purging Behaviors

Feeling moment before you purge: _____

_____

Words that best go with the picture that express your negative belief about yourself now: _____

_____

Floatback: *"Now, please bring up that picture of _____ (repeat disturbing experience) and those negative words ____ (state the NC). Now notice what feelings are coming up for you and where you are feeling them in your body, and just let your mind float back to an earlier time in your life—don't search for anything—just let your mind float back and tell me the earliest scene that comes to mind where you had similar thoughts of ___ (repeat NC) and feelings of ___ (repeat emotions) and where you feel it in your body."*

_____

_____

When you think about when you purge, what can you say that is positive about yourself: _____

_____

Where in your life have you felt the lack of ___ (state the PC): _____

_____

Restrictive Behaviors

Feeling moment before you restrict: _____

_____

Words that best go with the picture that express your negative belief about yourself now: _____

_____

Floatback: *"Now, please bring up that picture of _____ (repeat disturbing experience) and those negative words ____ (state the NC). Now notice what feelings are coming up for you and where you are feeling them in your body, and just let your mind float back to an earlier time in your life—don't search for anything—just let your mind float back and tell me the earliest scene that comes to mind where you had similar thoughts of ___ (repeat NC) and feelings of ___ (repeat emotions) and where you feel it in your body."*

_____

_____

When you think about when you restrict, what can you say that is positive about yourself: _____

_____

Where in your life have you felt the lack of ___ (state the PC): _____

_____

Family Behaviors

Parents' relationship with your body: _____

_____

Mother's relationship with her own body: _____

_____

Did someone in family suffer from an eating disorder: ☐ Yes ☐ No

Comment: _____

Targets Related to Symptomatology

Do you remember the first time you started to binge/purge/restrict: ☐ Yes ☐ No

Comment: _____

The last time: ☐ Yes ☐ No

Comment: _____

Case Conceptualization Worksheet—see chapter.

Phase 2: Preparation

Explain eating disorders and consequences   ☐ Yes ☐ No

"Eating disorders are persistent weight-controlling behaviors that damage physical health and psychological function. There are many risk factors implied in the onset and maintenance of eating disorders, but one of the most important is the impact of traumatic or difficult events that occurred during life. These events, in fact, can contribute to the development of maladaptive affect regulation strategies, which in turn may represent other risk factors for the development of this psychopathology."

Explanation of EMDR as in the Standard EMDR Protocol   ☐ Yes ☐ No

"When a trauma occurs it seems to be locked in the nervous system with the original picture, sounds, thoughts, and feelings. The eye movements we use in EMDR seem to unlock the nervous system and allow the brain to process the experience. That may be what is happening in REM or dream sleep—the eye movements may help to process the unconscious material. It is important to remember that it is your own brain that will be doing the healing and you are the one in control. With your permission, I'm going to _____ (state the type of BLS used)."

"Now I'll show you the procedure in order to decide which is the best distance for you and if you feel comfortable both with eye stimulation and tapping. Feel free to tell me if you don't feel comfortable and try to relax and be calm.

In order to help you just notice the experience and handle the intensity of the emotions, you can imagine riding on a train and the feelings and thoughts are just the scenery going by. If during the processing you have a problem or you feel you have to stop, please raise your hand and we will stop."

Work on Motivation

Part that wants to eat: _____

_____

Part that wants to feel better: _____

_____

"On a scale of 0% to 100%, where 0% is no difficulty and 100% is the most difficulty, how difficult is it for you to work on that target?"

_____ %

Physical sensations + Emotions linked to ___ (state what the poor motivation is) + BLS

Do every time patients feel they can't deal with difficult moments in the therapeutic process.

Parts Work: The Control History

"Everyone has different parts of the personality, and these parts play a fundamental role in your history and in the history of your disorder. You can have, for example, a very fragile part that needs to be protected and another part that has always acted to protect you. What part/s do you have?"

Part's name/representation: _____

Part is visible: _____ ☐ Yes ☐ No

Comment: _____

Part's age: _____

What happened to part: _____

_____

Was that the first time it happened? _____ ☐ Yes ☐ No

Comment: _____

Where or from whom did _____ (part) learn to control: _____

_____

Did anyone in your family use this way of controlling? _____ ☐ Yes ☐ No

Comment: _____

Has the food control aspect involved parents or others with whom you have a relationship? _____

☐ Yes ☐ No

Comment: _____

Task assigned to this part: _____

_____

Is ___ (she/he) protecting someone? _____ ☐ Yes ☐ No

Comment: _____

If the control part was no longer there, what would happen: _____

_____

Is ___ (she/he) protecting someone? _____ ☐ Yes ☐ No

Comment: _____

Are you able to see the part that ___(he/she) is protecting? _____ ☐ Yes ☐ No

Comment: _____

Can you describe it? _____ ☐ Yes ☐ No

Comment: _____

What is ___ (his/her) history: _____

_____

DISSOCIATIVE TABLE AT MEALTIME EXERCISE SCRIPT

Note: Be sure to read the comments in the chapter. This is only the script.

"Together, we must look for a way to allow your different parts to communicate. We all have parts or aspects of the self that at certain times compete to emerge, and this conflict contributes to the distress you may feel. We all have different parts that feel different emotions and have different longings. To be able to solve the difficult task connected with mealtime, it is helpful to identify and come into contact with the different parts of the self, so that they may help you in this endeavor.

Please think of a safe meeting place, like a room with a large table or anywhere else that works for you. _____

_____

Please ask your adult self to make ___ (himself/herself) comfortable in this safe place.

Now let's ask all the parts that represent the different aspects of yourself to come forth and _____ (make themselves comfortable, take a seat, etc.).

If the adult part could facilitate, I would like to meet each one of you, would that be OK? ☐ Yes ☐ No

Could your ____ (name the adult part) interact directly with the part and ask the following questions?" ☐ Yes ☐ No

How old are you? _____

What is your gender? _____

What do you look like? _____

What is your role and function for this person? _____

_____

Repeat for each part.

"I would like to thank the adult and all of you for letting me get to know you and for you to get to know each other more. Your working together will help what we are doing together.

I am glad that the _____ (control, in charge, etc.) part has come and I want ___ (her/him) to know that ____ (she/he) is very welcome. Please let us know if we are going too fast or we are asking you to do things you do not want or cannot do. Okay?"

The goal that we share is this person's well-being.

We will have to work on some difficult areas such as the importance of taking in additional calories so that you can survive. I know that this will be difficult. I am hoping that by working together, we can be successful.

Do we all agree that we need to discuss what happens at mealtimes and that we have to do something to increase food intake so that this situation is as positive as possible? ☐ Yes ☐ No

Which part/s of you do/does not want to eat? _____

_____

Which part/s of you want/wants to eat? _____

_____

Which part/s of you want/wants to feel better? _____

_____

_____

I would like to help you understand with ___ (the adult part or whatever you name this part) that saying no would involve further weight loss which would have very adverse consequences on your life and could jeopardize it.

How motivated do you think that you are to change so that we can figure out what to do next?" _____

_____

Say to the control part, "_____ (name of control part) *how are you feeling?"* _____

_____

Have you felt this feeling in the past?" ☐ Yes ☐ No

Comment: _____

"Are you willing to help find other ways to manage the situation if you believe that what we are proposing won't work?" ☐ Yes ☐ No

Comment: _____

"I understand how ___ (state the feeling such as distressed, anger) you are feeling. I am sure that you have had a good reason to act as you did in the past.

You are hearing things you have been told before and have every right to be skeptical; however, we are here now, and we want to help. What can we do to help you?

_____

_____

Do you think there is a way we could get along? You will always be with us; actually, we need you."
  ☐ Yes ☐ No

Comment: _____

"Would you consider giving us a sign to tell us when you feel it's too much for you and that you are not being respected?" ☐ Yes ☐ No

Comment: _____

"Are you afraid that some other part might step in and acquire too much power? Or is there some part that you do not trust?" ☐ Yes ☐ No

Comment: _____

"*Are you* _____ (state the control part's name) *concerned that if we intervene then it will jeopardize something or someone in your system?*"   ☐ Yes ☐ No

Comment: _____

"*If so, how can the other parts help you? What strategies might they adopt?*" _____

_____

_____

RESOURCE INSTALLATION SCRIPT

Skill/strength/resource needed with issue + Feelings and sensations—What do you notice and feel?

_____

_____

Skill/strength/resource + Sights + Sounds + Smells + Body Sensations—What do you notice?

_____

_____

Skill/strength/resource + Location of pleasant sensations in body + BLS

_____

_____

Cue word + Positive thoughts/associations + BLS

Feeling: _____

_____

Phase 3: Assessment

Target/Memory/Image: _____

_____

NC: _____

PC: _____

VOC: ___/7

Emotions: _____

SUD: ___/10

Sensation: _____

Phase 4: Desensitization

Apply the Standard EMDR Protocol for all targets.

Phase 5: Installation

Install the PC.

Original PC: ☐ Use original PC ☐ Use new PC
New PC (if new one is better): _____

VOC: _____/7

Incident + PC + BLS

Phase 6: Body Scan

Unresolved tension/tightness/unusual sensation: _____

_____

Unresolved tension/tightness/unusual sensation + BLS

Strengthen positive sensation using BLS.

If there is more discomfort, reprocess until discomfort subsides + BLS. Then repeat body scan.

VoC: ___/7

Phase 7: Closure

Most positive thing learned: _____

_____

PC: _____

+ BLS

Check with VOC:_____

Normal Closure: ☐ Yes ☐ No

"Things may come up or they may not. If they do, great. Write it down and it can be a target for next time. You can use a log to write down what triggers, images, thoughts or cognitions, emotions, and sensations occur; you can rate them on our 0-to-10 scale where 0 is no disturbance or neutral and 10 is the worst disturbance. Please write down the positive experiences, too.

If you get any new memories, dreams, or situations that disturb you, just take a good snapshot. It isn't necessary to give a lot of detail. Just put down enough to remind you so we can target it next time. The same thing goes for any positive dreams or situations. If negative feelings do come up, try not to make them significant. Remember, it's still just the old stuff. Just write it down for next time. Then use the tape or the Safe Base exercise to let as much of the disturbance go as possible. Even if nothing comes up, make sure to use the tape every day and give me a call if you need to."

Phase 8: Reevaluation

Noticed since last session:_____

_____

Current symptoms: _____

New material: _____

_____

SUD: ____/10

REFERENCES

American Psychiatric Association. (2013). *Diagnostic and statistical manual of mental disorders* (5th ed.). Arlington, VA: American Psychiatric Publishing.

Derogatis, L. R. (1990). SCL-90-R. *A bibliography of research reports 1975-1990*. Baltimore, MD: Clinical Psychometric Research.

Garner, D. M. (2004). *Eating disorder inventory-3 professional manual*. Odessa, FL: Psychological Assessment Resources.

Gratz, K. L., & Roemer, L. (2004). Multidimensional assessment of emotion regulation and dysregulation: Development, factor structure, and initial validation of the Difficulties in Emotion Regulation Scale. *Journal of Psychopathology and Behavioral Assessment, 26,* 41–54. doi:10.1023/B:JOBA.0000007455.08539.94

EMDR THERAPY PROTOCOL FOR EATING DISORDERS

3

Natalia Seijo

INTRODUCTION

Based on the author's years of experience working with eating disorders (EDs), the most adequate treatment is that which covers the areas that generate the disorder, instead of focusing on the symptom in an isolated manner. Without a doubt, EMDR therapy accomplishes this goal, since it works by going to the root of the trauma—where it all began—and repairing it. When speaking of trauma in EDs, we do not speak only of traumatic events, but also of attachment and developmental traumas, which are quite common in EDs.

The EMDR Protocol for Eating Disorders helps improve the way we understand these disorders and the recovery time of the people who suffer from them. This protocol combines work on trauma, attachment, and dissociation—three fields that are linked at the foundation of these disorders and that must be worked on in order to attain successful results in the long run.

The protocol is developed throughout the eight phases of treatment and is centered on three basic points:

- Identification and organization of the client's inner world
- Neutralization of the defenses
- Processing of the different traumas (big "T"; small "t"; adverse life experiences)

The final goal is achieved with the integration of the inner world, through the reprocessing of the traumas that originate the disorder.

DEFINITION

ICD-10 and Eating Disorders
In *International Statistical Classification of Diseases and Related Health Problems (ICD-10)*, eating disorders are codified within the "Behavioral syndromes associated with physiological disturbances and somatic factors." In particular, eating disorders are codified in the "F50 Eating Disorders" category, including the following disorders:

- *F50.0 Anorexia Nervosa (AN)*: Disorder characterized by the presence of deliberate weight loss, induced or maintained by the client.
- *F50.1 Atypical AN*: This term must be used in cases in which one or more main characteristics of AN are missing (F50.0), like amenorrhea or significant weight loss, but that otherwise present a pretty typical clinical picture. These clients are usually found in consultation and liaison psychiatry, as well as in primary care. Clients who have all the important symptoms of AN, but to a mild degree, can also be included here. This term must not be used for eating disorders that are similar to AN but which are due to a known somatic etiology.
- *F50.2 Bulimia Nervosa* (BN): Syndrome characterized by repeated episodes of excessive intake of food and by an exaggerated concern over the control of body weight, which makes the client

adopt extreme measures to mitigate weight gain deriving from the intake of food. This term should be restricted to the forms of the disorder that are related to AN by sharing the same pathologies. The disorder may be considered an effect of persistent AN (although the opposite sequence is also possible). At first glance, a previously anorexic client may appear to be getting better by gaining weight—and even recovering her menstruation if it is a woman—but then a malignant form of behavior characterized by overeating and vomiting emerges. Repeated vomiting may result in electrolyte balance disorders, in somatic complications (seizures, cardiac arrhythmia, or muscle weakness), and in further weight loss.

- *F50.3 Atypical BN*: This term must be used in those cases that lack one or more of the main characteristics of BN (F50.2), but which otherwise present a pretty typical clinical picture. Clients are usually of normal weight or even higher than normal, but present repeated episodes of excessive food intake followed by vomiting or purging. It is not rare to find partial syndromes accompanied by depressive symptoms (if these symptoms fulfill the criteria for a depressive disorder, a dual diagnosis must be made).
- *F50.4 Overeating Associated With Other Psychological Alterations*: Excessive food intake as a reaction to stressful events that gives way to obesity. Grieving, accidents, surgical interventions, and emotionally stressful events may result in "reactive obesity," especially in clients prone to weight gain. Obesity as the cause of psychological alterations must not be codified here. Obesity may make the client feel very sensitized about his or her appearance and trigger lack of confidence in relationships. The subjective assessment of bodily dimensions may be exaggerated. In order to codify obesity as the cause of psychological alteration, categories such as F38.8, other mood disorders (affective); F41.2, mixed anxiety depressive disorder; or F48.9, neurotic disorder not otherwise specified, plus an E66. code to indicate the type of obesity, must be used.
- *F50.5 Vomiting Associated With Other Psychological Alterations*: Besides BN, in which vomiting is self-induced, repeated vomiting may be present in dissociative disorders (conversion; F44.8); hypochondria (F45.2), in which vomiting may be one of the multiple bodily symptoms; and during pregnancy, where emotional factors may contribute to the appearance of recurring vomiting and nausea.

RESEARCH

This research studied the effects of "emotional eating" (EE; Halvgaard, 2015). The study was designed to examine whether treating the symptoms of EE with selected protocols and methods with EMDR psychotherapy would have a positive effect. Participants experienced an overall positive change in their eating behaviors.

The findings and the evaluation of the treatment indicate that there is a positive effect on eating behavior and affect regulation in the defined triggering situations. This effect also holds over time, at least when tested in 3 and 6 months.

The most effective part of the treatment seems to be the combination of the techniques of anchoring the feeling into the physiology and working on a deeper therapeutic level, offering an understanding of the underlying issues highlighted by the ego state work.

The conclusion is that it is possible to demonstrate a positive effect by applying EMDR therapy, and more specifically, the adjusted desensitization of triggers and urge reprocessing protocol, in the treatment of EE. The treatment was helpful in this case, and given that the client is typical of the population of individuals suffering from EE, it also seems reasonable to conclude that the development of obesity when driven by emotional avoidance could be reduced as well.

MEASURES

These are the measures used:

- Eating Disorder Inventory-3 (EDI-3; Garner, 2004)
- Body Attitude Test (BAT; Probst, Vandereycken, Van Coppenolle, & Vanderlinden, 1995)
- Fear of Negative Evaluation (FNE) Scale (Learly, 1983; Watson & Friend, 1969)

THE EMDR PROTOCOL FOR EATING DISORDERS SCRIPT NOTES

Phase 1: History Taking

The first thing to bear in mind when starting to work with a client with an ED is that underneath that which is shown through the disorder lies a hurt little girl or boy hoping to be found and helped. It is a simple guideline that will be important to keep in mind throughout the treatment.

A good case conceptualization will provide an outline, which will steer you toward the established goal. It will be necessary to gather the client's history in order to conceptualize the case. Notes will be taken on the areas that follow.

General Aspects: Diagnosis and Comorbidity

- *Psychopathological assessment*: Diagnosis received by a specialist medical professional. Medical monitoring and check-ups. Review of medical reports that can be provided.
- *Associated disorders*: Information on those disorders related to the ED with which the client may have been previously diagnosed.

Anamnesis

- *General data*: Referring to age, education, profession, civil status, and so on.
- *Genogram*: Graphically gathers family structure providing information on each family member, as well as the distribution and relationship among them. This graphical representation of the multigenerational family registers information on pathologies and EDs from family members up to the second generation.
- *Medical and psychological treatments*: Information regarding previously consulted professionals. Successful and nonsuccessful aspects of those treatments. This will provide information on what to do and not to do with the client.

Eating Disorder History

WEIGHT HISTORY

It will be important to inquire about current and past weight and height, and to determine the client's body mass index (BMI). Other important areas to explore are bowel movements, diets or meal regimes, and physical symptoms associated with the ED, such as the following:

- *Lanugo*: Body hair that covers the body due to weight loss in AN
- *Russell signs*: Calluses that frequently appear on the knuckles, by digging the teeth in over and over trying to provoke vomiting
- *Moon face*: Inflammation of the parotid glands, located beneath the jaw in people who purge frequently, creating the effect of a rounder face
- *Cold sores*: Sores that appear in the corners of the mouth, caused by the aggression produced in the area when purging

Some questions regarding amenorrhea and menstrual periods will be directed only at girls. The family's reaction toward this issue is important information since, sometimes, what happens during this stage in the client's life may be an important target on which to work.

HISTORY OF THE CURRENT EPISODE

The history of the current episode includes gathering all the information regarding what led to the situation as it is now.

- *Instances of restriction*: What led the client to restrict, where it was learned, and what was happening during that time?
- *Strange behavior concerning food*: It is common for there to be lying or omitting information regarding this issue, and on occasion, this is discovered throughout therapy. We will focus on obtaining this information through the client or a family member concerning if she or he hides food, throws it out, spits it out, or cuts it up excessively.

BINGEING AND/OR VOMITING EPISODES

When exploring binge eating, keep in mind that a binge is an excessive intake of food, to the point that a single intake can contain up to 2,500 calories, which is what a client can ingest throughout an entire day. In addition, this food intake must be performed in a short period of time.

It must be taken into account that when asking about binge eating, people can give different answers because often variations are found depending on the ED and how the client perceives the disorder. In cases such as AN (purgative type), the client will respond that he or she binges. However, bingeing in this ED may mean eating an apple, a yogurt, and a biscuit, for example. This disorder is based on restriction, and everything that goes beyond that could be considered bingeing.

In the case of binge eating disorder (BED), binges will be as in BN: intake of large amounts of food in a short period of time, as described previously. In hyperorexia, where the client binges constantly, it would be something like eating all day long, extending the binge for large periods of time. Either way, it will be important to have this information in mind to identify the food episodes and their triggers.

PURGING

Purging consists of the use of laxatives, diuretics, and so on.

CURRENT TRIGGERS

One of the focal points in the treatment of bingeing and vomiting is stabilizing these compensatory responses that pose a physical risk and generate dependency. Current triggers refer to those situations that predispose the client to bingeing and vomiting, such as loneliness, boredom, or sadness.

HOSPITALIZATIONS

This type of trauma has severe consequences in people with EDs who have been hospitalized, since these admissions are difficult because of the limitations to which they are subjected.

Hospitalization trauma is caused by the different hospital admissions that people with EDs are forced to go through at times. These admissions may be due to extreme underweight, as in AN, and also the chaos in regard to bingeing and vomiting in some BN clients and the risk this entails. Admissions may also be triggered by autolytic attempts, which can happen in times of crisis.

Although the reasons for admission may be different, it is helpful to process these hospitalization situations with the Standard EMDR Protocol to contribute to recovery. In instances of suicide attempts, both moments—what led to the attempt and the hospitalization itself—must be processed.

Some therapists consider it may be harmful to process hospitalization trauma, since some classic treatments used the fear of admission as a tool for improvement. In this author's clinical experience, fear does not seem to be a good option, as it results in unstable improvements and increased insecurity. The recommendation is to be able to relieve their inner world from all those experiences that have left an indelible mark.

Food History

HISTORY OF MEALTIMES

Mealtimes at home are important targets for EMDR reprocessing, since these times end up becoming conflictive, creating distress in the client, and not allowing improvements until they are worked on.

TIME SPENT IN FRONT OF THE PLATE

This point is important, especially in AN, in which the client may spend hour after hour sitting in front of the plate of food forced to eat what is given, as well as the inner denial to do so. Thus, the client tends to experience these times with much suffering, generating trauma. Each and every memory of this kind that emerges will be worked on as an EMDR target with the Standard EMDR Protocol.

OVERFEEDING ATTACHMENT FIGURES

In EDs, it is common to find attachment figures who feed the client disproportionately, substituting displays of affection with food. Thus, the client learns from childhood to eat when not hungry and without physical signs of satiation, thus satisfying the needs of the adult.

Attachment Issues

Through this information we may assess the attachment style of these clients. We must pay attention to issues such as attachment style of parents, separation or divorce, moves, feelings of being understood and validated, and role reversal.

ATTACHMENT TRAUMA

Adverse life experiences related to clients' bond with attachment figures occur frequently. Ask about instances when there was a lack of validation, support, or display of affection; the help of the attachment figures was needed, but no help was received; the client was negatively compared to other people; attachment figures showed perfectionism and rigidity; attachment figures were very critical; role reversal; and so on.

Trauma and Adverse Life Experiences History

On the one hand, trauma can result in a class of traumatic stress disorders with symptoms that last more than 1 month. There are various forms of posttraumatic stress disorders (PTSDs) depending on the time of onset and the duration of these stress symptoms. In the *acute* form, the duration of the symptoms is between 1 and 3 months. In the *chronic* form, symptoms last more than 3 months. With *delayed onset*, symptoms develop more than 6 months after the traumatic event.

- Acute, chronic, or delayed reactions to *traumatic events* such as military combat, assault, or natural disaster.
- An *anxiety disorder* precipitated by an experience of intense fear or horror while exposed to a traumatic (especially life-threatening) event. The disorder is characterized by intrusive recurring thoughts or images of the traumatic event; avoidance of anything associated with the event; a state of hyperarousal; and diminished emotional responsiveness. These symptoms are present for at least 1 month and the disorder is usually long term.
- An *anxiety disorder* that develops in reaction to physical injury or severe mental or emotional distress, such as military combat, violent assault, natural disaster, or other life-threatening events. Having cancer may also lead to PTSD. Symptoms interfere with day-to-day living and include reliving the event in nightmares or flashbacks; avoiding people, places, and things connected to the event; feeling alone and losing interest in daily activities; and having trouble concentrating and sleeping.
- *PTSD* is a real illness. You can get PTSD after living through or seeing a traumatic event, such as war, a hurricane, rape, physical abuse, or a bad accident. PTSD makes you feel stressed and afraid after the danger is over. It affects your life and the people around you. PTSD can cause problems like the following:
  - Flashbacks, or feeling like the event is happening again
  - Trouble sleeping or nightmares
  - Feeling alone
  - Angry outbursts
  - Feeling worried, guilty, or sad

On the other hand, psychological trauma derived from *adverse life experiences* is the individual's unique experience of an incident, a series of incidents, or a set of enduring conditions in which the individual's ability to integrate his or her emotional experience (i.e., the ability to stay present, to understand what is happening, to integrate feelings and give meaning to the experience) becomes overwhelmed.

TRAUMATIC EVENTS

Have the client compile the 10 worst moments related to the events of the trauma, such as accidents, loss, and grieving.

HUMILIATION TRAUMA

Explore humiliation trauma. Ask if the client has ever felt humiliated. Perhaps there were looks the child might have gotten from an adult during childhood or adolescence, or words that might have been said, which made him or her feel uncomfortable; these can produce humiliation trauma.

BETRAYAL TRAUMA

Betrayal Trauma Theory (Freyd, Deprince, & Gleaves, 2007) defines the degree to which a negative event represents a betrayal of the necessary trust and will influence the way in which those events are processed and remembered.

Betrayal trauma can be used to refer to a certain type of trauma regardless of the reaction to the trauma. It occurs when people or institutions—which the client depends on to survive—violate his or her confidence or well-being, physically and/or emotionally. Sexual abuse perpetrated by a caregiver is an example of betrayal trauma.

DIETING

It is common for people who suffer from these disorders to spend much of their lives on a diet, often from early childhood. Dieting becomes traumatic for the client and is associated with high levels of anxiety, frustration, sadness, and a feeling of helplessness. This actually results in the impossibility of dieting.

In case conceptualization, it will be important to gather information regarding diets. This item will provide information when processing one of the traumas called "diet trauma," which will be explained in more detail in the section about trauma in the protocol. The processing of these traumas will help people with EDs associated with continuous unsuccessful diets to effectively carry out a diet without the symptoms of anxiety and angst that often provoke an internal experience of inefficiency in the client.

Inquire about issues such as whether the client is on a diet or any feeding regime; the types of diets the client has tried and their effectiveness; first or earliest diet; feeding restrictions, if any; possible allergic reactions confirmed by medical tests; and diets the client has been on throughout life.

HIDDEN TRAUMA

Hidden trauma refers to the inability of the caregiver to modulate affective dysregulation. In childhood, many perceived threats stem from affective signs and caregiver accessibility rather than from the actual level of physical danger or risk to survival (Schuder & Lyons-Ruth, 2004).

Hidden trauma is very common in ED, so it is important to take it into account. It is often difficult for the client to remember, since these are subtle events that are usually played down, which are hurtful without being overt.

BODY HISTORY

In this section, collect precise information about the body, inquiring about the scars the client may notice regarding the yo-yo effect (heavy weight gain or loss), major restrictions, and so on. Ask in-depth questions about the rejection or lack of acceptance that the client feels about his or her own body and the existence of self-harming behaviors.

Phase 2: Preparation

This phase provides the structure upon which the rest of the treatment will be built. Dedicate as much time as each case requires. The structure of this work focuses on two basic points:

- Identifying the inner world of the client with an ED
- Smoothing and processing the defenses

People who suffer from EDs lack childhood experiences, and a vast majority are women. They have been treated as small adults since they can remember, forced to assume responsibilities that they were not supposed to assume. Due to external demands beyond what they could tolerate, their inner world becomes overwhelmed and collapses, triggering the development of parts in order to protect the system.

It is helpful to highlight that the therapeutic work will not focus on eliminating defenses, since this would intensify them, thus increasing the symptom, sensation, or disturbing emotion that contains it. From EMDR therapy, the focus is on changing and neutralizing the defense, validating the contributions and functions with which it has protected the system.

The way in which defenses are used to protect the inner system must be respected, even though it may not be the most adaptive way for the client in the present. It is important to remember how adequate the defense was in the past and the fact that it helped the client to get by or survive. It is important to bear in mind that defenses have a double function of defense/protection and resource at the same time.

Psychoeducation Regarding the Edge of Trauma and Somatic Identifiers

Providing psychoeducation is important at this point, because by anticipating what may happen, you are able to create an environment of trust and safety. Such an environment helps clients understand that they are in a situation where they can be themselves and work with what emerges, trusting that they will be held and, above all, that they can maintain an *inner locus of control*—difficult for them to achieve, but extremely important.

Start by offering psychoeducation on the edge of trauma. Using this concept, explain that you and your client will be paying attention to a line that will not be crossed until the client is prepared to do so. This line represents the edge of the trauma, which is reached when you begin to touch the traumas or adverse experiences that will need to be processed so the client may begin to improve and heal the underlying problem. This section of Phase 2 is a step that will help everything flow in an appropriate manner in Phase 3. Prepare the client by *dilating the edge of the trauma*, meaning that by respecting this line and helping the client develop an inner locus of control, you can progress little by little without the risk of dysregulation during sessions, thus creating *a safe base.*

Explain that the ideal is to always stay one or two steps before the edge of the trauma, so that you are preventing the appearance of unpleasant feelings or emotions that may create a negative experience and the risk of rejecting future work for fear of the pain that might arise.

In order to know when the client approaches the edge of the trauma, explain which somatic identifiers can give you a clue as to what is happening. Being able to identify the most common ones will help the clinician to see them more clearly. Some examples of somatic identifiers follow later in the text. These are indicative, though, and it will be important to check with your client to know what each defense actually contains.

- *Tension shown in different parts of the body* might reflect the repression of an emotion that wants to come out but is blocked.
- *Biting the lip* may be a sign of emotional control. It may happen when the client feels like crying and is trying to cut it off.
- *Withdrawing eye contact or severing it* at a specific moment might show that the client does not wish to receive or to be seen, or fears being exposed.
- *Speaking in the second or third person* might show a lack of integration.
- *Tension in the neck* might be an attempt to control what is happening during the process and is related to the feeling of loss of control.
- *Feeling sleepy* during processing says the client has exceeded his or her tolerance threshold to what is coming up, and it might be a way of showing that the processing is too intense.
- *Headaches* during processing may signal traumatic material that the client is reluctant to let out. It might be a sign that there is a dissociative part making an appearance.

Identifying the Inner World

The inner world can be defined as a set of what Liotti (1999) describes as the different internal representations of the self. These representations gradually become the foundation for the development of autonomous and complex mental structures, which van der Hart, Nijenhuis, and Steele (2006) calls dissociative parts.

It must be taken into account that parts—also referred to as states or representations of the self—develop toward one concept or another depending on the degree of dissociation that is present. So, in many cases, the parts of the inner world do not become autonomous. They would be like structures containing memories of adverse experiences that generate the current disturbing behaviors associated with food. It is precisely there where the professional must go in order to process and integrate.

The inner world represents the structure of the personality, and the different aspects or parts that make it up. Through these, people develop their internal experience, their information-processing style, in an inner world, their management of emotions, and their interaction style with others. Getting to know and shaping this structure helps both the therapist and the client in naming what had never been named.

When developing the internal world, the therapist must take into account three tools that also function as resources.

1. *Validate the client*: Validate the client throughout the whole process, since these individuals usually suffer from an absence of validation from an early age. Thus, the therapist—from his or her role as a "substitute safe attachment" figure—heals, but also fosters a safe foundation the client can lean on and trust.
2. *Promote compassion and understanding*: Promote compassion and understanding without judgment, since they rarely receive compassion from others, and, on occasion, they go through different treatments in which they do not always feel understood. This tool will help with the good development of the therapeutic relationship.
3. *Helping to organize the inner world and its parts*: Helping to organize the inner world and its parts, bearing in mind that in people who suffer from an ED, this internal world tends to be chaotic and it is precisely there where we must insist upon. In the section on parts, they will be named and their characteristics described in detail.

Once identified, it will be easy to compose the internal world, as if it were a jigsaw puzzle, piece by piece, so that everything makes sense in the client's eyes and, thus, promotes the aforementioned compassion.

Another important step during this phase is focused on psychoeducation, which will be a constant throughout treatment. During work with the inner world and the parts, psychoeducation will be essential in order to provide all the information the client requires or needs in order to trust the process.

IDENTIFYING PARTS, NEUTRALIZING DEFENSES, AND ACCESSING TRAUMA

At this stage of treatment, psychoeducation will focus on shaping the inner world. This will begin to organize it and allow us to work with the concept of each part or state as a way to reach and work with the traumas or adverse experiences contained within them.

Begin by naming the inner girls (Seijo, 2012):

- The little girl who never was
- The little girl who could not grow up
- The pathological critic
- The rejected self
- The hidden self
- The fatty self

Note: We refer to these parts as "girls" given that the majority of clients with ED are female. However, these names can easily be adapted when working with male ED clients.

Before starting to develop the parts along with their beliefs, it will be best to introduce psychoeducation regarding defenses, as to offer a more visual structure of the inner world and explore the therapeutic goals. This understanding will also promote compassion.

When mentioning defenses, we are talking about blockage points that prevent the natural flow during therapy or, specifically, the EMDR processing. Defense work begins in Phase 2 through psychoeducation, which helps the client understand the process. Defenses in ED are one of the key points to insist upon, since they can be the cause of therapeutic failure and/or possible abandonment.

In order to graphically explain how defenses are distributed in the internal world of the clients, *the artichoke metaphor* is used. Each layer of this artichoke would be the structure over which lies one or more parts of the inner world and the defense or defenses that accompany it. The layer, in turn, covers another layer, and all of them form a structure that protects the central nucleus, where the most vulnerable part lies. The clinician's understanding of this structure will help the work that will later be developed in detail during the protocol.

The treatment model is developed in a movement from the outside in, from the most external layers toward the most internal ones. By accessing each layer, a process is opened, following the pattern: part/defense/trauma (PDT), which explains that when parts of the internal system are activated, defenses are triggered. When these defenses are neutralized, they allow access to the trauma, which is then reprocessed with the Standard EMDR Protocol.

The process is similar to "weaving." Each layer takes us to the PDT scheme, through which defenses and different traumas are neutralized and reprocessed. The final result is the integration of the inner world and the normalization of food and the eating process.

In summary, the process would be as follows:

A layer is accessed → A part is activated → The defense appears → Work on the defense begins → The defense is neutralized → Access to trauma is gained → Standard processing with EMDR starts

The main defenses will be reprocessed with EMDR through the different subprotocols described in the defenses section. However, the defenses that must be neutralized first are the subtlest ones, such as the "what if ..." defense ("what if I face it and I can't"), the "everything is great" defense, pleasing the therapist so as not to go in too deep, and so on. If the inner layers are reached too soon, we run the risk that the client may feel threatened and drop out of therapy.

Once these defenses are neutralized, we begin working with the main ones: non-awareness of the disease, fear of improvement, hunger defense, and all of those that will be named further along in the protocol and with which we begin to work in Phase 2 and throughout the rest of the phases of treatment.

The Parts/States in EDs and Their Corresponding Beliefs

Each one of the previously named parts has its own basic belief, from which other beliefs may stem. In Phase 2, it is helpful to explain the beliefs of each one of the parts to the client.

THE BELIEF OF "THE CHILD WHO NEVER WAS" OR WORKING WITH CONTROL

This is a very dominant and damaged part that usually generates the most defenses. This part defends the inner world through exercising *control* and contains the pain and frustration of having to learn to do things alone. The part holds the belief *"Things must be done my way."*

Control may be reflected through food, especially in AN. Its origins are the trauma with which the client will connect and which we will work on through the Standard EMDR Protocol in order to heal the belief.

THE BELIEF OF "THE CHILD WHO COULD NOT GROW UP" OR WORKING WITH GUILT

This part failed to go through an adequate maturational development and shows some inappropriate behaviors for the client's age. This part defends the inner world through *guilt*. Not feeling seen connects with the belief *"One needs to get sick in order to get some attention."*

THE BELIEF OF "THE HIDDEN SELF" OR WORKING WITH SHAME AND FEAR

This part protects the inner system through *shame* and *fear*. The predominant emotion is fear, and work must be done with shame. This part holds the belief *"I cannot show myself or stand out because if I do, I will get hurt."*

THE BELIEF OF "THE PATHOLOGICAL CRITIC"/THE PIRANHA OR WORKING WITH PERFECTIONISM

This is the most hostile and confrontational part in the system, the inner critic or "Piranha" (Seijo, 2015). Clients immediately recognize this as the most active part in their inner world. This part or state defends the inner world through *criticism*, and work needs to be focused on perfectionism.

The origins are the traumas to which the client connects and which you can work on later using the Standard EMDR Protocol, in order to heal the belief *"Nothing is ever good enough,"* which is the foundation for this part.

Note: A subprotocol for working specifically on the Piranha is detailed later in text.

THE BELIEF OF "THE REJECTED SELF" OR WORKING WITH BODY IMAGE DISTORTION

This part contains the body image distortion, and work needs to be done at this level. Depending on the client, this may be displayed from a negative body image to a body dysmorphic disorder. This part holds the belief *"I never again want to be who I was."*

The rejected self is the dissociative part and the image distortion is the defense used by the rejected self. When we process the rejected self, we are processing both at the same time.

Note: A full protocol for working with this important part is explained in detail in Chapter 4 of this book.

THE BELIEF OF "THE FAT SELF" OR WORKING WITH REJECTION AND SUBMISSION

This dissociative part shows up most often in BED, hyperphagia, and obesity. This means that the body the client is currently rejecting is the actual body in the present moment, and which the client has usually had throughout the years. (For an in-depth explanation of this concept, please refer to the complete Rejected Self Protocol, developed in Chapter 4 of this book). This part is related to being overweight and becomes imprinted in the internal system. It is very resistant to change, generates many defenses—usually somatic—and is covered by layers. It represents the somatic defense of the hidden self in these disorders.

This part or state defends the inner world through *rejection and submission*. Work needs to be done on defectiveness, since the part holds the beliefs *"There is no place for me in this world"* and *"I am inadequate because I am fat."*

Psychoeducation on EMDR and the Three-Pronged Protocol

The Standard EMDR Protocol is based on the Three-Pronged Protocol: past, present, and future. The EMDR Three-Pronged Protocol is used to reprocess past traumatic experiences, work with present triggers, and address future concerns in order to bring the client to the highest level of adaptive response.

Subprotocol for Working With the "Piranha": The Metaphor for the Mechanism of Criticism

The Piranha metaphor (Seijo, 1999) was developed to help shape and explain one of the most intrusive parts of the inner world of people who suffer from ED and one that highly hinders treatment.

Throughout the years of working with people who suffer from EDs, the name "Piranha"—which came up 1 day as a way of naming something harmful inside of them—became something that fit in perfectly with their internal experience, was quickly accepted, and was effective in helping them. This was how the name was consolidated and became an essential part of the therapeutic work.

Self-criticism is inversely proportional to self-esteem, so when one grows, the other one diminishes. Thus, when self-criticism increases throughout the years due to negative reinforcement from the outside world, it can become pathological.

The negative development of self-criticism can be brought on by negative comments, actions, reactions, or behaviors from the family system, social surroundings, school, peer group, traumas, and so on. This, combined with the absence of validation that would provide adequate compensation, turns self-criticism into an internal enemy. This would be similar to an autoimmune disease on a psychological level, defending and protecting the inner world by attacking it.

The "Piranha" part is the first "voice" people with EDs identify. They describe an intense, harsh, and very critical "voice" that causes great distress and makes hurtful comments about their physique, food, behavior, and personality.

Comparison and humiliation are examples of what this part generates in the internal experience, that is, how the client perceives it internally.

This part tends to show itself adversely. However, its function, like the rest of the parts, is to protect the internal world. It is not a negative part, but the complete opposite; it is the way in which it learned to defend the inner world, which worked until now, although things may not be the same any more. When the client experiences the Piranha internally as very harmful, he or she often has difficulties understanding its protective function. Consequently, we must find a way to have it learn to be protective in a more adaptive and adequate way. As clinicians, we must bear this in mind, so that we don't find ourselves confused by the client's point of view.

PSYCHOEDUCATION ABOUT THE "PIRANHA"

Psychoeducation about the "Piranha" helps the client understand the protective function and identify how this part acts and communicates within the inner system, learning to recognize the origin of the distorted critical messages, which so greatly destabilize the internal world.
Certain goals are to be achieved:

- *Protective function*: It is important to take into consideration the *protective function* that this part has played in the inner world up until now, since it develops through the internalization of those negative comments that the client usually receives from his or her most critical attachment figures. Thus, the Piranha imitates the learned negative comments. The client may have trouble grasping this concept, so the most important thing to understand is that the Piranha avoids emotional pain by imitating the attachment figure whose comments were hurtful. The basic idea is that if internal self-criticism is more intense, external criticism will be less painful. Once the client becomes aware of this protective function, the thoughts about this part change and it normalizes. He or she understands better that the part is trying to heal when it shows up. The goal is for the Piranha to transform into healthy self-criticism and help regulate the inner world. In order to do this, we will guide the client to find where he or she learned to protect the self in this way, eliciting the memories that we will work on with the Standard EMDR Protocol.

- *Differentiating internal from external*: That is to say, what belongs to the client and what belongs to others. We must explain that those needs not covered by others are truly the needs that the client is not covering for herself. In order to work on this, we use current situations that act as triggers, so we activate the PDT pattern, which will take us to the memories we will process with the Standard EMDR Protocol. These memories represent where the client learned not to distinguish that internal and external are different. Differentiation is an internal experience that people with ED have not adequately learned in their development. The use of the concept of "membrane" helps them to clarify and develop it appropriately.
- *Establishing an internal safe place*: Developing an internal safe place that reestablishes trust and safety in their own internal world. Once the Piranha becomes a regulating healthy part, a more trusting inner space will generate, increasing self-respect and the capacity to make better decisions.
- *Differentiate healthy critic from the Piranha*: Identify different ways in which the Piranha communicates by differentiating the function of the healthy critic from the unhealthy and pathological one (Piranha). The Piranha communicates through cognitive distortions. Some of the strategies it uses are negative thinking habits, which make the client interpret reality in an unrealistic fashion. It makes the client see herself as she is not, neither physically nor emotionally nor psychologically, causing unnecessary suffering.

The most common distortions are described as follows. We must explain these to the client so that she can begin to identify them:

- *Personalization*: Through which the client owns situations and behaviors that are not related to her.
- *Polarized thinking*: This distortion causes a thinking process that resembles binary language. Through this distortion, reality becomes "black and white."
- *Filtering*: To explain filtering, we continue with the telescope metaphor that describes in a simple way how this distortion works.

THE TELESCOPE METAPHOR

The client may easily understand the mechanism of the Piranha—how it transforms reality—so that what has been distorted may be substituted and the client can have a more adequate experience of reality.

Being able to identify when and how this part shows up makes the client become aware of repairing the distortions of the Piranha. Clinical work will consist of helping the client translate these distortions or thoughts into healthy beliefs.

INTERVENTION

Once the client knows the strategies this part uses and is able to identify them, the goal now will be to neutralize them. To that end, we must ask questions focused on creating doubt about the internal experience of that part, which the client lives and experiences as real.

Once the client identifies, understands, and is able to manage this part, it is possible to get to the origin, which is connected to the client's history: *Who does this part resemble or who is it imitating?*

For this part of the work, a very valid instrument is a journal, in which notes can be taken on the messages from the Piranha. This helps the client to work on these messages during sessions. Where did the Piranha "feed" from? And where did it learn to do it that way? By doing so, the client comes to elaborate on the internal experience, identifying what causes that internal information and that which she had not been aware of until now.

Sometimes, this intervention creates defenses that generate different reactions among therapists:

- Some professionals decide to be *rescuers* in order to convince the client. However, the professional gets "lost" and worn out looking for how to do it.
- The other reaction is to *presume the client is a lost cause;* the therapist feels frustrated, and the client confirms what she brings.

The correct guideline will be to help the client identify this part, observing what triggers it and which part is triggered by it. This way, work would begin regarding neutralization of the defense in order to work with the part and everything else that is triggered, just as it is done with the PDT pattern. We would also validate the difficulties the client has encountered in order to find help and how positive it is to express it.

The therapist will, in turn, identify internally all those feelings and reactions that may be a part of the transference generated by the therapist–client relationship. We must not antagonize so that the defense can be neutralized. Thus, it will not be reinforced as part of the problem that leads them to being unable to work on what really generates the disorder.

Subprotocols for Working With Defenses

These protocols are used as a stabilizing tool—which is why we include them at the end of Phase 2—but we will use them as needed throughout the treatment. If one of these defenses shows up and could block the processing, we must then take a step back and process these defenses by using these different subprotocols, so we can continue moving forward with our work.

LACK OF ILLNESS AWARENESS DEFENSE

Clients deny having an ED, since they do not identify with those who suffer this illness. As rationale for the defense, they usually use those features that differentiate them from the ED. They are usually uncomfortable or upset when talking about the ED, showing a closed and noncooperative attitude, which usually generates frustration in the therapist. Under this defense lies a fear of getting well.

SOMATIC DEFENSES

Somatic defenses are symptoms, sensations, physical reactions, gestures, or somatizations through which the body communicates. They become activated during the therapeutic process when the internal system is compromised, usually due to emotional pain or a threatening trigger. As clinicians, we must pay attention to every part of the body that shows tension, contraction, pressure, shaking, tingling, muscle weakness, unrest, tiredness, pain, burning, and so on.

Anyway, each client has his or her own somatic language and being able to clarify it helps increase awareness.

ALEXITHYMIA DEFENSE

Alexithymia is characterized by difficulty verbalizing and recognizing emotions and using them as internal signals. It is included in the dissociative experience and generates a somatosensory deficit. The goal of working with alexithymia is reconnecting with the body. The underlying belief is *"If I don't feel, I won't suffer."*

HUNGER DEFENSE

This sensation is similar to hunger, but it is not physical hunger. The role of this defense is to cover up the underlying emotion, which clients believe they cannot confront because they feel they have no resources. The client eats to soothe the feeling of hunger and cover up the emotion believed to be intolerable.

Through working with this defense, the client will be able to differentiate between the hunger defense and the true physical hunger. By doing so, the client increases his or her sense of control, which is crucial when this defense is present.

FEAR-OF-IMPROVEMENT DEFENSE

It is the fear that appears as a defense against the possibility of improvement and of therapy being effective. This defense is very common in EDs, and in AN, it is one of the main defenses that prevents the development of treatment from the very beginning.

- *Anorexia*: With *anorexia*, the possibility of getting better may generate a fear of weight gain. The underlying belief is *"I'm worth anything only if I'm skinny,"* so the disorder ensures thinness. Getting better is associated with gaining weight, therefore, with being defective and unworthy.
- *BED*: With *BED*, the defense tends to show itself through the fear that if the client *"let's go of the food,"* he or she will lose the only safe haven that provides comfort and the element that enables him or her to connect to a secure foundation. Thus, this is what may be underneath this defense. The client will lose the element that connects with a secure foundation. Thus, fear of improvement will appear, sabotaging therapy. Bingeing has a "curtain" function, which covers up what hurts or bothers the client, so that she does not see it. Thus, if the client improves, the fear lies in seeing too much.

When several defenses appear at once, we must remember that the internal world is feeling threatened. In these cases, we must respect the defense and find the part that is blocking, through this defense, and we proceed to the PDT system, until we arrive at where the client learned it and connect with the trauma, which we will process using the Standard EMDR Protocol.

Phase 3: Assessment

Phase 3 begins when memories of "T" or "t" traumas come up while working with the PDT scheme. We then use the Standard EMDR Protocol.

In this phase, the belief that defines each of the different parts is a crucial aspect. For example, "The child who never was" holds beliefs related to "things are done my way" and "there are no limits except my own," which are based on control.

Another peculiarity to bear in mind during this phase is alexithymia. This dissociative-type defense—characterized by difficulty recognizing their own and other people's emotions—tends to be present in ED, especially in those disorders based on an avoidant attachment style, like AN and psychogenic vomiting. Thus, for these clients, describing their feelings will be a complicated task. Due to this difficulty, the person will not report adequate information about feelings, so it will not always be possible to assess the subjective unit of disturbance (SUD). Instead, proceed directly to processing with the negative cognition (NC) without the SUD. The client is asked to focus on any sensation or sign from the body, regardless of its intensity, and we begin to process. As integration increases, alexithymia decreases.

Targets

TARGETING FOOD

Use the following difficult moments as targets:

- Sitting at the table; that is, the client is in front of the plate of food
- Thinking about food

TARGETING CURRENT TRIGGERS

Use the following difficult moments as targets for current triggers:

- The uncontrollable urge to eat just before bingeing/purging begins
- Anticipating binge eating and vomiting
- Anxiety, boredom, and sadness
- Other triggers leading to bingeing and purging that are specific for each client

TARGETING HOSPITALIZATION TRAUMA

Use the following difficult moments as targets for hospitalization trauma:

- Nasogastric tube that ED clients must wear at all times
- Hardest moments of the hospitalization
- Eating in common dining rooms

TARGETING DIETING TRAUMA

Use the following worst moments as targets for dieting trauma:

- Earliest and most difficult moments related to dieting
- Effort and suffering when dieting

TARGETING TRAUMA AND ADVERSE LIFE EXPERIENCE AND ATTACHMENT ISSUES

Process those traumas indicated by the client in Phase 1 that have to do with events related to trauma or attachment issues.

Betrayal Trauma

In betrayal trauma the client is unable to trust the self or others.

Use the following as targets for betrayal trauma:

- The distrusting itself
- Events where learned to distrust

Hidden Trauma

Use the following as targets for hidden trauma:

- Hurtful and subtle double-meaning messages and verbal manipulations client identifies
- Gestures and silences that make the client feel ignored

Phase 4: Desensitization

One of the peculiarities of this phase is somatic processing. This type of processing lacks images and thoughts. During the processing, the client tends to repeat that "nothing comes up" over and over again. However, if we pay attention to the body, we will be able to identify the changes that are happening. This type of processing will be explained in further detail in the section on somatic defenses.

During the processing, it will be important to bear in mind dual attention, since given the different degrees of dissociation that accompany these disorders, past and present may be confused during reprocessing and the client may enter a dissociative state. In order to prevent this from happening, the client must be kept with one foot in the present and the other foot in the past, remembering that both the somatic memories that may come up in the form of physical sensations and the memories that appear on a cognitive level are part of a past that is already gone. According to the Adaptive Information Processing (AIP) model, both types of memories are dysfunctionally stored information, which we are trying to adequately reorganize with EMDR.

Another characteristic to bear in mind during this phase is that interweaves may be both cognitive and somatic (the latter will be explained in the somatic defenses section). Among the cognitive interweaves, one that we will use the most is psychoeducation: brief information that covers what is absent in the internal experience. Another useful interweave will be the validation of the own experience during reprocessing, as was previously stated in Phase 2.

Phase 5: Installation

This phase is necessary in order to reorganize the processing, due to the dispersion of information that may appear during reprocessing. Thus, when going back to the memory, the processing focuses again on a specific neural network, allowing all associated memories to be processed. This facilitates, at the same time, the integration of the internal world.

Phase 6: Body Scan

Just as in Phase 3, alexithymia may cause difficulty when checking the body. Thus, the information the client gives will be valued, even though it may not be precise. As the integration of the internal world of the client increases, the way the client feels about her body and the information she gives about it will also improve.

Phase 7: Closure

In this phase, the processing is reinforced and new insights are recognized. This is when we dedicate some time to the new emerging material, reinforcing it by increasing awareness of new insights and adding bilateral stimulation (BLS), which will help with integration.

Thus, the unhealthy relationship with food starts changing, so that food may stop being used to cover up frustrations, fears, or traumatic memories. Once processing is completed, food will no longer have its pathological function, and thus, it will simply be food.

As the different traumas and defenses are being processed, there is increased realization of how these are related to food issues and the disorder improves.

As the processing of traumatic events evolves, the integration of parts increases and voices decrease in intensity or disappear. At this point, we must be aware of what has been called "parts' grief." In this process, the client feels sad due to the internal silence after integration of the parts has taken place. There is additional sadness related to the realization of how much time has been lost, which will also need to be processed with standard procedures.

Phase 8: Reevaluation

In this session, the target from the previous session is reevaluated. Note that if a SUD has increased compared to the previous session, it is likely that the memory is associated with other memory channels. Often, what seemed like a very clear target in the session can be broken into several others in the next session.

THE EMDR PROTOCOL FOR EATING DISORDERS SCRIPT

Phase 1: History Taking

This section includes the actual questions that you will be asking your client.

General Aspects: Diagnosis and Comorbidity

Ask about the psychopathological assessment.

Say, *"Has any specialist given you a diagnosis for what is happening to you?"*

_____

_____

Ask about any associated disorders:

Say, *"Have you received any other diagnoses in the past?"*

_____

_____

Anamnesis

Ask about general data.

Say, *"I will now collect the information regarding your personal data such as age, education, marital status, and so on."*

_____

_____

Do a genogram.

Say, *"In order to have an outline of your family, I am going to do what we call a genogram, which means I will ask you about your parents, siblings, grandparents, and so on."*

Ask about medical and psychological treatments.

Say, *"Have you received previous psychological and medical treatments?"*

_____

_____

If the answer is "yes,"

Say, *"What about these treatments has worked and what has not worked?"*

_____

_____

Eating Disorder History

WEIGHT HISTORY

Say, *"I will now ask some questions about your height and weight, so we can calculate your BMI."*

Say, *"How tall are you?"*

_____

_____

Say, *"What is your current weight?"*

_____

_____

Say, *"What has been your maximum weight?"*

_____

_____

Say, *"What has been your minimum weight?"*

_____

_____

Say, *"How are your bowel movements? Have you had or do you have any constipation? What do you think the cause is?"*

_____

_____

Say, *"Are you currently following any type of diet or meal regime?"*

_____

_____

If the client's answer is "yes," ask for the name of the professional who follows-up on her diet.

Say, *"Please let me know the professional/dietician/nutritionist who follows up on your diet."*

_____

_____

Say, *"I'll ask you about some symptoms associated with eating disorders in case you recognize any of them."*

_____

_____

If the client suffers from AN, say the following:

> *"Have you noticed that you have more hair in your body, fine hair that appears in places where there was no hair before? It is called* lanugo.*"*

_____

_____

Say, *"Have you noticed that the palms of your hands have an unusual orange color?"*

_____

_____

Say, *"Have you noticed that you have an excess of energy despite the weight loss?"*

_____

_____

Say, *"Have you felt colder than usual, especially your hands and feet?"*

_____

_____

Say, *"Have you noticed dizziness or that your heart feels different?"*

_____

_____

One of the important criteria of AN is alexithymia, or the inability to identify and describe emotion in the self or identify or feel other people's emotions, so it will be important to ask the following questions:

Say, *"Have you noticed that you feel your emotions less, as if you had lost sensitivity?"*

_____

_____

Say, *"Have you noticed that you feel other people in your surroundings differently?"*

_____

_____

Say, *"Have you ever felt surprise observing that when you feel, you do so differently than other people? Have you asked yourself why?"*

_____

_____

Say, *"Have you ever considered yourself to be a cold person?"*

_____

_____

One of the clearest symptoms of AN is the lack of illness awareness or denial of it, so it is important to ask about it.

Say, *"Do you know what is happening to you; that is, are you aware of your illness?"*

_____

_____

If the answer is "no," we inquire further.

Say, *"What do you think is the reason you are here today?"*

_____

_____

If the answer is "yes," we inquire further.

Say, *"What do you think the disorder is?"*

_____

_____

If the client suffers from BN, say the following:

"How many times do you binge per day?"

_____

_____

Say, *"Do you vomit after bingeing or do you compensate for it in any other way?"*

_____

_____

Say, *"I'm going to ask you to show me your hands to see if you have calluses on your knuckles."*

_____

_____

Say, *"Have you noticed if you have* petechiae *under your eyes? They are tiny little red dots of blood."*

_____

_____

Say, *"Have you noticed if your heart beats faster or your heartbeat is irregular, as if you had tachycardia?"*

_____

_____

Say, *"Have you noticed whether the shape of your chin area has changed?"*

_____

_____

Say, *"Have you noticed whether you have small painful marks in the corners of your mouth that bleed occasionally?"*

_____

_____

If the client suffers from BED, say the following:

"Have you noticed any swelling in your body?"

_____

_____

Say, *"Have you noticed any abdominal pain?"*

_____

_____

Say, *"Have you noticed any leg pain?"*

_____

_____

Just for girls, say the following:

"It is important to have information about your menses, so I will ask you some questions about it."

_____

_____

Say, *"When did you get your period for the first time? What was your family's reaction to your first menstrual period?"*

_____

_____

Say, *"Has your period ever disappeared for some time? When did that happen?"*

_____

_____

Say, *"Do you currently have your period? Is it regular every month?"*

_____

_____

HISTORY OF THE CURRENT EPISODE

Say, *"When was the first or most significant time you remember starting to pay attention to food in a different way than simply eating?"*

_____

_____

Say, *"What happened in that moment in your life? And what about with food?"*

_____

_____

Say, *"Where did you learn to do it that way?"*

_____

_____

Say, *"What are your eating habits nowadays?"*

_____

_____

If the client does not provide enough information, complete that information with the family.

Say, *"Can you tell me the peculiarities of her eating habits?"*

_____

_____

RESTRICTION EPISODES

Say, *"I would like to know more about those moments of restriction. Could you describe those times at the dinner table during meals?"*

_____

_____

Say, *"Do you feel more disturbance? Do parts become more activated and conflict increases?"*

_____

_____

Say, *"Do you feel that you dissociate during mealtimes?"*

_____

_____

Say, *"After eating, do you feel guilty for having eaten?"*

_____

_____

Say, *"Do you feel more distrust during mealtimes?"*

_____

_____

BINGEING AND/OR VOMITING EPISODES

Say, *"Have you experienced or do you currently experience bingeing episodes?"*

_____

_____

Say, *"Could you describe the bingeing?"*

_____

_____

Say, *"How long have you been bingeing?"*

_____

_____

Say, *"How often do you binge?"*

_____

_____

Say, *"Does bingeing serve any function for you? Do you binge because you feel full, empty, sad, lonely, and so on?"*

_____

_____

Say, *"When is the first time you remember bingeing?"*

_____

_____

Say, *"Which are the earliest or most significant memories associated with vomiting?"*

_____

_____

Say, *"What was going on in your life at the time?"*

_____

_____

CURRENT TRIGGERS

Say, *"The general precipitants for a bingeing episode usually are those moments in which you feel sadness, boredom, or anxiety. Can you identify with any of these?"*

_____

_____

Say, *"In addition to these general triggers, there may also be other specific ones that trigger the episodes. What do you think are the current situations that lead you to binge, vomit, or compensate in some other way that I may not have asked about yet?"*

_____

_____

Say, *"Could you describe where you learned to do this?"*

_____

_____

PURGING

Say, *"Now I would like to ask you if you compensate the bingeing with vomiting."*

_____

_____

Say, *"Do you use any kind of medication like diuretics or laxatives?"*

_____

_____

HOSPITALIZATIONS

Say, *"Have you ever been hospitalized for your eating problems?"*

_____

_____

Say, *"Have you been to any medical center because of the disorder, even if you were not hospitalized, for example, emergency room or medical visits?"*

_____

_____

Food History

HISTORY OF MEALTIMES

Say, *"Let's talk about the meals at home. Who sat at the table during meals?"*

_____

_____

Say, *"How are mealtimes for you now?"*

_____

_____

Say, *"How are or were your family's eating habits? Do they usually eat fast or slow? Are there members of your family who eat differently?"*

_____

_____

Say, *"Who cooks or used to cook at home?"*

_____

_____

Say, *"How are your eating habits at home? Is the diet balanced in your opinion?"*

_____

_____

Say, *"Is there someone at home who is or has ever been on a diet?"*

_____

_____

TIME SPENT IN FRONT OF THE PLATE

Say, *"How much time do you spend at mealtimes?"*

_____

_____

Say, *"Do you spend a lot of time in front of the plate or do you finish up quickly?"*

_____

_____

OVERFEEDING

Say, *"Is there someone in your family who represents what is called an 'overfeeding figure', someone in your family who has fed you too much? For example, someone who fed you even when you said you were not hungry?"*

_____

_____

If the answer is "yes," say the following:

"How did this overfeeding figure feed you?"

_____

_____

Say, *"When did she/he do it?"*

_____

_____

Attachment Issues

Say, *"I would like to know about your relationship with your parents or the attachment figures you have grown up with, and I will ask you some questions about it. Please describe your attachment to your father. Is he a loving and close father, or is he cold and distant?"*

_____

_____

Say, *"How is the relationship between your parents?"*

_____

_____

Say, *"What kind of relationship do you have and have you had with each one of them?"*

_____

_____

Say, *"Please describe your attachment to your mother. Is she affectionate or the opposite?"*

_____

_____

Say, *"Are your parents married or divorced?"*

_____

_____

If they are divorced, say the following:

"Please describe the relationship with their respective partners."

_____

_____

ATTACHMENT TRAUMA

Say, *"Have you always lived in the same place or have you lived in different places during your childhood or adolescence?"*

_____

_____

Say, *"Who made you feel the most validated in your life? Who made you feel the most understood in your life?"*

_____

_____

Say, *"Who made you feel the least understood and validated in your life?"*

_____

_____

Say, *"What would you have needed to feel understood and validated?"*

_____

_____

Say, *"Who has been the person who has given you the most love?"*

_____

_____

Say, *"Who has made you feel safest?"*

_____

_____

Say, *"What is your father's typical expression?"*

_____

_____

Say, *"What is your mother's typical expression?"*

_____

_____

Say, *"Have you ever felt like the mother or father of your parents, as if you had a role that was not fit for you?"*

_____

_____

Say, *"Could you tell me of any times you remember in which your parents, or people who represented affection and security, have made you feel that you were not worthy?"*

_____

_____

Say, *"Have you felt that they did not offer you comfort when you needed it?"*

_____

_____

Say, *"Have you felt that they have been rigid or perfectionist with you, forcing you to meet high standards?"*

_____

_____

Say, *"Has anyone ever compared you to other people, leaving you in the worse position?"*

_____

_____

Trauma History

Say, *"We will now collect all the information regarding those events or adverse experiences that may have impacted you in some way and with which we will work throughout the therapy so that they stop affecting you in the way they have been affecting you so far."*

TRAUMATIC EVENTS

Say, *"Have you suffered any kind of accident that has had an emotional or physical impact?"*

_____

_____

Say, *"Have you ever suffered an important and difficult loss of a loved one?"*

_____

_____

Say, *"Have you suffered any major loss in your life that has caused you emotional pain?"*

_____

_____

HUMILIATION TRAUMA

Say, *"Now, let's explore the events or adverse experiences you have suffered in your life that may have been traumatic for you in some way."*

_____

_____

Say, *"I would like to know if you have ever felt any abuse of power that made you feel humiliated or submissive in some way?"*

_____

_____

BETRAYAL TRAUMA

Say, *"Have you ever felt betrayed by someone?"*

_____

_____

Say, *"Have you suffered any sexual abuse, touching, or inappropriate behavior in this regard?"*

_____

_____

Say, *"Have you ever felt that someone looked at you in a way that made you feel uncomfortable?"*

_____

_____

DIETING TRAUMA

Say, *"How many times have you been on a diet?"*

_____

_____

Say, *"When were you on a diet for the first time, and how old were you?"*

_____

_____

Say, *"Whose idea was it to go on a diet?"*

_____

_____

Say, *"What was the worst moment of all the diets you have been on?"*

_____

_____

Say, *"How would you define the worst moment about being on a diet?"*

_____

_____

Say, *"Was there a need for the diet? What was it?"*

_____

_____

Say, *"What happens inside of you at mealtimes?"*

_____

_____

HIDDEN TRAUMA

Say, *"Have you felt that you had to self-soothe or self-regulate? Or on the contrary, has there been someone there for you to help you do it?"*

_____

_____

If the answer is "No one has been there for me," keep asking.

Say, *"When did you realize that you did not feel seen by your parents or the people who looked after you when you needed to calm down and nobody was there for you?"*

_____

_____

Say, *"Have you ever felt that you needed to be seen and have your needs taken care of by your parents or the people who took care of you, but it did not happen?"*

_____

_____

Say, *"Have you felt emotionally understood and validated when feeling sad or angry?"*

_____

_____

BODY HISTORY

Say, *"What comes up for you when you think about your body?"*

_____

_____

Say, *"What words or adjectives would you use to define it?"*

_____

_____

Say, *"Are there any physical marks from the ED that worry you, like scars or stretch marks due to weight shift, flaccid skin, and so on?"*

_____

_____

Say, *"Have you received negative comments about your body?"*

_____

_____

If the answer is "yes," say the following:

"From whom?"

_____

_____

Say, *"Have you ever caused damage to your body because of feeling upset or needing to channel frustration?"*

_____

_____

If the answer is "yes," inquire about the kind of self-harming behavior.

Say, *"What did you do?"*

_____

_____

Phase 2: Preparation

Introducing the Preparation Phase

Say, *"We are going to start organizing the work that we will be doing throughout the sessions, so you can understand it and trust the process. We need for you and me to become a team, so you can feel that you're not alone in this.*

We will first identify the aspects or parts of you that are part of your inner world. Then, we will start neutralizing the potential defenses that may arise, which will let us know that we need to stop and check. This way, we will know that we are moving along at the right pace, and not too fast, especially with life or food issues that perhaps may be difficult for you to cope with.

In order to do so, we will respect your defenses, which give us very valuable information. We will neutralize them by using a resource that helps your inner world and parts; in this way, we will move forward little by little with our work.

The goal is for you to start feeling better. There may be some moments that are harder than others, but the important thing is to be able to extract a resource from those difficult moments, which will help us move forward."

_____

_____

Psychoeducation Regarding the Edge of Trauma and Somatic Identifiers

Say, *"The first thing we need is to be able to understand how your inner world works. For this, we must identify the sensations that will be letting us know that we are approaching the edge of the trauma, which is the line that establishes the point that can be reached at any given time in therapy. We will always remain one or two steps away from this edge of the trauma, so you can feel that the process is safe and have an inner sense of control that everything is okay.*

In order to know when we are approaching this edge of the trauma, we will explore which are the sensations or emotions you usually notice when you become dysregulated. For example, you could have the sensation of not feeling the body, or suddenly becoming very tired and sleepy, or not being present, or a rapid heartbeat. There may be sensations of this kind or similar that may indicate that we are approaching the edge. If so, let me know and we will stop and introduce a resource that will help you to feel calm and know that everything is okay."

Identifying the Inner World

Say, *"The structure of this next phase of our work focuses on two basic points: identifying the parts of your inner world and the defenses that normally protect these parts.*

The inner world represents your personality and could be explained as an orchestra. An orchestra is composed of musicians who are led by a conductor. When musicians play in unison and follow the conductor, the orchestra sounds great. However, when one of the musicians becomes unruly and refuses to play or wants to take over from the orchestra conductor or chooses to play an instrument different from the one he or she has been assigned, the orchestra will not sound good.

The same thing happens in your inner world when aspects or parts of you want to perform functions that are not appropriate; things do not work well inside. So, our job will be to organize every aspect of you that is not in its proper place. As the work develops, you will meet every part of you and this will help you understand much better what is happening to you and get out of the eating disorder from which you suffer."

Throughout the process, it is important to validate the client, promote compassion from understanding, and help organize the chaotic inner world and its parts, naming and describing them in detail.

Say, *"I see that it is difficult for you to understand what is happening inside, since you probably feel a certain chaos that often does not allow you to identify what is happening. In order for you to understand it better, I will introduce the different states or parts in which your inner world is divided, so you can organize your internal world."*

IDENTIFYING PARTS, NEUTRALIZING DEFENSES, AND ACCESSING TRAUMA

Say, *"In order to start organizing your inner world, we will begin by naming the parts and explaining what function and belief they have within you. These are the parts or states that I will explain in detail in a few minutes:*

- *The little girl who never was*
- *The little girl who could not grow up*
- *The pathological critic*
- *The rejected self*
- *The hidden self*
- *The fat self"*

Say, *"Just so you can understand better, these states or internal parts I just named generate defenses. Defenses are all those inner experiences that make us unable to continue processing at a certain point in time. These inner experiences may be an emotion, a thought, a sensation, or a movement arising from the body. Every part or state generates its own defense(s), which we will identify so we can neutralize them and move forward with our work, little by little and always trusting the process."*

Artichoke Metaphor

Say, *"The inner world could be represented by the artichoke metaphor that helps us see all the layers covering up the inner world, as a way to protect its most vulnerable part. When working with EMDR therapy, each of these layers contains the traumas, adverse experiences, and defenses that may arise. We will gradually process each one of these layers, until we reach the artichoke heart and repair what needs to be repaired. This is always done with great care, respecting the inner world and, above all, trusting the process.*

Once we start working with parts, you will see that each one has specific defenses, but so you can understand how this develops based on the artichoke metaphor, this will be explained in greater detail.

The model of treatment in EDs is developed from the outside in, starting at the outermost layers and moving inward. Each time a layer is accessed, we open a process that follows the pattern: part, defense, trauma (or the PDT system). When the parts of the inner system are activated, the defenses are triggered. The defenses are the way in which the parts learned to protect the system. The fear of making contact with what is difficult to remember activates the defenses in order to avoid the pain. By softening these defenses, accessing trauma or adverse life experiences and reprocessing these memories with the Standard EMDR Protocol become possible. For example, if the part of 'the child who never was' becomes activated and the defense of control appears, using the PDT system, we will ask the question, 'Where did this part of you learn to control in this way?' or 'Where did this part of you learn to protect you through control?' This question will give us access to the memories that are held by the part, which will be processed."

The Parts/States in EDs and Their Corresponding Beliefs

It is important to educate your client about the parts/states in EDs and their corresponding beliefs:

Say, *"Each one of the previously named parts has its own basic belief, from which other beliefs may stem. As we talk about each part, I will want to know whether/how much of this fits your experience."*

Say, *"When working with the parts/defense/trauma system, I will ask you to identify the triggers that activate it. This could be a current situation, a personal relationship, or an event that threatens the inner world. For each part, this threat will make a different defense emerge. The origin of this defense and its corresponding belief is the trauma with which you connect when we explore where you learned to defend your inner world in each specific way."*

THE BELIEF OF "THE CHILD WHO NEVER WAS" OR WORKING WITH CONTROL

Briefly explain this part to the client, stating the belief that goes along with it.

Say, *"'The child who never was' contains the pain and frustration of having to learn to do things alone. It represents the self-sufficient child who has been forced to grow up quickly and become an 'adult' in childhood. The child has learned to self-regulate and to have self-control through food and does things in _____ (his/her) own way. This part, which learned to defend the inner system through control, holds the belief 'Things must be done my way'."*

Say, *"Could you tell me how much of this fits with your experience?"*

_____

_____

Explore triggers.

Say, *"What makes this part of you become activated?"*

_____

_____

Continue to further explore this part.

Say, *"Tell me about this part; how old is it?"*

_____

_____

Say, *"When did this part start to exist?"*

_____

_____

Say, *"Where did you learn to feel like this?"*

_____

_____

Then inquire where this client learned to defend the inner world by exercising control.

Say, *"Could you describe where this part learned to defend you through control?"*

THE BELIEF OF "THE CHILD WHO COULD NOT GROW UP" OR WORKING WITH GUILT

Briefly explain this part to the client, stating the belief that goes along with it.

Say, *"'The child who could not grow up' failed to go through an adequate maturational development and shows some inappropriate behaviors for _____ (his/her) age. This is a lost child who does not know if talking is allowed or not and, through food, has found a way of being seen. This part defends the inner world through guilt such as 'Not being seen is my fault.' The main belief is 'One needs to get sick in order to get some attention.'"*

Say, *"Could you tell me how much of this fits with your experience?"*

_____

_____

Explore triggers.

Say, *"What makes this part of you become activated?"*

_____

_____

Further exploration of this part is as follows:

Say, *"Tell me about this part; how old is it?"*

_____

_____

Say, *"When did this part start to exist?"*

_____

_____

Say, *"Where did you learn to feel like this?"*

_____

_____

Then inquire where this client learned to defend the inner world through guilt.

Say, *"Could you describe where this part learned to defend you through guilt?"*

_____

_____

THE BELIEF OF "THE HIDDEN SELF" OR WORKING WITH SHAME AND FEAR

Briefly explain this part to the client, stating the belief that goes along with it.

Say, *"'The hidden self' protects the inner system by hiding, not exposing or showing, the self, since whenever this was done in the past, things became threatening or even dangerous. Staying in the shadows ends up being safer. This part develops early in life and somatizes what cannot be expressed otherwise. This part, which learned to defend the inner system through shame, holds the belief 'I cannot show myself or stand out because if I do, I will get hurt.'"*

Say, *"Could you tell me how much of this fits with your experience?"*

_____

_____

Explore triggers.

Say, *"What makes this part of you become activated?"*

_____

_____

Continue to further explore this part.

Say, *"Tell me about this part. How old is it?"*

_____

_____

Say, *"When did this part start to exist?"*

_____

_____

Say, *"Where did you learn to feel like this?"*

_____

_____

Then inquire where this client learned to defend the inner world through shame.

Say, *"Could you describe where this part learned to defend you through shame?"*

_____

_____

THE BELIEF OF "THE PATHOLOGICAL CRITIC"/THE PIRANHA OR WORKING WITH PERFECTIONISM

Briefly explain this part to the client, stating the belief that goes along with it.

Say, *"'The Piranha' is the inner critic, always judging and blocking your self-esteem, filtering reality, and letting in only the negative perspective. This part imitates, in the inner world, those who criticized and judged the child in real life, resulting in a constant comparison to others. This part, which learned to defend the inner system through criticism, holds the belief 'Nothing is ever good enough.'"*

Say, *"Could you tell me how much of this fits with your experience?"*

_____

_____

Explore triggers.

Say, *"What makes this part of you become activated?"*

_____

_____

Further exploration of this part is as follows:

Say, *"Tell me about this part; how old is it?"*

_____

_____

Say, *"When did this part start to exist?"*

_____

_____

Say, *"Where did you learn to feel like this?"*

_____

_____

Then, inquire where this client learned to defend the inner world through criticism.

Say, *"Could you describe where your 'Piranha' learned to defend you through criticism?"*

_____

_____

THE BELIEF OF "THE REJECTED SELF" OR WORKING WITH BODY IMAGE DISTORTION

Briefly explain this part to the client, stating the belief that goes along with it.

Say, *"'The rejected self' is a part of you from either the past or the present that you reject, and of which you are ashamed. This part may hold feelings of disgust or contempt, and it may have been there throughout the years as an imprinted image of what you never want to be again, and through which you see yourself when looking in the mirror."*

_____

_____

Say, *"Could you tell me how much of this fits with your experience?"*

_____

_____

Explore triggers.

Say, *"What makes this part of you become activated?"*

_____

_____

Further exploration of this part.

Say, *"Tell me about this part; how old is it?"*

_____

_____

Say, *"When did this part start to exist?"*

_____

_____

Say, *"Where did you learn to feel like this?"*

Then inquire where this client learned to feel rejected.

_____

_____

Say, *"What is the oldest or most significant memory in which you have felt or seen yourself rejected?"*

_____

_____

THE BELIEF OF "THE FAT SELF" OR WORKING WITH REJECTION AND SUBMISSION

Briefly explain this part to the client, stating the belief that goes along with it.

Say, *"'The fat self' covers the unmet needs through the body. Weight gain is the protective somatic defense of this part, so the client hides underneath this self or takes more space in the world because he or she does not feel seen. This part, which learned to defend the inner system through rejection and submission, holds the beliefs 'There is no place for me in this world' and 'I am inadequate because I am fat.'"*

_____

_____

Say, *"Could you tell me how much of this fits with your experience?"*

_____

_____

Explore triggers.

Say, *"What makes this part of you become activated?"*

Continue further exploration of this part.

Say, *"Tell me about your fat self; how old is it?"*

_____

_____

Say, *"When did your fat self start to exist?"*

_____

_____

Say, *"Have you ever felt not seen, or have you ever felt there is no place for you in the world?"*

_____

_____

Say, *"Where did you learn to feel like this?"*

_____

_____

Then inquire where this client learned to defend the inner world through weight gain.

Say, *"Could you describe where your fat self learned to defend you through gaining weight?"*

_____

_____

Psychoeducation on EMDR and the Three-Pronged Protocol

Before stepping into Phase 3, or before applying any of the subprotocols, offer a brief explanation about EMDR:

> Say, *"When a trauma occurs, it seems to get locked in the nervous system with the original picture, sounds, thoughts, and feelings. The eye movements we use in EMDR seem to unlock the nervous system and allow the brain to process the experience. That may be what is happening in REM or dream sleep—the eye movements may help to process the unconscious material. It is important to note that it is your own brain that will be doing the healing and that you are the one in control. When we process following the Three-Pronged Protocol, we are talking about the fact of the experiences of the past, which affect your present life; once they are processed, they stop affecting you and will not disturb you in the future."*

Subprotocol for Working With the "Piranha": The Metaphor for the Mechanism of Criticism

Once the Piranha is identified, along with where the client learned to develop this part or state, it will be necessary to stabilize the inner world. When we start this work, this part will most likely have a destabilizing effect due to the adverse experiences or traumas to which it is connected. For this reason, we first start working with this subprotocol, which has been specifically developed for this part.

> Say, *"I would now like to start working with this part of you, the most critical part of your inner world, which has been called Piranha because of how it behaves inside. This does not mean it is a negative part, this is not the case, even though it may seem so at times, but the way in which it shows up can be quite aggressive."*

PSYCHOEDUCATION ABOUT "THE PIRANHA"

> Say, *"We will start by getting to know this part a little better and offering you psychoeducation about how it behaves in your inner world and the function that it has."*

_____

_____

First, explain the protective function of this part.

> Say, *"The Piranha avoids emotional pain by imitating the attachment figure whose comments were hurtful. The basic idea is that if internal self-criticism is more intense, external criticism will be less painful. The goal is for the Piranha to transform into healthy self-criticism and help regulate the inner world."*

_____

_____

Second, teach them to differentiate the internal from the external worlds through the concept of a "membrane."

> Say, *"Those needs not covered by others are truly the needs that you are not covering for yourself. In order to differentiate what is internal from what is external, I would like you to imagine a* membrane *dividing the inner and outer worlds. By doing this, you can now realize that what is inside your membrane belongs to you and what is outside of the membrane belongs to the external world."*

_____

_____

Third, help clients identify the different ways in which the inner critic communicates.

> Say, *"The healthy critic has the role of regulating how you regard yourself, providing a point of view based on reality, and regulating self-esteem and self-concept in a way that develops acceptance. However, when the critic becomes unhealthy and turns into the Piranha part, it generates internal communication that is harmful for you."*

_____

_____

In order to better understand harmful communication from the Piranha, explain cognitive distortions.

> Say, *"In order to explain the personalization distortion, I shall use a real-life situation. Imagine you meet up with a friend, and during the conversation, he tells you that he's tired. If the Piranha uses this distortion at this moment, it's likely that you will start thinking that you are boring him. Focusing on this does not give you the option of thinking that he may be tired for many different reasons, but your being boring is more than likely not one of them."*

_____

_____

Say, *"One way of understanding the* polarized thinking distortion *might be how something white doesn't turn black because of a stain. There are many colors and ranges between them, and white is just one more color."*

_____

_____

_____

_____

Say, *"Filtering is another cognitive distortion that this part uses as a way of transforming internal experience. It could be described as if the Piranha put a filter in front of your senses. This is the way reality becomes filtered. Negative information would get filtered. The positive information is there, but it's about how this part filters it for you. It's as if in addition to filtering, it records and saves it for a more convenient time. We will pay attention to how it happens. For example, you go somewhere or speak to someone, and, after the situation occurs, the Piranha reminds you how inadequate you were. It may also associate this event with other past situations when you were as inadequate as in the previous one. This will make you feel bad and trigger feelings of inadequacy, harming your self-esteem."*

_____

_____

Say, *"Do you have any questions or comments about what I just explained to you?"*

_____

_____

THE TELESCOPE METAPHOR

The telescope metaphor can be explained through the following visualization exercise.

Say, *"Let me explain to you, by using a metaphor, how this Piranha part functions in your mind. Imagine a telescope that you aim toward the stars. How do you see them?"*

_____

_____

Say, *"Okay, so now imagine what happens if you turn the telescope around and look through the other end."*

_____

_____

Say, *"Okay, you see them farther away. Now, imagine the telescope once again and see what happens now if you change the telescope's lens for one that is cracked."*

_____

_____

Say, *"You are doing very well. Imagine the telescope again and see what happens if you change the lens to one that is cracked and also smeared with grease."*

_____

_____

Say, *"You would see blurry stains, wouldn't you? Well, you know what? That is how the Piranha makes you look at reality most of the time. That is one of the reasons why we have to change the cracked and stained lens for one that is only cracked, and once you are able to perceive something other than stains, we can change it for a crystal-clear lens, so that you can tell me you see the stars clearly, although far away. Then we'll be able to turn the telescope around and you'll be able to see them crystal clear."*

_____

_____

Say, *"In order to achieve this, it will be necessary to work with the Piranha's distortions and be able to recognize them. This will make it possible for you to differentiate what is your own from what is external and, thus, change the lenses. It is not a part or state against which we have to fight. Instead, it is a part of you that we will have to help heal because it's become unhealthy."*

_____

_____

INTERVENTION

Help to differentiate the Piranha in the following way:

Say, *"All the negative thoughts that come up about yourself and make you suffer come from the Piranha. Since people do not gratuitously harm themselves, there is something that is not healthy and we must help it become healthy, so you can get to see yourself as you truly are, accept yourself, and be okay with it."*

In order to neutralize the ploys used by the "Piranha" and obtain information about the beliefs:

Say, *"What thoughts did this part show you?"*

_____

_____

Say, *"What proof do you have that what it showed you is true?"*

_____

_____

Say, *"If someone you cared about had that thought, would you think the same?"*

_____

_____

Say, *"What alternative interpretations are there?"*

_____

_____

Say, *"What kind of distortion is it?"*

_____

_____

Say, *"How does that thought make you feel?"*

Say, *"If the thought were true, what is the worst that could happen?"*

Say, *"What do you think the Piranha is trying to cover up with what it shows you?"*

Say, *"If you could say something to the Piranha about how it has acted in that situation, what would you say to it?"*

Say, *"What other options regarding how it could act toward you would you suggest so that it does not make you feel this way?"*

Say, *"Could you describe where your 'Piranha' learned to defend you from criticism?"*

Say, *"Let us take each one of these memories and process them with the Standard EMDR Protocol so this part of you can become more integrated and develop into healthy criticism. We will work with the earliest or most significant memory that came up for you when I asked you where your 'Piranha' learned to defend you from criticism."*

Subprotocols for Working With Defenses

These subprotocols should be used as necessary throughout the treatment process, when defenses block the continuation of the process.

LACK OF ILLNESS AWARENESS DEFENSE

Look for exceptions, moments in which they noticed there was some kind of problem with food.

Say, *"Think of a time or times when you have realized that something is happening with food in your life."*

Work through the belief *"I have anorexia"* with BLS. The goal is to reduce the defense and locate the blocking point.

> Say, *"Now, I would like you to think of the sentence 'I have anorexia' (or 'I have bulimia' or 'I have a binge eating disorder,' whatever the case may be)."*

Do BLS.

Note: Do not ask for SUDs, since in many cases clients also have alexithymia, so they don't initially recognize feelings and emotions.

Explore the role of the defense following Jim Knipe's work (2015):

> Say, *"What is good about not identifying with the ED?"*

_____

_____

> Say, *"What is bad about not identifying with the ED?"*

_____

_____

SOMATIC DEFENSES AND REPROCESSING

One of the places where trauma dwells is the body. Trauma is stored on a somatic level. If you work on the area of the body where it was stored, you can help process and liberate all the traumatic material contained in it. The dissociative parts also contain and show themselves through somatic defenses. The work here consists of giving a voice to that defense that blocks the internal experience and identifying its function.

> Say, *"Allow yourself to notice what is coming up in the body right now that is preventing us from continuing to process. Describe to me what you are feeling and where you feel it in the body."*

_____

_____

We must then do a modified reprocessing, where we take a sensation, emotion, or pain instead of the standard image, and ask about the negative belief.

> Say, *"Focus on the sensation you are noticing in your body. If that sensation, pain, or bodily experience that is emerging could be expressed in words, what words would those be?"*

_____

_____

Do BLS.

> Say, *"What does that _____ (name sensation/pain/bodily experience) say about you?"*

_____

_____

> Or say, *"If _____ (name the sensation/pain/bodily experience) had words, what would it tell you?"*

Checking SUDs.

> Say, *"On a scale of 0 to 10, where 0 is no disturbance or neutral and 10 is the highest disturbance you can imagine, how disturbing does it feel now?"*

> 0   1   2   3   4   5   6   7   8   9   10

> (no disturbance)   (highest disturbance)

Do BLS.

If the client does not get to the belief, take the somatic reaction and assess it on a scale of 0 to 10, just with those two elements—the SUD and the somatic reaction—and do BLS.

> Say, *"Please focus on the physical reaction you are noticing and on a scale of 0 to 10, where 0 is no intensity or neutral and 10 is the highest intensity you can imagine, how intense does it feel now?"*

> 0   1   2   3   4   5   6   7   8   9   10

> (no intensity)   (highest intensity)

Do BLS.

Continue processing the sensations until they are no longer present and the disturbance has reached zero.

ALEXITHYMIA DEFENSE

Ask clients to describe how they experience "not feeling."

> Say, *"Could you please describe what you notice when you have the experience of 'not feeling'?"*

> _____

> _____

The defense starts deactivating by asking the following:

> Say, *"What happens inside of you when _____ (state what you experience when 'not feeling')?"*

> _____

> _____

Do BLS.

Once the defense lowers, explore the memories that generated this belief and work on them with the Standard EMDR Protocol.

> Say, *"When do you remember having to start not feeling in order to protect yourself?"*

> _____

> _____

Once the defense is deactivated, the client will be able to start reconnecting.

Note: Remember that when doing Phase 3 during the Standard EMDR Protocol, you may not be able to obtain emotions and SUD level.

HUNGER DEFENSE

Help the client to differentiate the defense of hunger from physical hunger.

Say, *"Does this sensation feel like physical hunger because you are really hungry, or is it something that is similar to hunger but it is not?"*

_____

_____

Say, *"How does this feel and where do you feel it?"*

_____

_____

Say, *"This feeling is what we call the hunger defense. Check and see if you can identify the emotion it is covering up."*

_____

_____

Say, *"In what situations does the defense of hunger appear?"*

_____

_____

Say, *"What happens when the defense appears?"*

_____

_____

Say, *"If there was no such defense, what would happen?"*

_____

_____

Ask the client to connect with the feeling of hunger and measure its intensity.

Say, *"Please, notice this sensation of hunger. On a scale of 0 to 10, where 0 is no sensation of hunger or neutral and 10 is the highest sensation of hunger you can imagine, how disturbing does it feel now?"*

0	1	2	3	4	5	6	7	8	9	10

(no sensation of hunger or neutral)   (highest sensation of hunger)

Do BLS.

FEAR-OF-IMPROVEMENT DEFENSE

Ask the client to describe what he or she is noticing inside.

Say, *"There seems to be something blocking the flow of therapy. Could you check inside and notice what is happening? Can you describe it for me?"*

_____

_____

Then name it "fear of improvement."

> Say, *"This defense is called fear of improvement and it has to do with being scared of the possibility of improving and therapy being effective. Could you please check inside and let me know if this is how it is for you?"*

The client is asked, once again, to locate that fear of improvement in the body, and then begin to process and gather information from what comes up after the sets of BLS. Sometimes they cannot describe where they feel the fear because people suffering from anorexia may have some degree of alexithymia.

> Say, *"Where do you notice the fear in your body?"*

_____

_____

> Say, *"Please, notice this fear. On a scale of 0 to 10, where 0 is no fear or neutral and 10 is the most fear you can imagine, how much fear do you feel now?"*

>   0   1   2   3   4   5   6   7   8   9   10

> (no fear)   (most fear)

Do three or four sets of BLS to neutralize the defense and introduce the belief to which that fear of improvement may be related.

For anorexia, say the following:

> Say, *"This fear is usually related to gaining weight and to the internal belief that 'I'm worthy only if I'm skinny.'"*

_____

_____

We ask the client to focus on that belief while we stimulate to see how true it is.

> Say, *"Could you please focus on the belief 'I'm worthy only if I'm skinny'?"*

Do BLS.

This belief is usually true, so we must search for its origin:

> Say, *"Where did you learn that you're worthy only if you're skinny?"*

_____

_____

A memory or cluster of memories is obtained, which leads us to the trauma that will be processed in Phase 3 using the Standard EMDR Protocol. Maybe the client will say she does not feel the belief is true. In this case, the client may be in denial and unable to see and recognize the belief for the same reason: fear of improvement. This defense may require several sessions until the original trauma is processed.

In bulimia and BED, say the following:

> Say, *"This fear is usually related to letting go of food and to the internal belief that 'without food, I have no support'."*

Ask the client to focus on that belief while we stimulate to see how true it is.

> Say, *"Could you please focus on the belief 'Without food, I have no support'?"*

_____

_____

Do BLS.

This belief is usually true, so search for its origin:

> Say, *"Where did you learn that without food, you have no support?"*

_____

_____

A memory or cluster of memories is obtained, which leads to the trauma that will be processed in Phase 3 using the Standard EMDR Protocol.

Other issues to explore in both bulimia and BED are the following:

LACK OF CONTROL WITH FOOD

> Say, *"In binge eating disorder, one of the first steps in treatment is stabilizing the state in which you find yourself regarding food. For this, we will first dedicate time to the issue of lack of control over food. So, when you see yourself at the table with food in front of you, how much do you feel in control in regard to food?"*

_____

_____

> Say, *"If that lack of control said something about you, what would it say?"*

_____

_____

The answer usually reveals the belief.

> Say, *"When was the first or the earliest time that you felt this 'lack of control' along with the words ____ (state the belief stated earlier)?"*

_____

_____

Using the Standard EMDR Protocol, target those memories that represent the lack of control so the client can retrieve the sensation of being in control.

THE URGE TO EAT

Target the exact moment that the feeling of desperation with food appeared and then apply BLS. The intention is to reduce the intensity of the urge.

> Say, *"Let's focus on the feelings that represent the urge you feel when you're about to binge. We are going to work with this. When you think about the moment when you're about to binge, focus on the exact moment that represents the urge to go and get the food. How do you feel that urge in the body and what sensation represents it?"*

_____

_____

Do BLS.

> Say, *"Thank you for focusing on this situation where you feel the urge to eat and please notice this urge to eat you feel on a scale of 0 to 10, where 0 is no urge to eat or*

neutral and 10 is the biggest urge you can imagine; how much urge to eat do you feel now?"

0	1	2	3	4	5	6	7	8	9	10

(no urge)   (highest urge)

Do BLS.

THE URGE TO VOMIT

Say, *"Let's focus on the feelings that represent the urge you feel when you're about to vomit. We are going to work with this. When you think about the moment when you're about to vomit, where do you feel that urge in the body?"*

_____

_____

Do BLS.

Say, *"Thank you for focusing on this situation where you feel the urge to vomit and please notice this urge to vomit you feel on a scale of 0 to 10, where 0 is no urge to vomit or neutral and 10 is the biggest urge you can imagine; how much urge to vomit do you feel now?"*

0	1	2	3	4	5	6	7	8	9	10

(no urge)   (most urge)

Do BLS.

Phase 3: Assessment

Target Selection

Select a target image (stationary picture) of the memory.

Say, *"What picture represents the most disturbing part of this incident now?"*

_____

_____

Obtaining the Negative Cognition and Positive Cognition

NEGATIVE COGNITION

Say, *"What words best go with the picture that express your negative belief about yourself now?"*

_____

_____

POSITIVE COGNITION

Say, *"When you bring up the picture of the incident, what would you like to believe about yourself now?"*

_____

_____

VALIDITY OF COGNITION

Say, *"When you bring up the picture of the incident, how true do those words _____ (clinician repeats the positive cognition [PC]) feel to you now on a scale of 1 to 7, where 1 feels completely false and 7 feels completely true?"*

1	2	3	4	5	6	7

(completely false)   (completely true)

Identify Emotions, SUD Level, and Location in the Body

EMOTIONS

Say, *"When you bring up the picture* (or incident) *and those words _____ (clinician states the NC), what emotion do you feel now?"*

_____

_____

SUBJECTIVE UNITS OF DISTURBANCE

Say, *"On a scale of 0 to 10, where 0 is no disturbance or neutral and 10 is the highest disturbance you can imagine, how disturbing does it feel now?"*

0	1	2	3	4	5	6	7	8	9	10

(no disturbance)   (highest disturbance)

LOCATION OF BODY SENSATION

Say, *"Where do you feel it* (the disturbance) *in your body?"*

_____

_____

Phase 4: Desensitization

Apply the Standard EMDR Protocol for All Targets

Say, *"Bring up the picture and the words _____ (clinician repeats the NC) and notice where you feel it in your body. Now follow _____ (state the BLS modality)."*

This procedure is to be repeated until SUDs = 0. Then the PC is installed. Each traumatic event associated with the problem that is not reprocessed during the normal course of the first target needs to be processed using the protocol discussed previously until SUDs reach an ecological 1 or 0 and the PC is installed.

Say, *"When you go back to the original incident, on a scale of 0 to 10, where 0 is no disturbance or neutral and 10 is the highest disturbance you can imagine, how disturbing does it feel now?"*

0	1	2	3	4	5	6	7	8	9	10

(no disturbance)   (highest disturbance)

If the SUD is 1 or higher, options are as follows:

Say, *"Look at the incident as it is now stored in your head. What aspect of it is most disturbing?"*

Or say, *"What is there in the picture that is causing the _____ (state the SUD level)? What do you see?"*

Say, *"Concentrate on that aspect. Okay, have you got it? Go with that."*

Do sets of eye movements or other BLS until SUD = 0.

Phase 5: Installation

Install the PC

Say, *"As you think of the incident, how do the words feel from 1 being completely false to 7 being completely true?"*

1	2	3	4	5	6	7

(completely false)   (completely true)

Say, *"Think of the event and hold it together with the words* _____ *(repeat the PC). Go with that."*

Continue this procedure until the validity of cognition (VOC) is 7.

Phase 6: Body Scan

Say, *"Close your eyes and keep in mind the original memory and the positive cognition. Then bring your attention to the different parts of your body, starting with your head and working downward. Any place you find any tension, tightness, or unusual sensation, tell me."*

If any sensation is reported, the therapist introduces BLS.

If it is a positive or comfortable sensation, BLS is used to strengthen the positive feelings.

If a sensation of discomfort is reported, this is reprocessed until the discomfort subsides. Finally, the VOC has to be checked.

Say, *"As you think of the incident, how do the words feel from 1 being completely false to 7 being completely true?"*

1	2	3	4	5	6	7

(completely false)   (completely true)

Check All Other Targets (Past Memories and Current Triggers)

See Phase 1: History Taking: Determine an appropriate and feasible treatment goal and decide whether it is still necessary to reprocess these experiences (SUD when bringing up the memory is greater than 0).

Say, *"Okay, let's check the next target that is in your list* _____ *(state the next target). On a scale of 0 to 10, where 0 is no disturbance or neutral and 10 is the highest disturbance you can imagine, how disturbing does it feel now?"*

0	1	2	3	4	5	6	7	8	9	10

(no disturbance)   (highest disturbance)

If the SUD is greater than 0, continue the procedure and start at Phase 8: Reevaluation.

Future Template Installation

If all targets (Phase 1: History Taking: Determine an Appropriate and Feasible Treatment Goal) as well as current triggers are processed, clients may still have to anticipate future situations in which the former phobic stimuli are present (e.g., at the table sitting in front of the plate situation) and in which they need to interact with these stimuli. To prepare for that, clients are asked to mentally progress in time to identify a specific mental image of a typical future situation by which the fear, prior to this session, certainly would have been triggered. This may be a situation that clients usually avoid because of fear or a situation that they, until now, are not able to enter or to undergo without fear.

Say, *"Okay, we have reprocessed all of the targets that we needed to that were on your list. Now let's anticipate what will happen when you are faced with* _____ *(state the anxiety-provoking object or situation). Think of a time in the future and identify a mental image or photo of a typical situation that would have triggered your fear prior to our work together. What would that be?"*

_____

_____

Say, *"I would like you to imagine yourself coping effectively with _____ (state the fear trigger) in the future. Please focus on the image; say to yourself, 'I can handle it'; notice the sensations associated with this future scene and follow my fingers (or any other BLS)."*

Say, *"To what extent do you believe you are able to actually handle this situation (VOC) on a scale of 1 to 7, where 1 feels completely false and 7 feels completely true?"*

1	2	3	4	5	6	7

(completely false)   (completely true)

The therapist continues with this procedure (instruction and VOC rating) until the future template is sufficiently installed (VOC = 7).

If there is a block, meaning that even after 10 or more installations the VOC is still below 7, there are more targets that need to be identified and addressed. The therapist should use the Standard EMDR Protocol to address these targets, before proceeding with the template (see worksheets in the Appendix). Also, evaluate whether clients need any new information, resources, or skills to be able to comfortably visualize the future coping scene. Introduce this needed information or skill.

Say, *"What would you need to feel confident in handling the situation?"*

_____

_____

Or say, *"What is missing from your handling of this situation?"*

_____

_____

Video Check

After the incorporation of a positive template for future action, the clinician asks clients to close their eyes and to run a mental video.

Say, *"This time, I'd like you to imagine yourself stepping into the future. Close your eyes and play a movie from the beginning until the end. Imagine yourself coping with any challenges that come your way. Notice what you are seeing, thinking, feeling, and experiencing in your body. While playing this movie, let me know if you hit any blocks. If you do, just open your eyes and let me know. If you don't hit any blocks, let me know when you have viewed the whole movie."*

If clients encounter a block and open their eyes, this is a sign for the therapist to instruct clients to say the following:

"Say to yourself, 'I can handle it' and follow my fingers (or other form of BLS)."

_____

_____

The mental videotape is repeated until it can be viewed entirely without distress.

Say, *"Please repeat the video until it can be viewed entirely without distress."*

_____

_____

To provide the clinician with an indication regarding clients' self-efficacy, have them rate their response on a VOC scale from 1 to 7. This procedural step may give the clinician feedback on the extent to which the goals are met.

Say, *"As you think of the incident, how do the words feel from 1 being completely false to 7 being completely true?"*

1	2	3	4	5	6	7

(completely false)   (completely true)

If clients are able to play the movie from start to finish with a sense of confidence and satisfaction, they are asked to play the movie once more from the beginning to the end, BLS is introduced, and the PC "I can handle it" is installed. In a sense, this movie is installed as a future template.

Say, *"Okay, play the movie one more time from beginning to end and say to yourself, 'I can handle it.' Go with that."*

_____

_____

Phase 7: Closure

Incomplete Session

The session is incomplete when there is still unresolved material:

- If there is still discomfort or the SUD score is greater than 1
- If the VOC score is less than 6
- If negative feelings persist in the body scan
- If the SUD is greater than 1, skip Phases 5 and 6

Congratulate the client for the work done and assess the need for stabilization techniques and relaxation, containment, and/or sensory orientation exercises.

Say, *"We're almost out of time and need to stop soon. You've done a good job and I really appreciate the effort you made. How do you feel?"*

_____

_____

Say, *"We will not go on with the installation of positive cognition or body scan because there is still material to be processed. However, we will do a containment exercise."*

Say, *"I would like for us to do a relaxation exercise before stopping. Would you like to do the _____ (suggest a form of relaxation, such as safe place)?"*

_____

_____

Complete Session

Once stabilized, say the following:

> *"Things may come up or they may not. If they do, great. Write them down and it can be a target for the next time. You can use a log to write down triggers, images, thoughts or cognitions, emotions, and sensations; you can rate them on our 0-to-10 scale, where 0 is no disturbance or neutral and 10 is the worst disturbance. Please write down the positive experiences, too. If you get any new memories, dreams, or situations that disturb you, just take a good snapshot. It isn't necessary to give a lot of detail. Just put down enough to remind you so we can target it the next time. The same thing goes for any positive dreams or situations. If negative feelings do come up, try not to make them significant. Remember, it's still just the old stuff. Just write it down for the next time. Then use the safe place exercise to let go of as much of the disturbance as possible. Even if nothing comes up, make sure to use the safe place every day and give me a call if you need to."*

Phase 8: Reevaluation

Evaluate whatever is left to be done.

Say, *"What have you been noticing since our last session?"*

_____

_____

Say, *"What are the current symptoms (if any) you have been noticing?"*

_____

_____

Say, *"What kind of progress have you noticed, especially in terms of the homework?"*

_____

_____

Say, *"As you think back on the target that we were working on last time, on a scale of 0 to 10, where 0 is no disturbance or neutral and 10 is the highest disturbance you can imagine, how disturbing does it feel now?"*

0	1	2	3	4	5	6	7	8	9	10

(no disturbance)   (highest disturbance)

If the disturbance level has increased, these reverberations need to be targeted or otherwise addressed.

Reprocessing an Incomplete Target

If the target was incomplete in the previous session, return to the incomplete target and continue reprocessing.

Say, *"Bring back to mind the incident _____ (state the incident) we worked on in the previous session. What comes up?"*

_____

_____

Say, *"What thoughts arise?"*

_____

_____

Say, *"What emotions arise?"*

_____

_____

Say, *"What physical sensations arise?"*

_____

_____

Accessing the Baseline

Say, *"On a scale of 0 to 10, where 0 is no disturbance or neutral and 10 is the highest disturbance you can imagine, how disturbing does it feel now?"*

    0   1   2   3   4   5   6   7   8   9   10

(no disturbance)   (highest disturbance)

Continue reprocessing.

Say, *"Go with that."*

Continue until Phases 4, 5, and 6 are complete. This is when the client has reached SUDs = 0 and VOC = 7 and the body scan presents no disturbances.

If target is complete, we recommend continuing with the treatment plan and reprocessing further targets.

SUMMARY

This chapter explains the EMDR Therapy Protocol for Eating Disorders, detailing everything the clinician must take into consideration in order to proceed step by step throughout the eight phases of treatment. The goal is to process those traumas and adverse experiences that are the foundation of these disorders, using the artichoke metaphor: working layer by layer from the outside in. Each and every layer holds a part, a defense, and a trauma or adverse life experience, as specified in the PDT system. Once the part is named and the defense is identified, it is possible to reach the targeted event/trauma and process it with the Standard EMDR Protocol. As these events are processed, clients integrate the parts of their inner world. This will be reflected directly in an improvement in their relationship with food and, as a result, the disorder will improve.

REFERENCES

Freyd, J., Deprince, A., & Gleaves, D. (2007). The state of betrayal trauma theory: Reply to McNally—Conceptual issues, and future directions. *Memory, 15*(3), 295–311. doi:10.1080/09658210701256514

Garner, D. M. (2004). *EDI 3: Easting disorder inventory-3: Professional manual*. Odessa, FL: Psychological Assessment Resources.

Halvgaard, K. (2015). Single case study: Does EMDR psychotherapy work on emotional eating? *Journal of EMDR Practice and Research, 9*(4), 188–197. doi:10.1891/1933-3196.9.4.188

Knipe, J. (2015). *EMDR toolbox. Theory and treatment of complex PTSD and dissociation*. New York, NY: Springer Publishing.

Learly, M. R. (1983). A brief version of the fear of negative evaluation scale. *Personality and Social Psychology, 9*, 371–385. doi:10.1177/0146167283093007

Liotti, G. (1999). Disorganization of attachment as a model for understanding dissociative psychopathology. In J. Solomon & C. George (Eds.), *Attachment disorganization* (pp. 291–317). New York, NY: Guilford Press.

Probst, M., Vandereycken, W., van Coppenolle, H., & Vanderlinden, J. (1995). The Body Attitude Test for patients with an eating disorder: Psychometric characteristics of a new questionnaire. *Eating Disorders: The Journal of Treatment & Prevention, 3*(2), 133–144. doi:10.1080/10640269508249156

Schuder, M. R., & Lyons-Ruth, K. (2004). "Hidden Trauma" in infancy: Attachment, fearful arousal, and early dysfunction of the stress response system. In J. D. Osofsky (Ed.), *Young children and trauma: Intervention and treatment* (pp. 69–104). New York, NY: Guilford Press.

Seijo, N. (2012). EMDR and eating disorders. *Revista Hispanoamericana de Psicotraumatología y Disociación, 4.*

Seijo, N. (2015). *Somatic defenses* (master's theses). Universidad Nacional de Educación a Distancia, Madrid, Spain.

van der Hart, O., Nijenhuis, E. R. S., & Steele, K. (2006). *The haunted self: Structural dissociation and the treatment of chronic traumatization.* New York, NY: W. W. Norton.

Watson, D., & Friend, R. (1969). Measurement of social-evaluative anxiety. *Journal of Consulting and Clinical Psychology, 33*(4), 448–457. doi:10.1037/h0027806

World Health Organization (1992). *The ICD-10 classification of mental and behavioural disorders: Clinical descriptions and diagnostic guidelines.* Geneva, Switzerland: World Health Organization.

Natalia Seijo
SUMMARY SHEET BY MARILYN LUBER

Name: _____ Diagnosis: _____

Medications: _____

Test Results: _____

☑ Check when task is completed, response has changed, or to indicate symptoms.

Note: This material is meant as a checklist for your response. Please keep in mind that it is only a reminder of different tasks that may or may not apply to your incident.

INTRODUCTION

Diagnoses *ICD-10*

☐ *F50.0 Anorexia Nervosa*: Disorder characterized by the presence of deliberate weight loss, induced or maintained by the client.

☐ *F50.1 Atypical Anorexia Nervosa*: This term must be used in cases in which one or more main characteristics of anorexia nervosa are missing (F50.0), like amenorrhea or significant weight loss, but that otherwise present a pretty typical clinical picture. These clients are usually found in consultation and liaison psychiatry as well as in primary care. Clients who have all the important symptoms of anorexia nervosa, but to a mild degree, can also be included here. This term must not be used for eating disorders that are similar to anorexia nervosa but which are due to a known somatic etiology.

☐ *F50.2 Bulimia Nervosa*: Syndrome characterized by repeated episodes of excessive intake of food and by an exaggerated concern over control of body weight, which makes the client adopt extreme measures to mitigate weight gain deriving from the intake of food. This term should be restricted to the forms of the disorder that are related to anorexia nervosa by sharing the same pathologies. The disorder may be considered an effect of persistent anorexia nervosa (although the opposite sequence is also possible). At first glance, a previously anorexic client may appear to be getting better by gaining weight—and even recovering her menstruation if it's a woman—but then a malignant form of behavior characterized by overeating and vomiting emerges. Repeated vomiting may result in electrolyte balance disorders, in somatic complications (seizures, cardiac arrhythmia, or muscle weakness), and in further weight loss.

☐ *F50.3 Atypical Bulimia Nervosa*: This term must be used in those cases that lack one or more of the main characteristics of bulimia nervosa (F50.2), but which otherwise present a pretty typical clinical picture. The clients usually have normal weight or even higher than normal, but present repeated episodes of excessive food intake followed by vomiting or purging. It is not rare to find partial syndromes accompanied by depressive symptoms (if these symptoms fulfill the criteria for a depressive disorder, a dual diagnosis must be made).

☐ *F50.4 Overeating Associated With Other Psychological Alterations*: Excessive food intake as a reaction to stressful events that gives way to obesity. Grieving, accidents, surgical interventions, and emotionally stressful events may result in "reactive obesity," especially in clients prone to weight gain. Obesity as the cause of psychological alterations must not be codified here. Obesity may make the client feel very sensitized about his or her appearance and trigger lack of confidence in intercliental relationships. The subjective assessment of bodily dimensions may be exaggerated. In order to codify obesity as the cause of psychological alteration, categories such as F38.8-, other mood disorders (affective); F41.2, mixed anxiety depressive disorder; or F48.9, neurotic disorder not otherwise specified, plus an E66.- code to indicate the type of obesity, must be used.

☐ *F50.5 Vomiting Associated With Other Psychological Alterations*: Besides bulimia nervosa, in which vomiting is self-induced, repeated vomiting may be present in dissociative disorders (conversion; F44.8-); in hypochondria (F45.2), in which vomiting may be one of the multiple bodily symptoms; and during pregnancy, where emotional factors may contribute to the appearance of recurring vomiting and nausea.

Measures

☐ Eating Disorder Inventory-2 (EDI-2; Garner, 1991)
☐ Body Attitude Test (BAT; Probst et al., 1995)
☐ Fear of Negative Evaluation (FNE) Scale (Learly, 1983; Watson & Friend, 1969)

EMDR PROTOCOL FOR EATING DISORDERS PROTOCOL

Phase 1: History Taking

General Aspects: Diagnosis and Comorbidity

Diagnosis: _____

Past diagnosis: _____

Anamnesis

Age: _____

Studies: _____

Marital status: _____

Do genogram: ☐ Yes ☐ No

Previous psychological and mental treatments: ☐ Yes ☐ No

Comment: _____

What treatments work and what do not: _____

Eating Disorder History

WEIGHT HISTORY

Height: _____

Minimum weight: _____

Maximum weight: _____

Comment: _____

Constipation or diarrhea: ☐ Yes ☐ No

Comment: _____

Following diet or meal regime: ☐ Yes ☐ No

Comment: _____

Name of nutritionist: _____

Questions for AN:

Lanuga—fine hair in places where none before:	☐ Yes ☐ No

Comment: _____

Palms an unusual orange color:	☐ Yes ☐ No

Comment: _____

Excess energy despite weight loss:	☐ Yes ☐ No

Comment: _____

Colder—especially hands and feet:	☐ Yes ☐ No

Comment: _____

Dizziness and heart feels different:	☐ Yes ☐ No

Comment: _____

You feel emotions less like losing sensitivity:	☐ Yes ☐ No

Comment: _____

You are aware of your illness:	☐ Yes ☐ No

Comment: _____

If no, what is the reason you are here: _____

If yes, what is the disorder: _____

Questions for BN

How many times binge a day: _____

You vomit after bingeing or compensate in other ways:	☐ Yes ☐ No

Comment: _____

Calluses on your knuckles:	☐ Yes ☐ No

Comment: _____

Petechiae/little red dots of blood under eyes:	☐ Yes ☐ No

Comment: _____

Heart beats faster or irregular like tachycardia:	☐ Yes ☐ No

Comment: _____

Shape of chin changed:	☐ Yes ☐ No

Comment: _____

Small painful marks in corners of mouth that bleed occasionally:	☐ Yes ☐ No

Comment: _____

If no, what is the reason you are here: _____

If yes, what is the disorder: _____

Questions for BED

Swelling in body:	☐ Yes ☐ No

Comment: _____

Abdominal pain: ☐ Yes ☐ No

Comment: _____

Leg pain: ☐ Yes ☐ No

Comment: _____

Menses for first time: _____

Family's reaction: _____

Period ever disappeared for some time: ☐ Yes ☐ No

Comment: _____

You get your period currently: ☐ Yes ☐ No

Comment: _____

It is regular every month: ☐ Yes ☐ No

Comment: _____

HISTORY OF THE CURRENT EPISODE

First/most significant paid attention to food rather than simply eating: _____

_____

What happened: _____

What about food: _____

Where you learned to do it that way: _____

Current eating habits: _____

Ask family about eating habits if not sufficient information: _____

_____

RESTRICTION EPISODES

Describe moments of restriction especially at dinner table: _____

_____

You feel more disturbance and parts activated and conflicts increase: ☐ Yes ☐ No

Comment: _____

Dissociate during meals: ☐ Yes ☐ No

Comment: _____

After eating you feel guilty for eating: ☐ Yes ☐ No

Comment: _____

You feel more distrust during meals: ☐ Yes ☐ No

Comment: _____

BINGEING AND/OR VOMITING EPISODES

Experienced bingeing currently or in past: ☐ Yes ☐ No

Comment: _____

Describe the bingeing: _____

_____

How long bingeing: _____

How often bingeing: _____

Bingeing serves a function such as feeling full, empty, sad, lonely, and so on: ☐ Yes ☐ No

Comment: _____

First time bingeing: _____

Earliest/most significant memories associated with vomiting: _____

_____

What went on in your life at that time: _____

_____

CURRENT TRIGGERS

Identify current triggers for bingeing: _____

_____

Situations that lead you to binge, vomit, or compensate in other ways: _____

_____

Where you learned to do this: _____

PURGING

You compensate bingeing with vomiting: ☐ Yes ☐ No

Comment: _____

Use medications like diuretics or laxatives: ☐ Yes ☐ No

Comment: _____

HOSPITALIZATIONS

Hospitalized for eating problems: ☐ Yes ☐ No

Comment: _____

Visited other medical centers because of the disorder, emergency room/medical visits: ☐ Yes ☐ No

Comment: _____

Food History

HISTORY OF MEALTIMES

Who sat at table during meals: _____

_____

How mealtimes are for you now: _____

_____

Describe family eating habits—fast or slow eating: _____

_____

Who cooks or used to cook at home: _____

_____

Your eating habits at home: _____

_____

Diet balanced or not: □ Yes □ No

Comment: _____

Someone at home who is or has been on a diet: □ Yes □ No

Comment: _____

TIME SPENT IN FRONT OF THE PLATE

Time spent at meals: _____

_____

Time in front of plate: □ A lot □ Finish quickly

Comment: _____

OVERFEEDING

Overfeeding figure in family who fed you too much: □ Yes □ No

Comment: _____

If yes, how you were fed: _____

_____

When done: _____

_____

Attachment Issues

Attachment to mother: □ Loving and close □ Cold and distant

Comment: _____

Relationship between parents: _____

_____

_____

Relationship with each parent now and before: _____

_____

_____

Attachment to father: □ Loving and close □ Cold and distant

Comment: _____

Parents: □ Married □ Divorced

Comment: _____

If divorced, describe relationship with respective partners: _____

_____

ATTACHMENT TRAUMA

Living situation during childhood and adolescence: ☐ Same place ☐ Distant place

Comment: _____

Who made you feel most validated and understood in your life: _____

_____

Who made you feel least validated and understood in your life: _____

_____

What needed to feel validated and understood in your life: _____

_____

Who gives you the most love: _____

_____

Who made you feel safest: _____

_____

Father's typical expression: _____

_____

Mother's typical expression: _____

_____

Who gives you the most love: _____

_____

You were a parentified child: ☐ Yes ☐ No

Comment: _____ _____

Times parents or significant people made you feel unworthy: _____

_____

Times parents or significant people did not give you comfort as you needed: _____

_____

Times parents or significant people rigid or perfectionist with you, forcing you to meet high standards: _____

_____

Times parents or significant people compared you to others, leaving you in worse position: _____

_____

Trauma History

TRAUMATIC EVENTS

You suffered any accident that left an emotional/physical impact: ☐ Yes ☐ No

Comment: _____

You suffered an important and difficult loss of a loved one: ☐ Yes ☐ No

Comment: _____

You suffered any major loss that caused you emotional pain: ☐ Yes ☐ No

Comment: _____

HUMILIATION TRAUMA

You suffered abuse of power that made you feel humiliated or submissive: ☐ Yes ☐ No

Comment: _____

BETRAYAL TRAUMA

You felt betrayed by someone: ☐ Yes ☐ No

Comment: _____

You suffered sexual abuse, touching, or inappropriate behavior: ☐ Yes ☐ No

Comment: _____

You felt someone looked at you in a way that made you feel uncomfortable: ☐ Yes ☐ No

Comment: _____

DIETING TRAUMA

Times on a diet: _____

First diet. How old: _____

_____

Whose idea to start dieting: _____

Worst moment of all diets on: _____

_____

Define the worst moment about being on a diet: _____ _____

_____

There was a need for a diet: ☐ Yes ☐ No

Comment: _____

What happens inside you at mealtimes: _____

_____

HIDDEN TRAUMA

You have had to self-soothe/self-regulate: ☐ Yes ☐ No

Comment: _____

If yes, you have had someone to help you to self-soothe/self-regulate: ☐ Yes ☐ No

Comment: _____

If no, when you realized there was no one to look after you to help you calm down: _____

_____

Needed to have needs taken care of but did not happen: ☐ Yes ☐ No

Comment: _____

Felt emotionally validated and understood when sad or angry: ☐ Yes ☐ No

Comment: _____

BODY HISTORY

What you think about when you think of your body: _____

_____

What words/adjectives you use to define your body: _____ _____

_____

Any physical marks from ED that worry you: ☐ Yes ☐ No

Comment: _____

You received negative comments about your body: ☐ Yes ☐ No

Comment: _____ _____

If yes, from whom: _____

_____

You cause damage to your body because upset or channeling frustration: ☐ Yes ☐ No

Comment: _____

If yes, what you did: _____

_____

Phase 2: Preparation

Introducing the Preparation Phase   ☐ Yes ☐ No

"We are going to start organizing the work that we will be doing throughout the sessions, so you can understand it and trust the process. We need you and me to become a team, so you can feel that you're not alone in this.

We will first identify the aspects or parts of you that are part of your inner world. Then, we will start neutralizing the potential defenses that may arise, which will let us know that we need to stop and check. This way, we will know that we are moving along at the right pace, and not too fast, especially with life or food issues that perhaps may be difficult for you to cope with.

In order to do so, we will respect your defenses, which give us very valuable information. We will neutralize them by using a resource that helps your inner world and parts; in this way, we will move forward little by little with our work.

The goal is for you to start feeling better. There may be some moments that are harder than others, but the important thing is to be able to extract a resource from those difficult moments, which will help us move forward."

Psychoeducation Regarding the Edge of Trauma and Somatic Identifiers   ☐ Yes ☐ No

"The first thing we need is to be able to understand how your inner world works. For this, we must iden-tify the sensations that will let us know that we are approaching the edge of the trauma, which is the line that establishes the point that can be reached at any given time in therapy. We will always remain one or two steps away from this edge of the trauma, so you can feel that the process is safe and have an inner sense of control that everything is okay.

In order to know when we are approaching this edge of the trauma, we will explore which are the sen-sations or emotions you usually notice when you become dysregulated. For example, you could have the sensation of not feeling the body, or suddenly becoming very tired and sleepy, or not being present, or a rapid heartbeat. There may be sensations of this kind or similar that may indicate that we are approaching the edge. If so, let me know and we will stop and introduce a resource that will help you to feel calm and know that everything is okay."

Identifying the Inner World

"The structure of this next phase of our work focuses on two basic points: identifying the parts of your inner world and the defenses that normally protect these parts.

The inner world represents your personality and could be explained as an orchestra. An orchestra is composed of musicians who are led by a conductor. When the musicians play in unison and follow the conductor, the orchestra sounds great. However, when one of the musicians becomes unruly and refuses to play or wants to take over from the orchestra conductor or chooses to play an instrument different from the one he or she has been assigned, the orchestra will not sound good.

The same thing happens in your inner world when aspects or parts of you want to perform functions that are not appropriate; things do not work well inside. So, our job will be to organize every aspect of you that is not in its proper place. As the work develops, you will meet every part of you, and this will help you understand much better what is happening to you and get out of the eating disorder from which you suffer."

Throughout the process, it is important to validate the client, promote compassion from understanding, and help organize the chaotic inner world and its parts, naming and describing them in detail.

"I see that it is difficult for you to understand what is happening inside, since you probably feel a certain chaos that often does not allow you to identify what is happening. In order for you to understand it better, I will introduce the different states or parts in which your inner world is divided, so you can organize your internal world."

IDENTIFYING PARTS, NEUTRALIZING DEFENSES, AND ACCESSING TRAUMA

"In order to start organizing your inner world, we will begin by naming the parts and explaining what function and belief they have within you. These are the parts or states that I will explain in detail in a few minutes: the little girl who never was; the little girl who could not grow up; the pathological critic; the rejected self; the hidden self; the fat self.

Just so you can understand better, these states or internal parts I just named generate defenses. Defenses are all those inner experiences that make us unable to continue processing at a certain point in time. These inner experiences may be an emotion, a thought, a sensation, or a movement arising from the body. Every part or state generates its own defense(s), which we will identify so we can neutralize them and move forward with our work, little by little and always trusting the process."

Artichoke Metaphor

"The inner world could be represented by the artichoke metaphor that helps us see all the layers covering up the inner world, as a way to protect its most vulnerable part. When working with EMDR therapy, each of these layers contains the traumas, adverse experiences, and defenses that may arise. We will gradually process each one of these layers until we reach the artichoke heart and repair what needs to be repaired. This is always done with great care, respecting the inner world and, above all, trusting the process. Once we start working with parts, you will see that each one has a specific defense, but so you can understand how this develops based on the artichoke metaphor, this will be explained in greater detail.

The model of treatment in EDs is developed from the outside in, starting at the outermost layers and moving inward. Each time a layer is accessed, we open a process that follows the pattern: part, defense, trauma, or the PDT system. When the parts of the inner system are activated, the defenses are triggered. The defenses are the way in which the parts learned to protect the system. The fear of making contact with what is difficult to remember activates the defenses in order to avoid the pain. By softening these defenses, accessing trauma or adverse life experiences and reprocessing these memories with the Standard EMDR Protocol becomes possible. For example, if the part of "the child who never was" becomes activated and the defense of control appears, using the PDT system, we will ask the question, "Where did this part of you learn to control in this way?" or "Where did this part of you learn to protect you through control?" This question will give us access to the memories that are held by the part, which will be processed."

The Parts/States in EDs and Their Corresponding Beliefs

"Each one of the previously named parts has its own basic belief, from which other beliefs may stem. As we talk about each part, I will want to know whether/how much of this fits your experience.

When working with the parts/defense/trauma system, I will ask you to identify the triggers that activate it. This could be a current situation, a client relationship, or an event that threatens the inner world. For each part, this threat will make a different defense emerge. The origin of this defense and its corresponding belief is the trauma with which you connect when we explore where you learned to defend your inner work in each specific way."

THE BELIEF OF "THE CHILD WHO NEVER WAS" OR WORKING WITH CONTROL

"'The child who never was' contains the pain and frustration of having to learn to do things alone. It represents the self-sufficient child, who has been forced to grow up quickly and become an 'adult' in childhood. The child has learned to self-regulate and to have self-control through food and does things in _____ (his/her) own way. This part, which learned to defend the inner system through control, holds the belief 'Things must be done my way'."

This explanation fits your experience: ☐ Yes ☐ No

Comment: _____

Triggers that activate this part: _____

_____

How old the part is: _____

When the part started to exist: _____

Where you learned to feel like this: _____

Describe when this part learned to defend you through control: _____

_____

_____

THE BELIEF OF "THE CHILD WHO COULD NOT GROW UP" OR WORKING WITH GUILT

"'The child who could not grow up' failed to go through an adequate maturational development and shows some inappropriate behaviors for ____ (his/her) age. This is a lost child who does not know if talking is allowed or not and, through food, has found a way of being seen. This part defends the inner world through guilt such as 'Not being seen is my fault.' The main belief is 'One needs to get sick in order to get some attention'."

This explanation fits your experience: ☐ Yes ☐ No

Comment: _____

Triggers that activate this part: _____

_____

How old the part is: _____

When the part started to exist: _____

Where you learned to feel like this: _____

Describe when this part learned to defend you through guilt: _____

_____

_____

THE BELIEF OF "THE HIDDEN SELF" OR WORKING WITH SHAME AND FEAR

"'The hidden self' protects the inner system by hiding, not exposing or showing the self, since whenever this was done in the past, things became threatening or even dangerous. Staying in the shadows ends up being safer. This part develops early in life and somatizes what cannot be expressed otherwise. This part, which learned to defend the inner system through shame, holds the belief 'I cannot show myself or stand out because if I do, I will get hurt'."

This explanation fits your experience: ☐ Yes ☐ No

Comment: _____

Triggers that activate this part: _____

How old the part is: _____

When the part started to exist: _____

Where you learned to feel like this: _____

Describe when this part learned to defend you through shame: _____

_____

_____

THE BELIEF OF "THE PATHOLOGICAL CRITIC/THE PIRANHA" OR WORKING WITH PERFECTIONISM

"'The Piranha' is the inner critic, always judging and blocking your self-esteem, filtering reality, and letting in only the negative perspective. This part imitates, in the inner world, those who criticized and judged the child in real life, resulting in a constant comparison to others. This part, which learned to defend the inner system through criticism, holds the belief 'Nothing is ever good enough'."

This explanation fits your experience: ☐ Yes ☐ No

Comment: _____

Triggers that activate this part: _____

_____

How old the part is: _____

When the part started to exist: _____

Where you learned to feel like this: _____

Describe when this part learned to defend you through criticism: _____

_____

_____

THE BELIEF OF "THE REJECTED SELF" OR WORKING WITH BODY IMAGE DISTORTION

"'The rejected self' is a part of you from either the past or the present that you reject and of which you are ashamed. This part may hold feelings of disgust or contempt, and it may have been there throughout the years as an imprinted image of what you never want to be again, and through which you see yourself when looking in the mirror."

This explanation fits your experience: ☐ Yes ☐ No

Comment: _____

Triggers that activate this part: _____

_____

How old the part is: _____

When the part started to exist: _____

Where you learned to feel like this: _____

Describe the oldest or most significant memory where you have felt or seen yourself rejected: _____

_____

_____

THE BELIEF OF "THE FAT SELF" OR WORKING WITH REJECTION AND SUBMISSION

"'The fat self' covers the unmet needs through the body. Weight gain is the protective somatic defense of this part, so the client hides underneath this self or takes more space in the world because he or she does not feel seen. This part, which learned to defend the inner system through rejection and submission, holds the beliefs, 'There is no place for me in this world' and 'I am inadequate because I am fat'."

This explanation fits your experience: ☐ Yes ☐ No

Comment: _____

Triggers that activate this part: _____

_____

How old the part is: _____

When the part started to exist: _____

Where you learned to feel like this: _____

Describe when this part learned to defend you through gaining weight: _____

_____

_____

Explanation of EMDR as in the Standard EMDR Protocol   ☐ Yes ☐ No

"When a trauma occurs, it seems to get locked in the nervous system with the original picture, sounds, thoughts, and feelings. The eye movements we use in EMDR seem to unlock the nervous system and allow the brain to process the experience. That may be what is happening in REM or dream sleep—the eye movements may help to process the unconscious material. It is important to note that it is your own brain that will be doing the healing and that you are the one in control. When we process following the Three-Pronged Protocol, we are talking about the fact of the experiences of the past, which affect your present life; once they are processed, they stop affecting you and will not disturb you in the future."

Subprotocol for Working With the "Piranha": The Metaphor for the Mechanism of Criticism

"I would now like to start working with this part of you, the most critical part of your inner world, which has been called Piranha because of how it behaves inside. This does not mean it is a negative part; this is not the case, even though it may seem so at times, but the way in which it shows up can be quite aggressive. The Piranha avoids emotional pain by imitating the attachment figure whose comments were hurtful. The basic idea is that if internal self-criticism is more intense, external criticism will be less painful. The goal is for the Piranha to transform into healthy self-criticism and help regulate the inner world.

Those needs not covered by others are truly the needs that you are not covering for yourself. In order to differentiate what is internal from what is external, I would like you to imagine a membrane dividing the inner and outer worlds. By doing this, you can now realize that what is inside your membrane belongs to you and what is outside of the membrane belongs to the external world.

The healthy critic has the role of regulating how you regard yourself, providing a point of view based on reality and regulating self-esteem and self-concept in a way that develops acceptance. However, when

the critic becomes unhealthy and turns into the Piranha part, it generates internal communication that is harmful for you.

In order to explain the personality distortion, I shall use a real-life situation. Imagine you meet up with a friend, and during the conversation, he tells you that he's tired. If the Piranha uses this distortion at this moment, it's likely that you will start thinking that you are boring him. Focusing on this does not give you the option of thinking that he may be tired for many different reasons, but your being boring is more than likely not one of them. One way of understanding the polarized thinking distortion might be how something white doesn't turn black because of a stain. There are many colors and ranges between them, and white is just one more color.

Filtering is another cognitive distortion that this part uses as a way of transforming internal experience. It could be described as if the Piranha put a filter in front of your senses. This is the way reality becomes filtered. Negative information would get filtered. Positive information is there, but it's about how this part filters it for you. It's as if in addition to filtering, it records and saves it for a more convenient time. We will pay attention to how it happens. For example, you go somewhere or speak to someone, and after the situation occurs, the Piranha reminds you how inadequate you were. It may also associate this event with other past situations when you were as inadequate as in the previous one. This will make you feel bad and trigger feelings of inadequacy, harming your self-esteem."

Questions/comments: _____

_____

THE TELESCOPE METAPHOR

"Let me explain to you, by using a metaphor, how this Piranha part functions in your mind. Imagine a telescope that you aim toward the stars. How do you see them?

Okay, so now imagine what happens if you turn the telescope around and look through the other end. Okay, you see them farther away. Now, imagine the telescope once again and see what happens now if you change the telescope's lens for one that is cracked.

You are doing very well. Imagine the telescope again and see what happens if you change the lens to one that is cracked and also smeared with grease. You would see blurry stains, wouldn't you? Well, you know what? That is how the Piranha makes you look at reality most of the time. That is one of the reasons why we have to change the cracked and stained lens for one that is only cracked, and once you are able to perceive something other than stains, we can change it for a crystal-clear lens, so that you can tell me you see the stars clearly, although far away. Then we'll be able to turn the telescope around and you'll be able to see them crystal clear. In order to achieve this, it will be necessary to work with the Piranha's distortions and be able to recognize them. This will make it possible for you to differentiate what is your own from what is external and, thus, change the lenses. It is not a part or state against which we have to fight. Instead, it is a part of you that we will have to help heal because it's become unhealthy."

INTERVENTION

"All the negative thoughts that come up about yourself and make you suffer come from the Piranha. Since people do not gratuitously harm themselves, there is something that is not healthy and we must help it become healthy, so you can get to see yourself as you truly are, accept yourself and be okay with it."

What thoughts Piranha showed you: _____

_____

What proof you have it is true: _____

_____

Alternative interpretations: _____

_____

What kind of distortion it is: _____

How the thought makes you feel: _____

_____

If true, the worst that could happen: _____

_____

What Piranha is covering up by what it shows you: _____

_____

What you would say about how Piranha acted in that situation: _____

_____

Other ways Piranha could act and speak to you: _____

_____

Describe where Piranha learned to defend you through criticism: _____

_____

What proof you have it is true: _____

_____

"Let us take each one of these memories and process them with the Standard EMDR Protocol so this part of you can become more integrated and develop into healthy criticism. We will work with the earliest or most significant memory that came up for you when I asked you where your 'Piranha' learned to defend you through criticism."

Subprotocols for Working With Defenses

(Use these subprotocols when necessary throughout treatment when defenses block the continuation of the process.)

LACK OF ILLNESS AWARENESS DEFENSE

"Think of a time or times when you have realized that something is happening with food in your life.

_____

_____

Think of that sentence ____ *(see the previous sentence)."* Do BLS to reduce the defense and locate the blocking point. _____

_____

Explore the defense.

"What is good about not identifying with the ED?" _____

_____

"What is bad about not identifying with the ED?" _____

_____

SOMATIC DEFENSES AND REPROCESSING

(This work gives voice to that defense that blocks the internal experience and identifies its function).

"Allow yourself to notice what is coming up in the body right now that is preventing us from continuing to process. Describe to me what you are feeling and where you feel it in the body." _____

_____

Sensation/Pain/Bodily experience + Express in words = _____

_____

+ BLS

"What does that _____ (name sensation/pain/bodily experience) *say about you?"* _____

Or say, *"If* _____ (name sensation/pain/bodily experience) *had words, what would it tell you?"*

_____

_____

SUD: ____/10

Do BLS. If no belief, use somatic reaction and assess:

SUD: ____/10

Belief/Somatic reaction + BLS

"Please focus on the physical reaction you are noticing and on a scale from 0 to 10, where 0 is no intensity or neutral and 10 is the highest intensity you can imagine, how intense does it feel now?"

____/10 Do BLS until SUD =0.

ALEXITHYMIA DEFENSE

(How client is "not feeling.")

Describe what you notice when "not feeling." _____

_____

To deactivate the defense:

"What happens inside of you when _____ (state what you experience when 'not feeling')?*"* _____

_____

Do BLS.

When defense lowers, explore the memories that generated this belief and use Standard EMDR Protocol (may not be able to get emotions and SUD). *"When do you remember having to start not feeling in order to protect yourself?"* _____

_____

When defense is deactivated, client can start to reconnect.

HUNGER DEFENSE (Differentiate defense of hunger from physical hunger)

"Does this sensation feel like physical hunger because you are really hungry or is it something that is similar to hunger but it is not?" _____

_____

"How does that feel and where do you feel it?" _____

_____

"This feeling is what we call the hunger defense. Check and see if you can identify the emotion it is covering up." _____

_____

"In what situations do the defense of hunger appear?" _____

_____

"What happens when the defense appears?" _____

_____

"If there was no such defense, what would happen?" _____ _____

_____

"Please, notice this sensation of hunger. On a scale from 0 to 10, where 0 is no sensation of hunger or neutral and 10 is the highest sensation of hunger you can imagine, how disturbing does it feel now?"

Do BLS.

FEAR OF IMPROVEMENT DEFENSE

"There seems to be something blocking the flow of therapy. Could you check inside and notice what is happening? Can you describe it for me?" _____

_____

_____

"This defense is called fear of improvement and it has to do with being scared of the possibility of improving and therapy being effective. Could you please check inside and let me know if this is how it is for you?" _____

_____

"Where do you notice the fear in your body?" _____

_____

"Please, notice this fear. On a scale from 0 to 10, where 0 is no fear or neutral and 10 is the most fear you can imagine, how much fear do you feel now?" ____/10

Do BLS to neutralize the defense and introduce the belief to which that fear of improvement may be related.

For anorexia: *"This fear is usually related to gaining weight and to the internal belief that 'I'm only worthy if I'm skinny'."*

____ (State Belief) + BLS
"Where did you learn that you're only worthy if you're skinny?" _____

_____

A memory or cluster of memories is obtained, which leads us to the trauma that will be processed in Phase 3 using the Standard EMDR Protocol. Maybe the client will say she does not feel the belief is true. In this case, the client may be in denial and unable to see and recognize the belief for the same reason: fear of improvement. This defense may require several sessions until the original trauma is processed.

In Bulimia and BED

"This fear is usually related to letting go of food and to the internal belief that 'Without food, I have no support.' Could you please focus on the belief 'Without food, I have no support'?" Do BLS.
This belief is usually true, so search for its origin: *"Where did you learn that without food, you have no support?"* _____

_____

A memory or cluster of memories is obtained, which leads to the trauma that will be processed in Phase 3 using the Standard EMDR Protocol.

Other issues to explore in both bulimia and BED are the following:

LACK OF CONTROL WITH FOOD

"In binge eating disorder (BED), one of the first steps in treatment is stabilizing the state in which you find yourself regarding food. For this, we will first dedicate time to the issue of lack of control over food. So, when you see yourself at the table with food in front of you, how much do you feel in control in regard to food?" _____

_____

*"If that lack of control said something about you, what would it say?"*_____

_____

The answer usually reveals the belief.

"When was the first or the earliest time that you felt this 'lack of control' along with the words ____ (state the belief from above)?" _____

_____

Using the Standard EMDR Protocol, target those memories that represent the lack of control so the client can retrieve the sensation of being in control.

THE URGE TO EAT

*"Let's focus on the feelings that represent the urge you feel when you're about to binge. We are going to work with this. When you think about the moment when you're about to binge, focus on the exact moment that represents the urge to go and get the food. How do you feel that urge in the body and what sensation represents it?"*_____

_____

Do BLS.

"Thank you for focusing on this situation where you feel the urge to eat and please notice this urge to eat you feel on a scale from 0 to 10, where 0 is no urge to eat or neutral and 10 is the biggest urge you can imagine. How much urge to eat do you feel now?" ___/10

THE URGE TO VOMIT

"Let's focus on the feelings that represent the urge you feel when you're about to vomit. We are going to work with this. When you think about the moment when you're about to vomit, where do you feel that urge in the body?" _____

_____

Do BLS.

"Thank you for focusing on this situation where you feel the urge to vomit and please notice this urge to vomit you feel on a scale from 0 to 10, where 0 is no urge to vomit or neutral and 10 is the biggest urge you can imagine. How much urge to vomit do you feel now?" _____/10

Do BLS.

Phase 3: Assessment

Target/Memory/Image: _____

_____

NC: _____

PC: _____

VOC: _____/7

Emotions: _____

SUD: ___/10

Sensation: _____

Phase 4: Desensitization

Apply the Standard EMDR Protocol for all targets

Image + NC + Sensations in body + BLS

Repeat until SUDs = 0 and VOC = 7/7

Phase 5: Installation

Install the PC.

Original PC: □ Use original PC □ Use new PC

New PC (if new one is better): _____

VOC: _____/7

Incident + PC + BLS

Phase 6: Body Scan

Unresolved tension/tightness/unusual sensation: _____

_____

Unresolved tension/tightness/unusual sensation + BLS

Strengthen positive sensation using BLS.

If there is more discomfort, reprocess until discomfort subsides + BLS. Then repeat body scan.

VOC: ___/7

Check other targets where SUDs are greater than 0. If the SUD is greater than 0, continue the procedure and start at Phase 8: Reevaluation.

Check All Other Targets (Past Memories and Current Triggers)

See Phase 1: History Taking: Determine an appropriate and feasible treatment goal and decide whether it is still necessary to reprocess these experiences (SUD when bringing up the memory is greater than 0).

SUDs = ____/10

If the SUD is greater than 0, continue the procedure and start at Phase 8: Reevaluation.

Future Template Installation

Installation of the Future Template (Image)
Image of coping effectively with/or in the fear trigger in the future: _____

_____

PC: (I can handle it) _____

Sensations: _____

+ BLS

VOC (able to handle the situation): ___/7

Install until VOC = 7

If continuing to be greater than 7, there are more targets to be identified and addressed and used with the Standard EMDR Protocol.

Blocks/Anxieties/Fears in future scene: _____

1. _____

2. _____

3. _____

Do BLS. If they do not resolve, ask for other qualities needed to handle the situation or what is missing.

1. _____

2. _____

3. _____

Use BLS. If blocks are not resolved, identify unprocessed material and process with Standard EMDR Protocol.

1. _____

2. _____

3. _____

Target/Memory/Image: _____

_____

NC: _____

PC: _____

VOC: _____/7

Emotions: _____

SUD: ___/10

Sensation: _____

Video Check (Future Template as Movie)

Say, *"This time, I'd like you to imagine yourself stepping into the future. Close your eyes, and play a movie from the beginning until the end. Imagine yourself coping with any challenges that come your way. Notice what you are seeing, thinking, feeling, and experiencing in your body. While playing this movie, let me know if you hit any blocks. If you do, just open your eyes and let me know. If you don't hit any blocks, let me know when you have viewed the whole movie."*

If block(s), say, "I can handle it," and BLS. Repeat until the client can go through the whole movie entirely without distress.

VOC: ___/7

If the client can play the movie from beginning to end with confidence and satisfaction, play the movie one more time from beginning to end + BLS: ☐ Yes ☐ No

Phase 7: Closure

Most positive thing learned: _____

_____

PC: _____

+ BLS
Check with VOC: _____

Incomplete session: ☐ Yes ☐ No
The session is incomplete when there is still unresolved material:

- If there is still discomfort or the SUD score is greater than 1
- If the VOC score is less than 6
- If negative feelings persist in the body scan
- If the SUD is greater than 1, skip Phases 5 and 6

Do relaxation exercise.

Complete session: ☐ Yes ☐ No
"Things may come up or they may not. If they do, great. Write them down and it can be a target for the next time. You can use a log to write down triggers, images, thoughts or cognitions, emotions, and sensations; you can rate them on our 0-to-10 scale, where 0 is no disturbance or neutral and 10 is the worst disturbance. Please write down the positive experiences, too. If you get any new memories, dreams, or situations that disturb you, just take a good snapshot. It isn't necessary to give a lot of detail. Just put down enough to remind you so we can target it the next time. The same thing goes for any positive dreams or situations. If negative feelings do come up, try not to make them significant. Remember, it's still just the old stuff. Just write them down for the next time. Then use the safe place exercise to let go of as much of the disturbance as possible. Even if nothing comes up, make sure to use the safe place every day and give me a call if you need to."

Phase 8: Reevaluation

Noticed since last session: _____

_____

Current symptoms: _____

New material: _____

SUD: ____/10

"When you think about the work we have done together, what do you feel is the most useful to you?"

Useful: _____

_____

Install if useful with BLS.

Gained: _____

_____

Noticed: _____

_____

Install if useful with BLS.

Noticed: _____

_____

Install if useful with BLS.

Noticed: _____

_____

Install if useful with BLS.

Positive target/memory/image: _____

_____

Sensations and emotions: _____

SUD: ___/10

Location of body sensation: _____

BLS, notice: _____

_____

BLS, learned: _____

_____

"Now, think about the image or memory, about the parts of your body where you feel the positive sensations, and about the word/phrase and put them altogether. Go with that."

BLS, notice: _____

_____

BLS, notice: _____

_____

REFERENCES

Garner, D. M. (2004). *EDI 3: Easting disorder inventory-3: Professional manual.* Odessa, FL: Psychological Assessment Resources.

Learly, M. R. (1983). A brief version of the fear of negative evaluation scale. *Personality and Social Psychology, 9*, 371–385. doi:10.1177/0146167283093007

Probst, M., Vandereycken, W., van Coppenolle, H., & Vanderlinden, J. (1995). The Body Attitude Test for patients with an eating disorder: Psychometric characteristics of a new questionnaire. *Eating Disorders: The Journal of Treatment & Prevention, 3*(2), 133–144. doi:10.1080/10640269508249156

Watson, D., & Friend, R. (1969). Measurement of social-evaluative anxiety. *Journal of Consulting and Clinical Psychology, 33*(4), 448–457. doi:10.1037/h0027806

THE REJECTED SELF EMDR THERAPY PROTOCOL FOR BODY IMAGE DISTORTION

4

Natalia Seijo

INTRODUCTION

Everything we have been told about who we are is connected to our physical appearance. Body image refers to the image we have created in our minds regarding our own body, that is to say, the way in which we see ourselves (Schilder, 1935). The lives of people with eating disorders (EDs) end up revolving around the *meaning* that lies behind this image.

The person's dissatisfaction is the result of a discrepancy between the *perceived self* and the *ideal self* (i.e., who the person would like to become). However, concern over the perception of the body begins when a *rejected self* is generated. This rejected self is the image of the self from the past that the person rejected, to which she compares herself and does not want to return ever again. When this point is reached, we start talking about *body image distortion*.

The author has observed that there are other defenses that are helpful with which to work other than the classical ones such as denial, regression, acting out, dissociation, compartmentalization, projection, reaction formation, repression, displacement, intellectualization, rationalization, undoing, sublimation, compensation, and assertiveness. Defenses can also be "the experiences from inside that block the therapeutic process at an emotional or cognitive level" (Seijo, 2015b). These are defenses because they do not allow the client to work in therapy. It is in this way that emotions can be seen as defenses.

The application of the rejected self protocol for body image distortion in EDs (Seijo, 2016) is quite straightforward. The protocol involves neutralizing the three main emotional defenses of rejection, shame, and worry and the body image distortion defense (also of a dissociative nature) that are blocking full awareness of the body and lie between the actual body image and the rejected self. This body image distortion is one of the most *resistant* defenses in treating clients with EDs. Through the application of this protocol in the treatment of EDs with EMDR therapy, the client learns to identify and process the part of the inner world that represents the rejected self. By doing this, two of the primary goals in regard to the actual body are achieved: first, developing awareness, and second, reaching the point of acceptance.

DIAGNOSES

The concept of body image implies a continuum. Depending on the degree of rejection toward the body, the person may shift from simply having a realistic self-image to having a negative self-image.

This is the continuum of body image:

Realistic body image >>> Negative body image >>> Body image disorder >>> Body dysmorphic disorder

The following are the definitions of these concepts:

- *Body image* (Schilder, 1935): The image we create in our minds regardless of our bodies
- *Negative body image* (Bell & Rushforth, 2008): The dissatisfaction regarding the body or parts of it

- *Body image distortion* (Thompson, 1990): A persistent state of dissatisfaction and worry related to some aspect of physical appearance that can lead to obsession
- *Body dysmorphic disorder (BDD), DSM-5*: A mental disorder characterized by an obsessive preoccupation that some aspect of one's own appearance is severely flawed and warrants exceptional measures to hide or fix it. In BDD's delusional variant, the flaw is imagined.

MEASURES

We know that clients have a distorted body image when their real image does not match the description of their self-image. There are different degrees of body image distortion, which will be described later. Using clinical judgment during history gathering, assess how far this described self-image is from reality and how often this has happened in the past.

Some questionnaires assess body image distortion, such as the body shape questionnaire, which measures:

- Alterations in proportions regarding body image and concept
- Alterations in perceptual accuracy
- Paralyzing feeling of ineffectiveness

It includes 34 items and is scored on a Likert scale from 1 to 6. The items are divided into four subscales:

- Body dissatisfaction
- Fear of gaining weight
- Low self-esteem due to appearance
- Desire to lose weight

THE REJECTED SELF EMDR THERAPY PROTOCOL FOR BODY IMAGE DISTORTION SCRIPT NOTES

Phase 1: History Taking and Case Conceptualization

History of Body Image Distortion

The body image distortion phenomenon is based on day-to-day life experiences. It is as if the representation of the body from the past remains static, impermeable to the effect of the passage of time and bodily experiences; it is as if there was a distorted cognitive filter that does not allow the person to see how he or she truly is.

In order to assess body image, how the person perceives the shape of his or her body (i.e., the image that has been created in his or her mind) must be taken into account. Thus, it is important to check how the person evaluates his or her body size and to gather information regarding the emotional aspects involved, such as the attitudes toward this self-image. This is the aspect we normally focus on when we speak of *negative* body image, also using the terms *dissatisfaction* or *rejection* of the body.

In order to gather information regarding body dissatisfaction, ask questions that will provide all the necessary data about how body dissatisfaction has developed and how it might have derived into body image distortion or BDD, if that is the case. Among other issues, at this stage inquire about the following:

- Information on how the body image was experienced in the family of origin
- Information on how parents related to their own bodies, which may have developed into implicit procedural learning
- Comments that the client may have received at home about his or her body
- Whether the client was compared to other people in relation to his or her body
- Through whose eyes the client may have learned to look at himself or herself (often, we see ourselves as other people saw us or as who we were told we were)

Identification and History of the Rejected Self

After exploring body dissatisfaction, move on to gathering the history about the rejected self. In order to do this, the first thing will be to define this concept. One way of doing it is using simple words that can automatically connect the clients with that part, which tends to appear rapidly. They are told to try and identify their rejected self, the part that they reject, the part of themselves they would never want to be again, and the part with whom they currently compare themselves. It is the part that the person is ashamed of. In order to begin working on this protocol, the clinician must know that processing the rejected self reaches directly into the most profound layers of trauma, be it of traumatic or attachment origins.

In the Body Image Distortion Protocol, two types of images can represent the rejected self:

- *Past body image distortion*: The rejected self part is like an image imprinted on the brain through which the current body image is seen, generating a great deal of distortion. Most of the time, the person sees that image of the *past* instead of seeing the present image of the true body. Hence, in disorders such as anorexia nervosa, when a woman looks in the mirror, she sees the parts of the body she rejects, and sometimes, it does not correspond to the actual image.
- *Present body image distortion*: It may be that when asked for the image of the rejected self, the image clients get is the image of the *present* and not of the past. When this occurs (e.g., after a pregnancy in which the person has great weight gain and becomes overweight, obesity provoked by a complication of an organic or psychological kind, or a car accident in which the body can find itself affected at the level of physical appearance), work will be done with the rejected self of the present in the same way as with the rejected self from the past.

The common difference between the image from the rejected self from the past and the rejected self of the present is that in the former, the work tends to be associated with *attachment traumas*. On the contrary, the latter tends to be associated with a *traumatic event*. Although in these cases we can find both types of trauma, it will be interesting to differentiate them in order to guide ourselves when conceptualizing and establishing a clear treatment plan.

In the phenomenon of body image distortion, daily experience does not change the person's idea about his or her body. The representation of the body from the past remains static—unaffected by the passage of time and bodily experiences—as the image of that "rejected self" from the past to which the person does not want to return ever again. The body image distortion goes along with a distorted cognitive filter, which may be seen in examples such as, "When I look at myself in the mirror, I don't see my lips as full as I would like them to be; so that's when I cut them so they swell up and I can have them as I wish them to be" or "I sleep each night wrapped up in plastic, so I can sweat and get rid of my abdominal fat; I won't stop until my hipbones are prominent."

The "rejected self" and the body image distortion manifest when the strongly rejected image from the past stands between the image he or she sees in the mirror and his or her current real image. Not wanting to be that person again generates intense concern. The mental representation of the "rejected self" could be, for example, her "15-year-old self" with the same flaws that he or she had at the time.

Toward this part of herself, the person feels rejection, shame, or concern. These emotions are the emotional defenses that maintain dissociation. Since she sees herself through the lens of this rejected self from the past, she is unable to see her body image objectively when the person looks in the mirror and does not see the reflection in the mirror; instead, she sees the body of the past, from when she was a teenager, that is not real and will never be real again.

When a client was asked about her rejected self, she described her 16-year-old self, with fat legs, flabby belly, and a big butt, even though she was in treatment for anorexia nervosa and her weight was 38 kilograms (183 pounds). She continues to feel ashamed and concerned, because she still sees her fat legs and flabby belly, just like that rejected image from the past, even though she is now 20 years old and nothing of what she sees in her body is real anymore. Due to her image distortion, what she sees in the mirror is the dissociated image from her rejected self of the past.

The appropriate time to start working with the rejected self is when the person is stabilized, when general defenses have been neutralized, and when judgments and critical comments from inside have been channeled and turned into more healthy and constructive comments. Once this step has been taken, frame the work with the rejected self and the body image distortion and follow the steps of the protocol that are described in the following sections.

Phase 2: Preparation

Resources

The resource work helps clients to connect better with the rejected self's vulnerability and to provide strength and empowerment. The results are that clients increase their sense of internal security, trust more in the process, and are assisted in neutralizing their defenses.

It is important for clients to have previously worked on the necessary resources. In this way, the client will be prepared to face difficult situations that may arise from this work.

Ironically, the most appropriate resources for this phase will be those based on exceptions in clients' lives, the situations that clients barely recognize and often need a great deal of help to recover from.

The clinician may ask questions about the following experiences:

- *Positive comments/affect*: Situations or moments—however brief—in the clients' history where they were able to see themselves without their habitual critical gaze. If they cannot find any exceptions, ask for times when others said something positive about their physique at any time throughout their lives. Aside from comments about the body, the exceptions can extend to positive affect about physical, cognitive, or emotional qualities that they can appreciate about themselves.
- *Loving eyes*: Resources related to the person who looked at the client with loving eyes without paying attention to his or her physical appearance
- *Ideal figure*: Resources that refer to an ideal figure that makes the client feel that it is okay to be just the way he or she is

In some cases, these qualities will probably compensate for shortcomings clients believe they have and will help us as clinicians. By working on them as resources, they give a solid and supportive foundation to neutralize and process the part of the rejected self.

Psychoeducation and Self-Care

Psychoeducation is offered in order to help the client create an internal locus of control and sense of self. This is done by promoting healthy and appropriate self-care through healthy eating and drinking habits, hygiene, sleeping habits, medical checkups, appropriate hydration, and so on.

These concepts must be recovered and developed once the rejected self is neutralized and integrated.

- *Self-concept:* The image each person has of his or her self, as well as the ability to self-recognize. Self-concept includes the evaluation of all parameters relevant to the person: from physical appearance to skills. Self-concept is not innate; it develops with experience and the image projected and perceived by others. It is dynamic, which means that it can be modified by new data.
- *Self-esteem:* Set of perceptions, thoughts, feelings, and behaviors directed toward ourselves, toward our way of being and behaving, toward the features of our bodies and our character. Ultimately, it is how we assess ourselves. The importance of self-esteem lies in that it affects our worth and our way of being. Respect becomes a fundamental construct because self-esteem is related to how we have been respected and how we learn to respect ourselves.

It is important to know that when working with the rejected self, the mother figure is the main issue that emerges as part of the processing. It is the reference figure, probably because it is the physical model from which to learn and model the self. When we work with the rejected self, we also process and repair the relationship with the attachment figure of the mother (Seijo, 2012).

Psychoeducation on the Three Defenses: Rejection, Shame, and Worry

Defenses are the mechanisms through which the internal system protects itself so the person can be "functional."

The body, or a part of the body, is often not felt as one's own; it feels strange. It is important to highlight dissociation as one of the defenses that tends to appear in body image distortion through the rejected self. It is usually a dissociative experience of the *psychoform type* (i.e., mental in nature), through which the clients perceive their bodies in unrealistic proportions.

During our work with body image distortion, the defenses to be processed first are the emotional ones described later in text, since they are the main ones that block the processing and acceptance of the rejected part.

- *Rejection*: Nonacceptance, confrontation, or opposition. It is the internal experience that causes avoidance toward the part.
- *Shame:* Not to show oneself in order to conceal that which is perceived as negative. This defense helps enable the avoidance of implicit memories associated with the rejected self.
- *Worry:* Protects from going back to being what was. It is an internal process that maintains the distortion, thus maintaining the nonacceptance and blocking the emotions and beliefs that may come up. The person feels worry that he or she could become the rejected self again.

Psychoeducation on EMDR

The Rejected Self Protocol, like the Standard EMDR Protocol, is based on the Three-Pronged Protocol: past, present, and future. The EMDR Three-Pronged Protocol is used to reprocess past adverse/traumatic experiences, work with present triggers, and address future concerns in order to bring the client to the highest level of adaptive response.

The Standard Three-Pronged Protocol developed by Francine Shapiro (1995, 2001, 2018) recommends that all traumatic incidents be sequentially reprocessed from the earliest to the present. The author has made some modifications to the Standard EMDR Protocol to better address the work with this dissociative part.

Bear in mind that despite working with the image of the past and the present, both of them will take us first to the past. Processing the traumas associated with the distortion will result in the neutralization of the imprinted image of the rejected self and will help attain a realistic body image in the future. Thus, self-concept and self-esteem are restructured at the same time and acceptance of the real body is achieved.

People with body image disorders usually present a rich constellation of attachment and trauma events throughout their lives associated with their bodies. Therefore, it is often necessary to start the therapeutic treatment from the perspective of working with defenses. When speaking of defenses, we are referring to blockage points that prevent the natural flow of the EMDR processing. Defense work begins in Phase 2 through psychoeducation, helping the person understand the process.

Defenses in EDs are one of the key points to insist upon, since they can be the cause of therapeutic failure and/or possible dropout from treatment.

In order to graphically explain how defenses are distributed in the inner world of these clients, use the "artichoke metaphor" (Seijo, 2015b). Each layer contains the part and the defenses whose function is to protect it when something is being triggered inside. The leaf, in turn, covers another leaf and all of them form a structure that protects the core, where the most vulnerable part resides. The metaphor describes the therapeutic development as a spiral moving from the outside in, from the outermost layers inward, to finally reach the heart of the "artichoke," where the pain of the wounded child remains. The process is similar to "weaving." The final result is the integration of the inner world and the normalization of body image.

This metaphor helps clients understand that when the rejected self is activated, defenses are triggered. When these defenses are neutralized, they allow access to the trauma, which is then reprocessed with the Standard EMDR Protocol. The clinician's understanding of this structure will help the work that will later be developed in detail during the protocol.

In summary, the process would be described as follows:

A layer is accessed. >>> The rejected self is activated. >>> The defense appears. >>> Work on the defense with the Rejected Self Protocol for body image distortion. >>> The defense is neutralized. >>> Access to trauma. >>> Standard processing with EMDR.

Phase 3: Assessment

Using the "Rejected Self" as an Established Treatment Plan Target

The rejected self is a dissociative part, and the body image distortion is the defense used by the rejected self. By processing the rejected self directly, it is possible to process both at the same time. After the rejected self and body image distortion—which is the person's dissociation from his or her own body in an attempt to avoid what the body is and what it conveys, feels, or expresses (Seijo, 2016)—have been identified, confirm the rejected self image.

Figure 4.1 describes how the rejected self and the body image distortion are organized in the inner system. The far left end of the diagram shows the true/real image of the client, who looks at his or her body in the mirror through the rejected self and, at the same time, is influenced by the ideal self the client has. When the client sees himself or herself in the mirror, what the client sees is the rejected self (the part that is rejected from the past). The client does not see the real body; what the client sees is the rejected self. This perception of the rejected self is influenced by the discrepancy between the real image of the self and the ideal self. The whole time the client is comparing the real body with the ideal body, because the real body is not the body the client wants. As a result of the comparison of the rejected self with the ideal self-image, a discrepancy between both images arises, the perceived one and the ideal one described in Figure 4.2. The rejected self image has the effect of reflecting back a distorted image of the body. This distortion is strongly influenced by the idea of an ideal self to which people constantly compare themselves in a negative way.

By applying this protocol, clients integrate the rejected self into the accepted self and become free to finally see the actual image of their own body that can be seen without distortion.

Figure 4.2 illustrates how body dissatisfaction appears when there is a discrepancy between the perceived self and the ideal self the person would like to be (Seijo, 2016). For example, it happens when clients look at themselves in the mirror and there is a discrepancy (i.e., an illogical or surprising lack of compatibility or similarity) between the perceived self (the body that clients see) and the ideal self (the unrealistic self concerning size and weight). As a result, body dissatisfaction can occur.

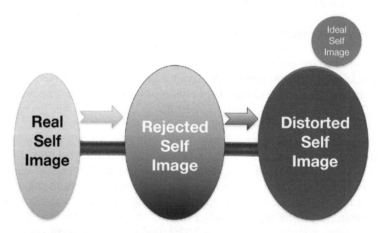

Figure 4.1   The rejected self image.

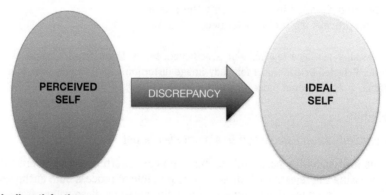

Figure 4.2   Body dissatisfaction.

Phase 4: Desensitization

Reprocessing Specific Features

When reprocessing begins, the target of the rejected self identified in Phase 2, clients will make associations to traumatic and adverse life experiences throughout their lives. The memories of these traumas are maintaining the dissociation of the rejected self in the inner world, and this protocol becomes a great way to identify them.

Use the Standard EMDR Protocol when the traumas that appear during reprocessing block and interrupt the flow of the Rejected Self Protocol. Then, reprocess these targets independently with the Standard EMDR Protocol and later continue with the Rejected Self Protocol to check if the image distortion continues and to assess if the rejected self seems more integrated and the processing is flowing again on its own. It is possible that even more processing of memories is needed because this protocol can open the window to adverse life experience related to this rejected part and the body. Sometimes, it will not always be necessary to work with the Standard EMDR Protocol, and the Rejected Self Protocol will be all that is needed to help integrate the rejected self.

Usually, after the defenses and the traumatic and adverse life experiences have been successfully reprocessed, clients will no longer feel rejection, shame, or worry. Instead, they will feel sorrow for the part of themselves they once rejected. This is a way to know that processing is taking place. Little by little, the defenses start weakening, making room for the other emotions that were always underneath.

When asking clients to connect with the rejected self, they often feel rejection, shame, and worry toward that past self. However, in certain disorders such as EDs—in which the person is overweight, for example—the rejected self may be the self of the present. In these cases, it is important to work in the present in order to get to the past.

Information to Consider During This Phase

It is common for the information that starts to come up to be related to the maternal figure. Maternal representations play a fundamental role in the construction of body image. The maternal attachment figure fulfills the functions of validation and acceptance of the self, which are the foundation of the construct of the self. Without recognition and validation, especially from the maternal figure, the concept of the self is built upon a base of insecurity and will seek external confirmation in order to be internally validated.

Criteria for target selection will follow the standard clustering method, which includes the first, worst, and most recent memories related to the present symptom with which the therapist and client work. In the case of multiple targets, choose those related to the symptoms that keep the rejected self dissociated in the inner world and facilitate the distortion of body image.

Just as is done in the Standard EMDR Protocol, in which we return to the original memory, in this protocol, go back to the image representing the rejected self and ask about the defenses. As the rejected self is processed, the adverse experiences that maintain the dissociation of this part are reprocessed and desensitized. Once the part becomes integrated, the distortion of the body image is neutralized and the client is then able to begin to see himself or herself in a more realistic way. In the next phase, install the new image of the client that begins to develop from that moment.

Phase 5: Installation

Strengthening Reprocessing With Knipe's "Loving Eyes" Protocol

During this phase, once defenses have been neutralized and the client has processed the sorrow for the part of the rejected self, apply Jim Knipe's Loving Eyes Protocol (Knipe, 2015) in order to promote increased acceptance of this part and enhance integration. It must be very clearly conveyed that the client and the part are the same person. Once this point in the protocol has been reached, the client has gone through an important transformation and is on the way to integration.

Phase 6: Body Scan

The body scan is performed exactly as in the Standard EMDR Protocol. The only difference is that, as it has been done throughout this protocol, the client returns to the image of the rejected self and pays attention to whether there is discomfort in any part of the body. The goal is to do reprocessing until the client feels fine with it and the SUD equals zero.

Phase 7: Closure

Ask the client if it is okay to leave it like this or if there is anything else he or she feels the part needs to hear or the client has to do. If all is well, close the session by instructing the client to write down what comes up in the days ahead and that the work will continue next session.

Phase 8: Reevaluation

When the client comes back to the next session, check again to see if he or she feels the rejected self part, if there is any rejection left, and if she or he feels that the part is integrated and the rejection processed.

It is possible that there will be work with the protocol needed over the course of a few sessions until the integration of the rejected self is achieved.

THE REJECTED SELF EMDR THERAPY PROTOCOL FOR BODY IMAGE DISTORTION SCRIPT

Phase 1: History Taking and Case Conceptualization

Please ask the client the following questions:

Body Image Distortion Questions

Say, *"How would you define your body?"*

_____

_____

Say, *"What emotions, feelings, or sensations are generated by your body?"*

_____

_____

Say, *"Have you ever dieted or changed the amount of food you eat in order to change the size of your body?"*

_____

_____

Say, *"How much satisfaction do you feel in relation to your body?"*

_____

_____

Say, *"What defects do you perceive in your body?"*

_____

_____

Say, *"How much time do you spend observing, judging, or covering the features of your body you dislike?"*

Note: Say "features" to avoid using the word "part" and prevent confusion with the rejected self part.

_____

_____

Say, *"How much have you been influenced by your body whenever you have had to relate to others or attend different social events throughout your life?"*

_____

_____

Say, *"Is there anyone in your family with the same problem?"*

_____

_____

Say, *"How was body image valued in your family of origin?"*

_____

_____

Say, *"How did your parents relate to their own bodies?"*

_____

_____

Say, *"Who used to look at you in the way you look at yourself nowadays?"*

_____

_____

Say, *"What comments have you received about your body throughout your life, both from your family and from other people?"*

_____

_____

Say, *"Did you ever compare your body to that of others, looking for the flaws in your own?"*

_____

_____

Say, *"How much does what you see in your body have to do with how other people see you?"*

_____

_____

Say, *"Which life experiences have been crucial for you in regard to your body?"*

_____

_____

Say, *"How old were you when you started paying attention to your body or to the possible defects you find in it, in a negative way?"*

_____

_____

Say, *"What was happening in your life the first time you were aware of your body dissatisfaction?"*

_____

_____

Identification of the "Rejected Self Questions"

Identify the rejected self. Most of the time, the image of the rejected self comes up immediately, since it always accompanies the client.

Say, *"I want to talk to you about the idea of 'the rejected self.' The rejected self is a part from the past or the present that you reject and of which you are ashamed. Take the time you need to allow this image of yourself to come to mind. This part may hold feelings of disgust or contempt, and it may have been there throughout the years as an imprinted image of what you never want to be again, and through which you see yourself when looking in the mirror."*

_____

_____

When the rejected self comes up, ask for detailed information.

Say, *"Can you identify your rejected self, the part you don't want to be anymore?"*

_____

_____

If the person answers that the rejected self is the body in the present, say the following:

"Can you identify the image of yourself you reject in the present?"

_____

_____

Say, *"Can you tell me about the part that you would never like to be again?"*

_____

_____

Say, *"Floating back and focusing on this rejected self, what is the oldest or most significant memory in which you have felt or seen yourself rejected?"*

_____

_____

Phase 2: Preparation

Resources

Say, *"What are some of your resources?"*

_____

_____

TIMES WHEN CLIENTS SEE THEMSELVES IN A POSITIVE LIGHT

Say, *"Please tell me what resources you have that show you in a positive light, without criticism."*

_____

_____

Say, *"What are some of the positive things people have said about your body?"*

_____

_____

_____

_____

Notice which traits or qualities were highlighted, validate them, and offer bilateral stimulation (BLS) to integrate them.

Say, *"*_____ (state highlighted traits and qualities) *are very helpful and important. Let's do some bilateral stimulation to integrate that. Go with that."*
Do BLS.

_____

_____

ATTACHMENT FIGURE WHO OFFERED THE MOST LOVE OR SECURITY

Say, *"Who was the person who made you feel the most loved and secure?"*

_____

_____

Say, *"Please describe who it was and how it was done."*

_____

_____

Say, *"What are the feelings that come up when you think about this?"*

_____

_____

Say, *"What traits in yourself do you think you may be able to learn to love like he or she does?"*

_____

_____

Ask how receiving love and security makes the client feel as a person; it generally helps to increase feelings of being worthy of love and often adds self-worth.

Say, *"What does having received love and security say to you about yourself as a person?"*

_____

Offer BLS so the client can integrate it.
Say, *"Go with that."*
Do BLS.

IDEAL FIGURE

Say, *"Please look for someone in your life you admire or who stands out because of his or her excellent self-concept or sense of self-esteem. Who might that be?"*

_____

_____

Underline the characteristics that show that these ideal figures love or respect themselves, so you can work on those same traits for the client.

Say, *"Observe what proves to you that this person has an excellent self-concept or sense of self-esteem. What do you notice?"*

_____

_____

Say, *"Imagine being able to see yourself having these same traits, fully accepting that these traits have been embodied and internalized, and are now yours. Notice how you see yourself."*

_____

_____

Offer BLS so it can be integrated.
Say, *"Go with that."*

Psychoeducation and Self-Care

Offer a clear explanation of the ideas of self-concept and self-esteem.

Say, *"I would like to talk to you about self-concept. Self-concept is the image each person has of himself or herself, as well as the ability to self-recognize. Self-concept includes an evaluation of all parameters relevant to the person: from physical appearance to skills. Self-concept is not innate; it develops with experience and the image projected and perceived by others. It is dynamic, which means that it can be modified by new data. After this work, the person changes the old information for the new information and feels better."*

Say, *"Let's go on to the idea of self-esteem. Self-esteem is a set of perceptions, thoughts, feelings, and behaviors directed toward ourselves, toward our way of being and behaving, toward the features of our bodies and our character. Ultimately, it is how we assess ourselves. The importance of self-esteem lies in that it affects our worth and our way of being. Respect becomes a fundamental construct because self-esteem is related to how we have been respected and how we learn to respect ourselves."*

We will obtain information about the client's self-esteem and self-concept with the following question:

Say, *"Where did you learn to see yourself in that way?"*

This question is crucial because it provides information that will help us to better understand the rejected self and will likely bring up memories from the past that will have to be processed later on with the Standard EMDR Protocol.

Psychoeducation on the Three Defenses: Rejection, Shame, and Worry

First offer a brief explanation about the three most common defenses in this work.

Say, *"There are three common defenses that usually appear when you imagine placing the rejected self in front of you: rejection, shame, or worry, or perhaps all three at once. These three defenses encompass the different emotions, feelings, and sensations you may feel toward your rejected self. These will be the defenses that we will neutralize in order to reach the compassion and acceptance of this part of you, a part that you have been rejecting all these years."*

REJECTION

Identify the rejection that the person is feeling and where it is felt in the body in regard to the part from the past identified as the rejected self.

Note: One of the three defenses prevents clients from accepting themselves. Since the image perceived is the rejected self of the past, it gets in the way of being able to see the actual body image. This is where the blockage appears.

Say, *"Imagine placing the part of you that represents your rejected self in front of you and tell me if and how you notice a sense of rejection."*

Say, *"Where do you feel it in the body?"*

_____

_____

Say, *"How would you describe the sensations?"*

_____

_____

SHAME

Identify the shame that is felt toward the rejected self.

Say, *"Can you identify the shame that you feel toward your rejected self?"*

_____

_____

Say, *"Where do you feel it in the body?"*

_____

_____

Say, *"Can you tolerate the feeling of shame?"*

_____

_____

WORRY

Do the same with the worry that the person feels while focusing on the rejected self. Clients are concerned that once again they could become who they were in the past, and this activates an alarm that can be used as feedback for the distortion.

Say, *"When you focus on your rejected self, are you worried that you may once again become that person with that body?"*

_____

_____

If the answer is "yes," say the following:

Say, *"Which emotions and/or sensations are generated by this worry about becoming that rejected self again?"*

_____

_____

Say, *"Where do you feel them in the body?"*

_____

_____

After identifying the defenses and seeing how they maintain the rejected self, focus again on resources to enable the client to process the rejected self—and everything that is connected to it—back in time.

Psychoeducation on EMDR

Before stepping into Phase 3, we will offer a brief explanation of EMDR.

> Say, *"When a trauma occurs it seems to get locked in the nervous system with the original picture, sounds, thoughts, and feelings. The eye movements we use in EMDR seem to unlock the nervous system and allow the brain to process the experience. That may be what is happening in REM or dream sleep—the eye movements may help to process the unconscious material. It is important to note that it is your own brain that will be doing the healing and that you are the one in control. When we process using the Three-Pronged Protocol, we are talking about the experiences of the past that affect your present life. After these past experiences are processed, they will stop affecting you negatively in the present and will not disturb you in the future."*

The Artichoke Metaphor

> Say, *"The inner world could be represented through an artichoke metaphor, which helps us see all the leaves/layers covering up the inner world in order to protect its most vulnerable part. When working with EMDR therapy, each of these leaves/layers contains the traumas, adverse experiences, and defenses that may arise. We will gradually process each one of these leaves/layers, until we reach the artichoke heart and repair what needs to be repaired. This is always done with great care, respecting the inner world and, above all, trusting in the process."*

Phase 3: Assessment

First, ask the client to focus on the rejected self and confirm the image that comes up.

> Say, *"We have identified _____ (describe what the client says about the rejected self) about the rejected self."*

_____

_____

> Say, *"Is this accurate?"*

_____

_____

> Say, *"We have identified _____ (describe what the client says about the distortion of the body image) about the distortion of your body image."*

_____

_____

> Say, *"Is this accurate?"*

_____

_____

Then, ask the client to feel/experience the defenses. Give clients enough time to check inside and answer if they feel one, two, or all three of the defenses, as well as their location in the body.

Say, *"When you put your rejected self in front of you, do you feel rejection, shame, or worry?"*

_____

_____

Once the person has identified the defenses, ask where they are felt in the body, and the level of disturbance when looking at the rejected self. Assess each of them on a scale from 0 to 10, 0 being no rejection, shame, or worry at all to 10 being complete rejection, shame, or worry.

Say, *"If you feel rejection, where do you feel it in your body?"*

_____

_____

Say, *"On a scale of 0 to 10, where 0 is no rejected feelings or neutral and 10 is the most rejection you can imagine, how disturbing does your rejection feel now?"*

0	1	2	3	4	5	6	7	8	9	10

(no rejected feelings/neutral)   (most rejection)

Say, *"If you feel shame, where do you feel the shame in your body?"*

_____

_____

Say, *"On a scale of 0 to 10, where 0 is no shameful feelings or neutral and 10 is the most shame you can imagine, how disturbing does your rejection feel now?"*

0	1	2	3	4	5	6	7	8	9	10

(no shameful feelings/neutral)   (most shame)

Say, *"If you feel worry, where do you feel the worry in your body?"*

_____

_____

Say, *"On a scale of 0 to 10, where 0 is no worry or neutral and 10 is the most worry you can imagine, how disturbing does your rejection feel now?"*

0	1	2	3	4	5	6	7	8	9	10

(no worry/neutral)   (most worry)

Say, *"If you feel all of them, tell me where you feel each one of them in your body."*

_____

_____

Say, *"On a scale of 0 to 10, where 0 is no worry, shame, or rejection, or neutral and 10 is the most worry, shame, or rejection you can imagine, how disturbing does your rejection, shame, or worry feel now?"*

0	1	2	3	4	5	6	7	8	9	10

(no rejection, worry, or shame/neutral)   (most rejection, worry, or shame)

Phase 4: Desensitization

Once the client tells us which defense he or she is feeling and its intensity, ask the client to focus on the image of the rejected self; connect with the one, two, or all three defenses; locate them in the body; and notice their intensity. You may process all the defenses at once here.

Say, *"Please focus on the image of your rejected self and connect with _____ (state the defense/s) and where you notice it in your body as well as its intensity."*

_____

_____

Say, *"Go with that."*

Do BLS.

Write down every big "T" or small "t" trauma associated with the rejected self. If these traumas seem to be interrupting the flow of the Body Image Distortion Protocol, we must stop and reprocess them using the Standard EMDR Protocol.

Say, *"What comes up now?"*

_____

_____

_____

_____

_____

Process using sets of BLS, letting the information flow until nothing is coming up or the information that arises has nothing to do with the matter in question. Then ask the client to go back to connecting with the rejected self and check once again on the defenses: rejection, shame, or worry. Wait for the answer and ask the client to focus on the rejected self and the defenses.

Say, *"Please connect with the rejected self again and tell me which of the defenses comes up: rejection, shame, or worry."*

_____

_____

Say, *"Okay. Please focus on your rejected self and _____ (state the defense's name). Go with that."*

Do BLS.

_____

_____

Process until nothing comes up.

Say, *"Now, let's return to thinking about the rejected self and check each of the three defenses. Do you notice any of the defenses of rejection, shame, or worry? Aside from these three defenses, are there any other emotions or feelings that we have not yet named?"*

_____

_____

Often when the client no longer feels rejection, shame, or worry, the underlying emotion that comes up is sorrow. Once defenses have been neutralized and the client can start to feel sorrow or compassion for the part of the rejected self, we can process this sadness by simply focusing on it and then having the person allow himself or herself to just feel it.

Say, *"Let yourself feel that sadness. Where are you feeling it in the body?"*

_____

_____

"Go with that."
Do BLS.
Process until nothing comes up or the client starts making positive associations.

Phase 5: Installation

Strengthening Reprocessing With Knipe's "Loving Eyes" Protocol

Once the sadness is processed, apply Knipe's Loving Eyes Protocol in order to integrate this part. This helps increase compassion toward this part, and compassion leads to integration.

Say, *"Imagine that you can look the rejected part in the eyes and imagine that the part looks back at you. Please allow yourself to see that this part's eyes are your eyes, because you and this part are the same person. It is the part of you that you have been rejecting for so long."*

_____

_____

Say, *"Go with that."*

Do BLS.

Phase 6: Body Scan

Say, *"Go back to the rejected self and scan your body from head to toe. Check if there is any uncomfortable sensation still remaining, or if everything is fine."*

_____

_____

If the body is clear, the procedure is complete. If it is not, process the point of disturbance, just focusing on that point.

FUTURE TEMPLATE

In order to work with the future template, check for the part that represented the rejected self in the past. Clients use the most adaptive information learned from experiences in the past and present with the goal of integrating this part into their life in the future once the rejected self is accepted and integrated.

Have the client imagine a future anticipated situation.
Install the Future Template.

Say, *"Okay, we have reprocessed all of the targets that we needed to do. Now, let's anticipate what will happen when you are faced with the picture of your body. What comes
up?"*

_____

_____

_____

_____

Say, *"I would like you to imagine yourself coping effectively with _____
(the picture of your body) in the future. Bring up this picture and say to yourself, 'I
can handle it,' and feel the sensations. Okay, have you got it? Follow my fingers (or any
other forms of BLS)."*

_____

_____

Say, *"Bring up the picture again, on a scale from 1 to 7, where 1 feels completely false and
7 feels completely true. To what extent do you think you can manage to really do it?"*

1	2	3	4	5	6	7

(completely false)   (completely true)

Install with sets of eye movements until a maximum level of validity of cognition (VOC) has been
achieved. If there is a block, meaning that even after 10 or more installations, the VOC is still below 7,
there are more targets that need to be identified and addressed. The therapist should use the Standard EMDR Protocol to address these targets before proceeding with the template (see worksheets in
Appendix A). Also, evaluate whether the client needs any new information, resources, or skills to be
able to comfortably visualize the future coping scene. Introduce this needed information or skill.

Say, *"What would you need to feel confident in handling the situation?"*

_____

_____

Or say, *"What is missing from your handling of your body?"*

_____

_____

Use BLS; if blocks are not resolved, identify unprocessed material and process with the Standard
EMDR Protocol.

Video Check (Future Template as Movie)

Say, *"This time, I'd like you to imagine yourself stepping into the scene of a future confrontation with your body for which the future template was meant. Close your eyes
and play a movie of this happening, from the beginning until the end. Imagine yourself
coping with any challenges that come your way. Notice what you are seeing, thinking,
feeling, and experiencing in your body. While playing this movie, let me know if you hit
any blocks. If you do, just open your eyes and let me know. If you don't hit any blocks,
let me know when you have viewed the whole movie."*

_____

_____

If the client encounters a block and opens her eyes, this is a sign for the therapist to instruct the client to say the following:

"Say to yourself 'I can handle it' and follow my fingers (introduce a set of eye movements)."

To provide the clinician with an indication regarding the client's self-efficacy, ask her to rate her response on a VOC scale from 1 to 7. This procedural step may give the clinician feedback on the extent to which the goals are met.

Say, *"As you think of your body, how do the words feel from 1 being completely false to 7 being completely true?"*

1	2	3	4	5	6	7

(completely false)   (completely true)

If the client is able to play the movie from start to finish with a sense of confidence and satisfaction, the client is asked to play the movie once more from the beginning to the end, BLS is introduced, and the positive cognition (PC) "I can handle it" is installed. In a sense, this movie is installed as a future template.

Say, *"Okay, play the movie one more time from beginning to end and say to yourself, 'I can handle it.' Go with that."*

Phase 7: Closure

Say, *"Is it okay to leave it like this or is there anything you feel the part needs to hear or that you need to do?"*

_____

_____

Say, *"Things may come up or they may not. If they do, great. Write it down and it can be a target for the next time. You can use a log to write down triggers, images, thoughts, cognitions, emotions, and sensations; you can rate them on our 0-to-10 scale, where 0 is no disturbance or neutral and 10 is the worst disturbance. Please write down the positive experiences, too."*

Say, *"If you get any new memories, dreams, or situations that disturb you, just take a good snapshot. It isn't necessary to give a lot of detail. Just put down enough to remind you so we can target it the next time. The same thing goes for any positive dreams or situations. If negative feelings do come up, try not to make them significant. Remember, it's still just the old stuff. Just write it down for the next time."*

_____

_____

Phase 8: Reevaluation

Say, *"When you think about the rejected self, what comes up for you now?"*

_____

_____

Say, *"Does it feel like there is any rejection left?"*

_____

_____

Say, *"Do you feel that this part of you is integrated and the rejection is processed?"*

_____

_____

If yes, say, *"Feel it,"* and do BLS.
If no, repeat the Rejected Self Protocol until the rejected self is accepted.

SUMMARY

Our body image develops from a process of implicit learning, meaning that we learn to see ourselves based on who we were told we were and how we see that others perceive themselves in our family environment. This shapes the way in which we end up seeing ourselves in the future, our body image, and our acceptance of it.

Once we develop this learning about our own image, the negative beliefs and ideas about it become resistant to change, given that what we learn early in life becomes more resistant to change (van der Kolk, 1986).

Through the Rejected Self Protocol, change becomes easier because defenses are neutralized and the memories that maintain the fixed image are reprocessed. By doing this, the body image becomes integrated into the whole person and it improves, based on the reality that clients will learn to accept with compassion and understanding that it is okay to be who they are.

Overall, the goals that lead to the therapeutic success are the following: identifying the body as one's own; accepting the body as one's own; processing the trauma contained in the rejected self, at both cognitive and emotional levels; substituting body image distortion for acceptance; learning to respectfully feel and take care of the body; and integrating this dissociative part that represents the rejected self and its defense (body image distortion).

REFERENCES

Bell, L., & Rushforth, J. (2008). *Overcoming body image disturbance. A program for people with eating disorders*. London, UK: Routledge.

Knipe, J. (2015). *EMDR toolbox. Theory and treatment of complex PTSD and dissociation*. New York, NY: Springer Publishing.

Schilder, P. (1935). *The image and appearance of the human body*. Oxford, UK: Kegan Paul.

Seijo, N. (2012). EMDR and eating disorders. *Revista hispanoamericana de psicotraumatología y Disociación, 4*.

Seijo, N. (2015a). Eating disorders and dissociation. *ESTD Newsletter, 4*(1), 9–15.

Seijo, N. (2015b). *Somatic defenses* (EMDR master's thesis). Universidad Nacional de Educación a Distancia, Madrid, Spain.

Seijo, N. (2016). The rejected self: Working with body image distortion in eating disorders. *ESTD Newsletter, 5*(4), 8–13.

Shapiro, F. (1995). *Eye movement desensitization and reprocessing (EMDR). Basic principles, protocols, and procedures*. New York, NY: Guilford Press.

Shapiro, F. (2001). *Eye movement desensitization and reprocessing (EMDR). Basic principles, protocols, and procedures* (2nd ed.). New York, NY: Guilford Press.

Shapiro, F. (2018). *Eye movement desensitization and reprocessing (EMDR). Basic principles, protocols, and procedures* (3rd ed.). New York, NY: Guilford Press.

Thompson, J. K. (1990). *Body image disturbance: Assessment and treatment*. New York, NY: Pergamon Press.

van der Kolk, B. (1986). *Psychological trauma*. Washington DC: American Psychiatric Publishing.

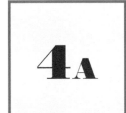

SUMMARY SHEET
The Rejected Self EMDR Therapy Protocol
for Body Image Distortion

Natalia Seijo
SUMMARY SHEET BY MARILYN LUBER

Name: _____ Diagnosis: _____

Medications: _____

Test Results: _____

☑ Check when task is completed, response has changed, or to indicate symptoms.

Note: This material is meant as a checklist for your response. Please keep in mind that it is only a reminder of different tasks that may or may not apply to your incident.

PHASE 1: HISTORY TAKING

Body Image Distortion Questions

Identification of the "Rejected Self" Questions

Definition of body: _____

_____

Emotions, feelings, sensations generated by your body: _____

_____

Have you dieted/changed the amount of food you eat to change body size: ☐ Yes ☐ No

Comment: _____

Satisfaction you feel in relation to your body: _____

_____

Defects perceived in your body: _____

_____

Amount of time spent observing, judging, or covering features of your body you dislike: _____

_____

How much influenced by your body when relating to others/attending different social events in your life: _____

_____

Anyone in family with same problem: _____

_____

How body image valued in family of origin: _____

_____

How parents related to own bodies: _____

_____

Who looked at you the way you do now: _____

_____

Comments received about your body from family and friends throughout life: _____

_____

You compared your body to others looking for your flaws: ☐ Yes ☐ No

Comment: _____

How much of what you see has to do with how others view you: _____

_____

Life experiences crucial for you concerning your body: _____

_____

Age when paid attention to body/defects in negative way: _____

_____

What was happening in your life when first aware of body dissatisfaction: _____

_____

Identification of the "Rejected Self" Questions

"I want to talk to you about the idea of "the rejected self." The rejected self is a part from the past or the present that you reject and of which you are ashamed. Take the time you need to allow this image of yourself to come to mind. This part may hold feelings of disgust or contempt, and it may have been there throughout the years as an imprinted image of what you never want to be again, and through which you see yourself when looking in the mirror.

Can you identify the rejected self?   ☐ Yes ☐ No

Comment: _____

If person identifies it in the present?

Can you identify the rejected self in the present?   ☐ Yes ☐ No

Comment: _____

Can you tell me about the part you would never want to be again?   ☐ Yes ☐ No

Comment: _____

Floating back and focusing on this rejected self, what is the oldest or most significant memory in which you have felt or seen yourself rejected: _____

_____

_____

PHASE 2: PREPARATION

Resources: _____
_____
_____

TIMES WHEN CLIENTS SEE THEMSELVES IN A POSITIVE LIGHT

Resources you have when you see yourself in a positive light: _____
_____
_____

Positive things people said about your body: _____
_____
_____
_____

_____ (state highlighted traits/qualities) + BLS

ATTACHMENT FIGURE WHO OFFERED THE MOST LOVE OR SECURITY

Person who made you feel most loved and secure: _____
_____

Describe who it was and how it was done: _____
_____
_____
_____

Feelings that come up when you think about this: _____
_____

Traits in yourself you think you may be able to learn to love like she or he does: _____
_____
_____

What does having received love and security say to you about yourself as a person: _____
_____
_____

_____ (state what it says about you) + BLS

IDEAL FIGURE

Someone in your life you admire because of his or her excellent self-concept/self-esteem: _____
_____

Observe proofs that this person has excellent self-concept/self-esteem: _____
_____

Traits in yourself you think you may be able to learn to love like she or he does: _____
_____
_____

See yourself having these same traits, fully accepting that these traits have been embodied and internalized and are now yours. Notice how you see yourself: _____

_____

_____

_____ (state what you noticed) + BLS

Psychoeducation and Self-Care   ☐ Yes ☐ No

"I would like to talk to you about self-concept. Self-concept is the image each person has of himself or herself, as well as the ability to self-recognize. Self-concept includes the evaluation of all parameters relevant to the person: from physical appearance to skills. Self-concept is not innate; it develops with experience and the image projected and perceived by others. It is dynamic, which means that it can be modified by new data. After this work, the person changes the old information for the new information and feels better.

    Let's go on to the idea of self-esteem. Self-esteem is a set of perceptions, thoughts, feelings, and behaviors directed toward ourselves, toward our way of being and behaving, toward the features of our bodies and our character. Ultimately, it is how we assess ourselves. The importance of self-esteem lies in that it affects our worth and our way of being. Respect becomes a fundamental construct because self-esteem is related to how we have been respected and how we learn to respect ourselves."

Where did you learn to see yourself in that way? _____

_____

_____

This question is crucial because it provides information that will help us to better understand the rejected self and will likely bring up memories from the past that will have to be processed later on with the Standard EMDR Protocol.

Psychoeducation on the Three Defenses: Rejection, Shame, and Worry   ☐ Yes ☐ No

"There are three common defenses that usually appear when you imagine placing the rejected self in front of you: rejection, shame, or worry, or perhaps all three at once. These three defenses encompass the different emotions, feelings, and sensations you may feel toward your rejected self. These will be the defenses that we will neutralize in order to reach the compassion and acceptance of this part of you, a part that you have been rejecting all these years."

REJECTION

Identify the rejection that the person is feeling and where it is felt in the body in regard to the part from the past identified as the rejected self.

Note: One of the three defenses prevents clients from accepting themselves. Since the image perceived is the rejected self of the past, it gets in the way of being able to see the actual body image. This is where the blockage appears.

Someone in your life you admire because of his or her excellent self-concept/self-esteem: _____

Imagine placing the part of you that represents your rejected self in front of you; tell me if and how you notice a sense of rejection: _____

_____

Location in body: _____

Describe sensations: _____

_____

SHAME

Identify shame you feel toward rejected self: _____

_____

Location in body: _____

Can you tolerate shame feelings: ☐ Yes ☐ No

Comment: _____

WORRY

Do the same with the worry that the person feels while focusing on the rejected self. Clients are concerned that once again they could become who they were in the past, and this activates an alarm that can be used as feedback for the distortion.

Focus on the rejected self; are you worried you will become that person with that body:

☐ Yes ☐ No

Comment: _____

If yes, identify emotions/sensations generated by the worry about becoming the rejected self again:

_____

_____

Location in body: _____

Can you tolerate shame feelings: ☐ Yes ☐ No

Comment: _____
After identifying the defenses and seeing how they maintain the rejected self, focus again on resources to enable the client to process the rejected self—and everything that is connected to it—back in time.

Psychoeducation on EMDR   ☐ Yes ☐ No

Before stepping into Phase 3, we will offer a brief explanation of EMDR.

"When a trauma occurs, it seems to get locked in the nervous system with the original picture, sounds, thoughts, and feelings. The eye movements we use in EMDR seem to unlock the nervous system and allow the brain to process the experience. That may be what is happening in REM or dream sleep—the eye movements may help to process the unconscious material. It is important to note that it is your own brain that will be doing the healing and that you are the one in control. When we process using the Three-Pronged Protocol, we are talking about the experiences of the past that affect your present life. After these past experiences are processed, they will stop affecting you negatively in the present and will not disturb you in the future."

The Artichoke Metaphor   ☐ Yes ☐ No

"The inner world could be represented through an artichoke metaphor, which helps us see all the layers covering up the inner world in order to protect its most vulnerable part. When working with EMDR therapy, each of these layers contains the traumas, adverse experiences, and defenses that may arise. We will gradually process each one of these layers, until we reach the artichoke heart and repair what needs to be repaired. This is always done with great care, respecting the inner world and, above all, trusting in process.

PHASE 3: ASSESSMENT

Identify rejected self: _____

_____

_____ ☐ Accurate ☐ Inaccurate

Identify distortion of body image: _____

_____

_____ ☐ Accurate ☐ Inaccurate

Feel or experience the defenses

Rejection: ☐ Yes ☐ No   Location of rejection in body: _____ SUD: ___/10 _____

Shame: ☐ Yes ☐ No   Location of rejection in body: _____ SUD: ___/10 _____

Worry: ☐ Yes ☐ No   Location of rejection in body: _____ SUD: ___/10 _____

PHASE 4: DESENSITIZATION

Focus on the image of rejected self + (state defense/s) + location in body + intensity of feeling + BLS

List of big "T" and small "t" traumas associated with the rejected self:

_____

_____

_____

_____

Focus on rejected self: Which defenses come up?   ☐ Rejection ☐ Shame ☐ Worry

Focus on rejected self + ___ (state defense) + BLS until nothing comes up

_____

_____

_____

Check if any defenses come up: ☐ Rejection ☐ Shame ☐ Worry

_____

_____

Other emotions noticed (often sadness): _____

_____

Focus on ___ (state emotion) + Location in body + BLS until client makes positive associations.

_____

_____

PHASE 5: INSTALLATION

Strengthening Reprocessing With Knipe's "Loving Eyes" Protocol

Imagine that you can look the rejected part in the eyes and imagine that the part looks back at you. Please allow yourself to see that this part's eyes are your eyes, because you and this part are the same person. It is the part of you that you have been rejecting for so long + BLS.

_____

_____

PHASE 6: BODY SCAN

Rejected self + Scan your body from head to toe

Unresolved tension/tightness/unusual sensation: _____

_____

Unresolved tension/tightness/unusual sensation + BLS

Strengthen positive sensation using BLS.

If there is more discomfort, reprocess until discomfort subsides + BLS. Then repeat body scan.

PHASE 7: CLOSURE

Anything the part needs to hear/you need to do: ☐ Yes ☐ No

Comment: _____

"Things may come up or they may not. If they do, great. Write it down and it can be a target for the next time. You can use a log to write down triggers, images, thoughts, cognitions, emotions, and sensations; you can rate them on our 0-to-10 scale, where 0 is no disturbance or neutral and 10 is the worst disturbance. Please write down the positive experiences, too."

"If you get any new memories, dreams, or situations that disturb you, just take a good snapshot. It isn't necessary to give a lot of detail. Just put down enough to remind you so we can target it the next time. The same thing goes for any positive dreams or situations. If negative feelings do come up, try not to make them significant. Remember, it's still just the old stuff. Just write it down for the next time."

PHASE 8: REEVALUATION

Rejected self + What comes up for you now: _____

_____

Any rejection left: ☐ Yes ☐ No

Comment: _____

Is this part integrated and the rejection processed: ☐ Yes ☐ No

Comment: _____

TRANSFORMING RELATIONSHIP DISTORTION WITH EMDR THERAPY

According to the National Domestic Violence Hotline (2018), "Domestic violence (also called intimate partner violence (IPV), domestic abuse or relationship abuse) is a pattern of behaviors used by one partner to maintain power and control over another partner in an intimate relationship." IPV can happen to anyone regardless of age, ethnicity, religion, sexual orientation, or gender. It can happen to people who are married, single, living together, or dating. It does not discriminate by socioeconomic status or education levels.

King (2008) in the *Journal of Midwifery & Women's Health* in a special issue on "The Effects of Violence and Trauma on Women's Health created a fact sheet about this type of violence. It states that you are being abused if someone

- Kicks, shoves, slaps, punches, shakes, pinches, pulls your hair, or physically harms you in any way
- Forces you to have sex against your will or makes you have sex in ways that are painful or ways that make you feel bad about yourself
- Keeps you away from friends or relatives or does not allow you to work or needs to know where you are all the time
- Says things to you that make you feel bad about yourself or calls you names in front of your children or others
- Threatens to hurt your children if you do not do what he or she wants
- Hurts your dog, cat, or other pets to punish or scare you
- Threatens to take your children if you leave him or her
- Threatens to kill himself or herself if you leave

King goes on to report that there is a cycle to IPV:

- *Phase 1*: When life begins to get tense and you can feel that something negative is going to happen so you begin to walk on eggshells.
- *Phase 2*: The eruption occurs, and that is when the screaming; hurting you, your children, and your pets; as well as breaking things happen.
- *Phase 3*: The "honeymoon" happens and everything seems to go back to normal. The abuser apologizes and promises to never do it again. There is peace for several days and then the pressure begins to build and you are back at Phase 1.

Often, it is difficult for victims of IPV to get away, or they get lulled back into feeling it will be okay to return after Phase 3. However, the cycle continues and the idealized view the victim has of the perpetrator gets shattered over and over again, only to return to its idealized form when the abuser apologizes and everything seems to return to normal.

There are few cases and studies concerning the use of EMDR and IPV for these clients. Carpenter (1999) worked with five battered women who received the shelter program and the EMDR treatment and five battered women who completed the shelter program but did not undergo the EMDR treatment. Both showed reduced posttraumatic stress disorder (PTSD), state anxiety, and depression scores; however, those with EMDR showed more improvement within these measures.

Stapleton, Taylor, and Admundson (2007) concluded that exposure therapy was more effective than EMDR in treating IPV-related PTSD. However, there was incomplete case information, and the two cases that were compared were substantially different. It does not seem that this was a valid comparison between EMDR and exposure therapy. Stowasser (2007) showcased another case study in her chapter "EMDR and Family Therapy in the Treatment of Domestic Violence," where she discusses the interface between EMDR and therapy of social action. The therapy of social action is a blended application of strategic and structural family therapy. It is a 12-step approach to working with perpetrators, victims, and their families. When used in conjunction with EMDR, it "appears to be a powerful combination for the treatment of Domestic Violence." In 2009, Phillips, Freund, Fordiani, Kuhn, and Ironson treated a woman who was a victim of domestic violence and who continued to have symptoms of PTSD 10 years after separating from her husband. She had nine actual sessions of EMDR, and they concluded that EMDR treatment was beneficial to the client as her PTSD symptoms decreased and her scores on outcome measures increased, which was a positive result. It was most helpful to elicit and process her memories of traumatic incidents and her negative self-referencing beliefs.

In 2012, Tarquinio, Schmitt, Tarquinio, Rydberg, and Spitz conducted a pilot study on EMDR and victims of domestic abuse. Thirty-six women were divided into three treatment groups: 12 received EMDR treatment, 12 received eclectic psychotherapy, and 12 were assigned to a control group. They found that women in the EMDR group displayed significantly reduced PTSD and anxiety compared to the eclectic group, and even more significantly reduced scores on PTSD, depression, and anxiety measures when compared to the control group. The effects were maintained at the 6-month follow-up. Also, the effect sizes for Impact Event Scale (IES) and State-Trait Anxiety Inventory for Adults (STAI) scores were larger for the EMDR condition subjects. This study met the authors' expectations and "confirm[s] the advantages and the potential of EMDR." Another study by Tarquinio, Schmitt, and Tarquinio (2012) offered five women subjects treatment between three and nine 60-minute EMDR sessions. Assessments were completed at pre-, post-, and 6-month follow-up to see if EMDR could reduce PTSD, anxiety, and depressive symptoms. Results demonstrated that there was a significant decrease in PTSD, anxiety, and depression scores that were maintained after 6 months. They concluded, "EMDR therapy seems to offer a promising therapeutic, social, and clinical response for this population, which is often difficult to treat." Tarquinio, Schmitt, Tarquinio, Rydberg, et al. (2012) did another study called "Benefits of Eye Movement Desensitization and Reprocessing: Psychotherapy in the Treatment of Female Victims of Intimate Partner Rape." In this study, six female patients were the victims of intimate partner rape. They completed the following measures: Hospital Anxiety and Depression Scale, IES, and subjective units of disturbance (SUDs). They had interviews before and after the treatment to assess the presence of PTSD symptoms. Results showed a "significant and gradual decrease in scores on these measures." Ultimately, EMDR led to a significant decrease in PTSD symptoms. These are all a positive trend for the use of EMDR therapy in the treatment of those who are dealing with domestic violence and IPV.

Jim Knipe has been working with the idea of defensive avoidance and embedded strong positive affect for more than 25 years. He began to write about it in the EMDR Network Newsletter (1995) and later wrote a chapter in Phillip Manfield's edited book, *Extending EMDR: A Casebook of Innovative Applications*, which he called "It was a Golden Time—Treating Narcissistic Vulnerability" (1998). His main query was how to work with the very powerful rooted positive affect that compelled his patients to engage in certain behaviors that were captivating but maladaptive and kept them in dangerous relationships, unable to move out. Intrigued, he presented at the 1998 EMDR International Association Conference with Phil Manfield and Elizabeth Snyker and continued to record his findings in the EMDRIA Newsletter (Knipe, 1999). He wrote another chapter to explore this subject and titled it "Targeting Positive Affect to Clear the Pain of Unrequited Love, Codependence, Avoidance and Procrastination" for Robin Shapiro's *EMDR Solutions* (2005). Knipe created the "EMDR Toolbox" and presented it throughout the world (2006, 2007a, 2007b, 2008a, 2008b, 2008c) to share with other clinicians. In Knipe (2009a, 2009b, 2009c, 2009d), he published four chapters for *Eye Movement Desensitization and Reprocessing (EMDR) Scripted Protocols: Special Populations*. They were on dysfunctional positive affect and addressed the following: assisting clients with unwanted avoidance defenses, procrastination, clearing the pain of unrequited love, and codependence or obsession with self-defeating behavior. In addition, Mosquera and Knipe have described procedures for therapeutically targeting dysfunctional positive affect held within an idealized, narcissistic "false self" (Mosquera & Knipe, 2015) and as a distortying element that can be addresses in the treatment of many recipients of IPV (Mosquera & Knipe, 2017).

This work is the precursor for his chapter with Dolores Mosquera in this volume. He also wrote *EMDR Toolbox: Theory and Treatment of Complex PTSD and Dissociation* (2015).

Mosquera is the director of the Institute for the Study of Trauma and Personality Disorders (INTRA-TP) in A Coruña, Spain—a three-clinic private institution initially founded in 2000 as LOGPSIC. She collaborates with two different domestic violence programs—one works with victims and the other with perpetrators. She is a recognized expert on personality disorders, complex trauma, and dissociation and has written 15 books and many articles on these subjects. In 2017, Mosquera and Knipe teamed up to write "Idealization and Maladaptive Positive Emotion: EMDR Therapy for Women Who Are Ambivalent About Leaving an Abusive Partner" for the *Journal of EMDR Practice and Research*, which is a precursor of the chapter in this section.

In Part II, "Transforming Relationship Distortion With EMDR Therapy," Mosquera and Knipe wrote Chapter 5, "EMDR Therapy and Physical Violence Injury: 'Best Moments' Protocol." This protocol is used only when the patient is expressing ambivalent feelings about whether or not to leave an abusive relationship. If clients are not ambivalent, it would not be appropriate to do this work, and it would be best to use the Standard EMDR Protocol.

The key to working with patients who have maladaptive positive emotion is to examine the distorted way they view their partner. Despite the partner's violent behavior, the patient holds firm to an overly positive viewpoint of the perpetrator and focuses on the rare "positive moments" that have happened in their relationship while minimizing the continuing threats and intermittent violence. In fact, it is almost as if the victim does not have full awareness of the violence. Because of their use of idealization and maladaptive positive emotion in these serious situations, their behavior can be life threatening. In this work, the authors process the distorted affect associated with idealized targets. This way of conceptualizing the "urge" to engage in addictive behavior began with Popky in his DeTUR method (1995, 2009) and then moved on to the positive feeling that follows.

The key with this population is to have patients focus on the best memories possible and use a "Level of Positive Affect (LOPA)" to assess the amount of positive affect and sensation. The positive statement is different than in the Standard EMDR Protocol. In this work the positive statement is a distorted cognition because of this idealization. As the processing occurs, the idealization decreases and the reality of the situation comes into focus. It is a very helpful protocol for therapists to have in their toolbox.

A summary sheet accompanies this chapter to remind clinicians of the important aspects of the chapter and to give a place to include the data of patients. There is a CD version of this text to use in the field or to enter data.

REFERENCES

Carpenter, M. N. (1999). Eye movement desensitization and reprocessing in battered women: Alleviation of post-traumatic stress disorder. *Journal of Midwifery & Women's Health, 53*, 6. Retrieved from Proquest Dissertations and Theses database (UMI No. 1394355).

Knipe, J. (1995). Targeting defensive avoidance and dissociated numbing. *EMDR Network Newsletter, 5*(2), 6–7.

Knipe, J. (1998). It was a golden time—Treating narcissistic vulnerability. In P. Manfield (Ed.), *Extending EMDR: A casebook of innovative applications* (pp. 232–255). New York, NY: W. W. Norton.

Knipe, J. (1999). Strengthening affect tolerance and adult perspective through construction of imagined dissociative avoidance. *EMDRIA Newsletter, 4*(2), 10, 25.

Knipe, J. (2002). A tool for working with dissociative clients. *EMDRIA Newsletter, 7*(2), 14–16.

Knipe, J. (2005). Targeting positive affect to clear the pain of unrequited love, codependence, avoidance, and procrastination. In R. Shapiro (Ed.), *EMDR solutions: Pathways to healing* (pp. 189–212). New York, NY: W. W. Norton.

Knipe, J. (2006, June). *EMDR toolbox: Video examples of methods of targeting avoidance, procrastination, affect dysregulation, the pain of being "dumped" by a lover, and a shame-based ego state in a client with an identity disorder*. Invited presentation at the EMDR European Conference, Istanbul, Turkey.

Knipe, J. (2007a, February). *EMDR toolbox: Video examples of methods of targeting avoidance, procrastination, affect dysregulation, the pain of being "dumped" by a lover, and a shame-based ego state in a client with an identity disorder*. Invited presentation at the EMDR Denmark Conference, Copenhagen, Denmark.

Knipe, J. (2007b, April). *EMDR toolbox: Video examples of methods of targeting avoidance, procrastination, affect dysregulation, the pain of being "dumped" by a lover, and a shame-based ego state in a client with an identity disorder.* Invited presentation at the Japan EMDR Association Annual Conference, Kyoto, Japan.

Knipe, J. (2007c). *Loving eyes: Procedures to therapeutically reverse dissociative processes while preserving emotional safety.* In C. Forgash & M. Copeley (Eds.), *Healing heart of trauma and dissociation.* New York, NY: Springer Publishing.

Knipe, J. (2008a, April). *EMDR toolbox: Video examples of methods of targeting avoidance, procrastination, affect dysregulation, the pain of being "dumped" by a lover, and a shame-based ego state in a client with an identity disorder.* Invited presentation at the EMDR Netherlands Annual Conference, Amsterdam, the Netherlands.

Knipe, J. (2008b, June). *EMDR toolbox: Video examples of methods of targeting avoidance, procrastination, affect dysregulation, the pain of being "dumped" by a lover, and a shame-based ego state in a client with an identity disorder.* Invited presentation at the EMDREA Conference, London, England.

Knipe, J. (2008c, June). *The CIPOS method—Procedures to therapeutically reduce dissociative processes while preserving emotional safety.* EMDREA Conference, London, England.

Knipe, J. (2009a). Dysfunctional positive affect: To assist clients with unwanted avoidance defenses. In M. Luber (Ed.), *Eye movement desensitization and reprocessing (EMDR) scripted protocols: Special populations* (pp. 451–452). New York, NY: Springer Publishing.

Knipe, J. (2009b). Dysfunctional positive affect: Procrastination. In M. Luber (Ed.), *Eye movement desensitization and reprocessing (EMDR) scripted protocols: Special populations* (pp. 453–458). New York, NY: Springer Publishing.

Knipe, J. (2009c). Dysfunctional positive affect: To clear the pain of unrequited love. In M. Luber (Ed.), *Eye movement desensitization and reprocessing (EMDR) scripted protocols: Special populations* (pp. 459–462). New York, NY: Springer Publishing.

Knipe, J. (2009d). Dysfunctional positive affect: Codependence or obsession with self-defeating behavior. In M. Luber (Ed.), *Eye movement desensitization and reprocessing (EMDR) scripted protocols: Special populations* (pp. 463–466). New York, NY: Springer Publishing.

Knipe, J. (2015). *EMDR toolbox: Theory and treatment of complex PTSD and dissociation.* New York, NY: Springer Publishing.

Mosquera, D., & Knipe, J. (2015). Understanding and treating narcissism with EMDR therapy. *Journal of EMDR, Practice and Research, 9*(1), 46–63. doi:10.1891/1933-3196.9.1.46

Mosquera, D., & Knipe, J. (2017). Idealization and maladaptive positive emotion: EMDR therapy for women who are ambivalent about leaving an abusive partner. *Journal of EMDR Practice and Research, 11*(13), 54–66. doi:10.1891/1933-3196.11.1.54

The National Domestic Violence Hotline. (2018). What is domestic violence? Retrieved from http://www.thehotline.org/is-this-abuse/abuse-defined/0

Phillips, K. M., Freund, B., Fordiani, J., Kuhn, R., & Ironson, G. (2009). EMDR treatment of past domestic violence: A clinical vignette. *Journal of EMDR Practice and Research, 3*(3), 192–197. doi:10.1891/1933-3196.3.3.192

Popky, A. (1995). *The use of EMDR with addictive disorders.* EMDR Network Annual Meeting, Sunnyvale, CA.

Popky, A. (2009). The Desensitization of Triggers and Urge Reprocessing (DeTUR) protocol. In M. Luber (Ed.), *Eye movement desensitization and reprocessing (EMDR) scripted protocols: Special populations* (pp. 489–515). New York, NY: Springer Publishing.

Stapleton, J. A., Taylor, S., & Admundson, G. J. G. (2007). Efficacy of various treatments in battered women: Case studies. *Journal of Cognitive Psychotherapy, 21*, 91–102. doi:10.1891/088983907780493287

Stowasser, J. E. (2007). EMDR and family therapy in the treatment of domestic violence. In F. Shapiro, F. W. Kaslow, & L. Maxfield (Eds.), *Handbook of EMDR and family therapy processes* (pp. 243–261). Hoboken, NJ: John Wiley & Sons.

Tarquinio, C., Brennstuhl, M.-J., Rydberg, J. A., Schmitt, A., Mouda, F., Lourel, M., & Tarquinio, P. (2012, October). [Eye movement desensitization and reprocessing (EMDR) therapy in the treatment of victims of domestic violence: A pilot study]. *Revue Europenne de Psychologie Applique, 62*(4), 205–212. doi:10.1016/j.erap.2012.08.006 [French]

Tarquinio, C., Schmitt, A., & Tarquinio, P. (2012, March). Violences conjugales et psychothérapie Eye movement desensitization reprocessing (EMDR): études de cas. *L & Evolution Psychiatrique, 77*(1), 97–108. doi:10.1016/j.evopsy.2011.11.002

Tarquinio, C., Schmitt, A., Tarquinio, P., Rydberg J.-A., & Spitz, E. (2012, April–June). Intérêt de la psychothérapie "Eye movement desensitization reprocessing" dans le cadre de la prise en charge de femmes victimes de viols conjugaux. *Sexologies, 21*(2), 92–99. doi:10.1016/j.sexol.2011.05.001

EMDR THERAPY AND PHYSICAL VIOLENCE INJURY: "BEST MOMENTS" PROTOCOL

Dolores Mosquera and Jim Knipe

INTRODUCTION

Many victims of prolonged intimate partner violence (IPV) enter psychotherapy in order to find a way to escape from a dangerous relationship, and for these clients, it is typically appropriate to focus within the therapy sessions on strategies for keeping safe and creating an action plan for safely ending the relationship. Other clients, though, who have been victims of violence may have had little experience in safe, healthy relationships. Many idealize or fixate on isolated "positive moments" that have occurred in the relationship and minimize the importance of persistent threats and episodic violence. Some have learned to associate control and jealousy with love: "My partner does that because he/she loves me so much." Many victims feel guilty when their partner is arrested and/or incarcerated, and quickly forget or focus away from the risks and past violent incidents. They frequently will wish to drop charges and go back to their abusive relationships. In this way, idealization and maladaptive positive emotion in IPV situations are serious, potentially life-threatening issues—issues that can be understood and treated within the Adaptive Information Processing (AIP) model.

Idealization and maladaptive positive emotion are often overlooked in psychotherapy (Mosquera & Knipe, 2015), where the emphasis is usually placed on working through negative emotions related to adverse and traumatizing experiences (Gonzales & Mosquera, 2012).

IDEALIZED MOMENTS: DYSFUNCTIONALLY STORED INFORMATION/MALADAPTIVE POSITIVE AFFECT

Accessing disturbing memories of traumatic experiences is not the only way to target dysfunctionally stored information (DSI). When dealing with IPV, strong investment in an unrealistic positive image of a perpetrating partner can block full conscious access to memories of specific traumatic experiences, preventing the resolution of the memories of violence. Full awareness of abuse memories is blocked by overly valued memories of the "best moments" with the abusive "other." Consequently, the victim is unable to realize the danger of the situation, and therapeutic progress is impaired (Mosquera & Knipe, 2017).

In order to expand our possibilities of intervention with EMDR therapy, it is important to think from a broad conceptualization of the experiential "information" that is dysfunctionally stored. The concept of DSI, described in the AIP model, can be viewed as being broader in nature than memories for adverse experiences and can include dysfunctional defenses such as strong emotional investment in an inaccurate and overly idealized image of a relationship partner.

This approach, which has been described previously as an EMDR-related treatment for codependence (Knipe, 2005, 2009), involves "processing" distorted and dysfunctional positive affect associated with idealized images. This approach, using focused sets of bilateral stimulation (BLS) to target dysfunctional positive affect, was first described and pioneered by Popky, with his DeTUR method

(1995, 2005), for treating addictive disorders—both substance addictions and behavioral "addictions." A behavioral addiction can be defined as a behavioral sequence of the following:

1. Specific situational or experiential "triggers," which activate a strong urge and then lead to an addictive behavior
2. The addictive behavior, which results immediately in an experience of positive affect
3. And then, at a later time (immediately or perhaps the next day), negative affect of low self-esteem and shame, anxiety, and feelings of helplessness ("My addiction is bigger than I am!")

Often, there is initially a degree of dissociative disconnect—a lack of full co-conscious access—between (2) and (3). With repeated occurrences, this behavioral sequence can become strongly entrenched in what Hase and colleagues (2008) have described as an "Addiction Memory"—an implicit memory of positive affect that arises in consciousness as an urge to initiate and repeat the addictive sequence. People can develop a substance addiction to alcohol, drugs, and also endogenous (self-generated) chemicals such as endorphins and dopamine that accompany out-of-control behavioral addictions (e.g., gambling, compulsive shopping, pornography, video games, etc.). Effective EMDR targeting, for clients with an addictive disorder, can begin with the following:

- The *urge* to engage in the addictive behavior (Hase, 2006; Knipe, 2014; Popky, 2005)
- The *positive feeling* that immediately accompanies the addictive behavior (Knipe, 1998, 2005, 2010; Miller, 2010; Popky, 1995)
- The *anxiety and shame* that may occur at a later point after a compulsive dysfunctional behavior (Greenwald, 2000)
- After an *addictive relapse* (Hase, 2006)

Any of these targets can be the entry point for useful therapeutic processing, and, for the therapist, the choice of targets really depends on accessibility and considerations of client safety and preference.

This model of addiction can be used in treating the problem of codependence—a strong emotional "investment" in continuing to hold an unrealistically positive image of a relationship partner. Because of this distorted image of the partner, the person continues to return repeatedly to a dysfunctional, abusive relationship. Sometimes clients describe their ambivalent experience as a type of "compulsion" or "addiction." As one woman said, "I never took any drugs or anything like that, but I am pretty sure the feeling is similar." That emotional investment may be driven by memories of a subset of genuinely positive experiences. These positive memories may be emotionally satisfying in themselves, and this positive feeling may block and prevent full awareness of other disturbing and traumatic events that have occurred within that relationship or within previous relationships. In these instances, the effectiveness of the standard EMDR therapy is likely to be impaired because the full conscious access to the disturbing memories is blocked (Mosquera & Knipe, 2017).

It can be useful, in these instances, to ask the client to think of a highly positive memory that is representative of the idealized image of the partner. There may be positive cognitions (PCs) associated with that visual memory image, such as "He really loves me!" or "I am lovable" or "He is strong and is protecting me." The client may be asked for a LOPA score, 0 to 10, associated with the positive memory, and the location of the positive affect in physical sensations can be determined. Then, these elements of positive visual image, positive cognition, and positive emotion and body sensations can be combined with sets of BLS (see the script for detailed steps of how to apply the procedure). To the extent that the positive image of the partner is unrealistic and idealized, that idealization is likely to diminish with continued sets of BLS, resulting in the client being able to have a clearer and more objective understanding of the negatives in the relationship (as well as an objective perspective regarding any positive elements). This will allow the client to make much better decisions regarding issues of safety and whether to discontinue the relationship.

DIAGNOSES

The use of this "best moment" intervention is not determined by the client's diagnosis, but by the extent that the client is perceiving the partner in a distorted, overly positive way. This type of distortion can occur across many diagnostic categories.

RESEARCH

This intervention has been used successfully by the authors, their colleagues, and supervises, but has not been evaluated in a clinical trial.

MEASURES

The measure used for this procedure is the LOPA score, where "on a scale of 0 to 10, where zero is no good feeling or sensation or neutral and 10 is the most positive you can imagine, how nice does it feel now?"

EMDR THERAPY FOR THE BEST MOMENTS PROTOCOL: PROCESSING THE IDEALIZED IMAGE OF THE PERPETRATING OTHER SCRIPT NOTES

Assessing the Current State of the Client

EMDR therapy for the Best Moments Protocol is recommended whenever some of the following indicators of dysfunctional positive affect exist for the client:

- Thinking about dropping charges, following a clearly abusive and/or life-threatening incident
- Missing the perpetrator and not being able to recall negative experiences
- Not realizing the severity of events
- Lacking the understanding of the danger of the situation
- Continuing codependency issues

For many situations of posttraumatic stress resulting from IPV, the Standard EMDR Protocol is likely to be the treatment of choice. A representative memory image of an abusive incident can be identified, along with negative self-referencing cognitions such as "I am helpless" or "I can't say what I really feel" and alternative positive cognitions, such as "I am able to protect myself," "I deserve to be treated with respect," or "I am easily able to say what I really feel, with complete respect for both myself and other people." For many clients who have been through traumatic IPV, EMDR Phases 3 to 7 can be very useful in helping the client attain whatever adaptive resolution is appropriate for the situation. Alternatively, the procedures described in this chapter can be used when standard processing is blocked by an idealization defense.

Preparation Prior to the Best Moments Protocol

During the preparation phase, it is important to do the following:

- Establish a strong therapeutic alliance between the therapist and the patient
  Goal: Through accurate, communicated empathetic attunement, the client can come to an awareness of emotional safety when in the therapist's office, and this sense of safety can then be a resource to fortify the client in coming to a realization regarding traumatic events.
- Educate the client through psychoeducation about AIP and interpersonal violence
  Goal: To reformulate the client's presenting problems in terms of dysfunctional positive affect.
- Anticipate and explain possible changes and phases that may take place during the therapy process
  Goal: Anticipate potential "difficulties" as part of this process, to help clients understand the rationale for the work and feel safe. Introduce psychoeducation about frequent responses in survivors of domestic violence; for example, missing the perpetrator, wanting to drop charges, or minimizing what happened and blaming oneself.

Annex: Processing Idealization-Related Moments

In cases of domestic violence, we can also target moments related to the idealization, such as moments when they miss the perpetrator or have unrealistic feelings of inadequacy/self-blame. In these cases, we can use the Standard EMDR Protocol.

We have found that the inclusion of targeting of idealization defenses such as "best moments" often has a transformative effect in the treatment of IPV survivors. Other idealization-related targets can be selected in these cases, as illustrated in the following examples:

Example 1: *Maintaining the idealization*: A 56-year-old woman whose husband tried to kill her and her parents and burn them alive had many difficulties when she tried to sleep at night. She understood that she couldn't be with the perpetrator anymore and that he was in jail for attempted murder. Still she felt lonely and missed him. When we explored the worst part of the situation for her, she said: "When I go to bed and he is not there anymore. I can't sleep, I miss him and I can't even sleep inside the sheets because he is not there."

In this instance, the client was maintaining the idealization, and longed to have the perpetrator back, because he was perceived as a solution to the problem of the fear of abandonment. If things get stuck with the Standard EMDR Protocol, there may be a need for an internal dialogue between the part that longs for him and the part that more realistically sees him as a danger and a bad partner. Sets of BLS can facilitate this healing dialogue.

Example 2: After targeting the best moment with a 48-year-old woman referred by a program of victims of domestic violence, the therapist and the client explored other problematic aspects that interfered with the client functioning in daily life. The client said: "When I think about them happy together (perpetrator and new partner), I feel so bad!" The client hadn't seen them together, but she had imagined this so many times that she even had an imagined mental picture for it. Although this was not a real memory, it had become maladaptively encoded information that could be targeted per se.

> *Target*: The selected target was the "idea of him, with her, happy" (the image was a representation of this idea, which she had played in her mind over and over).
>
> *Negative cognition* (NC): The negative belief was easy to identify for the client: "I am guilty. It is my fault." These NCs seemed almost equivalent to the client, and therefore, they were both accepted, essentially, as one NC.
>
> *Positive cognition* (PC): The PC was not so easy to identify. When the client was asked what she would rather think, she gave a positive cognition that was other-referencing, not self-referencing. She said, "He is happy with me." After an extended discussion, the client accepted a PC suggested by the therapist: The opposite of "I am guilty" or "It is not my fault" was suggested as a starting point. The therapist suggested another PC—"I am innocent"—but the client preferred "It is not my fault."

By processing this DSI (the idealized image of the ex-boyfriend), the client was able to differentiate her overly positive view of the moments they lived together from the reality (i.e., attain adaptive resolution). During the processing, she connected to thinking about the trial she would have to attend on the following week: "He is going to laugh at me," "It will be another failure." These thoughts were simply channels of information on the way to resolution. Later on, during the processing, she had an important realization: "He always put me down, but it was really the other way around. He did not deserve me." This session was productive, but was incomplete, since some disturbance was left. However, following this session, the client was able to think with more clarity about the situation, and she started taking better care of herself. The client was able to go to trial the following week, feeling more secure and proud when she realized that an important change had taken place. In a subsequent session, she said: "I could hold my head up. I knew it was not my fault the whole time I was there."

EMDR PROTOCOL FOR THE BEST MOMENTS SCRIPT: PROCESSING THE IDEALIZED IMAGE OF THE PERPETRATING OTHER

Phase 1: History Taking and Case Conceptualization

The "best moments" intervention should be considered when the client, during the time of initial history taking and treatment planning, expresses mixed feelings (ambivalent confusion and disturbance) regarding whether to leave a repeatedly violent relationship. For clients who are not ambivalent, this procedure would not be appropriate or needed.

Case Conceptualization

The client is conceptualized as having an unresolved conflict between personality parts: One part idealizes the partner and another part holds traumatic memories of the violent mistreatment. The idealization is experienced with unrealistic but strong positive affect, and prevents the client from having full realization of what occurred during the violence and the implications of that violence for the relationship. By targeting and resolving the idealization defense, the memory of violence becomes fully accessible and available for effective standard EMDR processing.

Phase 2: Preparation

Explanation of EMDR and AIP

Say, *"When a trauma occurs, it seems to get locked in the nervous system with the original picture, sounds, thoughts, and feelings. The eye movements we use in EMDR seem to unlock the nervous system and allow the brain to process the experience. That may be what is happening in REM or dream sleep—the eye movements may help to process the unconscious material. It is important to note that it is your own brain that will be doing the healing and that you are the one in control."*

Explanation of Stuck Issues

Say, *"Some people have difficulties in realizing the danger they are in. It is like they know at a rational level but something emotional does not allow them to think it through and see the situation with clarity. There may be confusion, and as a result, the person may remain in contact with the danger. In some cases, the problem is related to idealized moments like in your case. Perhaps that is what is happening with you, and if we can work with this, it might help you not feel so confused. We can try it and see if it helps.* _____ *(give a specific example about the case)."*

Anticipate Possible Disruptive Changes That May Occur

Say, *"This can be hard. It can be very difficult to reevaluate or let go of cherished moments. I will be here with you to help out. It is possible that when we target idealized moments, you will have contact with difficult issues. The idea is for you to be able to become clear about the reality of your situation and what are the best choices to meet the larger therapy goals you have described to me and be in contact with the reality. Processing won't take away anything you need or anything that is important. It will just help you make the choices that are best for you so that you are in contact with the reality and more aware of what your choices are and the adaptive information you need to be able to access."*

Use normal resources for preparation.

Phase 3: Assessment

When there is a clear idealization of the perpetrating other, we search for the "best moment." General steps to follow:

Incident

Say, *"When you think of* _____ *(perpetrator's name), can you remember happy times, or loving times?"*

_____

_____

If the client says, "Yes," say the following:

> *"When you are missing _____ (him or her), and longing to be with _____ (him or her), again, what are the times with _____ (him or her) that you are remembering?"*

_____

_____

_____

Picture

Say, *"Is there a time, or a moment, that stands out as still being an especially positive memory, maybe the best memory?"*

_____

_____

Positive Feeling

If yes, say the following:

> *"When you think of that time, or that moment, do you have a good feeling, even right now?"*

_____

_____

Note: If the client identifies a "best moment," but then says, "I have mixed positive and negative feelings about it right now," say the following:

> *"Can you just put your negative feelings off to the side right now, and focus on the positive feelings that you still have, when you think of that moment?"*

_____

_____

If the client says that his or her "best moment" brings up only negative feelings, that may be an indication that the client is now beginning to relinquish an unrealistic idealized image of the abusive partner. However, the therapist still may need to check to see if the idealized image is continuing to distort the client's perception of the relationship, to some degree. If an element of idealization is still occurring, the therapist and client can then find another "best moment" that represents that remaining idealization.

Get cognitions associated with the positively valanced memory image (best moment). This type of PC is not the same as the PCs used in the standard EMDR trauma procedures. These are statements about self or about the other that are distorted because of the idealization (e.g., "When I am with him, I am safe." Or "When he smiles at me, it proves he really loves me").

> Say, *"As you think about that picture and the nice sensation in your body, is there a positive statement about _____ (him or her), or about yourself, that comes up for you now?"*

_____

_____

LOPA

The LOPA score may be very high (e.g., 8–10), which would reflect the high degree of idealized distortion in the client's image of the perpetrator.

> Say, *"On a scale of 0 to 10, where 0 is no good feeling or sensation of niceness or neutral and 10 is the most nice you can imagine, how nice does it feel now?"*

> 0   1   2   3   4   5   6   7   8   9   10

> (no good feeling or sensation of niceness)   (the most nice you can imagine)

Ask for the body location of the 0–10 LOPA score.

Location of Body Sensation

> Say, *"Where do you feel it* (the disturbance) *in your body?"*

_____

_____

Continue with the rest of the Standard EMDR Protocol.

Phase 4: Desensitization

Reprocess, by asking the client to hold in mind the image of the "best moment," the dysfunctional positive cognitions about self or about the perpetrator, and the location of positive sensations in the body, and then initiate sets of BLS.

> Say, *"Now, remember, it is your own brain that is doing the healing and you are the one in control. I will ask you to mentally focus on the target and to _____* (state the BLS you are using). *Just let whatever happens, happen, and we will talk at the end of the set. Just tell me what comes up and don't discard anything as unimportant. Any new information that comes to mind is connected in some way. If you want to stop, just raise your hand."*

> Then say, *"Bring up the picture of the best moment and the words _____* (state the dysfunctional positive PC about self or perpetrator) *and notice where you feel it in your body. Now follow _____* (state the BLS)*."*

As the processing continues, the idealization (maladaptive or dysfunctional positive information) is very likely to decrease in intensity and the reality of the situation (adaptive information) will become increasingly available. The reality-based information about the perpetrator may contain positive moments that are not distorted, but with processing the client will be better able to put these moments into a more realistic perspective (i.e., along with the very negative moments) so that good decisions about the relationship will be facilitated.

For some clients, the idealization will be so strong that it initially overrides the awareness of the horror of the abuse. Other clients may feel an uncomfortable ambivalence, due to conflicting internal agendas: wanting to maintain the dysfunctional idealized image of the partner while also having posttraumatic images and disturbance from violent incidents.

Phase 5: Installation

During the processing of the idealization image, the client may become aware of personal strengths and resources, such as "I can stand up for myself" or "I have the right and the ability to take action to protect myself." These PCs will be resources that can be installed during the continuing processing of the idealization and/or traumatic events that have occurred in the relationship.

Phase 6: Body Scan

At the end of the "best moment" targeting, when the client gives a verbal report that indicates his or her previous idealization of the partner has now shifted, the therapist should check to see if some positive physical sensations connected with the idealization still remain to be processed. If such sensations are still present, continuing sets of BLS will be likely to bring them to a more realistic adaptive resolution. For example, "I did enjoy those times with him, and it is okay for me to remember how that felt, but I see now that I didn't see the whole picture, the price I had to pay."

Phase 7: Closure

It is important to close the session enhancing realization, with questions such as the following:

Say, *"What have you realized today after the work we did?"*

_____

_____

Or say, *"How can the work we did help you from now on?"*

_____

_____

Phase 8: Reevaluation

Reevaluate like any other target.

It is important to pay attention to the following questions when the client returns after doing EMDR work.

Say, *"When you think of whatever is left of the problem that we worked on last time, how disturbing is it now on a scale of 0 to 10, where 0 is no disturbance or neutral and 10 is the highest disturbance you can imagine?"*

0   1   2   3   4   5   6   7   8   9   10

(no disturbance)   (highest disturbance)

Say, *"Have you noticed any other material associated with the original memory since the last session?"*

Check changes to see if the initial ambivalence and dysfunctional positive affect are still there.

Say, *"You did some very good work last time, sorting out your mixed feelings about him and about the relationship. Did you think about it more after the session? Were there moments when you felt confused again, even a little bit?"*

_____

_____

If there were any moments like that, say the following:

"Let's take a look to see what went on with that. Please tell me what moment we should target."

_____

_____

Then, the identified moments can be targeted, using these procedures.

SUMMARY

Individuals who repeatedly return to an abusive and dangerous relationship can often benefit from standard EMDR therapy, to resolve their confusion, resolve feelings of shame and helplessness, and make positive choices. Some return to the relationship because of a fear of violent consequences if they attempt to leave, and in these situations, the procedures described in this chapter would not be appropriate—instead, therapy in these instances is better focused on creating an action plan to successfully and safely leave a dangerous situation. However, a subset of individuals, who return to a relationship following violence, may be blocked in utilizing the therapeutic power of EMDR by their strong emotional investment in an unrealistic positive image of the abusive partner. The authors have described a procedure to assist such clients in removing this block to processing, through identifying and targeting a "best moment" memory that represents the distorted idealized image of the partner and of the relationship.

REFERENCES

Gonzalez, A., & Mosquera, D. (2012). *EMDR and dissociation*: *The progressive approach*. Ed Createspace. Spanish Edition: *EMDR y Disociación*: *El Abordaje Progresivo*. Madrid: Ed. Pléyades.

Greenwald, R. (2000, April). A trauma-focused individual therapy approach for adolescents with conduct disorder. *International Journal of Offender Therapy and Comparative Criminology, 44*(2), 146–163. doi:10.1177/0306624X00442002

Knipe, J. (1998). It was a golden time. . . . Treating narcissistic vulnerability. In P. Manfield (Ed.), *Extending EMDR*: *A casebook of innovative applications* (1st ed., pp. 232–255). New York, NY: W. W. Norton.

Knipe, J. (2005). Targeting positive affect to clear the pain of unrequited love, codependence, avoidance, and procrastination. In R. Shapiro (Ed.), *EMDR solutions*: *Pathways to healing* (pp. 189–212). New York, NY: W. W. Norton.

Knipe, J. (2009). Dysfunctional positive affect: Codependence or obsession with self-defeating behavior. In M. Luber (Ed.), *EMDR scripted protocols*: *Special populations* (pp. 463–466). New York, NY: Springer Publishing.

Knipe, J. (2010). *Shame is my safe place*. EMDRIA Annual Conference, Minneapolis, MN.

Knipe, J. (2014). *EMDR toolbox*: *Theory and treatment of complex PTSD and dissociation*. New York, NY: Springer Publishing.

Miller, R. (2010).The feeling-state theory of impulse-control disorders and case the impulse-control disorder protocol. *Traumatology, 16*(3), 2–10. doi:10.1177/1534765610365912

Mosquera, D., & Knipe, J. (2015). Understanding and treating narcissism with EMDR therapy. *Journal of EMDR, Practice and Research, 9*(1), 46–63. doi:10.1891/1933-3196.9.1.46

Mosquera, D., & Knipe, J. (2017). Idealization and maladaptive positive emotion: EMDR therapy for women who are ambivalent about leaving an abusive partner. *Journal of EMDR, Practice and Research, 11*(1), 54–66. doi:10.1891/1933-3196.11.1.54

Popky, A. (1995). *The use of EMDR with addictive disorders*. EMDR Network Annual Meeting, Sunnyvale, CA.

Popky, A. J. (2005). DeTUR, an urge reduction protocol for addictions and dysfunctional behaviours. In R. Shapiro (Ed.), *EMDR solutions* (pp. 167–188). New York, NY: W-W. Norton.

Dolores Mosquera and Jim Knipe
SUMMARY SHEET BY MARILYN LUBER

Name: _____ Diagnosis: _____

Medications: _____

Test Results: _____

☑ Check when task is completed, response has changed, or to indicate symptoms.

Note: This material is meant as a checklist for your response. Please keep in mind that it is only a reminder of different tasks that may or may not apply to your incident.

DIAGNOSES

The use of this "best moment" intervention is not determined by the client's diagnosis, but by the extent that the client is perceiving the partner in a distorted, overly positive way. This type of distortion can occur across many diagnostic categories.

MEASURES

Level of Positive Affect (LOPA): ___1/10

EMDR THERAPY AND PHYSICAL VIOLENCE INJURY: "BEST MOMENTS" SCRIPTED PROTOCOL NOTES

EMDR Therapy for the Best Moments Protocol is recommended whenever some of the following indicators of dysfunctional positive affect exist for the client:

- ☐ Thinking about dropping charges, following a clearly abusive and/or life-threatening incident
- ☐ Missing the perpetrator and not being able to recall negative experiences
- ☐ Not realizing the severity of events
- ☐ Lacking understanding of the danger of the situation
- ☐ Continuing codependency issues

EMDR THERAPY AND PHYSICAL VIOLENCE INJURY: "BEST MOMENTS" SCRIPTED PROTOCOL

Phase 1: History Taking

- The "best moments" intervention should be considered when the client, during the time of initial history taking and treatment planning, expresses mixed feelings (ambivalent confusion and disturbance) regarding whether to leave a repeatedly violent relationship. For clients who are not ambivalent, this procedure would not be appropriate or needed.

Case Conceptualization

The client is conceptualized as having an unresolved conflict between personality parts: One part idealizes the partner and another part holds traumatic memories of the violent mistreatment. The idealization is experienced with unrealistic but strong positive affect, and prevents the client from having the full realization of what occurred during the violence and the implications of that violence for the relationship. By targeting and resolving the idealization defense, the memory of violence becomes fully accessible and available for effective standard EMDR processing.

Phase 2: Preparation

Explanation of EMDR as in the Standard EMDR Protocol   ☐ Yes ☐ No

"When a trauma occurs, it seems to be locked in the nervous system with the original picture, sounds, thoughts, and feelings. The eye movements we use in EMDR seem to unlock the nervous system and allow the brain to process the experience. That may be what is happening in REM or dream sleep—eye movements may help to process the unconscious material. It is important to remember that it is your own brain that will be doing the healing and you are the one in control."

Explanation of Stuck Issues   ☐ Yes ☐ No

"Some people have difficulties in realizing the danger they are in. It is like they know at a rational level, but something emotional does not allow them to think it through and see the situation with clarity. There may be confusion, and as a result, the person may remain in contact with the danger. In some cases, the problem is related to idealized moments, like in your case. Perhaps that is what is happening with you, and if we can work with this, it might help you not feel so confused. We can try it, and see if it helps _____ (give a specific example about the case)."

Anticipate Possible Disruptive Changes That May Occur   ☐ Yes ☐ No

"This can be hard. It can be very difficult to reevaluate or let go of cherished moments. I will be here with you to help out. It is possible that when we target idealized moments, you will have contact with difficult issues. The idea is for you to be able to become clear about the reality of your situation, and what are the best choices to meet the larger therapy goals you have described to me and be in contact with the reality. Processing won't take away anything you need or anything that is important. It will just help you make the choices that are best for you so that you are in contact with the reality and more aware of what your choices are and the adaptive information you need to be able to access."

Use the normal resources for preparation.

Phase 3: Assessment

"When you think of _____ (perpetrator's name), can you remember happy times, or loving times?"

_____

"When you are missing _____ (him or her), and longing to be with _____ (him or her) again, what are the times with _____ (him or her) that you are remembering?"

_____

_____

Most positive target/memory/image: _____

_____

Positive feeling: _____

If mixed emotions:

"Can you just put your negative feelings off to the side right now, and focus on the positive feelings that you still have, when you think of that moment?"   □ Yes □ No

If no, and client idealizing the perpetrator, find another best moment.

_____

_____

PCs here are different than the usual PC and are statements about self or other that are distorted because of the idealization, that is, "When I am with him, I am safe."

"As you think about that picture and the nice sensation in your body, is there a positive statement about _____ (him or her), *or about yourself, that comes up for you now?"*

_____

_____

LOPA: ___/10

Sensation:_____

Continue with the rest of the Standard EMDR Protocol.

Phase 4: Desensitization

Apply the Standard EMDR Protocol for all targets

Image of the "best moment" + Dysfunctional PC + Location of positive body sensations + BLS

Phase 5: Installation

Install the PC.

Original PC: □ Use original PC □ Use new PC

New PC (if new one is better): _____

VOC: ____/7

Incident + PC + BLS

Phase 6: Body Scan

Unresolved positive physical sensations: _____

_____

Unresolved positive physical sensations + BLS

Strengthen more adaptive resolution using BLS.

If there is more discomfort, reprocess until discomfort subsides + BLS. Then repeat body scan.

VOC: ___/7

Phase 7: Closure

What you realized after work done: _____

_____

How work can help you from now on: _____

_____

PC: _____

Phase 8: Reevaluation

LOPA: ____/10

Noticed since last session: _____

_____

Any confusion remaining: ☐ Yes ☐ No

Comment: _____

New material to target: _____

_____

Use "best moments" protocol or Standard EMDR Protocol as needed.

SHIFTING CHRONIC PAIN EXPERIENCE USING EMDR THERAPY

The American Academy of Pain Medicine (2018) defines pain in this way:

> While acute pain is a normal sensation triggered in the nervous system to alert you to possible injury and the need to take care of yourself, chronic pain is different. Chronic pain persists. Pain signals keep firing in the nervous system for weeks, months, even years. There may have been an initial mishap—sprained back, serious infection, or there may be an ongoing cause of pain—arthritis, cancer, ear infection, but some people suffer chronic pain in the absence of any past injury or evidence of body damage. Many chronic pain conditions affect older adults. Common chronic pain complaints include headache, low back pain, cancer pain, arthritis pain, neurogenic pain (pain resulting from damage to the peripheral nerves or to the central nervous system itself).

According to the Global Industry Analysts (PRWeb, 2011), a recent market research report indicated that more than 1.5 billion people worldwide suffer from chronic pain and that approximately 3% to 4.5% of the global population suffers from neuropathic pain, with the incidence rate increasing as people age. In the United States, chronic pain affects over 100 million Americans (Institute of Medicine Report, 2011).

Other facts that show the impact of chronic pain are the following:

- The total annual incremental cost of healthcare due to pain ranges from $560 billion to $635 billion (in 2010 dollars) in the United States, which combines the medical costs of pain care and the economic costs related to disability days and lost wages and productivity (Institute of Medicine Report, 2011).
- More than half of all hospitalized patients experienced pain in the last days of their lives, and although therapies are present to alleviate most pain for those dying of cancer, research shows that 50% to 75% of patients die in moderate to severe pain (Connors et al., 1995).
- An estimated 20% of American adults (42 million people) report that pain or physical discomfort disrupts their sleep a few nights a week or more (National Sleep Foundation, 2000).
- When asked about four common types of pain, respondents of a National Institute of Health Statistics survey indicated that low-back pain was the most common (27%), followed by severe headache or migraine pain (15%), neck pain (15%), and facial ache or pain (4%; National Centers for Health Statistics, 2006).

Chronic pain has been a subject of conversation in EMDR therapy circles from its start. Ray Blanford and Carol Blanford (1991) reported in the EMDR Network Newsletter about the first pain protocol. Based on observation, the authors had clients move their bodies into positions that maximized the pain and then focused on the memories needed to reprocess (they did not specify if the memories were pain related or not). They used eye movements while the client was in a position to maximize pain until the pain reached a low level or was gone. Then, the next point of pain was identified as it often moved to a new location. It was reprocessed until the pain reduced or was no longer there. They added in self-EMDR for times when an unforeseen activity reestablished the old pain pathway, but they did not advocate self-EMDR's use in new areas. They cautioned that it was important to address secondary gains and to help clients make room for a new experience of being pain free. This was part of the early exploration when practitioners were looking into how EMDR therapy could assist their patients with whatever problems they had.

In 1993, Bruce Eimer (1993a, 1993b) created an in-depth treatment that he called the "Chronic Pain Protocol," which became the inspiration for further protocols on pain management and phantom limb pain. Ultimately, his protocol was based on Cheek and LeCron's (1968) assessment of the client's "pain complex" and the "coping complex" and the Standard EMDR Protocol. In his 21-step protocol, he focused on the pain itself as the patient targeted the actual physical attributes of pain, He introduced the concept of "antidote images" to help shift the negative images that patients used to represent pain. By 1994 and 1995, Eimer reported getting excellent results with his pain patients and presented his findings at EMDR International Association conferences.

In 1995, Hassard wrote his paper, "Investigation of Eye Movement Desensitization in Pain Clinic Patients," for *Behavioral and Cognitive Psychotherapy*. He worked with 27 pain patients referred for EMD. Of the 19 that finished, 12 were successful and 7 were complete failures, who dropped out before the end of treatment. There was an overall decrease, with some return of symptoms on a 3-month follow-up. Tesarz et al. (2014) criticized this report because Hassard had not formally learned EMDR and just "initiated the procedure based on the published description." Tesarz et al. concluded in their review on chronic pain, "The weakest effects on pain intensity were observed in the only study in which the therapist had no direct training in EMDR and may support the recommendation that EMDR treatment requires special training."

Following Funabiki's (1993) observation that surgical experience was traumatic, Christine Rost (2003) in her article "EMDR in the Treatment of Chronic Pain," published in the journal *Zeitschrift für Psychotraumatologie und Psychologische Medizin*, hypothesized the importance of trauma in the chronic pain patient's treatment and how EMDR therapy can be used to support recovery.

According to the Amputee Coalition, "Phantom limb pain (PLP) refers to ongoing painful sensations that seem to be coming from the part of the limb that is no longer there. The limb is gone, but the pain is real.... It is believed that nearly 80% of the amputee population world has experienced this kind of pain" (2018, paras. 1–2). Levin (1992) was the first to report working successfully with phantom limb pain in one session. The patient had lost his finger as a result of an industrial accident. Later, in 1996, Linda Vanderlaan (2000) treated a 15-year-old girl with phantom limb pain, 8 days after her surgery following an EMDR Basic training in Bogota, Columbia. The training was for staff of Forjar, an NGO that focused on abandoned children who have AIDS or cancer. After EMDR, she no longer had phantom limb pain. Sandra Wilson, Bob Tinker, and Lee Becker saw a presentation about Vandarlaan's work at EMDRIA's 1996 conference and were inspired to do a pilot study using the case series approach with seven amputees. Most patients' phantom limb pain disappeared within three sessions. In Germany, they used brain imaging to see the pre- and post-EMDR conditions of patients with phantom limb pain (Wilson, Tinker, Becker, Hofmann, & Cole, 2000). They went on to publish a chapter, "The Phantom Limb Pain Protocol (Wilson & Tinker, 2009)," in Robin Shapiro's *EMDR Solutions* and another in 2009 *Eye Movement Desensitization and Reprocessing (EMDR) Scripted Protocols: Special Populations.* Their protocol includes history taking and rapport building, targeting the trauma, and fully targeting the pain itself with their phantom pain scale (PPS), which measures the range of pain on a 0 to 10 scale, similar to the subjective units of disturbance that are part of the Standard EMDR Protocol.

Wilensky reported his findings with five cases of patients with PLP in the *EMDRAC Newsletter* (2000) and the *Journal of Brief Therapy* (2006). Four of the five patients completed the treatment and reported that the pain was "completely eliminated" or reduced to 1/10. The client who stopped treatment had reduced his pain by half and found it tolerable to live with it and was not interested in pursuing any further interventions. He targeted the accident as well as other earlier related memories or beliefs. The treatment also resulted in an increased positive sense of self. Navy commander Mark Russell (2008) thought this work would be important for the military because of the large number of service members with PLP after surviving combat-related trauma. His report on an active duty patient who suffered a traumatic leg amputation took four sessions of EMDR. The patient's PLP, as well as his PTSD and depression symptomatology, was eliminated. He concluded that the results were promising and more research was needed.

Since 1997, Mark Grant has been speaking and writing about pain management, as well as creating CDs to help with chronic pain. He began by presenting on *EMDR in a Multi-Modal Approach to Chronic Pain* (1997a) at the EMDR International Conference. He went on to create a manual for clinicians, *Pain Control with EMDR* (1997b) that was later updated into a treatment manual in 2009. In 2002, Grant and Threlfo reported on three cases in their article, *EMDR In the Treatment of Chronic Pain,* that appeared in the *Journal of Clinical Psychology*. They found that all their subjects reported substantially lower pain levels, a decrease in negative affect and were able to manage their pain levels. They concluded that the results indicated that EMDR "may be efficacious" and supported more research. In 2009, he wrote *Change your Brain, Change your Pain* (2009b) where he described how pain affects the brain, and strategies for changing the pain. In Pain Control with EMDR, found in Luber's *EMDR Scripted Protocols: Special Populations* (2009c), he modified the Standard EMDR Protocol to support his pain populations' needs by assessing and educating his patients about pain, targeting the pain by eliciting a description of the physical sensations, either installing a PC or substituting "antidote imagery," and introducing a future template to manage future pain episodes. In 2016, he wrote *"The New Change Your Brain, Change Your Pain."* His website, www.overcomingpain.com was one of the first EMDR-related websites to deal with overcoming physical, emotional, or a combination of both types of pain.

In 2010, De Roos, Veenstra, de Jongh et al. published the "Treatment of Chronic Phantom Limb Pain Using a Trauma-Focused Psychological Approach," with the Standard EMDR Protocol and the "EMDR Pain Control Protocol for Present Pain." In this uncontrolled observational clinical trial that used a pretest/posttest design with a 3-month follow-up at variable time points, four of the 10 participants were pain free at the 3-month follow-up and six improved. After a long-term follow-up, three were pain free and two had reduced pain. For the two nonresponders, they viewed their amputations as life saving and therefore did not experience them as traumatic. De Roos and Veenstra (2009) also contributed to *Eye Movement Desensitization and Reprocessing (EMDR) Scripted Protocols: Special Populations* with their chapter, "EMDR Pain Protocol for Current Pain." In this chapter they distinguished three kinds of EMDR targets: traumatic memories, pain-related memories, and current pain. They gave guidance on what to do when patients find it difficult to focus on processing or are unable to see or report changes. They included suggestions on different types of interweaves to facilitate the work.

Gerhardt (2016) investigated the utility of EMDR therapy for patients who have chronic pain. There were 40 patients with chronic back pain and psychological trauma. They were randomized with two conditions: TAU or EMDR therapy + TAU with follow-ups at 2 weeks after the study and 6 months later. The major outcome was a reduction in pain, measured by pain intensity, disability, and treatment satisfaction. Forty percent of the EMDR group + TAU improved clinically and evaluated their situation as satisfactory clinically. However, in the control group, no patients showed any clinical improvement. The authors decided that EMDR is a safe and effective therapy treatment to decrease pain intensity and disability with chronic back pain.

In 2017, Rostaminejad, Behnammoghadam, Rostaminejad, Behnammoghadam, and Bashti did a randomized-controlled trial with 60 patients with amputations and divided them randomly into two experimental and control groups at the Clinical Rehabilitation Unit in the city of Yasuj. The experimental group received EMDR therapy in 12 one-hour, individual sessions and completed the SUDs and a pain rating scale pre and post the intervention. The authors identified four targets for reprocessing: memory of the event that caused the injury, memory of the amputation, memories of difficulties functioning because of the amputation, and the physical pain sensations themselves. For both groups there were 1- and 24-month follow-ups. There was no change in the control group at either interval. However, for the experimental group, differences were statistically significant (p less than .001) using a repeated-measures analysis of variance. Because of these results and their maintenance at the 24-month follow-up, the authors recommended EMDR for the treatment of PLP. They concluded, "The results of this randomized-controlled trial confirm the efficacy of EMDR therapy as an efficient and long-lasting treatment for PLP."

The first chapter in this section, "EMDR Therapy and Chronic Pain Conditions," is by Jonas Tesarz, Günter H. Seidler, and Wolfgang Eich. Tesarz, Seidler, and Eich (2015) are among the most active researchers and clinicians who are looking into the use of EMDR therapy with chronic pain. They did a systematic review of the effects of EMDR treatment in chronic pain patients (Tesarz et al., 2014) and found only 12 studies that met their Platinum Standard (Hertlein & Ricci, 2004). Through this review they came to the conclusion that "although the results of our study suggest that EMDR may be a safe and promising treatment option in chronic pain conditions, the small number of high-quality studies leads to insufficient evidence for definite treatment recommendations." However, in their evaluation of the work done, they came up with some interesting observations. They noted from van der Kolk and Fisler's 1995 work on "Dissociation and the Fragmentary Nature of Traumatic Memories—Overview and Exploratory Study" that "the neurobiological similarities found in patients who suffered from PTSD and chronic pain disorders encouraged scientists to explore the utilization of EMDR in the treatment of chronic pain, even in the absence of psychological trauma," thus giving a nod to supporting the use of EMDR therapy in areas beyond trauma. Despite the diversity in the study results, there were promising results for PLP (De Roos et al., 2010; Schneider, Hofmann, Rost, & Shapiro, 2008; Wilensky, 2006), *headache* (Konuk,

Epzdemir, Hacıomeroglu Ateken, Aydın, & Yurtsever, 2011; Marcus, 2008; Mazzola et al., 2009), and *chronic musculoskeletal pain* (Allen, 2004; Grant & Threlfo, 2002) as pain decreased with EMDR and the results were maintained over time. This is unlike cognitive behavioral therapy (CBT), a method that shows low effects on pain intensity (Morley, 2011; Williams, Eccleston, & Morley, 2012).

EMDR seems to have "a direct impact on the underlying pain processing corticolimbic levels" to effect the pain experience itself. Tesarz et al. believe that because EMDR treats "the affective aspects of pain" when "targeting the affective distress and associated distressing events that are coupled with pain itself [EMDR] will ameliorate pain." In his study, Wilensky observed that "the sooner the pain is treated, the more quickly remission can be achieved" and that often other memories that contribute not only to patients' physical pain but their emotional pain as well seem to be needed to reduce chronic pain. He also noted that there were no severe safety concerns. Although there could be transient increases in distress, the initial treatment can be followed by long-lasting pain relief (Allen, 2004; de Roos et al., 2010; Konuk et al., 2011). Tesarz and his colleagues thought that the findings of the review were so promising that there was "an urgent need for well-designed studies with adequate control groups to assess specific pain conditions using standardized EMDR intervention of sufficient treatment length."

Their contribution to this volume reviews the research on chronic pain, and they use a "standardized and scientifically validated procedure" to treat chronic pain from their 2015 study. They also caution the importance of modifying what we know to fit the patient. They included a wide range of measures in their evaluation of their patients with pain.

During Phases 1 and 2, they make sure to support clients by following the acronym DISH: create distance, provide information, create security, and provide hope. They work with three types of therapy protocols: Trauma-Associated Memories Protocol (TAP), Pain-Associated Memories Protocol (PAP), and Current Pain Sensation Memories Protocol (CUP). They give a list of the most used negative cognitions (NCs) and positive cognitions (PCs) that chronic pain patients use. They also give guidelines on responding to patients during the desensitization phase to help clinicians ask the types of questions needed to understand what is underneath some of the patients' answers and to make sure that patients leave the session in a positive frame of mind. Using "antidote imagery" is one way to support a positive conclusion for patients. Reevaluation includes checking on changes in pain perception and any new material that came up as well as progress noted.

According to the Migraine Research Foundation (migraineresearchfoundation.org, 2018), migraine affects 39 million people in the United States and 1 billion worldwide. It is the third most prevalent illness in the world and the sixth most disabling. Eighty-five percent of migraine sufferers are women. More than 90% of sufferers are unable to work or function normally during their migraine. The attack is typically a severe throbbing recurring pain, usually on one side of the head. In about one-third of attacks, both sides are affected. Attacks are often accompanied by one or more of the following disabling symptoms: visual disturbances; nausea; vomiting; dizziness; extreme sensitivity to sound, light, touch, and smell; and tingling or numbness in the extremities or face. Attacks usually last between 4 and 72 hours. Medication overuse is the most common reason why episodic migraine turns chronic. Over 20% of chronic migraine sufferers are disabled, and the likelihood of disability increases sharply with the number of comorbid conditions. Treatment and research for migraine sufferers would be an important contribution to those with migraines throughout the world.

Kimie and Tsuneo (1999) published the first known case of a successfully treated migraine in the *Japanese Journal of Psychosomatic Medicine*. The title was "A Case of Toilet Phobia Accompanied With a Migraine Attack Successfully Treated by EMDR." However, the person whose name has frequently been connected to treating migraines is Steven Marcus. He has presented at conferences in the United States and Europe on his "Integrated EMDR Protocol" for migraines. In Phase 1 of his treatment, he teaches acute headache relief; Phase 2 consists of a multisession headache treatment; and Phase 3 is about a home treatment program for patients after having had 35 successful full Phase 1 and Phase 2 treatments. Marcus (2008) reported on a study with 43 patients diagnosed with classic or common migraine who were randomly assigned to Phase 1 of integrated EMDR treatment or a standard medication treatment. In Phase 1, he used the bilateral stimulation (BLS) of the Standard EMDR Protocol and integrated it with diaphragmatic breathing and cranial compression for a migraine-specific treatment to help treat a migraine in progress. "Both standard care medication and integrated EMDR treatment groups demonstrated reduced migraine pain levels immediately at posttreatment, 24 hours, 48 hours, and 7 days. However, integrated EMDR treatment reduced or eliminated migraine pain with greater rapidity and showed significantly greater improvement compared to standard care medication immediately posttreatment."

The Turkish team of authors for the second chapter in this section, "EMDR Therapy Treatment for Migraine," started work in this area in the mid-millenium. Their motivation was the prevalence of chronic migraine headaches in Turkey; for women it was 21% of the population and 11% for men. They noted that the term "chronic" meant that the problem was not solvable, and although medication and behavioral interventions reduced the pain, there is a large population of those with migraines who were resistant to these measures. They were inspired to work with this intractable population when learning about the neurobiological similarities found in patients who suffer from posttraumatic stress disorder (PTSD) and chronic pain and studying the work of Grant (1997b) on chronic pain and Marcus (2008) on headaches. In 2011, Konuk et al. reported a pilot study at GaziosmanpaSa Hospital in Istanbul to test the effectiveness of using EMDR therapy to treat migraine sufferers by reprocessing their traumas, especially related to their headaches. In the 11 participants (nine women and two men), there were decreases in headache frequency and duration with no reduction in pain intensity, including a significant decrease in the use of painkillers and ER visits. These results were maintained at a 3-month follow-up. Their conclusion was that there was preliminary evidence that EMDR therapy may be "effective and useful as an alternative treatment for migraine."

In their chapter, our Turkish colleagues point out that adverse life events are etiologically related to chronic pain (Raphael, Chandler, & Ciccone, 2004), and as Grant (2001) states, "If chronic pain is somehow a product of trauma, then this would have implications for the understanding and treatment of pain." Patients have neurological, psychiatric, and psychological assessments, including self-administered assessment scales. History taking concerning the headache and its triggers is important while stressing the importance of following medication use, doctors' visits, treatment, and filling out weekly forms. They teach the Trigger Point Therapy Technique (DeLaune, 2008) to decrease the head pain if a migraine attack is triggered during the therapy. They use the Three-Pronged Protocol, which includes working with the traumatic and stressful events connected with the onset, and the migraines as traumatic themselves; the triggers that start or increase the migraine; and the future template for each of the activating triggers.

According to the Mayo Clinic (www.mayoclinic.org/diseases-conditions/fibromyalgia/symptoms-causes/syc-20354780, 2018), fibromyalgia is a "disorder characterized by widespread musculoskeletal pain accompanied by fatigue, sleep, memory and mood issues." Researchers believe that fibromyalgia increases painful feelings by changing the way the brain processes pain signals. These symptoms can begin after physical trauma, surgery, infection, or significant psychological stress. Other times, the symptoms occur over time without any one event to trigger it. Women are more likely to develop it, and although there is no cure for fibromyalgia, the symptoms can be controlled with medications, exercise, relaxation, and stress-reduction techniques.

There is a scarcity of research on fibromyalgia. In 2004, Friedberg reported on a study in the *Complementary Therapy in Nursing and Midwifery* using EMD for a pilot study to investigate the effectiveness of EMD for the relief of pain, fatigue, anxiety, and depression in fibromyalgia. Six Caucasian women participated in two treatment sessions. Using in-session measures including thermal biofeedback monitoring and SUDs rating for pain, stress, and fatigue, four of the six were considered treatment responders. At the end of the treatment, pre- to post-measures showed that the fibromyalgia impact decreased by 12.6%.

Royle (2008) reported on "EMDR as a Therapeutic Treatment for Chronic Fatigue Syndrome," which is similar to fibromyalgia but not the same. Chronic pain and fatigue are common symptoms of both chronic fatigue syndrome and fibromyalgia. The difference is that in fibromyalgia, fatigue often takes a backseat to debilitating muscle pain. In chronic fatigue syndrome, people have an overwhelming lack of energy, but can also experience some pain. Dennis Thompson Jr. for Everyday Health (www.everydayhealth.com/fibromyalgia/fibromyalgia-and-chronic-fatigue-syndrome.aspx, 2018) reports that the U.S. Centers for Disease Control and Prevention estimate that there are about 5 million people in the United States with fibromyalgia. The Arthritis Foundation estimates that 50% to 70% of people with fibromyalgia also fit the criteria of chronic fatigue. Royle describes a case study with a 49-year-old man who had chronic fatigue syndrome (CFS) for approximately 6 years. After nine sessions of EMDR, where he targeted his feelings of exhaustion and his negative cognition, "I am a failure," prior to his diagnosis of CFS, he reported that "his energy levels were significantly higher, his need for sleep had reduced (from 15–20 hours to 9.5 hours in a 24-hour period), and he was able to resume employment." His CFS had not returned after a 12-month follow-up. She noted that EMDR therapy may be useful in treating CFS.

Tricia Teneycke (2012) wrote her dissertation on "Utilizing the Standard Trauma-Focused EMDR Protocol in the Treatment of Fibromyalgia" for Antioch University. She decided to use the Standard EMDR Protocol with her three female participants to see if it was sufficient to reduce chronic physical and psychological symptoms of fibromyalgia. She reported that pre- and post-measures for posttraumatic stress, depression, and pain decreased along with the participants' pain and symptoms of fibromyalgia. She also reported that they had improved sleep, communication with family, and sexual functioning. These results support the use of the Standard EMDR Protocol with fibromyalgia patients who have a history of trauma.

In 2014, Konuk, Zat, Kavakçı, and Akyuz discussed "EMDR in the Treatment of Fibromyalgia" at the *EMDR Europe Association Annual Conference*. They reported on a single-case research design with a client with fibromyalgia that resulted in a decrease in symptoms that remained clear at the 3-month follow-up. Kavakçı, Semyz, Kaptanoglu, and Ozer (2012)'s work was also reported at the presentation. His group's study, "EMDR Treatment of Fibromyalgia, a Study of Seven Cases," was published in the *Anatolian Journal of Psychiatry*. Paper-and-pencil measures were used to quantify trigger points, pain levels, depression, PTSD, sleep quality, and anger. After treatment with EMDR, there was a significant decrease in all but the score for anger management. Following the treatment, only one of the six patients met the requirement for fibromyalgia.

The third chapter in this section by Konuk, Zat, and Kavakçı is "Fibromyalgia Syndrome Treatment With EMDR Therapy." As in their chapter on migraines, they noted the connection between adverse life experience and chronic pain/fibromyalgia. They decided to design an "EMDR Therapy Protocol for Fibromyalgia" when some patients reported a return of their pain in the Kavakçı et al. study. They do neurological, psychiatric, and psychological assessments for each patient with a variety of measures. Creating resources helps patients with their pain. Therapists give patients the language so that they can conceptualize their fibromyalgia by showing the link between trauma and fibromyalgia pain and how the pain starts after trauma/s and continue/s with adverse life experiences that link to the memory networks connected to the trauma. Targets include the first works and most recent memories related to fibromyalgia, any other traumatic memories related or unrelated to fibromyalgia (FMS) throughout its course, memories before the FMS, triggers, and future template.

Each chapter has a companion summary sheet and a CD version for data entry to remind you of the steps of these protocols.

REFERENCES

Allen, T. M. (2004). *Efficacy of EMDR and chronic pain management*. Chicago, IL: Argosy University.

American Academy of Pain Medicine. (2018). *What is Chronic Pain?* Retrieved from American Academy of Pain Medicine website: http://www.painmed.org/patientcenter/facts-on-pain/#chronic

Amputee Coalition. (2018). Managing phantom pain. Retrieved from https://www.amputee-coalition.org/limb-loss-resource-center/resources-for-pain-management/managing-phantom-pain

Blanford, R., & Blanford, C. (1991, December). EMDR used as a treatment in chronic pain. *EMDR Network Newsletter, 1*(2), 8.

Cheek, D. B., & LeCron, L. M. (1968). *Clinical hypnotherapy*. New York, NY: Grune and Stratton.

Connors, A. F., Dawson, N. V., Desbiens, N. A., Fulkerson Jr., W. J., Goldman, L., Knaus, W. A., ... Ransohoff, D. (1995). A controlled trial to improve care for seriously ill hospitalized patients. The Study to Understand Prognoses and Preferences for Outcomes and Risks of Treatments (SUPPORT). *Journal of the American Medicial Association, 274*(20), 1591–1598. doi:10.1001/jama.1995.03530200027032

DeLaune, V. (2008). *Trigger point therapy for headaches & migraines: Your self-treatment workbook for pain relief*. Oakland, CA: New Harbinger.

De Roos, C., & Veenstra, S. (2009). EMDR pain protocol for current pain. In M. Luber (Ed.), *EMDR scripted protocols: Special populations* (pp. 537–548). New York, NY: Springer Publishing.

De Roos, C., Veenstra, A., de Jongh, A., den Hollander-Gijsman, M., van der Wee, N., Zitman, F., & van Rood, Y. (2010). Treatment of chronic phantom limb pain using a trauma-focused psychological approach. *Pain Research and Management, 15*(2), 65–71. doi:10.1155/2010/981634

Eimer, B. (1993a, Spring). Desensitization and reprocessing of chronic pain with EMDR. *EMDR Network Newsletter, 2*(2), 13–17.

Eimer, B. (1993b, Winter). EMDR for chronic pain. *EMDR Network Newsletter, 2*(2), 4–7

Eimer, B. (1994). *Chronic pain*. EMDR Conference, San Jose, CA.

Eimer, B. (1995, June). *EMDR applications for pain management*. EMDRIA Conference, Santa Monica, CA.

Friedberg, F. (2004). Eye movement desensitization in fibromyalgia: A pilot study. *Complementary Therapy in Nursing and Midwifery, 10*(4), 245–249. doi:10.1016/j.ctnm.2004.06.006

Funabiki, D. (1993). Preparation for cardiac catheterization. *EMDR Network Newsletter, 3*(3), 8–10.

Gerhardt, A. (2016). Eye movement desensitization and reprocessing vs. treatment-as-usual for non-specific chronic back pain patients with psychological trauma: A randomized controlled pilot study. *Frontiers in Psychiatry, 7*, 201. doi: 10.3389/fpsyt.2016.00201

Grant, M. (2001) Understanding and treating chronic pain as trauma, with EMDR. Retrieved from https://www.researchgate.net/profile/Mark_Grant4/publication/265746746_UNDERSTANDING _AND_TREATING_CHRONIC_PAIN_AS_TRAUMA_WITH_EMDR/links/551a3a750cf2f51a6fea2d88/ UNDERSTANDING-AND-TREATING-CHRONIC-PAIN-AS-TRAUMA-WITH-EMDR.pdf

Grant, M. (2009a). *Pain control with EMDR: Treatment manual.* Oakland, CA: New Harbinger Publications.

Grant, M. (2009b). Change your brain, change your pain. Australia. Retrieved from http://www .overcomingpain.com

Grant, M. (2009c). Pain control with EMDR. In M. Luber (Ed.), *EMDR scripted protocols: Special populations* (pp. 517–536). New York: Springer Publishing.

Grant, M. (2012). *Pain control with EMDR: Treatment manual* (2nd ed.). Oakland, CA: New Harbinger Publications.

Grant, M. (2016). The new change your brain, change your pain. Australia. Retrieved from http:// www.overcomingpain.com

Grant, M., & Threlfo, C. (2002). EMDR in the treatment of chronic pain. *Journal of Clinical Psychology, 58*(12), 1505–1520. doi:10.1002/jclp.10101

Hassard, A. (1995). Investigation of eye movement desensitization in pain clinic clients. *Behavioral & Cognitive Psychotherapy, 23*(2), 177–185. doi:10.1017/S1352465800014429

Hertlein, K. M., & Ricci, R. J. (2004). A systematic research synthesis of EMDR studies: Implementation of the platinum standard. *Trauma, Violence & Abuse, 5*(3), 285–300. doi:10.1177/1524838004264340

Institute of Medicine Committee on Advancing Pain Research, Care, and Education and Board on Health Sciences Policy. (2011). *Relieving pain in America, A blueprint for transforming prevention, care, education, and research.* Washington, DC: National Academies Press. Retrieved from https:// www.nap.edu/read/13172/chapter/1

Kavakçı, O., Semyz, M., Kaptanoglu, E., & Ozer, Z. (2012). [EMDR treatment of fibromyalgia, a study of seven cases]. *Anatolian Journal of Psychiatry/Anadolu Psikiyatri Dergisi, 13*(1), 75–81. Turkish

Kimie, T., & Tsuneo, K. (1999, June). [A case of toilet phobia accompanied with a migraine attack successfully treated by EMDR]. *Japanese Journal of Psychosomatic Medicine, 39*(5), 398.

Konuk, E., Epzdemir, H., Hacıomeroglu Ateken, S., Aydın, Y. E., & Yurtsever, A. (2011). EMDR treatment of migraine. *Journal of EMDR Practice and Research, 5*(4), 166–176. doi:10.1891/1933-3196.5.4.166

Konuk, E., Zat, Z., Kavakçı, O., & Akyuz, T. (2014, June). *EMDR in the treatment of fibromyalgia.* EMDR Specialty Presentations (Emre Konuk, Chair). Presentation at the 15th EMDR Europe Association Conference, Edinburgh, Scotland.

Levin, C. (1992, December). The heart of EMDR. *EMDR Network Newsletter, 2*(2), 18.

Marcus, S. V. (2008). Phase 1 of integrated EMDR: An abortive treatment for migraine headaches. *Journal of EMDR Practice and Research, 2*(1), 15–25. doi:10.1891/1933-3196.2.1.15

Mayo Clinic. (2018). Fibromyalgia. Retrieved from https://www.mayoclinic.org/diseases-conditions/ fibromyalgia/symptoms-causes/syc-20354780

Mazzola, A., Calcagno, M. L., Goicochea, M. T., Pueyrrodòn, H., Leston, J., & Salvat, F. (2009). EMDR in the treatment of chronic pain. *Journal of EMDR Practice and Research, 3*(2), 66–79. doi:10.1891/1933-3196.3.2.66

Migraine Research Foundation. (2018). Retrieved from https://migraineresearchfoundation.org

Morley, S. (2011, March). Efficacy and effectiveness of cognitive behaviour therapy for chronic pain: Progress and some challenges. *Pain,* (3 Suppl), S99–S106. doi:10.1016/j.pain.2010.10.042

National Centers for Health Statistics. (2006). *Health, United States, 2006 with chartbook on trends in the Health of Americans* (pp. 68–87). Hyattsville, MD: Author. Retrieved from http://www.cdc.gov/ nchs/data/hus/hus06.pdf

National Sleep Foundation. (2000). Sleep in America poll. Retrieved from http://www.sleepfoundation .org

PRWeb. (2011). Global pain management market to reach US$60 billion by 2015, according to a new report by Global Industry Analysts, Inc. Retrieved from http://www.prweb.com/pdfdownload/ 8052240.pdf

Raphael, K. G., Chandler, H. K., & Ciccone, D. S. (2004). Is childhood abuse a risk factor for chronic pain in adulthood? *Current Pain and Migraine Reports, 8*, 99–1110. doi:10.1007/s11916-004-0023-y

Rost, C. (2003). EMDR in derbehandlung von chronischem schmerz [EMDR in the treatment of chronic pain]. *Zeitschrift für Psychotraumatologie und Psychologische Medizin, ZPPM, 1*(3), 7–15.

Rostaminejad, A., Behnammoghadam, M., Rostaminejad, M., Behnammoghadam, Z., & Bashti, S. (2017). Efficacy of eye movement desensitization and reprocessing on the phantom limb pain of patients with amputations within a 24-month follow-up. *International Journal of Rehabilitation Research, 40*(3), 209–214. doi:10.1097/MRR.0000000000000227

Royle, L. (2008). EMDR as a therapeutic treatment for chronic fatigue syndrome (CFS). *Journal of EMDR Practice and Research, 2*(3), 226–232. doi:10.1891/1933-3196.2.3.226

Russell, M. (2008). Treating traumatic amputation-related phantom limb pain: A case study utilizing eye movement desensitization and reprocessing (EMDR) within the armed services. *Clinical Case Studies, 7*(2), 136–153. doi:10.1177/1534650107306292

Schneider, J., Hofmann, A., Rost, C., & Shapiro, F. (2008, Jan-Feb). EMDR in the treatment of chronic phantom limb pain. *Pain Medicine, 9*(1), 76–82. doi:10.111/j1526-4637.2007.00299.x

Teneycke, T. (2012, December). Utilizing the standard trauma-focused EMDR protocol in the treatment of fibromyalgia (Doctoral disseration). Antioch University, Culver City, CA. Retrieved from http://aura.antioch.edu/cgi/viewcontent.cgi?article=1027&context=etds&sei-redir=1&referer=http%3A%2F%2Fwww.bing.com%2Fsearch%3Fq%3Demdr%2520dissertations%26qs%3Dn%26form%3DQBRE%26pq%3Demdr%2520dissertations%26sc%3D0-15%26sp%3D-1%26sk%3D%26cvid%3D461a577507e943edbac7f0c9d4a20139#search=%22emdr%20dissertations%22

Tesarz, J., Leisner, S., Gerhardt, A., Janke, S., Seidler, G. H., Eich, W., & Hartmann, M. (2014), Effects of eye movement desensitization and reprocessing (EMDR) treatment in chronic pain patients: A systematic review. *Pain Medicine, 15*, 247–263. doi: 10.1111/pme.12303

Tesarz, J. Seidler, G. H., & Eich, W. (2015). *Treatment of pain with EMDR* (in German). Stuttgart: Klett-Cotta.

Thompson Jr., D. The common threads of fibromyalgia and chronic fatigue syndrome. Retrieved from https://www.everydayhealth.com/fibromyalgia/fibromyalgia-and-chronic-fatigue-syndrome.aspx

Tinker, R. H., & Wilson, S. A. (2005). The phantom limb pain protocol. In R. Shapiro (Ed.), *EMDR solutions: Pathways to healing* (pp. 147–159). New York: W. W. Norton.

van der Kolk, B. A., & Fisler, R. (1995). Dissociation and the fragmentary nature of traumatic memories: Overview and exploratory study. *Journal of Traumatic Stress, 8*(4), 505–525. doi:10.1007/bf02102887

Vanderlaan, L. L. (2000, December). The resolution of phantom limb pain in a 15-year old girl using eye movement desensitization and reprocessing. *EMDRIA Newsletter*, (Special Edition), 31–34.

Wilensky, M. (2000). Phantom limb pain. *EMDRAC Newsletter, 4*(2), 2.

Wilensky, M. (2006). Eye movement desensitization and reprocessing (EMDR) as a treatment for phantom limb pain. *Journal of Brief Therapy, 5*(1), 31–44. doi: 10.1186/1471-2474-14-256

William, A. C., Eccleston, C., & Morley, S. (2012, November). Psychological therapies for the management of chronic pain (excluding headache) in adults. *Cochrane Database of Systematic Reviews, 11*, CD007407. doi:10.1002/14651858.CD007407.pub3

Wilson, S. A., & Tinker, R. (2009). EMDR and phantom limb pain research protocol. In M. Luber (Ed.), *EMDR scripted protocols: Special populations* (pp. 559–574). New York, NY: Springer Publishing.

Wilson, S. A., Tinker, R., Becker, L. A., Hofmann, A., & Cole, J. W. (2000, September). *EMDR treatment of phantom limb pain with brain imaging (MEG)*. Paper presented at the annual meeting of the EMDR International Association, Toronto, Canada.

EMDR THERAPY AND CHRONIC PAIN CONDITIONS

Jonas Tesarz, Günter H. Seidler, and Wolfgang Eich

INTRODUCTION

Psychosocial factors play a significant role in the development and persistence of chronic pain. Particularly for patients with high degrees of emotional distress, significant fear-avoidance behavior, or relevant psychological comorbidity, classic pain-psychotherapeutic approaches are often inadequate. The psychotherapeutic attention paid to patients affected by pain had long focused mainly on dysfunctional coping strategies and maladaptive behavioral patterns. This neglected the fact that distressing life events and/or emotional distress can also have a central impact on the sensation and processing of pain for patients with chronic pain. It is well known that physical pain alongside the purely sensory experience of pain generally always also comes with a significant emotional dimension. This emotional dimension not only determines fundamental aspects such as how severe or distressing a pain is felt to be, but also significantly influences the persistence of the pain symptoms. Recent studies show that in the context of pain chronification in the brain, there is a shift away from the classic pain-processing regions of the brain and toward the emotional networks of the brain (Hashmi et al., 2013). This "emotional" shift is to blame for the fact that, similar to flashback symptoms in posttraumatic stress disorder (PTSD), pain can settle in and never go away. The acknowledgment that pain can become chronic through maladaptive emotional processing forms the pathophysiological basis for applying EMDR therapy in treating chronic pain: With this in mind, EMDR therapy, as an established "procedure for exposing emotional response" from trauma therapy, can be used specifically to process emotional distress in patients suffering from chronic pain with the clear objective of processing this dysfunctional "emotional shift." In addition to this EMDR-specific element of "desensitization and reprocessing," EMDR contains numerous other pain-relief therapeutic elements that are not specific to EMDR (e.g., exposure, relaxation and hypnotic techniques, improving coping abilities, cognitive restructuring, etc.), which can be adjusted to the respective individual requirements of the patient due to the patient-centered nature of EMDR. Against this backdrop, it is no surprise that EMDR is increasingly being used to treat patients with chronic pain (Tesarz et al., 2014).

RESEARCH

Summarizing the current state of the evidence regarding EMDR therapy in the treatment of chronic pain, a recent systematic review demonstrated significant and clinically relevant improvements in pain intensity with high effect sizes and sustained improvements in the follow-up assessments (Tesarz et al., 2014). In this systematic review, two controlled trials and 10 observational studies met the inclusion criteria. All of these studies assessed pain intensity. In addition, five studies measured disability, eight studies depression, and five studies anxiety. Controlled trials demonstrated significant improvements in pain intensity with high effect sizes. The pre-/post-treatment effect size calculations of the observational studies revealed that the effect sizes varied considerably depending on the underlying pain conditions and lengths of treatment. Promising results were reported for phantom limb pain (de Roos et al., 2010; Schneider, Hofmann, Rost, & Shapiro, 2008; Wilensky, 2006), headache (Konuk, Epözdemir, Atçeken, Aydin, & Yurtsever, 2011; Marcus, 2008; Mazzola et al., 2009), and chronic musculoskeletal pain conditions (Allen, 2004; Grant & Threlfo, 2002). Moreover, when evaluating the stability of treatment effects, most of the results were either maintained or showed even further improvements at the follow-up assessments, thus providing some preliminary evidence that EMDR may be effective over the long term. One interesting finding was that treatment success varied with the length of treatment. In particular, studies characterized by treatment duration of fewer than five sessions showed only small improvements in pain. Notably, in those studies in which the number of treatment sessions was not pre-set, but was instead based on treatment success, the mean number of treatment sessions varied between six and eight. Such data suggest that treatment duration of six sessions or more may be more favorable for the use of EMDR in the treatment of chronic pain conditions. Interestingly, Wilensky (2006) observed that the number of sessions necessary for treatment success was correlated with the amount of time since the initial accident. He suggested that the sooner the pain is treated, the more quickly remission can be achieved. Although it would be valuable to further investigate these observations systematically, this observation indicates that more than a few sessions of EMDR may be required to alleviate pain.

In the authors' own study, a 10-session EMDR short-term intervention to treat patients with nonspecific chronic back pain was used. Within this randomized-controlled pilot study, 20 patients with EMDR treatment were compared to 20 patients with treatment as usual (TAU). Results showed that EMDR compared to TAU shows moderate effects on pain intensity and disability, respectively. Evaluation on an individual patient basis showed that 53% of the patients in the EMDR group rated their overall situation as improved at a clinically relevant level, with strong effects on pain intensity and disability, while this was the case in zero patients of the control group. This is a high effect with a number needed to treat of about two. No severe safety concerns were observed with the use of EMDR in this study. These results suggest that EMDR is a safe and promising treatment option in chronic pain conditions for a significant number of chronic pain patients (Gerhardt et al., 2016).

MEASURES

Standardized and validated questionnaires, to complement history, are part of the essential documentation for every pain treatment plan. For the assessment of the pain and pain-related symptoms, the following questionnaires are useful:

- *Pain intensity*: Pain intensity can be measured using a numerical rating scale, ranging from 0, "no pain," to 10, "worst pain imaginable."
- *Pain location*: Pain location and the spatial pain distribution patterns can be assessed sufficiently using pain drawings. For this purpose, the patient is asked to complete a body pain diagram, marking all areas where pain is experienced. Afterward, however, the pain diagram should be discussed jointly by the patient and the therapist to rule out any misunderstandings (Harkness, Macfarlane, Silman, & McBeth, 2005). Based on the assessment of the pain drawings, pain symptomatology can be classified as "chronic widespread pain" (defined as pain that simultaneously exists as axial pain, upper and lower segment pain, and left- and right-sided pain) or chronic local pain (chronic widespread pain criteria not fulfilled) according to the American College of Rheumatology criteria.
- *Pain quality and pain affect*: Pain quality refers to the specific physical sensations associated with pain. Pain affect is the degree of emotional arousal caused by the sensory experience of pain. The affective and sensory dimensions of pain can be measured using the Pain Perception Scale (SES). The SES is the standard instrument of the German chapter of the International Association for the Study of Pain. The SES consists of 10 items on a sensory subscale (e.g., "throbbing," "wrenching," or "stinging") and 14 items on an affective subscale (e.g., "exhausting," "fearful," or "unbearable"). The response format is a four-stage format (0 "not appropriate"; 1 "somewhat appropriate"; 2 "generally appropriate"; 3 "fully appropriate"). The sensory score of the SES is the mean of all sensory items; the affective score of the SES is the mean of all affective items (Geissner, 1996).
- *Disability/impairment*: Assess the severity of chronic pain problems by using the chronic pain grade (CPG). It measures pain intensity and disability in regard to work and daily activities via patients' self-reports. The CPG comprises six items that can be answered on an 11-point numerical rating scale ranging from "0" to "10." The number of days during which the patient experienced a disability during the past 3 months is assessed. Pain severity can be graded in four hierarchical classes (Grade I, low disability—low intensity; Grade II, low disability—high intensity; Grade III, high disability—moderately limiting; Grade IV, high disability—severely limiting; Von Korff, Ormel, Keefe, & Dworkin, 1992).

- *Anxiety and depression*: The severity of anxiety and depression can be determined by the use of the Hospital Anxiety and Depression Scale (HADS-D). The HADS was especially developed for patients with somatic diseases and thus excludes physical symptoms. Each scale consists of seven items that measure anxiety and depression via the patient's self-report with a four-stage response format (Hermann, Buss, & Snaith, 2011).
- *Early stress exposure*: The Childhood Trauma Questionnaire (CTQ) measures early stress exposure, or maltreatment during childhood and adolescence. The CTQ consists of five subscales ("emotional abuse," "physical abuse," "sexual abuse," "emotional neglect," and "physical neglect"; D. P. Bernstein et al., 2003).
- *Severity of trauma-associated symptoms*: The severity of trauma-associated symptoms can be assessed with the Posttraumatic Diagnostic Scale (PDS-D; Griesel, Wessa, & Flor, 2006). The PDS symptom severity score includes 17 items and is widely used for the assessment of posttraumatic symptom severity. Each item corresponds to one of the PTSD symptoms specified in the *Diagnostic and Statistical Manual of Mental Disorders (DSM-IV,* 1994*)* and ratings range from 0 ("never") to 3 ("5 times per week or more/very severe/nearly always"). The PDS-D assesses the frequency of current PTSD symptoms in the past 4 weeks related to the most stressful life event. For analysis, the authors used the PDS-D sum score (range 0 to 54) to estimate the severity of trauma-associated symptoms.
- *Dissociative symptoms*: Dissociative symptoms can be assessed by the Dissociative Experiences Scale (DES) for the assessment of dissociative symptoms in daily life (E. M. Bernstein & Putnam, 1986; Spitzer, Mestel, Klingelhöfer, Gänsicke, & Freyberger, 2004). It is a 28-item self-report questionnaire developed for screening dissociative experiences including disturbances in memory, identity, awareness, and cognition, not occurring under the influence of alcohol or drugs. It includes three subscales: amnesia, absorption, and depersonalization-derealization. The possible response options increase by increments of 10% ("this never happens") to 100% ("this always happens").
- *Health-related quality of life*: The health-related quality of life can be measured with the 12-Item Short Form Health Survey (SF-12). The SF-12 consists of 12 items on eight scales ("physical functioning," "role limitations due to physical problems," "bodily pain," "general health," "vitality," "social functioning," "role limitations due to emotional problems," and "perceived mental health"). Response categories vary from 2 to 6 and can be transformed to scale scores ranging from 0 ("the worst") to 100 ("the best"; Bullinger & Kirchberger, 1998).
- *Resilience factors*: Resilience is a personality characteristic that moderates the negative effects of stress and promotes adaptation. Thus, it avoids any potentially negative effects of stress. Resilience can be measured with the Resilience Scale (RS-11; Röhrig, Schleußner, Brix, & Strauß, 2006). The RS-11 comprises two factors—"acceptance of self and life" and "personal competence"—with a seven-point response format ranging from 1, "disagree," to 7, "agree." Thus, scores can range from 7 to 77, with higher scores reflecting higher resilience.

EMDR PAIN PROTOCOL FOR CHRONIC PAIN CONDITIONS SCRIPT NOTES

The following sections present a standardized and scientifically validated procedure for treating chronic pain using EMDR (Tesarz, Seidler, & Eich, 2015). The procedure is articulated clearly in the structure and follows the concept of eight phases of therapy created by Francine Shapiro (Shapiro, 2001). At this point, however, one should be reminded of Roger Solomon's (Solomon, 1999) guiding principle: "EMDR is not a 'stand-alone' method!" which emphasizes that an EMDR-centered pain treatment should always be integrated into a comprehensive ("multimodal") therapy concept adjusted to meet patients' individual needs. Furthermore, one should recognize that there is no one correct pain protocol for all types of chronic pain syndromes. This also means that there is no one correct procedure. In the authors' experience, it can be necessary—and useful—to continually modify the classic procedure to be able to satisfy the individual needs and requirements of the individual patient. The observations and formulation proposals presented in the following sections serve as a guide in this context.

Phase 1 and 2: History Taking and Preparation

Important Treatment Elements

In the initial phase, in addition to collecting information and excluding patients with potential EMDR therapy contraindications, establishing a viable therapeutic relationship and preparing for future desensitization are of paramount importance. Since EMDR can be quite a sensitive and emotionally invasive procedure, particular attention is focused on establishing adequate physical and mental stability of the patient during the initial phase of the therapy. This is similar to the procedure in classic trauma therapy. The *aim* is to keep current pain levels at a tolerable level and under sufficient control before the actual processing can commence. Mark Grant (2009) suggests that—unlike in classic trauma therapy, where the focus is on creating adequate patient security during the initial phase—for pain patients, in addition to this element of security, the aspect of being able to distance oneself from the pain ("detachment") and the development of a more positive perspective ("sow seeds of hope") have important roles to play. To better satisfy these specific requirements, four central treatment elements must be worked out in EMDR therapy for pain patients, which we can summarize briefly using the acronym "DISH."

- *Creating distance*: Improve the ability to distance oneself from the pain.
  Similar to PTSD treatment, from the beginning of therapy, introduce pain patients to the idea of considering their pain from a more "detached" and distanced point of view. For example, instead of asking the question "How do you feel today?" or "How are you today?" ask "How does the pain make you feel today?"
- *Providing information*: Educate patients on EMDR and pain.
  Educate the patient on EMDR and pain based on his or her specific needs. Address the following themes that are common for pain patients: the neurophysiological basis of pain perception and modulation, the relationship between pain and (psychological) traumatization, and the effect of EMDR on pain and pain perception.
- *Creating security*: Strengthen inner security and stability and develop positive body-based resources. Chronic pain can influence the security and stability needs of patients negatively as often they experience a loss of control, feel betrayed by their own body, and/or feel helpless and dependent. In contrast to patients with PTSD, pain patients usually do *not* feel threatened by external forces. Pain patients' experience of threat is through their own bodies such as physical discomfort, loss of physical integrity and function, and/or inadequate pain control. Therefore, a special emphasis should be placed on physically based resources, especially resources concerning "physical well-being" and "physical relaxation" techniques.
- *Providing hope*: Develop hope and (treatment) motivation. Pain patients are worried and disappointed when numerous different treatment attempts repetitively fail and the pain continues. Resignation, however, reduces the quality of life and worsens psychological responses such as anxiety and depression, hampering the patients' more autonomous dealing with their pain and even exaggerating and maintaining the pain. Strengthen the patients' motivation by supporting their developing individualized strategies for the control of their pain, such as the use of heat and/or ice packs, relaxation or distraction techniques, optimized pharmacological management, and physiotherapeutic exercises. Special attention should be paid to restore the patients' quality of life by teaching them how to pace themselves better, as well as strategies on how to start up again everyday activities, despite their pain and all its limitations.

Targeting Sequences, Protocols, and Case Conceptualization

Another important question concerns which EMDR therapy targets are to be processed using EMDR—that is, which stressful memories, thoughts, feelings, and sensations. Any memory that is currently distressing qualifies. It is important to distinguish between memories associated with trauma, memories associated with pain, and current pain (de Roos & Veenstra, 2009) and find which types are relevant to the patient. Based on these three different types of targets, there are *three different therapy protocols*:

1. TAP (for trauma-associated memories)
2. PAP (for pain-associated memories)
3. CUP (for current pain sensation memories)

Should the therapy start with the initially triggering trauma, if present, or should it focus first directly on the pain? No conclusive statement can be made in this regard. The authors have neither comparative studies nor clear recommendations. However, the following procedure for case conceptualization has been proposed (see also Figure 6.1).

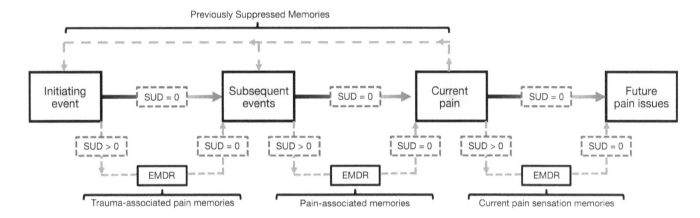

Figure 6.1   Decision tree for focus selection and treatment planning.
When the pain is associated with an initiating traumatic and a current distressing event (SUD > 0), use the EMDR therapy to start desensitizing and reprocessing the trauma-associated pain memories of this initiating traumatic event, and afterward target all pain-associated memories of subsequent events until the subjective degree of distress of these memories reaches "zero" (SUD = 0). After distressing memories and thoughts of the initiating and subsequent events are processed and in those cases in which no distressing memories or thoughts can be identified initially, current pain sensation is focused. In cases where patients uncover new, previously suppressed events during pain processing, reactive memories can again be addressed and processed further as therapy progresses. Finally, future pain issues as future pain crises or potential pain triggers can be targeted.
SUD, subjective units of distress.

1. *Traumatic/distressing events*: Where the pain is associated with traumatic and distressing events (still today!), start by desensitizing and reprocessing these events for the following reasons:
   ○ EMDR can demonstrably and quickly reduce posttraumatic stress, leading to a quick improvement in the patient's general condition and thus creating a good starting point for further therapy.
   ○ The pain can represent a somatosensory symptom of PTSD (in the sense of flashback pain or as memory pain). Thus, the treatment of the triggering trauma can represent a causal therapeutic approach because the PTSD can be the origin of the pain symptomatology, thus elevating the PTSD to the cause of the pain.
2. *Pain-associated memories*: In cases where either no traumatic event can be identified as the trigger or the traumatic event has been reprocessed successfully in the meantime, the distressing memories and thoughts associated with the pain should be processed for the following reasons:
   ○ Distressing memories associated with the pain can intensify the pain.
   ○ Distressing thoughts play a key role in the development and persistence of maladaptive behavioral patterns.
3. *Current pain sensation memories:* After distressing memories and thoughts are processed and in those cases in which no distressing memories or thoughts can be identified initially, focus on the pain using the CUP. Expect a positive effect on the pain symptoms for the following reasons:
   ○ EMDR leads to a direct modulation of the pain perception (Gerhardt et al., 2016; Hekmat, Groth, & Rogers, 1994).
   ○ EMDR triggers a global relaxation response in the patient.
   ○ The pain-specific EMDR protocol can lead to an increase in the interoceptive and somatosensory expressiveness. With the resulting improved differentiation ability of somatosensory and emotional reactions, maladaptive emotional processes (e.g., the avoidance or suppression of one's primary or adaptive emotions, which then activates neural pathways that trigger, augment, or maintain pain and other symptoms) can be modulated positively.
   ○ As a result of the protocol, cognitive restructuring can be induced and effective coping strategies can be implemented.

In keeping with the importance of completing all aspects of chronic pain, the authors include the following types of targets that are also included in most Standard EMDR Protocols.

4. *Previously suppressed memories*: In cases where patients uncover new, previously suppressed events during pain processing, reactive memories can again be addressed and processed further as therapy progresses using the Standard EMDR Protocol or the modified protocol for the following reason:
    ○ Previously suppressed memories can have a relevant impact on the pain.
5. *Future pain issues*: The Standard EMDR Protocol or the absorption exercise can be used to alleviate future pain crises and potential pain triggers. One can expect a positive effect on the pain symptoms for the following reasons:
    ○ Maladaptive behavioral patterns can be prevented effectively by modulating dysfunctional fear and avoidance reactions.
    ○ Helps to strengthen individual coping abilities.

Phase 3: Assessment/Evaluation Phase

After Phases 1 and 2 are completed, assessment and reprocessing can begin (Phases 3–4). Start by selecting the initial target and then assessing the positive and negative cognitions, emotions, and sensations. If the pain is associated with a (recalled) distressing event, it is advisable to make this recollected situation the focus of the processing (PAP). However, if an association with a distressing situation cannot be established, to select the pain itself as the primary therapy target (CUP) is justified. In cases where patients report central, yet allegedly pain-independent traumatic events, which in this case have urgent priority, it is often more useful to process them using the Standard EMDR protocol (TAP) first, before turning toward the allegedly pain-specific targets. In the authors' experience, patients usually come to their central topics by themselves during processing, and an active directing or suppression of these by the therapist—for example, by attempting to limit the patients' associations or the conscious omission of specific memories—is often not beneficial to the process. If topics other than the specific pain are currently central to the patient, then the focus on pain-specific states is often made much more complicated.

Note: One exception can be patients with complex traumatization and interwoven traumas on a vast scale. It may be a good idea here to restrict the therapeutic focus and target the topic of pain from the very start.

The aim of the assessment phase is also to ensure that the patient is given every possible opportunity to develop an intensive, emotional access to the pain sensation to be processed. Patients are asked to describe as precisely as possible how they perceive the pain at this particular time, for example, in the categories "size," "shape," "color," "temperature," and "character." Some patients are often unable to adequately describe their pain in words or images at the start. In these cases, one can also ask them to draw a picture of their pain. The "artistic talents" of patients are unimportant here; what is important is that an "auxiliary tool" can be found together with patients to focus and specify the pain in an effective manner. The primary concern of the pain descriptions is to establish an "inner connection to the pain." The authors begin this way with every pain partient to ensure that the focus is on the pain.

Selecting the Assessment Components

These are the assessment components:

- *Cognitive assessment*: Based on the prioritized negative cognition (NC), a positive cognition (PC) is formulated along with a current assessment of the subjective truth content of this PC by the patient.
- *NC*: The therapist asks the patient to formulate a negative self-cognition that is associated with the therapy target to be processed. The therapist should ensure that the patient makes a statement about himself or herself and does so in the "I" form, where possible ("I am . . .", "I have . . ."). An important criterion for whether a NC is suitable for the subsequent EMDR process is that a clear relationship between the cognition and the distressing memory or pain exists and that an adequate emotional resonance with the patient is produced. It is worth noting when it comes to processing pain and pain-associated memories that the emotion and interoceptive sensations take up a clearly more central status than the accompanying NC. Experience has shown that the same status cannot be attributed to the identification and articulation of an NC when focusing on the pain (in the

context of the pain protocol) compared with the classic trauma therapy, and Grant therefore suggests considering the formulation of a NC only as an "optional" possibility (Grant, 2009).

- *PC*: The therapist asks the patient to formulate a positive self-cognition that is associated with the pain perception to be processed. Furthermore, patients should use the "validity of cognition" (VOC) scale to rate just how accurate this self-cognition is estimated to be at the precise moment in question.

Negative Cognition	Positive Cognition
Self-Efficacy and Control	
I do not have the pain under control.	I can learn to influence my pain.
I am helpless.	I can (learn to) help myself.
I'm paralyzed/unable to move.	I have enough opportunities to be active again.
I am powerless/cannot do what I want.	I have enough opportunities/alternatives/prospects.
Self-Esteem and Identity	
I'm worthless/useless.	I am valuable.
I am not good enough.	I'm okay as I am.
I am weak.	I am strong.
I cannot stand it/I can no longer bear this.	I can learn how to deal with this.
I am sick/defective/I cannot function properly any more.	I'm fine the way I am/a good person/valuable/brave/…
I am a loser.	I do my best/the best that I can.
I'm crazy.	I'm normal (just stressed).
Independency and autonomy	
I'll end up in a wheelchair.	I am independent and self-employed.
I'll lose my job/I'll never be able to go back to work.	I am competent/efficient/strong.
I cannot support my family.	I am important to my family as I am! I can support my family as I am!
Guilt and Responsibility	
It's my fault.	I did the best I could.
I did everything wrong.	I did the best I could.
I deserve to suffer.	I'm fine the way I am/I did the best I could.

These are the types of NCs and PCs above that patients with chronic pain report.

- *Emotional assessment*: Identifying and verbalizing the associated distressing feelings together with a current assessment of the subjective degree of distress by the patient is important. After assessing and validating the pain-associated self-cognition, the therapist proceeds to elicit the emotional state in light of the initial topic. It should be noted that for pain patients the focus is often less on the degree of emotional distress and more on the pain-induced degree of distress, so that here, instead of the "subjective units of distress" (SUDs) scale, the assessment of the degree of distress lends itself based on the numerical "subjective units of pain" (SUPs) scale.
- *Location of body sensation/interoceptive assessment*: Identifying and localizing the physical sensations associated with the distressing memory.

Phase 4: Desensitization

During Phase 4, provide brief preliminary information about the effectiveness of BLS to adumbrate the subsequent desensitization. The principle of reprocessing using BLS is based definitively on patients resorting to the "state" to be processed (initial image/sensation plus the associated NC and the accompanying affect) and turning attention both inwardly (pain/physical feeling) and outwardly to the safe and secure "here and now" (i.e., to eye movements or an alternative BLS). Ask patients to imagine the pain with the distressing memories and the associated negative sensations, feelings, and cognitions, while eye movement sequences (or other BLSs) are being carried out simultaneously. BLS usually takes place repetitively between 40 and 60 sets in the desensitizing and reprocessing phase. Of note, however, the variation between and among individuals can be extremely wide. During the first stimulation (approximately 30–40 sets), pay particular attention to patients' body-based cues such as breathing, facial expressions, and muscle tone so that the therapist can intervene or inquire about emotions as necessary. If the patient is struggling to find the NC, this can be omitted in individual cases, especially at the beginning. An individual stop signal should also be agreed upon with the patient in advance; this allows patients to signal the therapist unambiguously that the situation is currently becoming overwhelming. In such cases, other stabilizing measures may first have to be practiced before processing can continue such as imaginative resources (safe place, happy place, light beam, antidote imagery, etc.).

It is good practice to read the rationale for EMDR as kind of an "opening ritual" immediately before starting desensitization. This "explanatory text" can serve as a type of distant signal to adumbrate the subsequent BLS.

Moreover, it is important to take into account that the desensitization process in pain patients can be sometimes very different in nature than those seen in the treatment of PTSD patients. Usually, the desensitization process runs more or less automatically with only little interventions from the therapist. Then, the therapist should let the process go as far as possible without intervening too much. In such cases, the patient needs to be guided only discreetly to follow his or her internal processes (e.g., with the words "Go with that!" or "Concentrate on that!"). This procedure is then continued until there are no new changes. Then, the focus should turn back to the original target (e.g., the current pain) to assess if there has been any change in the pain.

Many chronic pain patients, however, initially have problems in focusing on the internal process to activate and change the pain. In the authors' experience, the greatest difficulty in desensitization lies in the fact that many pain patients often fail initially to perceive their feelings as "neutral" without cognitively analyzing or evaluating them directly. In such cases, therapists should not be content with statements such as "It feels better" or "It is okay," but should always explicitly request more detail in such cases: "What feels better?" "How does it feel?" "Where are these feelings? Please describe in more detail!" and so on.

If therapists receive more specific information, they should use it to guide and encourage patients further ("Simply, notice it and let whatever happens happen!"), so that the patient is able to get an idea of what is meant by a neutral, observant, and nonjudgmental attitude. As soon as positive changes are produced, the therapist should then request the "details" and simultaneously install this information bilaterally: "What feels better?" "How does it feel better?" "What has changed? What is now in place of the pain? Describe it in precise terms!" If the pain continues to change, therapists will further strengthen patients by reiterating the following after each BLS: "Notice it and allow what happens to happen." The therapist will continue with the BLS as long as it takes to reduce the patient's SUD/SUP degree of distress to a level deemed acceptable. The primary aim is to reduce the SUD to zero. In a certain percentage of patients, however, this is not possible in one session and by focusing on one single target. In these patients, it is important to reinforce every improvement the patient reports. In the authors' experience, it is typical of pain patients that even if the pain is gone completely within the desensitization phase, patients will say that their SUD is still above "0" because they are unsure if the pain will come back! Two weeks later, for example, in the reevaluation, they report that the SUD value has now fallen to zero!

This phase of desensitization and reprocessing is highly variable but also unpredictable due to the associative way of processing. This repeatedly places particular demands on therapists. Therefore, therapists should be allowed to employ a certain degree of flexibility, so they can react appropriately to unexpected reactions. On the one hand, the therapist should always act as neutral and unobtrusive as possible, but, on the other hand, in the case of looping, targeted interventions may be helpful sometimes. Only in this way can one succeed in providing the patient with the required level of support without, at the same time, blocking his or her own processing methods in the patient's adaptive information-processing system. Nevertheless, deliberate application of specific interventions by the therapist can sometimes add value to the process. This is especially true if the EMDR process threatens to come to a standstill or to go around in circles as in looping.

When the process is looping or is going around in circles (two sets without changes), try the following:

- Change the BLS (extend the set, change the direction of eye movements, change the type of stimulation)
- Focus (revisit the initial target)
- Use the affect bridge (return to early experiences connected affectively)
- Focus on a different modality (e.g., for sensation, say, "Where exactly in your body do you feel that?" or for sound, say, "What were you hearing at the time?")

- Physical and imaginative resources (safe place, happy place, light beam, antidote imagery, etc.)
- Distancing, perspective change ("If you look at the scene now from a distance/as an adult ...")
- Support (encouragement, permission, acknowledgment)

If nothing more distressing comes to light, if the situation or status needs to be checked again, or if the session draws to a close, a reevaluation of the degree of distress should be carried out. To this end, patients are asked to return to the target or to the initial pain and to reevaluate the associated degree of distress. When the subjective degree of distress/pain reaches "zero" (SUD/SUP = 0) and the positive cognition is totally true (VOC = 7), one should proceed to Phase 5: Installation. In addition, if a patient reports a stable, positive change during processing, consider installing it, even if distress is greater than 0 when a session concludes. This is why when reprocessing chronic pain (or the distressing memories associated with the pain), installing PCs and/or positive body experiences is so important. In all other cases, either continue the processing or—if, for example, the session has drawn to a close—find an alternative positive conclusion (e.g., installation of a PC based on a positive physical resource or antidote imagery).

Phase 5: Installation

The installation phase occurs when the SUDs = 0 at the end of the desensitization phase. Reevaluate the positive cognition after SUD = 0. If the subjective distress caused by the pain or the processed memory has reduced sufficiently during processing, the next step is to reevaluate and install the changes that have been achieved. To this end, the attention of the patient must again switch to the target and the PC must be called to mind and reviewed. Since the process of desensitization and reprocessing is often associated not only with the individual degree of distress but also with a change of perspective, it is good practice to reexamine the consistency of the PC after processing has taken place. This occurs with the patient first being asked whether the original PC chosen at the start is still appropriate or whether there has been a better positive "I" statement in the meantime, which the patient sees as more consistent with respect to the initial target.

Note: When processing sensations of pain, achieving a complete reduction in the pain is often impossible. While processing pain-independent, distressing material (TAP), it is important therapeutically to start the installation phase only when the subjective degree of distress is at SUD = 0 and the PC is completely consistent (VOC = 7). However, when processing chronic pain (PAP/CUP), it may be sometimes beneficial to install a positive (body) state directly with the patient when a stable, positive change is reported during processing, even if the level of distress is greater than 0 when a session concludes.

Phase 6: Body Scan

If patients' pain and distress is no longer decreasing and no further improvements can be made, invite patients on a "mindful journey of the body" before concluding the EMDR work of a session. It frequently happens that patients acquire access to positive body resources during the body scan, as when patients perceive a pleasant feeling of warmth in the abdominal area, a feeling of freedom and wideness in the chest, or a more relaxed posture. In such cases, the positive body resources should be further strengthened by focusing the patient on this sensation with a brief series of slow bilateral stimuli.

Phase 7: Closure

In addition to debriefing, the closure phase of an EMDR session should usually comprise some preparation for possible aftereffects of the session. It may also involve planning further exercises that patients can do on their own between the individual therapy sessions.

Give patients ample opportunity during the debriefing to examine striking experiences that are unsettling or threatening. Point out that the adaptive information process triggered during the EMDR session can also continue after the session with an interim intensification of pain and intrusive memories (especially if the pain is associated with a trauma or when distressing events have been processed). Associated memory material can appear in dreams, feelings, ideas, and also in the form of physical sensations (e.g., pains). Encourage patients to write down any thoughts, memories, and dreams that they might have as it can support patients in distancing themselves from the distressing material, as well as serve as a basis and starting point in dealing with the resulting material in the next session.

Further, it is important to ensure patients are in a secure and balanced mental state at the end of the session. As far as possible, patients should always leave a therapy session in a positive state of mind. This cannot be repeated often enough! If necessary, use any of the resource exercises (such as a positive body resource, the happy place exercise, the light beam technique, the safe place, etc.) to ensure patients' well-being before leaving the session.

Phase 8: Checking and Reevaluation

During the next session, if patients process a distressing target successfully, check whether the target remains clear or whether new material has surfaced. Reevaluate the SUDs and VOC for the PC as well.

When the SUD = 0 the initial target has been processed; now continue with Phases 5 to 7. When the SUD is greater than 0, revisit the target and continue the reprocessing. However, note that with chronic pain, distress levels do not always attain a level of SUD = 0. Therefore, appreciate and re-inforce any relief from and reduction in pain. The desire to be healthy and free of pain often blocks minor changes from being appreciated or observed, and this prevents proper progress. It can help to inquire about positive changes in sleep behavior, physiological tension level, and general activity level of patients, to make them aware of these organic changes and to allow assumptions that may be incorrect—for example, that nothing has changed—to be modified somewhat. In cases where com-plete freedom from pain cannot be achieved after the pain and the triggering memories have been processed, present and future triggers of the symptoms as well as potential relapses (future projection) should also be targeted and processed.

If the pain symptoms have been reduced sufficiently and the previously distressing memories no longer produce any emotional or physical reactions, the primary aim of the therapy is achieved. In addition, if dysfunctional behavioral patterns, cognitive attitudes, and emotional processing schemes have disappeared, assume that the dysfunctional memory content has been processed completely and the therapy can be concluded.

EMDR PAIN PROTOCOL FOR CHRONIC PAIN CONDITIONS SCRIPT

The following sections present the three protocol scripts used for treating chronic pain patients. Phase 1: History Taking and Phase 2: Preparation, however, are done in the same manner for all three protocol scripts. Afterward, use the following protocols for the different types of issues explained later in text:

- TAP: To focus on trauma-associated memories of previous traumatic events
- PAP: To target all pain-associated memories
- CUP: To focus on the current pain sensations

Phase 1: History Taking

Take a full pain history (see, e.g., the *Guide to Pain Management* of the International Association for the Study of Pain; Powell, Downing, Ddungu, & Mwangi-Powell, 2010). For the purpose of this chapter, the most essential questions about pain and its association with traumatic events are selected. They include a determination of the following: location; description; intensity; duration; alleviating and ag-gravating factors; and any associative factors, and their impact upon the patient's life. These compo-nents are most commonly embodied in the "PQRST" approach: provokes and palliates, quality, region and radiation, severity, and time (or temporal). General questions common for every intake are left out and should be included by therapists according to their own needs.

Description of Pain Quality and Intensity

Say, *"How does the pain feel exactly?"*

_____

_____

Say, *"What words would you use to describe your pain? Is it sharp, burning, shooting, hot, cold, electrical, whining, and so on?"*

_____

_____

Say, *"On a scale of 0 to 10, where 0 is no pain or neutral and 10 is the worst pain you can imagine, choose the number that fits the pain now."*

0   1   2   3   4   5   6   7   8   9   10

(no pain)   (most pain)

Say, *"On a scale of 0 to 10, where 0 is no pain or neutral and 10 is the worst pain you can imagine, choose the number that fits during the last week."*

0   1   2   3   4   5   6   7   8   9   10

(no pain)   (most pain)

Say, *"On a scale of 0 to 10, where 0 is no pain or neutral and 10 is the worst pain you can imagine, choose the number that fits the pain during the last month."*

0   1   2   3   4   5   6   7   8   9   10

(no pain)   (most pain)

Location and Spatial Extent of Pain

Say, *"Where is the pain exactly?"*

_____

_____

Say, *"Draw a picture of the pain at this moment. Draw the whole body, if necessary, from the front and from the back, and draw the pain in the body with another color (or colors)."*

Say, *"Above this pain, are there any additional pain sites? Add this pain to the body drawing!"*

_____

_____

Symptom Development: Onset and Temporal Pattern

Say, *"When did your pain start?"*

_____

_____

Say, *"How often does it occur? Is it present all the time, or are you sometimes pain free at night or during the day? Does the pain intensity change during the day?"*

_____

_____

Say, *"Has its intensity changed since the beginning? Let's draw a time line of the course of your pain from when it started until now. The horizontal line represents the time and the vertical line represents the pain from 0 to 10."*

Help the patient draw the time line on a piece of paper.

Aggravating and Relieving Factors and Coping Behavior

Say, *"What helps the pain to decrease?"*

_____

_____

Say, *"What can make the pain worse?"*

_____

_____

Say, *"How does the pain react to warmth, moving, distraction, rest, and so forth?"*

_____

_____

Say, *"What else do you do to cope with your pain?"*

_____

_____

Say, *"Are there any current stressful circumstances in your life?"*

_____

_____

Say, *"How do you cope with this stress?"*

_____

_____

Say, *"How do you cope with the emotional aspects of your ordeal; for example, do you get angry, depressed, and so forth?"*

_____

_____

Say, *"What type of supports do you have in the form of family or friends?"*

_____

_____

Diagnoses and Previous Treatments

Say, *"What diagnoses were made by the physicians that you have seen so far?"*

_____

_____

Say, *"What type of treatments have you tried to relieve your pain and how effective was (were) it (they)?"*

_____

_____

Say, *"Were they effective or are they still effective?"*

_____

_____

Say, *"What medications do you use and what is the dosage that you take for each of your medications?"*

_____

_____

Patients may not know their diagnosis or they may not accept it. If the patient does not know the diagnosis, say the following:

"What is your understanding of the problem?"

_____

_____

If the patient does not accept the diagnosis, you will need to review the patient's medical history and discuss his or her options regarding further investigations.

Say, *"Please tell me what you have done so far to understand what is going on with you concerning your pain."*

_____

_____

Say, *"What do you see your options are concerning any further medical investigations?"*

_____

_____

Addictive Behaviors

Say, *"Do you feel that you cannot stop using a medicine?"*

_____

_____

If using opiates or benzodiazepines, say the following:

"Would you be willing to stop using this or to decrease the use of your medicine before trying EMDR?"

_____

_____

Effects on Functioning

Say, *"How does the pain affect your physical functioning?"*

_____

_____

Say, *"How does the pain affect your social functioning?"*

_____

_____

Say, *"How does the pain affect your mood and your ability to pay attention or concentrate (emotional and cognitive functioning)?"*

_____

_____

Say, *"What do you do to reduce the pain to make it bearable (behavioral functioning)?"*

_____

_____

History of Trauma and Pain-Related Incidents

Say, *"Did the pain start with a traumatic event?"*

_____

_____

Say, *"Did you have any health problems prior to the trauma?"*

_____

_____

Say, *"Does the pain remind you of another specific event?"*

_____

_____

Say, *"Did you have any traumatic experiences before the start of the pain?"*

_____

_____

Say, *"Did you have any traumatic medical experiences?"*

_____

_____

Say, *"Please make a drawing of the time line of the course of your pain* (see the list of potential targets in the next section). *Let's put in the major issues or events related to your pain."*

_____

_____

Ask for specific posttraumatic stress–related symptoms:

Say, *"Have you noticed any posttraumatic stress–related symptoms? For example,*

Are you reexperiencing the event through repeated, distressing memories, or dreams, or by feeling as if the event were happening again such as flashbacks or a sense of reliving it, or by intense physical and/or emotional distress when you are exposed to things that remind you of the event?"

_____

_____

"Or, do reminders of the event affect you in a way that you avoid thoughts, feelings, or conversations about it, or activities and places or people who remind you of it?"

_____

_____

"Or, do you lose interest for the significant activities in your life, or do you feel detached from other people or that your range of emotions is restricted?"

_____

_____

"Or, are you troubled by problems with sleeping, irritability or outbursts of anger, problems concentrating, feeling "on guard," or an exaggerated startle response?"

_____

_____

Fill in this history with any other normal history-taking information that you think is important for you to have or is mandated. The need to take a complete history may also need to be balanced against the need to engage the patient and generate relief, particularly if the patient presents in crisis. Rather than an isolated event, the history taking and assessment of pain is an ongoing process that can continue throughout therapy rather than something that is necessarily completed in a single session. The patient's pain should therefore be assessed on a regular basis throughout the entire treatment.

Phase 2: Preparation

After you have identified potential EMDR targets in the history taking phase, you have to choose the order in which targets will be desensitized (see also Figure 6.1) and the type of BLS (visual, auditory, or tactile). For this purpose, create a list including title/keywords of the events, date, current level of distress, and the intended order, and check out different stimulation types (visual, auditory, or tactile). Furthermore, before starting the actual desensitization, provide some brief preliminary information about the effect and process of EMDR, and arrange an individual stop signal with the patient.

Say, *"Today, I am going to ask you to remember the most stressful situations that you have and we will put it into this chart. We can start with about five situations, and if there are more or less, that is fine. You do not have to go into all of the details because we will do that later. Just give me the headline!"*

_____

_____

Say, *"How old were you when you had that distressing experience?"*

_____

_____

Say, *"On a scale of 0 to 10, where 0 is no disturbance or neutral and 10 is the highest disturbance you can imagine, how disturbing does it feel now?"*

| 0 | 1 | 2 | 3 | 4 | 5 | 6 | 7 | 8 | 9 | 10 |

(no disturbance)   (highest disturbance)

List of Potential Targets

Target	SUD	Date	Priority
1.			
2.			
3.			
4.			
5.			

Explanation of EMDR Therapy to the Patient

A comprehensive rationale for treatment contributes both to the degree of cooperation of the patient and to the effect of treatment. A simple text with which the rationale of treatment can be explained is the following:

Say, *"The memories of very distressing and painful events often appear as if frozen in the nervous system. This applies to all images, sounds, thoughts, feelings, body sensations, and all other impressions that a person has recorded in such a distressing situation. The bilateral stimulation that we use in EMDR treatment can reopen the path into the nervous system and the neural networks and allow the brain to process such painful experiences. What is important is that you constantly keep in mind during this process that it is your own brain that brings about the healing. And that you know that you are ultimately in control of the whole event. There is nothing in this process that has to be, or that is right or wrong. Simply allow to happen whatever is going to happen!"*

Teach Patients How to Use Language to Describe Pain

There are not that many words available with regard to pain, and as a rule, patients are not accustomed to speaking about their pain in these words. In those patients with a moderate or minimal capacity for verbalization and visualization, it is more difficult to monitor the EMDR process during the desensitization phase and continue to keep the process in motion. Therefore, it is important, in the preparation phase, for the therapist to teach patients how to use language to describe pain. For example, it is possible to suggest words that describe the quality or intensity of the pain by giving examples of visualized pain.

Say, *"Not many words are available to describe pain, and most patients are not accustomed to talk about their pain. However, finding words to communicate about your pain helps you to concentrate on your pain during the EMDR procedure and helps me, your therapist, to follow the course of the information you are processing. You can describe the quality or intensity of your pain in words, images, or a combination of both."*

From the intake, the therapist knows if the patient is able to find words or images describing the pain. If so, continue the protocol. If not, it is important to take extra time here to teach the patient how to use language to describe pain. For example,

Say, *"Some patients describe their pain, for example, as a wall of flames, a buckle around the foot, or an apple with spikes. There are many different ways pain can manifest itself! How would you describe your pain?"*

_____

_____

Develop the DISH Skills

In addition to the ability of verbalizing and visualizing the pain, the aspect of being able to distance one-self from the pain ("creating distance"), to regain the experience of control and hope by the receiving of sufficient information ("providing information"), the regaining of security ("creating security"), and the development of a more positive perspective ("providing hope") constitute important points of the preparation phase. To better satisfy these specific requirements, four central treatment elements must be worked out in EMDR therapy for pain patients, which we can summarize briefly using the acronym "DISH."

D: CREATING DISTANCE

Instruct patients to appraise their pain from a third-person perspective. This can help patients feel significantly less emotional pain when they envision the memory using a third-person perspective than when using a first-person perspective.

Say, *"How does the pain make you feel today?"*

_____

_____

If patients have difficulties in describing their pain from a third-person perspective, say the following:

"Zoom out until you see yourself within the scene, then zoom out even further so you can see the scene unfold as if you were a stranger that happened to pass by. Describe the 'strangers' pain while maintaining the third-person perspective. Make sure to employ a third-person perspective whenever you find yourself reflecting on the experience!"

_____

_____

I: PROVIDING INFORMATION

Comprehensive information about the neurophysiological basis of pain perception and modulation is important. Give some information about the differences between nociception and pain.

Note: The authors adapt the pain education information to the individual needs of the patient. For scientific purposes, however, they have manualized the pain education material so that in the pain studies, every patient receives the same information.

Say, *"In pain research a distinction is made between the sensory nervous system's response to certain harmful or potentially harmful stimuli, on the one hand, and the resulting pain sensation, on the other hand. This sensory nervous system response to certain harmful or potentially harmful stimuli is called* nociception. *The sensation of pain is always a complex subjective sensation, having the character of an unpleasant warning signal, which usually forces us to interrupt our current activities. Of note, pain is always a conscious sensation. Therefore, the process of nociception has to be clearly distinguished from the experience of pain. Nociception refers to the activity of peripheral receptors (also called "nociceptors") that do lead to the painful stimulus. If, for example, someone is pinched strongly on the ear, nociceptors of the ear are activated immediately. This signal is then routed and processed in the direction of the brain. If the signal is strong enough, it penetrates into consciousness and we perceive this nociceptive activity as pain. Pain is always linked to consciousness. Thus, if a person who is unconscious is pinched on the ear even though the nociceptors of the ear are activated, the person will perceive no pain—at least as long as the person is unconscious.*

In this way, nociception is not a conscious perception, but an activity of neuronal cells so that if this activity penetrates into consciousness, it can result in pain. Accordingly, the neuronal cells that contribute to the development of pain are called the 'nociceptive system'. A central component of this nociceptive system is the so-called pain network in the brain. This pain network, also called 'pain matrix', consists of different neuronal cell populations, which are interconnected with each other and process in a computer-like manner all the information they get. As a result of this process, a sensation arises that we perceive as pain."

Give some information on pain processing and pain memory.

Say, *"Of note, there is a strong overlap between the pain matrix with the emotional networks of the brain. Therefore, the experience of pain is a response evoked by nociception and emotional processes together. The objective physiological processes (= nociception) are fundamentally supplemented by subjective, mental processes. Scientists have shown that the nociceptive system sends a permanent 'background noise' of nociceptive signals toward the pain matrix. Thus, the pain matrix constantly receives potentially painful signals. Nevertheless, we usually do not feel pain as the pain matrix usually filters the incoming signals out in an efficient manner. That is because the activity of the pain matrix depends not only on nociceptive activity but also on non-nociceptive activity, such as emotions, attention, previous experiences, and so on. Considering all this additional information, the pain matrix processes the incoming nociceptive information and either puts it away unconsciously or leads to a conscious perception: the pain. The pain matrix thus acts as a kind of filter, which can filter out unimportant pain signals so that they cannot come into consciousness. If this filter is weakened, this can lead to an increased sensitivity to pain. This filter-like processing system can be thought of as a kind of volume control on a radio, by which the pain can be made loud or quiet. If the pain filter is exhausted, this can mean that the pain level is pushed up to a damagingly loud sound.*

*Overall, it is important to keep in mind that the emergence of a conscious perception of pain is not necessarily linked to the existence of a peripheral nociceptive stimulus. **The pain matrix can be triggered even in the absence of such a stimulus by numerous other information (feelings, attention, previous experience, etc.).** In such cases, no structural damage can be found in the examinations or medical imaging despite the obvious presence of pain. This is especially true for already longstanding pain conditions—so called 'chronic pain'—where the structural damage has ceased long ago and no longer activates peripheral receptors for a long time. **Nevertheless, due to the longstanding and profound prior experience of pain, a kind of pain memory in the pain matrix has developed, which now continuously recalls the pain.** A very impressive example of a pain memory can be seen in phantom limb pain patients: Years after amputations, patients feel pain in a limb that no longer exists. Here, the source of the pain lies in the nervous system itself."*

Give information on endogenous pain regulation and the descending pain inhibitory system.

Say, *"Besides the ability of pain conduction, the human nervous system possesses a complex system of endogenous pain regulation. So everyone knows the anecdotes of sportsmen and women who have continued activity despite an injury that (theoretically) should have caused them to stop: the cyclist who has open bone fragments piercing through the skin after an accident or the boxer fighting with a broken hand, and so on. In the cut and thrust of competition, the pain system can "shut the gate," and leave athletes completely pain free in spite of injured tissue.*

The reason for this is the so-called 'descending pain inhibitory system' of the brain, which acts as a kind of 'gatekeeper' for pain signals coming from the periphery before sending them up to the brain. This system is highly effective, and is also important for normal pain perception. Scientists have shown that these pain inhibitory pathways are constantly active. Even at rest and under normal conditions, they exert their inhibitory influence on the incoming signals from the body. If the activity of this endogenous pain-regulating system is disturbed, for example, by an extreme level of stress, this can lead to the situation that stimuli that are usually not perceived as painful can now no longer be filtered out and thus become painful.

Of note, the activity of the body's own pain-regulating system can be influenced by a wide range of different factors (e.g., stress, sleep, physical activity). Importantly, recent studies also demonstrated a powerful influence of stressful experiences and psychological trauma on this system. By the way, this is considered sufficient reason why chronic pain is a common symptom after psychological trauma."

Include information on the relationship between pain and psychological traumatization.

Say, "As I have already said, the endogenous pain-regulating system is able to modulate the incoming nociceptive signals from the periphery in a powerful way. This is not only the case for acute events but especially true for persisting pain conditions. This is usually referred to as 'pain memory' (or 'pain engram'), which is activated by acute stimulization and remains effective even when the initial peripheral causes of pain are already eliminated. That such a mechanism of pain memory exists may have a biological origin: Pain as a warning sign indicates a potentially threatening condition for the organism. Usually the longer a threat persists, the stronger and more dangerous it is for the individual. It therefore makes sense that the longer the pain persists, the stronger the intensity of the pain becomes. In line with this, the endogenous pain-regulating system has efficient mechanisms to exaggerate the pain as a possible signal that the organism is still in danger. This is the only way of ensuring that the affected person will do everything necessary to eliminate the imminent threat of damage. Against this background, it is not surprising that acute pain often becomes chronic, at least when it is not adequately controlled.

As much as this may be useful from an evolutionary point of view, the more harmful these mechanisms are for the physical comfort of the affected individual, the more the nervous system will take it that something is amiss when acute pain is not handled adequately. Thus, even a relatively harmless event such as the pain of a herniated disc, if treated quickly, could be easily forgotten but can move into chronic pain. The pain has left its memory traces in the brain, and these traces can cause pain now so that the memory of pain *becomes entirely independent of whether the tissue is irritated or not.*

Not only pain, but also other threatening or dangerous situations can stimulate our brain in this way. This may lead to the development of a so-called 'trauma-pain-memory network.' The more threatening the situation is, the more intense and pronounced the memories may be. As a result of the trauma, the brain is put into a 'maladaptive' memory state so that the traumatic situation induces a massive pathological sensory input. It seems that above a certain intensity of fear, anger, shame, or pain, our brain is not able to deal with it and it switches into a kind of 'emergency mode'. In such cases, specific parts of experience—images, sounds, smells, feelings, thoughts, and perceptions—are no longer integrated adaptively into the overall composite of the memory network. Instead of that, the distressing memory seems to become 'frozen' on a neurological level. This results in the development of pathological networks, so-called trauma–pain networks *that can lead to further physical symptoms. The result is a kind of vicious circle because pain can be triggered by the trauma–pain network, which in turn maintains and expands the trauma–pain network.*

It is now known that traumatic and painful experiences can lead very easily to the development of pathological pain networks. This phenomenon is known as 'hypermnesia,' derived from the Greek terms mnesis = 'memory' and hyper = 'too much', meaning something like 'excessive memory ability'. In the biology of evolution, however, this strong memory capacity for pain and traumatic events appears quite useful, because traumatic and painful situations are generally dangerous and threatening events that should be prevented as best as possible. With the aim of avoiding the recurrence of such existentially threatening events in the future, it therefore might have been evolutionarily quite appropriate that traumatic experiences automatically engrave themselves deeply into the memory and induce a state of increased perception (also for pain!) and alert to escape next time by an earlier recognition of the danger. So, you can imagine that it would have been beneficial for the survival of stone-age hunters that, when they had just escaped the clutches of a saber-toothed tiger, they developed a profound memory (hypermnesia) of it and a sensitized state of perception. This could help to detect and prevent such events in the future earlier. Against this background, chronic pain syndromes can be considered as an 'undesirable side effect' of such former self-protection mechanisms. In the face of such a priming caused by dangerous situations, not only external circumstances but also internal states such as unpleasant body sensations and pain experiences are imprinted in our memory. The pain must be 'remembered' over and over again, so that the person concerned does not put himself or herself into such a situation again. In addition, the trauma induces a state of hyperexcitability that leads to increased tension in the muscles, as an attack of a saber-toothed tiger had to be expected at any moment. Of note, however, a constant tension of the muscles can lead secondarily to muscular (tension) pain. This can then be noticed as muscular back pain, neck pain, headache, and so on."

Talk about information about the effect of EMDR on pain and pain perception.

Say, *"EMDR stands for 'eye movement desensitization and reprocessing' therapy and is a well-established method of psychotherapy that was originally developed for the processing of emotional stress caused by psychological trauma. Meanwhile, EMDR is internationally recognized as one of the most effective methods to treat posttraumatic stress disorders and associated emotional distress.*

EMDR therapy is a technique that is able to stimulate the nervous system so that the endogenous healing process is promoted. The brain's information-processing system naturally moves toward mental health. If the system is blocked or imbalanced by the impact of pain memories, the pain festers and can cause intense suffering. Once the block is removed, healing resumes. Using the detailed protocols and procedures learned in EMDR training sessions, clinicians help patients activate their natural healing processes. EMDR stimulates the pain-processing system in a way that dysfunctional pain memories are adaptively resolved. The eye movements and other bilateral modalities, with which we work in EMDR, allow us to open the responsible neuronal pain networks. This allows the brain to process the pain memories sufficiently and to activate the powers of self-healing. And even in the cases in which the pain memories cannot fully be eliminated, EMDR is usually able to induce a profound state of relaxation, which always acts as an analgesic. In addition, EMDR can be used to empower our personal strengths, self-awareness, and sensitivity for the body and, therefore, the way we move, walk, and behave."

Give some information about the EMDR procedure.

Say, *"The EMDR treatment itself always follows a specified treatment protocol that is passed through step by step by the patient during each therapy session. One of the key elements of EMDR is 'bilateral stimulation'. During treatment, you will be asked to think or talk about your pain and related memories, as well as possible triggers and painful emotions, while simultaneously focusing on my moving fingers or another form of bilateral stimulus. In a typical EMDR therapy session, we will focus on emotional distressing memories and associated negative emotions, beliefs, and body sensations while you will simultaneously track my moving fingers with yours eyes as it moves back and forth. However, bilateral stimulation does not have to be limited to eye movements; we also have other forms of external stimuli that can be used in EMDR therapy (e.g., alternating hand taps or a sound that pans back and forth from ear to ear).*

It is important that you always keep in mind that when using EMDR, your own brain causes the healing. Your nervous system knows just what to do and what it needs. It is therefore not necessary to do or want to change anything actively! Just let whatever happens, happen, and observe whatever may happen!"

S: CREATING SECURITY

Identify and develop skills to be able to manage the pain crises sufficiently and to strengthen the sense of pain control and inner security.

Say, *"What can you do to reduce your pain?"*

_____

_____

Say, *"How do you cope with your pain?"*

_____

_____

Say, *"What kind of things have you tried so far?"*

_____

_____

Say, *"What was helpful?"*

_____

_____

Where the pain is associated with psychological trauma (such as child physical or sexual abuse, combat-related injuries, industrial accidents, etc.), patients may have safety issues.

Say, *"Is there anywhere you can go or anything you can do where you feel safe from the trauma or pain? Some people feel better when they are doing something they enjoy that takes their mind off the pain; some people like listening to the soothing sounds of nature, such as the ocean, or rain on a roof; other people feel better when they can talk to someone who understands. What do you do that makes you feel safe?"*

_____

_____

Place a special emphasis on physically based resources.

Say, *"Close your eyes and focus your attention on your body. Can you detect any positive physical sensation in your body? Is there any place in your body that feels good—or at least neutral? Please let me know which part of your body feels best at the moment."*

_____

_____

Say, *"Now think of your pain once again, and also the positive thoughts and positive physical feeling. Go with that."*

Do sets of BLS.

_____

_____

Install a PC based on antidote imagery.

Say, *"Now try to think of something that can ease your pain or something that gives you a feeling of relaxation and relief. Allow your thoughts and your imagination to run free. This can be completely unrealistic and a fantasy. Find an image, a thought, or a fantasy that can help ease your pain."*

_____

_____

Say, *"What do you see now?"*

_____

_____

Say, *"Again, think of your pain together with the pain-relieving image and also remember the positive thoughts. Go with that."*

_____

_____

Do sets of BLS.

Patients need to accept that they need to pace themselves differently.

Say, *"When you have chronic pain, it is important that you learn how to pace yourself so that you're not constantly aggravating your pain. Pacing yourself means stopping whatever you're doing when the pain starts to come on. It may mean changing your expectations; instead of finishing tasks in one go, they may need to be broken down and completed in bite-sized chunks."*

_____

_____

Assist your patient to create an emergency kit!

Say, *"It is often helpful to have some of what I call quick strategies to help manage your pain more effectively. For example, many chronic pain sufferers have their own strategies to handle their pain. Though every single point for its own does not so far appear sufficient enough to eliminate the pain, they may together play a key role in controlling the pain. Thus, let's develop together an emergency kit that provides a list of your individual coping skills for your use!"*

_____

_____

H: PROVIDING HOPE

During the preparation phase, it is important to develop hope and (treatment) motivation (Grant, 2009; Figure 6.2).

Say, *"Even though it can feel sometimes like the pain is never ending, there is always hope; things change, nothing lasts forever. "*

_____

_____

Also, point out the things that they are still doing despite their pain and all its limitations.

Relaxation exercises	• Progressive muscle relaxation (PMR)
	• Autogenic training (AT)
Imagination exercises	• Positive body resource
	• Imaginative place of well-being
Real (concrete) resources and opportunities of distraction	• Positive things (e.g., favorite music, perfume, photo)
	• Positive activities (written down on paper)
	• Phone number of friends
Counter-irritation techniques	• Porcupine ball
	• Chili, tiger balm, ABC heat pad
	• Ice water bath
Physical resources	• Hot water bottle
	• Cherry stone pillow
	• TENS devices (transcutaneous electrical nerve stimulation)
Medications	• OTC pain-reliever pills/drops (acetaminophen or nonsteroidal anti-inflammatory drugs)
	• Individual prescription pain medications
Emergency phone numbers	• Phone numbers of a carefully selected pain hospital and/or the doctor of choice

Figure 6.2 Emergency kit with pain control skills.[a]
[a]Gradual application recommended.
An emergency kit with individual pain control skill contains quick strategies for pain management. It usually provides a list of your individual coping skills for a staggered application.
OTC, over the counter.

Say, *"It is also important for you to think about _____ (state what they can do despite their pain). You know that is really impressive that even though you have all of this pain, you can succeed at _____ (state their success)!"*

_____

_____

Choice of Bilateral Stimulation (Visual, Auditory, or Tactile)

Visual, auditory, or tactile stimuli can be used for processing. Thus far, there is no scientific support for the hypothesis that one of the three types of stimuli has a greater affect than the others, so patients can choose the one that is fit for them.

Say, *"We will be doing sets of bilateral stimulation to stimulate the dysfunctional pain memory networks. For this, visual, auditory, or tactile stimuli can be used. An approved technique is tracking my moving fingers with your eyes as it moves back and forth. However, bilateral stimulation does not have to be limited to eye movements. If it is more comfortable for you, we can also use other forms of external stimuli (e.g., alternating hand taps or a sound that pans back and forth from ear to ear). Let us first experimentally try out different kinds of stimuli."*

_____

_____

Stop Signal

The more intense the pain becomes, the more difficult it is for patients to concentrate on the pain for a long period of time; in this case, the patient's attention shifts to dealing with the pain or even to surviving. If the pain becomes too intense, patients are instructed to use a stop signal and together you can determine whether continuing the EMDR session is feasible and bearable.

> Say, *"The degree of distress is unlikely to reach unbearable levels. If it does, simply raise your hand* (therapist shows the stop signal using hand) *so that we can interrupt the exercise!"*

_____

_____

TRAUMA-ASSOCIATED MEMORIES PROTOCOL (TAP) SCRIPT

Phase 3: Assessment

Target Selection

Select a target image (stationary picture) from the most distressing memories of the traumatic event:

Incident

> Say, *"Which event has triggered your pain? If you now think of the distressing situation, what do you experience?"*

_____

_____

Picture

> Say, *"What picture represents the most disturbing part of this incident now? Also, what are the pictures that begin and end your memory?"*

_____

_____

NEGATIVE COGNITION

The therapist asks the patient to formulate a negative self-cognition that is associated with the therapy target to be processed. If the patient talks about feelings and not cognitions at this point, the following question is often useful:

> Say, *"What words best go with the picture that express your negative belief about yourself now?"*

> Say, *"What does that say about you as a person?"*

_____

_____

POSITIVE COGNITION

> Say, *"When you bring up that picture or _____ (state the issue), what would you like to believe about yourself now?"*

_____

_____

VALIDITY OF COGNITION

Say, *"When you think of the incident* (or picture) *and the associated pain, how true do those words* _____ (clinician repeats the PC) *feel to you now on a scale of 1 to 7, where 1 feels completely false and 7 feels completely true?"*

1   2   3   4   5   6   7

(completely false)   (completely true)

EMOTIONS

IDENTIFICATION OF AND FOCUS ON THE ASSOCIATED AFFECT:

Say, *"When you bring up the picture or* _____ (state the issue) *and those words* _____ (clinician states the NC), *what emotion do you feel now?"*

_____

_____

SUBJECTIVE UNITS OF DISTURBANCE

Say, *"On a scale of 0 to 10, where 0 is no disturbance or neutral and 10 is the highest disturbance you can imagine, how disturbing does it feel now?"*

0   1   2   3   4   5   6   7   8   9   10

(no disturbance)   (highest disturbance)

LOCATION OF BODY SENSATION

Say, *"Where do you feel it* (the disturbance) *in your body?"*

_____

_____

Continue with the rest of the Standard EMDR Protocol.

Phase 4: Desensitization

Remind patient about the stop signal.

Say, *"The degree of distress is unlikely to reach unbearable levels. However, if it does, simply raise your hand* (therapist shows the stop signal using hand) *so that we can interrupt the exercise!"*

Start desensitization by informing the patient about the effects of BLS.

Say, *"The memories of very distressing and painful events often appear as if frozen in the nervous system. This applies to all images, sounds, thoughts, feelings, body sensations, and all other impressions that a person has recorded in such a distressing situation. The bilateral stimulation that we use in EMDR treatment can reopen the path into the nervous system and the neural networks and allow the brain to process such painful experiences. What is important is that you constantly keep in mind during this process that it is your own brain that brings about the healing and that you know that you are ultimately in control of the whole event. There is nothing in this process that has to be or that is right or wrong. Simply allow to happen whatever is going to happen!"*

Tell patients about the importance of feedback.

Say, *"Please tell me again briefly what you are feeling right now and what is going on inside you. Sometimes things will change, and sometimes they won't. There are no 'supposed to's'! or 'it should be like this!' Simply allow to happen whatever is going to happen!"*

Use dual focus by concentrating on the traumatic memory and the associated negative thoughts and feelings, as well as the simultaneous feeling of the related physical sensations and the bilateral stimuli.

Say, *"Imagine the initial scene together with the associated distressing feeling and _____ (state the negative self-statement/NC). Are you connecting with this? If so, please give me a quick nod. Pay attention to where you feel this in your body and at the same time _____ (state BLS)! Simply be aware of what is happening without evaluating it, and simply allow to happen whatever is going to happen!"*

Do a set of BLS.

Say, *"Now take a deep breath!"*

Say, *"What do you feel now?"*

_____

_____

Say, *"Simply take it in!"*

Say, *"What do you notice now?"*

_____

_____

Reevaluating the degree of distress:

Say, *"On a scale of 0 to 10, where 0 is no disturbance or neutral and 10 is the highest disturbance you can imagine, how disturbing does it feel now?"*

0	1	2	3	4	5	6	7	8	9	10

(no disturbance)   (highest disturbance)

If the SUD is greater than 0, ask what the patient is feeling and focus on the sensations/feelings. Use BLS.

Ask about the distress.

Say, *"What is currently preventing the distress from going to 0?"*

_____

_____

Say, *"If you concentrate on the _____ (state SUD), what is behind this number?"*

_____

_____

Say, *"What do you notice?"*

_____

_____

Say, *"What sensations are present?"*

_____

_____

Say, *"That is very good! Be aware of this and continue ____ (state BLS). Allow whatever is going to happen, to happen!"*

_____

_____

Do sets of BLS.

Incomplete Processing

Often, with pain patients, processing does not shift in one session. Here are some ways to close the session as needed. Find a positive resolution to an incomplete processing session. Install a PC based on a positive physical resource.

Say, *"Close your eyes and focus your attention on your body. Can you detect any positive physical sensation in your body? Is there any place in your body that feels good—or at least neutral? Please let me know which part of your body feels best at the moment."*

_____

_____

Say, *"Now think of your pain once again, and also the positive thoughts and positive physical feeling!"*

_____

_____

Install a PC based on antidote imagery.

Say, *"Now try to think of something that can ease your pain or something that gives you a feeling of relaxation and relief. Allow your thoughts and your imagination to run free. This can be completely unrealistic and a fantasy. Take an image, a thought, or a fantasy that can help ease your pain."*

_____

_____

Say, *"What do you see now?"*

_____

_____

Say, *"Again, think of your pain together with the pain-relieving image and also remember the positive thoughts! Go with that."*

_____

_____

Do sets of BLS.

Reevaluate the PC.

Say, *"Is the sentence* _____ (therapist repeats the PC) *still appropriate, or has there been another positive statement in the meantime that better reflects how you now feel?"*

_____

_____

Say, *"Now, remember, it is your own brain that is doing the healing and you are the one in control. I will ask you to mentally focus on the target and to* _____ (state the BLS you are using). *Just let whatever happens, happen, and we will talk at the end of the set. Just tell me what comes up and don't discard anything as unimportant. Any new information that comes to mind is connected in some way. If you want to stop, just raise your hand."*

Then say, *"Bring up the picture and the words* _____ (clinician repeats the NC) *and notice where you feel it in your body. Now follow* _____ (state the BLS)."*

_____

_____

SUBJECTIVE UNITS OF DISTURBANCE

Say, *"On a scale of 0 to 10, where 0 is no disturbance or neutral and 10 is the highest disturbance you can imagine, how disturbing does it feel now?"*

0	1	2	3	4	5	6	7	8	9	10

(no disturbance)   (highest disturbance)

This procedure is to be repeated until the SUDs = 0.

Say, *"When you go back to the original image or incident, notice the words* _____ (repeat the NC), *the emotion, and body sensation and* _____ (state the BLS)."*

_____

_____

Then the PC is installed.

Note: Each traumatic event associated with the problem that is not reprocessed during the normal course of the first target needs to be processed using this protocol until the SUDs reach an ecological 1 or 0 and the PC is installed.

Continue with sets of BLS until the SUD level reaches 0.

Phase 5: Installation

Note: This is used for complete versus incomplete processing, as shown previously.

Say, *"When you bring up that original incident, does your original positive belief* (repeat the PC) _____ *still fit or is there now a better statement or positive belief about yourself?"*

_____

_____

_____

If the patient accepts the original PC, the clinician should check the VOC rating to see if it has improved.

Say, *"As you think about the original incident and those words* _____ (repeat the selected PC), *how do the words feel to you now on a scale of 1 to 7, where 1 is completely false and 7 is completely true?"*

1	2	3	4	5	6	7
(completely false)				(completely true)		

Installation of the Positive Cognition

Say, *"Think of the event and hold it together with the words* _____ (repeat the PC). *Go with that."* Add BLS.

_____

_____

Continue this procedure until the VOC reaches 7.

Link the Positive Cognition and the Target, and Install

Say, *"Think about the original incident or event and hold it together with the words* _____ (repeat the PC) *and follow my fingers."* Add BLS.

_____

_____

Do sets of BLS as long as the patient reports new positive associations, sensations, or emotions. Check VOC, after each set of BLS, until the PC is fully installed (VOC = 7).

Remember to check for a blocking belief, if the VOC does not reach a 7.

Phase 6: Body Scan

Say, *"Close your eyes and keep in mind the original memory and the positive cognition. Then bring your attention to the different parts of your body, starting with your head and working downward. Any place you find any tension, tightness, or unusual sensation, tell me."*

_____

_____

If any sensation is reported, the clinician adds BLS.

If it is a positive or comfortable sensation, the clinician uses BLS to strengthen the positive feelings.

If a sensation of discomfort is reported, reprocess the body sensation until the discomfort subsides.

Say, *"Close your eyes and once again try to recall the original memory. Also try to recall the positive thoughts* (the therapist repeats the PC). *Now focus your attention back on your body. Starting with your head, slowly let your attention move down your body from top to bottom. Do you notice any tension, stinging, pulling, or any other unusual sensation anywhere?"*

_____

_____

If patients report no changes or only minor changes at the end of the treatment, omit the body scan, because old distressing memories can often be activated through the remaining pain. Try a cognitive interweave, for example,

"Are you really sure that there is no difference there?"

_____

_____

If the patient affirms this,

Say, *"Okay! Do you know what is preventing your pain from changing?"*

_____

_____

If not, instead of the body scan, focus on a positive conclusion, such as an "antidote imagery" exercise.

ANTIDOTE IMAGERY

When patients report differences in pain or changes in the way it is perceived, ask questions to build up an antidote image out of the change.

Say, *"So what's come in the pain's place? What's there now where the pain was before?"*

_____

_____

Sometimes, when the pain doesn't change of its own accord, it may be necessary to instruct patients to do the following:

Say, *"Think of something that could take the pain away or make it better; don't worry about whether it seems realistic or not, just let your imagination run wild."*

_____

_____

Once you obtain something concrete (e.g., smooth, softer, smaller, etc.), restimulate.

If change continues after a couple of more sets, ask the following:

"What's that like? What does it remind you of?"

_____

_____

Phase 7: Closure

Encourage patients to write down upcoming material:

Say, *"Things may come up or they may not. If they do, great. Write them down and it can be a target for the next time. It isn't necessary to give a lot of detail. Just put down enough to remind you so we can target it the next time. You can use a log to write down triggers, images, thoughts, cognitions, emotions, and sensations; you can rate them on our 0-to-10 scale, where 0 is no disturbance or neutral and 10 is the worst disturbance. Please write down the positive experiences, too."*

_____

_____

Prepare patients to deal with the upcoming material:

Say, *"If negative feelings do come up, try not to make them significant. Remember, it's still just the old stuff. If necessary, you can use the Safe Place exercise or one of the other skills we talked about to let as much of the disturbance go as possible. Even if nothing comes up, make sure to use the exercises every day and give me a call if you need to!"*

_____

_____

Phase 8: Reevaluation

It is important to pay attention to the following questions when the patient returns after doing EMDR work.

Ask for the period since the last session.

Say, *"Let's look back over the period of time since our last session. What have you noticed? Have you perceived any changes in your pain since the last session?"*

_____

_____

Say, *"Have you noticed any other material associated with the original memory since the last session?"*

_____

_____

Say, *"What kind of progress have you noticed, especially in terms of the homework?"*

Ask for SUD.

Say, *"As you think back on the target that we were working on last time, on a scale of 0 to 10, where 0 is no disturbance or neutral and 10 is the highest disturbance you can imagine, how disturbing does it feel now?"*

0	1	2	3	4	5	6	7	8	9	10

(no disturbance)　　　　　　　　　　　　　　　(highest disturbance)

If the disturbance level has increased, these reverberations need to be targeted or otherwise addressed.

Ask for VOC (validity of PC):

Say, *"When you think of the incident* (or picture), *how true do those words* _____ (clinician repeats the PC) *feel to you now on a scale of 1 to 7, where 1 feels completely false and 7 feels completely true?"*

1	2	3	4	5	6	7

(completely false)　　　　　　　(completely true)

PAIN-ASSOCIATED MEMORIES PROTOCOL (PAP) SCRIPT

Phase 3: Assessment

Target Selection

Select a target image (stationary picture) from the distressing memories of traumatic events with subjective reference to pain symptoms.

INCIDENT

Say, *"Which event has triggered your pain? If you now think of the distressing situation connected with the pain, what do you experience?"*

_____

_____

PICTURE

Say, *"What picture represents the most disturbing part of this pain incident now?"*

_____

_____

NEGATIVE COGNITION

The therapist asks the patient to formulate an NC that is associated with the *situation connected with the pain*.

Say, *"What words best go with the picture that express your negative belief about yourself now that is associated with the situation connected with the pain?"*

_____

_____

Or, say, *"What does that say about you as a person today?"*

_____

_____

POSITIVE COGNITION

Ask the patient to formulate a PC that is associated with the situation connected with the pain.
Say, *"When you bring up that picture or _____ (state the issue) connected with the pain, what would you like to believe about yourself now?"*

_____

_____

VALIDITY OF COGNITION

Say, *"When you think of the incident (or picture) and the situation associated with the pain, how true do those words _____ (clinician repeats the PC) feel to you now on a scale of 1 to 7, where 1 feels completely false and 7 feels completely true?"*

1   2   3   4   5   6   7

(completely false)   (completely true)

EMOTIONS

Identify and focus on the associated affect:

> Say, *"When you bring up the picture of* _____ (state the issue) *and those words* _____ (clinician states the NC), *what emotion do you feel now?"*

If the distressing traumatic event is closely associated with the primary pain, substitute the pain for the trauma-related emotion.

> Say, *"When you bring up the picture of* _____ (state the issue) *and those words* _____ (clinician states the NC), *what type of pain do you feel now?"*

_____

_____

SUBJECTIVE UNITS OF PAIN

Rate the current pain level with the SUP scale.

> Say, *"On a scale of 0 to 10, where 0 is no pain or neutral and 10 is the maximum pain you can imagine, how disturbing does the pain feel now?"*

0	1	2	3	4	5	6	7	8	9	10

(no pain)   (maximum pain)

LOCATION OF BODY SENSATION

> Say, *"Where do you feel the pain in your body?"*

_____

_____

Continue with the rest of the Standard EMDR Protocol.

Phase 4: Desensitization

Remind the patient about the stop signal.

> Say, *"When we are doing our processing, the degree of distress is unlikely to reach unbearable levels. If it does, simply raise your hand* (therapist shows the stop signal using hand) *so that we can interrupt the exercise."*

> Start desensitization by informing the patient about the effects of BLS.

> Say, *"The memories of very distressing and painful events often appear as if frozen in the nervous system. This applies to all images, sounds, thoughts, feelings, body sensations, and all other impressions that a person has recorded in such a distressing situation. The bilateral stimulation that we use in EMDR treatment can reopen the path into the nervous system and the neural networks and allow the brain to process such painful experiences. What is important is that you constantly keep in mind during this process that it is your own brain that brings about the healing and that you know that you are in control of the whole event. There is nothing in this process that has to be or that is right or wrong. Simply allow to happen whatever is going to happen!"*

> Tell patients about the importance of feedback.

> Say, *"Please tell me again briefly what you are feeling right now. Please let me know what is going on inside you. Sometimes things change, sometimes they don't. There are no*

'supposed to's,' or 'It should be like this!' Simply allow to happen whatever is going to happen!"

_____

_____

Use dual focus by concentrating on the pain-associated memory and the pain that the memory brings up, the associated negative thoughts and feelings, as well as the simultaneous feeling of the related physical sensations. Then do BLS.

Say, *"Imagine the initial scene together with the negative thoughts and the pain associated with the memory. Are you really experiencing it? If so, please give me a quick nod. Pay attention to where you feel this in your body and at the same time _____ (state the BLS). Simply be aware of what is happening without evaluating it, and simply allow whatever is going to happen, to happen!"*

Do a set of BLS.

Say, *"Now take a deep breath."*

Say, *"What do you feel now?"*

_____

_____

Say, *"Simply take it in."*

Say, *"What do you notice now?"*

_____

_____

Reevaluating the degree of distress:

Say, *"On a scale of 0 to 10, where 0 is no pain or neutral and 10 is the maximum pain you can imagine, how disturbing does the pain feel now?"*

0	1	2	3	4	5	6	7	8	9	10
(no pain)								(maximum pain)		

If the SUD is greater than 0, ask what the patient is feeling and focus on the sensations/feelings. Use BLS.

Ask about the distress.

Say, *"What is currently preventing the distress from going to 0?"*

_____

_____

Say, *"If you concentrate on the ___ (state the SUD level), what is behind this number?"*

_____

_____

Say, *"What do you notice?"*

_____

_____

Say, *"What sensations are present?"*

_____

_____

Say, *"Be aware of this and continue to _____ (state the BLS). Allow whatever is going to happen, to happen!"*

_____

_____

Do sets of BLS.

This procedure is to be repeated until the SUDs = 0.

Say, *"On a scale of 0 to 10, where 0 is no pain or neutral and 10 is the maximum pain you can imagine, how disturbing does the pain feel now?"*

0   1   2   3   4   5   6   7   8   9   10

(no pain)   (maximum pain)

Say, *"When you go back to the original image or incident of the pain connected to the situation, notice the words _____ (repeat the NC), the emotion, and the body sensation _____ (state the BLS)."*

_____

_____

Then the PC is installed.

Note: Each traumatic event associated with the problem that is not reprocessed during the normal course of the first target needs to be processed using this protocol until the SUDs reach an ecological 1 or 0 and the PC is installed.

Continue with sets of BLS until the SUD level reaches 0.

Incomplete Processing

Often, with pain patients, processing does not shift in one session. Here are some ways to close the session as needed.

POSITIVE PHYSICAL RESOURCE

Find a positive conclusion to an incomplete processing session. Install a PC based on a positive physical resource.

Say, *"Close your eyes and focus your attention on your body. Can you detect any positive physical sensation in your body? Is there any place in your body that feels good—or at least neutral? Please let me know which part of your body feels best at the moment."*

_____

_____

Say, *"Now think of your pain once again, and also the positive thoughts and positive physical feeling. Go with that."*

Do sets of BLS.

_____

_____

ANTIDOTE IMAGERY

Install a PC based on antidote imagery.

> Say, *"Now try to think of something that can ease your pain or something that gives you a feeling of relaxation and relief. Allow your thoughts and your imagination to run free. This can be completely unrealistic and a fantasy. Find an image, a thought, or a fantasy that can help ease your pain."*

> Say, *"What do you see now?"*

> Say, *"Again, think of your pain together with the pain-relieving image and also remember the positive thoughts. Go with that."*

Do sets of BLS.

Phase 5: Installation

Note: This is used for complete versus incomplete processing, as shown previously.

> Say, *"When you bring up that original incident associated with pain, does your original positive belief* (repeat the PC) _____ *still fit, or is there now a better statement or positive belief about yourself?"*

If the patient accepts the original PC, the clinician should check the VOC rating to see if it has improved.

> Say, *"As you think about the original incident associated with pain and those words _____* (repeat the selected PC), *how do the words feel to you now on a scale of 1 to 7, where 1 is completely false and 7 is completely true?"*

> 1   2   3   4   5   6   7
>
> (completely false)   (completely true)

Installation of the Positive Cognition

> Say, *"Think of the event associated with the pain and hold it together with the words _____* (repeat the PC). *Go with that."* Add BLS.

Continue this procedure until the VOC reaches 7.

Link the positive cognition and the target and install.

Say, *"Think about the original incident associated with the pain or event and hold it together with the words _____ (repeat the PC) and follow my fingers."* Add BLS.

_____

_____

Do sets of BLS as long as the patient reports new positive associations, sensations, or emotions. Check VOC after each set of BLS, until the PC is fully installed (VOC = 7).

Remember to check for a blocking belief if the VOC does not reach a 7.

Phase 6: Body Scan

If a distressing sensation is reported, reprocess the body sensation until the discomfort subsides.

Say, *"Close your eyes and once again try to recall the original memory associated with the pain. Also try to recall the positive thought _____ (state the PC). Now focus your attention back on your body. Starting with your head, slowly let your attention move down your body from top to bottom. Do you notice any tension, stinging, pulling, or any other unusual sensation anywhere?"*

_____

_____

If any sensation is reported, the clinician adds BLS.

If it is a positive or comfortable sensation, the clinician uses BLS to strengthen the positive feelings.

Phase 7: Closure

Encourage patients to write down upcoming material:

Say, *"Things may come up or they may not. If they do, great. Write them down and it can be a target for the next time. It isn't necessary to give a lot of detail. Just put down enough to remind you so we can target it the next time. You can use a log to write down triggers, images, thoughts, cognitions, emotions, and sensations; you can rate them on our 0-to-10 scale, where 0 is no disturbance or neutral and 10 is the worst disturbance. Please write down the positive experiences, too."*

_____

_____

Prepare patients to deal with the upcoming material:

Say, *"If negative feelings do come up, try not to make them significant. Remember, it's still just the old stuff. If necessary, you can use the imagination exercises or one of the other skills we talked about to let as much of the disturbance go as possible. Even if nothing comes up, make sure to use the exercises every day and give me a call if you need to!"*

_____

_____

Prepare patients to deal with possible after-effects of the session:

Say, *"As EMDR stimulates the pain memory networks, the pain may even increase tempo-rarily. If so, don't worry—this may even be a sign of successful processing. If negative sensations do come up, however, try not to make them significant. If necessary, you should use skills we talked about to control the pain as much as possible. Even if nothing comes up, make sure to use the exercises every day and give me a call if you need to!"*

_____

_____

Phase 8: Reevaluation

Each session should begin by reviewing the patient's experience of his or her pain and the related distress over the period since the last session. Against this background, it is important to pay attention to the following questions when the patient returns after doing EMDR work the session before.

Ask about the period since the last session.

Say, *"Let's look back over the period of time since our last session. What have you noticed? Have you perceived any changes in your pain since the last session?"*

_____

_____

Say, *"Have you noticed any other material associated with the original memory since the last session?"*

_____

_____

Say, *"What kind of progress have you noticed, especially in terms of the homework?"*

_____

_____

Rate the current pain level with the SUP scale.

Say, *"On a scale of 0 to 10, where 0 is no pain or neutral and 10 is the maximum pain you can imagine, how disturbing does the pain associated with the incident feel now?"*

0	1	2	3	4	5	6	7	8	9	10

(no pain)   (maximum pain)

   If the pain level has remained unchanged or increased, continue with EMDR processing.

Ask for VOC (validity of PC):

Say, *"As you think about the pain associated with the incident and those words _____ (repeat the selected PC), how do the words feel to you now on a scale of 1 to 7, where 1 is completely false and 7 is completely true?"*

1	2	3	4	5	6	7

(completely false)   (completely true)

Continue with EMDR processing until the SUP = 0 or an ecological value and the VOC = 7.

CURRENT PAIN SENSATION MEMORIES PROTOCOL (CUP) SCRIPT

Phase 3: Assessment

Target Selection

Select a target image (stationary picture) concerning the current pain or previous (worst/first/last) pain crises.

Incident

Say, *"Please describe how your pain feels today. It would be helpful if you described the pain in words using the various senses."*

_____

_____

Say, *"If the pain had a size, what size would it be?"*

_____

_____

Say, *"If the pain had a shape, what shape would it have?"*

_____

_____

Say, *"If the pain had a color, what color would it be?"*

_____

_____

Say, *"Does the pain feel warm or cold?"*

_____

_____

Say, *"If the pain had a voice, what would it say?"*

_____

_____

PICTURE

Say, *"What picture represents the most disturbing part of your pain now?"*

_____

_____

The following are examples of the types of NCs and PCs seen with patients who are in chronic pain.

NEGATIVE COGNITION

The therapist asks the patient to formulate an NC with respect to the current pain.

Note: The formulation of an NC is optional when the focus is on the *current pain*.

Say, *"With respect to the pain, what words best go with the picture that express your negative belief about yourself now?"*

_____

_____

POSITIVE COGNITION

Say, *"When you bring up that picture or _____ (state the issue) concerning your current pain, what would you like to believe about yourself now?"*

_____

_____

VALIDITY OF COGNITION

Ask the patient to formulate a PC that is associated with the current pain.

Say, *"When you think of the image and the current pain, how true do those words _____ (clinician repeats the PC) feel to you now on a scale of 1 to 7, where 1 feels completely false and 7 feels completely true at this precise moment?"*

1	2	3	4	5	6	7

(completely false)   (completely true)

EMOTIONS

Identify the emotions associated with the current pain.

Say, *"When you think of your current pain and (if appropriate) those words _____ (clinician states the NC), what emotion/s do you feel now?"*

_____

_____

SUBJECTIVE UNITS OF PAIN

Rate the current pain level with the SUP scale.

Say, *"On a scale of 0 to 10, where 0 is no pain or neutral and 10 is the maximum pain you can imagine, how disturbing does the pain feel now?"*

0	1	2	3	4	5	6	7	8	9	10

(no pain)   (maximum pain)

LOCATION OF BODY SENSATION

Say, *"Where do you feel the pain in your body?"*

_____

_____

Continue with the rest of the Standard EMDR Protocol.

Phase 4: Desensitization

Remind the patient about the stop signal.

> Say, *"When we are doing our processing, the degree of distress is unlikely to reach unbearable levels. If it does, simply raise your hand* (therapist shows the stop signal using hand) *so that we can interrupt the exercise."*

> Start desensitization by informing the patient about the effects of BLS.

> Say, *"The memories of very distressing and painful events often appear as if frozen in the nervous system. This applies to all images, sounds, thoughts, feelings, body sensations, and all other impressions that a person has recorded in such a distressing situation. The bilateral stimulation that we use in EMDR treatment can reopen the path into the nervous system and the neural networks and allow the brain to process such painful experiences. What is important is that you constantly keep in mind during this process that it is your own brain that brings about the healing and that you know that you are in control of the whole event. There is nothing in this process that has to be or that is right or wrong. Simply allow to happen whatever is going to happen!"*

Tell patients about the importance of feedback.

> Say, *"Please tell me again briefly what you are feeling right now. Please let me know what is going on inside you. Sometimes things change, sometimes they don't. There are no 'supposed to's,' or 'It should be like this!' Simply allow to happen whatever is going to happen!"*

_____

_____

Use dual focus by concentrating on the pain-associated memory and the pain that the memory brings up, the associated negative thoughts and feelings, as well as the simultaneous feeling of the related physical sensations. Then do BLS.

> Say, *"Imagine the initial image together with the associated distressing feeling and the negative self-statement* (negative cognition). *Are you really experiencing it? If so, please give me a quick nod. Pay attention to where you feel this in your body and at the same _____* (state the BLS). *Simply be aware of what is happening without evaluating it, and simply allow to happen whatever is going to happen!"*

Do a set of BLS.

> Say, *"Now take a deep breath."*

> Say, *"What do you feel now?"*

_____

_____

> Say, *"Simply take it in."*

> Say, *"What do you notice now?"*

_____

_____

Reevaluating the degree of pain:

> Say, *"On a scale of 0 to 10, where 0 is no pain or neutral and 10 is the maximum pain you can imagine, how disturbing does the pain feel now?"*

0	1	2	3	4	5	6	7	8	9	10

(no pain)   (maximum pain)

If the SUP is greater than 0, ask what the patient is feeling and focus on the sensations/feelings. Use BLS.

Ask about the distress.

Say, *"What is currently preventing the distress from falling to 0?"*

_____

_____

Say, *"If you concentrate on the ___ (state the SUP level), what is behind this number?"*

_____

_____

Say, *"What do you notice?"*

_____

_____

Say, *"What sensations are present?"*

_____

_____

Say, *"Be aware of this and continue to _____ (state the BLS). Allow whatever is going to happen to happen!"*

_____

_____

Do sets of BLS.

This procedure is to be repeated until the SUPs = 0.

Say, *"On a scale of 0 to 10, where 0 is no pain or neutral and 10 is the maximum pain you can imagine, how disturbing does the pain feel now?"*

0	1	2	3	4	5	6	7	8	9	10

(no pain)   (maximum pain)

Say, *"When you go back to the original image or incident of the pain connected to the situation, notice the words _____ (repeat the NC), the emotion, and the body sensation _____ (state the BLS)."*

_____

_____

Then the PC is installed.

Note: Each traumatic event associated with the problem that is not reprocessed during the normal course of the first target needs to be processed using this protocol until the SUDs reach an ecological 1 or 0 and the PC is installed.

Continue with sets of BLS until the SUD level reaches 0.

Incomplete Processing

Often, with pain patients, processing does not shift in one session. Note ways to close the session.

POSITIVE PHYSICAL RESOURCE

Find a positive conclusion to an incomplete processing session. Install a PC based on a positive physical resource.

> Say, *"Close your eyes and focus your attention on your body. Can you detect any positive physical sensation in your body? Is there any place in your body that feels good—or at least neutral? Please let me know which part of your body feels best at the moment."*

_____

_____

> Say, *"Now think of your pain once again, and also the positive thoughts and positive physical feeling. Go with that."*

Do sets of BLS.

_____

_____

ANTIDOTE IMAGERY

Install a PC based on antidote imagery.

> Say, *"Now try to think of something that can ease your pain or something that gives you a feeling of relaxation and relief. Allow your thoughts and your imagination to run free. This can be completely unrealistic and a fantasy. Find an image, a thought, or a fantasy that can help ease your pain."*

_____

_____

> Say, *"What do you see now?"*

_____

_____

> Say, *"Again, think of your pain together with the pain-relieving image and also remember the positive thoughts. Go with that."*

_____

_____

Do sets of BLS.

Reevaluate the PC.

Phase 5: Installation

Note: This is used for complete versus incomplete processing, as shown previously.

> Say, *"When you bring up that current pain, does your original positive belief* (repeat the PC) _____ *still fit or is there now a better statement or positive belief about yourself?"*

_____

_____

If the patient accepts the original PC, the clinician should check the VOC rating to see if it has improved.

Say, *"As you think about the current pain and those words _____ (repeat the selected PC), how do the words feel to you now on a scale of 1 to 7, where 1 is completely false and 7 is completely true?"*

1	2	3	4	5	6	7

(completely false)   (completely true)

Installation of the Positive Cognition

Say, *"Think of the current pain and hold it together with the words _____ (repeat the PC). Go with that."* Add BLS.

_____

_____

Continue this procedure until the VOC reaches 7.

Link the Positive Cognition and the Target and Install

Say, *"Think about the current pain and hold it together with the words _____ (repeat the PC) and follow my fingers."* Add BLS.

_____

_____

Do sets of BLS as long as the patient reports new positive associations, sensations, or emotions. Check VOC after each set of BLS, until the PC is fully installed (VOC = 7).

Remember to check for a blocking belief if the VOC does not reach a 7.

Phase 6: Body Scan

If a distressing sensation is reported, reprocess the body sensation until the discomfort subsides.

Say, *"Close your eyes and once again try to recall the current pain. Also try to recall the positive thought _____ (state the PC). Now focus your attention back on your body. Starting with your head, slowly let your attention move down your body from top to bottom. Do you notice any tension, stinging, pulling, or any other unusual sensation anywhere?"*

_____

_____

If any sensation is reported, the clinician adds BLS.

If it is a positive or comfortable sensation, the clinician uses BLS to strengthen the positive feelings.

Phase 7: Closure

Encourage patients to notice any change:

Say, *"We cannot predict with any accuracy how long the changes that you have experienced today will last. Sometimes the pain never returns; sometimes it returns but is weaker! If you notice any problems or difficulties, take note of them, so that we can work on them during the next session!"*

_____

_____

Encourage patients to write down upcoming material:

Say, *"Things may come up or they may not. If they do, great. Write them down and it can be a target for the next time. It isn't necessary to give a lot of detail. Just put down enough to remind you so we can target it the next time. You can use a log to write down triggers, images, thoughts, cognitions, emotions, and sensations; you can rate them on our 0-to-10 scale, where 0 is no disturbance or neutral and 10 is the worst disturbance. Please write down the positive experiences, too."*

_____

_____

Prepare patients to deal with possible after-effects of the session:

Say, *"As EMDR stimulates the pain memory networks, the pain even may increase temporarily. If so, don't worry; this may even be a sign of successful processing. If negative sensations do come up, however, try not to make them significant. If necessary, you should use skills we talked about to control the pain as much as possible. Even if nothing comes up, make sure to use the exercises every day and give me a call if you need to!"*

_____

_____

Phase 8: Reevaluation

Each session should begin by reviewing the patients' experience of their pain and related distress over the period since the last session. It is not uncommon for the image of the pain to change between sessions, as the patients' experience changes, especially if some progress is being made. Against this background, it is important to pay attention to the following questions when the patient returns after doing EMDR work the session before.

Ask for the period since the last session.

Say, *"Let's look back over the period of time since our last session. What have you noticed? Have you perceived any changes in your pain since the last session?"*

_____

_____

Say, *"Have you noticed any other material associated with the original memory since the last session?"*

_____

_____

Say, *"What kind of progress have you noticed, especially in terms of the homework?"*

_____

_____

Ask for SUP.

Rate the current pain level with the SUP scale.

Say, *"On a scale of 0 to 10, where 0 is no pain or neutral and 10 is the maximum pain you can imagine, how disturbing does the pain associated with the incident feel now?"*

0	1	2	3	4	5	6	7	8	9	10

(no pain)   (maximum pain)

If the pain level has remained unchanged or increased, continue with EMDR processing.

Ask for VOC (validity of PC):

> Say, *"As you think about the pain associated with the incident and those words* _____
> (repeat the selected PC), *how do the words feel to you now on a scale of 1 to 7, where
> 1 is completely false and 7 is completely true?"*
>
> 1   2   3   4   5   6   7
>
> (completely false)   (completely true)

Continue with EMDR processing until the SUP = 0 or an ecological value and the VOC = 7.

TERMINATION OF EMDR TREATMENT

According to the Standard EMDR Protocol, processing is repeated, usually until the patient reports no further disturbance for the memory (SUD = 0) and a VOC of 6 or 7, and no further changes in image, cognition, affect, or sensation are perceived. In processing pain memories, however, the end point is not always as clear. As already mentioned, it is often not certain that the score of the pain intensity (SUP) can finally become "zero." Thus, it has been suggested to set the criterion of completing EMDR for current pain as the consecutive achievement of the same SUP score three times (at the end of the session; de Roos & Veenstra, 2009). However, as there are no clear standards, the termination of EMDR treatment should always be adjusted to the situational factors as well as the specific needs of the individual patient.

SUMMARY

The idea behind this EMDR Therapy Protocol and the Chronic Pain Control Protocol for the treatment of chronic pain conditions is to desensitize all of the emotional distress associated with the pain and after that to focus on the pain itself. Outside of EMDR, there is growing evidence that in the context of pain chronification in the brain, there is a shift away from the classic pain-processing regions of the brain and toward the emotional networks of the brain (Hashmi et al., 2013). EMDR, as an established procedure for exposing emotional response from trauma therapy, is suggested to specifically process this dysfunctional emotional shift. For this purpose, the EMDR procedure combines the use of well-established psychotherapeutic methods (including imaginal exposure and cognitive and self-control techniques) and the use of specific EMDR elements, such as bilateral sensory stimulation (e.g., left-right eye movements or bilateral hand-tapping induced by the therapist's fingers) and the principle of dual focus of attention. This procedure is suggested to facilitate information processing of emotionally distressing memories (e.g., traumatic events or pain sensations), and thereby causes a decrease in the emotional distress related to these memories. Important targets for EMDR processing in chronic pain conditions are disturbing memories, current pain perceptions, and anticipated future painful situations together with the associated cognitions, emotions, and bodily sensations.

According to this protocol, the EMDR condition starts with a comprehensive assessment of the patient's history to identify relevant traumatic and pain-related memories causing emotional distress and dysfunctional emotional response, discussing the patient's explanatory model, and subsequently providing psychoeducation to develop a better understanding of the links between trauma, pain, emotional response, and the principles of EMDR. Subsequently, desensitizing and reprocessing starts by first targeting the most emotionally distressing memories; afterward, all pain-associated memories of subsequent events are focused until the subjective degree of distress of these memories drops down. After distressing memories and thoughts are processed, current pain sensations are focused. Toward the end, future pain issues as future pain crises or potential pain triggers are targeted by the installation and reinforcement of EMDR-based skills to cope with future distressing or painful events.

A recent scientific evaluation of this protocol indicates that this EMDR approach for the treatment of chronic pain conditions is a safe and promising treatment option in chronic pain conditions for a significant number of chronic pain patients (Gerhardt et al., 2016).

REFERENCES

Allen, T. M. (2004). *Efficacy of EMDR and chronic pain management.* Chicago, IL: Argosy University.

American Psychiatry Association (1994). *Diagnostic and statistical manual of mental disorders (DSM-IV).* Washington, DC: American Psychiatry Association.

Bernstein, D. P., Stein, J. A., Newcomb, M. D., Walker, E., Pogge, D., Ahluvalia, T., ... Zule, W. (2003). Development and validation of a brief screening version of the Childhood Trauma Questionnaire. *Child Abuse and Neglect, 27*(2), 169–190. doi:10.1016/s0145-2134(02)00541-0

Bernstein, E. M., & Putnam, F. W. (1986). Development, reliability, and validity of a dissociation scale. *Journal of Nervous and Mental Disease, 174*(12), 727–735. doi:10.1097/00005053-198612000-00004

Bullinger, M., & Kirchberger, I. (1998). *SF-36 Fragebogen zum Gesundheitszustand: Handanweisung.* Göttingen, Germany: Hogrefe.

de Roos, C., & Veenstra, A. C. (2009). EMDR pain protocol for current pain. In M. Luber (Ed.), *Eye movement desensitization and reprocessing (EMDR): Special populations.* New York, NY: Springer Publication.

de Roos, C., Veenstra, A. C., de Jongh, A., den Hollander-Gijsman, M., van der Wee, N. J., Zitman, F. G., & van Rood, Y. R. (2010). Treatment of chronic phantom limb pain using a trauma-focused psychological approach. *Pain Research and Management, 15*(2), 65–71. doi:10.1155/2010/981634

Geissner, E. (1996). *Die Schmerzempfindungs-Skala (SES): Handanweisung.* Göttingen, Germany: Hogrefe.

Gerhardt, A., Leisner, S., Hartmann, M., Janke, S., Seidler, G., Eich, W., & Tesarz, J. (2016). Eye movement desensitization and reprocessing vs. treatment-as-usual for non-specific chronic back pain patients with psychological trauma: A randomized controlled pilot study. *Frontiers in Psychiatry, 7*(201), 1–10. doi:10.3389/fpsyt.2016.00201

Grant, M. (2009). *Pain control with EMDR* (3rd revised ed.). Charleston, SC: CreateSpace.

Grant, M., & Threlfo, C. (2002). EMDR in the treatment of chronic pain. *Journal of Clinical Psychology, 58*(12), 1505–1520. doi:10.1002/jclp.10101

Griesel, D., Wessa, M., & Flor, H. (2006). Psychometric qualities of the German version of the Posttraumatic Diagnostic Scale (PDSD). *Psychological Assessment, 18,* 262–268. doi:10.1037/1040-3590.18.3.262

Harkness, E. F., Macfarlane, G. J., Silman, A. J., & McBeth, J. (2005). Is musculoskeletal pain more common now than 40 years ago?: Two population-based cross-sectional studies. *Rheumatology, 44*(7), 890–895. doi: 10.1093/rheumatology/keh599

Hashmi, J., Baliki, M., Huang, L., Baria, A., Torbey, S., Hermann, K., ... Apkarian, A. (2013). Shape shifting pain: Chronification of back pain shifts brain representation from nociceptive to emotional circuits. *Brain, 136*(9), 2751–2768. doi:10.1093/brain/awt211

Hekmat, H., Groth, S., & Rogers, D. (1994). Pain ameliorating effect of eye movement desensitization. *Journal of Behavior Therapy and Experimental Psychiatry, 25*(2), 121–129. doi:10.1016/0005-7916(94)90004-3

Hermann, C., Buss, U., & Snaith, R. P. (2011). *Hospital Anxiety and Depression Scale - Deutsche Version. Ein Fragebogen zur Erfassung von Angst und Depressivität in der somatischen Medizin.* Bern, Switzerland: Verlag Hans Huber.

Konuk, E., Epözdemir, H., Atçeken, Ş. H., Aydin, Y. E., & Yurtsever, A. (2011). EMDR treatment of migraine. *Journal of EMDR Practice and Research, 5*(4), 166–176. doi:10.1891/1933-3196.5.4.166

Marcus, S. V. (2008). Phase 1 of integrated EMDR: An abortive treatment for migraine headaches. *Journal of EMDR Practice and Research, 2*(1), 15–25. doi:10.1891/1933-3196.2.1.15

Mazzola, A., Calcagno, M. L., Goicochea, M. T., Pueyrredòn, H., Leston, J., & Salvat, F. (2009). EMDR in the treatment of chronic pain. *Journal of EMDR Practice and Research, 3*(2), 66–79. doi:10.1891/1933-3196.3.2.66

Powell, R., Downing, J., Ddungu, H., & Mwangi-Powell, F. (2010). Pain history and pain assessment. In A. Kopf & N. Patel (Eds.), *Guide to pain management in low-recourse setting* (pp. 67–78). Seattle, WA: International Association for the Study of Pain.

Röhrig, B., Schleußner, C., Brix, C., & Strauß, B. (2006). Die Resilienzskala (RS): Ein statistischer vergleich der kurz- und Langform anhand einer onkologischen patientenstichprobe. [The Resilience Scale (RS): A statistical comparison of the short and long version based on a patient population]. *Psychotherapie Psychosomatik Mededizinische Psychologie, 56*(07), 285–290. doi:10.1055/s-2006-932649

Schneider, J., Hofmann, A., Rost, C., & Shapiro, F. (2008). EMDR in the treatment of chronic phantom limb pain. *Pain Medicine, 9*(1), 76–82. doi:10.1111/j.1526-4637.2007.00299.x

Shapiro, F. (2001). *Eye movement desensitization and reprocessing (EMDR): Basic principles, protocols, and procedures* (2nd ed.). New York, NY: Guilford Press.

Solomon, R. (1999). Utilization of EMDR in crisis intervention. *EMDRIA Newsletter, 4*(3), 11.

Spitzer, C., Mestel, R., Klingelhöfer, J., Gänsicke, M., & Freyberger, H. J. (2004). Screening und veränderungsmessung dissoziativer psychopathologie: Psychometrische charakteristika der kurzform des fragebogens zu dissoziativen symptomen (FDS-20). [Screening and measurement of change of dissociative psychopathology: psychometric properties of the short version of the Fragebogen zu Dissoziativen Symptomen (FDS-20)]. *Psychotherapie Psychosomatik Mededizinische Psychologie, 54*(03/04), 165–172. doi:10.1055/s-2003-814783

Tesarz, J., Leisner, S., Gerhardt, A., Janke, S., Seidler, G., Eich, W., & Hartmann, M. (2014). Effects of eye movement desensitization and reprocessing (EMDR) treatment in chronic pain patients: A systematic review. *Pain Medicine, 15*(2), 247–263. doi:10.1111/pme.12303

Tesarz, J., Seidler, G. H., & Eich, W. (2015). *Treatment of pain with EMDR (in German)*. Stuttgart, Germany: Klett-Cotta.

Von Korff, M., Ormel, J., Keefe, F. J., & Dworkin, S. F. (1992). Grading the severity of chronic pain. *Pain, 50*(2), 133–149. doi: 10.1016/0304-3959(92)90154-4

Wilensky, M. (2006). Eye movement desensitization and reprocessing (EMDR) as a treatment for phantom limb pain. *Journal of Brief Therapy, 5*(1), 31–44. doi: 10.1186/1471-2474-14-256

Jonas Tesarz, Günter H. Seidler, and Wolfgang Eich
SUMMARY SHEET BY MARILYN LUBER

Name: _____ Diagnosis: _____

Medications: _____

Test Results: _____

☑ Check when task is completed, response has changed, or to indicate symptoms.

Note: This material is meant as a checklist for your response. Please keep in mind that it is only a reminder of different tasks that may or may not apply to your incident.

MEASURES

- ☐ Pain intensity (0–10)
- ☐ Pain location
- ☐ Pain Perception Scale (SES)
- ☐ Chronic pain grade (CPG)
- ☐ Hospital Anxiety and Depression Scale (HADS-D)
- ☐ Childhood Trauma Questionnaire (CTQ)
- ☐ Posttraumatic Diagnostic Scale (PDS-D)
- ☐ Dissociative Experiences Scale (DES)
- ☐ 12-Item Short-Form Health Survey (SF-12)
- ☐ Resilience Scale (RS-11)

EMDR THERAPY AND CHRONIC PAIN CONDITIONS SCRIPTED PROTOCOL NOTES

- ☐ *Creating Distance*: Improve the ability to distance oneself from the pain.For example, instead of asking the question "How do you feel today?" or "How are you today?" ask "How does the pain make you feel today?"
- ☐ *Providing Information*: Educate patients on EMDR and pain. Address the following themes that are common for pain patients: the neurophysiological basis of pain perception and modulation, the relationship between pain and (psychological) traumatization, and the effect of EMDR on pain and pain perception.
- ☐ *Creating Security*: Strengthen inner security and stability and develop positive body-based resources. Chronic pain can influence the security and stability needs of the patient negatively as often patients experience a loss of control, feel betrayed by their own body, and/or feel helpless and dependent. In contrast to patients with PTSD, pain patients usually do *not* feel threatened by external forces. Pain patients' experience of threat is through their own bodies

such as physical discomfort, loss of physical integrity and function, and/or inadequate pain control. Therefore, special emphasis should be placed on physically based resources, especially resources concerning "physical well-being " and "physical relaxation" techniques.

☐ *Providing Hope*: Develop hope and (treatment) motivation. Pain patients are worried and disappointed when numerous different treatment attempts repetitively fail and the pain continues. Strengthen the patients' motivation by supporting their developing individualized strategies for the control of their pain, such as the use of heat and/or ice packs, relaxation or distraction techniques, optimized pharmacological management, and physiotherapeutic exercises. Special attention should be paid to restore the patients' quality of life by teaching them how to pace themselves better, as well as strategies on how to start up again everyday activities, despite their pain and all its limitations.

CASE CONCEPTUALIZATION—TARGETS

☐ *1. Traumatic/Distressing events*: Trauma Associated Memories Protocol (TAP). Where the pain is associated with traumatic and distressing events (still today!), start by desensitizing and reprocessing.

☐ *2. Pain-associated memories*: Pain Associated Memories Protocol (PAP). In cases where either no traumatic event can be identified as the trigger or the traumatic event has been reprocessed successfully in the meantime, the distressing memories and thoughts associated with the pain should be processed.

☐ *3. Current pain sensation memories*: Current Pain Sensation Memories Protocol (CUP). After distressing memories and thoughts are processed and in those cases in which no distressing memories or thoughts can be identified initially, focus on the pain using the CUP. Expect a positive effect on the pain symptoms.

☐ *4. Previously suppressed memories*: In cases where patients uncover new, previously suppressed events during pain processing, reactive memories can again be addressed and processed further as therapy progresses using the Standard EMDR Protocol or the modified protocol.

☐ *5. Future pain issues*: The Standard EMDR Protocol or the absorption exercise can be used to alleviate future pain crises and potential pain triggers. One can expect a positive effect on the pain symptoms.

Self-Efficacy and Control	
I do not have the pain under control.	I can learn to influence my pain.
I am helpless.	I can (learn to) help myself.
I'm paralyzed/unable to move.	I have enough opportunities to be active again.
I am powerless/cannot do what I want.	I have enough opportunities/alternatives/prospects.
Self-Esteem and Identity	
I'm worthless/useless.	I am valuable.
I am not good enough.	I'm okay as I am.
I am weak.	I am strong.
I cannot stand it/I can no longer bear this.	I can learn how to deal with this.
I am sick/defective/I cannot function properly any more.	I'm fine the way I am/a good person/valuable/brave/ …
I am a loser.	I do my best/the best that I can.
I'm crazy.	I'm normal (just stressed).
Independency and autonomy	
I'll end up in a wheelchair.	I am independent and self-employed.
I'll lose my job/I'll never be able to go back to work.	I am competent/efficient/strong.
I cannot support my family.	I am important to my family as I am! I can support my family as I am!
Guilt and Responsibility	
It's my fault.	I did the best I could.
I did everything wrong.	I did the best I could.
I deserve to suffer.	I'm fine the way I am/I did the best I could.

Phase 4: Desensitization

Many chronic pain patients, however, initially have problems in focusing on the internal process to activate and change the pain. In the authors' experience, the greatest difficulty in desensitization lies in the fact that many pain patients often fail initially to perceive their feelings as "neutral" without cognitively analyzing or evaluating them directly. In such cases, therapists should not be content with statements such as "It feels better" or "It is okay," but should always explicitly request more detail in such cases: "What feels better?" or "How does it feel?" or "Where are these feelings? Please describe in more detail!," and so on.

If a patient reports a stable, positive change during processing, consider installing it even if distress is greater than 0 when a session concludes. This is why when reprocessing chronic pain (or the distressing memories associated with the pain) installing positive cognitions and/or positive body experiences is so important. In all other cases, either continue the processing or—if, for example, the session has drawn to a close—find an alternative positive conclusion (e.g., installation of a positive cognition based on a positive physical resource or antidote imagery).

EMDR THERAPY AND CHRONIC PAIN CONDITIONS SCRIPTED PROTOCOL

Phase 1: History Taking

Description of Pain Quality and Intensity

Describe pain: _____

_____

Words to describe pain: _____

_____

Worst pain you can imagine now: ____/10

Worst pain you can imagine during the last week: ____/10

Worst pain you can imagine during the last month: ____/10

Location and Spatial Extent of Pain

Where is the pain: _____

Draw a picture of the pain: _____

Any additional pain sites to add to body drawing: _____

Symptom Development: Onset and Temporal Pattern

When pain started: _____

_____

How often: _____

_____

Plot intensity change from beginning with time line: _____

Aggravating and Relieving Factors and Coping Behavior

What helps decrease pain: _____

_____

What makes pain worse: _____

_____

Pain response to warmth, moving, distraction, rest, and so on: _____

_____

What else done to cope with pain: _____

_____

Current stressful circumstances in your life: ☐ Yes ☐ No

Comment: _____

How you cope with this stress: _____

_____

How you cope with emotional aspects of ordeal: _____

_____

What family and friend support you have: _____

_____

Diagnoses and Previous Treatments

Your diagnoses so far: _____

_____

Treatments for pain relief and how effective: _____

_____

_____

Were they effective/still effective: ☐ Yes ☐ No

Comment: _____

Medications and dosage: _____

_____

If diagnosis not known:

What is your understanding of the problem: _____

_____

What have you done to understand what is going on with your pain: _____

_____

What are your options for further medical investigations: _____

_____

Addictive Behaviors

You feel you can't stop using a medicine: ☐ Yes ☐ No

Comment: _____

Would you be willing to stop using this/decrease usage before starting EMDR: ☐ Yes ☐ No

Comment: _____

Effects on Functioning

How pain affects physical functioning: _____

_____

How pain affects social functioning: _____

_____

How pain affects your mood and ability to pay attention or concentrate: _____

_____

What you do to reduce pain to make it bearable: _____

_____

History of Trauma and Pain-Related Incidents

Pain started with traumatic event: ☐ Yes ☐ No

Comment: _____

Health problems prior to trauma: ☐ Yes ☐ No

Comment: _____

Pain reminds you of another specific event: ☐ Yes ☐ No

Comment: _____

Any traumatic experiences before start of pain: ☐ Yes ☐ No

Comment: _____

Any traumatic medical experiences: ☐ Yes ☐ No

Comment: _____

Draw time line of course of pain with major issues or events related to pain: _____

_____

Ask for specific PTS-related symptoms:

Reexperiencing event through repeated, distressing memories, or dreams, or by feeling as if the event were happening again: ☐ Yes ☐ No

Comment: _____

Reminders of event causes you to avoid thoughts, feelings/conversations about it, or activities and places or people who remind you of it: ☐ Yes ☐ No

Comment: _____

You lose interest for significant activities in your life/feeling detached from other people/range of emotion is restricted: ☐ Yes ☐ No

Comment: _____

Troubled by problems with sleeping, irritability/outbursts of anger, problems concentrating, feeling on guard/exaggerated startle response: ☐ Yes ☐ No

Comment: _____

Phase 2: Preparation

Targets of Most Stressful Situations Headline	SUD	Date	Priority
1.			
2.			
3.			
4.			
5.			

Explanation of EMDR Therapy to the Patient ☐ Yes ☐ No

"The memories of very distressing and painful events often appear as if frozen in the nervous system. This applies to all images, sounds, thoughts, feelings, body sensations, and all other impressions that a person has recorded in such a distressing situation. The bilateral stimulation that we use in EMDR treatment can reopen the path into the nervous system and the neural networks and allow the brain to process such painful experiences. What is important is that you constantly keep in mind during this process that it is your own brain that brings about the healing. And that you know that you are ultimately in control of the whole event. There is nothing in this process that has to be or that is right or wrong. Simply allow to happen whatever is going to happen!"

Teach Patients How to Use Language to Describe Pain ☐ Yes ☐ No

"Not many words are available to describe pain, and most patients are not accustomed to talk about their pain. However, finding words to communicate about your pain helps you to concentrate on your pain during the EMDR procedure and helps me, your therapist, to follow the course of the information you are processing. You can describe the quality or intensity of your pain in words, images, or a combination of both.

Some patients describe their pain, for example, as a wall of flames, a buckle around the foot, or an apple with spikes. There are many different ways."

Develop DISH Skills

D: Creating Distance ☐ Yes ☐ No

How pain makes you feel: _____

_____

"Zoom out until you see yourself within the scene, then zoom out even further so you can see the scene unfold as if you were a stranger that happened to pass by. Describe the 'strangers' pain while maintaining the third-person perspective. Make sure to employ a third-person perspective whenever you find yourself reflecting on the experience!"

I: Providing Information ☐ Yes ☐ No

"In pain research a distinction is made between the sensory nervous system's response to certain harmful or potentially harmful stimuli, on the one hand, and the resulting pain sensation, on the other hand. This sensory nervous system response to certain harmful or potentially harmful stimuli is called nociception. The sensation of pain is always a complex subjective sensation, having the character of an unpleasant warning signal that usually forces us to interrupt our current activities. Of note, pain is always a conscious sensation. Therefore, the process of nociception has to be clearly distinguished from the experience of pain. Nociception refers to the activity of peripheral receptors (also called 'nociceptors') that do lead to the painful stimulus. If, for example, someone is pinched strongly on his or her ear, nociceptors of the ear are activated immediately. This signal is then routed and processed in the direction of the brain. If the signal is strong enough, it penetrates into consciousness and we perceive this nociceptive activity as pain. Pain is always linked to consciousness. Thus, if a person who is unconscious is pinched on the ear even though the nociceptors of the ear are activated, the person will perceive no pain—at least as long as the person is unconscious.

In this way, nociception is not a conscious perception, but an activity of neuronal cells so that if this activity penetrates into consciousness, it can result in pain. Accordingly, the neuronal cells that contribute to the development of pain are called the 'nociceptive system.' A central component of this nociceptive system is the so-called 'pain network' in the brain. This pain network, also called 'pain matrix,' consists of different neuronal cell populations that are interconnected with each other and that process in a computer-like manner all the information they get. As a result of this process, a sensation arises that we perceive as pain."

Give some information on pain processing and pain memory.

"Of note, there is a strong overlap between the pain matrix with the emotional networks of the brain. Therefore, the experience of pain is a response evoked by nociception and emotional processes together.

The objective physiological processes (= nociception) are fundamentally supplemented by subjective mental processes. Scientists have shown that the nociceptive system sends a permanent 'background noise' of nociceptive signals toward the pain matrix. Thus, the pain matrix constantly receives potentially painful signals. Nevertheless, we usually do not feel pain as the pain matrix usually filters the incoming signals out in an efficient manner. That is because the activity of the pain matrix depends not only on nociceptive activity but also on non-nociceptive activity, such as emotions, attention, previous experiences, and so on. Considering all this additional information, the pain matrix processes the incoming nociceptive information and either puts it away unconsciously or leads to a conscious perception: the pain. The pain matrix thus acts as a kind of filter that can filter out unimportant pain signals, so that they cannot come into consciousness. If this filter is weakened, this can lead to an increased sensitivity to pain. This filter-like processing system can be thought of as a kind of volume control on a radio, by which the pain can be made loud or quiet. If the pain filter is exhausted, this can mean that the pain level is pushed up to a damagingly loud sound.

*Overall, it is important to keep in mind that the emergence of a conscious perception of pain is not necessarily linked to the existence of a peripheral nociceptive stimulus. **The pain matrix can be triggered even in the absence of such a stimulus by numerous other information (feelings, attention, previous experience, etc.).** In such cases, no structural damage can be found in the examinations or medical imaging despite the obvious presence of pain. This is especially true for already longstanding pain conditions—so called 'chronic pain'—where the structural damage has ceased long ago and no longer activates peripheral receptors for a long time. **Nevertheless, due to the longstanding and profound prior experience of pain, a kind of pain memory in the pain matrix has developed, which now continuously recalls the pain.** A very impressive example of a pain memory can be seen in phantom limb pain patients: Years after amputations, patients feel pain in a limb that no longer exists. Here, the source of the pain lies in the nervous system itself."*

Give information on endogenous pain regulation and the descending pain inhibitory system.

"Besides the ability of pain conduction, the human nervous system possesses a complex system of endogenous pain regulation. So everyone knows the anecdotes of sportsmen and women who have continued activity despite an injury that (theoretically) should have caused them to stop: the cyclist who has open bone fragments piercing through the skin after an accident or the boxer fighting with a broken hand, and so on. In the cut and thrust of competition, the pain system can 'shut the gate' and leave athletes completely pain free in spite of injured tissue.

*The reason for this is the so-called '**descending pain inhibitory system**' of the brain, which acts as a kind of '**gatekeeper**' for pain signals coming from the periphery before sending them up to the brain. This system is highly effective and is also important for normal pain perception. Scientists have shown that these pain inhibitory pathways are constantly active. Even at rest and under normal conditions, they exert their inhibitory influence on the incoming signals from the body. If the activity of this endogenous pain-regulating system is disturbed (e.g., by an extreme level of stress), this can lead to the situation that stimuli that are usually not perceived as painful can now no longer be filtered out and thus become painful.*

Of note, the activity of the body's own pain-regulating system can be influenced by a wide range of different factors (e.g., stress, sleep, physical activity). Importantly, recent studies also demonstrated a powerful influence of stressful experiences and psychological trauma on this system. By the way, this is considered sufficient reason why chronic pain is a common symptom after psychological trauma."

Include information on the relationship between pain and psychological traumatization.

"As I have already said, the endogenous pain-regulating system is able to modulate the incoming nociceptive signals from the periphery in a powerful way. This is not only the case for acute events but especially true for persisting pain conditions. This is usually referred to as 'pain memory' (or 'pain engram'), which is activated by acute stimulation and remains effective even when the initial peripheral causes of pain are already eliminated. That such a mechanism of pain memory exists may have a biological origin: Pain as a warning sign indicates a potentially threatening condition for the organism. Usually the longer a threat persists, the stronger and more dangerous it is for the individual. It therefore makes sense that the longer the pain persists, the stronger the intensity of the pain becomes. In line with this, the endogenous pain-regulating system has efficient mechanisms to exaggerate the pain as a possible signal that the organism is still in danger. This is the only way of ensuring that the affected person

will do everything necessary to eliminate the imminent threat of damage. Against this background, it is not surprising that acute pain often becomes chronic, at least when it is not adequately controlled.

As much as this may be useful from an evolutionary point of view, the more harmful these mechanisms are for the physical comfort of the affected individual, the more the nervous system will take it that something is amiss when acute pain is not handled adequately. Thus, even a relatively harmless event such as the pain of a herniated disc, if treated quickly, could be easily forgotten but can move into chronic pain. The pain has left its memory traces in the brain, and these traces can cause pain now so that the memory of pain becomes entirely independent of whether the tissue is irritated or not.

Not only pain, but also other threatening or dangerous situations can stimulate our brain in this way. This may lead to the development of a so-called 'trauma-pain-memory network.' The more threatening the situation is, the more intense and pronounced the memories may be. As a result of the trauma, the brain is put into a 'maladaptive' memory state so that the traumatic situation induces a massive patho-logical sensory input. It seems that above a certain intensity of fear, anger, shame, or pain, our brain is not able to deal with it and it switches into a kind of 'emergency mode.' In such cases, specific parts of experience—images, sounds, smells, feelings, thoughts, and perceptions—are no longer integrated adaptively into the overall composite of the memory network. Instead of that, the distressing memory seems to become 'frozen' on a neurological level. This results in the development of pathological net-works, so-called trauma–pain networks that can lead to further physical symptoms. The result is a kind of vicious circle, because pain can be triggered by the trauma–pain network, which in turn maintains and expands the trauma–pain network.

It is now known that traumatic and painful experiences can lead very easily to the development of pathological pain networks. This phenomenon is known as 'hypermnesia,' derived from the Greek terms mnesis = 'memory' and hyper = 'too much,' meaning something like 'excessive memory ability.' In the biology of evolution, however, this strong memory capacity for pain and traumatic events appears quite useful because traumatic and painful situations are generally dangerous and threatening events that should be prevented as best as possible. With the aim of avoiding the recurrence of such existentially threatening events in the future, it therefore might have been evolutionarily quite appropriate that traumatic experiences automatically engrave themselves deeply into the memory and induce a state of increased perception (also for pain!) and alert to escape the next time by an earlier recognition of the danger. So, you can imagine that it would have been beneficial for the survival of stone-age hunters that, when they had just escaped the clutches of a saber-toothed tiger, they developed a profound mem-ory ('hypermnesia') of it and a sensitized state of perception. This could help to detect and prevent such events in the future earlier. Against this background, chronic pain syndromes can be considered as an 'undesirable side effect of such former self-protection mechanisms.' In the face of such a priming caused by dangerous situations, not only external circumstances but also internal states such as unpleasant body sensations and pain experiences are imprinted in our memory. The pain must be 'remembered' over and over again, so that the person concerned does not put himself or herself into such a situation again. In addition, the trauma induces a state of hyperexcitability that leads to increased tension in the muscles, as an attack of a saber-toothed tiger had to be expected at any moment. Of note, however, a constant tension of the muscles can lead secondarily to muscular (tension) pain. This can then be noticed as muscular back pain, neck pain, headache, etc."

Talk about information about the effect of EMDR on pain and pain perception.

"EMDR stands for 'Eye Movement Desensitization and Reprocessing' and is a well-established method of psychotherapy that was originally developed for the processing of emotional stress caused by psycho-logical trauma. Meanwhile EMDR is internationally recognized as one of the most effective methods to treat posttraumatic stress disorders and associated emotional distress.

EMDR is a technique that is able to stimulate the nervous system so that the endogenous healing process is promoted. The brain's information processing system naturally moves toward mental health. If the system is blocked or imbalanced by the impact of pain memories, the pain festers and can cause intense suffering. Once the block is removed, healing resumes. Using the detailed protocols and procedures learned in EMDR training sessions, clinicians help patients activate their natural healing processes. EMDR stimulates the pain processing system in a way that dysfunctional pain memories are adaptively resolved. The eye movements and the other bilateral modalities, with which we work in EMDR, allow us to open the responsible neuronal pain networks. This allows the brain to process the pain memories suf-ficiently and to activate the powers of self-healing. And, even in the cases in which the pain memories

cannot fully be eliminated, EMDR is usually able to induce a profound state of relaxation, which always acts as an analgesic. In addition, EMDR can be used to empower our personal strengths, self-awareness, and sensitivity for the body and therefore the way we move, walk, and behave."
Give some information about the EMDR procedure.

"The EMDR treatment itself always follows a specified treatment protocol that is passed through step by step by the patient during each therapy session. One of the key elements of EMDR is 'bilateral stimulation.' During treatment, you will be asked to think or talk about your pain and related memories, as well as possible triggers and painful emotions while simultaneously focusing on my moving fingers or another form of bilateral stimuli. In a typical EMDR therapy session, we will focus on emotional distressing memories and associated negative emotions, beliefs, and body sensations while you will simultaneously track my moving finger with your eyes as it moves back and forth. However, bilateral stimulation does not have to be limited to eye movements; we also have other forms of external stimuli that can be used in EMDR therapy (e.g., alternating hand taps or a sound that pans back and forth from ear to ear).

It is important that you always keep in mind that when using EMDR your own brain causes the healing. Your nervous system knows just what to do and what it needs. It is therefore not necessary to do or want to change anything actively! Just let happen whatever happens and observe whatever may happen!"

S: Creating Security   ☐ Yes ☐ No

What you do to reduce pain: _____

_____

How you cope with your pain: _____

_____

Things you have tried so far: _____

_____

What was helpful: _____

_____

"Is there anywhere you can go or anything you can do where you feel safe from the trauma or pain? Some people feel better when they are doing something they enjoy that takes their mind off the pain; some people like listening to the soothing sounds of nature, such as the ocean, or rain on a roof; other people feel better when they can talk to someone who understands. What do you do that makes you feel safe?"

_____

_____

Place a special emphasis on physically based resources.

"Close your eyes and focus your attention on your body. Can you detect any positive physical sensation in your body? Is there any place in your body that feels good—or at least neutral? Please let me know which part of your body feels best at the moment."

_____

_____

Pain + Positive thoughts + Positive feelings + BLS

_____

_____

"Now try to think of something that can ease your pain or something that gives you a feeling of relaxation and relief. Allow your thoughts and your imagination to run free. This can be completely unrealistic and a fantasy. Find an image, a thought, a fantasy that can help ease your pain."

_____

_____

Pain + Pain-relieving image + Positive thoughts + BLS

_____

_____

_____

"When you have chronic pain, it is important that you learn how to pace yourself so that you're not constantly aggravating your pain. Pacing yourself means stopping whatever you're doing when the pain starts to come on. It may mean changing your expectations; instead of finishing tasks in one go, they may need to be broken down and completed in bite-sized chunks.

It is often helpful to have some of what I call quick strategies to help manage your pain more effectively. For example, many chronic pain sufferers have their own strategies to handle their pain. Though every single point for its own does not so far appear sufficient enough to eliminate the pain, they may play together a key role in controlling the pain. Thus, let´s try to develop together a kind of emergency kit that provides a list of your individual coping skills for a staggered application!"

H: Providing Hope   ☐ Yes ☐ No

"Even though it can feel sometimes like the pain is never ending, there is always hope, things change, nothing lasts forever.

It is also important for you to think about _____ (state what they can do despite their pain). *You know that is really impressive that even though you have all of this pain, you can succeed at _____ (state their success)!"*

Choice of Bilateral Stimulation (Visual, Auditory, or Tactile)   ☐ Yes ☐ No

"We will be doing sets of bilateral stimulation to stimulate the dysfunctional pain memory networks. For this, visual, auditory, or tactile stimuli can be used. An approved technique is tracking my moving fingers with your eyes as they move back and forth. However, bilateral stimulation does not have to be limited to eye movements. If it is more comfortable for you, we can also use other forms of external stimuli (e.g., alternating hand taps or a sound that pans back and forth from ear to ear). Let us first experimentally try out different kinds of stimuli."

Stop Signal   ☐ Yes ☐ No

The more intense the pain becomes, the more difficult it is for patients to concentrate on the pain for a long period of time; in this case, the patient's attention shifts to dealing with the pain or even to surviving. If the pain becomes too intense, patients are instructed to use a stop signal and together you can determine whether continuing the EMDR session is feasible and bearable.

"The degree of distress is unlikely to reach unbearable levels. If it does, simply raise your hand (therapist shows the stop signal using hand) *so that we can interrupt the exercise."*

Phase 3: Assessment

Trauma-Associated Pain Memories Protocol (TAP) Script

Event that triggered pain: _____

_____

Target/Memory/Image: _____

_____

NC: _____

PC: _____

VOC: ___/7

Emotions: _____

SUD: ___/10

Sensation: _____

Continue with the rest of the Standard EMDR Protocol.

Phase 4: Desensitization

Apply the Standard EMDR Protocol for all targets.

When incomplete session:

"Close your eyes and focus your attention on your body. Can you detect any positive physical sensation in your body? Is there any place in your body that feels good–or at least neutral? Please let me know which part of your body feels best at the moment."

_____

Pain + Positive thoughts + Positive physical feeling

+ Something that can ease your pain/gives you a feeling of relaxation and relief/something unrealistic and a fantasy to help ease your pain

_____

_____

Pain + Pain-relieving image + Positive thoughts + BLS

Install the PC.

Original PC: ☐ Use original PC ☐ Use new PC

New PC (if new one is better): _____

VOC: _____/7

Incident + PC + BLS

Phase 5: Installation

Install the PC.

Original PC: ☐ Use original PC ☐ Use new PC

New PC (if new one is better): _____

VOC: _____/7

Incident + PC + BLS

Phase 6: Body Scan

Unresolved tension/tightness/unusual sensation: _____

_____

Unresolved tension/tightness/unusual sensation + BLS

Strengthen positive sensation using BLS.

If there is more discomfort, reprocess until discomfort subsides + BLS. Then repeat body scan.

VOC: ___/7

"Close your eyes and once again try to recall the original memory. Also try to recall the positive thoughts (therapist repeats the positive cognition). *Now focus your attention back on your body. Starting with your head, slowly let your attention move down your body from top to bottom. Do you notice any tension, stinging, pulling, or any other unusual sensation anywhere?"*

Phase 7: Closure

Most positive thing learned: _____

_____

PC: _____

+ BLS

Check with VOC

Normal closure: ☐ Yes ☐ No

Phase 8: Reevaluation

Noticed since last session: _____

_____

Current symptoms: _____

New material: _____

_____

SUD: ____/10

PAIN-ASSOCIATED MEMORIES PROTOCOL (PAP) SCRIPT

Select a target image from the distressing memories of traumatic events with subjective reference to pain symptoms.

Most disturbing target/memory/image of the pain incident: _____

_____

Negative cognitions   positive cognitions

NC: _____

PC: _____

VOC: ___/7

Emotions: _____

Subjective units of pain (SUP): ___/10

Sensation: _____

Phase 4: Desensitization

Apply the Standard EMDR Protocol for all targets.

Incomplete processing:

POSITIVE PHYSICAL RESOURCE

Close eyes + Focus on body + Positive physical sensation in body + Place in body that feels good

_____

Pain + Positive thoughts + Positive physical feelings + BLS

ANTIDOTE IMAGERY

Something that can ease your pain/gives you a feeling of relaxation and relief/something unrealistic and a fantasy to help ease your pain

_____

_____

Pain + Pain-relieving image + Positive thoughts + BLS

Phase 5: Installation

Install the PC.

Original PC: □ Use original PC □ Use new PC

New PC (if new one is better): _____

VOC: _____/7

Incident + PC + BLS

Phase 6: Body Scan

Unresolved tension/tightness/unusual sensation: _____

_____

Unresolved tension/tightness/unusual sensation + BLS

Strengthen positive sensation using BLS.

If there is more discomfort, reprocess until discomfort subsides + BLS. Then repeat body scan.

VOC: ___/7

"Close your eyes and once again try to recall the original memory. Also try to recall the positive thoughts (therapist repeats the positive cognition). Now focus your attention back on your body. Starting with your head, slowly let your attention move down your body from top to bottom. Do you notice any tension, stinging, pulling, or any other unusual sensation anywhere?"

Phase 7: Closure

Most positive thing learned: _____

_____

PC: _____

+ BLS

Check with VOC _____

Normal closure: □ Yes □ No

Encourage patients to write down upcoming material:

"Things may come up or they may not. If they do, great. Write it down and it can be a target for next time. It isn't necessary to give a lot of detail. Just put down enough to remind you so we can target it next time. You can use a log to write down triggers, images, thoughts, cognitions, emotions, and sensations; you can rate them on our 0-to-10 scale where 0 is no disturbance or neutral and 10 is the worst disturbance. Please write down the positive experiences, too."

Prepare patients to deal with the upcoming material:

"If negative feelings do come up, try not to make them significant. Remember, it's still just the old stuff. If necessary, you can use the imagination exercises or one of the other skills we talked about to let as much of the disturbance go as possible. Even if nothing comes up, make sure to use the exercises every day and give me a call if you need to!"

Prepare patients to deal with possible after-effects of the session:

"As EMDR stimulates the pain memory networks, the pain may even increase temporarily. If so, don't worry—this may even be a sign of successful processing. If negative sensations do come up, however, try not to make them significant. If necessary, you should use skills we talked about to control the pain as much as possible. Even if nothing comes up, make sure to use the exercises every day and give me a call if you need to."

Phase 8: Reevaluation

Noticed since last session: _____

_____

Current symptoms: _____

New material: _____

SUP: ____/10

CURRENT PAIN SENSATION MEMORIES PROTOCOL (CUP) SCRIPT

Select a target image (stationary picture) concerning the current pain or previous (worst/first/last) pain crises.

"Please describe how your pain feels today. It would be helpful if you described the pain in words using the various senses." _____

_____

Size: _____

Shape: _____

Color: _____

Warm or cold: _____

If pain had a voice: _____

(See list of NCs and PCs in Pain Associated Memories Protocol [PAPs] Script earlier in text.)

NC: _____

PC: _____

VOC: ___/7

Emotions: _____

SUP: ___/10

Sensation: _____

Phase 4: Desensitization

Apply the Standard EMDR Protocol for all targets.

Incomplete processing:

POSITIVE PHYSICAL RESOURCE

Close eyes + Focus on body + Positive physical sensation in body + Place in body that feels good

_____

Pain + Positive thoughts + Positive physical feelings + BLS

ANTIDOTE IMAGERY

Something that can ease your pain/gives you a feeling of relaxation and relief/something unrealistic and a fantasy to help ease your pain

_____

_____

Pain + Pain-relieving image + Positive thoughts + BLS

Phase 5: Installation

Install the PC.

Original PC: ☐ Use original PC ☐ Use new PC

New PC (if new one is better): _____

VOC: _____/7

Incident + PC + BLS

Phase 6: Body Scan

"Close your eyes and once again try to recall the current pain. Also try to recall the positive thoughts (therapist repeats the positive cognition). *Now focus your attention back on your body. Starting with your head, slowly let your attention move down your body from top to bottom. Do you notice any tension, stinging, pulling, or any other unusual sensation anywhere?"*

If negative, add BLS until it comes down.

If positive, add BLS to strengthen the positive feelings.

Phase 7: Closure

Most positive thing learned: _____

_____

PC: _____

+ BLS

Check with VOC _____

Normal closure: ☐ Yes ☐ No

Encourage patients to notice any change:

"We cannot predict with any accuracy how long the changes that you have experienced today will last. Sometimes the pain never returns; sometimes it returns but is weaker! If you notice any problems or difficulties, take note of them, so that we can work on them during the next session!"

Encourage patients to write down upcoming material:

"Things may come up or they may not. If they do, great. Write it down and it can be a target for next time. It isn't necessary to give a lot of detail. Just put down enough to remind you so we can target it next time. You can use a log to write down triggers, images, thoughts, cognitions, emotions, and sensations; you can rate them on our 0-to-10 scale where 0 is no disturbance or neutral and 10 is the worst disturbance. Please write down the positive experiences, too."

Prepare patients to deal with the upcoming material:

"If negative feelings do come up, try not to make them significant. Remember, it's still just the old stuff. If necessary, you can use the imagination exercises or one of the other skills we talked about to let as much of the disturbance go as possible. Even if nothing comes up, make sure to use the exercises every day and give me a call if you need to!"

Prepare patients to deal with possible after-effects of the session:

"As EMDR stimulates the pain memory networks, the pain may even increase temporarily. If so, don't worry—this may even be a sign of successful processing. If negative sensations do come up, however, try not to make them significant. If necessary, you should use skills we talked about to control the pain as much as possible. Even if nothing comes up, make sure to use the exercises every day and give me a call if you need to."

Phase 8: Reevaluation

Noticed since last session, especially any changes in pain: _____

_____

_____

Any material associated with the original memory: _____

_____

Current symptoms: _____

New material: _____

_____

SUP: ____/10

If unchanged or increased, continue EMDR processing.

VOC: _____/7

Termination of EMDR treatment:

Usually SUD = 0 and VOC = 6-7/7 and no further changes in image, cognition, or affect/sensation perceived.

The endpoint for processing pain is not always clear. It does not always go to zero.

Criterion of completing EMDR for current pain = the same SUP score three times at end of session.

EMDR THERAPY TREATMENT FOR MIGRAINE

Emre Konuk, Hejan Epözdemir, Zeynep Zat, Sirin
Haciomeroglu Atceken, and Asena Yurtsever

INTRODUCTION

Migraine has been related to mental illness in the medical field for more than a century (Lake, Rains, Penzien, & Lipchik, 2005; Marcus, 2008). The characteristics of migraine are head pain and neurological, gastrointestinal, and autonomic symptoms (Curry & Green, 2007). During migraine attacks, one or more of the following symptoms might occur:

- Loss of vision
- Nausea
- Vomiting
- Dizziness
- Sensitivity to sound, light, and smell
- Tingling/numbing in the extremities of the face

It has also been noted that migraine causes disruption in family, household, social, and work activities (Lake et al., 2005). According to the Migraine Research Foundation (2018), migraine is the third most common illness in the world. An estimated 12% of the population suffers from migraine.

Before it was studied systematically, the association between migraine and psychopathology was often discussed clinically (Silberstein, Lipton, & Dalessio, 2001). Many studies have revealed that psychiatric illnesses such as depression and anxiety occur more often among migraine patients compared to the general population (Lake et al., 2005). A great number of studies state that migraines are strongly related to mood and anxiety disorders such as depression, anxiety, panic, and bipolar disorders (Beghi et al., 2007; Hamelsky & Lipton, 2006; Kececi, Dener, & Analan, 2003). In fact, the presence of psychiatric problems is a risk factor for transforming the migraine into its chronic form. An 8-year follow-up study by Guidetti et al. (1998) of 100 young adults with migraine examined the association between psychiatric illness on initial evaluation and migraine status at follow-up. The study concluded that a migraine with adolescent onset varies its features over time, and often the migraine will decrease or improve.

A wide variety of treatments are available for migraine, including both medication and a variety of other therapies. Nonmedication treatments involve a lot of modalities such as behavioral therapy, diet modification, hypnotherapy, and biofeedback.

It is important to note that the concept that chronic pain is etiologically related to adverse life events has a long history in the literature (Raphael, Chandler, & Ciccone, 2004). Grant (2001) states, "If chronic pain is somehow a product of trauma, then this would have implications for the understanding and treatment of pain."

EMDR therapy sees chronic pain, including migraine pain, as involving a disturbing somatic component, combined with the emotional reaction to the pain that gets stored in the brain. Therefore, the treatment with EMDR therapy for pain integrates the processing of pain-related events accompanied by the disturbing emotional and body sensations related with the pain (Marcus, 2008).

RECENT RESEARCH WITH EMDR AND MIGRAINE

Recent studies are providing early evidence for the use of EMDR therapy for chronic pain patients (Grant, 2000; Grant & Threlfo, 2002; Schneider, Hofmann, Rost, & Shapiro, 2008; Wilensky, 2006). These are promising findings for further study of the use of EMDR therapy with migraine patients.

Chronic daily migraine is defined as migraine that lasts 15 days or more in a month. Relying on the literature, the EMDR Migraine Protocol was developed focusing on traumas associated with migraine and pain and tailored to the needs of migraine patients. In 2011, Konuk, Epözdemir, Haciömeroğlu Atçeken, Aydin, and Yurtsever conducted and published a pilot study to study this protocol. For this pilot study, neurologists and psychiatrists examined a number of patients, and after their evaluation, 11 Turkish patients were diagnosed with chronic daily migraine; this group fit the criteria for the sample. The EMDR Migraine Protocol was used with the participants. Before and after the EMDR intervention, daily ratings were recorded that included migraine frequency, duration, and intensity; medication intake; and hospital emergency room (ER) visits. The study showed that there is a significant reduction in migraine frequency, duration, medication intake, and hospital ER visits. According to results, the frequency and duration of migraine decreased significantly. Although there was some decrease in pain intensity, it was not statistically significant. Also, findings show that there were 24 ER visits in the 3 months before treatment, but none after the treatment. In addition, the pain medication used by participants decreased from 129 pills to 24 pills per month after the treatment. The effects of the treatment continued at 3-month follow-up. These results are evidence for the effectiveness of the EMDR Migraine Protocol; however, further research is needed.

MEASURES: ASSESSMENT AND INVENTORIES

This protocol was developed to enable the therapist to use EMDR therapy in the treatment of chronic pain. However, clients may have various psychiatric or psychological symptoms as well, so therapists need to use their clinical judgment concerning what to treat first. For example, the client may have frequent panic attacks and migraines. In these cases, therapists must decide where to begin treatment: traumas related to the migraine or panic attacks. This protocol is for working with migraines exclusively. Therefore, therapists need to ensure that their client is able to focus on EMDR therapy work with migraines first before tackling their panic.

The client history/assessment for treatment using the EMDR Migraine Protocol includes three phases:

1. *Neurological assessment*: Use of the EMDR Migraine Protocol is for patients who have been diagnosed with a primary migraine, tension, or cluster headache.
   NB: This excludes patients suffering from neurological disorders such as organic causes (brain tumor, head trauma, etc.), epilepsy, multiple sclerosis, and so on.
2. *Psychiatric assessment*: After the neurological assessment, if necessary, patients may be examined by a psychiatrist to rule out severe psychopathologies:
   a. Clinical judgment about using EMDR therapy
   b. Either the psychiatrist or the therapist thinks that the patient is not an appropriate candidate at this time for the following reasons:
      ○ Patients who have to first deal with another disorder or problem clinically
         □ Psychosis
         □ Recent unresolved traumatic events
         □ Severe personality disorders (e.g., borderline, antisocial)
         □ Unresolved loss
         □ Severe depression and/or suicidal risk
         □ Ongoing violence
         □ Alcohol or substance abuse/dependence
         □ Sleep disorders
         □ Eating disorders
         □ Mental retardation
         □ Patients who are pregnant and in their first trimester
3. *Psychological assessment.* After neurological and psychiatric examinations, a clinician evaluates the patients accepted for migraine treatment. The psychological assessment consists of psychological testing. For all psychological testing, instruments are self-administered.

a. *Migraine Assessment Scale (HAS;* see the Appendices 7.1 and 7.2):
   i. HAS is the most precise measure of the frequency, severity, and duration of attacks, usage of medication, and frequency of emergency visits on a daily basis (necessary).
   ii. HAS II (weekly) is a short version but less precise and is used once a week—within the sessions—to measure the previous week's average migraine (intensity, frequency, and duration).

   The DBE Migraine Project Team developed both scales.

b. The Subjective Pain Level (SPL) scale assesses the level of pain on a scale of 0 to 10.
c. The goal of the Migraine Disability Assessment Program (MIDAS) is to improve the management of the migraine (suggested; https://headaches.org/wp-content/uploads/2018/02/MIDAS.pdf).
d. The Symptom Assessment-45 Questionnaire (SA-45) measures psychiatric symptomatology and is available from Multi-Health Systems Inc. (suggested; www.mhs.com/product.aspx?gr=cli&prod=sa45&id=overview).
e. The World Health Organization Quality-of-Life BREF (WHOQOL-BREF) is an international cross-cultural quality-of-life instrument (suggested; www.who.int/substance_abuse/research_tools/whoqolbref/en).

MIGRAINE FROM A TRAUMA PERSPECTIVE

General Information

Assess demographic information; migraine history; family history; health, work, and marital/relationship status; children; friends; social life; and other details. Check for family medical history, including migraines.

Case Formulation

Our clinical experiences indicate that when we work on traumas with EMDR therapy, the clients' migraines decrease. This clinical result shows that there may be a link between chronic migraine and traumatic experience(s). From the Adaptive Information Processing (AIP) perspective, psychopathology is based on traumas. This is valid for chronic migraine as well. It begins with trauma and continues to develop with it. This is how the memory network develops.

EMDR is a three-pronged approach that is used for case formulation and treatment planning with the EMDR Therapy Protocol for Chronic Migraine including the past, present triggers, and future template. History taking is crucial to access the information that is needed.

Treatment Planning

When the assessment is over, patients who are eligible for this program are evaluated and their treatment is planned. During case formulation, the following are taken into consideration:

- Results of assessment: Client history, case planning, and treatment plan are factors to be considered.
- Other observers of the patient's migraine attack impressions, such as the psychiatrist and neurologist, for instance, head traumas, epilepsy, organic disorders, and so on.
- History of the migraine: Any other traumatic memories that may be relevant to the patient's migraines apart from traumas that fall into a hierarchical sequence as following:
  - Other early traumas that clinically may be relevant to the patient's migraines, such as unresolved sexual abuse and physical or psychological violence
  - Migraine history in other family members and relevant traumatic memories

Use the Three-Pronged Protocol, which includes the following:

- *Past*: Use this hierarchy to structure EMDR therapy past trauma processing:
  - Traumatic/stressful events that are connected with migraines or relatively close to the first remembered migraine by the client and the therapist.
  - Migraines can be traumatic in themselves. Consequently, if no traumatic experiences are related to the migraines, ask if the migraines are traumatic.

- Use the Standard EMDR Protocol with them and check the SUD level.
- Start with the worst memory, if necessary; continue with the first, then the most recent incident.
- *Present triggers*: After working with the main traumas that are connected with the migraine, work with the stimuli that trigger migraines. Use the following hierarchy to structure EMDR therapy for present trigger processing:
  - List triggers and/or incidents that initiate or increase the migraine. Start with the most frequently experienced trigger.
  - For each trigger, find the most disturbing event/incident to work with the Standard EMDR Protocol.
- *Future template*: Use the future template with each of the triggers that activates client migraines.

Therapy Goals

If you have chronic migraine pain, almost all of life is organized around pain. This includes family life, relationship with a partner, children, work, entertainment, friends, social life, and so on. Therefore, the treatment plan needs to include not only getting rid of your pain but also organizing the future when the client does not have pain. The therapist may ask the client to think and dream about the future without the migraine.

EMDR TREATMENT FOR MIGRAINE PROTOCOL SCRIPT NOTES

Phase 1: History Taking

When you begin Phase 1, it is important to get the history of the patient, including descriptive information. Pay close attention to the history of the client's migraine:

- Frequency, including the first attack
- Severity of attacks
- Duration
- Ongoing symptoms
- Type and shape of migraine
- What was occurring prior to the first attack
- Negative effects on social, familial, and work life

Ask for a trauma history:

- Traumatic events that took place relatively close to the first migraine
- Traumatic events that the therapist and client connect to the migraine
- Traumatic experiences during the first, worst, and most recent migraine

It is important to track what triggers the migraine:

- Stress of daily life
- Foods and drinks
- Sleepless night
- Menstrual period and/or hormonal factors
- Seasonal
- Temperature
- Barometric pressure
- Environmental factors (noise, traffic, etc.)

Phase 2: Preparation

It is important to inform the client about the following basic elements of the preparation:

- EMDR therapy
- Using medication as prescribed
- Visiting the doctor as advised

- Treatment and what is expected
- Filling out the session or weekly forms of HAS and SPL assessments
- Traumas or problems not thought to be related to migraines will not be dealt with in the beginning of treatment

Another element taught during the preparation phase is the trigger-point therapy technique (DeLaune, 2008). This protocol assumes that chronic migraines are related to past traumas. It is reasonable to assume that while working with past trauma, a migraine attack or pain may be triggered. In this event, use this technique when the pain level is 5 to 6 out of 10. In the experience of the treatment as well as research team, if the pain does not reach too high a level, it takes only several minutes to reduce the pain to 0 or even a 1 to 2 out of 10. Then, the EMDR therapy can resume. Make sure to ask the pain level before the beginning of each session, in case other interventions are needed before beginning EMDR therapy. Also, often clients will not report their migraines, so it is important to ask about migraines throughout the session as well. It is helpful to finish a session with a relaxation that has proven to be helpful to the client in the past.

Phase 2 is the time to introduce EMDR therapy. This includes teaching about the general procedures, including sitting position, type of bilateral stimulation (BLS), stop sign, and metaphors commonly used in distancing the client from the memory in EMDR. Also, teach resources such as the safe place and/or resource development and so on.

Phase 3: Assessment/Choice of Targets

When beginning to work with EMDR, note that the Standard EMDR Protocol is used during the session. The order of traumas to process set up in the "Planning the Tasks and Putting Traumas Into a Hierarchical Sequence," discussed later in text, is followed. During EMDR sessions, if any new traumatic experience comes up, take a note of the new experience. When the work with the traumatic experience is done, check the strength of the new traumatic experience's connection with the patient's migraine and then decide where to put the new experience in the hierarchy.

This is the hierarchy to use:

- Past
  - Traumatic events close to the first remembered migraine
  - Trauma of the migraine itself
    - Worst migraine
    - First migraine
    - Most recent migraine
- Present triggers
  - Related to the traumas worked on in the past traumas section earlier in text that are connected to the migraine
  - Increase or start the migraine
- Future template
  - Use the image as a future template: imagining positive outcomes (Shapiro, 2009). Imagining positive outcomes seems to assist the learning process. In this way, clients learn to enhance optimal behaviors, to connect them with a positive cognition, and to support generalization. The assimilation of this new behavior and thought is supported by the use of BLS into a positive way to act in the future.

Phases 4 Through 7: Desensitization Through Closure

Follow the Standard EMDR Protocol, focusing on the migraine issues, present triggers, and future concerns.

Phase 8: Reevaluation

During the eighth phase, do the following:

- Reevaluate what has come up in the client's life since the last session
- Reevaluate the target worked on in the previous session. If the individual target has been resolved, move on to check the next target in the hierarchy. If not, finish processing the target from the past session.

EMDR THERAPY TREATMENT FOR MIGRAINE PROTOCOL SCRIPT

Phase 1: Client History

Results of Neurological, Psychiatric, and Psychological Assessments

Use the results of the full assessment to inform choices for treatment and the use of the EMDR Therapy Treatment for Migraine Protocol. Check any relevant information later in the text.
Results of neurological assessment:

- Tension
- Migraine
- Cluster
- Not appropriate

Results of psychiatric assessment:

- Another disorder/problem clinically first
- Pregnant in the first trimester
- Psychosis
- Recent unresolved traumatic events
- Severe personality disorders (e.g., borderline, antisocial)
- Unresolved loss
- Severe depression and/or suicidal risk
- Ongoing violence
- Alcohol or substance abuse/dependence
- Sleep disorders
- Eating disorders
- Mental retardation

Results of psychological testing:

- HAS
- HAS II
- SPL Scale
- Migraine Disability Assessment Program (MIDAS)
- The World Health Symptom Assessment-45 Questionnaire (SA-45)
- The World Health Organization Quality of Life BREF (WHOQOL-BREF)

Results of psychological assessment:

Descriptive Information

Say, *"What is your full name?"*

_____

Say, *"What is your age?"*

_____

Say, *"What is your date of birth?"*

_____

Say, *"What is your family status? Are you single, married, divorced, partnered?"*

_____

Say, *"What education have you had?"*

_____

Say, *"With whom do you live?"*

_____

Say, *"In the event of an emergency, who would I contact?"*

_____

Say, *"Are you currently employed and/or in school? Or are you retired or out of work? If employed, what is your job description?"*

_____

History of Migraine

Say, *"When did you first begin to have migraines?"*

_____

Say, *"What was going on in your life prior to your first migraines?"*

_____

Say, *"How have your migraines developed over time? Are they the same intensity? Did they get worse? Did they get better?"*

_____

_____

Say, *"What are the symptoms that you have during a migraine?"*

_____

_____

Say, *"Currently, how often are you experiencing them? Do they occur daily, every few days, weekly, monthly?"*

_____

_____

Say, *"On a scale of 0 to 10, where 10 is the worst pain and 0 is no pain, how severe are your migraines? Are they always at that severity or do they change?"*

_____

_____

Say, *"For the most part, how long do your migraines last?"*

_____

_____

Say, *"Who made the diagnosis and when? What's the diagnosis of your migraine?"*

_____

_____

Say, *"Can you describe the way you experience your migraine* (e.g., pounding, heaviness, pressure, one or two sides)?*"*

_____

Say, *"How do your migraines affect your social life?"*

_____

_____

_____

_____

Say, *"How do your migraines affect your family life?"*

_____

_____

_____

_____

Say, *"How do your migraines affect your work life?"*

_____

_____

_____

_____

Say, *"Are there any ways that your migraine affords you an opportunity to not do something that you do not want to do (secondary gain)?"*

_____

_____

_____

_____

Traumatic/Stressful Events

Say, *"Were there any traumatic/stressful events that took place relatively close to the first migraine?"*

_____

_____

_____

_____

Say, *"In your opinion, are there any traumatic/stressful events that may cause your migraines to begin?"*

_____

_____

_____

Say, *"Are there any other traumatic/stressful events that might be connected to the migraine that you can think of?"*

_____

_____

_____

_____

Say, *"Did you have any traumatic/stressful experience/s in, around, and/or during your first migraine?"*

_____

_____

_____

Say, *"Did you have any traumatic/stressful event(s) in, around, and/or during your worst migraine?"*

_____

_____

_____

_____

Say, *"Did you have a traumatic/stressful experience/s in, around, and/or during your most recent migraine?"*

_____

_____

_____

Traumatic Memories Relevant to Patient's Migraine

Say, *"Are there other traumatic memories that you have had in your life that might be relevant to your migraines?"*

_____

_____

_____

_____

Say, *"Are there other traumatic memories that you have had in your life that are connected to any type of abuse or violence to yourself and/or witnessed and/or recounted to you that affected you?"*

_____

_____

_____

_____

Say, *"Are there other traumatic memories that have happened to you concerning family members or friends that might be relevant to your migraines?"*

_____

_____

_____

_____

Triggers

Say, *"Please tell me about the stress or difficulties that generally trigger your migraines."*

_____

_____

_____

_____

Say, *"Are there any particular foods that precipitate/cause a migraine?"*

_____

_____

_____

_____

Say, *"Are there particular beverages that precipitate/cause a migraine?"*

_____

_____

_____

_____

Say, *"Do migraines cause you to have sleepless nights, and/or do you get migraines if you do not have enough sleep or too much sleep?"*

_____

_____

_____

_____

Say, *"Do you notice any hormonal factors connected with your migraine? Some women experience migraines before/during their menstrual cycles."*

_____

_____

_____

_____

Say, *"Have you noticed whether you have more migraines during certain seasons or changes in weather?"*

_____

_____

_____

_____

Say, *"Are your migraines connected in any way to changes in heat, cold, and/or humidity?"*

_____

_____

_____

_____

Say, *"Do particular environmental factors such as noise, traffic, and so on precipitate migraines?"*

_____

_____

_____

_____

Say, *"Do you notice that you have more migraines when certain people in your life are around?"*

_____

_____

_____

_____

Say, *"Are there any other events, situations, or stimulations that trigger your migraines?"*

_____

_____

_____

_____

Medical Treatment

Say, *"When you have a migraine, what have people in the medical profession prescribed, such as usage of painkillers or treatment such as antidepressants?"*

_____

_____

_____

_____

Phase 2: Preparation Phase

During the preparation phase, it is important to inform the patient about EMDR.

Say, *"When a disturbing event occurs, it can get locked in the brain with the original picture, sounds, thoughts, feelings, and body sensations. This material can combine factual material with fantasy and with images that stand for the actual event or feelings about it. EMDR seems to stimulate the information and allows the brain to process the experience. That may be what is happening in REM or dream sleep—eye movements (tones, tactile) may help to process the unconscious material. It is your own brain that will be doing the healing and you are the one in control."*

At the same time, it is important to introduce to the client the ethical rules that are valid for the present context and to inform the patient about the program/course of treatment.

Say, *"It is important that you use your medication and see your doctor as frequently as he/ she asks you to. Please fill out the forms as we have agreed, so that we keep track of your migraine. In this treatment, we will see each other for _____ (state the length of your treatment; ours is 15 sessions)."*

Say, *"I will be scheduling weekly sessions with you as often as possible. They will last 50 minutes. Will you be able to follow through with this plan?"*

_____

Say, *"Some of the traumas and problems that we have talked about together, such as ____ (note appropriate traumas and problems), will not be dealt with during your migraine treatment because they do not seem to be related to your migraines. If, however, we find that they are, we can always address them. When your migraine treatment is complete, we can always come back to them if you are still concerned about any of them."*

And also inform the patient about the need to fill out the session or weekly forms of the HAS and the SPL assessment.

Say, *"I want to tell you about some of the things I am going to ask you to do that will be helpful to both you and me during your migraine treatment. First, I will be asking you to fill out the session and weekly forms of the Migraine Assessment Scale, or HAS, which measures the frequency, severity, and duration of your migraines; your medication usage; and any emergency visits you might have in between sessions. Would you be willing to do this?"* ☐ Yes ☐ No

Say, *"Also, before we begin our EMDR sessions, I will ask you to tell me your Subjective Pain Level (SPL), which assesses the level of pain you have on a scale of 0 to 10, where 10 is the most severe pain and 0 is no pain or neutral. Would you agree to that?"*

☐ Yes ☐ No

Phase 3: Assessment/Choice of Targets

A. Past Trauma Memories

1. Traumatic/Stressful Events Close to the First Remembered Migraine

Say, *"Earlier, we identified the relevant past traumatic events related to your migraine. The ones that I have noted down are the following."*

List of Traumatic Events Close to the First Remembered Migraine

_____

_____

_____

Say, *"Are there any others that you can think of before we start our EMDR processing?"*

_____

_____

Say, *"We generally tend to begin with the first experience. Is that okay for you?"*

_____

INCIDENT

Say, *"Focus on the _____ (state the issue\event)."*

_____

_____

PICTURE

Say, *"What picture represents the most traumatic part of the entire incident _____ (state the issue)?"*

_____

_____

NEGATIVE COGNITION (NC)

Say, *"What words best go with the picture that express your negative belief about yourself now?"*

_____

_____

POSITIVE COGNITION (PC)

Say, *"When you bring up that picture or _____ (state the issue), what would you like to believe about yourself now?"*

_____

_____

VALIDITY OF COGNITION (VOC)

Say, *"When you think of _____ (state the issue or picture), how true do those words _____ (clinician repeats the PC) feel to you now on a scale of 1 to 7, where 1 feels completely false and 7 feels completely true?"*

1	2	3	4	5	6	7

(completely false)   (completely true)

Sometimes, it is necessary to explain further.

Say, *"Remember, sometimes we know something with our head, but it feels differently in our gut. In this case, what is the gut-level feeling of the truth of _____ (clinician states the PC), from 1 (completely false) to 7 (completely true)?"*

1	2	3	4	5	6	7

(completely false)   (completely true)

EMOTIONS

Say, *"When you bring up the picture _____ (state the issue) and those words _____ (clinician states the NC), what emotion do you feel now?"*

_____

_____

SUBJECTIVE UNITS OF DISTURBANCE (SUDs)

Say, *"On a scale of 0 to 10, where 0 is no disturbance or neutral and 10 is the highest disturbance you can imagine, how disturbing does it feel now?"*

0	1	2	3	4	5	6	7	8	9	10

(no disturbance)   (highest disturbance)

LOCATION OF BODY SENSATIONS

Say, *"Where do you feel it (the disturbance) in your body?"*

_____

_____

Use Phases 4 through 7 for each incident. Work with past issues, checking to see if other targets have been processed or still need to be processed with the Standard EMDR Protocol. Continue to process past issues until they are no longer an issue.

    2. Trauma of the Migraine Itself
        a. Worst Migraine

Say, *"Earlier, we talked about the trauma of the migraine that you have had, and we identified the first migraine and the trauma related to that experience."*

_____

_____

_____

_____

INCIDENT

Say, *"Focus on the _____ (state the worst migraine)."*

_____

_____

_____

PICTURE

Say, *"What picture represents the most traumatic part of the entire incident _____ (state the issue)?"*

_____

_____

NEGATIVE COGNITION

Say, *"What words best go with the picture that express your negative belief about yourself now?"*

_____

_____

POSITIVE COGNITION

Say, *"When you bring up that picture or _____ (state the issue), what would you like to believe about yourself now?"*

_____

_____

VALIDITY OF COGNITION

Say, *"When you think of* _____ (state the issue or picture), *how true do those words* _____ (clinician repeats the PC) *feel to you now on a scale of 1 to 7, where 1 feels completely false and 7 feels completely true?"*

1	2	3	4	5	6	7

(completely false)   (completely true)

Sometimes, it is necessary to explain further.

Say, *"Remember, sometimes we know something with our head, but it feels differently in our gut. In this case, what is the gut-level feeling of the truth of* _____ (clinician states the PC), *from 1* (completely false) *to 7* (completely true)?"*

1	2	3	4	5	6	7

(completely false)   (completely true)

EMOTIONS

Say, *"When you bring up the picture* _____ (state the issue) *and those words* _____ (clinician states the NC), *what emotion do you feel now?"*

_____

_____

SUBJECTIVE UNITS OF DISTURBANCE

Say, *"On a scale of 0 to 10, where 0 is no disturbance or neutral and 10 is the highest disturbance you can imagine, how disturbing does it feel now?"*

0	1	2	3	4	5	6	7	8	9	10

(no disturbance)   (highest disturbance)

LOCATION OF BODY SENSATIONS

Say, *"Where do you feel it* (the disturbance) *in your body?"*

_____

_____

Use Phases 4 through 7 for each incident. Work with past issues, checking to see if other targets have been processed or still need to be processed with the Standard EMDR Protocol. Continue to process past issues until they are no longer an issue.

b. First Migraine

Say, *"Earlier, we identified the traumatic nature of your worst migraine."*

_____

_____

_____

_____

INCIDENT

Say, *"Focus on the _____ (state the first migraine)."*

_____

_____

PICTURE

Say, *"What picture represents the most traumatic part of the entire incident _____ (state the issue)?"*

_____

_____

NEGATIVE COGNITION

Say, *"What words best go with the picture that express your negative belief about yourself now?"*

_____

_____

POSITIVE COGNITION

Say, *"When you bring up that picture or _____ (state the issue), what would you like to believe about yourself now?"*

_____

_____

VALIDITY OF COGNITION

Say, *"When you think of _____ (state the issue or picture), how true do those words _____ (clinician repeats the PC) feel to you now on a scale of 1 to 7, where 1 feels completely false and 7 feels completely true?"*

1	2	3	4	5	6	7

(completely false)   (completely true)

Sometimes, it is necessary to explain further.

Say, *"Remember, sometimes we know something with our head, but it feels differently in our gut. In this case, what is the gut-level feeling of the truth of _____ (clinician states the PC), from 1 (completely false) to 7 (completely true)?"*

1	2	3	4	5	6	7

(completely false)   (completely true)

EMOTIONS

Say, *"When you bring up the picture _____ (state the issue) and those words _____ (clinician states the NC), what emotion do you feel now?"*

_____

_____

SUBJECTIVE UNITS OF DISTURBANCE

Say, *"On a scale of 0 to 10, where 0 is no disturbance or neutral and 10 is the highest disturbance you can imagine, how disturbing does it feel now?"*

0   1   2   3   4   5   6   7   8   9   10

(no disturbance)   (highest disturbance)

LOCATION OF BODY SENSATIONS

Say, *"Where do you feel it* (the disturbance) *in your body?"*

_____

_____

Use Phases 4 through 7 for each incident. Work with past issues, checking to see if other targets have been processed or still need to be processed with the Standard EMDR Protocol. Continue to process past issues until they are no longer an issue.

c. Most Recent Migraine

Say, *"Earlier, we identified the trauma of your most recent migraine."*

_____

_____

_____

_____

INCIDENT

Say, *"Focus on the _____* (state the most recent migraine).*"*

_____

_____

PICTURE

Say, *"What picture represents the most traumatic part of the entire incident _____* (state the issue)*?"*

_____

_____

NEGATIVE COGNITION

Say, *"What words best go with the picture that express your negative belief about yourself now?"*

_____

_____

POSITIVE COGNITION

Say, *"When you bring up that picture or* _____ (state the issue), *what would you like to believe about yourself now?"*

_____

_____

VALIDITY OF COGNITION

Say, *"When you think of* _____ (state the issue or picture), *how true do those words* _____ (clinician repeats the PC) *feel to you now on a scale of 1 to 7, where 1 feels completely false and 7 feels completely true?"*

| 1 | 2 | 3 | 4 | 5 | 6 | 7 |

(completely false)   (completely true)

Sometimes, it is necessary to explain further.

Say, *"Remember, sometimes we know something with our head, but it feels differently in our gut. In this case, what is the gut-level feeling of the truth of* _____ (clinician states the PC), *from 1 (completely false) to 7 (completely true)?"*

| 1 | 2 | 3 | 4 | 5 | 6 | 7 |

(completely false)   (completely true)

EMOTIONS

Say, *"When you bring up the picture* _____ (state the issue) *and those words* _____ (clinician states the NC), *what emotion do you feel now?"*

_____

_____

SUBJECTIVE UNITS OF DISTURBANCE

Say, *"On a scale of 0 to 10, where 0 is no disturbance or neutral and 10 is the highest disturbance you can imagine, how disturbing does it feel now?"*

| 0 | 1 | 2 | 3 | 4 | 5 | 6 | 7 | 8 | 9 | 10 |

(no disturbance)   (highest disturbance)

LOCATION OF BODY SENSATIONS

Say, *"Where do you feel it* (the disturbance) *in your body?"*

_____

_____

Use Phases 4 through 7 for each incident. Work with past issues, checking to see if other targets have been processed or still need to be processed with the Standard EMDR Protocol. Continue to process past issues until they are no longer an issue.

Phase 4: Desensitization

To begin, say the following:

> *"Now, remember, it is your own brain that is doing the healing and you are the one in control. I will ask you to mentally focus on the target and to follow my fingers (or any other BLS you are using). Just let whatever happens, happen, and we will talk at the end of the set. Just tell me what comes up, and don't discard anything as unimportant. Any new information that comes to mind is connected in some way. If you want to stop, just raise your hand."* Then say, *"Bring up the picture and the words _____ (clinician repeats the NC) and notice where you feel it in your body. Now follow my fingers with your eyes (or other BLS)."*

Phase 5: Installation

Say, *"How does _____ (repeat the PC) sound?"*

_____

_____

Say, *"Do the words _____ (repeat the PC) still fit, or is there another positive statement that feels better?"*

_____

_____

If the client accepts the original PC, the clinician should ask for a VOC rating to see if it has improved:

Say, *"As you think of the incident, how do the words feel, from 1 (completely false) to 7 (completely true)?"*

1	2	3	4	5	6	7

(completely false)   (completely true)

Say, *"Think of the event and hold it together with the words _____ (repeat the PC)."*

Do a long set of BLS to see if there is more processing to be done.

Phase 6: Body Scan

> Say, *"Close your eyes and keep in mind the original memory and the positive cognition. Then bring your attention to the different parts of your body, starting with your head and working downward. Any place you find any tension, tightness, or unusual sensation, tell me."*

_____

_____

Phase 7: Closure

> Say, *"Things may come up or they may not. If they do, great. Write them down and it can be a target for the next time. You can use a log to write down what triggers your headaches (e.g., alcohol, running, bath, food, lack of sleep, tiredness, loud music) and other images, thoughts or cognition, emotions and sensations; you can rate them on our 0-to-10 scale, where 0 is no disturbance or neutral and 10 is the worst disturbance. Please write down the positive experiences, too."*

> *"If you get any new memories, dreams, or situations that disturb you, just take a good snapshot. It isn't necessary to give a lot of detail. Just put down enough to remind you so we can target it the next time. The same thing goes for any positive dreams or situations. If negative feelings do come up, try not to make them significant. Remember, it's*

still just the old stuff. Just write it down for the next time. Then use the tape or the safe place exercise to let as much of the disturbance go as possible. Even if nothing comes up, make sure to use the tape every day and give me a call if you need to."

PRESENT TRIGGERS

List of Triggers

List by the frequency of triggers, starting with the most frequently experienced trigger. For each trigger, find the worst incident/moment/picture that caused the migraine, and target that.

Trigger 1:

Worst incident: _____

_____

Trigger 2:

Worst incident: _____

_____

Trigger 3:

Worst incident: _____

_____

Trigger 4:

Worst incident: _____

_____

INCIDENT

Say, *"Tell me the worst incident you have experienced with _____ (state the trigger)."*

_____

_____

_____

PICTURE

Say, *"What picture represents the most traumatic part of the entire incident _____ (state the incident)?"*

_____

_____

NEGATIVE COGNITION

Say, *"What words best go with the picture that express your negative belief about yourself now?"*

_____

_____

POSITIVE COGNITION

Say, *"When you bring up that picture or* _____ (state the trigger), *what would you like to believe about yourself now?"*

_____

_____

VALIDITY OF COGNITION

Say, *"When you think of the* _____ (state the trigger or picture), *how true do those words* _____ (clinician repeats the PC) *feel to you now on a scale of 1 to 7, where 1 feels completely false and 7 feels completely true?"*

1   2   3   4   5   6   7

(completely false)   (completely true)

Sometimes, it is necessary to explain further.

Say, *"Remember, sometimes we know something with our head, but it feels differently in our gut. In this case, what is the gut-level feeling of the truth of* _____ (clinician states the PC), *from 1 (completely false) to 7 (completely true)?"*

1   2   3   4   5   6   7

(completely false)   (completely true)

EMOTIONS

Say, *"When you bring up the picture* _____ (state the trigger) *and those words* _____ (clinician states the NC), *what emotion do you feel now?"*

_____

_____

SUBJECTIVE UNITS OF DISTURBANCE

Say, *"On a scale of 0 to 10, where 0 is no disturbance or neutral and 10 is the highest disturbance you can imagine, how disturbing does it feel now?"*

0   1   2   3   4   5   6   7   8   9   10

(no disturbance)   (highest disturbance)

LOCATION OF BODY SENSATION

Say, *"Where do you feel it* (the disturbance) *in your body?"*

_____

_____

Continue with Phases 4 through 7 for each trigger. Process all of the relevant triggers, checking after the completion of each one to see if other targets need to be processed. If so, continue the processing until all are completed and then move on to the next step.

FUTURE TEMPLATE

Say, *"I would like you to imagine yourself coping effectively with the trigger* _____ (such as meeting the boss, doing a presentation, etc.) *in the future. With the positive belief* _____ (state the positive belief, such as "I can do it," "I can manage it") *and your new sense of* _____ (state the quality, i.e., relaxed, strength, clarity, confidence, calm), *imagine stepping into this scene.*

Notice what you see and how you are handling the situation.

Notice what you are thinking, feeling, and experiencing in your body."

_____

_____

_____

Again, here is the opportunity to catch any disturbance that may have been missed.

Say, *"Are there any blocks, anxieties, or fears that arise as you think about this future scene?"*

_____

_____

_____

If yes, say the following:

Say, *"Then focus on these blocks and follow my fingers* (or any other BLS).*"*

Say, *"What do you get now?"*

_____

_____

_____

If the blocks do not resolve quickly, evaluate if the client needs any new information, resources, or skills to be able to comfortably visualize the future coping scene. Introduce needed information or skills.

Say, *"What would you need to feel confident in handling the situation?"*

Or say, *"What is missing from your handling of this situation?"*

_____

_____

If the block still does not resolve and the client is unable to visualize the future scene with confidence and clarity, use direct questions, the affect scan, or the floatback technique to identify old targets related to blocks, anxieties, or fears. Remember, the point of the Three-Pronged Protocol is not only to reinforce positive feelings and behavior in the future, but also to catch any unresolved material that may be getting in the way of an adaptive resolution of the issue (s). Use the Standard EMDR Protocol to address these targets before proceeding with the template.

If there are no apparent blocks and the client is able to visualize the future scene with confidence and clarity, say the following:

"Please focus on the image, the positive belief, and the sensations associated with this future scene and follow my fingers (or any other BLS).*"*

_____

_____

Process and reinforce the positive associations with BLS. Do several sets until the future template is sufficiently strengthened.

Say, *"Go with that."*

_____

_____

Then say, *"Close your eyes and keep in mind the image of the future and the positive cognition. Then bring your attention to the different parts of your body, starting with your head and working downward. Any place you find any tension, tightness, or unusual sensation, tell me."*

_____

_____

If any sensation is reported, do BLS.

Say, *"Go with that."*

If it is a positive or comfortable sensation, do BLS to strengthen the positive feelings.

Say, *"Go with that."*

If a sensation of discomfort is reported, reprocess until the discomfort subsides.

Say, *"Go with that."*

When the discomfort subsides, check the VOC.

Say, *"When you think of the incident* (or picture), *how true do those words* _____ (clinician repeats the PC) *feel to you now on a scale of 1 to 7, where 1 feels completely false and 7 feels completely true?"*

1	2	3	4	5	6	7

(completely false)   (completely true)

Continue to use BLS until you reach a VOC = 7 or there is an ecological resolution. When the image as future template is clear and the PC is true, move on to the movie as a future template.

Movie as a Future Template or Imaginal Rehearsing

During this next level of future template, clients are asked to move from imagining this one scene or snapshot to imagining a movie about coping in the future, with a beginning, a middle, and an end. Encourage clients to imagine themselves coping effectively in the face of specific challenges, triggers, or snafus. Therapists can make some suggestions of things in order to help inoculate them with future problems. It is helpful to use this type of future template after clients have received needed education concerning social skills and customs, assertiveness, and any other newly learned skills.

Say, *"This time, I'd like you to close your eyes and play a movie, imagining yourself coping effectively with* _____ (state where the client will be) *in the future. With the new positive belief* (state the positive belief) *and your new sense of* _____ (strength, clarity, confidence, calm), *imagine stepping into the future. Imagine yourself coping with any challenges that come your way. Make sure that this movie has a beginning, a middle, and an end. Notice what you are seeing, thinking, feeling, and experiencing in your body. Let me know if you hit any blocks. If you do, just open your eyes and let me know. If you don't hit any blocks, let me know when you have viewed the whole movie."*

_____

_____

If the client hits blocks, address as discussed earlier with BLS until the disturbance dissipates.

Say, *"Go with that."*

If the material does not shift, use interweaves, new skills, information, resources, direct questions, and any other ways to help your clients access information that will allow them to move on. If these options are not successful, usually it means that there is earlier material still unprocessed; the floatback and affect scan are helpful in these cases to access the material that keeps clients stuck.

If clients are able to play the movie from start to finish with a sense of confidence and satisfaction, ask them to play the movie one more time from beginning to end and introduce BLS.

Say, *"Okay, play the movie one more time from beginning to end. Go with that."*

Use BLS.

In a sense, you are installing this movie as a future template.

After clients have fully processed their issue(s), they might want to work on other positive templates for the future in other areas of their lives using the future templates discussed earlier in text.

If new material comes ups during the reevaluation phase after the current anxiety and behavior were processed, target this material as soon as possible to make sure that the whole event, including its past issues, current triggers, and future issues, has been fully reprocessed.

Phase 8: Reevaluation

The therapist goes through the HAS with the patient. If a migraine occurred, check for triggers.

Say, *"Can you remember any event or incident that is a trigger that initiated your migraine?"*

_____

_____

If triggers are identified, the therapist works with them.

SUMMARY

Migraines are the third most common illness in the world, with 12% of the world population suffering from this type of chronic headache. Migraine disrupts family, social, and work activities. There is also a connection between psychiatric illnesses such as anxiety disorders and depression. Often, when there is a psychiatric problem, there is more of a possibility of it converting to its chronic form. Because chronic pain is etiologically related to adverse life events (traumatic experiences), the authors believe that EMDR therapy could be of use and created the EMDR Chronic Migraine Protocol. A pilot study found that there was a significant reduction in migraine frequency and duration, emergency visits, and medication use. There was also a decrease in pain intensity, although not statistically significant. EMDR therapy includes the Three-Pronged Protocol and an in-depth history of the client's migraine and trauma. More research is needed to support this new protocol.

REFERENCES

Beghi, E., Allais, G., Cortelli, P., D'Amico, D., De Simone, R., d'Onofrio, F., . . . Bussone, G. (2007). Migraine and anxiety–depressive disorder comorbidity: The HADAS study. *Neurological Sciences, 28*(2), S217–S219. doi:10.1007/s10072-007-0780-6

Curry, K., & Green, R. (2007). Prevalence and management of migraine in a university undergraduate population. *Journal of the American Association of Nurse Practitioners, 19*(7), 378–382. doi:10.1111/j.1745-7599.2007.00237.x

DeLaune, V. (2008). *Trigger point therapy for headaches & migraines: Your self-treatment workbook for pain relief.* Oakland, CA: New Harbinger.

Grant, M. (2000). EMDR: A new treatment for trauma and chronic pain. *Complementary Therapies in Nursing and Midwifery, 6*(2), 91–94. doi:10.1054/ctnm.2000.0459

Grant, M. (2001). Understanding and treating chronic pain as trauma, with EMDR. Retrieved from https://www.researchgate.net/profile/Mark_Grant4/publication/265746746_UNDERSTANDING _AND_TREATING_CHRONIC_PAIN_AS_TRAUMA_WITH_EMDR/links/551a3a750cf2f51a6fea2d88/ UNDERSTANDING-AND-TREATING-CHRONIC-PAIN-AS-TRAUMA-WITH-EMDR.pdf

Grant, M., & Threlfo, C. (2002). EMDR in the treatment of chronic pain. *Journal of Clinical Psychology, 58*, 1505–1520. doi:10.1002/jclp.10101

Guidetti, V., Galli, F., Fabrizi, P., Giannantoni, A. S., Napoli, L., Bruni, O., & Trillo, S. (1998). Migraine and psychiatric comorbidity: Clinical aspects and outcome in an 8-year follow-up study. *Cephalalgia, 18*(7), 455–462. doi:10.1046/j.1468-2982.1998.1807455.x

Hamelsky, S. W., & Lipton, R. B. (2006). Psychiatric comorbidity of migraine. *Headache: The Journal of Head and Face Pain, 46*(9), 1327–1333. doi:10.1111/j.1526-4610.2006.00576.x

Kececi, H., Dener, S., & Analan, E. (2003). Co-morbidity of migraine and major depression in the Turkish population. *Cephalalgia, 23*(4), 271–275. doi:10.1046/j.1468-2982.2003.00518.x

Konuk, E., Epözdemir, H., Haciömeroğlu Atçeken, Ş., Aydin, Y. E., & Yurtsever, A. (2011). EMDR treatment of migraine. *Journal of EMDR Practice and Research, 5*(4), 166–176. doi:10.1891/1933-3196.5.4.166

Lake, A. E., Rains, J. C., Penzien, D. B., & Lipchik, G. L. (2005). Migraine and psychiatric comorbidity: Historical context, clinical implications, and research relevance. *Headache: The Journal of Head and Face Pain, 45*(5), 493–506. doi:10.1111/j.1526-4610.2005.05101.x

Marcus, S. V. (2008). Phase 1 of integrated EMDR: An abortive treatment for migraine headaches. *Journal of EMDR Practice and Research, 2*(1), 15–25. doi:10.1891/1933-3196.2.1.15

Migraine Research Foundation. (2018). Raising money for migraine research. Retrieved from http:// migraineresearchfoundation.org/resources/migraine-in-the-news

Raphael, K. G., Chandler, H. K., & Ciccone, D. S. (2004). Is childhood abuse a risk factor for chronic pain in adulthood? *Current Pain and Migraine Reports, 8*, 99–1110. doi:10.1007/s11916-004-0023-y

Schneider, J., Hofmann, A., Rost, C., & Shapiro, F. (2008). EMDR in the treatment of chronic phantom limb pain. *Pain Medicine, 9*(1), 76–82. doi:10.1111/j.1526-4637.2007.00299.x

Shapiro, F. (scripted by M. Luber). (2009). Current anxiety and behavior. In M. Luber (Ed.), *Eye Movement Desensitization and Reprocessing (EMDR) scripted protocols: Basics and special situations* (pp. 138–140). New York, NY: Springer Publishing.

Silberstein, S. D., Lipton, R. B., & Dalessio, D. J. (Eds.). (2001). *Wolff's migraine and other head pain.* Oxford, UK: Oxford University Press.

Wilensky, M. (2006). Eye movement desensitization and reprocessing (EMDR) as a treatment for phantom limb pain. *Journal of Brief Therapy, 5*(1), 31–44. doi:10.1186/1471-2474-14-256

APPENDIX 7.1

(Konuk et al., 2011)

MIGRAINE ASSESSMENT FORM (SESSION)

Date ..../..../...... ...../

Name-Surname:_____ `

1. How many times did you have a migraine during the past week?

...../..... times

---

2. During the past week, how many days did you have a migraine?

1   2   3   4   5   6   7

---

3. Did you make any visits to the ER last week because of your migraine?

O Yes   O No   If yes, how many times?   .... times

---

4. Did you use medication to alleviate your migraine?

O Yes   O No   If yes, how many?.........

---

5. What was the rate of your **most intense** migraine this past week (circle the number)?

10 EXCRUCIATING: My migraines reach a point that I can't function in any way.

9

8 VERY PAINFUL: It makes it difficult to concentrate, but I can do tasks requiring attention.

7

6 PAINFUL: It hurts, but I can carry out what I need to do.

5

4 LITTLE PAIN: Most of the time I can ignore the pain.

3

2 VERY LITTLE PAIN: I notice my migraine only if I concentrate on it.

1

0 NO PAIN

---

6. What was the average length of your migraines during the past week?

Duration:.........   (hour).........   (minute)

---

7. During the past week how long did your **most intense** migraine last?

Duration:.........   (hour).........   (minute)

APPENDIX 7.2

(Konuk et al., 2011)

MIGRAINE ASSESSMENT FORM (WEEKLY)

DATES: ....../....../.......... ..../......./.......

Name-Surname:

....

Instruction: This form is prepared for you to keep a record of the number, intensity, and duration of your migraines and the number of pills that you use after your migraines. Please use the following "Migraine Intensity Scale" ranging from 0 to 10 to evaluate the intensity of your migraines.

Migraine Intensity Scale

⑩ A LARGE AMOUNT OF PAİN..... My head aches to the point that I can't do anything about it.

⑨

⑧ VERY PAINFUL........................... It makes it difficult to concentrate but I can do tasks requiring attention.

⑦

⑥ PAINFUL.................................... My head hurts, but I can carry out what I need to do.

⑤

④ SLIGHT PAIN............................. Most of the time I can ignore the pain.

③

② SOME PAIN................................ I notice my migraine only if I concentrate on it.

①

⓪ NO MİGRAİNE

1. How many times did you have a migraine on Monday? . . . . (times)
   a. What was the average **intensity** of those migraines?

      ⓪ ① ② ③ ④ ⑤ ⑥ ⑦ ⑧ ⑨ ⑩

   b. What was the average **duration** of those migraines?

      ⓪ ① ② ③ ④ ⑤ ⑥ ⑦ ⑧ ⑨ ⑩

   c. What was the **intensity of your most painful** migraine?

      ⓪ ① ② ③ ④ ⑤ ⑥ ⑦ ⑧ ⑨ ⑩

   d. What was the **duration of your most painful** migraine?

      Duration: .... (hours) .... (minutes)

   e. Did you use any pills to stop your pain?

      ○ Yes ○ No If your answer is "Yes," how many did you use? . . ..

   f. Did you make any visits to the emergency room because of your migraine?

      ○ Yes ○ No

2. How many times did you have a migraine on Tuesday? . . . . (times)

    a. What was the average <u>**intensity**</u> of those migraines?

       ⓪ ① ② ③ ④ ⑤ ⑥ ⑦ ⑧ ⑨ ⑩

    b. What was the average <u>**duration**</u> of those migraines?

       ⓪ ① ② ③ ④ ⑤ ⑥ ⑦ ⑧ ⑨ ⑩

    c. What was the <u>**intensity of your most painful**</u> migraine?

       ⓪ ① ② ③ ④ ⑤ ⑥ ⑦ ⑧ ⑨ ⑩

    d. What was the <u>**duration of your most painful**</u> migraine?

       Duration: . . . . (hours) . . . . (minutes)

    e. Did you use any pills to stop your pain?

       ○ Yes ○ No If your answer is "Yes," how many did you use? . . . .

    f. Did you make any visits to the emergency room because of your migraine?

       ○ Yes ○ No

3. How many times did you have a migraine on Wednesday? . . . . (times)

    a. What was the average <u>**intensity**</u> of those migraines?

       ⓪ ① ② ③ ④ ⑤ ⑥ ⑦ ⑧ ⑨ ⑩

    b. What was the average <u>**duration**</u> of those migraines?

       ⓪ ① ② ③ ④ ⑤ ⑥ ⑦ ⑧ ⑨ ⑩

    c. What was the <u>**intensity of your most painful**</u> migraine?

       ⓪ ① ② ③ ④ ⑤ ⑥ ⑦ ⑧ ⑨ ⑩

    d. What was the <u>**duration of your most painful**</u> migraine?

       Duration: . . . . (hours) . . . . (minutes)

    e. Did you use any pills to stop your pain?

       ○ Yes ○ No If your answer is "Yes," how many did you use? . . . .

    f. Did you make any visits to the emergency room because of your migraine?

       ○ Yes ○ No

4. How many times did you have a migraine on Thursday? . . . . (times)

    a. What was the average <u>**intensity**</u> of those migraines?

       ⓪ ① ② ③ ④ ⑤ ⑥ ⑦ ⑧ ⑨ ⑩

    b. What was the average <u>**duration**</u> of those migraines?

       ⓪ ① ② ③ ④ ⑤ ⑥ ⑦ ⑧ ⑨ ⑩

    c. What was the <u>**intensity of your most painful**</u> migraine?

       ⓪ ① ② ③ ④ ⑤ ⑥ ⑦ ⑧ ⑨ ⑩

    d. What was the **duration of your most painful** migraine?

       Duration: . . . . (hours) . . . . (minutes)

    e. Did you use any pills to stop your pain?

       ○ Yes ○ No If your answer is "Yes," how many did you use? . . . .

    f. Did you make any visits to the emergency room because of your migraine?

       ○ Yes ○ No

5. How many times did you have a migraine on Friday? . . . . (times)

   a. What was the average **intensity** of those migraines?

   ⓪ ① ② ③ ④ ⑤ ⑥ ⑦ ⑧ ⑨ ⑩

   b. What was the average **duration** of those migraines?

   ⓪ ① ② ③ ④ ⑤ ⑥ ⑦ ⑧ ⑨ ⑩

   c. What was the **intensity of your most painful** migraine?

   ⓪ ① ② ③ ④ ⑤ ⑥ ⑦ ⑧ ⑨ ⑩

   d. What was the **duration of your most painful** migraine?

   Duration: . . . . (hours) . . . . (minutes)

   e. Did you use any pills to stop your pain?

   ◯ Yes ◯ No If your answer is "Yes," how many did you use? . . . .

   f. Did you make any visits to the emergency room because of your migraine?

   ◯ Yes ◯ No

6. How many times did you have a migraine on Saturday? . . . . (times)

   a. What was the average **intensity** of those migraines?

   ⓪ ① ② ③ ④ ⑤ ⑥ ⑦ ⑧ ⑨ ⑩

   b. What was the average **duration** of those migraines?

   ⓪ ① ② ③ ④ ⑤ ⑥ ⑦ ⑧ ⑨ ⑩

   c. What was the **intensity of your most painful** migraine?

   ⓪ ① ② ③ ④ ⑤ ⑥ ⑦ ⑧ ⑨ ⑩

   d. What was the **duration of your most painful** migraine?

   Duration: . . . . (hours) . . . . (minutes)

   e. Did you use any pills to stop your pain?

   ◯ Yes ◯ No If your answer is "Yes," how many did you use? . . . .

   f. Did you make any visits to the emergency room because of your migraine?

   ◯ Yes ◯ No

7. How many times did you have a migraine on Sunday? . . . . (times)

   a. What was the average **intensity** of those migraines?

   ⓪ ① ② ③ ④ ⑤ ⑥ ⑦ ⑧ ⑨ ⑩

   b. What was the average **duration** of those migraines?

   ⓪ ① ② ③ ④ ⑤ ⑥ ⑦ ⑧ ⑨ ⑩

   c. What was the **intensity of your most painful** migraine?

   ⓪ ① ② ③ ④ ⑤ ⑥ ⑦ ⑧ ⑨ ⑩

   d. What was the **duration of your most painful** migraine?

   Duration: . . . . (hours) . . . . (minutes)

   e. Did you use any pills to stop your pain?

   ◯ Yes ◯ No If your answer is "Yes," how many did you use? . . . .

   f. Did you make any visits to the emergency room because of your migraine?

   ◯ Yes ◯ No

Emre Konuk, Hejan Epözdemir, Zeynep Zat, Sirin
Haciomeroglu Atceken, and Asena Yurtsever
SUMMARY SHEET BY MARILYN LUBER

Name: _____ Diagnosis: _____

☑ Check when task is completed, response has changed, or to indicate symptoms or diagnosis.

Note: This material is meant as a checklist for your response. Please keep in mind that it is only a reminder of different tasks that may or may not apply to your client.

EMDR TREATMENT FOR MIGRAINE PROTOCOL SCRIPT

Phase 1: Client History

Assessment

1. *Neurological Assessment*

   ☐ Tension
   ☐ Migraine
   ☐ Cluster
   ☐ Not appropriate

2. *Psychiatric Assessment*

   ☐ Another disorder/problem clinically first
   ☐ Pregnant in the first trimester
   ☐ Psychosis
   ☐ Recent unresolved traumatic events
   ☐ Severe personality disorders (e.g., borderline, antisocial)
   ☐ Unresolved loss
   ☐ Severe depression and/or suicidal risk
   ☐ Ongoing violence
   ☐ Alcohol or substance abuse/dependence
   ☐ Sleep disorders
   ☐ Eating disorders
   ☐ Mental retardation

3. *Psychological Assessment*

   ☐ Psychological Testing
   ☐ Headache Assessment Scale (HAS)
   ☐ HAS II
   ☐ Subjective Pain Level (SPL) Scale

☐ Migraine Disability Assessment Program (MIDAS)
☐ Symptom Assessment-45 Questionnaire (SA-45)
☐ The World Health Organization Quality of Life BREF (WHOQOL-BREF)

Intake Questions

Descriptive Information

Name: _____

Age: _____

Date of birth: _____

Family status: ☐ Single   ☐ Married   ☐ Divorced   ☐ Partnered

Education: _____

Live with: _____

Emergency contact: _____

☐ Employed   ☐ Not employed   ☐ Retired   ☐ In school

If employed, job description: _____

History of Migraine

Date of first migraine: _____

Events prior to first migraine: _____

Discuss development of migraines over time: _____

_____

Discuss intensity over time: _____

Worse or better over time: _____

Symptoms: _____

_____

Frequency: ☐ Daily   ☐ Every few days   ☐ Weekly   ☐ Monthly

Severity of SUP: ____/10 _____

Range over time: _____

Length of migraines: _____

Who made the diagnosis and when: _____

_____

Describe experience of migraine: ☐ Pounding   ☐ Heaviness   ☐ Pressure   ☐ One side

☐ Two sides _____

Effect on social life: _____

Effect on family life: _____

Effect on work life: _____

Secondary gain: _____

Traumatic or stressful events: _____

Traumatic memories relevant to patient migraine: _____

Triggers: _____

Medical treatment: _____

A. Treatment Planning

1. CASE FORMULATION INCLUDES THE FOLLOWING:

a. ☐ Results of assessment (history, case planning, treatment plan)
b. ☐ R/O/postpone EMDR with clients with the following issues:

   o Psychosis
   o Recent unresolved traumatic events
   o Severe personality disorders (e.g., borderline, antisocial)
   o Unresolved loss
   o Severe depression and/or suicidal risk
   o Ongoing violence
   o Alcohol or substance abuse/dependence
   o Sleep disorders
   o Eating disorders
   o Mental retardation

c. ☐ Team members' concerns _____
d. ☐ Traumatic memories relevant to patient migraine concerning the following:

   o Early traumas clinically relevant to migraines such as unresolved abuse or violence
   o Migraine history or relevant traumatic memories in other family members

2. THREE-PRONGED PROTOCOL

a. ☐ *Past Memories*: (hierarchy for EMDR past trauma processing: worst, first, most recent)

   o Traumatic/stressful events connected with migraines or close to the first migraine
   o Specific migraines that were traumatic
   o Start: worst, first, most recent
   o Use the Standard EMDR Protocol

b. ☐ *Present Triggers*: (hierarchy for stimuli that trigger migraines)

   o List triggers initiating or increasing migraine
   o Start: most frequent trigger
   o Find most disturbing event
   o Use the Standard EMDR Protocol

c. ☐ *Future Template:*

   o Use the future template with each trigger that stimulates migraine

Phase 2: Preparation

1. General rules
      Inform the patient about EMDR
      Ethical issues
      Informing the patient about the program
      Weekly sessions
2. Introduce HAS and SPL assessment
3. Introduce EMDR
4. Teach resources
      Trigger-Point Therapy Technique

Phase 3: Assessment

    A. Past
        1. Traumatic events close to the first remembered attack
        2. Trauma of the migraine itself
            a. Worst migraine
            b. First migraine
            c. Most recent migraine
    B. Present triggers
    C. Future template

Phases 4 Through 7: Desensitization Through Closure

Follow the Standard EMDR Protocol, focusing on the migraine issues, present triggers, and future concerns.

Phase 8: Reevaluation

Client's life since the last session
Reevaluate the last target

EMDR TREATMENT FOR MIGRAINE PROTOCOL SCRIPT

Phase 1: Client History

Descriptive Information

Full name: _____

Age: _____ DOB: _____

Family status: ☐ Never married   ☐ Married   ☐ Divorced   ☐ Partnered

Highest education level: _____

With whom you live: _____

Emergency contact: _____

Employed: ☐ Yes ☐ No   Student: ☐ Yes ☐ No

If Yes, job description: _____

History of Migraine

Migraine first began: _____

Circumstances prior to first migraine: _____

Development of migraine over time: _____

_____

Same intensity?   ☐ Yes ☐ No

Symptoms during migraine: _____

Frequency: ☐ Daily   ☐ Every few days   ☐ Weekly   ☐ Monthly

SUDs: ___/10   ☐ Same level of severity   ☐ Severity changes

Length of migraine after onset: _____

Name of healthcare practitioner making diagnosis: _____

Date of diagnosis: _____

Diagnosis: _____

Description of migraine: ☐ Pounding   ☐ Heaviness   ☐ Pressure   ☐ One side   ☐ Two sides
☐ Other: _____

Effect of migraine on social life: _____

Effect of migraine on family life: _____

Effect of migraine on work life: _____

Secondary gain: _____

Traumatic/Stressful Events

Traumatic/Stressful events close to first migraine: _____

_____

Traumatic/Stressful event triggers of migraines: _____

_____

Traumatic/Stressful event connected to migraines: _____

_____

Traumatic/Stressful experiences in, around, and/or during first migraine: _____

_____

Traumatic/Stressful experiences in, around, and/or during worst migraine: _____

_____

Traumatic/Stressful experiences in, around, and/or during most recent migraine: _____

_____

Traumatic Memories Relevant to Patient Migraine

Other traumatic/stressful events relevant to migraine: _____

_____

Other traumatic/stressful events connected to any type of abuse/violence to yourself and/or witnessed and/or recounted to you: _____ _

_____

Other traumatic/stressful events concerning family or friends relevant to migraine: _____

_____

Triggers

Migraine triggers:

Foods precipitating migraine: _____

Beverages precipitating migraine: _____

Sleepless nights: ☐ Yes ☐ No

Not enough sleep: ☐ Yes ☐ No

Too much sleep: ☐ Yes ☐ No

Hormonal factors connected with migraines: ☐ Yes ☐ No

Seasons/Changes in weather: ☐ Yes ☐ No

Changes in heat, cold, and/or humidity: ☐ Yes ☐ No

Environmental factors (noise, traffic, etc.):   ☐ Yes ☐ No

When certain people in life around: ☐ Yes ☐ No

Other events/situations/stimulations triggering migraines: _____

_____

_____

_____

Medical Treatment

Prescription drugs prescribed for migraines: ☐ Painkillers   ☐ Antidepressants

☐ Other: _____

Phase 2: Preparation

Inform Patient About EMDR

"When a disturbing event occurs, it can get locked in the brain with the original picture, sounds, thoughts, feelings, and body sensations. This material can combine factual material with fantasy and with images that stand for the actual event or feelings about it. EMDR seems to stimulate the information and allows the brain to process the experience. That may be what is happening in REM or dream sleep—eye movements (tones, tactile) may help to process the unconscious material. It is your own brain that will be doing the healing and you are the one in control."

Ethical Issues and Informing the Patient About the Program

Weekly Sessions

"It is important that you use your medication and see your doctor as frequently as is requested. Please fill out the forms as we have agreed, so that we can keep track of your migraines. In this program, we will see each other for _____ (state the length of treatment). I will be scheduling weekly sessions with you as often as possible. They will last 50 minutes. Will you be able to follow through with this plan?"   ☐ Yes☐ No

"Some of the traumas and problems that we have talked about together such as ____ (note appropriate traumas and problems) will not be dealt with during your migraine treatment because they do not seem to be related to your migraines. If, however, we find that they are, we can always address them. Also, when your migraine treatment is complete, we can always come back to them if you are still concerned about any of them."

Introduce HAS and SPL Assessment: *"I want to tell you about some of the things I am going to ask you to do that will be helpful to both you and me during your migraine treatment. First, I will be asking you to fill out the session and weekly forms of the Migraine Assessment Scale, or HAS, which measures the frequency, severity, and duration of your attacks; your medication usage; and any emergency visits you might have in between sessions. Would you be willing to do this?"*   ☐ Yes ☐ No

"Also, before we begin our EMDR sessions, I will ask you to tell me your Subjective Pain Level (SPL), which assesses the level of pain you have on a scale of 0 to 10, where 10 is the most severe pain and 0 is no pain or neutral. Would you agree to that?"   ☐ Yes ☐ No

Phase 3: Assessment

A. Past Trauma Memories

1. TRAUMATIC/STRESSFUL EVENTS CLOSE TO THE FIRST REMEMBERED ATTACK

List of Traumatic Events Close to the First Remembered Attack

Target: _____

Picture/Image: _____

Negative cognition (NC): _____

Positive cognition (PC): _____

Validity of cognition (VOC): _____/7

Emotions: _____

Subjective units of disturbance (SUDs): ____/10

Location of Body Sensation: _____

2. TRAUMA OF THE MIGRAINE ATTACK ITSELF

a. Worst Migraine Attack

Target: _____

Picture/Image: _____ _____

Negative cognition (NC): _____

Positive cognition (PC): _____

Validity of cognition (VOC): _____/7

Emotions: _____

Subjective units of disturbance (SUDs): ____/10

Location of body sensation: _____

b. First Migraine

Target: _____

Picture/Image: _____

Negative cognition (NC): _____

Positive cognition (PC): _____

Validity of cognition (VOC): _____/7

Emotions: _____

Subjective units of disturbance (SUDs): ____/10

Location of body sensation: _____

c. Most Recent Migraine

Target: _____

Picture/Image: _____

Negative cognition (NC): _____

Positive cognition (PC): _____

Validity of cognition (VOC): _____/7

Emotions: _____

Subjective units of disturbance (SUDs): ____/10

Location of body sensation: _____

Phase 4: Desensitization

Introduce according to the Standard EMDR Protocol.

If SUD = 1 or more, continue processing.

If SUD continues to be 0 after two sets of BLS, go to the installation phase.

Phase 5: Installation

PC: □ Completed

New PC (if new one is better): _____

VOC: _____/7

Incident + PC + BLS

Continue Installation Phase with BLS until material becomes increasingly adaptive. If VOC = 6 or less, check and see if there is a limiting belief: *"Which thoughts or concerns prevent you from feeling those words as completely true?"* _____

Note: If the limiting belief is not resolved quickly, explore to see whether there are any limiting beliefs or unidentified/unprocessed memory/ies/networks that are causing this difficulty. _____

The session is then considered incomplete; therefore, return to the incomplete target and continue the installation process in the next session.

Phase completed   □ Yes □ No

Phase 6: Body Scan

"Close your eyes, and keep in mind the original memory and the words _____ (state the positive belief). Then bring your attention to different parts of your body, starting with your head and working downward. Any place you find any tension, tightness, or any unusual feeling, let me know."

Note: If the client reports any negative feeling, do a set of BLS until it disappears. If the client reports positive feelings, continue with BLS in order to strengthen them.

Phase 7: Closure

"Things may come up or they may not. If they do, great. Write them down and it can be a target for the next time. You can use a log to write down what triggers your headaches (e.g., alcohol, running, bath, food, lack of sleep, tiredness, loud music) and other images, thoughts or cognition, emotions and sensations; you can rate them on our 0-to-10 scale, where 0 is no disturbance or neutral and 10 is the worst disturbance. Please write down the positive experiences, too.

If you get any new memories, dreams, or situations that disturb you, just take a good snapshot. It isn't necessary to give a lot of detail. Just put down enough to remind you so we can target it the next time. The same thing goes for any positive dreams or situations. If negative feelings do come up, try not to make them significant. Remember, it's still just the old stuff. Just write it down for the next time. Then use the tape or the safe place exercise to let as much of the disturbance go as possible. Even if nothing comes up, make sure to use the tape every day and give me a call if you need to."

PRESENT TRIGGERS

List of Triggers

Trigger 1:

Worst incident: _____

_____

Trigger 2:

Worst incident: _____

_____

Trigger 3:

Worst incident: _____

_____

Trigger 4:

Worst incident: _____

Phase 8: Reevaluation

SUDS of incident/s processed: _____/10

New material: _____

_____

Reprocessed necessary targets:　　　　　　　　　　　　　　☐ Completed

FUTURE TEMPLATE

1. *Create a Future Template*

IMAGE AS FUTURE TEMPLATE: IMAGINING POSITIVE OUTCOMES

Incorporate a detailed template for dealing adaptively with an appropriate future situation [e.g., coping with a similar situation, or coping with present triggers/reminders (see earlier in text)].

Image of coping effectively with/or goal in future: _____

_____

PC: _____

New quality/attribute needed: _____

What you see as handling the situation: _____

Thinking, feeling, and experiencing in body: _____

Blocks/anxieties/fears in future scene: _____

1. _____
2. _____
3. _____

Do BLS. If they do not resolve, ask for other qualities needed to handle the situation.

Other new information, resources, or skills to comfortably visualize coping in the future:

1. _____
2. _____
3. _____

If blocks are not resolved, identify the unprocessed material and process with the Standard EMDR Protocol:

1. _____
2. _____
3. _____

Target/Memory/Image: _____

_____

NC: _____

PC: _____

VOC: _____/7

Emotions: _____

SUD: ___/10

Sensation: _____

If there are no blocks, move on.

Future image + PC + Sensations associated with future scenes + BLS

Do a body scan. (Close eyes + Image of future + PC + Attention to different parts of your body + Report tension, tightness/unusual sensation): _____

If there is a sensation, process until the sensation subsides and the VOC = 7/ecological resolution and move on to the movie as a future template.

VOC: _____/7

Image as a future template: □ **Completed**

MOVIE AS A FUTURE TEMPLATE OR IMAGINAL REHEASING

Close your eyes and play a movie adaptively coping with a difficult situation with a beginning, a middle, and an end.

Coping effectively with problem/in the location: _____

PC: _____

New quality/attribute: _____

Step into the future and imagine coping with *any* challenges. The movie has a beginning, a middle, and an end.

Thinking, feeling, and experiencing in body: _____

Blocks/Anxieties/Fears in future scene:

1. _____

2. _____

3. _____

If blocks, use BLS until disturbance dissipates or check for other qualities/resources needed.

Other qualities/resources needed:

1. _____

2. _____

3. _____

If blocks are not resolved, identify the unprocessed material and process with the Standard EMDR Protocol:

1. _____

2. _____

3. _____

Target/Memory/Image: _____

_____

NC: _____

PC: _____

VOC: _____/7

Emotions: _____

SUD: ___/10

Sensation: _____

If the client can play the movie from beginning to end with confidence and satisfaction, play the movie one more time from beginning to end + BLS: ☐ Completed

Movie as a future template: ☐ Completed

FIBROMYALGIA SYNDROME TREATMENT WITH EMDR THERAPY

Emre Konuk, Zeynep Zat, and Önder Kavakçı

INTRODUCTION

What Is Fibromyalgia?

Fibromyalgia, or the fibromyalgia syndrome (FMS), is a chronic pain disorder characterized by fatigue, muscle pain, tenderness, and sleep difficulties (Yunus, 2002). This syndrome is also referred to as "soft-tissue rheumatism." Fibromyalgia is a disorder that intrudes upon the daily lives of people and is a worldwide phenomenon (Häuser et al., 2009). Population-based research shows that "the estimated prevalence of chronic widespread pain (CWP) is 7% to 11%, and that fibromyalgia syndrome (FMS) . . . [affects] 1% to 5%" of the general population (Eich et al., 2008).

According to the diagnostic criteria set by the American College of Rheumatology (ACR), people with FMS have a medical problem characterized by pain in the following areas: the axial skeleton, the right and left sides of the bodies, the waist, and at least 11 to 18 tender points in the body (Häuser et al., 2009). Badash (2013) reports that fibromyalgia might also include other symptoms such as concentration and memory problems, thinking problems, labile mood, depression, anxiety, nervousness, fatigue, sleep problems, morning stiffness, painful menstrual cramps, urinary symptoms, irritable bowel syndrome, heartburn, headaches, jaw pain, numbness, tender trigger points, and tingling in the hands, arms, feet, and legs. Most of them report that they feel "blue" or "down." As a result of the ACR's focus on pain areas and not on psychological symptoms, FMS is not classified under any *Diagnostic and Statistical Manual of Mental Disorders* (*DSM*) criteria. Namely, it is not seen as a psychiatric problem. Because FMS has no relevant organic pathology, it is placed in the realm of medically unexplained physical symptoms (MUPS; Tynes & Spiegel, 2013).

Fibromyalgia differs by gender and age. According to Bennett and McGain (1995), women are in the high-risk group for developing fibromyalgia compared to men. Bartels et al. (2009) note that the ratio of men to women developing fibromyalgia is 1:9. Bennett and McGain (1995) reported that the prevalence of fibromyalgia in the general U.S. population is 3.4% for women and 0.5% for men. It is possible that genetic factors have a role to play in developing fibromyalgia. According to Badash (2013), people who have a family member with fibromyalgia could be at a higher risk for developing this disorder.

Antidepressants, painkillers, muscle relaxants, and physiotherapy are known as the common medical treatment. In general, besides medical treatment, the following interventions have been helpful in reducing pain in fibromyalgia patients: pain and sleep management; psychological support; exercise such as aerobics, water therapy, and yoga; acupuncture; breathing techniques; cognitive behavioral therapy; aromatherapy; and nutritional supplements. Badash (2013), however, states that there is no established cure for fibromyalgia and the treatment methods only help reduce the pain and other symptoms of this syndrome.

Life experiences such as important life events, divorces, accidents, adverse childhood traumatic events, and so on, may be the precipitants or part of the picture of the development of fibromyalgia (Imbierowicz & Egle, 2003; van Houdenhove & Egle, 2004). It is important to note that the concept that chronic pain in adulthood is etiologically related to adverse life events has a long history in the literature (Raphael, Chandler, & Ciccone, 2004). Grant (2001) states, "If chronic pain is somehow a product of trauma, then this would have implications for the understanding and treatment of pain."

Adverse childhood experiences (ACEs), including neglect, abuse, and other negative life experiences, are a significant social health problem. Many research studies show that there is a high incidence of ACEs in individuals with adult onset of a wide range of illnesses, diseases, and disorders, including cancer, heart disease, lung disease, liver disease (Felitti et al., 1998; Giedd & Rapoport, 2010; Kendall-Tackett, 2009; Middlebrooks & Audage, 2008), chronic pain (Gatchel, Peng, Peters, Fuchs, & Turk, 2007), chronic fatigue syndrome (Brooks, Cronholm, & Strawn, 2012; Maloney et al., 2006), and fibromyalgia (Brooks et al., 2012; Imbierowicz & Egle, 2003). Other researchers (Felitti et al., 1998; Imbierowicz & Egle, 2003) also indicate that individuals with five or more ACEs are more likely to develop FMS. As a result of these findings, there seems to be a significant link between ACEs and developing fibromyalgia in adulthood (Fay, 2015).

RESEARCH, EMDR, AND CHRONIC PAIN

Recent studies have provided early evidence for the use of EMDR therapy for chronic pain patients (Grant, 2000; Grant & Threlfo, 2002; Schneider, Hofmann, Rost, & Shapiro, 2008; Wilensky, 2006). EMDR therapy is being used for other pain conditions including fibromyalgia (Gerhardt, Eich, Seidler, & Tesarz, 2013) and phantom limb pain (Russell, 2008; Schneider et al., 2008; Tinker & Wilson, 2005; Wilensky, 2006).

Schneider et al. (2008) conducted a study of EMDR treatment with inpatient and outpatient clients with phantom limb pain, including extensive follow-up. The investigation demonstrated that after 3 to 15 EMDR sessions, there was "a significant decrease or elimination of phantom pain, reduction in depression and posttraumatic stress disorder (PTSD) symptoms to subclinical levels, and significant reduction or elimination of medications related to the phantom pain and nociceptive pain at long-term follow-up." The researchers also argued that the reprocessing of traumatic memories was the reason for the success of this treatment. Based on these trends, EMDR treatment holds great promise for working with patients with fibromyalgia as it provides physical and emotional relief by processing adverse life experiences and traumatic memories.

Likewise, Grant and Threlfo (2002) examined the effectiveness of the EMDR Chronic Pain Protocol with adults who suffer from chronic pain and found out that the patients' pain levels and negative affect decreased, while their ability to control their pain increased following treatment. In 2013, Gerhardt et al. concluded, "Early reports show that EMDR either significantly reduces the intensity of pain or even completely eliminates chronic pain in various pain conditions, including phantom limb pain, fibromyalgia and migraine." As a result of a critical review of papers focused on the feasibility and effectiveness of EMDR in the treatment of chronic pain, in 2012, Kavakçı, Semiz, Kaptanoğlu, and Özer conducted another study investigating the effectiveness of EMDR in the treatment of fibromyalgia. EMDR treatment was used with seven patients diagnosed with fibromyalgia, between 22 and 41 years. The clients were asked about the traumas they experienced from the beginning of their illness, and those traumas were processed with EMDR therapy. After the prescribed five to eight sessions of EMDR treatment, they found, "None of the patients met the FMS criteria but one patient and EMDR therapy was effective in the treatment of these patients with FMS" (Kavakçı et al., 2012). These are promising findings for further study of the use of EMDR therapy with FMS patients. After communicating with the lead researcher, the authors found out that some of the clients reported that their pain was back. As a result, the authors designed an EMDR Therapy Protocol for Fibromyalgia focusing on traumas related to fibromyalgia and pain and tailored to the needs of FMS patients.

Note: This protocol is based on clinical work with patients with FMS. More research is required to gain more understanding of the effectiveness of EMDR in the treatment of fibromyalgia specifically.

EMDR AND FIBROMYALGIA PROTOCOL NOTES

Phase 1: History Taking

Phase 1 includes three aspects:

1. Medical Assessment

Make sure that clients have had a medical assessment and the physician has given an FMS diagnosis. This is important to ensure that clients have only FMS pain and no other pain related to medically unexplained symptoms, such as temporomandibular joint disorders (TMJ) syndrome, both tension and migraine headaches, or any other physical problem.

2. Psychiatric Assessment

Reviews indicate that FMS is highly comorbid with depression, anxiety, posttraumatic stress disorder, and panic disorder (Buskila & Cohen, 2007). Therefore, it is advised to refer clients for a psychiatric consult to assess for the following concerns:

- Comorbid psychiatric problems where it is important to deal with another disorder or problem first
- Necessary medication and medication regulation
- Appropriate candidate at this time because:
  - The patient is pregnant and has a risk of miscarriage
  - Uncontrolled epileptic seizures may occur

3. Psychological Assessment

Apart from history taking, the EMDR therapist may wish to assess the client by using valid and reliable assessment tools related to FMS pain on a regular basis (e.g., weekly) and also psychological tools before and after treatment, as needed. This enables the clinician to follow the improvements of the client throughout the therapy process and for follow-up.

ASSESSMENT TOOLS

Adverse Childhood Experience (ACE) Questionnaire

The ACE Questionnaire assesses the adverse life experience of the client according to 10 different categories and gives a trauma score. Basically, it focuses on the relationship between childhood traumas and physical and mental diseases in adulthood. The ACE Study was conducted with over 17,000 Americans, in collaboration with the Centers for Disease Control and Prevention and Kaiser Permanente. The questionnaire asked questions relevant to participants who had experienced "recurrent physical and emotional abuse, sexual abuse, an alcohol or drug abuser in the house, an incarcerated parent/s or household member, chronically depressed, mentally ill, institutionalized, or suicidal family member, violent mother, one or no parents, physical and/or emotional neglect situations" before the age of 18. According to the ACE Study's findings, childhood traumas caused serious health problems, such as cancer, heart attack, stroke, diabetes, exhaustion, and so on (WHO Adverse Childhood Experiences International Questionnaire [ACE-IQ], n.d.-a).

Visual Analog Scale (VAS)

The VAS measures the intensity of pain in adult populations who suffer from rheumatic diseases. On the scale, there is a continuum showing "no pain" on the left side of the line and "pain as bad as it could possibly be" on the right side of the line. Participants/patients are asked to place a mark on the line indicative of their pain symptom(s) (Hawker, Mian, Kendzerska, & French, 2011).

Beck Depression Inventory (BDI)

The BDI measures the severity of depression in adolescents and adults. It is a self-report scale consisting of 21 questions with multiple choices. The BDI is one of the most widely used scales for measuring the severity of depression (Beck, Ward, Mendelson, Mock, & Erbaugh, 1961).

Trauma Symptom Checklist-40 (TSC-40)

TSC-40 measures the symptoms in adults related to childhood or adulthood traumatic experiences. It has 40 self-report questions and six subscales, which are anxiety, depression, dissociation, sexual abuse trauma index, sexual problems, and sleep disturbance. The participants rate questions from 0 (never) to 3 (often; Briere & Runtz, 1989).

Pittsburgh Sleep Quality Index (PSQI)

PSQI measures the person's sleep quality and disturbances during a 1-month period. PSQI is a self-rated scale and has questions addressing the following seven areas: sleep quality, sleep latency, sleep duration, habitual sleep efficiency, sleep disturbances, use of sleeping medication, and day-time dysfunction. PSQI is used in clinical and research settings (Buysse, Reynolds, Monk, Berman, & Kupfer, 1989).

The World Health Organization Quality of Life (WHOQOL)

WHOQOL is an inventory that assesses the quality of life. It was developed by the WHOQOL Group, which was determined by the World Health Organization throughout 15 international centers. The goal was to translate the inventory into other languages and adapt it to different cultures. It basically assesses physical and psychological health, social relationship, and environment of an individual according to his or her culture (WHO Quality of Life-BREF [WHOQOL-BREF], n.d.-b).

Fibromyalgia Impact Questionnaire (FIQ)

The FIQ is a self-administered questionnaire that was designed for assessing the functionality of the person. In the FIQ, physical functioning, anxiety, stiffness, fatigue, pain, morning tiredness, depression, and absence from work are assessed over the past week (Burckhardt, Clark, & Bennett, 1991).

Fibromyalgia Diagnostic Criteria

The American College of Rheumatology Fibromyalgia Diagnostic Criteria is an inventory that assesses the widespread pain index and symptom severity of the patient on at least 11 tender points of 19 areas. In 2010, the American College of Rheumatology endorsed a new set of criteria for diagnosing fibromyalgia. They published those criteria in the *Arthritis Care and Research* journal (Wolfe et al., 2010). According to those criteria, patients have fibromyalgia if they meet the following criteria:

- A widespread pain index (WPI) score of 7 or higher and a symptom severity scale (SS) score of 5 or higher. Or, you have a WPI score of 3 to 6 and an SS score of 9 or higher.
- Symptoms at a similar level for at least 3 months.
- No other disorder explains symptoms.

Phase 2: Preparation Phase

After Phase I, where the assessment and treatment planning occur, the preparation phase begins. These are the basic elements of the preparation phase.

General Information

Assess demographic information, family history, health, work, marital/relationship status, children, friends, social life, and so on. Check for family history of fibromyalgia.

Definition of Fibromyalgia Pain History

Assess the developmental history of the onset of fibromyalgia pain and the frequency, severity, and duration of pain.

Treatment Goals

As a result of chronic pain, clients cannot pursue their lives in the ways they would want. For example, often, because of the pain, they cannot socialize with their loved ones, work properly, have good times with their spouse and children, or even sleep soundly, despite having tried many different treatments. As a result of the impact of chronic pain over time, people who suffer from FMS feel helpless, inadequate, and hopeless. It is very helpful to ask them to think about what life would be like when the FMS ends by imagining the picture of their preferred future, as a way to motivate them to feel more hopeful. Among the most common responses are "I want to have no pain, to be able to sleep well, to be able to socialize more, to do housework, to carry bags without pain, and to comfortably hold my baby."

Ethical Issues

The therapist introduces the client to the general ethical rules about psychotherapy and EMDR. EMDR therapists specifically inform clients about confidentiality, time, and money and issues that are relevant for the present situation.

Informing the Patient About the Treatment Process and EMDR

It is helpful for clients to understand the process of their therapy and know about EMDR therapy, trauma/adverse life experiences, possible linkages between past traumas and present complaints, and the reason to work with traumas for FMS treatment. Therefore, it is important to inform the patients about the rationale of reprocessing the traumas throughout the therapy, give information about EMDR as in the Standard EMDR Protocol, and discuss the structure of the therapy process (i.e., usually weekly sessions are scheduled for 50/90 minutes, or more frequently per week if indicated and possible). Inform clients about measures of assessment as needed.

Resources

FMS patients are usually hypervigilant. They find it very difficult to relax even for a short time due to their pain. You can help them feel safe and relaxed by assisting them in creating resources such as the Safe Place exercises, the resource development exercise, and relaxation exercises.

Phase 4: Assessment

Treatment Plan/How to Choose the Target

Clients come to talk about complaints in therapy and they hope to resolve them. They do not use the language of trauma, EMDR, or Adaptive Information Processing (AIP). In this case, they want to "get rid of" fibromyalgia pain. Formulating problems and symptoms in terms of trauma, EMDR, and AIP is the job of the EMDR therapist. The AIP model needs to be used to show the link between trauma and fibromyalgia pain. The hypothesis is as follows: Fibromyalgia pain starts after trauma(s) and continues with adverse life experiences that often link to the memory networks connected to trauma.

As always, the guide is based on the Standard EMDR Protocol: past, present (triggers), and future (future template). Therefore, in order to design a treatment plan based on the AIP model, gathering the client's history is crucial for a well-formed case conceptualization and treatment plan. During the assessment, ask about when the experience occurred as well as rate it using the Subjective Units of Disturbance (SUD) scale. Assess the client's experiences concerning the following:

- First traumatic memory related to fibromyalgia pain
  - Earliest
  - Worst
  - Recent
- Other traumatic memories related or unrelated to fibromyalgia throughout the FMS
- Traumatic memories (after the first fibromyalgia pain) related or unrelated to fibromyalgia
- Traumatic memories before fibromyalgia pain
- Triggers
- Future template

Use this hierarchy to target the memories from the treatment plan.

Note: Please remember! Whenever the memory is reprocessed, go back and check the SUDs for each memory on the list. Note the changes and revise the treatment plan, as appropriate.

Phases 4 to 8: Desensitization Re-evaluation

Use the Standard EMDR Protocol for stages 4 through 8 to work with each memory. When you finish working with the past, continue to the present.

PRESENT TRIGGERS

After working with the main traumas connected to the FMS pain, work with the conditions that trigger FMS pain and traumas that seem to be unrelated to FMS. List triggers and/or incidents from the highest SUD score to the lowest SUD score. Then, start with the trigger with the highest SUD score and continue with the most frequently experienced trigger. After completing these triggers, work with what is left. For each trigger, find the most disturbing event/incident (which has the highest SUD level) to work with the Standard EMDR Protocol.

FUTURE TEMPLATE

Use the future template with each of the triggers that trigger the patient's FMS.

Throughout your treatment, if any traumatic experience comes up during reprocessing, note the new memory. After processing the trauma, check the strength of the patient's fibromyalgia pain; then decide where to put the new traumatic experience in the treatment plan. This means that during the course of therapy, the plan may be revised.

FIBROMYALGIA SYNDROME TREATMENT WITH EMDR THERAPY SCRIPT

Phase 1: History Taking

General Information

Say, *"What is your full name?"*

_____

Say, *"What is your age?"*

_____

Say, *"What is your date of birth?"*

_____

Say, *"What is your family status? Are you single, married, divorced, partnered?"*

_____

Say, *"What education have you had?"*

_____

Say, *"With whom do you live?"*

_____

Say, *"In the event of an emergency, who would I contact?"*

_____

Say, *"Are you currently employed and/or in school? If so, what is your job description?"*

_____

History of Fibromyalgia Syndrome

Say, *"When did you first begin to have the pain in your body?"*

_____

Say, *"How have your pain experiences developed over time? Is there any change in the intensity? Did it get worse? Did it get better?"*

_____

_____

Say, *"Currently, how often are you experiencing this type of pain? Does it occur daily, every few days, weekly, monthly?"*

_____

_____

Say, *"How does your pain affect your social life?"*

_____

_____

_____

_____

Say, *"How does your pain affect your family life?"*

_____

_____

_____

_____

Say, *"How does your pain affect your work life?"*

_____

_____

_____

_____

Say, *"What other problems do you have besides your pain?"*

_____

_____

_____

_____

Say, *"Are there any ways that your pain gives you an opportunity to* not *do something that you do not want to do?"*

_____

_____

Traumatic/Stressful

FIRST/EARLIEST MEMORY(IES)

Say, *"Were there any traumatic/stressful events that took place relatively close to the **first/earliest time** you had fibromyalgia pain in your body?"*

_____

_____

_____

_____

Note: There may be many traumatic memories that coincide with the time before the client's pain onset. Write them all down with the SUD and NC.

Say, *"On a scale of 0 to 10, where 0 is no disturbance or neutral and 10 is the highest disturbance you can imagine, how disturbing does it feel now?"*

0   1   2   3   4   5   6   7   8   9   10

(no disturbance)   (highest disturbance)

Say, *"In your opinion, are there any traumatic/stressful events or a process that may have **caused** your pain to begin?"*

_____

_____

_____

WORST TRAUMATIC/STRESSFUL EVENT(S)

Say, *"What is the **worst traumatic/stressful event(s)** or a process in, around, and/or during the times you have FMS pains?"*

_____

_____

_____

_____

Say, *"On a scale of 0 to 10, where 0 is no disturbance or neutral and 10 is the highest disturbance you can imagine, how disturbing does it feel now?"*

0   1   2   3   4   5   6   7   8   9   10

(no disturbance)   (highest disturbance)

RECENT TRAUMATIC/STRESSFUL EXPERIENCES

Say, *"Are there any other **more recent** traumatic/stressful experiences you recently encountered that trigger your pain?"*

_____

_____

Say, *"On a scale of 0 to 10, where 0 is no disturbance or neutral and 10 is the highest disturbance you can imagine, how disturbing does it feel now?"*

0   1   2   3   4   5   6   7   8   9   10

(no disturbance)   (highest disturbance)

OTHER TRAUMATIC MEMORIES RELATED OR UNRELATED TO THE FIBROMYALGIA THROUGHOUT THE FMS

Say, *"Are there any other significant traumatic/stressful events related to or not related to FMS pain that has occurred during the FMS?"*

_____

_____

Say, *"On a scale of 0 to 10, where 0 is no disturbance or neutral and 10 is the highest disturbance you can imagine, how disturbing does it feel now?"*

0	1	2	3	4	5	6	7	8	9	10

(no disturbance)   (highest disturbance)

OTHER SIGNIFICANT TRAUMATIC/STRESSFUL EVENTS BEFORE THE ONSET OF FIBROMYALGIA PAIN

Say, *"Are there any other significant traumatic/stressful events from early childhood or early times that may be related to FMS pain?"*

_____

_____

Say, *"On a scale of 0 to 10, where 0 is no disturbance or neutral and 10 is the highest disturbance you can imagine, how disturbing does it feel now?"*

0	1	2	3	4	5	6	7	8	9	10

(no disturbance)   (highest disturbance)

Say, *"What is the negative cognition for _____ (state the memory)."*

_____

_____

Triggers

Say, *"Please tell me about the stress or difficulties that generally trigger your pain."*

_____

_____

_____

_____

If the client does not mention the triggers, you may check for the following points specifically:

Say, *"Have there been any hormonal factors* (e.g., menstrual cycles) *that trigger your pain?"*

_____

_____

Say, *"Do certain seasons or changes in the weather affect your pain level?"*

_____

_____

Say, *"Do changes in heat, cold, and/or humidity affect your pain?"*

_____

_____

Say, *"Does overexertion, illness, injury, or traveling affect your pain?"*

_____

_____

Say, *"Does noise, traffic, and so on, trigger your pain?"*

_____

_____

Say, *"Do certain people in your life affect your pain?"*

_____

_____

Say, *"Do any other events, situations, or stimulations trigger your pain?"*

_____

_____

Treatment Goals

Say, *"Please tell me what you would like to achieve and to change in your life on the completion of this therapy."*

_____

_____

Say, *"Please tell me how life would be different for you if you did not have pain."*

_____

_____

Phase 2: Preparation Phase

Introduction to EMDR Therapy

Inform the patient about the treatment process and EMDR.

Say, *"When a disturbing event occurs, it can get locked in the brain with the original picture, sounds, thoughts, feelings, and body sensations. This material can combine factual material with fantasy and with images that stand for the actual event or feelings about it. EMDR seems to stimulate the information and allows the brain to process the experience. That may be what is happening in REM or dream sleep—the eye movements (tones, tactile) may help to process the unconscious material. It is your own brain that will be doing the healing and you are the one in control."*

_____

_____

Say, *"It is important that you use your medication and see your doctor as frequently as he requires. In this therapy process, we will see each other for _____ (state the course of treatment if there is a restriction)."*

_____

_____

Say, *"We will start working with the traumas that seem to be related to your FMS. Some of the traumas and problems that we have talked about together such as ____ (note appropriate traumas and problems) will not be dealt with during your treatment because they do not seem to be related to your fibromyalgia syndrome. If, however, we find that they are, we can always address them. When your fibromyalgia syndrome treatment is complete, we can always come back to them if you are still concerned about any of them."*

_____

_____

Introduce the Measurement Scales

Say, *"I want to tell you about some of the things I am going to ask you to do that will be helpful to both you and me during your fibromyalgia syndrome treatment. First, I will be asking you to fill out the psychometric tests before and after the treatment. Here is the list of them: the Beck Depression Inventory (BDI), the Posttraumatic Diagnostic Scale (PDS), Pittsburgh Sleep Quality Index (PSQI), and the State-Trait Anger Scale (STAS). You will fill out only the Visual Analog Scale every week. You will fill out the ACE Questionnaire only before the treatment. Would you be willing to do this?"*

_____

_____

If yes, say, *"Please remember to fill the psychometric tests as we have agreed, so that we keep track of your fibromyalgia syndrome."*

_____

_____

Resources

It is important to support clients by assisting them in creating resources such as the Safe Place, resource development, relaxation, the Four Element Protocol, and lightstream exercises. Finish sessions using these relaxation techniques that have already been practiced with the patient.

Say, *"What would you need to not feel helplessness?"*

_____

_____

Say, *"Think of a time when you managed to get out of a very difficult situation. Please focus on how you managed to cope. Now focus on the sensations and feelings. Go with that."*

_____

_____

Phase 3: Assessment

Treatment Plan

Use this hierarchy to structure EMDR past trauma processing:

- First traumatic memory related to fibromyalgia pain
- Traumatic memories related or unrelated to fibromyalgia throughout the FMS
- Traumatic memories before fibromyalgia pain
- Triggers
- Future template

It is helpful for the EMDR therapist to use the fibromyalgia treatment plan. The Standard EMDR Protocol is used during the session for the chosen targets. If any new traumatic experience comes up, note it down. When processing is done, check the strength of its connection with the patient's fibromyalgia pain and then decide where to put the new experience in the hierarchy.

PAST TRAUMA MEMORIES

Traumatic/Stressful Events Related to the First Remembered FMS Memory

Find the earliest traumatic memory related to FMS; for example, "I failed my university exam, then I had my first experience of FMS."

> Say, *"Okay. We have gathered information. Now, we will need to target the memories according to our treatment plan (hierarchy). We generally tend to begin with* **the first experience**. *Is that okay for you?"*

_____

If the client says okay,

> Say, *"Okay. Now, we will do the protocol."*

_____

Incident

> Say, *"Focus on the* _____ *(state the issue/event)."*

_____

_____

Picture

> Say, *"What picture represents the most traumatic part of the entire incident* _____ *(state the issue)?"*

_____

_____

Negative Cognition (NC)

> Say, *"What words best go with the picture that express your negative belief about yourself now?"*

_____

_____

Positive Cognition (PC)

Say, *"When you bring up that picture or _____ (state the issue), what would you like to believe about yourself now?"*

_____

_____

Validity of Cognition (VOC)

Say, *"When you think of _____ (state the issue or picture), how true do those words _____ (clinician repeats the PC) feel to you now on a scale of 1 to 7, where 1 feels completely false and 7 feels completely true?"*

1	2	3	4	5	6	7

(completely false)   (completely true)

Sometimes, it is necessary to explain further.

Say, *"Remember, sometimes we know something with our head, but it feels differently in our gut. In this case, what is the gut-level feeling of the truth of _____ (clinician states the PC), from 1 (completely false) to 7 (completely true)?"*

1	2	3	4	5	6	7

(completely false)   (completely true)

Emotions

Say, *"When you bring up the picture _____ (state the issue) and those words _____ (clinician states the NC), what emotion do you feel now?"*

_____

_____

Subjective Units of Disturbance

Say, *"On a scale of 0 to 10, where 0 is no disturbance or neutral and 10 is the highest disturbance you can imagine, how disturbing does it feel now?"*

0	1	2	3	4	5	6	7	8	9	10

(no disturbance)   (highest disturbance)

Location of Body Sensation

Say, *"Where do you feel it (the disturbance) in your body?"*

_____

_____

Use Phases 4 through 7 for each incident. Work with past issues, checking to see if other targets have been processed or still need to be processed with the Standard EMDR Protocol. Continue to process past issues until they are no longer an issue.

Worst Traumatic/Stressful Events Related to FMS

Say, *"Earlier, we identified the worst relevant past traumatic event related to FMS. Now, we will work on it."*

Incident

Say, *"Focus on the _____ (state the issue/event)?"*

_____

_____

Picture

Say, *"What picture represents the most traumatic part of the entire incident _____ (state the issue)?"*

_____

_____

Negative Cognition

Say, *"What words best go with the picture that express your negative belief about yourself now?"*

_____

_____

Positive Cognition

Say, *"When you bring up that picture or _____ (state the issue), what would you like to believe about yourself now?"*

_____

_____

Validity of Cognition

Say, *"When you think of _____ (state the issue or picture), how true do those words _____ (clinician repeats the PC) feel to you now on a scale of 1 to 7, where 1 feels completely false and 7 feels completely true?"*

1	2	3	4	5	6	7

(completely false)   (completely true)

Sometimes, it is necessary to explain further.

Say, *"Remember, sometimes we know something with our head, but it feels differently in our gut. In this case, what is the gut-level feeling of the truth of _____ (clinician states the PC), from 1 (completely false) to 7 (completely true)?"*

1	2	3	4	5	6	7

(completely false)   (completely true)

Emotions

Say, *"When you bring up the picture _____ (state the issue) and those words _____ (clinician states the NC), what emotion do you feel now?"*

_____

_____

Subjective Units of Disturbance

Say, *"On a scale of 0 to 10, where 0 is no disturbance or neutral and 10 is the highest disturbance you can imagine, how disturbing does it feel now?"*

0	1	2	3	4	5	6	7	8	9	10

(no disturbance)   (highest disturbance)

Location of Body Sensation

Say, *"Where do you feel it* (the disturbance) *in your body?"*

_____

_____

Use Phases 4 through 7 for each incident. Work with past issues, checking to see if other targets have been processed or still need to be processed with the Standard EMDR Protocol. Continue to process past issues until they are no longer an issue.

Most Recent Traumatic/Stressful Events Related to the FMS

Say, *"We generally tend to work with the **most recent experience** related to FMS. Is that okay for you?"*

_____

Incident

Say, *"Focus on the* _____ (state the issue/event).*"*

_____

_____

Picture

Say, *"What picture represents the most traumatic part of the entire incident* _____ (state the issue)?*"*

_____

_____

Negative Cognition

Say, *"What words best go with the picture that express your negative belief about yourself now?"*

_____

_____

Positive Cognition

Say, *"When you bring up that picture or* _____ (state the issue), *what would you like to believe about yourself now?"*

_____

_____

Validity of Cognition

Say, *"When you think of* _____ (state the issue or picture), *how true do those words* _____ (clinician repeats the PC) *feel to you now on a scale of 1 to 7, where 1 feels completely false and 7 feels completely true?"*

1	2	3	4	5	6	7

(completely false)   (completely true)

Sometimes, it is necessary to explain further.

Say, *"Remember, sometimes we know something with our head, but it feels differently in our gut. In this case, what is the gut-level feeling of the truth of* _____ (clinician states the PC), *from 1* (completely false) *to 7* (completely true)*?"*

1	2	3	4	5	6	7

(completely false)   (completely true)

Emotions

Say, *"When you bring up the picture* _____ (state the issue) *and those words* _____ (clinician states the NC), *what emotion do you feel now?"*

_____

_____

Subjective Units of Disturbance

Say, *"On a scale of 0 to 10, where 0 is no disturbance or neutral and 10 is the highest disturbance you can imagine, how disturbing does it feel now?"*

0	1	2	3	4	5	6	7	8	9	10

(no disturbance)   (highest disturbance)

Location of Body Sensation

Say, *"Where do you feel it* (the disturbance) *in your body?"*

_____

_____

Use Phases 4 through 7 for each incident. Work with the past issues, checking to see if the other targets have been processed or still need to be processed with the Standard EMDR Protocol. Continue to process the past issues until they are no longer an issue.

Other Traumatic Memories Throughout the FMS Related/Unrelated to FMS Pain

Say, *"Earlier, we talked about the traumas that seem related or unrelated to your FMS and occurred during the FMS. How much does each one disturb you from 0 to 10, where 0 is no disturbance or neutral and 10 is the highest disturbance you can imagine?"*

_____

_____

Say, *"We will work with the highest score. Therefore, we will work with* _____ (state the target memory). *Is that okay with you?"*

_____

_____

Incident

Say, *"Focus on the _____ (state the issue/event)."*

_____

_____

Picture

Say, *"What picture represents the most traumatic part of the entire incident _____ (state the issue)?"*

_____

_____

Negative Cognition

Say, *"What words best go with the picture that express your negative belief about yourself now?"*

_____

_____

Positive Cognition

Say, *"When you bring up that picture or _____ (state the issue), what would you like to believe about yourself now?"*

_____

_____

Validity of Cognition

Say, *"When you think of _____ (state the issue or picture), how true do those words _____ (clinician repeats the PC) feel to you now on a scale of 1 to 7, where 1 feels completely false and 7 feels completely true?"*

1	2	3	4	5	6	7

(completely false)   (completely true)

Sometimes, it is necessary to explain further.

Say, *"Remember, sometimes we know something with our head, but it feels differently in our gut. In this case, what is the gut-level feeling of the truth of _____ (clinician states the PC), from 1 (completely false) to 7 (completely true)?"*

1	2	3	4	5	6	7

(completely false)   (completely true)

Emotions

Say, *"When you bring up the picture _____ (state the issue) and those words _____ (clinician states the NC), what emotion do you feel now?"*

_____

_____

Subjective Units of Disturbance

Say, *"On a scale of 0 to 10, where 0 is no disturbance or neutral and 10 is the highest disturbance you can imagine, how disturbing does it feel now?"*

0	1	2	3	4	5	6	7	8	9	10

(no disturbance)   (highest disturbance)

Location of Body Sensation

Say, *"Where do you feel it* (the disturbance) *in your body?"*

_____

_____

   Use Phases 4 through 7 for each incident. Work with past issues, checking to see if other targets have been processed or still need to be processed with the Standard EMDR Protocol. Continue to process past issues until they are no longer an issue.

TRAUMATIC MEMORIES BEFORE FIBROMYALGIA

Check with the ACE Scale. It gives a very clear picture of the traumatic events that took place when the child is between 0 and 18 years old; that is, when he or she is in the family.

Say, *"Earlier, we talked about the traumas that happened before the beginning of FMS. When talking about the history of your traumas, you mentioned traumatic events that took place before the onset of your FMS. We will work with _____* (state the target memory). *Is that okay with you?"*

_____

_____

Incident

Say, *"Focus on the _____* (state the issue/event).*"*

_____

_____

Picture

Say, *"What picture represents the most traumatic part of the entire incident _____* (state the issue)*?"*

_____

_____

Negative Cognition

Say, *"What words best go with the picture that express your negative belief about yourself now?"*

_____

_____

Positive Cognition

Say, *"When you bring up that picture or* _____ (state the issue), *what would you like to believe about yourself now?"*

_____

_____

Validity of Cognition

Say, *"When you think of* _____ (state the issue or picture), *how true do those words* _____ (clinician repeats the PC) *feel to you now on a scale of 1 to 7, where 1 feels completely false and 7 feels completely true?"*

1	2	3	4	5	6	7

(completely false)   (completely true)

Sometimes, it is necessary to explain further.

Say, *"Remember, sometimes we know something with our head, but it feels differently in our gut. In this case, what is the gut-level feeling of the truth of* _____ (clinician states the PC), *from 1 (completely false) to 7 (completely true)?"*

1	2	3	4	5	6	7

(completely false)   (completely true)

Emotions

Say, *"When you bring up the picture* _____ (state the issue) *and those words* _____ (clinician states the NC), *what emotion do you feel now?"*

_____

_____

Subjective Units of Disturbance

Say, *"On a scale of 0 to 10, where 0 is no disturbance or neutral and 10 is the highest disturbance you can imagine, how disturbing does it feel now?"*

0	1	2	3	4	5	6	7	8	9	10

(no disturbance)   (highest disturbance)

Location of Body Sensation

Say, *"Where do you feel it* (the disturbance) *in your body?"*

_____

_____

Use Phases 4 through 7 for each incident. Work with past issues, checking to see if other targets have been processed or still need to be processed with the Standard EMDR Protocol. Continue to process past issues until they are no longer an issue.

Phase 4: Desensitization

Introduce Phase 4, or the desensitization phase, to the client.

In this phase, the EMDR therapist starts using bilateral stimulation (BLS) while clients focus on the targeted memory. Some of the clients may have hesitation about feeling pain in their body while working on the memory. It is important that clients remain calm. The clinician may remind clients that they can use the stop signal. Moreover, the clinician may give information about dual awareness to the client. It is also important to encourage the client to process body sensations. For this purpose, the EMDR therapist may ask clients to pay attention to their body sensations than continues BLS. It is also important to suggest clients take a deep breath after each set, to support coming back to a relaxed state after processing traumatic/disturbing material.

The work in Phase 4 follows the Standard EMDR Protocol.

To begin, say the following:

Say, *"Now, remember, it is your own brain that is doing the healing and you are the one in control. I will ask you to mentally focus on the target and to _____ (state BLS you are using). Just let whatever happens, happen, and we will talk at the end of the set. Just tell me what comes up, and don't discard anything as unimportant. Any new information that comes to mind is connected in some way. If you want to stop, just raise your hand."*

Then say, *"Bring up the picture and the words _____ (clinician repeats the NC) and notice where you feel it in your body. Now follow _____ (state the BLS)."*

_____

_____

This procedure is to be repeated until SUDs = 0. Then the PC is installed. Each traumatic event associated with the problem that is not reprocessed during the normal course of the first target needs to be processed using this protocol until the SUDs reach an ecological 1 or 0 and the PC is installed.

Phase 5: Installation

Say, *"Let's start with the _____ (state the targeted memory) memory."*

_____

_____

Say, *"I'd like you to bring up that image, those negative words _____ (repeat the NC), notice where you are feeling it in your body, and follow my fingers (or alternative BLS)."*

_____

_____

Say, *"Take a deep breath. Let it go. What do you notice now?"*

_____

_____

Say, *"That's fine, just notice and go with that."*

_____

_____

Process the memory until the SUD level drops to 0.

Say, *"What body sensations go with that?"*

_____

_____

Say, *"Just notice. Go with that."*

_____

_____

Say, *"Take a deep breath. Let it go. What do you notice now?"*

_____

_____

Say, *"That's fine, just go with that."*

_____

_____

Work with the triggers related to the traumas worked on in the "Past Traumas" section earlier in the text that are connected to fibromyalgia and fibromyalgia pain. Also, include any other triggers that increase or start the pain.

PRESENT TRIGGERS

List of Triggers

List by the frequency of triggers, starting with the most frequently experienced trigger. For each trigger find the worst incident that caused the pain and then target that.

   1. Trigger: _____

      Worst incident: _____

      _____

   2. Trigger: _____

      Worst incident: _____

      _____

   3. Trigger: _____

      Worst incident: _____

      _____

   4. Trigger: _____

      Worst incident: _____

      _____

Start with the trigger that is experienced most frequently and then work through the list.

Incident

Say, *"Tell me the worst incident you have experienced with* (state the trigger).*"*

_____

_____

_____

Picture

Say, *"What picture represents the most traumatic part of the entire incident _____* (state the incident)?*"*

_____

_____

Negative Cognition

Say, *"What words best go with the picture that express your negative belief about yourself now?"*

_____

_____

Positive Cognition

Say, *"When you bring up that picture or _____* (state the trigger), *what would you like to believe about yourself now?"*

_____

_____

Validity of Cognition

Say, *"When you think of the _____* (state the trigger or picture), *how true do those words _____* (clinician repeats the PC) *feel to you now on a scale of 1 to 7, where 1 feels completely false and 7 feels completely true?"*

1	2	3	4	5	6	7

(completely false)   (completely true)

Sometimes, it is necessary to explain further.

Say, *"Remember, sometimes we know something with our head, but it feels differently in our gut. In this case, what is the gut-level feeling of the truth of _____* (clinician states the PC), *from 1* (completely false) *to 7* (completely true) *?"*

1	2	3	4	5	6	7

(completely false)   (completely true)

Emotions

Say, *"When you bring up the picture _____* (state the trigger) *and those words _____* (clinician states the NC), *what emotion do you feel now?"*

_____

_____

Subjective Units of Disturbance

Say, *"On a scale of 0 to 10, where 0 is no disturbance or neutral and 10 is the highest disturbance you can imagine, how disturbing does it feel now?"*

0	1	2	3	4	5	6	7	8	9	10

(no disturbance)   (highest disturbance)

Location of Body Sensation

Say, *"Where do you feel it* (the disturbance) *in your body?"*

_____

_____

    Continue with Phases 4 through 7 for each trigger. Process all of the relevant triggers, checking after the completion of each one to see if other targets need to be processed. If so, continue the processing until all are completed and then move on to the next step.

Phase 5: Installation

Say, *"When you bring up that original incident, does your original positive cognition _____* (repeat PC) *still fit or is there now a better statement?"* (Is the client now able to see further down the tracks?)

_____

_____

Say, *"Think about the original incident and those words _____* (repeat the selected PC). *From 1, completely false, to 7, completely true, how true do they feel now?"*

_____

_____

Say, *"Think about the original incident and those words _____* (repeat the selected PC) *and follow my fingers."*

Say, *"What do you get now?"*

_____

_____

Say, *"That's fine, just notice and go with that."*

_____

_____

Do sets of BLS (same speed and approximate duration as in desensitization) as long as the client reports new positive associations, sensations, or emotions and install the PC until the VOC = 7.

Check VOC after each set of BLS until the PC is fully installed (VOC=7).

FUTURE TEMPLATE

Use the future template for each trigger. A future template is the future projection of a desired emotional and behavioral response.

Image as Future Template: Imagining Positive Outcomes (Shapiro, 2009)

Imagining positive outcomes seems to assist the learning process. In this way, clients learn to enhance optimal behaviors, to connect them with a PC, and to support generalization. The assimilation of this new behavior and thought is supported by the use of BLS into a positive way to act in the future.

Say, *"I would like you to imagine yourself coping effectively with* _____ (state the goal) *in the future. With the positive belief* _____ (state the positive belief) *and your new sense of* _____ (state the quality, i.e., strength, clarity, confidence, calm), *imagine stepping into this scene.*

Notice what you see and how you are handling the situation.

Notice what you are thinking, feeling, and experiencing in your body."

_____

_____

Again, here is the opportunity to catch any disturbance that may have been missed.

Say, *"Are there any blocks, anxieties, or fears that arise as you think about this future scene?"*

_____

_____

If yes, say the following:

Say, *"Then focus on these blocks and follow my fingers* (or any other BLS)."

Say, *"What do you get now?"*

_____

_____

If the blocks do not resolve quickly, evaluate if the client needs any new information, resources, or skills to be able to comfortably visualize the future coping scene. Introduce needed information or skills.

Say, *"What would you need to feel confident in handling the situation?"* Or say, *"What is missing from your handling of this situation?"*

_____

_____

If the blocks still do not resolve and the client is unable to visualize the future scene with confidence and clarity, use direct questions, the affect scan, or the floatback technique to identify old targets related to blocks, anxieties, or fears. Remember, the point of the Three-Pronged Protocol is not only to reinforce positive feelings and behavior in the future, but also to catch any unresolved material that may be getting in the way of an adaptive resolution of the issue(s). Use the Standard EMDR Protocol to address these targets before proceeding with the template.

If there are no apparent blocks and the client is able to visualize the future scene with confidence and clarity, say the following:

"Please focus on the image, the positive belief, and the sensations associated with this future scene and follow my fingers (or any other BLS).*"*

_____

_____

Process and reinforce the positive associations with BLS. Do several sets until the future template is sufficiently strengthened.

Say, *"Go with that."*

_____

_____

Then say, *"Close your eyes and keep in mind the image of the future and the positive cognition. Then bring your attention to the different parts of your body, starting with your head and working downward. Any place you find any tension, tightness, or unusual sensation, tell me."*

_____

_____

If any sensation is reported, do BLS. Say, *"Go with that."*

If it is a positive or comfortable sensation, do BLS to strengthen the positive feelings.

Say, *"Go with that."*

If a sensation of discomfort is reported, reprocess until the discomfort subsides.

Say, *"Go with that."*

When the discomfort subsides, check the VOC.

Say, *"When you think of the incident* (or picture), *how true do those words* _____ (clinician repeats the PC) *feel to you now on a scale of 1 to 7, where 1 feels completely false and 7 feels completely true?"*

1	2	3	4	5	6	7

(completely false)   (completely true)

Continue to use BLS until VOC = 7 or there is an ecological resolution. When the image as future template is clear and the PC is true, move on to the movie as a future template.

Movie as a Future Template or Imaginal Rehearsing

During this next level of future template, clients are asked to move from imagining this one scene or snapshot to imagining a movie about coping in the future, with a beginning, a middle, and an end. Encourage clients to imagine themselves coping effectively in the face of specific challenges, triggers, or snafus. Therapists can make some suggestions of things in order to help inoculate them with future problems. It is helpful to use this type of future template after clients have received needed education concerning social skills and customs, assertiveness, and any other newly learned skills.

Say, *"This time, I'd like you to close your eyes and play a movie, imagining yourself coping effectively with* _____ (state where the client will be) *in the future. With the new positive belief* (state the positive belief) *and your new sense of* _____ (strength, clarity, confidence, calm), *imagine stepping into the future. Imagine yourself coping with* any *challenges that come your way. Make sure that this movie has a beginning, a middle, and an end. Notice what you are seeing, thinking, feeling, and experiencing in your body. Let me know if you hit any blocks. If you do, just open your eyes and let me know. If you don't hit any blocks, let me know when you have viewed the whole movie."*

_____

_____

If the client hits blocks, address as mentioned earlier with BLS until the disturbance dissipates.

Say, *"Go with that."*

If the material does not shift, use interweaves, new skills, information, resources, direct questions, and any other ways to help your clients access information that will allow them to move on. If these options are not successful, usually it means that there is earlier material still unprocessed; the floatback and affect scan are helpful in these cases to access the material that keeps clients stuck.

If clients are able to play the movie from start to finish with a sense of confidence and satisfaction, ask them to play the movie one more time from beginning to end and introduce BLS.

Say, *"Okay, play the movie one more time from beginning to end. Go with that."*

Use BLS.

In a sense, you are installing this movie as a future template.

After clients have fully processed their issue(s), they might want to work on other positive templates for the future in other areas of their lives using these future templates.

Phase 6: Body Scan

This phase is particularly important for clients with FMS. Make sure that body sensations are processed sufficiently.

Say, *"Close your eyes and keep in mind the original memory and the _____ (repeat the PC). Then bring your attention to different parts of your body, starting with your head and working downward. Any place you find tension, tightness, or unusual sensation, tell me."*

_____

_____

Say, *"What do you get now?"*

_____

_____

Say, *"That's fine; just notice and go with that."*

_____

_____

If the client cannot deal with the negative body sensations, ask the following types of questions:

Say, *"What is the shape of pain? What color is it? Where is it exactly? What is it made from? How does it smell? Is it intensive or light? and so on."*

_____

_____

Say, *"That's fine; just notice and go with that."*

Say, *"What do you get now?"*

_____

_____

Say, *"Okay, that is fine. Now, imagine that you have a remote control in your hand. What would you like to do with it to the pain* (describe the pain with its qualifications stated by the client)*?"*

_____

_____

Say, *"What do you get now?"*

_____

_____

Say, *"That's fine; just notice and go with that."*

Reprocess any negative sensation or strengthen the positive sensation with standard sets of BLS. Reprocessing of the chosen target is not considered complete until the body scan is clear of all negatively associated sensations. Positive sensations should be reinforced with standard sets of BLS.

Phase 7: Closure

Ask the client the SUD level, the VOC level, and body sensations. Be sure that SUD = 0, VOC = 7, and the body scan is clear.

Say, *"You have done very good work today. How are you feeling?"*

_____

_____

Say, *"As you review your experience in our session today, what positive statement can you make to express what you have learned or gained?"*

_____

_____

If SUD is greater than 0, VOC is less than 7, and there is no clear body scan, do not take SUD; check PC, take VOC, or do body scan, but then use the instructions for unfinished targets.

Say, *"Unfortunately, as the time is up, we have to stop now."*

If the client needs to do any stabilization, you may use one or more of following strategies:

A. Calm/Safe Place
B. Relaxation exercise

Say, *"You have done some good work today. How are you feeling?"*

_____

_____

Say, *"As you consider your experience today, what positive statement can you make to express what you have learned or gained?"*

_____

_____

Use these instructions at the end of each session whether it is a finished or an unfinished target.

Say, *"Processing may continue after our session. You may or may not notice new insights, thoughts, memories, physical sensations, or dreams. Please make a note of whatever you notice. We will talk about that at our next session. Remember to use one of the self-control techniques (Safe Place, Four Elements) as needed."*

Phase 8: Reevaluation

On review, it is important to make sure that the targeted memory/ies is/are properly processed.

Say, *"Is there any pain in your body?"*

If there is pain, check for triggers:

Say, *"Have you had any event or incident that triggered and initiated your pain since our last session?"*

_____

_____

If triggers are identified, the therapist works with them.

Say, *"Are there any of the symptoms in the following list?"*

Anxiety	☐ Yes ☐ No
Concentration and memory problems	☐ Yes ☐ No
Depression	☐ Yes ☐ No
Fatigue	☐ Yes ☐ No
Headaches	☐ Yes ☐ No
Irritable bowel syndrome	☐ Yes ☐ No
Morning stiffness	☐ Yes ☐ No
Painful menstrual cramps	☐ Yes ☐ No
Sleep problems, numbness	☐ Yes ☐ No
Tingling in hands, arms, feet, and legs	☐ Yes ☐ No
Tender points	☐ Yes ☐ No
Urinary symptoms	☐ Yes ☐ No

_____

_____

Say, *"Do you think you achieved the treatment goal of this therapy?"*

_____

_____

Say, *"What are the differences in your social life between the times you had before therapy and now?"*

_____

_____

Say, *"What have you learned about yourself by completing this process?"*

_____

_____

Assess the client using the following assessment tools post the EMDR intervention:

- ACE Questionnaire: _____
- Visual Analog Scale (VAS): _____
- Beck Depression Inventory (BDI): _____
- Posttraumatic Diagnostic Scale (PDS): _____
- Pittsburgh Sleep Quality Index (PSQI): _____
- State-Trait Anger Scale (STAS): _____

SUMMARY

FMS is a chronic pain disorder (e.g., fatigue, muscle pain, tenderness, and sleep difficulties) that affects 1% to 5% of the general population. Fibromyalgia might also include other symptoms such as concentration and memory problems, labile mood, depression, anxiety, sleep problems, painful menstrual cramps, and numbness. Because FMS has no relevant organic pathology, it is placed in the realm of medically unexplained physical symptoms. Recent studies are providing early evidence for the use of EMDR therapy for chronic pain patients. Also, EMDR therapy is being used for other pain conditions, including fibromyalgia. Therefore, the authors created the EMDR Fibromyalgia Syndrome Protocol that includes the Three-Pronged Protocol and an in-depth history of the client's FMS and trauma. More research is needed to support this new protocol.

REFERENCES

Badash, M. (2013). Symptoms of fibromyalgia. Retrieved from http://www.lahey.org/Departments _and_Locations/Departments/Ophthalmology/Ebsco_Content/Astigmatism.aspx?chunkiid=19458

Bartels, E., Dreyer, L., Jakopsen, S., Jespersen, A., Bliddal, H., & Danneskiold-Samsøe, B. (2009). [Fibromyalgia, diagnosis and prevalence. Are gender differences explainable?] *Ugeskr Laeger, 171*(49), 3588–3592. [Article in Danish]

Beck, A. T., Ward, C. H., Mendelson, M., Mock, J., & Erbaugh, J. (1961). An inventory for measuring depression. *Archives of General Psychiatry, 4*, 561–571. doi:10.1001/archpsyc.1961.01710120031004

Bennett, R., & McGain, G. (1995). Coping successfully with fibromyalgia. *Treatment & Research Information, 29*(5), 12.

Block, A., Kremer, E. F., & Fernandez, E. (1999). *Handbook of pain syndromes: Biopsychosocial perspectives.* Mahwah, NJ: Lawrence Erlbaum Associates.

Briere, J., & Runtz, M. (1989). The Trauma Symptom Checklist (TSC-33) early data on a new scale. *Journal of Interpersonal Violence, 4*(2), 151–163. doi:10.1177/088626089004002002

Brooks, R. K., Cronholm, P. F., & Strawn, J. R. (2012). Physiologic changes associated with violence and abuse exposure: An examination of related medical conditions. *Trauma, Violence, & Abuse, 13*(1), 41–56. doi:10.1177/1524838011426152

Burckhardt, C. S., Clark, S. R., & Bennett, R. M. (1991). The fibromyalgia impact questionnaire: Development and validation. *The Journal of Rheumatology, 18*(5), 728–733.

Buskila, D., & Cohen, H. (2007). Comorbidity of fibromyalgia and psychiatric disorders. *Current Pain and Headache Reports, 11*(5), 333–338. doi:10.1007/s11916-007-0214-4

Buysse, D. J., Reynolds III, C. F., Monk, T. H., Berman, S. R., & Kupfer, D. J. (1989). The Pittsburgh Sleep Quality Index: A new instrument for psychiatric practice and research. *Psychiatry Research, 28*(2), 193–213. doi:10.1016/0165-1781(89)90047-4

Eich, W., Häuser, W., Friedel, E., Klement, A., Herrmann, M., Petzke, F., . . . Henningsen, P. (2008). Definition, klassifikation und diagnose des fibromyalgiesyndroms. *Der Schmerz, 22*(3), 255–266. doi:10.1007/s00482-008-0671-7

Fay, S. D. (2015). *Relationship between adverse childhood experiences and illness perceptions among individuals with fibromyalgia* (Walden Dissertations and Doctoral Studies). Walden University Dissertations and Doctoral Studies, Minneapolis, MN. Retrieved from http://scholarworks.waldenu .edu/cgi/viewcontent.cgi?article=1212&context=dissertations

Felitti, V. J., Anda, R. F., Nordenberg, D., Williamson, D. F., Spitz, A. M., Edwards, V. E., Koss, M. P., & Marks, J. S. (1998, May). Relationship of childhood abuse and household dysfunction to many of the leading causes of death in adults: The Adverse Childhood Experiences (ACE) Study. *American Journal of Preventive Medicine, 14*(4), 245–258. doi:10.1016/S0749-3797(98)00017-8

Gatchel, R. J., Peng, Y. B., Peters, M. L., Fuchs, P. N., & Turk, D. C. (2007). The biopsychosocial approach to chronic pain: Scientific advances and future directions. *Psychological Bulletin, 133*(4), 581–624. doi:10.1037/0033- 2909.133.4.581

Gerhardt, A., Eich, W., Seidler, G., & Tesarz, J. (2013). Eye movement desensitization and reprocessing in chronic pain conditions. *OA Musculoskeletal Medicine, 1*(1), 1–7. doi:10.13172/2052-9287-1-1-524

Giedd, J. N., & Rapoport, J. L. (2010). Structural MRI of pediatric brain development: What have we learned and where are we going? *Neuron, 67*(5), 728–734. doi:10.1016/j.neuron.2010.08.040

Grant, M. (2000). EMDR: A new treatment for trauma and chronic pain. *Complementary Therapies in Nursing and Midwifery, 6*(2), 91–94. doi:10.1054/ctnm.2000.0459

Grant, M. (2001). Understanding and treating chronic pain as trauma, with EMDR. UND Retrieved from https://www.researchgate.net/profile/Mark_Grant4/publication/265746746_UNDERSTANDING_ AND_TREATING_CHRONIC_PAIN_AS_TRAUMA_WITH_EMDR/links/551a3a750cf2f51a6fea2d88/ UNDERSTANDING-AND-TREATING-CHRONIC-PAIN-AS-TRAUMA-WITH-EMDR.pdf

Grant, M., & Threlfo, C. (2002). EMDR in the treatment of chronic pain. *Journal of Clinical Psychology, 58*, 1505–1520. doi:10.1002/jclp.10101

Häuser, W., Eich, W., Herrmann, M., Nutzinger, D. O., Schiltenwolf, M., & Henningsen, P. (2009). Fibromyalgia syndrome classification, diagnosis, and treatment. *Deutsches Arzteblatt International, 106*(23), 383–391. doi:10.3238/arztebl.2009.0729b

Hawker, G. A., Mian, S., Kendzerska, T., & French, M. (2011). Measures of adult pain: Visual Analog Scale for Pain (VAS Pain), Numeric Rating Scale for Pain (NRS Pain), McGill Pain Questionnaire (MPQ), Short-Form McGill Pain Questionnaire (SF-MPQ), Chronic Pain Grade Scale (CPGS), Short Form-36 Bodily Pain Scale (SF-36 BPS), and Measure of Intermittent and Constant Osteoarthritis Pain (ICOAP). *Arthritis Care & Research, 63*(S11), S240–S252. doi:10.1002/acr.20543

Imbierowicz, K., & Egle, U. T. (2003). Childhood adversities in patients with fibromyalgia and somatoform pain disorder. *European Journal of Pain, 7*(2), 113–119. doi:10.1016/S1090-3801(02)00072-1

Kavakçı, Ö., Semiz, M., Kaptanoğlu, E., & Özer, Z. (2012). EMDR treatment of fibromyalgia, a study of seven cases. *Anatolian Journal of Psychiatry, 13*(1), 75–81. Turkish.

Kendall-Tackett, K. (2009). Psychological trauma and physical health: A psychoneuroimmunology approach to etiology of negative health effects and possible interventions. *Psychological Trauma: Theory, Research, Practice, and Policy, 1*(1), 35–48. doi:10.1037/a0015128

Maloney, E. M., Gurbaxani, B. N., Jones, J. F., de Souza Coelho, L., Pennachin, C., & Goertzel, B. N. (2006). Collaborative study: Chronic fatigue syndrome—Research report. Chronic fatigue syndrome and high allostatic load. *Pharmacogenomics, 7*(3), 467–473. doi:10.2217/14622416.7.3.467

Middlebrooks, J. S., & Audage, N. C. (2008). *The effects of childhood stress on health across the lifespan*. Atlanta, GA: Centers for Disease Control and Prevention, National Center for Injury Prevention and Control. Retrieved from http://www.cdc.gov/ncipc/pub-res/pdf/Childhood_Stress.pdf

Raphael, K. G., Chandler, H. K., & Ciccone, D. S. (2004). Is childhood abuse a risk factor for chronic pain in adulthood? *Current Pain and Headache Reports, 8*, 99–1110. doi:10.1007/s11916-004-0023-y

Russell, M. (2008). Treating traumatic amputation-related phantom limb pain: A case study utilizing eye movement desensitization and reprocessing (EMDR) within the armed services. *Clinical Case Studies, 7*(2), 136–153. doi:10.1177/1534650107306292

Schneider, J., Hofmann, A., Rost, C., & Shapiro, F. (2008). EMDR in the treatment of chronic phantom limb pain. *Pain Medicine, 9*, 76–82. doi:10.1111/j.1526-4637.2007.00299.x

Shapiro, F. (scripted by M. Luber). (2009). Current Anxiety and Behavior. In M. Luber (Ed.), *Eye Movement Desensitization and Reprocessing (EMDR) scripted protocols: Basics and special situations* (pp. 138–140). New York, NY: Springer Publishing.

Tinker, R. H., & Wilson, S. A. (2005). The phantom limb pain protocol. In R. Shapiro (Ed.), *EMDR solutions: Pathways to healing* (pp. 147–159). New York, NY: W. W. Norton.

Tynes, L. L., & Spiegel, J. C. (2013). Considerations in comorbid irritable bowel syndrome and fibromyalgia: A case report and review. *University of Toronto Medical Journal, 90*(2), 40–42.

van Houdenhove, B., & Egle, U. T. (2004). Fibromyalgia: A stress disorder? *Psychotherapy and Psychosomatics, 73*(5), 267–275. doi:10.1159/000078843

Wilensky, M. (2006). Eye movement desensitization and reprocessing (EMDR) as a treatment for phantom limb pain. *Journal of Brief Therapy, 5*(1), 31–44. doi:10.1186/1471-2474-14-256

Wolfe, F., Clauw, D. J., Fitzcharles, M., Goldenberg, D. L., Katz, R. S., Mease, P., . . . Yunus, M. B. (2010). The American College of Rheumatology preliminary diagnostic criteria for fibromyalgia and measurement of symptom severity. *Arthritis Care & Research, 62*(5), 600–610. doi:10.1002/acr.20140

World Health Organization. (n.d.-a). Adverse Childhood Experiences International Questionnaire (ACE-IQ). Retrieved from http://www.who.int/violence_injury_prevention/violence/activities/adverse_childhood_experiences/en

World Health Organization. (n.d.-b). WHO Quality of Life-BREF (WHOQOL-BREF). Retrieved from http://www.who.int/substance_abuse/research_tools/whoqolbref/en

Yunus, M. B. (2002). Gender differences in fibromyalgia and other related syndromes. *The Journal of Gender-Specific Medicine, 5*(2), 42–47.

Emre Konuk, Zeynep Zat, and Önder Kavakçı
SUMMARY SHEET BY MARILYN LUBER

Name: _____ Diagnosis: _____

Medications: _____

Test Results: _____

☑ Check when task is completed, response has changed, or to indicate symptoms.

Note: This material is meant as a checklist for your response. Please keep in mind that it is only a reminder of different tasks that may or may not apply to your incident.

INTRODUCTION

☐ What Is Fibromyalgia?

Fibromyalgia or fibromyalgia syndrome (FMS) is a chronic pain disorder characterized by fatigue, muscle pain, tenderness, and sleep difficulties (Yunus, 2002). This syndrome is also referred to as "soft-tissue rheumatism."

DIAGNOSES

According to the diagnostic criteria set by the American College of Rheumatology (ACR), people with FMS have a medical problem characterized by pain in the following areas:

- ☐ Axial skeleton
- ☐ Right and left sides of the bodies
- ☐ Waist
- ☐ At least 11 to 18 tender points in the body (Häuser et al., 2009).

Badash (2013) reports that fibromyalgia might also include other symptoms:

- ☐ Concentration and memory problems
- ☐ Thinking problems
- ☐ Labile mood
- ☐ Depression
- ☐ Anxiety
- ☐ Nervousness
- ☐ Fatigue
- ☐ Sleep problems
- ☐ Morning stiffness
- ☐ Painful menstrual cramps
- ☐ Urinary symptoms

☐ Irritable bowel syndrome
☐ Heartburn, headaches
☐ Jaw pain, numbness
☐ Tender trigger points
☐ Tingling in the hands, arms, feet, and legs.
☐ "Blue" or "down" (most report)

MEASURES

Fibromyalgia Syndrome Treatment With EMDR Therapy Scripted Protocol

Notes

Phase 1: History Taking

1. Medical Assessment

- Get medical assessment
- Physician gives FMS diagnosis

2. Psychiatric Assessment

Assess for the following concerns:
- Comorbid psychiatric problems where it is important to deal with another disorder or problem first
- Necessary medication and medication regulation
- Appropriate candidate at this time because:
  ▪ The patient is pregnant and has a risk of miscarriage
  ▪ Uncontrolled epileptic seizures may occur

3. Psychological Assessment

- A qualified EMDR clinician evaluates the patient.

Assessment tools to use:

☐ ACE Questionnaire
☐ Visual Analog Scale (VAS)
☐ Beck Depression Inventory (BDI)
☐ Trauma Symptom Checklist-40 (TSC-40)
☐ Pittsburgh Sleep Quality Index (PSQI)
☐ The World Health Organization Quality of Life (WHOQOL)
☐ Fibromyalgia Impact Questionnaire (FIQ)
☐ Fibromyalgia Diagnostic Criteria

Phase 2: Preparation Phase

☐ General Information
☐ Definition of Fibromyalgia Pain History
☐ Treatment Goals
☐ Ethical Issues
☐ Informing the Patient about the Treatment Process and EMDR
☐ Resources

Phase 3: Assessment

Treatment Plan

During case formulation/treatment planning, the following are taken into consideration:

☐ Results of assessing history
☐ Observations of other professionals. Assess the relevance of the following issues:

- Psychosis
- Recent unresolved traumatic events
- Severe personality disorders (e.g., borderline, antisocial)
- Unresolved loss
- Severe depression and/or suicidal risk
- Ongoing violence
- Alcohol or substance abuse/dependence
- Sleep disorders
- Eating disorders
- Mental retardation
- Somatoform disorder
  - ☐ History of fibromyalgia: Other relevant traumatic memories to the patient's pain apart from the following:
  - Other early traumas relevant to the patient's pain such as unresolved sexual abuse and physical or psychological violence.
  - Fibromyalgia history and relevant traumatic memories of other family members

Use the Three-Pronged Protocol

☐ PAST MEMORIES

Options to use:

- ☐ First memory, then worst, most recent memories, and triggers.
- ☐ Worst memory, then first memory, and, then, most recent incident and triggers

If not related to FMS traumatic experiences, focus on the pain itself with the Standard EMDR Protocol. There are no traumatic experiences that are related to the FMS pain; ask if the FMS pain experiences themselves are traumatic. _____

- ☐ Worst FMS pain memory (that has the highest SUD level); then the first FMS pain memory, most recent incident, and triggers.
- ☐ If necessary, work with traumas that seem to be unrelated to FMS.

☐ PRESENT TRIGGERS

- ☐ Work with conditions that trigger FMS pain, traumatic FMS pain, and traumas that seem to be unrelated to fibromyalgia syndrome. Structure EMDR present triggers in the following way:
- List triggers and/or incidents that initiate or increase the FMS pain.
- Start with the most frequently experienced trigger.
- For each trigger, find the most disturbing event/incident (that has the highest SUD level) to work with the Standard EMDR Protocol.

☐ FUTURE TEMPLATE

- ☐ Use the future template with each of the triggers that stimulate the patient's FMS.
- ☐ Use the Standard EMDR Protocol for reprocessing targets. Use order to process as mentioned previously.
- ☐ After processing, check the strength of the patient's fibromyalgia pain, and then place it in the treatment plan.

EMDR SCRIPTED PROTOCOL

Phase 1: History Taking

Full name: _____

Age: _____

Date of birth: _____

Family status: ☐ Single   ☐ Married   ☐ Separated   ☐Divorced   ☐ Partnered

Highest education: _____

Who does the patient live with: _____

Emergency contact: _____

☐Employed   ☐ Unemployed   ☐ Student

Job description: _____

History of Fibromyalgia

First pain: _____

Life events prior to first pain: _____

Development of pain over time: _____

Change in intensity: ☐ Yes ☐ No

Worse: ☐ Yes ☐ No

Better: ☐ Yes ☐ No

What parts are painful?

Painful tender points: ☐ Yes ☐No

Triggers: ☐ Yes ☐ No

Deep muscle pain: ☐ Yes ☐ No

Chronic headaches: ☐ Yes ☐ No

Back pain: ☐ Yes ☐ No

Shoulder or neck pain: ☐ Yes ☐ No

Pain #:___/10

Stays at severity or changes: _____

Pain when press on: _____

Frequency of pain: ☐ Daily ☐ Every few days ☐ Weekly ☐ Monthly

Effects on social life: _____

Effects on family life: _____

Effects on work life: _____

Secondary gain (opportunity to not do something you don't want to do): _____

Stays at severity or changes: _____

Traumatic/Stressful Events

First/Earliest target/memory/image: _____

_____

SUD: ___/10

NC: _____

Traumatic/stressful events that caused the beginning of pain: _____

_____

Worst traumatic/stressful events: _____

_____

SUD: ___/10

NC: _____

More recent traumatic/stressful experiences: _____

_____

SUD: ___/10

Traumatic/stressful events related to FMS pain: _____

_____

NC: _____

SUD: ___/10

NC: _____

Pain as Trauma

First memory of fibromyalgia pain: _____

_____

SUD: ___/10

NC: _____

Worst fibromyalgia pain: _____

_____

SUD: ___/10

NC: _____

More recent fibromyalgia pain memory: _____

_____

SUD: ___/10

Traumatic/stressful events related to FMS pain: _____

NC: _____

SUD: ___/10

NC: _____

Other significant traumatic/stressful fibromyalgia pain: _____

_____

SUD: ___/10

NC: _____

Other traumatic/stressful life events: _____

_____

SUD: ___/10

Triggers

Pain triggers: _____

_____

Hormonal factors: ☐ Yes ☐ No

Comment: _____

Certain seasons/weather changes: □ Yes □ No

Comment: _____

Heat/cold/humidity: □ Yes □ No

Comment: _____

Overexertion/illness/injury/traveling: □ Yes □ No

Comment: _____

Noise/traffic/etc.:   □ Yes □ No

Comment: _____

Certain people: □ Yes □ No

Comment: _____

Other events/situations/stimulations trigger pain: □ Yes □ No

Comment: _____

Information relevant to endemic/widespread FMS symptoms

Lack of sleep/changes in sleep routine: □ Yes □ No

Other symptoms you have during pain: _____

_____

Anxiety: □ Yes □ No

Concentration and memory problems: □ Yes □ No

Depression: □ Yes □ No

Fatigue: □ Yes □ No

Headaches: □ Yes □ No

Irritable bowel syndrome: □ Yes □ No

Morning stiffness: □ Yes □ No

Painful menstrual cramps: □ Yes □ No

Sleep problems, numbness: □ Yes □ No

Tingling in hands, arms, feet, and legs: □ Yes □ No

Tender points: □ Yes □ No

Urinary symptoms: □ Yes □ No

Assess the client using the following assessment tools before the EMDR intervention:

    □ ACE Questionnaire: _____

    □ Visual Analog Scale (VAS): _____

    □ Beck Depression Inventory (BDI): _____

    □ Trauma Symptom Checklist (TSC-40): _____

    □ Pittsburgh Sleep Quality Index (PSQI): _____

    □ Fibromyalgia Impact Questionnaire (FIQ): _____

    □ The World Health Organization Quality of Life (WHOQOL)

    □ Fibromyalgia Diagnostic Criteria

Phase 2: Preparation

Informed consent: ☐ Yes ☐ No

Ethical issues: ☐ Yes ☐ No

Treatment goals: _____

_____

Explanation of EMDR as in the Standard EMDR Protocol   ☐ Yes ☐ No

"When a disturbing event occurs, it can get locked in the brain with the original picture, sounds, thoughts, feelings, and body sensations. This material can combine factual material with fantasy and with images that stand for the actual event or feelings about it. EMDR seems to stimulate the information and allows the brain to process the experience. That may be what is happening in REM or dream sleep—eye movements (tones, tactile) may help to process the unconscious material. It is your own brain that will be doing the healing and you are the one in control.

I will be scheduling weekly sessions with you as often as possible. They will last 50/90 minutes. Will you be able to follow through with this plan?"   ☐ Yes ☐ No

"It is important that you use your medication and see your doctor as frequently as he or she requires. In this therapy process, we will see each other for _____ (state the course of treatment if there is a restriction).

We will start working with the traumas that seem to be related to your FMS. Some of the traumas and problems that we have talked about together such as ____ (note appropriate traumas and problems) will not be dealt with during your treatment because they do not seem to be related to your fibromyalgia syndrome. If, however, we find that they are, we can always address them. When your fibromyalgia syndrome treatment is complete, we can always come back to them if you are still concerned about any of them."

Introduce the scales _____ ☐ Yes ☐ No

*"I want to tell you about some of the things I am going to ask you to do that will be helpful to both you and me during your fibromyalgia syndrome treatment. First, I will ask you to fill out the psychometric tests every week. Here is the list: ACE Questionnaire, Visual Analog Scale (VAS), Beck Depression Inventory (BDI), The Posttraumatic Diagnostic Scale (PDS), Pittsburgh Sleep Quality Index (PSQI), and State-Trait Anger Scale (STAS). Would you be willing to do this?"*_____ ☐ Yes ☐ No

"Please remember to fill out the psychometric tests as we have agreed, so that we keep track of your fibromyalgia syndrome."

Resources: ☐ Yes ☐ No ☐Safe Place

Phase 3: Assessment

Traumatic Events Related to FMS

First—list traumatic events related to the first remembered fibromyalgia. Choose the first experience.

_____

_____

_____

Target/memory/image: _____

_____

NC: _____

PC: _____

VOC: ___/7

Emotions: _____

SUD: ___/10

Sensation: _____

Worst—list traumatic events related to the worst remembered fibromyalgia. Choose the worst experience.

_____

_____

_____

Target/memory/image: _____

_____

NC: _____

PC: _____

VOC: ___/7

Emotions: _____

SUD: ___/10

Sensation: _____

Most Recent Traumatic/Stressful Events Related to the FMS

Most recent—list traumatic events related to the most recent remembered fibromyalgia. Choose the worst experience.

_____

_____

_____

Target/memory/image: _____

_____

NC: _____

PC: _____

VOC: ___/7

Emotions: _____

SUD: ___/10

Sensation: _____

FMS Pain as Trauma

Worst FMS Pain Experience

Target/memory/image: _____

_____

NC: _____

PC: _____

VOC: ___/7

Emotions: _____

SUD: ___/10

Sensation: _____

First FMS Pain Experience

Target/memory/image: _____

_____

NC: _____

PC: _____

VOC: ___/7

Emotions: _____

SUD: ___/10

Sensation: _____

Most Recent FMS Pain Experience

Target/memory/image: _____

_____

NC: _____

PC: _____

VOC: ___/7

Emotions: _____

SUD: ___/10

Sensation: _____

Other—list traumatic/stressful events unrelated to the worst remembered fibromyalgia.

_____

_____

_____

Target/memory/image: _____

_____

NC: _____

PC: _____

VOC: ___/7

Emotions: _____

SUD: ___/10

Sensation: _____

Triggers That Trigger the Pain or Memories Associated With the Pain

Target/memory/image: _____

_____

NC: _____

PC: _____

VOC: ___/7

Emotions: _____

SUD: ___/10

Sensation: _____

Phase 4: Desensitization

Apply the Standard EMDR Protocol for all targets.

Phase 5: Installation

Install the PC

Original PC: ☐ Use original PC ☐ Use new PC

New PC (if new one is better): _____

VOC: ____/7

Incident + PC + BLS

Phase 6: Body Scan

Unresolved tension/tightness/unusual sensation: _____

_____

Unresolved tension/tightness/unusual sensation + BLS

Strengthen positive sensation using BLS.

If there is more discomfort, reprocess until discomfort subsides + BLS. Then repeat body scan.

VOC: ___/7

PRESENT TRIGGERS

Situations, Events, or Stimuli Triggers

☐ Trigger 1:

Most disturbing part: _____

☐ Trigger 2:

Most disturbing part: _____

☐ Trigger 3:

Most disturbing part: _____

☐ Trigger 4:

Most disturbing part: _____

Target: _____

Picture/Image: _____

Negative cognition (NC): _____

Note: If difficulty: *"In your worst moments, when you are remembering some aspect of the event, what thoughts or negative beliefs do you have about yourself?"*_____

Positive cognition (PC): _____

Validity of cognition (VOC): ____/7

Emotions: _____

Subjective units of disturbance (SUD): ____/10

Location of body sensation: _____

FUTURE TEMPLATE

Installation of the Future Template (Image)

Image of coping effectively with or in the fear trigger in the future: _____

_____

PC: (I can handle it) _____

Sensations: _____

+ BLS

VOC (able to handle the situation): ___/7

Install until VOC = 7

If continuing to be greater than 7, there are more targets to be identified and addressed and used with the Standard EMDR Protocol.

Blocks/anxieties/fears in future scene: _____

1. _____

2. _____

3. _____

Do BLS. If they do not resolve, ask for other qualities needed to handle the situation or what is missing.

1. _____

2. _____

3. _____

Use BLS. If blocks are not resolved, identify unprocessed material and process with the Standard EMDR Protocol.

1. _____

2. _____

3. _____

Target/memory/image: _____

_____

NC: _____

PC: _____

VOC: ___/7

Emotions: _____

SUD: ___/10

Sensation: _____

Video Check (Future Template as a Movie)

Say, *"This time, I'd like you to imagine yourself stepping into the future. Close your eyes, and play a movie from the beginning until the end. Imagine yourself coping with any challenges that come your way. Notice what you are seeing, thinking, feeling, and experiencing in your body. While playing this movie, let me know if you hit any blocks. If you do, just open your eyes and let me know. If you don't hit any blocks, let me know when you have viewed the whole movie."*

If block/s, say, *"I can handle it,"* and BLS. Repeat until the client can go through the whole movie entirely without distress.

VOC: ___/7

If the client can play the movie from beginning to end with confidence and satisfaction, play the movie one more time from beginning to end + BLS: ☐ Yes ☐ No

Phase 7: Closure

Most positive thing learned: _____

_____

_____

PC: _____

+ BLS

Check with VOC: _____

Normal Closure: ☐ Yes ☐ No

Phase 8: Reevaluation

Noticed since last session: _____

_____

Current symptoms: _____

New material: _____

_____

SUD: ___/10

"When you think about the work we have done together, what do you feel is the most useful to you?"

Useful: _____

Install if useful with BLS.

Gained: _____

_____

Noticed: _____

_____

Install if useful with BLS.

Noticed: _____

_____

Install if useful with BLS.

Noticed: _____

_____

Install if useful with BLS.

Positive target/memory/image: _____

_____

Sensations and emotions: _____

SUD: ___/10

Location of body sensation: _____

BLS, notice: _____

_____

BLS: learned: _____

_____

"Now, think about the image or memory, about the parts of your body where you feel the positive sensations, and about the word/phrase and put them all together. Go with that."

BLS, notice: _____

_____

BLS, notice: _____

_____

TREATING MALADAPTIVE SELF-CARE BEHAVIORS USING EMDR THERAPY

As the world spins faster and faster and there are more and more self-improvement plans, quality-of-life suggestions, and apps for all kinds of ways to take care of ourselves, it seems harder and harder to find the time to implement or do all of the things that amount to self-care.

When it comes to psychotherapists, self-care is often put on the back burner to the more important tasks of taking care of our clients. How long does it take for us to put our feet on the ground and breathe or go out for that walk in the sunshine or take a moment after that last patient to use Neil Daniels's "Self-Care for EMDR Practitioners" to rid us of the residual feelings of anger, frustration, regret, or hopelessness that creep up when patients hit a nerve or an old unresolved memory network (2009a, 2009b, 2014)? Self-care for therapist issues has been addressed but is sparse concerning practitioners in private and agency practice (Butler, 2016; Calof, 1995; Cooper, 1995; Dworkin, 2009a, 2009b; Friedman, 2000; Horne, 2014; Luber, 2009a, 2009b, 2014, 2016; McCall, 2017; Schubbe, 2011) or in response to man-made and natural disasters (Alter-Reid, 2014; Brivio & Bergamaschi, 2008; Farrell, 2014; Jarero, 2012; Jarero & Uribe, 2014; Luber, 2014). In fact, the Green Cross Academy of Traumatology created "Standards of Self Care Guidelines" (Green Cross Academy of Traumatology, 2005) to support respect for the dignity and worth of the self, the practitioner's responsibility for self-care, and the understanding that without self-care, clinicians cannot effectively perform their work. Levis and Pollack (2017a, 2017b) in their presentations "From Quicksand to Terra Firma: An EMDR Therapy Paradigm Shift from Vicarious Trauma to Vicarious Resilience" and "Resilient Client, Resilient Therapist: An Adventure in EMDR Therapy" look at both the therapist and the client perspective with many ideas of how to support both.

If we have a hard time, no wonder our patients find it difficult—if not impossible—to take care of themselves. Most of the authors of chapters in the EMDR Scripted Protocol series discuss different ways to self-soothe or develop resources in the preparation phase, such as Arne Hofmann's "The Absorption Technique" (Hofmann, 2009) or Elan Shapiro's "Four Elements Exercise for Stress Management" (Shapiro, 2009). Wesselmann, Schweitzer, and Armstrong (2016) in their section on developing attachment resources such as "Messages of Love Exercise" or the "Magical Cord of Love" exercise (as well as others) focus on helping parents who have never learned to soothe their children experience ways to do so with the therapist's support, and, in so doing, learn to self-soothe themselves as well as teach their children the skills they will need as adults. Marshall and Gilman (2016), working with the 9-1-1 responders population, include teaching how to manage heart rate variability to help them reduce and manage their hypervigilance that comes as a response to their job. The Barcelona Group of Amann et al. (2016), understanding the nature of patients with bipolar disorder (and other chronic disorders), include subprotocols in the preparation phase to deal with the types of issues that create difficulties for treatment success. They include the following:

- The EMDR Therapy Mood-Stabilizing Protocol for Bipolar Disorder
- The EMDR Therapy Illness Awareness Protocol
- The EMDR Therapy Adherence Enhancer Protocol
- The EMDR Therapy Prodromal Symptoms Protocol
- The EMDR De-idealization Manic Symptoms Protocol

As patients acquire the skills to use these protocols effectively, they are better able to handle the difficulties of their disorder.

The Ostacoli, Bertinoi, Negro, Carletto, and Luber (in press) group helps patients create a first-aid kit that includes the following:

- Body techniques
- Installation of positive experiences from the person's life
- Self-care techniques such as "Taking care of yourself" and "Being thankful"
- Positive self-connection such as "Drawing a picture of oneself and focusing on positive abilities/convictions," "Construct a relational bridge between the disease, the sick body and your 'self'"
- The logbook that is used to find what is useful during the session, at home to record pleasant experiences, and during the session to install valued experiences
- Homework to listen to on a recording regarding what has been done in the session to support the integration of the work done together
- Exercises to reinforce the adaptive parts of the self, such as to "Reinforce the sense of self-efficacy by strengthening the 'inner observer'" or "reinforce self-esteem by anchoring to strength and courage"

They turn evaluations of the EMDR process and the first-aid kit into a way to reinforce their self-worth. Then, they end treatment by asking patients to write a letter to themselves about "Taking care of myself in an affectionate way." Throughout this chapter, it is clear that patients are being taught to care for themselves in a very supportive way.

In this section, Carol Forgash and the Spanish team of Dolores Mosquera, Paula Baldomir Gago, Ana Cris Eiriz, and Raquel Fernández Dominguez are focusing on ways to help our patients discover how to do the self-care that they find difficult or impossible to do. Often, they need our help.

The issue that this section's first chapter represents, "The Impact of Complex PTSD and Attachment Issues on Personal Health," is one that is close to Carol Forgash's heart, and she has been writing and presenting about it since the millennium (Forgash, 2006, 2007; Monahan & Forgash, 2000). The basics of self-care and mental and physical hygiene are often elusive for our patients with complex posttraumatic stress disorder (CPTSD) and attachment problems and go far beyond just finding the time to take the moment to attend to themselves. In this chapter, Forgash points out the connection between adverse childhood experiences such as abuse, neglect, attachment deficits, and ruptures that often lead to addictive behaviors and an increase in dissociative responses that put their physical and mental health in jeopardy. This manifests in their difficulty in self-soothing and self-regulation and knowing how to take care of their personal health and hygiene. She also points out that PTSD depresses the immune system.

When injuries, accidents, or illnesses occurred in patients' families of origin, the adults either overdramatized, barely reacted, or ignored what happened. In this way, patients learned to not respond to what happened to them in their early family upbringing and continue to respond the same way in their current lives. They are unable to ask for help—because they never learned how to do so. One aspect of this is when Richard Kluft (1990) alerted practitioners to a situation he called "the sitting duck syndrome" or how patients often put themselves in situations of repetitive re-victimization in their relationships and often with healthcare practitioners. To add to their alienation, healthcare practitioners do not know about PTSD and dissociation, and are at a loss when our patients present themselves in their offices with their many symptoms, often of unknown origin.

Forgash proposes a phased treatment approach and underlines how important it is for clinicians to take a complete health history and to do it at a pace that is not overwhelming to patients. Phase 2 supports stabilization work so patients can work with their trauma memories and remove their dissociative and PTSD symptomatology. Throughout working with CPTSD patients, it is important to support the normalization of their responses and repair attachment problems through the use of the patient–therapist rapport as they explore the past. Often, ego state therapy is crucial to the working out of these issues. She addresses the hierarchy of targets and the types of negative and positive cognitions that often occur. She is always making sure to pace her patients so they do not get overwhelmed. As patients gain realistic control over their lives, they can begin living in a healthy manner and finding their own worth and sense of efficacy. Then, they are ready to attend to their healthcare from the perspective of a healthy adult.

In the 10th and last chapter in this volume, "EMDR Therapy Self-Care Protocol," Mosquera, Baldomir, Eiriz, and Fernández Dominguez write about their work with their patients at the Institute for the Study of Research and Treatment of Trauma and Personality Disorders (INTRA-TP) in A Coruña, Spain. They note that this protocol is an adjunct to the work that they do. They try to do this intervention in the beginning of treatment or parallel to support patients in actualizing their development. Anabel González and Dolores Mosquera developed this model for self-care (González & Mosquera, 2012; Mosquera, 2004; Mosquera & González, 2014). In their work, they include physical self-care and learning to tend to mental and emotional needs. They created a questionnaire to elicit the medical history that includes the types of questioning important for this patient group. Their work is based on the idea that children who grow up in neglectful and abusive surroundings are not able to take in healthy self-care patterns and learn to take care of themselves. They simply have no models (Chu, 1998; Ryle & Kerr, 2002). They note that it is important to assess for PTSD, trauma and adverse life events, dissociative disorders, and suicidal ideation. They suggest that this protocol not be used with patients who are suicidal as more work needs to be done to understand the patients' internal system before using it with patients with a dissociative disorder.

They describe seven EMDR self-help protocols and psychoeducational worksheets, as follows:

1. EMDR Therapy Self-Care Psychoeducational Protocol for Understanding Self-Care
2. EMDR Therapy Self-Care Psychoeducational Protocol for Learning How to Take Care of Ourselves (includes Psychoeducational Worksheet on How Do We Learn to Take Care of Ourselves, recommended as homework assignment)
3. EMDR Therapy Self-Care Psychoeducational Protocol on Relapse Prevention (includes Psychoeducational Worksheet on Relapse Prevention to give to the client at the end of treatment)
4. EMDR Therapy Self-Care Protocol for Developing Resources
5. EMDR Therapy Self-Care Protocol for Self-Harm and Self-Destructive Behaviors (includes Psychoeducational Script on the Function and Management of Self-Harm and Self-Destructive Behaviors, as well as a worksheet recommended as homework assignment); this protocol is to be used when in risk of self-harm and self-destructive behaviors
6. EMDR Therapy Self-Care Protocol to Develop and Install Positive Alternative Behaviors; this protocol is to be used when in risk of self-harm and self-destructive behaviors
7. EMDR Therapy Self-Care Protocol for Working With the Inner Child; we may skip protocols 5 and 6 when there is no imminent risk of self-harm and self-destructive behaviors

They choose which protocol to work with depending on the needs of patients. During the preparation phase, they have created steps A–G for the following: to support the therapeutic alliance, to work with the protocols and worksheets, to explain EMDR therapy, to install positive resources, to support stabilization, to reformulate the presenting problem in terms of their lack of learning how to do self-care habits, and to prevent relapse.

This section on treating maladaptive self-care behaviors using EMDR therapy is filled with important information, procedures, and protocols to address issues that are expressed earlier in the text. A summary sheet that serves as a checklist showing the important steps needed for clinicians' work accompanies each of these chapters, with a CD version format also available to provide mobile access.

REFERENCES

Alter-Reid, K. (2014). Community trauma: A blueprint for support and treatment for Trauma Recovery Network (TRN) responders from the Newtown, CT, tragedy. In M. Luber (Ed.), *Implementing EMDR early mental health interventions for man-made and natural disasters: Models, scripted protocols, and summary sheets* (pp. 495–502). New York, NY: Springer Publishing.

Amann, B. L., Batalla, R., Blanch, V., Capellades, D., Carvajal, M. J., Fernandez, I., ... Luber, M. (2016). The EMDR therapy protocol for bipolar disorder. In M. Luber (Ed.), *Eye movement desensitization and reprocessing (EMDR) therapy scripted protocols and summary sheets: Anxiety, obsessive-compulsive, and mood-related conditions treating* (pp. 223–264). New York, NY: Springer Publishing.

Brivio, R., & Bergamaschi, L. (2008, January). *Human and organizational aspects affecting the wellbeing in rescue-working activity: EMDR (Eye movement desensitization and reprocessing), Mirror Neuron and Stress Inoculation: The role of training methods, practice and simulation for psychological risks prevention and management in emergency workers.* International Workshop Reinforce Rescuers' Resilience by Empowering a Well-Being Dimension Workshop, Turin, Italy.

Butler, C. M. (2016). Healer, heal thyself: A commonsense look at the prevention of compassion fatigue. In M. Luber (Ed.), *Eye movement desensitization and reprocessing (EMDR) therapy scripted protocols and summary sheets: Treating trauma-and stressor-related conditions* (pp. 269–283). New York, NY: Springer Publishing.

Calof, D. (1995, June). *The self of the therapist: An experiential clinic for clinicians working with abuse recovery issues.* Paper presented at the International EMDR Annual Conference Sponsored by the EMDR Institute, Inc. and the EMDR International Association, Santa Monica, CA.

Chu, J. A. (1998). *Rebuilding shattered lives: The responsible treatment of complex post-traumatic and dissociative disorders.* New York, NY: Wiley.

Cooper, A. (1995, June). *EMDR with victims of trauma: Protecting your client, protecting yourself.* Workshop presented at the International EMDR annual conference sponsored by the EMDR Institute, Inc. and the EMDR International Association, Santa Monica, CA.

Daniels, N. (2009a). Self-care for EMDR practitioners. In M. Luber (Ed.), *Eye movement desensitization and reprocessing (EMDR) scripted protocols: Basics and special situations* (pp. 399–400). New York, NY: Springer Publishing.

Daniels, N. (2009b). Self-care for EMDR practitioners. In M. Luber (Ed.), *Eye movement desensitization and reprocessing (EMDR) scripted protocols: Special populations* (pp. 615–616). New York, NY: Springer Publishing.

Daniels, N. (2014). Self-care for EMDR practitioners. In M. Luber (Ed.), *Implementing EMDR early mental health interventions for man-made and natural disasters: Models, scripted protocols, and summary sheets* (pp. 491–492). New York, NY: Springer Publishing.

Dworkin, M. (2009a). The clinician awareness questionnaire in EMDR. In M. Luber (Ed.), *Eye movement desensitization and reprocessing (EMDR) scripted protocols: Basics and special situations* (pp. 401–408). New York, NY: Springer Publishing.

Dworkin, M. (2009b). The clinician awareness questionnaire in EMDR. In M. Luber (Ed.), *Eye movement desensitization and reprocessing (EMDR) scripted protocols: Special populations* (pp. 617–624). New York, NY: Springer Publishing.

Farrell, D. (2014). Vicarious trauma and EMDR. In M. Luber (Ed.), *Implementing EMDR early mental health interventions for man-made and natural disasters: Models, scripted protocols, and summary sheets* (pp. 507–524). New York, NY: Springer Publishing.

Forgash, C. (2006). *Integrating EMDR and ego state treatment: Addressing dissociation and PTSD in adult sexual abuse survivors and their negative impact on physical health.* Presentation at the 22nd EMDR International Association Conference, Los Angeles, CA.

Forgash, C. (2007). *The negative impact of complex PTSD on health: An EMDR/ego state treatment plan.* Presentation at the 22nd EMDR International Association Conference, Dallas, TX.

Friedman, M. J. (2000). PTSD diagnosis and treatment for mental health clinicians. In M. J. Scott & S. Palmer (Eds.), *Trauma and post-traumatic stress disorder* (pp. 1–14). New York, NY: Cassell Books.

González, A., & Mosquera, D. (2012). Working with self-care patterns: A structured procedure for EMDR therapy. *Revista Iberoamericana de Psicotraumatología y Disociación, 4, 2.*

Green Cross Academy of Traumatology. (2005). Standards of self care guidelines. Retrieved from http://greencross.org/about-gc/standards-of-care-guidelines

Hofmann, A. (2009). The absorption technique. In M. Luber (Ed.), *Eye movement desensitization and reprocessing (EMDR) scripted protocols: Special populations* (pp. 275–280). New York, NY: Springer Publishing.

Horne, B. (2014, May). *The joy of EMDR: Implications for the therapist.* Presentation at the EMDR Canada Annual Conference, Quebec City, QC, Canada.

Jarero, I. (2012, June). *Interventions on vicarious traumatization and compassion fatigue. In preconference 3: Self-care of therapists. An experiential workshop to learn to take care of ourselves.* Presentation at the 13th EMDR Europe Association Conference, Madrid, Spain.

Jarero, I., & Uribe, S. (2014). Worst case scenarios in recent trauma response. In M. Luber (Ed.), *Implementing EMDR early mental health interventions for man-made and natural disasters: Models, scripted protocols, and summary sheets* (pp. 533–538). New York, NY: Springer Publishing.

Kluft, R. P. (1990). Incest and subsequent revictimization: The case of the therapist-patient sexual exploitation, with a description of the sitting duck syndrome. In R. P. Kluft (Ed.), *Incest-related syndromes of adult psychopathology* (pp. 263–287). Washington, DC: American Psychiatric Press.

Levis, R. V., & Pollock, A. (2017a, April 21). *From quicksand to terra firma: An EMDR therapy paradigm shift from vicarious trauma to vicarious resilience.* Presentation at the EMDR Canada Annual Conference, Banff, AB, Canada.

Levis, R. V., & Pollock, A. (2017b, August 26). *Resilient client, resilient therapist: An adventure in EMDR therapy.* Presentation at the 22nd EMDR International Association Conference, Bellevue, WA.

Luber, M. (2009a). EMDR and clinician self-care. In M. Luber (Ed.), *Eye movement desensitization and reprocessing (EMDR) scripted protocols: Basics and special situations* (pp. 397–398). New York, NY: Springer Publishing.

Luber, M. (2009b). EMDR and clinician self-care. In M. Luber (Ed.), *Eye movement desensitization and reprocessing (EMDR) scripted protocols: Special populations* (pp. 611–614). New York, NY: Springer Publishing.

Luber, M. (2014). EMDR and clinician self-care: Recent trauma response. In M. Luber (Ed.), *Implementing EMDR early mental health interventions for man-made and natural disasters: Models, scripted protocols, and summary sheets* (pp. 486–489). New York, NY: Springer Publishing.

Luber, M. (2016). Self-care for clinicians. In M. Luber (Ed.), *Eye movement desensitization and reprocessing (EMDR) therapy scripted protocols and summary sheets: Treating trauma-and stressor-related conditions* (pp. 265–267). New York, NY: Springer Publishing.

Marshall, J., & Gilman, S. G. (2016). Reaching the unseen first responder with EMDR therapy: Treating 911 trauma in emergency telecommunicators. In M. Luber (Ed.), *Eye movement desensitization and reprocessing (EMDR) therapy scripted protocols and summary sheets: Treating trauma-and stressor-related conditions* (pp. 185–216). New York, NY: Springer Publishing.

McCall, K. (2017, April). *Vicarious trauma: Healing the EMDR therapist.* Presentation at the Western NY EMDR Regional Network Conference. Buffalo, NY.

Monahan, K., & Forgash, C. (2000). Enhancing the health care experiences of adult female survivors of childhood sexual abuse. *Women and Health, 30*(4), 27–41. doi:10.1300/J013v30n04_03

Mosquera, D. (2004). *Rough Diamonds II. Psychoeducational and treatment manual for borderline personality disorder. Structured program for professionals* (1st ed., rev.). Madrid, Spain: Pléyades, S.A. (Published in Spanish)

Mosquera, D., & González, A. (2014). *Borderline personality disorder and EMDR therapy.* Madrid, Spain: Pléyades, S.A. (English edition in Amazon Imprint)

Ostacoli, L., Bertinoi, G, Negro, M., Carletto, S., & Luber, M. (in press). EMDR Protocol for Patients Affected by Multiple Sclerosis. In M. Luber (Ed.), *Eye Movement Desensitization and Reprocessing (EMDR) scripted protocols and summary sheets: Treating medical-related issues.* New York, NY: Springer Publishing.

Ryle, A., & Kerr, I. B. (2002). *Introducing cognitive analytic therapy: Principles and practice by Ryle.* West Sussex, England: Wiley-Blackwell.

Schubbe, O. (2011, June). *Self care during the EMDR session: The application of the standard protocol for working with counter-transference.* Presentation Presented at the 12th EMDR Europe Association Conference, Vienna, Austria.

Shapiro, E. (2009). Four elements exercise for stress management. In M. Luber (Ed.), *Eye movement desensitization and reprocessing (EMDR) scripted protocols: Basics and special situations* (pp. 73–80). New York, NY: Springer Publishing.

Wesselmann, D. Schweitzer, C., & Armstrong, S. (2016). Child attachment trauma protocol. In M. Luber (Ed.), *Eye movement desensitization and reprocessing (EMDR) therapy scripted protocols and summary sheets: Treating trauma-and stressor-related conditions* (pp. 9–36). New York, NY: Springer Publishing.

THE IMPACT OF COMPLEX PTSD AND ATTACHMENT ISSUES ON PERSONAL HEALTH: AN EMDR THERAPY APPROACH

Carol Forgash

INTRODUCTION

Complex trauma is prevalent in the general therapy population and is rooted in early neglect and traumas of long duration, resulting in posttraumatic stress disorder (PTSD), dissociative disorders, attachment problems, and personality disorders. When these clients present themselves to the medical community by way of their family doctor or specialist, their psychological and physical symptoms are often misdiagnosed. They are seeking help for the severe symptoms of dissociation, PTSD, depression, and anxiety, as well as illnesses and pain. Articles on the correlation between poor health and sexual and physical abuse survivors focus on issues such as anxiety, phobias, loss of control, and powerlessness. The topic of dissociation, generally thought to be a typical symptom for complex trauma clients and clearly significantly related to healthcare treatment avoidance, has been absent from the literature concerning this population until recently. Attachment issues are now thought to be related to health problems as well. These issues are a legacy of adverse childhood experiences (ACE) in the life of the survivor. ACEs such as abuse, neglect, attachment deficits, and ruptures have a serious, negative effect on clients' health. These early experiences often lead to the adoption of behaviors that put the person at an additional risk for health problems, that is, substance abuse, eating disorders, smoking, and other compulsive behaviors. These ACEs also increase dissociative symptoms and vulnerability to PTSD. This will subsequently have negative effects on the immune system.

Additionally, ACE survivors (many with complex/chronic PTSD) frequently have no consistent experience in the management of affective and dissociative symptoms. Addressing this set of problems becomes an important emphasis of the work during the stabilization phase of EMDR therapy. The author wants to help her clients develop more stability, not merely to get to the "processing" phase quickly, but to increase self-efficacy, trust in the therapy relationship, and ensure that self-development is taking place.

Issues for the complex trauma/ACE survivor client, which can be targeted with EMDR therapy, include the following:

- Serious illness
- Chronic conditions such as migraines
- Untreated medical or dental symptoms
- Untreated substance abuse
- Lack of skills related to hygiene and healthcare
- Other health risk behaviors
- Avoidance of health treatment
- Lack of follow through

Finally, current accidents, illnesses, hospitalizations, and so on, may be related to and may trigger flashbacks to earlier traumatic events. These current symptoms and conditions, even with medical care, may not resolve without EMDR treatment of first the early trauma, and then the current issues.

These clients often are characterized by a chaotic/unstable family of origin, which can result in insecure, avoidant, and/or disorganized attachment styles. There may have been early losses and breaks in attachment. As a result of the neglect that they experience, these clients may lack skills in a number of basic areas, especially in regard to healthcare and hygiene. This cycle of abuse, neglect, attachment deficits, and ruptures has a negative effect on clients' health and often put them at an additional risk for health problems such as substance abuse, eating disorders, smoking, and other compulsive behaviors. They may present with issues concerning trust, self-hatred, and a fear of abandonment, in addition to the posttraumatic symptomatology. As a result, they have no consistent experience in receiving comfort from significant others that results in a lack of capacity for self-soothing. They often have no skill or training in managing affect. Furthermore, these clients often suffer from flashbacks with no one to witness and provide support. On a practical level, it is easy to understand that hygiene practices may never have been modeled—if practiced at all. Additionally, medical care may have been inconsistent during their abusive and neglectful childhoods.

If this were not enough, it is important to note that PTSD depresses the immune system. PTSD may be a result of health and iatrogenic events, such as untreated illnesses or procedures that might have been very painful. If the parent or physician did not explain to the child how the medical problem was going to be treated, the child may have been traumatized or there may have been malpractice issues. Another issue involves hospitalizations, where parents could not stay overnight with the child, leading to feelings of abandonment.

Another set of problems for complex trauma clients involves difficult-to-diagnose illnesses or conditions. They are typically called medically unexplained symptoms (MUS), such as the following:

- Respiratory illness
- Musculoskeletal complaints
- Chronic pain
- Fibromyalgia
- Chronic fatigue
- Eating disorders
- Headaches
- Irritable bowel syndrome (IBS)
- Gynecological problems, including pregnancy
- Regional pain syndromes
- Pseudo-neurological symptoms
- Sleep disorders

They are also prevalent among ACE survivors and can be treated with EMDR therapy.

For treatment planning, it is necessary to explore the roots of the CPTSD clients' health problems that emanate from their early neglect and/or abuse. Often, specific injuries, accidents, and illnesses occur, and their family either overreacts, underreacts, or ignores the symptoms. Often, when the child victims present in the physician's office or at the emergency room, there is no linking of their symptoms with the probable cause of abuse. By the time they reach adulthood, their reactions to their bodies and health needs have become more complex. ACE/complex trauma survivors may not have "normal" reactions to pain: either under- or overreacting or misinterpreting the pain. They may not notice symptoms of illness or tooth decay. They use dissociation to detach from their body and may have different thresholds of pain tolerance while dissociated. This creates problems when they try to explain medical/dental issues to a health practitioner who has no knowledge about PTSD and dissociation.

Felitti et al. (1998) note in the ACE study that there is a relationship between adult health status and childhood abuse and neglect. Childhood stressors are strongly related to development and the prevalence of risk factors for disease, health, and social well-being throughout the life span. Acute or prolonged stress increases cortisol production; this is adaptive for acute trauma, but over time becomes maladaptive and impairs the immune system, which, in turn, impairs healing. Cortisol levels become chronically decreased, resulting in illnesses such as rheumatoid arthritis (RA), fibromyalgia, chronic fatigue syndrome, thyroid diseases, Crohn's disease, and IBS (Bergmann, 2012). Furthermore, new research exploring neurotransmitters and hormones such as oxytocin show that these may be dysregulated by early human relational trauma and maltreatment, resulting in the development of dissociative, somatoform, and interpersonal disorders.

CPTSD clients rarely link their current difficulties with their treatment for prior trauma. This often results in increased traumatization in medical settings. Often, their level of anxiety mystifies them when they think about dealing with the healthcare profession. They may dissociate and/or have flashbacks in the medical/dental/therapy office; they have many issues about authority figures that may impact their relationships with physicians and dentists. This is complicated by their not being able to ask for help and experiencing confusion and/or disorientation if they try to focus on the problem.

Many CPTSD survivors do not believe they deserve good health and are ridden with shame and guilt. In fact, healthcare treatment can be so triggering that they avoid it for years, resulting in serious health problems.

Dissociation is a way that the CPTSD client copes with triggers and perceived threat or danger (Chefetz, 2015). Symptoms include the following:

- Hyper- or hypo-arousal/numbing
- "Out of body" experiences
- Not being present in the body
- Losing time
- "Going away" when stressed
- Depersonalization/derealization
- Looking "different" in the session
- Presenting with a childish voice
- Speaking about themselves in the third person
- Becoming disoriented
- Hearing "voices"

Depending on the degree of the continuum of dissociative symptoms, a CPTSD client may be diagnosed with a dissociative disorder. Somatic dissociation is not often talked about, but is not infrequent. According to Scaer (2007), clients using somatic dissociation may experience perceptual alterations and somatic symptoms such as shape, color, size, pain, functioning postural changes, sensations, and/or numbing. Often, they experience depersonalization of a body part and have fragmented images of the experiences of the traumatic event that produced the pain or injury. Their current injury may be in the same areas as an earlier accident or traumatic event such as abuse, but they may have amnesia for that earlier event.

These clients have complex problems and are difficult to treat. During the history-taking phase, it is essential to take a complete health history. It is important when taking the history to get the history of treatment, traumatic events, medications, and surgeries, as many current problems are based on earlier traumas (including medical issues and accidents). The site of the current medical problem is often the site of the earlier problem. It is important to treat earlier trauma, or treatment will be ineffective (Scaer, 2005). Of necessity, this history-taking phase may be lengthy, and must be paced carefully, due to the chance of overwhelming the client.

COMPLEX PTSD, PERSONAL HEALTH, AND EMDR THERAPY SCRIPT NOTES

CASE Conceptualization Overview

The treatment plan for EMDR therapy with CPTSD clients who are presenting with complex health issues includes the use of a phased treatment approach to provide stabilization/reduce symptoms of dissociation and deal with affect management problems. Phase 1 requires a good history taking, and having the client discuss current problems with a focus on health issues and trauma history, and then completing a Dissociative Experiences Scale and ACE questionnaire. In Phase 2, any needed stabilization work will be taught. After teaching and practicing many individualized interventions and skills, clinicians can safely desensitize and reprocess trauma memories and eliminate the dissociative and PTSD symptoms that impede these clients from dealing with health issues (Forgash, 2009).

In Phases 3 to 6, when making these treatment-planning decisions, remember it is a cooperative process. Phases 7 and 8 continue throughout the work.

In Phase 1, please note that it is necessary to obtain a complete history that includes many realms. At the same time, this has to be carefully timed as the CPTSD client may easily be triggered during history taking, or even casual conversation. Some of this important material may emerge over a long time as a trusting relationship develops. The therapist needs to be attuned to make sure that the pacing fits the client's needs. Therefore, expect historical material to come up in later phases of work. Determine if health issues are related to the following:

- Developmental/attachment trauma
- ACE trauma

- Shock trauma: actual abuse, injury, environmental incidents (this could also include medical treatment with negative results [iatrogenic])
- Normal health issues that the client is lacking skills to deal with
- History of family illnesses/self-destructive patterns (substance abuse, etc.)
- Chronic health problems
- Pain issues

It is important that decisions between therapist and client are jointly determined; giving back as much control as possible to the client is essential.

During Phases 1 to 3, the focus is on normalization of symptoms and the repair of attachment deficits while building client/internal system/therapist rapport and exploring historical material. Remember, during the history-taking phase, clients can become easily triggered. Therapists need to use their attunement skills to make sure of the pace of history taking.

It is often necessary to use an ego state (or parts) approach with complex trauma clients due to earlier dissociation and fragmentation of parts (Forgash, 2017; Knipe, 2008). There needs to be a system agreement among parts or ego states for the client to work on their problems. Part/s of the system may need to be "present" at the sessions (see Forgash & Copley [2008] for more information on how to work with dissociated parts of the personality or ego states, and Forgash [2009a], pp. 204–215, for a well-formulated explanation of working with dissociative clients and their part systems). With CPTSD clients, be sure to assess for readiness prior to proceeding with processing phase work. Then, select the appropriate targets by determining the past traumatic events, current issues, the main touchstone memories, negative cognitions (NCs), blocking beliefs, and needs of the client (and the ego state system) regarding attachment issues, trauma, health, illness, and pain.

Which targets take precedence? There may be several discussions to come to consensus:

- Adverse life experiences/small "t" trauma clusters concerning health and losses from earlier times
- Current life issues and illnesses
- Large "T" trauma, current and past
- Recent incidents/illnesses/injuries
- Health problems related to similar/earlier incidents

Certain types of *NC and positive cognition (PC)* come up frequently in this population:

- Avoidance of treatment due to prior interactions with healthcare providers
  NC: "I am not safe. I am not worth it."
  PC: "I am safe now. I'm worth it."
- History of being labeled and misinterpreted
  NC: "It is all in my head."
  PC: "My medical problems are real. I'm worth listening to."
- History of abandonment
  NC: "I am always going to be alone. I will die alone."
  PC: "I deserve support. I can start to connect with people."
- Fear of exams/procedures provoking flashbacks/dissociation
  NC: "I am crazy. No one will understand me."
  PC: "I can advocate for myself and be understood."
- Chronic illness/pain
  NC: "It will never get any better. I am going to die."
  PC: "I can cope with my situation."
- Losses, including identity
  NC: "I have lost too much."
  PC: "I can find a way to still be myself. I'm still able to have a life."

Introduce dissociative and affect management strategies to help clients stay in the optimum window of arousal:

- Resource development and installation
- Ego-building activities (see Phillips M. in Forgash & Copley, 2008)

- Mindfulness activities
- Learning to control stressful feelings and pain (Grant, 2009)
- Healing imagery (Siegel, 1988; Simonton, 1978)
- Positive body resource exercise (Levine, 2010)
- Cocoon of light healing exercise; meditation practices (Borysenko, 1988)
- Safety/distancing work (containers, affect dial/screen work; Back-of-the-Head scale; journaling, drawing, mapping [Forgash, 2009a; Forgash & Copley, 2008])
- Heart coherence exercise (Servan-Schreiber, 2004)

With current health problems, link up with any past trauma memories, similar feelings, thoughts, and beliefs. Treatment of current injuries/illnesses is more effective if old related traumas are desensitized and reprocessed; otherwise, many symptoms may not resolve after medical treatment.

Make sure to look for earlier traumas that are behind current beliefs as many serious life events emerge when the person has to deal with life-threatening illness. Always work with the medical team. Always be attentive to the client's physical condition and pace the work accordingly. Always end the session with debriefing and self-soothing work.

Always use the Standard EMDR Protocol except for the following variations: For complex trauma/dissociative clients, dissociated ego states may need to work together on a target, or several ego states with the same issue may work together to promote internal connection and cohesion. For example, the client may have had painful, traumatic medical procedures at different ages in childhood. Those child states may decide to process one of those events (first, worst, most recent) together. After that one has been processed, explore if some of the other events still need processing. Sometimes, processing one event generalizes to the others. If not, process each event (Forgash & Copley, 2008).

Other targets of importance include mourning past losses, missed opportunities, and regrets, as well as remorse about poor health. Remember that complex trauma clients may need to frequently return to stabilization phase work during Phases 4 to 8. This is typical and not client "failure." It should be normalized. Additionally, therapists need to take responsibility and work on pacing and readiness with the client. Remind them of skills they now have. Remind them of the stop sign, that they can determine how long they can process in any given session. This respectful treatment will often ease the path through the processing phases.

As you proceed through the processing phases, some of the most important work with a physically ill person concerns the present and future. There may be concerns, anxiety, and fear about life changes, re-occurrences, financial issues, and so on. Work is complete when the client can tackle once-feared problems, possible procedures, new tasks, and goals.

In this phase, clients work to regain realistic control of their lives, achieve healthy functioning, and enjoy as much efficacy in life domains as is possible. They work on gaining positive self-worth and identity and a sense of empowerment even if full recovery is not possible. They may try on new healthy behaviors and activities. The client often reports seeing old events and relationships from more of an adult perspective. Additionally, they express feelings of competence and can attend to their healthcare needs as an adult.

Future Template Work

What skills need to be learned and practiced? Rehearsals of any projected future situation (physical therapy, other rehabilitation, diagnostic testing, family occasions, returning to work, becoming well again, etc.) can be the focus of sessions. Work is not complete until clients can tackle once-feared problems, possible procedures, and new tasks. Clients can imagine behaviors such as speaking up and asking questions assertively, going for diagnostic procedures, attending an annual checkup or having an OB/GYN exam, learning how to use "aids" or prostheses, taking on new roles, and so on. Note any distress, and process until no distress is noted.

COMPLEX PTSD, PERSONAL HEALTH, AND EMDR THERAPY SCRIPT

Phase 1: History Taking

Health and Trauma History

Always explain the need for a health and trauma history for client and family members, such as a health genogram.

Say, *"I am interested in knowing about your health history. Is it OK to ask you some questions about this area? Remember, I want to go at your pace. Please stop me at any time."*

Say, *"I'd like to ask you, first, some questions on childhood experiences, which may be linked to your present issues, including health problems. These are the questions that appear on the ACE questionnaire. ACE stands for adverse childhood experiences. I think that your responses will help us clarify some of your issues. There is only one score per question, even if the events occurred more than once."*

ADVERSE CHILDHOOD EXPERIENCE (ACE) QUESTIONNAIRE

Say, *"Did a parent or other adult in the household often or very often swear at you, insult you, put you down, or humiliate you? Or act in a way that made you afraid that you might be physically hurt?"*

☐ If Yes, enter 1 ☐ If No, there is no score _____ Score

Say, *"Did a parent or other adult in the household often or very often push, grab, slap, or throw something at you? Or ever hit you so hard that you had marks or were injured?"*

☐ If Yes, enter 1 ☐ If No, there is no score _____ Score

Say, *"Did an adult or person at least 5 years older than you ever touch or fondle you or have you touch his or her body in a sexual way? Or attempt or actually have oral, anal, or vaginal intercourse with you?"*

☐ If Yes, enter 1 ☐ If No, there is no score _____ Score

Say, *"Did you often or very often feel that no one in your family loved you or thought you were important or special? Or your family didn't look out for each other, feel close to each other, or support each other?"*

☐ If Yes, enter 1 ☐ If No, there is no score _____ Score

Say, *"Did you often or very often feel that you didn't have enough to eat, had to wear dirty clothes, and had no one to protect you? Or your parents were too drunk or high to take care of you or take you to the doctor if you needed it?"*

☐ If Yes, enter 1 ☐ If No, there is no score _____ Score

Say, *"Was a biological parent ever lost to you through divorce or abandonment or for another reason?"*

☐ If Yes, enter 1 ☐ If No, there is no score _____ Score

Say, *"Was your mother or stepmother often or very often pushed, grabbed, slapped, or had something thrown at her or kicked, bitten, hit with a fist, or hit with something hard? Or ever repeatedly hit over at least a few minutes or threatened with a gun or knife?"*

☐ If Yes, enter 1 ☐ If No, there is no score _____ Score

Say, *"Did you live with anyone who was a problem drinker or alcoholic, or who used street drugs?"*

☐ If Yes, enter 1 ☐ If No, there is no score _____ Score

Say, *"Was a household member depressed or mentally ill, or did a household member attempt suicide?"*

☐ If Yes, enter 1 ☐ If No, there is no score _____ Score

Say, *"Did a household member go to prison?"*

☐ If Yes, enter 1 ☐ If No, there is no score _____ Score

Since the ACE report was written almost 20 years ago, other researchers have come to see that questions on poverty and community violence and bullying may also affect health.

Say, *"Did you grow up in poverty?"*

☐ If Yes, enter 1 ☐ If No, there is no score _____ Score

Say, *"Did anyone outside your home bully you?"*

☐ If Yes, enter 1 ☐ If No, there is no score _____ Score

Say, *"Was there violence in your community?"*

☐ If Yes, enter 1 ☐ If No, there is no score _____ Score

Total Score: _____

To obtain your ACE score, add up your "Yes" answers. The ACE score gives information to help you develop goals for your treatment, and for specific targets to process.

Note: You may use your own questions instead of what follows. You will certainly work to match your language to your client. Also, much of this information will be revealed as the relationship develops. However, it may be easier for a new therapist, or one who has not focused on health issues before, to utilize the questions. Like all other history taking with these clients, pacing is critical. Speed is irrelevant! Additionally, many clients will not be comfortable sharing material that may be shaming or guilt producing. They also may have dissociated much of their early history. You can assure them that speed is not of the essence here—their comfort is most important. Teach them the stop sign in the early phase work. It is very empowering and helps trust develop.

> Say, *"I am going to ask you some questions and I would like us to go at a pace that is comfortable for you. Please hold your hand up if you want to stop, like this* (demonstrate). *Do you have any questions or concerns?"*

_____

_____

During the next sessions, or when comfortable for the client:

Say, *"Tell me about any health issues in your childhood. Were you ill in your early years?"*

_____

_____

Say, *"Did you have many fevers growing up?"*

_____

_____

Say, *"Did you have any serious falls?"*

_____

_____

Say, *"When you fell, did they result in fractures?"*

_____

_____

Say, *"Were you ever hospitalized?"*

_____

_____

If so, say, *"Please describe what happened."*

_____

_____

The definition of iatrogenic is "physician induced or caused." This may have to be carefully explained.

Say, *"Did you have any recurrent illnesses and/or situations that were iatrogenic* (which means that the physician induced or caused problems?)*"*

_____

_____

Say, *"Did you have any painful conditions?"*

_____

_____

Say, *"What are your current problems including pain and disability?"*

_____

_____

Say, *"Have you had any serious illnesses or surgeries?"*

_____

_____

Say, *"How has your mental health been?"*

_____

_____

Say, *"Have you ever been in therapy before?"*

_____

_____

Say, *"Have you had any problems with drugs, alcohol, or eating disorders?"*

_____

_____

If yes, *"Please tell me about it."*

_____

_____

Say, *"Can you tell me about the health of close family members? Have any of them had serious illnesses, substance abuse, eating disorders, mental health issues, and medical and dental problems?"*

_____

_____

Say, *"Were there any deaths in your family, especially when you were a child?"*

_____

_____

If so, say, *"Please tell me about them."*

_____

_____

Say, *"Were there ever people with whom you were close in your immediate family who went away or came and went frequently?"*

_____

_____

Health Practices

Say, *"Were you taught regular basic hygienic routines such as brushing your teeth, washing your hands, and so on?"*

_____

_____

Say, *"Did you go regularly to the doctor and dentist when you were young?"*

_____

_____

If yes, ask the following:

Say, *"What were those visits like for you?"*

_____

_____

If no, ask the following:

Say, *"Why do you think that you didn't go regularly or at all?"*

_____

_____

Say, *"When did you have your last dental and medical exams?"*

_____

_____

Reinforce that your work together will help them to make changes.

Say, *"I am asking these questions today so that our work together can help you make the changes that you have said you want."*

Tell the client that you will be asking questions about some difficult areas.

Say, *"I will be asking questions about some difficult areas."*

Tell the client that you understand that many of these issues were attempts to solve problems stemming from early trauma.

Say, *"It is important to know that many of the issues you have were attempts to solve problems stemming from early trauma."*

Other Health Risk Behaviors

Say, *"Sometimes people go through periods where they had some risky health habits like using drugs or alcohol, having unprotected sex, having an eating disorder, or cutting. Have you had some of these problems?"*

_____

_____

AVOIDANCE OF HEALTH TREATMENT

Say, *"Do you have a history of avoiding medical care?"*

_____

_____

LACK OF FOLLOW THROUGH

Say, *"Has it been a problem following up on the doctor's suggestions or taking medications?"*

_____

_____

Use your own words and ask about the following:

CURRENT ACCIDENTS

Say, *"Have you had any accidents recently?"*

_____

_____

ILLNESSES

Say, *"Have you had any illnesses recently?"*

_____

_____

HOSPITALIZATIONS

Say, *"Have you been hospitalized recently?"*

_____

_____

Note: ACE clients may present with issues concerning trust, self-hatred, and a fear of abandonment, in addition to the posttraumatic symptomatology. As a result of these, they have no consistent experience in receiving comfort from significant others that results in a lack of capacity for self-soothing. They often have no skill or training in managing affect. Pay attention to pacing, and normalize their responses.

Say, *"There are categories of problems that are called medically unexplained symptoms (MUS). Please let me know if you have any of the following conditions. If so, we can explore how they have impacted you and determine how we can work on the issues that result from these problems."*

Note: This discussion may take place in segments depending on client willingness, fatigue, and so on.

Say, *"Have you ever been ill with any of the following?"*

☐ Respiratory illness
☐ Musculoskeletal and joint complaints
☐ Chronic pain
☐ Fibromyalgia
☐ Chronic fatigue
☐ Eating disorders
☐ Headaches
☐ Irritable bowel syndrome
☐ Gynecological problems including pregnancy
☐ Regional pain syndromes
☐ Pseudo-neurological symptoms
☐ Sleep disorders
☐ Rheumatoid arthritis
☐ Thyroid diseases
☐ Crohn's disease

Note: These are some symptoms of dissociation. Over time, explore these symptoms. Normalize them as being common results of being traumatized as a child.

Say, *"The symptoms I am going to ask you about next are common results of being traumatized as a child. Adults, when faced with danger, can often utilize 'fight' or 'flight.' Unfortunately, a child can do neither and what is left is the 'freeze' position and then dissociation. Have you experienced any of the following symptoms?"*

☐ *Hyper- or hypo-arousal/numbing*
☐ *"Out of body" experiences or not being present in the body*
☐ *Losing time*
☐ *"Going away" when stressed*
☐ *Depersonalization/observing yourself from outside your body*
☐ *Derealization/having a sense that things aren't real inside or outside your body*
☐ *Looking "different" in session*
☐ *Hearing "voices"*

Say, *"Sometimes, you may use something we call somatic dissociation to help you. Do you experience the following?"*

☐ *Perceptual alterations such as unusual pain in certain parts of your body; experiencing sensations in parts of the body that were injured, abused, or painful at other times in your life*
☐ *Somatic symptoms such as shape, color, size, pain, change in functioning of an extremity, and postural changes, sensations, and/numbing*

Client's Supports, Skills, and Strengths

Say, *"Who are the supports in your life currently?"*

_____

_____

Say, *"Who were the supports in your life in the past? I'd like to learn about your relationships with family and friends."*

_____

_____

Note: Some clients cannot acknowledge their skills and strengths early in treatment. They find it difficult to maintain positive affect. This can be a normal reaction to childhood *trauma.*

Say, *"Tell me about your skills and strengths."*

_____

_____

Phase 2: Preparation

Psychoeducation on Trauma-Informed Psychotherapy

This work will take several sessions or longer to communicate these very important concepts or information with clients. Some of it could be "triggering" or upsetting. Slow is best. People who have physical illness tire easily and have less energy, focus, and retention.

Clients need basic information about their conditions, the psychosomatic issues, and their rights. Convey that you are well informed about trauma/health issues and know why some people are reluctant health consumers.

Say, *"Lots of times when people have had difficult childhoods, illnesses, injuries, and abusive experiences, they have a lot of trouble trusting others, and that can include health practitioners. You may have had painful procedures and illnesses and, also, you may have worked with doctors who have not listened to you. If you have discomfort dealing with your health problems because of any of these issues, I hope that you will share them with me and I can help you overcome them."*

Psychoeducation About Patient Rights

Discuss *client rights.*

Say, *"Clients have rights as health consumers. Every one of your health providers should give you and discuss with you the Client Bill of Rights. You need to read it and ask questions about anything you don't understand."*

_____

_____

Psychoeducation About Becoming a Proactive Health Consumer

Teach the client how to become a *proactive health consumer.*

Say, *"One of the things you can do is bring a friend or family member with you to the doctor's office. When you are not feeling well, it's easier to misunderstand or be confused. You can make up a list of questions and concerns to discuss at the visit. Or we can do that as well."*

_____

_____

Give information about *resources* that help deal with illness/problems and trauma issues.

Say, *"In our community you will find associations such as the _____ (state the one that is appropriate: American Cancer Society, AA, the American Heart Association, etc.). They offer many kinds of services and education. It might be helpful for you to contact them. Would you be interested in speaking with them?"*

_____

_____

Psychoeducation About General Health, Stress and Pain, Normalizing Trauma Symptoms, and Their Effects on Health and Stress Reduction Work

Introduce general concepts about *improving health, stress, and pain, and normalizing trauma symptoms and their effects* on health and stress reduction work.

> Say, *"We know that trauma, stress, and pain all have an effect on health. What do you do in your life now to help yourself be healthy? Have you tried exercise, meditation, relaxing imagery? We can work on some of these strategies in the office."*

_____

_____

Psychoeducation About Psychosomatic Symptoms

> Say, *"Psychosomatic problems or conditions are generally affected by stress. Do you think that stress is a factor in your situation?"*   ☐ Yes ☐ No

> *"If so, how does it affect you?"*

_____

_____

Psychoeducation About Goal Setting, Hopes, and Plans

Explore *goal setting, hopes, and plans.*

Note: This can be a very informal discussion. As you talk, be aware of possible negative core beliefs and possible targets for EMDR processing.

> Say, *"Having health issues can make you fatigued, so we will make sure to go at your pace. Always let me know when you want to take a break. Let's explore some goals for us to work on."*

_____

_____

Explanation of EMDR as in the Standard EMDR Protocol

Introduce EMDR therapy and explain the AIP concepts, function, and types of bilateral stimulation in your usual style, when appropriate.

> Say, *"When a trauma occurs, it seems to be locked in the nervous system with the original picture, sounds, thoughts, and feelings. The eye movements we use in EMDR seem to unlock the nervous system and allow the brain to process the experience. That may be what is happening in REM or dream sleep—the eye movements may help to process the unconscious material. It is important to remember that it is your own brain that will be doing the healing and you are the one in control."*

> Say, *"BLS, or bilateral stimulation, is a component of EMDR therapy. It consists of eye movements, auditory tones, or tactile tapping. I'll show them all to you. We generally start with eye movements."*

> Say, *"EMDR therapy is an evidence-based therapy that is rated as highly effective in the treatment of trauma. As physical illnesses take a toll on the mind and body, they can be conceptualized as traumatic. Therefore, they are appropriate for EMDR treatment."*

Positive Healing Resources

Teach positive healing resources such as progressive muscle relaxation, slow deep breathing, and yoga breathing.

Say, *"These are strategies that will help you be calm and relaxed. You'll find a couple that you like and can practice at home in-between sessions. I will teach them to you now."*

PROGRESSIVE MUSCLE RELAXATION

Say, *"This is a gentle way to achieve relaxation. Just imagine the muscles in your head, scalp, and face feeling calm and relaxed, soft and loose. Now do the same with the muscles in your neck, shoulders, chest, arms, and back. Notice how that feels. Keep going slow until you reach your toes. Can you describe what that feels like? What are you noticing?"*

Note: If it seems safe and timely, introduce the idea of resourcing with BLS.

Say, *"Let's do a few sets of BLS to enhance your response."*

_____

_____

SLOW DEEP BREATHING

Say, *"Often when we are ill, stressed, and sleep deprived, we take shallow breaths and it's hard to relax. Here's another way to relax. Put one hand on your belly and notice what it feels like when you take a nice slow deep breath. As you inhale, notice your belly filling up with that breath and getting flat when you exhale. Try it a few times and see what you notice."*

_____

_____

_____

YOGA BREATHING

Say, *"Here is another easy breathing exercise. Watch me, and then you can try it. I'll breathe in and count to 4. Then I'll hold my breath to the count of 4 and breathe out to the count of 4.*

Now you try it. If 4 is too long, try counting to 3. Do that three times.

What did you notice when you tried that?"

_____

_____

COCOON OF LIGHT MEDITATION

Say, *"Find a comfortable position. With this exercise, we work with light as well as the breath. Take some slow gentle breaths. As you inhale, imagine a healing light of any color you like coming from the universe above, a spiritual place, or any source. Imagine the light forming a cocoon surrounding your entire body. Notice how that feels. If you like, you can imagine the cocoon of light entering your body and filling it with the same healing light. You can keep this light around you and keep gently breathing as long as you like."*

CALM SPACE

Teach the Calm Space exercise to your clients.

Say, *"Think about being in a place that feels calm and relaxing. Just notice what you see, feel, and even hear. You may notice emotions and physical sensations that feel comfortable. Let yourself enjoy them, and _____ (state BLS)."*

Do slow BLS.

Say, *"What do you notice now?"*

_____

_____

Say, *"Think of a word that represents your calm place. Focus on that and _____ (state BLS)."*
Do slow BLS.

Crisis Work: Immediate Need for Health Treatment in Any Phase

Teach how to deal with an upcoming visit to the medical/healthcare provider office, with medical and dental procedures, and so on. You are still working in Phases 1 to 3 and processing work has not begun. Remember, many CPTSD clients are avoidant of medical treatment.

Say, *"We've talked a little about going to the _____ (whatever health situation is upcoming). You've been feeling anxiety about keeping the appointment, and have described avoiding and not following up on healthcare before. Do you have a sense of why this happens?"* (Explore for future EMDR processing.)

_____

_____

Say, *"What do you think will help you get through this more easily? Please share your needs and concerns."*

_____

_____

_____

Utilize imaginal rehearsal of an office visit if appropriate (may be repeated as future template work). Introduce and use BLS if safe.

Say, *"Imagine the steps of making an appointment, asking questions of the doctor, telling the doctor your needs and concerns, having the work done, and seeing it go well. If there are problems, we'll try again."*

Say, *"How did you do?"*

_____

_____

If the client is still avoidant, introduce the "Constructive Avoidance of Present-Day Situations" exercise. This is an opportunity to introduce the concept of parts, ego states, and so on. The goal is to teach parts to stay safe when the client or "adult" has to do "adult tasks" such as visit a healthcare provider. This technique can be taught to all clients who become overly stressed in these situations.

Say, *"All of us have different parts of our personality. When we have a discussion in our heads, or are aware of two sides of a conflict, we can say that our parts are talking, or arguing. The argument could be about keeping the appointment. It might have to do with an old trauma. Later on, when the time is right, we can process these with EMDR. For now, the goal is to help you get through this _____ (state what client is preparing for) with more comfort."*

For dissociative clients:

Say, *"Due to the many traumatic events in your early life, many of your parts may not feel safe in a medical/dental setting and you are feeling their desire to avoid the situation. We can help them feel more comfortable."*

CONSTRUCTIVE AVOIDANCE OF PRESENT-DAY SITUATIONS SCRIPT

Note: This protocol assumes that clients have already established a home base (Forgash, 2009b) and workplace (Forgash, 2009c).

> Say, *"Okay, now that you have been working with your calm place for a while, let us put it to use in this situation of _____ (state the current situation that the client is concerned about). Bring up the calm place and just spend a little time there. We can teach your parts about a calm place that they can have for themselves. Can you suggest a place that they might like for their calm place? It could be a house in the country or on the beach. Imagine showing your parts that place and have them visit the ____ (state the place). Show them the family room and kitchen. Ask them what they would like in the place. Tell them that you can use it for meetings, for fun, whatever they would like."*

> _____

> _____

Option:
If a real event is going to occur relatively soon, use the real event.

> Say, *"If no real event is going to occur soon, you can make one up just for practice. What would you like to use for a practice situation?"*

> _____

> _____

> Say, *"Chances are some of your parts or ego states are not ready to deal with this situation. How about this? The day of the appointment, they will remain at their calm place while you deal with the present situation and go to _____ (state the current situation that the client is concerned about)."*

> _____

Let's invite them to listen in as we work on this.

> Say, *"I would like to tell you about a new way to work with _____ (state the upcoming situation)."*

> Say, *"This is just an imaginary practice session. You can remind parts that they don't have to listen if they don't want to. Is that all right with everyone?"*

> _____

> _____

If appropriate, say the following:

> Say, *"Tell them that they have the choice of watching what will happen on a screen or not watching. Or you could ask them what would they like to do while they are at their calm place and you are at _____ (state where you will be, such as doctor, dentist, etc.)."*

> _____

> _____

Say, *"Okay, tell the parts that you will always, when possible, tell them when you are go-ing to have a situation that you have to deal with but for which they don't need to be present. They can stay at the calm place."*

_____

_____

Say, *"Remind them that they are always with you, but by staying 'at the calm place,' they don't have to 'be' at the* _____ *(state the kinds of situations that they might have to encounter) or even pay attention to the situation while it is happening."*

_____

_____

Say, *"Also, you might tell them that you will always let them know when the situation or event has been completed. If you would like, you can ask them what they think about this idea."*

_____

_____

Say, *"Another choice is to let the parts know that sometimes they might want one part to take care of everyone while you are at the* _____ *(state where you will be). Who could that be? Does anyone want to volunteer?"*

_____

_____

Say, *"Tell the parts in words they can understand what is going to occur. For example, if you are going for a dental checkup and you know that in the past you have felt some anxiety but not too much, let them know this is what usually happens. Otherwise, use a practice situation."*

_____

_____

Say, *"Let's practice by imagining together that* _____ *('I am go-ing to the dentist in 2 weeks' or use as an example any appropriate task that needs to be done). It's only for* _____ *(a checkup or state the purpose).* _____ *('The dentist will just look at my teeth and take an x-ray' or state the appropriate task.) What would you like to do at home while I'm getting my* _____ *(checkup or state the activity)?"*

_____

_____

Say, *"Tell them, if they like, that they can watch the TV screen now and you can show them what the* _____ *(checkup or state the activity) will look like."*

_____

_____

Say, *"Anyone who doesn't want to watch doesn't have to. Remind them that they can say,'s Stop!' at any time. Play a short movie* _____ *(of going to the dentist,* sitting in the waiting room, or state the appropriate task). *Going into the* _____ (office or other relevant area). *Telling the* _____ (dentist or relevant person) *that you want them to 'Stop!' when you put your hand up and to always tell you what will be happening.* _____ (show the dentist looking at your teeth and the hygienist taking an x-ray or whatever relevant action). *Let them see you are leaving* _____ (the office or the relevant area). *Ask them what they noticed about how things went. You can go ahead and do that now."*

_____

_____

Say, *"Do you have any questions before you start?"*

_____

_____

Say, *"Is there anything else they need to help them be okay that day?"*

_____

_____

Say, *"If all is well, ask them what feels good about what they did today."*

_____

_____

This can be enhanced with a few short sets of BLS.

Say, *"When the day of the appointment arrives, tell the parts, 'I'll tell you when I'm leaving to go there and I'll let you know when I leave the* _____ (dentist's office or wherever they are going). *Is that okay with all of you?'"*

_____

_____

Say, *"Remind them that there will be opportunities to practice at the next session and at home. Ask if there are any more questions, and if there are, go ahead and discuss them."*

_____

_____

Debrief with a relaxation exercise and reminder to practice at home.

Say, *"Is there anything else that happened today that you feel is important and we should address, or are there any parts who have something to say or have questions?"*

_____

_____

Say, *"Okay, let's end with a relaxation exercise. You can choose from the ones that we have worked on before such as your safe or comfortable space, progressive muscle relaxation, slow deep breathing, yoga breathing (breathe in to the count of 4, hold to the count of 4,* breathe out to the count of 4), *finding the relaxed place in the body and gently focusing on that place or another one that you would find helpful, or any other relaxation exercises. Which one would you like to do today?"*

_____

_____

When the client chooses one, go through the closing exercise. Always use this as a time to check in with the system to make sure that everyone is okay before leaving the session. This is a good safety measure and models for everyone how to take care of themselves.

After doing the closing exercise, say the following:

"Okay, I would like to check in with everyone to make sure that all of you are okay before you leave the session. How are you doing?"

_____

_____

Say, *"I would like to remind you before you leave that you can practice this exercise at home this week."*

_____

Phase 3: Assessment

Note: For complex trauma/dissociative clients, dissociated ego states may need to work together on a target. Or several ego states with the same issue may work together to promote internal connection and cohesion.

Say, *"From what you have told me, you were traumatized by _____* (state if it was abuse, rape, abandonment, etc.) *several times. Let's talk with the parts and see if it would be helpful if those parts who were traumatized in the same ways would like to work."*

_____

_____

Say, *"Let's talk about the traumas we need to reprocess concerning your personal health. We can talk about current health issues and old childhood traumas and decide the sequence of processing."*

List of Traumas to Reprocess

_____

_____

_____

Choose the target with which to begin and do the assessment.

Example:

Say, *"We've been talking about your current medical problems and how that affects you. With which concern would you like to begin?"*

_____

_____

Say, *"What happens when you think of* _____ *(state the issue)?"*

_____

_____

Say, *"Or you may want to bring up the earliest time you had this* _____ *(state the issue)."*

_____

_____

Or say, *"When you think of* _____ *(state the issue), what do you get?"*

_____

_____

Picture

Say, *"What picture represents the entire* _____ *(state the issue)?"*

_____

_____

Say, *"What picture represents the most traumatic part of* _____ *(state the issue)?"*

_____

_____

Negative Cognition

Say, *"What words best go with the picture that express your negative belief about yourself now?"*

_____

_____

Positive Cognition

Say, *"When you bring up that picture or* _____ *(state the issue), what would you like to believe about yourself, now?"*

_____

_____

Validity of Cognition (VOC)

Say, *"When you think of* _____ *(state the issue or picture), how true do those words* _____ *(clinician repeats the PC) feel to you now on a scale of 1 to 7, where 1 feels completely false and 7 feels completely true?"*

1	2	3	4	5	6	7
(completely false)				(completely true)		

Sometimes, it is necessary to explain further.

Say, *"Remember, sometimes we know something with our head, but it feels differently in our gut. In this case, what is the gut-level feeling of the truth of* _____ *(clinician states the PC), from 1 (completely false) to 7 (completely true)?"*

1	2	3	4	5	6	7

(completely false)   (completely true)

Emotions

Say, *"When you bring up the picture or* _____ *(state the issue) and those words* _____ *(clinician states the NC), what emotion do you feel now?"*

_____

_____

Subjective Units of Disturbance (SUD)

Say, *"On a scale of 0 to 10, where 0 is no disturbance or neutral and 10 is the highest disturbance you can imagine, how disturbing does it feel now?"*

0	1	2	3	4	5	6	7	8	9	10

(no disturbance)   (highest disturbance)

Location of Body Sensation

Say, *"Where do you feel it* (the disturbance) *in your body?"*

_____

_____

Say, *"Please list the adverse life experiences/small 't' traumas we need to reprocess."*

List of Adverse Life Experiences/Small "t" Traumas to Reprocess

_____

_____

_____

_____

Choose the target with which to begin and do the assessment as earlier.

Say, *"Please list the important losses we need to reprocess."*

List of Important Losses

_____

_____

_____

_____

_____

Choose the target with which to begin and do the assessment as earlier.

> Say, *"Please list the missed opportunities, regrets, and remorse about poor health we need to reprocess."*

List of Missed Opportunities, Regrets, and Remorse About Poor Health

_____

_____

_____

_____

Choose the target with which to begin and do the assessment as earlier.

> Say, *"Please list the harmful habits we need to reprocess."*

List of Harmful Habits

_____

_____

_____

Choose the target with which to begin and do the assessment as earlier.

Phase 4: Desensitization

Note: Due to fatigue, confusion, and disorientation due to illness, plus the possibility of dissociation, it's often necessary to work in small segments and to let the client know that it is perfectly normal for him or her to ask to stop. Go over the stop sign. It may take many sessions to complete a target. This is common and needs to be normalized, as well.

> Say, *"Now, remember, it is your own brain that is doing the healing and you are the one in control. I will ask you to mentally focus on the target and to follow my fingers (or any other BLS you are using). Just let whatever happens, happen, and we will talk at the end of the set. Just tell me what comes up, and don't discard anything as unimportant. Any new information that comes to mind is connected in some way. If you want to stop, just raise your hand. Often, it is helpful to work in small segments. We can decide that as we go."*

> Then say, *"Bring up the picture and the words _____ (clinician repeats the NC) and notice where you feel it in your body. Now follow my fingers with your eyes (or other BLS)."*

_____

_____

Additionally and equally important is to look for signs of dissociation such as looking away, shutting down, being unable to communicate, and so on. This will necessitate using stabilization interventions to bring the person back to present orientation. When this occurs in a processing session, these are the types of phrases you can use to support the processing with your client. Say any of these phrases as you will learn which work best with each client:

- *"What are you feeling in your body?"*
- *"Where are you right now?"*
- *"Let's use the Back-of-the-Head scale."**
- *"Is there a part who needs to talk right now?"*

---

* Note: "Back-of-the-Head scale" refers to Knipe (2008).

Or use physically based strategies as the following:

- *"Tap your feet."*
- *"Here, catch this ball."*
- *"Listen to the clock ticking."*

Then, if possible, return to processing and say any of the following:

Say, *"Do you feel present in your body now?"*

_____

_____

Or, say, *"What did you notice when we worked on helping you come back to the present?"*

_____

_____

Or, say, *"What are you noticing now?"*

_____

_____

Say, *"Let's go back to the target or the processing."*

_____

_____

If necessary, close down the session with a relaxation exercise that can include the ego states.

Say, *"You have worked very hard today. Why don't you go back to a calm place and help the parts who were here today go back to their calm place? Remind them that this is a private place for them totally unknown to anyone but you and them. Let them know that you will check in occasionally and that we'll continue working together at the next session."*

_____

_____

Phase 5: Installation

Say, *"How does* _____ *(repeat the PC)* sound?"

_____

_____

Say, *"Do the words* _____ *(repeat the PC)* still fit, or is there another positive state-ment that feels better?"

_____

_____

If the client accepts the original PC, the clinician should ask for a VOC rating to see if it has improved:

Say, *"As you think of the incident, how do the words feel, from 1 (completely false) to 7 (completely true)?"*

1	2	3	4	5	6	7

(completely false)   (completely true)

Say, *"Think of the event and hold it together with the words _____ (repeat the PC)."*

_____

_____

Do a long set of BLS to see if there is more processing to be done.

Phase 6: Body Scan

Say, *"Close your eyes and keep in mind the original memory and the PC. Then bring your attention to the different parts of your body, starting with your head and working downward. Any place you find any tension, tightness, or unusual sensation, tell me."*

Phase 7: Closure

Say, *"Things may come up or they may not. If they do, great. Write it down and it can be a target for the next time. You can use a notebook or journal to write down triggers, images, thoughts or cognitions, emotions, and sensations; you can rate them on our 0-to-10 scale, where 0 is no disturbance or neutral and 10 is the worst disturbance. Please write down the positive experiences, too."*

Say, *"If you get any new memories, dreams, or situations that disturb you, just take a good snapshot. It isn't necessary to give a lot of detail. Just put down enough to remind you so we can target it the next time. The same thing goes for any positive dreams or situations. If negative feelings do come up, try not to make them significant. Remember, it's still just the old stuff. Just write it down for the next time. Then use the tape or the Safe Place exercise to let as much of the disturbance go as possible. Even if nothing comes up, make sure to use the tape every day and give me a call if you need to."*

Phase 8: Reevaluation

Present Stimuli That Trigger the Disturbing Memory or Reaction

List the situations that elicit the symptom(s). Examples of situations, events, or stimuli that trigger clients could be the following: another trauma, the sound of a car backfiring, or being touched in a certain way.

Say, *"What are the situations, events, or stimuli that trigger your trauma _____ (state the trauma)? Let's process these situations, events, or stimuli triggers one by one."*

_____

_____

Fears About Present and Future Due to Permanent Physical Damage Trigger List

Say, *"What are the fears you have about the present and future due to permanent physical damage?"*

_____

_____

Say, *"What are the problems that trigger you?"*

_____

_____

Problems Trigger List

_____

_____

_____

Target or Memory

Say, *"What situation, event, or stimulus that triggers you would you like to use as a target today?"*

_____

Picture

Say, *"What picture represents the _____ (state the situation, event, or stimulus) that triggers you?"*

_____

If there are many choices or if the client becomes confused, the clinician assists by asking the following:

Say, *"What picture represents the most traumatic part of the _____ (state the situation, event, or stimulus) that triggers you?"*

When a picture is unavailable, the clinician merely invites the client to do the following:

Say, *"Think of the _____ (state the situation, event, or stimulus) that triggers you."*

Negative Cognition

Say, *"What words best go with the picture that express your negative belief about yourself now?"*

_____

Positive Cognition

Say, *"When you bring up that picture or the _____ (state the situation, event, or stimulus) that triggers you, what would you like to believe about yourself now?"*

_____

Validity of Cognition

Say, *"When you think of the _____ (state the situation, event, stimulus, or picture that triggers you), how true do those words _____ (clinician repeats the positive cognition) feel to you now on a scale of 1 to 7, where 1 feels completely false and 7 feels completely true?"*

1	2	3	4	5	6	7

(completely false)   (completely true)

Sometimes, it is necessary to explain further.

> Say, *"Remember, sometimes we know something with our head, but it feels differently in our gut. In this case, what is the gut-level feeling of the truth of* _____ (clinician states the PC), *from 1* (completely false) *to 7* (completely true)?"

> 1   2   3   4   5   6   7

> (completely false)   (completely true)

Emotions

> Say, *"When you bring up the picture* (or state the situation, event, or stimulus) *that triggers you and those words* _____ (clinician states the NC), *what emotion do you feel now?"*

_____

Subjective Units of Disturbance

> Say, *"On a scale of 0 to 10, where 0 is no disturbance or neutral and 10 is the highest disturbance you can imagine, how disturbing does it feel now?"*

> 0   1   2   3   4   5   6   7   8   9   10

> (no disturbance)   (highest disturbance)

Location of Body Sensation

> Say, *"Where do you feel it* (the disturbance) *in your body?"*

_____

Continue to process the triggers according to the Standard EMDR Protocol.

FUTURE TEMPLATE SCRIPT

Fears of Being Alone and Unsupported List

> Say, *"Please note any fears you have of your illness or medical condition reoccurring."*

_____

_____

Fears of Recurrence of the Illness or Medical Condition

> Say, *"Please note any fears you have of your illness or medical condition reoccurring."*

_____

_____

Check the Significant People and Situations of the Presenting Issues for Any Type of Distress

It is helpful to check to see if all the material concerning the issue upon which the client has worked is resolved or if there is more material that has escaped detection so far. The future template is another place to find if there is more material that needs reprocessing.

Significant People

When the client's work has focused on a significant person, ask the following:

> Say, *"Imagine yourself encountering that person in the future _____ (suggest a place where the client might see this person). What do you notice?"*

_____

_____

Watch the client's reaction to see if more work is necessary. If a client describes a negative feeling in connection with this person, check to see if it is reality based.

> Say, *"Is _____ (state the person's name) likely to act _____ (state the client's concern)?"*

_____

_____

If the negative feeling is not matching the current reality, say the following:

> *"What do you think makes you have negative feelings toward _____ (state the person in question)?"*

_____

_____

If the client is unsure, use the floatback technique or affect scan to see what other earlier material may still be active.

> Say, *"Please bring up that picture of ____ (state image) and those negative words_____, ____ (repeat client's disturbing image and NC); notice what feelings are coming up for you, where you are feeling them in your body; and just let your mind float back to an earlier time in your life—don't search for anything—just let your mind float back and tell me the first scene that comes to mind where you had similar:*
>
> *Thoughts of ___ (repeat NC)*
> *Feelings of ___ (repeat emotions stated previously)*
> *In your ____ (repeat places in the body where the client reported feelings)."*

If the negative feelings are appropriate, it is important to reevaluate the clusters of events concerning this person and access and reprocess any remaining maladaptive memories. (See Past Memory Worksheet.)

_____

_____

Significant Situations

> Say, *"Please list the skills needed to be learned and practiced."*

SKILLS NEEDED TO BE LEARNED AND PRACTICED LIST

_____

_____

_____

Say, *"Please list any projected future situations of concern such as physical therapy, other rehabilitation, diagnosis, testing, family occasions, returning to work, becoming well again, and so on."*

PROJECTED FUTURE SITUATION LIST

(Physical therapy, other rehabilitation, diagnosis, testing, family occasions, returning to work, becoming well again, etc.)

_____

_____

_____

It is important to have the client imagine being in significant situations in the future; this is another way of accessing material that may not have been processed.

Say, *"Imagine a videotape or film of how _____ (state the current situation client is working on) and how it would evolve _____ (state the appropriate time frame) in the future. When you have done that, let me know what you have noticed."*

_____

If there is no disturbance, reinforce the positive experience.

Say, *"Go with that."*

Do BLS.

Reinforce the PC with the future situation with BLS as it continues the positive associations. For further work in the future, see later in the text.

If there is a disturbance, assess what the client needs: more education, modeling of appropriate behavior, or more past memories for reprocessing.

Say, *"On a scale of 0 to 10, where 0 is no disturbance or neutral and 10 is the highest disturbance you can imagine, how disturbing does it feel now?"*

0   1   2   3   4   5   6   7   8   9   10

(no disturbance)   (highest disturbance)

Anticipatory Anxiety

When the SUD is above 4, or when the desensitization phase is not brief, the clinician should look for a present trigger and its associated symptom and develop another targeting sequence plan using the Three-Pronged Protocol. (See worksheets on Past Memories and Present Triggers.)

When there is anticipatory anxiety at an SUD level of no more than 3 to 4 maximum, it is possible to proceed with reprocessing using the future template. The desensitization phase should be quite brief.

Say, *"What happens when you think of _____ (state the client's anticipatory anxiety or issue)?"*

_____

Or say, *"When you think of _____ (state the client's anticipatory anxiety or issue), what do you get?"*

_____

_____

Picture

Say, *"What picture represents the entire _____ (state the client's anticipatory anxiety or issue)?"*

_____

_____

If there are many choices or if the client becomes confused, the clinician assists by asking the following:

Say, *"What picture represents the most traumatic part of _____ (state the client's anticipatory anxiety or issue)?"*

_____

_____

Negative Cognition

Say, *"What words best go with the picture that express your negative belief about yourself now?"*

_____

_____

Positive Cognition

Say, *"When you bring up that picture or_____ (state the client's anticipatory anxiety or issue), what would you like to believe about yourself now?"*

_____

_____

Validity of Cognition

Say, *"When you think of _____ (state the client's anticipatory anxiety or issue) or picture, how true do those words _____ (clinician repeats the PC) feel to you now on a scale of 1 to 7, where 1 feels completely false and 7 feels completely true?"*

1	2	3	4	5	6	7

(completely false)   (completely true)

Emotions

Say, *"When you bring up the picture or _____ (state the client's anticipatory anxiety or issue) and those words _____ (clinician states the NC), what emotion do you feel now?"*

Subjective Units of Disturbance

Say, *"On a scale of 0 to 10, where 0 is no disturbance or neutral and 10 is the highest disturbance you can imagine, how disturbing does it feel now?"*

0	1	2	3	4	5	6	7	8	9	10

(no disturbance)   (highest disturbance)

Location of Body Sensation

Say, *"Where do you feel it* (the disturbance) *in your body?"*

_____

_____

Use the Standard EMDR Protocol.

Video Check (Future Template as Movie)

Say, *"This time, I'd like you to imagine yourself stepping into the scene of a future confrontation with the object or the situation for which the future template was meant* (e.g., to focus on illness/future challenges). *Close your eyes and play a movie of this happening, from the beginning until the end. Imagine yourself coping with any challenges that come your way. Notice what you are seeing, thinking, feeling, and experiencing in your body. While playing this movie, let me know if you hit any blocks. If you do, just open your eyes and let me know. If you don't hit any blocks, let me know when you have viewed the whole movie."*

_____

_____

If the client encounters a block and opens her eyes, this is a sign for the therapist to instruct the client to say the following:

"Say to yourself 'I can handle it' and follow my fingers (introduce a set of eye movements)."

To provide the clinician with an indication regarding the client's self-efficacy, ask her to rate her response on a VOC scale from 1 to 7. This procedural step may give the clinician feedback on the extent to which the goals are met.

Say, *"As you think of the incident, how do the words feel from 1 being completely false to 7 being completely true?"*

| 1 | 2 | 3 | 4 | 5 | 6 | 7 |

(completely false)   (completely true)

If the client is able to play the movie from start to finish with a sense of confidence and satisfaction, the client is asked to play the movie once more from the beginning to the end, BLS is introduced, and the PC, "I can handle it," is installed. In a sense, this movie is installed as a future template.

Say, *"Okay, play the movie one more time from beginning to end and say to yourself, 'I can handle it.' Go with that."*

_____

_____

SUMMARY

The intent of this chapter is to provide information that will help EMDR therapists enhance their ability to provide effective EMDR treatment for clients diagnosed with complex trauma who are also dealing with current health problems. The use of the ACE questionnaire, which provides much needed information on childhood abuse, neglect, attachment disorders, PTSD, and dissociation, is highlighted. This questionnaire, when combined with a broad developmental and health history, will be very helpful in case conceptualization and development of targets for work in Phases 4 to 7. Additionally, the author describes the links between the ACE issues and later health risks and problems that make these clients difficult to treat. Add to these issues with trust and relationship problems, and it is easy to recognize why these clients have had historical problems with accessing good healthcare. They deserve the best that we can give them.

Working with complex trauma clients who are also dealing with illness can be stressful, frustrating, and exhausting. It is important for us to be supported as we do this important, but difficult work. It is vital to seek consultation, peer support, and other aids (i.e., attending conferences, reading) to help us thrive in our work.

REFERENCES

Bergmann, U. (2012). *Neurobiological foundations for EMDR practice.* New York, NY: Springer Publishing.

Borysenko, J. (1988). *Stress reduction through visual imagery.* Presentation in Long Island, New York, NY.

Chefetz, R. (2015). *Intensive psychotherapy for persistent dissociative processes: The fear of feeling real.* New York, NY: W. W. Norton.

Felitti, V. J., Anda, R. F., Nordenberg, D., Williamson, D. F., Spitz, A. M., Edwards, V., . . . Marks, J. S. (1998). Relationship of childhood abuse and household dysfunction to many of the leading causes of death in adults. *American Journal of Prevention Medicine, 14*(4), 245–258. doi:10.1016/s0749-3797(98)00017-8

Forgash, C. (2009a). Stabilization phase of trauma treatment. In M. Luber (Ed.), *EMDR scripted protocols: Special populations* (pp. 209–233). New York, NY: Springer Publishing.

Forgash, C. (2009b). Home base. In M. Luber (Ed.), *EMDR scripted protocols: Special populations* (pp. 217–220). New York, NY: Springer Publishing.

Forgash, C. (2009c). Workplace or conference room. In M. Luber (Ed.), *EMDR scripted protocols: Special populations* (pp. 217–220). New York, NY: Springer Publishing.

Forgash, C. (2017). Breaking the ACE cycle of poor health. Distance learning course. Retrieved from https://advancededucationalproductions.com/the-ace-adverse-childhood-experiences-study-and-emdr/

Forgash, C., & Copley, M. (2008). *Healing the heart of trauma and dissociation with EMDR and ego state therapy.* New York, NY. Springer Publishing.

Grant, M. (2009). *Change your brain, change your pain.* Vermont South, Vic, Australia: Book POD.

Knipe, J. (2008). Loving eyes. In C. Forgash & M. Copeley (Eds.), *Healing the heart of trauma and dissociation with EMDR and ego state therapy* (pp. 109–203). New York, NY: Springer Publishing.

Levine, P. (2010). *In an unspoken voice. How the body releases trauma and restores goodness* (pp. 73–83). Berkeley, CA: North Atlantic Books.

Scaer, R. (2005). *The trauma spectrum.* New York, NY: W. W. Norton.

Scaer, R. (2007). *The body bears the burden* (2nd ed.). New York, NY: Routledge.

Servan-Schreiber, D. (2004). *The instinct to heal: Curing stress, anxiety and depression without drugs and without talk therapy.* Emmaus, PA: Rodale.

Siegel, B. (1988). *Love, medicine and miracles.* New York, NY: Harper.

Simonton, C. (1978). *Getting well again.* New York, NY: Bantam.

Carol Forgash
SUMMARY SHEET BY MARILYN LUBER

Name: _____ Diagnosis: _____

Medications: _____

Test Results: _____

☑ Check when task is completed, response has changed, or to indicate symptoms.

☑ **Note:** This material is meant as a checklist for your response. Please keep in mind that it is only a reminder of different tasks that may or may not apply to your incident.

INTRODUCTION

Issues for the complex trauma/ACE survivor client, which can be targeted with EMDR therapy, include the following:

- ☐ Serious illness
- ☐ Untreated medical or dental symptoms
- ☐ Untreated substance abuse
- ☐ Lack of skills related to hygiene and healthcare
- ☐ Other health risk behaviors
- ☐ Avoidance of health treatment
- ☐ Lack of follow through
- ☐ Current accidents
- ☐ Illnesses
- ☐ Hospitalizations

Another set of problems for complex trauma patients involves difficult-to-diagnose illnesses or conditions. They are typically called medically unexplained symptoms (MUS) such as the following:

- ☐ Respiratory illness
- ☐ Musculoskeletal complaints
- ☐ Chronic pain
- ☐ Fibromyalgia
- ☐ Chronic fatigue
- ☐ Eating disorders
- ☐ Headaches
- ☐ Irritable bowel syndrome
- ☐ Gynecological problems including pregnancy

- ☐ Regional pain syndromes
- ☐ Pseudo-neurological symptoms
- ☐ Sleep disorders

Dissociation is a way that the CPTSD client copes. Symptoms include the following (Forgash, 2009a):

- ☐ Hyper- or hypo-arousal/numbing
- ☐ "Out of body" experiences
- ☐ Not being present in the body
- ☐ Losing time
- ☐ "Going away" when stressed
- ☐ Depersonalization/derealization
- ☐ Looking "different" in session
- ☐ Hearing "voices"

Somatic Dissociation

- ☐ Perceptual alterations
- ☐ Somatic symptoms
- ☐ Depersonalization of body part
- ☐ Fragmented images of the traumatic event that produced the pain or injury
- ☐ Current injury may be in same areas as earlier accident/traumatic event but may have amnesia

CPTSD, PERSONAL HEALTH, AND EMDR THERAPY SCRIPT NOTES

When making treatment-planning decisions, remember it is a cooperative process. Determine if health issues are related to the following:

- ☐ Developmental/attachment trauma
- ☐ Shock trauma (including iatrogenic shock treatment)
- ☐ Normal health issues that the client is lacking skills to deal with
- ☐ Family illnesses/patterns
- ☐ Chronic health problems
- ☐ Pain issues

Which targets take precedence?

- ☐ Adverse life experiences/small "t" trauma clusters concerning health and losses from earlier times
- ☐ Current life issues and illnesses
- ☐ Large "T" trauma, current and past
- ☐ Recent incidents/illnesses/injuries
- ☐ Health problems related to similar/earlier incidents

Certain types of *negative and positive cognitions* come up frequently in this population:

- ☐ Avoidance of treatment due to prior interactions with healthcare providers
  NC: "I am not safe. I am not worth it."
  PC: "I am safe now. I'm worth it."
- ☐ History of being labeled and misinterpreted
  NC: "It is all in my head."
  PC: "My medical problems are real. I'm worth listening to."
- ☐ History of abandonment
  NC: "I am always going to be alone. I will die alone."
  PC. "I deserve support. I can start to connect with people."
- ☐ Fear of exams/procedures provoking flashbacks/dissociation
  NC: "I am crazy. No one will understand me."
  PC: "I can advocate for myself and be understood."
- ☐ Chronic illness/pain
  NC: "It will never get any better. I am going to die."
  PC: "I can cope with my situation."

☐ Losses, including identity
  NC: "I have lost too much."
  PC: "I can find a way to still be myself. I'm still able to have a life."

Introduce dissociative and affect management strategies to help the client stay in the optimum window of arousal.

☐ Resource development and installation
☐ Ego-building activities
☐ Mindfulness activities
☐ Learning to control stressful feelings and pain (Grant, 2009)
☐ Healing imagery (Siegel, 1988; Simonton, 1978)
☐ Positive body resource exercise (Levine, 2010)
☐ Cocoon of light healing exercise; meditation practices
☐ Safety/distancing work (containers, affect dial/screen work); Back-of-the-Head scale; journaling, drawing, mapping [Forgash & Copley, 2008])
☐ Heart coherence exercise (Servan-Schreiber, 2004)

CPTSD, PERSONAL HEALTH, AND EMDR THERAPY SCRIPT

Adverse Childhood Experience (ACE) Questionnaire Score = _____

See the questionnaire in the chapter for questions.

General Medical Questions:

Health issues in early childhood: _____

_____

Fevers: ☐ Yes ☐ No

Comment: _____

Serious falls: ☐ Yes ☐ No

Comment: _____

Hospitalizations: ☐ Yes ☐ No

Describe if yes: _____

_____

Recurrent illnesses and/or situations that the physician induced or that cause problems:

☐ Yes ☐ No

Comment: _____

Painful conditions: ☐ Yes ☐ No

Comment: _____

Current problems including pain and disability: _____

_____

Serious illnesses or surgeries: ☐ Yes ☐ No

Describe mental health: _____

_____

Been in therapy: ☐ Yes ☐ No

Comment: _____

Drugs, alcohol, or eating disorders: ☐ Yes ☐ No

Comment: _____

Health of close family members (serious illness, substance abuse, eating disorder, mental health issue, medical or dental problems): _____

_____

_____

_____

_____

Deaths in family, especially when child: _____ ☐ Yes ☐ No

Comment: _____

Close friends or family went away or came and went frequently: ☐ Yes ☐ No

Comment: _____

HEALTH PRACTICES QUESTIONS

Taught regular basic hygienic routines: ☐ Yes ☐ No

Comment: _____

Went regularly to doctor and dentist when young: ☐ Yes ☐ No

Comment: _____

Last dental and medical exams: _____

_____

OTHER HEALTH RISK BEHAVIORS

"Some risky health habits include using drugs or alcohol, having unprotected sex, any eating disorders, or cutting. Have you had some of these problems?":   ☐ Yes ☐ No

Comment: _____

AVOIDANCE OF HEALTH TREATMENT

History of avoiding medical care?:   ☐ Yes ☐ No

Comment: _____

LACK OF FOLLOW THROUGH

Problem following doctor's suggestions or taking medications?:   ☐ Yes ☐ No

Comment: _____

CURRENT ACCIDENTS

Recent accidents?:   ☐ Yes ☐ No

Comment: _____

ILLNESSES

Recent illnesses?:   ☐ Yes ☐ No

Comment: _____

HOSPITALIZATIONS

Recent hospitalizations?:   ☐ Yes ☐ No

Comment: _____

"Have you ever been ill with any of the following?"

- ☐ Respiratory illness
- ☐ Musculoskeletal and joint complaints
- ☐ Chronic pain
- ☐ Fibromyalgia
- ☐ Chronic fatigue
- ☐ Eating disorders
- ☐ Headaches
- ☐ Irritable bowel syndrome
- ☐ Gynecological problems including pregnancy
- ☐ Regional pain syndromes
- ☐ Pseudo-neurological symptoms
- ☐ Sleep disorders
- ☐ Rheumatoid arthritis
- ☐ Thyroid diseases
- ☐ Crohn's disease

Check if you have these symptoms:

Hyper/hypo-arousal/numbing: ☐ Yes ☐ No

Describe: _____

_____

"Out of Body" experiences: ☐ Yes ☐ No

Describe: _____

_____

Not being present in the body: ☐ Yes ☐ No

Describe: _____

_____

Losing time: ☐ Yes ☐ No

Describe: _____

_____

"Going away" when stressed: ☐ Yes ☐ No

Describe: _____

_____

Depersonalization/derealization: ☐ Yes ☐ No

Describe: _____

_____

Looking "different" in session: ☐ Yes ☐ No

Describe: _____

_____

Hearing "voices": ☐ Yes ☐ No

Describe: _____

_____

Perceptual alterations: ☐ Yes ☐ No

Describe: _____

_____

Somatic Symptoms: ☐ Yes ☐ No

Describe: _____

_____

Client's Supports, Skills, and Strengths

Current supports in life: _____

_____

Past supports in life: _____

_____

Describe your skills and strengths: _____

_____

Phase 2: Preparation

Psychoeducation

"This work will take several sessions or longer to communicate these very important concepts or information with patients. Some of it could be 'triggering' or upsetting. Slow is best. People who have physical illness tire easily and have less energy, focus, and retention."

Psychoeducation About Patient Rights: ☐ Yes ☐ No

"Clients have rights as health consumers. Every one of your health providers should give you and discuss the Client Bill of Rights. You need to read it and ask questions about anything you don't understand."

Psychoeducation About Becoming a Proactive Health Consumer: ☐ Yes ☐ No

"One of the things you can do is bring a friend or family member with you to the doctor's office. When you are not feeling well, it's easier to misunderstand or be confused. You can make up a list of questions and concerns to discuss at the visit. Or we can do that as well.

In our community you will find associations such as the (state the one that is appropriate: American Cancer Society, AA, the American Heart Association, etc.). *They offer many kinds of services and education. It might be helpful for you to contact them. Would you be interested in speaking with them?"*

Psychoeducation About General Health, Stress and Pain, Normalizing Trauma Symptoms, and Their Effects on Health and Stress Reduction Work: ☐ Yes ☐ No

"We know that trauma, stress, and pain all have an effect on health. What do you do in your life now to help yourself be healthy? Have you tried exercise, meditation, or relaxing imagery? We can work on some of these strategies in the office.

Psychoeducation About Psychosomatic Symptoms: ☐ Yes ☐ No

Psychosomatic problems or conditions are generally affected by stress. Do you think that stress is a factor in your situation?   ☐ Yes ☐ No

If so, how does it affect you? _____

_____

Psychoeducation About Goal Setting, Hopes, and Plans: ☐ Yes ☐ No

"Having health issues can make you fatigued, so we will make sure to go at your pace. Always let me know when you want to take a break. Let's explore some goals for us to work on."

Explanation of EMDR as in the Standard EMDR Protocol: ☐ Yes ☐ No

"When a trauma occurs, it seems to be locked in the nervous system with the original picture, sounds, thoughts, and feelings. The eye movements we use in EMDR seem to unlock the nervous system and allow the brain to process the experience. That may be what is happening in REM or dream sleep—the eye movements may help to process the unconscious material. It is important to remember that it is your own brain that will be doing the healing and you are the one in control.

BLS, or bilateral stimulation, is a component of EMDR therapy. It consists of eye movements, auditory tones, or tactile tapping. I'll show them all to you. We generally start with eye movements.

EMDR therapy is an evidence-based therapy that is rated as highly effective in the treatment of trauma. As physical illnesses take a toll on the mind and body, they can be conceptualized as traumatic. Therefore, they are appropriate for EMDR treatment."

Positive Healing Resources

PROGRESSIVE MUSCLE RELAXATION

"This is a gentle way to achieve relaxation. Just imagine the muscles in your head, scalp, and face feeling calm and relaxed, soft, and loose. Now do the same with the muscles in your neck, shoulders, chest, arms, and back. Notice how that feels. Keep going slow until you reach your toes. Can you describe what that feels like? What are you noticing? + BLS."

SLOW DEEP BREATHING

"Often when we are ill, stressed, and sleep deprived, we take shallow breaths and it's hard to relax. Here's another way to relax. Put one hand on your belly and notice what it feels like when you take a nice slow deep breath. As you inhale, notice your belly filling up with that breath and getting flat when you exhale. Try it a few times and see what you notice."

YOGA BREATHING

"Here is another easy breathing exercise. Watch me, and then you can try it. I'll breathe in and count to 4. Then I'll hold my breath to the count of 4 and breathe out to the count of 4. Now you try it. If 4 is too long, try counting to 3. Do that three times. What did you notice when you tried that?"

COCOON OF LIGHT MEDITATION

"Find a comfortable position. With this exercise, we work with light as well as the breath. Take some slow gentle breaths. As you inhale, imagine a healing light of any color you like coming from the universe above, a spiritual place, or any source. Imagine the light forming a cocoon surrounding your entire body. Notice how that feels. If you like, you can imagine the cocoon of light entering your body and filling it with the same healing light. You can keep this light around you and keep gently breathing as long as you like."

CALM SPACE

Teach the Calm Space exercise to your clients.

"Think about being in a place that feels calm and relaxing. Just notice what you see, feel, and even hear. You may notice emotions and physical sensations that feel comfortable. Let yourself enjoy them, and follow my fingers. (Slow BLS) What do you notice now?" _____

_____

"Think of a word that represents your calm place." _____

Focus on that + BLS

Crisis Work: Immediate Need for Health Treatment in Any Phase

☐ Visit to medical/healthcare provider office

☐ Imaginal rehearsal of an office visit, if appropriate

Note: This protocol assumes that clients have already established a home base (Forgash, 2009b) and workplace (Forgash, 2009c).

Constructive Avoidance of Present-Day Situations Accomplished: ☐ Yes ☐ No

Real/practice situation: _____

_____

Let clients know whether it is a real/practice situation: ☐ Real ☐ Practice

Ego states not ready to go will remain at calm place: ☐ Yes ☐ No

_____

Invite all to the calm place to learn about a new way to deal with present-day situations.

Choice of watching on screen/what would they like to do while client is at ___ (state). _____

_____

Tell parts when a situation will be coming up and they can stay home: ☐ Yes ☐ No

Tell parts always with you, but can stay at "home:"   ☐ Yes ☐ No

Tell parts will let them know when the situation is over: ☐ Yes ☐ No

Thinking: _____

Or there might be one part who takes care of everyone while you are at the ___ (state):

☐ Yes ☐ No

Who would the parts want to take care of them while you are at the __ (state)? _____

Tell them what to expect when ___ (state). _____

_____

Practice

Imagine going to __ (state the appointment you are going to) + What you would like to do at home while I am _____ (state)

State the activity: _____

Imagine it: _____

_____

Movie of activity going to do:

Parts participating: _____

Parts not participating: _____

Imagine ___ (state activity) + ___ (state what will happen) + What would you like to do when I am ___ (state activity)?_____

Practice activity and saying, "Stop!" (to relevant person) when they need to: ☐ Yes ☐ No

Let them see you leaving: ☐ Yes ☐ No

Questions

Anything else that needs to be okay: ☐ Yes ☐ No

What feels good about what they did: _____

Use BLS.

Day of activity/appointment

Tell when leaving to go: ☐ Yes ☐ No

Tell when leaving the ___ (state where went): ☐ Yes ☐ No

Agreement to do this: ☐ Yes ☐ No

Opportunities to practice at the next session and at home.

Debrief

Anything else to address or parts with questions/something to say: _____

_____

Relaxation Exercise

___ Calm place ____ Progressive muscle relaxation ___ Slow deep breathing ___ Yoga breathing ____

Finding the relaxed place in the body _____ Other

Check in with everyone to make sure okay: ☐ Okay ☐ Not okay

_____

Practice this exercise at home this week.

Phase 3: Assessment

List of Traumas to Reprocess

_____

_____

_____

Target/Memory/Image: _____

_____

NC: _____

PC: _____

VOC: ___/7

Emotions: _____

SUD: ___/10

Sensation: _____

List of Adverse Life Experiences/Small "t" Traumas to Reprocess

_____

_____

_____

Target/Memory/Image: _____

_____

NC: _____

PC: _____

VOC: ___/7

Emotions: _____

SUD: ___/10

Sensation: _____

List of Important Losses

_____

_____

_____

Target/Memory/Image: _____

_____

NC: _____

PC: _____

VOC: ___/7

Emotions: _____

SUD: ___/10

Sensation: _____

List of Missed Opportunities, Regrets, and Remorse About Poor Health

_____

_____

_____

Target/Memory/Image: _____

_____

NC: _____

PC: _____

VOC: ___/7

Emotions: _____

SUD: ___/10

Sensation: _____

List of Harmful Habits

_____

_____

_____

Target/Memory/Image: _____

_____

NC: _____

PC: _____

VOC: ___/7

Emotions: _____

SUD: ___/10

Sensation: _____

Phrases to bring the client into present orientation:

- ☐ *"What are you feeling in your body?"*
- ☐ *"Where are you right now?"*
- ☐ *"Let's use the Back-of-the Head scale."*
- ☐ *"Is there a part who needs to talk right now?"*

Or use physically based strategies as the following:

- ☐ *"Tap your feet."*
- ☐ *"Here, catch this ball."*
- ☐ *"Listen to the clock ticking."*

Phase 4: Desensitization

Apply the Standard EMDR Protocol for all targets.

Phase 5: Installation

Install the PC.

Original PC: ☐ Use original PC ☐ Use new PC

New PC (if new one is better): _____

VOC: ___/7

Incident + PC + BLS

Phase 6: Body Scan

Unresolved tension/tightness/unusual sensation: _____

_____

Unresolved tension/tightness/unusual sensation + BLS

Strengthen positive sensation using BLS.

If there is more discomfort, reprocess until discomfort subsides + BLS. Then repeat body scan.

VOC: ___/7

Phase 7: Closure

"Things may come up or they may not. If they do, great. Write it down and it can be a target for next time. You can use a log to write down triggers, images, thoughts or cognitions, emotions, and sensations; you can rate them on our 0-to-10 scale, where 0 is no disturbance or neutral and 10 is the worst disturbance. Please write down the positive experiences, too.

If you get any new memories, dreams, or situations that disturb you, just take a good snapshot. It isn't necessary to give a lot of detail. Just put down enough to remind you so we can target it next time. The same thing goes for any positive dreams or situations. If negative feelings do come up, try not to make them significant. Remember, it's still just the old stuff. Just write it down for the next time. Then use the tape or the Safe Place exercise to let as much of the disturbance go as possible. Even if nothing comes up, make sure to use the tape every day and give me a call if you need to."

Phase 8: Reevaluation

Noticed since last session: _____

_____

Current symptoms: _____

---

* **Note:** "Back-of-the-Head scale" refers to Knipe (2008, 2009).

New material: _____

_____

SUD: ____/10

PRESENT TRIGGERS

Situations, Events, or Stimuli Triggers

☐ Trigger 1:

Most disturbing part: _____

☐ Trigger 2:

Most disturbing part: _____

☐ Trigger 3:

Most disturbing part: _____

☐ Trigger 4:

Most disturbing part: _____

Target: _____

Picture/Image: _____

Negative cognition (NC): _____

Note: If difficulty: *"In your worst moments, when you are remembering some aspect of the event, what thoughts or negative beliefs do you have about yourself?"* _____

Positive cognition (PC): _____

Validity of cognition (VOC): ____/7

Emotions: _____

Subjective units of disturbance (SUD): ____/10

Location of body sensation: _____

Fears About Present and Future Due to Permanent Physical Damage Trigger List

☐ Trigger 1:

Most disturbing part: _____

☐ Trigger 2:

Most disturbing part: _____

☐ Trigger 3:

Most disturbing part: _____

☐ Trigger 4:

Most disturbing part: _____

Target: _____

Picture/Image: _____

Negative cognition (NC): _____

Note: If difficulty: *"In your worst moments, when you are remembering some aspect of the event, what thoughts or negative beliefs do you have about yourself?"* _____

Positive cognition (PC): _____

Validity of cognition (VOC): _____/7

Emotions: _____

Subjective units of disturbance (SUD): ____/10

Location of body sensation: _____

Problems Trigger List

☐ Trigger 1:

Most disturbing part: _____

☐ Trigger 2:

Most disturbing part: _____

☐ Trigger 3:

Most disturbing part: _____

☐ Trigger 4:

Most disturbing part: _____

FUTURE TEMPLATE

Fears of Being Alone and Unsupported List

_____

_____

_____

_____

Fears of Recurrence of the Illness or Medical Condition List _____

_____

_____

Significant People and Situations of the Presenting Issues for Any Type of Distress List _____

_____

_____

Use floatback as needed:

Floatback: *"Please bring up that picture of* ____ (state image), *and those negative words*_____,
_____ (repeat client's disturbing image and NC)*; notice what feelings are coming up for you, where you are feeling them in your body, and just let your mind float back to an earlier time in your life—don't search for anything—just let your mind float back and tell me the first scene that comes to mind where you had similar:*

Thoughts of ___ (repeat NC)

Feelings of ___ (repeat emotions stated earlier)

In your ____ (repeat places in the body where the client reported feelings)."

Skills Needed to Be Learned and Practiced List

_____

_____

Projected Future Situation List

_____

_____

Do the installation for whatever is needed from these lists.

Installation of the Future Template (Image)

Image of coping effectively with or in the fear trigger in the future: _____

_____

PC: (I can handle it) _____

Sensations: _____

+ BLS

VOC (able to handle the situation): ___/7

Install until VOC = 7

If continuing to be greater than 7, there are more targets to be identified, addressed, and used with the Standard EMDR Protocol.

Blocks/Anxieties/Fears in future scene: _____

1. _____

2. _____

3. _____

Do BLS. If they do not resolve, ask for other qualities needed to handle the situation or what is missing.

1. _____

2. _____

3. _____

Use BLS. If blocks are not resolved, identify unprocessed material and process with the Standard EMDR Protocol.

1. _____

2. _____

3. _____

Target/Memory/Image: _____

_____

NC: _____

PC: _____

VOC: ___/7

Emotions: _____

SUD: ___/10

Sensation: _____

Video Check (Future Template as Movie)

"This time, I'd like you to imagine yourself stepping into the future. Close your eyes, and play a movie from the beginning until the end. Imagine yourself coping with any challenges that come your way. Notice what you are seeing, thinking, feeling, and experiencing in your body. While playing this movie, let me know if you hit any blocks. If you do, just open your eyes and let me know. If you don't hit any blocks, let me know when you have viewed the whole movie."

If block/s, say, *"I can handle it,"* and BLS. Repeat until the client can go through the whole movie entirely without distress.

VOC: ___/7

If the client can play the movie from beginning to end with confidence and satisfaction, play the movie one more time from the beginning to end + BLS: ☐ Yes ☐ No

REFERENCES

Forgash, C. (2009a). Stabilization phase of trauma treatment. In M. Luber (Ed.), *EMDR scripted protocols: Special populations* (pp. 209–233). New York, NY: Springer Publishing.

Forgash, C. (2009b). Home base. In M. Luber (Ed.), *EMDR scripted protocols: Special populations* (pp. 217–220). New York, NY: Springer Publishing.

Forgash, C. (2009c). Workplace or conference room. In M. Luber (Ed.), *EMDR scripted protocols: Special populations* (pp. 217–220). New York, NY: Springer Publishing.

Forgash, C., & Copley, M. (2008). *Healing the heart of trauma and dissociation with EMDR and ego state therapy*. New York, NY. Springer Publishing.

Grant, M. (2009). *Change your brain, change your pain*. Vermont South, Vic, Australia: Book POD.

Levine, P. (2010). *In an unspoken voice. How the body releases trauma and restores goodness* (pp. 73–83). Berkeley, CA: North Atlantic Books.

Servan-Schreiber, D. (2004). *The instinct to heal: Curing stress, anxiety and depression without drugs and without talk therapy*. Emmaus, PA: Rodale.

Siegel, B. (1988). *Love, medicine and miracles*. New York, NY: Harper.

Simonton, C. (1978). *Getting well again*. New York, NY: Bantam.

EMDR THERAPY SELF-CARE PROTOCOL

10

Dolores Mosquera, Paula Baldomir Gago, Ana Cris Eiriz, and Raquel Fernández Domínguez

Note: This protocol is intended as an adjunct to therapeutic treatments including other types of interventions. By using this protocol, the authors attempt to structure the intervention in the beginning of treatment, or parallel to treatment. Good self-care is useful and necessary for improving clients' strengths as well as ensuring optimal development and a more successful treatment.

INTRODUCTION

Basic Self-Care Notions

The EMDR therapy model of self-care for clients was developed by González and Mosquera (González & Mosquera, 2011; Mosquera, 2004; Mosquera & González, 2014) to describe an optimal way for clients to take care of themselves in different areas of functioning.

Typically, self-care has been reduced to physical self-care, namely, food, sleep, and exercise. However, the concept is much broader (González & Mosquera, 2011; Mosquera, 2004; Mosquera & González, 2014). When speaking about self-care, in addition to physical self-care, it is important to take into consideration the person's mental and emotional needs, including the following:

- Realistic view of self
- Protecting self from any harmful figures
- Maintaining appropriate boundaries while interacting with others
- Recognition and validation of own emotions
- Finding time to dedicate to self
- Asking for and being capable of accepting help
- Treating self well, enhancing rather than destroying well-being

Where Do We Learn to Take Care of Ourselves?

Self-care patterns originate in childhood. From this overview of self-care, it is understood that we learn to take care of ourselves when our caregivers (usually our attachment figures) do the following:

- Look at us with unconditional acceptance
- Realize how we are feeling and what is happening to us
- Share pleasant moments
- Fully accept us when we are feeling upset or angry

People who grow up in neglectful and abusive environments have not internalized healthy self-care patterns (Chu, 1998; Knipe, 2015; Ryle & Kerr, 2002). That is, they have not learned to take care of themselves because, as children, no one looked after them appropriately. Therefore, they lack healthy self-care models that allow them to learn behaviors or attitudes of appreciation and attention toward themselves.

If caregivers are negligent, abusive, or uninterested, children may internalize these attitudes toward their own inner experiences, particularly those experiences that do not receive external validation. For example, a child who is seen as "good" and valued only to the extent that he or she is quiet and "does not bother" will not ask for much and will not show his or her needs or feelings.

A tool that will help us evaluate and reflect with the patient on self-care, understanding it from this point of view, is the questionnaire (based on González, Mosquera, Leeds, & Knipe, 2012) presented in the Phase 1 Section: History Taking (see the text that follows).

RESEARCH

This intervention has been used successfully by the authors, their colleagues, and supervisors, but has not been evaluated in a clinical trial.

EMDR SELF-CARE PROTOCOL SCRIPT NOTES

Assessing the Current State of the Client

The EMDR self-care protocol is recommended whenever some of the following indicators of deficient self-care patterns exist:

- Little understanding of the relevance of self-care
- Lack of compliance with prescribed medication
- Unhealthy lifestyle habits
- Substance abuse
- Self-harm
- Previous suicide attempts

Note: The EMDR self-care protocol is not recommended when *active suicidal ideation* is present.

Also, it is important to take into consideration issues such as the presence of personality disorders and complex trauma in clients because specific psychoeducation might be needed. Thus, it is crucial to assess for the presence of the following:

- Posttraumatic stress disorder (PTSD)/trauma/life events
- Dissociative disorders

In these cases, knowledge of the client's internal system will be needed before trying this type of intervention.

Phase 1: History Taking

During Phase 1, it is important to gather information regarding the client's childhood in detail concerning the following issues:

- Family situation during childhood (family members in the family unit, with whom and where did the client live, how much time did the client spend with each family member)
- Attachment style
- Disruption of family bonds or cut-off from certain family members (moving, death in the family, separation from certain family member, etc.)
- Style of physical and emotional caregiving received through childhood
- Possible traumatic situations in childhood (family member's physical illness, family member's psychological illness, presence of addictions in the family, witnessing a situation of self-harm and/or aggression by some family member, etc.)

In order to gather this type of information, we recommend the use of the Family Childhood Experiences Scale (EARLY) by González, Mosquera, and Leeds (2010) and González, Mosquera, Knipe, Leeds, and Santed (2017).

Assessing the Client's Self-Care Pattern Questionnaire in Order to Apply EMDR

On the basis of the answers to the Pattern "Self-Care Questionnaire," the therapist and client must decide which will be the specific self-care issues to work on first, always prioritizing at any given time the behaviors that are a risk for the client's life or for other people's lives. These areas include:

- Physical self-care
- Needs and obligations
- Personal recognition/realistic view of self
- Protecting myself/boundaries
- Time for myself
- Asking for help, allowing myself to be helped
- Recognizing and validating own emotions
- Treating self right

Note: See questionnaire's final section "Treating Myself Right" to make sure that behaviors that are a risk for the client's life or other people's lives are addressed first.

Phase 2: Preparation

The Seven EMDR Therapy Self-Help Protocols

In this phase, we will include the use of the following protocols, besides psychoeducational protocols and psychoeducational worksheets, to enhance client self-care. They will be described in depth in the following section.

1. EMDR Therapy Self-Care Psychoeducational Protocol for Understanding Self-Care
2. EMDR Therapy Self-Care Psychoeducational Protocol for Learning How to Take Care of Ourselves, which includes Psychoeducational Worksheet on How Do We Learn to Take Care of Ourselves, recommended as homework assignment
3. EMDR Therapy Self-Care Psychoeducational Protocol on Relapse Prevention, which includes Psychoeducational Worksheet on Relapse Prevention to give to the client at the end of treatment
4. EMDR Therapy Self-Care Protocol for Developing Resources
5. EMDR Therapy Self-Care Protocol for Self-Harm and Self-Destructive Behaviors, which includes Psychoeducational script on the Function and Management of Self-Harm and Self-Destructive Behaviors, as well as a worksheet recommended as a homework assignment (This protocol is to be used when in risk of self-harm and self-destructive behaviors.)
6. EMDR Therapy Self-Care Protocol to Develop and Install Positive Alternative Behaviors (This protocol is to be used when in risk of self-harm and self-destructive behaviors.)
7. EMDR Therapy Self-Care Protocol for Working With the Inner Child (We may skip protocols 5 and 6 when there is no imminent risk of self-harm and self-destructive behaviors.)

As previously mentioned, we must prioritize at any given time the behaviors that present a risk for the client's life or for other people's lives:

- If clients intended to engage in high-risk behaviors toward themselves, it would be important to work in session addressing self-harm and other destructive behaviors.
- If there were high-risk behaviors toward others, it would be important to identify potential targets associated with these behaviors to process them using protocols 4 and 5.

If there is no threat to self or other, continue with the EMDR Self-Care Protocol, including history gathering, preparation, and processing.

During the preparation phase, it is important to follow these steps:

STEP A: *Therapeutic Alliance*: Establish a good alliance between therapist and client.

Goal: Safety and enough trust to be able to work with attachment issues.

STEP B: *Psychoeducation for Self-Care:* Use psychoeducation/adaptive information regarding the most essential elements of self-care.

Goals:

- To understand the essential elements of healthy self-care and emotional regulation, so that clients recognize their own regulation style learned during childhood. Some of the key elements of healthy self-care are looking at ourselves with the "best possible eyes," looking at ourselves with "realistic eyes," identifying and properly regulating our own emotions, recognizing and validating our own needs, being able to adequately protect ourselves, and achieving a balance between meeting our needs and those of others. This is achieved through the **EMDR Therapy Self-Care Psychoeducational Protocol for Understanding Self-Care**.
- Help clients reflect on their perspective about their own learning, their emotional self-regulation capacities, and the childhood experiences that may have influenced the development of their self-care skills (without going into detailed traumatic memories). It is important to insist that it is not their fault and at the same time help them become aware of the consequences of those learnings. This is achieved through the **EMDR Therapy Self-Care Psychoeducational Protocol for Learning How to Take Care of Ourselves.** We then give clients the **Psychoeducational Worksheet on How Do We Learn to Take Care of Ourselves** as a homework assignment, and it will be discussed in the following session.
- Anticipate possible changes and phases that may take place during the therapy process by introducing the stabilization phase and the "apparent" improvements, stability phase, and "apparent block-age" of the "true improvement" phase, along with its expected moments of discomfort and crisis as previously noted (Mosquera, 2013). Knowing what to expect from the process and anticipating potential "relapses" as part of this process helps the person feel safer. Here, we use the **EMDR Therapy Self-Care Psychoeducational Protocol on Relapse Prevention**. The therapist explains this information at the beginning of treatment so that clients can become familiar with and identify the common stages. There is a specific psychoeducational worksheet that can be given to clients at the end of treatment to prevent relapses (EMDR Therapy Self-Care Psychoeducational Sheet on Relapse Prevention).

The first method developed as an urge-reduction protocol was the DeTUR protocol (Popky, 1993, 2009). It involves three specific phases such as identifying and installing important positive resources, and particularly a positive image of a day in the future after the person has become free of the addiction, desensitizing the urge affect associated with situational triggers of use, which is measured on a scale of 0 to 10, where 0 is no level of urger and 10 the highest level of urge. Once the LOU has reached zero, it combines the image of a trigger with the positive body sensations. In this procedure the LOU measurement are used in different moments. The EMDR Therapy Self-Care Protocol for Self-Harm and Self-Destructive Behaviors is based on Popky's idea or working with urges.

STEP C: *Explain EMDR Therapy*: Explain the concepts and EMDR procedures, as well as the basis of its usefulness.
Goals: To introduce the following concepts:

- *Adaptive Information Processing Theory (AIP)*: The human brain is prepared to process positive and negative events, to maintain mental balance. Negative events that are not spontaneously processed become blocked information, which EMDR processes adaptively by connecting it with other experiences stored in the rest of the neural networks. This results in adaptive resolution, and these events can then become part of regular memory and learning. Thus, symptoms caused by blocked information diminish or disappear. Under regular conditions, the innate AIP system assimilates recent experiences into existing neural networks, where they become integrated and connected with information that is already stored in these networks. This connection to previous information allows us to make sense of the experience, promotes learning, and helps guide us in the future (Shapiro, 2001).
- *Dual Attention*: The patient finds a balance between the emotional experience of suffering and observing the free associations that take place during processing, while remaining present. Eye movements (EMs) help the patient go through the experience while being in the present paying attention to the EMs.
- *Bilateral Stimulation*: Introducing different ways of doing bilateral stimulation and choosing one
- *Informed Consent*: Going over the informed consent form and asking the client to sign it

STEP D: *Install Positive Resources.* Install positive resources as necessary. We may include the Safe Place (Shapiro, 2001) as well as other procedures specifically designed for working on self-care, using the **EMDR Therapy Self-Care Protocol for Developing Resources.**
Goals:

* Positively reinforcing all those aspects indicating how clients are taking care of themselves adequately up to now
* Installing any insight related with the ability to take care of oneself
* Installing personalized resources to facilitate practicing self-care on specific items

STEP E: *Stabilization.* Stabilize the client, if necessary. As previously mentioned, we must prioritize at any given time the behaviors that present a risk for the client's life or for other people's lives. As previously explained, if there is no threat to self or others, we may skip this step and move on to Protocol #6.
Goal: To develop adaptive coping skills through psychoeducation and the use of two specific EMDR protocols for the management of self-harm and self-destructive behaviors:

* **EMDR Self-Care Protocol for Self-Harming and Other Self-Destructive Behaviors.** This protocol addresses self-harm and other self-destructive behaviors to assist clients to reduce impulses to carry out self-destructive behaviors in the present. This is done through the following steps:
  * *Psychoeducation*: Teach clients about the function and management of self-harm and destructive behaviors so that they can reformulate these behaviors by understanding that their attempts to self-regulate/use certain types of self-regulating strategies can be linked back to how they learned to regulate in such ways when they were younger. For this, we shall use the **Psychoeducational Script on the Function and Management of Self-Harm and Self-Destructive Behaviors.**
  * We then give clients the **Psychoeducational Worksheet on the Function and Management of Self-Harm and Self-Destructive Behaviors** for them to take home, complete, and bring back the following session.
* **EMDR Therapy Self-Care Protocol to Develop and Install Positive Alternative Behaviors:** This protocol assists the development and installation of positive alternative behaviors to increase clients' capacities to carry out positive behaviors in moments of distress, thus increasing their emotional self-regulation capacities.

STEP F: *Reformulating Presenting Problem.* Reformulating the client's presenting problem in terms of how the client learned his or her self-care habits is essential. For this, we use the **EMDR Therapy Self-Care Protocol for Working With the Inner Child.**
There are seven steps to address the needs of the inner child:

1. Identify how the adult has learned his/her self-care habits.
2. Describe the image of the child.
3. Explore dissociative phobias. Check the adult's feelings toward the child.
4. Connect the adult with the image of the child.
   a. Promote empathy in the adult: Help the adult understand the child's feelings and needs.
5. Identify needs and/or missing experiences.
   a. Identify the possible needs of the child.
   b. Explore the adult's capacity to meet the child's needs.
   c. Locate body sensations. Facilitate connection.
   d. Reinforce connection and integration.
6. Install change.
7. Closure
   a. Promote realization.
   b. Close the session.

Phases 3–8: Assessment-Reevaluation

If specific memories that should be reprocessed with the Standard EMDR Protocol come up during the different self-help protocols in Phase 2, we move on to Phases 3 to 8, following the Standard EMDR Protocol and working on past, present, and future as usual.

Figure 10.1 shows you at a glance the process to be followed through the eight phases.

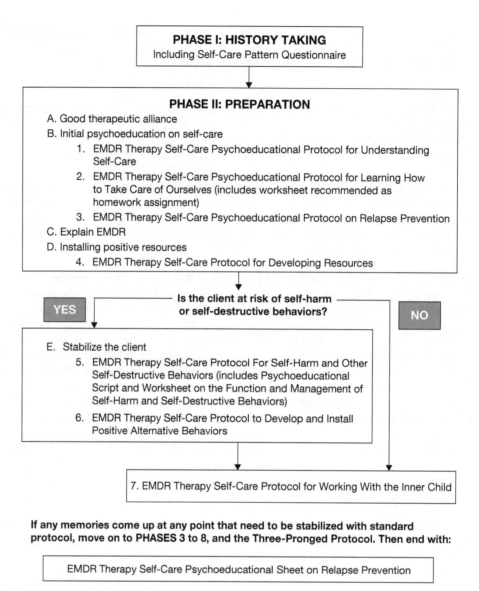

Figure 10.1 Using the EMDR self-care protocol.

STEP G: *Relapse Prevention.* The **EMDR Therapy Self-Care Psychoeducational Sheet on Relapse Prevention** is a specific psychoeducation sheet that can be given to clients at the end of treatment to prevent relapses.

There are many different variables influencing the therapeutic process, which make predicting its course quite difficult. However, in the authors' experience, some general phases have been observed that are common to different cases and situations. Anticipating and knowing these phases builds safety and security both in the client and in the family.

When someone has been feeling bad for some time, one of the main issues is the person's own lack of control over his or her discomfort, added to not knowing what to expect. Thus, offering a certain degree of "control" and anticipating possible relapses as part of the therapeutic process becomes essential in these cases.

Keeping in mind that each person and each situation is different, the authors have observed three phases, which are described in detail in the script section of the chapter:

- Stabilization and "Apparent Improvement" Phase
- Stability and "Apparent Stagnation" Phase
- "Actual Improvement" Phase

The goal is to anticipate possible changes and phases that may take place during the therapy process by introducing the stabilization phase and the "apparent" improvements, stability phase, and "apparent blockage" and the "true improvement" phase, along with its expected moments of discomfort and crisis as previously noted (Mosquera, 2004, 2017). Knowing what to expect from the process and anticipating potential "relapses" as part of this process helps the person feel safer. The therapist can explain this at the beginning of treatment so clients can be familiar with and identify the frequent phases.

EMDR THERAPY SELF-CARE PROTOCOL SCRIPT

Phase 1: Client History

The following questions are based on the Family Childhood Experiences Scale (EARLY). Usually, the authors read these items out loud to patients (González, Mosquera, & Leeds, 2010).

Client History Questions

NUCLEAR FAMILY

Say, *"Please tell me about the family in which you grew up."*

_____

_____

ATTACHMENT STYLE

Say, *"Did you ever feel rejected as a child? Tell me about it."*

_____

_____

Say, *"Did you ever feel that your parents or any other family members were threatening with you in any way—maybe for discipline or even jokingly* (i.e., threaten to leave; send you from home; silent treatment; memories of threats or abusive behavior)*? How old were you? What was the frequency?"*

_____

_____

Say, *"Is this threatening behavior still affecting you? Does it influence you when you parent your own children?"*

_____

_____

Say, *"Are there experiences like that with people outside the family?"*

_____

_____

LOSSES

Say, *"Do you remember losing important figures growing up? If so, how did this affect you or your caregivers?"*

_____

_____

PHYSICAL AND EMOTIONAL CAREGIVING

Say, *"Did you feel loved as a child?"*

_____

_____

Say, *"Do you feel your needs were met?"*

_____

_____

TRAUMATIC SITUATIONS

Say, *"Can you tell me about any specific traumatic memories that have affected you from ages 0 to 15?"*

_____

_____

Assessing the Client's Self-Care Pattern in Order to Apply EMDR

It is important to assess the client's self-care pattern to ascertain whether it is appropriate to apply EMDR or not. For this purpose, we use the **Client's Self-Care Pattern Questionnaire** (see the appendix at the end of the chapter).

Say, *"I am going to ask you some questions and I would appreciate if you would respond with 'Yes' or 'No' to this questionnaire. Do you have any questions? Please add more detail when you are answering the question if you would like to do so."*

SELF-CARE QUESTIONNAIRE

(Use qualitative scoring)

PHYSICAL SELF-CARE

☐ Yes ☐ No   I sleep as much as I need.

Comment: _____

☐ Yes ☐ No   I eat appropriately.

Comment: _____

☐ Yes ☐ No   I exercise often.

Comment: _____

☐ Yes ☐ No   I go to the doctor whenever I need to go.

Comment: _____

☐ Yes ☐ No   I rigorously attend all medical checkups.

Comment: _____

☐ Yes ☐ No   I take care of my physical appearance daily, even if I don't feel well.

Comment: _____

MY NEEDS AND OBLIGATIONS

☐ Yes ☐ No   I can ask for what I need.

Comment: _____

☐ Yes ☐ No   I am able to dedicate time to pleasurable activities.

Comment: _____

☐ Yes ☐ No   I can prioritize my needs before the needs of others.

Comment: _____

☐ Yes ☐ No   I can reach a balance between my own self-care and my caring for others and obligations.

Comment: _____

☐ Yes ☐ No   I am aware of when I need to stop and rest.

Comment: _____

PERSONAL RECOGNITION/REALISTIC VIEW OF SELF

☐ Yes ☐ No   Others should be there for me when I need them.

Comment: _____

☐ Yes ☐ No   I have values that I don't see in others.

Comment: _____

☐ Yes ☐ No   I take very good care of people, but they don't value me or recognize everything that I do.

Comment: _____

☐ Yes ☐ No   I have an ability to care for others that very few people have.

Comment: _____

☐ Yes ☐ No   I always feel like I'm being treated unfairly and I don't understand why.

Comment: _____

☐ Yes ☐ No   I get upset or angry when others don't respond immediately to my needs; I would never do that.

Comment: _____

PROTECTING MYSELF/BOUNDARIES

☐ Yes ☐ No   I have relationships with people that take care of me and treat me well.

Comment: _____

☐ Yes ☐ No   I cannot tolerate long relationships or situations that hurt me; I am able to stop them.

Comment: _____

☐ Yes ☐ No   I am able to say no when people ask me for something that I know is not good for me.

Comment: _____

☐ Yes ☐ No   I am able to say no when people ask me to do something that I don't want to do.

Comment: _____

☐ Yes ☐ No   I can establish/protect my personal space from people that try to invade it, when I feel uncomfortable.

Comment: _____

☐ Yes ☐ No   When I have to stand up for my rights, I don't doubt myself and people cannot make me doubt easily.

Comment: _____

TIME FOR MYSELF

☐ Yes ☐ No   I dedicate time in my life for enjoyable or fun activities.

Comment: _____

☐ Yes ☐ No   I see my friends often.

Comment: _____

☐ Yes ☐ No   I have time for myself.

Comment: _____

☐ Yes ☐ No   I avoid isolating from people, even when I feel bad.

Comment: _____

☐ Yes ☐ No   There is a balance between the time I dedicate to myself and the time I dedicate to other people.

Comment: _____

ASKING FOR HELP/ALLOWING MYSELF TO BE HELPED

☐ Yes ☐ No   I am able to share my problems and receive support from others.

Comment: _____

☐ Yes ☐ No   I am able to ask for help and allow myself to be helped whenever I need it.

Comment: _____

☐ Yes ☐ No   I take care of others just like I feel that others take care of me.

Comment: _____

☐ Yes ☐ No   There is a balance between what I give and what I receive.

Comment: _____

☐ Yes ☐ No   I don't do things for others out of obligation; I do them because I make a decision and want to do it.

Comment: _____

RECOGNIZING AND VALIDATING MY OWN EMOTIONS

☐ Yes ☐ No   I believe my emotions are useful for my self-care.

Comment: _____

☐ Yes ☐ No   All emotions, including anger, sadness, and fear, are positive.

Comment: _____

☐ Yes ☐ No   I pay attention to my emotions and how I feel.

Comment: _____

☐ Yes ☐ No   I recognize the type of emotion I'm feeling at any given moment.

Comment: _____

☐ Yes ☐ No   I feel overwhelmed by my emotions.

Comment: _____

☐ Yes ☐ No   When I feel bad, I am able to think of alternatives that can help me feel better.

Comment: _____

☐ Yes ☐ No   Whenever I feel bad about something, I become aware of it and try to do something
to improve it.

Comment: _____

TREATING MYSELF RIGHT/CORRECTLY

☐ Yes ☐ No   I do things that I know are beneficial for me.

Comment: _____

☐ Yes ☐ No   Sometimes I behave in self-harming ways.

Comment: _____

☐ Yes ☐ No   I consider that I deserve to treat myself right.

Comment: _____

☐ Yes ☐ No   Sometimes, I drink or take some kind of drug to feel better.

Comment: _____

☐ Yes ☐ No   Sometimes I take medication to numb myself.

Comment: _____

☐ Yes ☐ No   When I'm not feeling well, I get angry at myself for feeling like this, I blame myself,
or beat myself up constantly.

Comment: _____

☐ Yes ☐ No   When I'm not feeling well, I do things that make me feel even worse.

Comment: _____

Note: If clients indicate a threat to self or others, it is important to work on addressing self-harm and/
or other destructive behaviors.

Phase 2: Preparation

STEP A: Create a Therapeutic Alliance

As a first step, it is important to create a good therapeutic alliance with your client.
STEP B: Use Psychoeducation Guidelines

Use psychoeducation guidelines containing adaptive information regarding the most essential elements of self-care.

1. EMDR Therapy Self-Care Psychoeducational Protocol for Understanding Self-Care

> Say, *"The concept of self goes beyond good nutrition and adequate sleep for all of us. Good
> self-care has three core elements: (1) a positive attitude toward ourselves such as accept-
> ing and appreciating ourselves, (2) avoiding self-harm or self-defeating behaviors, and*

(3) taking specific actions that provide benefits, growth, or value to ourselves. Let's talk about some of the key elements of healthy self-care."

a. Looking at Ourselves With the "Best Possible Eyes."

Say, *"The first one is looking at ourselves with the 'best possible eyes.' What do you think this means?"*

_____

_____

Address the client's response and include the following explanation as needed:

Say, *"It is like being your own best friend or treating yourself as you would treat someone who you really care about, with empathy, affection, and loyalty. What do you think about that?"*

_____

_____

b. Looking at Ourselves With "Realistic Eyes."

Say, *"The next one is looking at ourselves with 'realistic eyes.' What do you think that means?"*

_____

_____

Address the client's response and include the following explanation as needed:

Say, *"If we believe that we are always right, we are unable to assume when we are wrong, or we always focus on what others are doing wrong or what they need to change, we are not looking at ourselves or the world in a realistic way. It is important to assume our share of responsibility for our lives and be able to put ourselves in other people's shoes. If we need to think that we are perfect or better than others in order to accept ourselves, we will encounter many problems in relationship to ourselves and others. It is important to feel that we are 'good enough,' just as we are. What do you think about that?"*

_____

_____

c. Identifying and Regulating/Managing Emotions.

Say, *"The next one is learning how to identify or regulate/manage emotions. Emotional regulation is the ability to modulate our emotional responses. What does that mean to you?"*

_____

_____

Address the client's response and include the following explanation as needed:

Say, *"This is related not only to the ability to reduce intense activation states, but also to the degree of emotional connection. The emotional reaction is not just a matter of how much emotion a person feels, but what he or she does with it. Many people have great difficulties identifying and managing their emotions because they have been taught to value emotions as positive, those that are more pleasant to feel, such as joy, or negative, those that are less pleasant to experience, such as anger, fear, or sadness. So, when they feel any of the emotions in the second group, they try to get rid of them. By doing this, people lose the opportunity to understand what they need. All emotions are positive, and they all have a role/function and help protect the person; therefore, the goal is not to avoid them, but to learn how to manage them properly. Any thoughts about this?"*

_____

_____

d. Recognizing and Validating Our Own Needs.

Say, *"The fourth element is recognizing and validating our own needs. What does that mean to you?"*

_____

_____

Address the client's response and include the following explanation as needed:

Say, *"This means being aware of our needs and paying attention to the most basic sensations. A child who grows up feeling that his or her core emotional and/or physical needs are being ignored or shamed cannot learn to distinguish between different feelings and needs. This leads to confusion regarding emotions. When this happens, we need to learn to identify our feelings and emotions, pay attention to them, and consider them as relevant and important. If we can do this, we may feel that we are entitled to satisfy our needs and find the resources to have them met, including the possibility of seeking help from others and accepting it. What are your thoughts about that?"*

_____

_____

e. Protecting Ourselves Adequately.

Say, *"The fifth element is protecting ourselves adequately. What do you think that is about?"*

_____

_____

Address the client's response and include the following explanation as needed:

Say, *"This would be related to the need for understanding healthy boundaries and being able to establish them. When caregivers do not recognize the limits of the child and/or fail to set healthy boundaries, not only will the future adult feel guilty for needing to set limits, but he or she may also actually lack an internal model to recognize the need for those boundaries. What does that mean to you?"*

_____

_____

f. Achieving a Balance Between Our Needs and Those of Others.

> Say, *"The last one is achieving a balance between our needs and those of others. What do you think that is about?"*

_____

_____

Address the client's response and include the following explanation as needed:

Say, *"Some people struggle with a 'black and white' or 'all or nothing' thinking because the healthy ways to find a balance between conflicting needs have not been learned. People who did not learn to detect their needs or their own relevance may focus on the needs of others and ignore their own. Moreover, some people are so focused on their needs that they are not able to think of others and this causes problems in their relationships. Finding a balance between these two aspects is crucial."*

_____

_____

2. EMDR Therapy Self-Care Psychoeducational Protocol for Learning How to Take Care of Ourselves

It is important that clients learn self-care for themselves.

> Say, *"I think it is important that you learn about your emotions, how you can handle them and to recognize the strengths and weaknesses of your regulation style that you learned in childhood. To help with this idea I am going to read you a story."*

> Say, *"Four 5-year-old girls (Susana, María, Laura, and Teresa) are running around playing. All four trip and fall, scratching their knees. They go home and each one gets a different response."*

Susana

"When Susana sees her bloody knees, she runs home crying. Her mother looks at her lovingly and says, 'Poor little girl, it hurts, doesn't it?' She gives the girl a hug and says, 'I'll clean up your wound. Yes, of course it hurts! We'll get a Band-Aid. Come and sit on my lap for a bit. We'll sing a song that will make you feel better.' In a short while, the little girl will want to go back out and play and her mother asks if her knee still hurts. Smiling, she says 'No,' while running out the door to play.

What does Susana learn?"

_____

_____

Address the client's response and include the following explanation as needed:

Say, *"Yes, _____ (state whatever was mentioned by the client). She also learned:*

- *My emotions are important.*
- *I can identify and name what I feel.*
- *I respect my feelings.*
- *When I feel bad, I believe my feelings are valid.*
- *I am able to pay attention to my needs.*

And, she may also learn about others' emotions:

- *Other people's emotions are important.*
- *I am able to identify, tolerate, and empathize with other people's emotions without making them mine.*

Does that make sense to you?"

María

> Say, *"María goes home and her mother is busy in the kitchen. María, with tears in her eyes from the shock and the pain, tells her, 'I fell down and hurt myself.' Her mother comes toward her without a word, grabs some Band-Aids and hydrogen peroxide, makes her sit down and cleans up her wound. Meanwhile, María tries to find her mother's eyes but, since there is no response, she focuses on how her mother is cleaning up her wound, appearing calmer. When her mother is done, she says, 'Go and wash up, we are about to have dinner,' and walks away, going back to her chores. María turns around, wipes off her tears and goes up to her room.*

What does María learn?"

Address the client's response and include the following explanation as needed:

> Say, *"Yes, _____ (state whatever was mentioned by the client). She also learned:*

- *I don't know what I feel.*
- *My emotions are not important.*
- *Emotions don't seem to be useful.*

And, she may also learn about others and their feelings:

- *I have trouble understanding other people's feelings.*
- *When others feel bad, I focus on myself.*

Does that make sense to you?"

Laura

> Say, *"Laura runs home crying as her mother runs out looking for her. She heard the girls screaming and thought that something very serious must have happened. When she sees her, she grabs her by the arms, yelling at her, 'Haven't I told you a thousand times to be careful? I'm going to have a heart attack because of you. Come on, go home.' Laura is very upset and keeps crying. Her mother says, 'Don't cry, little girl, it's nothing. . . . Come on, don't cry anymore, it makes you look ugly.'*

What does Laura learn?"

Address the client's response and include the following explanation as needed:

> Say, *"Yes, _____ (state whatever was mentioned by the client). She also learned:*

- *My emotions overwhelm me (and overwhelm others).*
- *I feel guilty for feeling this way.*

- *I don't know what to do with my emotions.*
- *I desperately seek others, but even if they respond, I am unable to calm down. (At times, I even get angry at them when they try to help me.)*
- *It takes me a long time to feel better.*

And, she may also learn about others' emotions:

- *Other people's emotions overwhelm me.*
- *I don't know how to relate to others in difficult situations.*
- *When people feel bad, I think it's their fault or they deserve it.*
- *When others don't calm down quickly, I get anxious or angry.*

Does that make sense to you?"

Teresa

> Say, *"Teresa got very scared with the fall and cannot stop crying. When she gets home her mother says, 'You're always falling down, you're clumsy and useless.' Teresa cries louder. Her mother is even more upset and shouts, 'Shut up! You're such a crybaby! I don't know who you took after!' The girl scratches herself and continues crying, more and more dysregulated. Her mother comes up, slaps her, and screams, 'Do you want more?' Teresa falls down due to the impact, freezes, and stops crying.*

What does Teresa learn?"

Address the client's response and include the following explanation as needed:

> Say, *"Yes, _____ (state whatever was mentioned by the client). She also learned:*

- *Showing emotions is dangerous.*
- *If I ask for help, I may get hurt.*
- *I deserve what is happening to me; it's my fault that I'm like this.*

And, she may also learn about others and their emotions:

- *I don't understand emotions or their use.*
- *Only weak people cry.*
- *I despise weakness, vulnerability, and fear.*
- *I don't need anyone.*
- *It's better not to feel anything.*

Does that make sense to you?"

Give them the **Psychoeducational Worksheet on How Do We Learn to Take Care of Ourselves** (see the appendix) as homework, and it will be discussed in the following session.

> Say, *"Here is a brief worksheet for you to read at home about what we have been discussing today. At the end, you will find some questions for you to reflect on at home concerning what you have read. Do you have any questions? We will discuss it more during the next session."*

3. EMDR Therapy Self-Care Psychoeducational Protocol on Relapse Prevention

Say, *"I would like you to be aware of a common situation that we encounter in therapy: fear of change. In many cases, when somebody feels better, he or she can get frightened or feel pressured because that individual not used to feeling better. We usually find that the therapeutic process follows three different phases:*

'Stabilization and Apparent Improvement' Phase: When someone has been feeling bad for some time, not knowing what is happening, finding an explanation that makes sense and feeling understood usually has a very positive effect in the initial stabilization. The word 'apparent' means that feeling good is temporary and variable and that it is probable that the discomfort will return as long as the work on all the aspects and events that have generated the disturbance are not finished.

'Stability and Apparent Stagnation' Phase: This phase is usually the longest and, in general, the least tolerable, both for you and your family. Once treatment is started and the first stabilization takes place, it is time to start working on adversities and traumatic events step by step. Throughout this phase of the process, therapeutic work takes place at an internal level. Thus, it is common that changes are not externalized or visible if only behaviors are assessed. This is why people usually see it as stagnation because they are expecting visible and more significant changes. This phase also includes the presence of relapses, which may initially be assessed as a step back, but truly are part of the process. The goal is for those relapses to be less intense and frequent over time.

'Actual Improvement' Phase: This would be the final phase of the process, in which improvement is clearly externalized and becomes more visible through behavior. Once adversities and traumatic events have been worked on therapeutically, you may normally use those resources and functioning alternatives acquired throughout the process that are more efficient, less harmful, and more functional."

Say, *"I will give you a worksheet on this process once your treatment is finished, for you to keep so you can go over it when needed, to avoid relapses."* (You will find the **Psychoeducational Sheet on Relapse Prevention** in the appendix.)

_____

_____

STEP C: Explanation of EMDR

Explain the concepts and *EMDR* procedures and the basis of EMDR therapy's usefulness. Include information about Adaptive Information Processing (AIP) theory, dual attention, bilateral stimulation, informed consent, and safe place.

Say, *"I want to tell you about EMDR therapy. When a trauma occurs, it seems to get locked in the nervous system with the original picture, sounds, thoughts, and feelings. The eye movements we use in EMDR seem to unlock the nervous system and allow the brain to process the experience. That may be what is happening in REM or dream sleep—the eye movements may help to process the unconscious material. It is important to note that it is your own brain that will be doing the healing and that you are the one in control."*

STEP D: Installing Positive Resources

The next step involves installing positive resources as necessary. This can include the Safe Place (Shapiro, 2001) and other procedures specifically designed for working on self-care.

4. EMDR Therapy Self-Care Protocol for Developing Resources

Reinforce aspects that indicate how clients take care of themselves adequately up to now such as setting adequate boundaries during the week, asking for help, and accepting it.
Get the description to install the positive sensation.

Say, *"This week you were able to set boundaries with _____ (state the person client set limits with). This is something that you wanted to do for a long time but couldn't. How did it feel to do this?"*

_____

_____

Install any insight related to the ability of taking care of oneself. Get the description to install the positive sensation.

Say, *"This week you realized how important it was to find time for yourself. Can you tell me how it felt when you realized this?"*

_____

_____

Install personalized resources in order to facilitate practicing self-care on specific items.

Say, *"What would be a resource that you experienced this week that helped you facilitate your self-care practice?"*

_____

_____

Installing these resources assists the development and installation of positive alternative behaviors to increase clients' capacities to carry out positive behaviors in moments of distress, thus increasing their emotional self-regulation capacities.

STEP E: Stabilization

Stabilize the client, if necessary. As mentioned earlier, we must prioritize at any given time the behaviors that present a risk for the client's life or for other people's lives.

5. EMDR Therapy Self-Care Protocol for Self-Harm and Self-Destructive Behaviors

This includes a psychoeducational script on the function and management of self-harm and self-destructive behaviors, as well as a worksheet recommended as a homework assignment, before applying the actual protocol.

Say, *"This is called the 'EMDR Self-Care Protocol for Self-Harm and Other Self-Destructive Behaviors' and the idea behind it is to help you address self-harm and other self-destructive behaviors so that you can reduce your impulses to carry out self-destructive behaviors in the present. Is that something you might be interested in?"*

_____

_____

Say, *"I would like to talk about how self-harm and destructive behaviors work so that you can understand how they evolve and how you learned them.*

Cuts, scratches, or compulsive, abusive, or self-destructive behaviors often lead to a temporary sense of calm and even euphoria, although they later have the opposite effect and generate discomfort and guilt (i.e., finding yourself feeling even worse than before the destructive act).

Sometimes self-harm happens because we cannot find words to express the intensity of our suffering and need to communicate it, 'get it out'; other times, because we need to make it visible in order to ask for help; and at still other times because the emotions are too intense and painful and we have not learned to identify, accept, tolerate, handle, or express them appropriately, as we mentioned in the previous informative session. Other reasons for self-destructive behavior include guilt, frustration, anger directed at oneself, or simply wanting to 'feel alive,' disconnect from the suffering or discomfort, or 'escape from our body.' Ironically, people sometimes resort to self-destructive behaviors as a comforting strategy to cope with discomfort.

This, which at first may seem like a strange and eccentric behavior, makes sense if we see it as learned behavior, as a way to regulate our own emotions. Whether the goal is feeling relief, self-punishment, or feeling alive, in all cases there is a significant emotional component that needs to be regulated or stopped: those who self-punish need a lesson; those who self-injure to feel alive need something to let them know they really exist, that they do feel; those who do it for relief need an escape because they have the feeling they are going to explode at any moment.

We could say that by not having acquired adaptive skills to calm down and manage stress or frustration, people resort to action because it is less complicated than trying to understand and express feelings. It is important to be aware that action brings relief, while verbalizing and sharing requires a big effort and a repertoire of skills that are often lacking, so resorting to action serves as a mean of communication.

For many, it is easier to tolerate physical pain than emotional pain, especially when they do not know why they feel so overwhelmed by a certain moment or situation. Physical pain is tangible, and it can be seen, shown, understood, transmitted, and even cured, but emotional pain is truly difficult to share and show. Showing emotional pain requires tears, screams, tremors, agitation, words, action, and the like—something visible or 'listenable' that allows those around us to visualize what we feel. If we cancel the physical or behavioral responses, it is particularly complicated to perceive or imagine what the other person is feeling. Try to imagine an expressionless person who is explaining what he is feeling without any gesture or movement to accompany this explanation. It would be cold, distant, and unreal. And this is what can lead many people to behave this way: the need to express feelings and the difficulties in doing so in a verbal or para-verbal way (nonverbal language such as gestures, postures, facial expressions, tone of voice, etc.).

It is important to find alternative ways to address these feelings without doing oneself any harm. One way to do this, for example, is learning to distract ourselves. Many people find it helpful to talk or write about feelings, take a walk, or do strenuous exercise."

We then give the **Psychoeducational Worksheet on the Function and Management of Self-Harm and Self-Destructive Behaviors** to the client, so he or she can fill it out at home.

Say, *"When people are feeling bad, generally, they cannot control their emotions and it is common to resort to self-destructive behaviors because they do not see any other way out. It is important to have resources to divert your attention and focus on possible alternatives, avoiding physical or psychological harm.*

These resources must be planned in advance because during the 'bad moments' it will be much harder to stop and think 'What would be better to do instead of _____?' A strategy that may be useful is to ask the question(s), 'What would I tell the person I love the most if he or she felt like I am feeling?' or 'What would I recommend they do?'

I'd like you to have this worksheet, take it home with you, and complete it. A series of questions are presented to gather important information about the type and function/motive of the self-destructive behavior and potential less harmful alternatives that may help regulate moments of intense discomfort. Check any answer that applies in your case. Next week, we'll use it for our work in session."

Then, we move on to installing additional resources, if needed. This is used only when self-harming behaviors are present.

IDENTIFY AND INSTALL POSITIVE RESOURCES

Say, *"One day in the future, when you don't need to 'hurt yourself' anymore _____ (state the type of self-destructive behavior that is riskier for the client), what kind of good things would that day have that you don't have today?"*

_____

_____

Identify positive image, positive cognition, and associated physical sensations.

Say, *"What is the positive image that represents what you would have?"*

_____

_____

Say, *"When you bring up that picture or the ___ (state the situation, event, or stimulus), what are the positive words that come up for you now?"*

_____

_____

Say, *"Notice that positive day and the positive words that go with that and ____ (state the bilateral stimulation that you are using). Go with that."*

Do BLS.

SEARCH FOR TRIGGERS

Say, *"What is your biggest current trigger for wanting to 'hurt yourself'? You may think of four or five, but choose the strongest one. Describe the image for that trigger."*

Trigger: _____

Image: _____

ASSESS THE LEVEL OF URGE

Say, *"Bring up the picture of that trigger along with any words, tastes, smells, or sounds that go with it. How strong is the level of urge (LoU) to hurt yourself right now, from 0 to 10, where 0 is no urge and 10 is the strongest?"*

0	1	2	3	4	5	6	7	8	9	10

(no urge)   (strongest urge)

Say, *"Where are you feeling that number in your body?"*

_____

_____

PROCESS THE URGE

Say, *"Be aware of that feeling in your body, the physical sensations you are noticing here and now. You have not decided to do it, just notice that you want to do it. Be aware of how much you want it. Go with that."*

Do a few sets of BLS.

CHECK

Say, *"Go back to the image. Assess the urge now. What is different?"*

_____

_____

Say, *"Go with that."*

Do a few sets of BLS.

Say, *"What do you get now?"*

_____

_____

Do a few sets of BLS.

INSTALLATION

If the LoU reaches 0, say the following:

"Think about the positive moments related to these 'self-destructive behaviors.' Is there anything left of that urge to 'hurt yourself'? Notice that this is how zero feels. Go with that."

_____

_____

Do a few sets of BLS.

Say, *"What would you say about yourself now? (PC) What do you notice in your body when you think of _____ (state the PC)?"*

_____

_____

Say, *"Notice it while keeping those words in mind. Go with that."*

Do a few sets of BLS.

DESENSITIZE EACH TRIGGER

Say, *"Bring up the picture of that trigger along with any words, tastes, smells, or sounds that go with it. How strong is the LoU to hurt yourself right now, from 0 to 10, where 0 is no urge and 10 is the strongest?"*

0	1	2	3	4	5	6	7	8	9	10

(no urge)   (strongest urge)

Repeat for each trigger.

6. EMDR Therapy Self-Care Protocol to Develop and Install Positive Alternative Behaviors

PREPARATION

Use the chart of alternative behaviors created by the client from the information in the **Worksheet on the Function and Management of Self-Harm and Self-Destructive Behaviors**.

Review the chart with the client to install those alternatives that have worked as positive resources. It is possible that you will have to repeat the EMDR Protocol for Self-Harming and Other Self-Destructive Behaviors if the client carried out any serious self-destructive behavior since the last session.

> Say, *"These are the resources/alternative behaviors that you thought would be better to do instead of ____* (state self-harming or other self-destructive behaviors) *where you would be depending only on yourself. Let's review them and see if we must modify, expand, or eliminate any item."*

> Say, *"These are the resources/alternative behaviors that you thought would be better to do instead of ____* (state self-harming or other self-destructive behaviors) *where you would be depending on others. Let's review them and see if we must modify, expand, or eliminate any item."*

INSTALLATION

Identify Positive Resources for Installation: The positive resource will be the one chosen that week by the client to substitute for the destructive behavior, which should be included in the chart from the worksheet.

> Say, *"Now that you selected a resource that you find useful, we can reinforce it."*

> Say, *"Think about _____* (state the chosen resource).*"*

Identify Positive Image

> Say, *"Describe the situation from this week in which you were telling me that you felt ____* (state the negative emotion described by the client), *that you were able to reduce the urge to ____* (state self-destructive behavior), *and where you also ____* (state alternative positive behavior).*"*

> _____

> _____

Identify the Positive Cognition (PC)

> Say, *"Think about the positive moments associated with having regulated your discomfort through a positive behavior. What are the positive words you would say about yourself now?"*

> _____

> _____

Assess the Validity of Cognition (VOC)

> Say, *"When you think of the incident* (or picture) *how true do those words _____* (clinician repeats the positive cognition) *feel to you now on a scale of 1 to 7, where 1 feels completely false and 7 feels completely true?"*

> 1   2   3   4   5   6   7
>
> (completely false)   (completely true)

Identify Associated Physical Sensations for Installation

> Say, *"Be aware of that _____* (state sensation in body) *in your body, the physical sensations you are noticing here and now. Go with that."*

Do several sets of BLS. Continue until VOC reaches 6 or 7.

Future Template

> Say, *"Think about some future moments in which you think it would be helpful to feel this sensation while you maintain the belief _____* (state PC). *Go with that."*

Do several sets of BLS.

Say, *"What do you get now?"*

_____

_____

Say *"Stop in each one of those moments so you can clearly feel the PC."*

_____

_____

STEP F: Reformulating the client's presenting problem in terms of how the client learned his or her self-care habit is essential.

7. EMDR Therapy Self-Care Protocol for Working With the Inner Child

I. IDENTIFYING HOW THE ADULT LEARNED SELF-CARE HABITS

Say, *"Where do you think you learned to _____ (state maladaptive self-care habit such as binging when feeling lonely/not allowing yourself to ask for help/judging and criticizing yourself when you feel sad or angry)?"*

_____

_____

It is important to be specific about the client's self-care problem selected as the focus for the current session. It is important to use the client's words.

Say, *"Do you remember any experience in your childhood that may be related to how you learned to take care of yourself in such ways?"*

_____

_____

Note for Therapist: There are many targets that can be used such as selecting a memory, a certain look/expression from the caregiver, a sentence or word from the caregiver, and so on.

II. DESCRIBING THE IMAGE OF THE CHILD

Say, *"Can you see the child that you were, who learned to _____ (state maladaptive behavior)?"*

_____

_____

We are going to work with the child as a whole, not just with the life history or specific experiences:

Say, *"Are you able to see that child?"*

_____

_____

Say, *"What do you see?"*

_____

_____

Say, *"How old is _____ (he/she)?"*

_____

_____

Say, *"What is _____ (he/she) doing?"*

_____

_____

Say, *"How is _____(his/her) body posture, _____(his/her) gestures?"*

_____

_____

The goal is to help the client build an image of the child that is as clear as possible.

Note for the Therapist: If the adult has trouble seeing the child, it is important to identify if this is a dissociative phobia or any other difficulty related to the lack of self-care experiences.

III. EXPLORING DISSOCIATIVE PHOBIAS. CHECKING THE ADULT'S FEELINGS TOWARD THE CHILD

Say, *"When you think about the child, how do you feel about _____ (state him/her)?"*

_____

_____

If the client says something negative and feels rejection, disgust, anger, or fear, process the dissociative phobia. The guidelines are that *if the client feels any negative feeling toward the child, this would be considered a dissociative phobia.*

When the client says something positive (curiosity, tenderness, or compassion), go to Step IV, "Connecting the adult with the image of the child."

Note for the Therapist: To explore dissociative phobias, it may be enough to explore the adult's reaction toward the image of the child. The following indicators can be helpful (based on González & Mosquera, 2011; Mosquera & González, 2014).

When the adult describes the image of the child, it is important to look for disconnection, overconnection, and/or high mental autonomy. It is important to help clinicians be aware of these three elements, which are frequent in dissociative cases where child parts have a first-person perspective and high mental autonomy. The following questions help with that.

When the client cannot see the child (disconnection), help him or her connect by asking questions such as the following:

Say, *"How do you think _____ (he/she) may have felt?"*

_____

_____

Say, *"Look at _____ (his/her) posture; what do you think may be happening to _____ (him/her)?"*

_____

_____

When the client becomes too emotionally involved and overwhelmed (overconnection), offer emotional psychoeducation by stating the following:

Say, *"Did you know that to help someone we do not have to feel exactly how they feel? Did you know that to think about the different ways of helping others we must remain calm and not feel things with the same intensity as those we are trying to help?"* _____

_____

_____

Or ask, *"How could you help the child with ___ (his/her) pain without feeling all the pain ___ (she/he) is feeling?"*

_____

_____

Whenever the child shows an autonomy that surprises the adult such as hiding or he or she does not want to speak to the adult (high mental autonomy, where the child has a first-person perspective), a negotiation process among dissociative parts must take place.

IV. CONNECTING THE ADULT WITH THE IMAGE OF THE CHILD. PROMOTING EMPATHY: HELPING THE ADULT THINK ABOUT THE CHILD'S FEELINGS

Say, *"Can you, without judging, see ____ (his/her) face, the look in ____ (his/her) eyes?"*

_____

_____

Say, *"Go with that."*

Do several sets of BLS.

Any negative memory that may come up during this process should be reprocessed with the Standard EMDR Protocol.

Say, *"What does ____ (he/she) convey through the look in ____ (his/her) eyes?"*

_____

_____

Say, *"Can you pick up on ____ (his/her) feelings through the look in ____ (his/her) eyes?"*

_____

_____

Say, *"Go with that."*

Do several sets of BLS.

Say, *"How do you think ____ (he/she) is feeling?"*

_____

_____

Note for the Therapist: Search for profound emotional pain (sometimes you may see a smiling face because this is what the child learned to show to protect him- or herself, but we must guide the client to go beyond that).

Recheck the feelings of the adult toward the child:

> Say, *"How does it make you feel, as your adult self here with me, to see this child who is feeling so* ____ (state how child is feeling)?"

_____

_____

If there is rejection or discomfort, we must process the defense.

> Say, *"On a scale of 0 to 10, where 0 is no disturbance or neutral and 10 is the highest disturbance you can imagine, how disturbing does it feel now?"*

0	1	2	3	4	5	6	7	8	9	10

(no disturbance)   (highest disturbance)

> Say, *"Go with that."*

Do several sets of BLS, until SUD = 0.

V. IDENTIFYING AND MEETING NEEDS AND/OR MISSING EXPERIENCES

Identify the Possible Needs of the Child.

> Say, *"What do you feel* ___ (he/she) *needs?"*

_____

_____

Provide psychoeducation, if needed, about childhood needs at the age of the inner child with whom we are working: physical touch, containment, company, play, and so on.

If the client is unable to find an answer that satisfies the child, we may help him reflect by asking things such as the following:

> Say, *"What may a child need when* ___ (he/she) *is crying because* ___ (he/she) *is sad?"*

_____

_____

If we are aware that the client knows a child of that age in his environment, we can use that example, or ask:

> *"What would you need to do as an adult if this kid you know were here with us and was crying because* ___ (he/she) *is scared of* ___ (state what he/she is scared of)?"

_____

_____

With our help, we try to facilitate the client reaching an empathic and validating response toward the child.

Explore the Adult's Feeling of Being Able to Meet the Child's Needs.

> Say, *"Do you feel able to give it to him?"*

_____

_____

If so, *"Imagine the adult that you are _____* (state adaptive response of adult such as hugging the child/holding his or her hand/telling him he or she is not alone) *and see what you notice."*

Do several sets of BLS.

If the client does not feel able to do so, say the following:

"Do you notice something in your body that says you can't do it?"

_____

_____

Say, *"On a scale of 0 to 10, where 0 is no disturbance or neutral and 10 is the highest disturbance you can imagine, how disturbing does it feel now?"*

0	1	2	3	4	5	6	7	8	9	10

(no disturbance)   (highest disturbance)

Do a set of BLS until the SUD reaches 0.

Note for the Therapist: When the adult response is one of wanting to get close to the child, showing a need for physical contact, it will be necessary to ask him to check if the child would be ready/willing to have this physical contact or if, for the time being, some other type of closeness would be enough. If so, remind the adult that this child has been very lonely and that we must respect his rhythm. For now, it could be enough with maintaining an accepting eye contact/sitting together/sitting side by side/sitting in front of each other, and the like. Explain that respecting the child's rhythm will be the best way to show him acceptance and caregiving. The therapist, through the adult, will give that same accepting message, saying things like the following:

Say, *"Can you please tell the child that we will respect his rhythm, that ___ (he/she) will be the one in charge of the work we do, and that we will listen to ___ (him/her) and take ___ (him/her) into consideration because ___ (he/she) is important?"*

Locate bodily feelings and facilitate connection.

Say, *"If you could locate the child in your body, where do you feel ___ (he/she) would live?"*

_____

_____

Say, *"Can you notice the child's emotion in your body?"*

_____

_____

Say, *"Where do you notice it?"*

_____

_____

Say, *"What is the physical sensation that goes along with that emotion?"*

_____

_____

Say, *"Go with that."*

Do several sets of BLS.

Reinforce Connection and Integration.

Ask the adult to allow the child to feel the emotion and explore where the adult notices the physical sensation that belongs to the child's emotion, then propose that the adult places his/her hands over the part of the body where the emotion of the child is felt:

Say, *"Can you place your adult hands over the part of your body where you notice that sensation or emotion of the child?"*

_____

_____

Say, *"Can you offer the child the ___ (state either caregiving/love/containment or anything appropriate for the client) that your adult hands are conveying?"*

_____

_____

Say, *"Go with that."*

Do several sets of BLS.

Say, *"If your hands could convey that sensation through words, what message would they give to the child?"*

_____

_____

Say, *"Go with that."*

Do several sets of BLS.

Note for the Therapist: Find simple words that the child can understand given his or her age, for example, *"I am here with you," "I see you and I feel you," "I'll take care of you," "You're important for me,"* and so on.*"

Say, *"It may be the first time that the child shares this emotion; it is a very exciting and important moment. Can you notice the connection between the both of you?"*

_____

_____

Say, *"Go with that."*

Do several sets of BLS.

Say, *"Check and see how the child feels when ___ (he/she) notices that the adult is there for ___ (him/her), check and see how the adult feels when ___ (he/she) notices that ___ (he/she) can comfort the child."*

_____

_____

Say, *"Go with that."*

Do several sets of BLS.

VI. INSTALLING THE CHANGE

Say, *"Look again into the eyes of the child. What do you see? Has something changed? What is different now?"*

_____

_____

If there is any change, regardless of how small, ask the client to notice the difference in the emotion/thought/body.

Say, *"OK. Notice the difference."*

Say, *"Go with that."*

Do several sets of BLS.

If a positive emotion comes up, point it out and validate it.

Say, *"Notice that ____ (state positive emotion)."*

_____

_____

Repeat the client's words when referring to that positive emotion.

Say, *"Where do you notice it in your body?"*

_____

_____

Say, *"Yes, just notice that."*

Do several sets of BLS.

VII. CLOSURE

Promoting Realization.

Promote reflection.

Say, *"What are you noticing while doing this exercise?"*

_____

_____

Say, *"What meaning do you give to what you just experienced?"*

_____

_____

Say, *"Do you understand more about yourself right now?"*

_____

_____

Say, *"Do you understand more about your problem and how to get over it?"*

_____

_____

Please enhance any new form of awareness with BLS.

Closing the Session.

Use psychoeducation as needed about what happened in the session, clarifying any doubts the client may have.

Say, *"What have you realized today?"*

_____

_____

Say, *"How do you think this can help you?"*

_____

_____

If you see that the client is ready, ask him or her to repeat the exercise at home connecting his or her hands to the physical sensation of the child's emotion.

Say, *"Do you think this is an exercise that you can practice at home?"*

_____

_____

Use the calm/safe place exercise, which was done in previous sessions, and ask the adult and child to go together to the safe place, if appropriate for closure.

Say, *"Can you think of your safe place?"*

_____

_____

Say, *"Can you share this safe place with the child?"*

_____

_____

Or say, *"Can you show this safe place to the child and ask him or her to join you?"*

_____

_____

Say, *"Go with that."*

Do several sets of BLS.

Phases 3 to 8: Assessment–Reevaluation

For any negative traumatic memories that must be reprocessed, use the Standard EMDR Protocol. **STEP G:** Give the **EMDR Therapy Self-Care Psychoeducational Script on Relapse Prevention** psychoeducation sheet to clients at the end of treatment to prevent relapses (see the appendix).

Say, *"Please read the psychoeducation sheet about relapse prevention."*

After the client has read it, say the following:

Say, *"What are your thoughts about this?"*

_____

_____

SUMMARY

The work explained in the chapter helps clients relate to themselves in a more compassionate way by learning a completely new method of looking at themselves with acceptance, comprehension, and care. This type of work helps repair attachment wounds and introduces new adaptive information that clients lack, which is a great preparation for future processing of traumatic events.

REFERENCES

Chu, J. A. (1998). *Rebuilding shattered lives: The responsible treatment of complex post-traumatic and dissociative disorders.* New York, NY: John Wiley & Sons.

González, A., & Mosquera, D. (2011). Working with self-care patterns: A structured procedure for EMDR therapy. *Revista Iberoamericana de Psicotraumatología y Disociación, 4,* 3.

González, A., Mosquera, D., Knipe, J., Leeds, A., & Santed, M. (2017). *The self-care patterns scale* (Unpublished Document).

González, A., Mosquera, D., & Leeds, A. (2010). *Childhood experiences questionnaire* (Unpublished Document).

González, A., Mosquera, D., Leeds, A., & Knipe, J. (2012). *Self-care Scale.* Unpublished document.

Knipe, J. (2015). *EMDR toolbox: Theory and treatment of complex PTSD and dissociation.* New York, NY: Springer Publishing.

Mosquera, D. (2004). *Rough diamonds II. Psychoeducational and treatment manual for borderline personality disorder. Structured program for professionals* (1st ed. rev.). Madrid, Spain: Pléyades, S.A. (Published in Spanish).

Mosquera, D. (2013). *Rough diamonds II. Psychoeducational and treatment manual for borderline personality disorder. Structured program for professionals* (2nd ed. rev.) Madrid, Spain: Pléyades, S.A. (Published in Spanish).

Mosquera, D. (2017). *The discovery of the self: Enhancing reflective thinking, emotional regulation and self-care in borderline personality disorder.* North Charleston, SC: CreateSpace.

Mosquera, D., & González, A. (2014). *Borderline personality disorder and EMDR therapy.* Pléyades, S.A. (English edition in Amazon Imprint).

Popky, A. J. (1993). *Smoking protocol.* Paper presented at the EMDR Institute Annual Conference, Sunnyvale, CA.

Popky, A. J. (2009). The desensitization of triggers and urge reprocessing (DeTUR) protocol. In M. Luber (Ed.), *Eye Movement Desensitization and Reprocessing (EMDR) scripted protocol: Special populations* (pp. 489–511). New York, NY: Springer Publishing.

Ryle, A., & Kerr, I. B. (2002). *Introducing cognitive analytic therapy. Principles and practice.* New York, NY: John Wiley & Sons.

Shapiro, F. (2001). *Eye movement desensitization and reprocessing. Basic principles, protocols and procedures* (2nd ed.). New York, NY: Guilford Press.

Appendix 10.1

EMDR THERAPY SELF-CARE PSYCHOEDUCATIONAL WORKSHEET ON "HOW DO WE LEARN TO TAKE CARE OF OURSELVES?"

Relational patterns usually are passed on from generation to generation, but we may be able to make changes if we become aware of them. Many factors can interfere with a parent's ability to realize what his or her child feels and needs, to see him as an autonomous being with his own emotions and thoughts, or to accept him as he is while at the same time helping him to become "his better self."

This warm connection and the ability to unconditionally accept the child, without projecting onto him our own desires or fears, occurs in varying degrees in different families. If the child "is seen," that is, someone has identified his needs, considered them important, and gave back to the child a positive and realistic image of himself, he is likely to learn how to look at himself in a realistic and positive way, identify his needs and those of others, and take care of himself in a healthy way.

If the internal experience of the child—particularly all or some of his emotions—are punished or not recognized by a caregiver, the child will learn to imitate and internalize the adult's negative attitudes. This can be very obvious in families where there is mistreatment or abuse, and may occur in less obvious ways in dedicated and concerned families. Certain emotions may not be well tolerated in some families, for example, being angry may not be acceptable and may even be punished.

If caregivers are negligent, abusive, or uninterested, the child may learn and internalize these attitudes toward his or her own inner experiences, or toward some of them in particular. For example, if a child got scolded for crying, when he feels sad now as an adult, he may tell himself similar negative words—those he was repeatedly told at home. If a child got beaten up when he did something wrong, it is likely that now as an adult, he will beat himself up internally when he makes a mistake though he may not be fully aware of the things he is telling himself.

Caregivers with high levels of physical or psychological discomfort, blocked by personal problems and difficulties, will find it difficult or impossible to connect, validate, and manage/calm the emotions of the child. A caregiver who is not feeling well may not have enough energy for the child's demands for attention. Therefore, he will not provide the child with enough learning opportunities for developing an appropriate and sufficiently large emotional vocabulary. As this child grows up, he will easily develop a tendency to ignore his own needs and focus on those of others, learning that having needs is "bad" or "selfish."

When caregivers are not healthy models or do not accept, attend, or attach importance to the experiences of their children, the consequences may be different from those generated by direct abuse. However, in both cases they will affect a person's self-image and attitudes toward the self, including self-care patterns. Therefore, it is important to think about where we learned to take care of ourselves as we do, without blaming or judging.

Questions to reflect on what you have read:

1. Reflect on what you just read.

   _____

   _____

   _____

2. Do you think you are able to identify the emotions you are feeling? Do you recognize their relevance or do you avoid them? Do you try to understand what makes you feel like this or do you ignore it?

   _____

   _____

   _____

3. Do you think you are able to identify your needs? Do you recognize their relevance or do you tend to prioritize other people's feelings?

_____

_____

4. Where do you think you learned to take care of yourself as you do?

_____

_____

EMDR THERAPY SELF-CARE PSYCHOEDUCATIONAL WORKSHEET ON THE FUNCTION AND MANAGEMENT OF SELF-HARM AND SELF-DESTRUCTIVE BEHAVIORS

Self-harm and self-destructive behaviors have different functions, which can vary from person to person, or even in the same person in different situations.

This type of behavior causes an initial feeling of well-being, leading to a temporary feeling of calm and even euphoria. However, it is common for the discomfort to return, even more intensely, because the initial discomfort is usually attached to feelings of guilt or loss of control. That is, the final effect is often the opposite: finding yourself feeling even worse than before performing the self-destructive act.

So, we need to look for and learn new ways to help you relieve your discomfort that are less harmful and more durable and effective over time.

A series of questions are presented to gather important information about the type and function/ motive of the self-destructive behavior and potential less harmful alternatives that may help regulate moments of intense discomfort. Check any answer that applies in your case:

1. How do you usually harm yourself?

- Cutting
- Burning
- Hitting
- Substance abuse: alcohol or drugs
- Personal negligence
- Eating compulsively
- Shopping compulsively
- Unhealthy relationships
- Isolation
- Other: _____

2. What type of emotions trigger self-destructive behaviors in your case?

- Anger
- Anxiety
- Fear
- Guilt
- Confusion
- Shame
- Sadness
- Emptiness
- Lack of emotions or bodily sensations
- Other: _____

3. Which of the following are reasons to harm yourself?

- Feeling alive
- Calling for attention
- Expressing my inner pain
- Asking for help
- Self-punishment
- Feeling/noticing the body
- Other: _____

4. Which skills can you use to decrease your chances of carrying out any self-destructive behaviors?

- Talking to someone about any neutral subject
- Talking to someone about my feelings
- Writing about my feelings
- Remembering or going over exercises I have learned

- Reading
- Relaxation techniques, yoga, meditation, and so on.
- Going for a walk
- Taking a bath
- Physical exercise, dancing
- Artistic work: drawing, painting, sculpting, and so on.
- Counting in sevens backward starting from a high number
- Other: _____

5. Given the previous information, make a list of personal alternatives that you think you could *use before hurting yourself*. We will divide this list of positive alternatives to resort to before hurting yourself in two: one for those that depend only on you, which will be more easily attainable, and a second one in which we can include those that also depend on others. These will not be as reliable, precisely because they will not depend only on you.

DEPENDS ONLY ON ME	DEPENDS ON OTHERS
1.	1.
2.	2.
3.	3.
4.	4.
5.	5.

The purpose of this table is for you to have it handy in times of distress (on the bedroom or bathroom door, or where you usually carry out those behaviors that are destructive or harmful for your self-care). The reason for having it clearly visible is because if you are not feeling well, it will be hard to start looking for personal notes, other exercises you have done, and such. It is useful to record the things that work so you can check them out in times of confusion and great distress.

EMDR THERAPY SELF-CARE PSYCHOEDUCATIONAL SHEET ON RELAPSE PREVENTION

There are many different variables influencing the therapeutic process, which make predicting its course quite difficult. However, in our experience, we have observed some general phases, common in different cases and situations. Anticipating and knowing these phases builds safety and security both in the client and in the family.

When someone has been feeling bad for some time, one of the main issues is the person's own lack of control over his or her discomfort, added to not knowing what to expect. Thus, offering of a certain degree of "control" and anticipating possible relapses as part of the therapeutic process becomes essential in these cases.

Generally, and always from a flexible point of view, remembering that each person and each situation is different, we may speak about three phases: (1) the stabilization and "apparent improvement" phase, (2) the stability and "apparent stagnation" phase, and (3) the "actual improvement" phase.

1. Stabilization and "Apparent Improvement" Phase

When someone has been feeling bad for some time, not knowing what is happening, finding an explanation that makes sense usually has a very positive effect in the initial stabilization.

Feeling understood, understanding what is happening, knowing that they're not "the only person" going through this, and, overall, recovering hope when it was already lost are aspects influencing this "apparent improvement."

The word "apparent" does not mean the improvement is fake; it means that feeling good is temporary and variable and that we must expect the discomfort to return as long as we do not finish working on all the aspects and events that have generated the disturbance. We also talk about "apparent" because the intensity and duration of this well-being can be assessed as unrealistic, given that this intensity does not match the treatment; that is, it is impossible to have a lasting improvement when we have not started the treatment itself.

2. Stability and "Apparent Stagnation" Phase

This phase is usually the longest (since here is where most of the therapeutic work takes place) and, in general, the least tolerable, both for the client and for the family, if they do not understand what is happening.

Once treatment is started and the first stabilization takes place (intensity of suicidal ideation is reduced or stops altogether, self-harming behaviors are not as frequent and intense, and/or emotional instability becomes stabilized), it is time to start working on adversities and traumatic events step by step.

Throughout this phase of the process, therapeutic work takes place at an internal level, understanding and changing functioning patterns and working on processing traumatic events. Thus, it is common that changes are not externalized or visible if we only assess the person's behaviors. This is why clients and family members usually see it as stagnation because they are expecting visible and more significant changes.

This phase also includes the presence of relapses, which may initially be assessed as a step back, but truly are part of the process. We want those relapses to be less intense and frequent over time, and, if analyzed in depth, we will see that their foundation is not the same. Anticipating these relapses, as we said, generates safety and security in the client and the family. If it is not seen like this, there will be a tendency to feel hopeless, thinking that everything was an illusion and that the changes have not been real.

3. "Actual Improvement" Phase

This would be the final phase of the process in which improvement is clearly externalized and becomes more visible through behavior.

Once adversities and traumatic events have been worked on therapeutically, the person may normally use those resources and functioning alternatives acquired throughout the process that are more efficient, less harmful, and more functional.

This phase is mostly characterized by emotional stability, with unstable moments becoming much more sporadic and less intense.

Dolores Mosquera, Paula Baldomir Gago, Ana Cris Eiriz, and
Raquel Fernández Domínguez
SUMMARY SHEET BY MARILYN LUBER

Name: _____ Diagnosis: _____

Medications: _____

Test Results: _____

☑ Check when task is completed, response has changed, or to indicate symptoms.

Note: This material is meant as a checklist for your response. Please keep in mind that it is only a reminder of different tasks that may or may not apply to your incident.

EMDR SELF-CARE SCRIPTED PROTOCOL NOTES—SEE CHAPTER

Note: The EMDR self-care protocol is NOT recommended when *active suicidal ideation* is present.

EMDR THERAPY SELF-CARE SCRIPTED PROTOCOL

Phase 1: History Taking

Client History Questions

NUCLEAR FAMILY

Family grew up in: _____

_____

_____

ATTACHMENT STYLE

Rejected as child: ☐ Yes ☐ No

Comment: _____

_____

Threatening parents or family members: ☐ Yes ☐ No

Comment: _____

_____

Threatening behavior still affecting you: □ Yes □ No

Comment: _____

_____

Threatening behavior influencing your parenting: □ Yes □ No

Comment: _____

_____

Threatening experiences outside the family: □ Yes □ No

Comment: _____

_____

LOSSES

Loss of important figure growing up: □ Yes □ No

Comment on effect on you and caregivers: _____

_____

PHYSICAL AND EMOTIONAL CAREGIVING

Felt loved as a child: □ Yes □ No

Comment: _____

_____

Felt needs met: □ Yes □ No

Comment: _____

_____

TRAUMATIC SITUATIONS

Specific traumatic memories affecting you at ages 0 to 15

_____

_____

_____

_____

_____

_____

Assessing the Client's Self-Care Pattern in Order to Apply EMDR

See Questionnaire

Phase 2: Preparation

- **STEP A:** *Create a Good Therapeutic Alliance.* Therapeutic alliance with your client.
- **STEP B:** *Use Psychoeducation Guidelines*
- Use psychoeducation guidelines containing adaptive information regarding the most essential elements of self-care. The seven self-care protocols.
  - *1. EMDR Therapy Self-Care Psychoeducational Protocol for Understanding Self-Care*

  "The concept of self goes beyond good nutrition and adequate sleep for all of us. Good self-care has three core elements: (1) a positive attitude toward ourselves such as accepting and appreciating ourselves, (2) avoiding self-harm or self-defeating behaviors, and (3) taking specific actions that

provide benefits, growth, or value to ourselves. Let's talk about some of the key elements of healthy self-care."

a. Looking at Ourselves With the "Best Possible Eyes."

"The first one is looking at ourselves with the 'best possible eyes.' What do you think this means?"

_____

_____

Address the client's response and include the following explanation as needed: *"It is like being your own best friend or treating yourself as you would treat someone who you really care about, with empathy, affection, and loyalty. What do you think about that?"* _____

b. Looking at Ourselves With "Realistic Eyes."

"The next one is looking at ourselves with 'realistic eyes.' What do you think that means?"

_____

_____

Address the client's response and include the following explanation as needed: *"If we believe that we are always right, we are unable to assume when we are wrong, or we always focus on what others are doing wrong or what they need to change, we are not looking at ourselves or the world in a realistic way. It is important to assume our share of responsibility for our lives and be able to put ourselves in other people's shoes. If we need to think that we are perfect or better than others to accept ourselves, we will encounter many problems in relationship to ourselves and others. It is important to feel that we are 'good enough,' just as we are. What do you think about that?"* _____

c. Identifying and Regulating/Managing Emotions.

"The next one is learning how to identify and regulate/manage emotions. Emotional regulation is the ability to modulate our emotional responses. What does that mean to you?"

_____

_____

Address the client's response and include the following explanation as needed:

"This is related not only to the ability to reduce intense activation states, but also to the degree of emotional connection. The emotional reaction is not just a matter of how much emotion a person feels, but what he or she does with it. Many people have great difficulties identifying and managing their emotions because they have been taught to value emotions as positive, those that are more pleasant to feel, such as joy, or negative, those that are less pleasant to experience, such as anger, fear, or sadness. So, when they feel any of the emotions in the second group, they try to get rid of them. By doing this, people lose the opportunity to understand what they need. All emotions are positive, they all have a role/function and help protect the person; therefore, the goal is not to avoid them, but to learn how to manage them properly. Any thoughts about this?"

☐ Yes ☐ No

Comment: _____

d. Recognizing and Validating Our Own Needs.

"The fourth element is recognizing and validating our own needs. What does that mean to you?" ____

_____

Address the client's response and include the following explanation as needed:

"This means being aware of our needs and paying attention to the most basic sensations. A child who grows up feeling that his or her core emotional and/or physical needs are being ignored or shamed cannot learn to distinguish between different feelings and needs. This leads to confusion regarding emotions. When this happens, we need to learn to identify our feelings and emotions, pay attention to them, and consider them as relevant and important. If we can do this, we may feel that we are entitled

*to satisfy our needs and find the resources to have them met, including the possibility of seeking help from others and accepting it. What are your thoughts about that?"*_____

e. Protecting Ourselves Adequately.

"The fifth element is protecting ourselves adequately. What do you think that is about?" _____

_____

Address the client's response and include the following explanation as needed:

*"This would be related to the need for understanding healthy boundaries and being able to establish them. When caregivers do not recognize the limits of the child and/or fail to set healthy boundaries, not only will the future adult feel guilty for needing to set limits, but he or she may also actually lack an internal model to recognize the need for those boundaries. What does that mean to you?"*_____

f. Achieving a Balance Between Our Needs and Those of Others.

"The last one is achieving a balance between our needs and those of others. What do you think that is about?" _____

_____

Address the client's response and include the following explanation as needed:

> *"Some people struggle with a 'black and white' or 'all or nothing' thinking because the healthy ways to find a balance between conflicting needs have not been learned. People who did not learn to detect their needs or their own relevance may focus on the needs of others and ignore their own. Moreover, some people are so focused on their needs that they are not able to think of others and this causes problems in their relationships. Finding a balance between these two aspects is crucial."*

_____

2. EMDR Therapy Self-Care Psychoeducational Protocol for Learning How to Take Care of Ourselves

"I think it is important that you learn about your emotions, how you can handle them, and to recognize the strengths and weaknesses of your regulation style that you learned in childhood. To help with this idea, I am going to read you a story.

Four 5-year-old girls (Susana, María, Laura, and Teresa) are running around playing. All four trip and fall, scratching their knees. They go home and each one gets a different response.

*Susana: When Susana sees her bloody knees, she runs home crying. Her mother looks at her lovingly and says, 'Poor little girl, it hurts, doesn't it?' She gives the girl a hug and says, 'I'll clean up your wound. Yes, of course it hurts! We'll get a Band-Aid. Come and sit on my lap for a bit. We'll sing a song that will make you feel better.' In a short while, the little girl will want to go back out and play and her mother asks if her knee still hurts. Smiling, she says 'No,' while running out the door to play. What does Susana learn?"*_____

_____

Address the client's response and include the following explanation as needed: *"Yes, _____ (state whatever was mentioned by the client). She also learned:*

- *My emotions are important.*
- *I can identify and name what I feel.*
- *I respect my feelings.*
- *When I feel bad, I believe my feelings are valid.*
- *I am able to pay attention to my needs."*

And, she may also learn about others' emotions:

- *"Other people's emotions are important.*
- *I am able to identify, tolerate, and empathize with other people's emotions without making them mine. Does that make sense to you?"*   ☐ Yes ☐ No

Comment: _____

"María: María goes home and her mother is busy in the kitchen. María, with tears in her eyes from the shock and the pain, tells her, 'I fell down and hurt myself.' Her mother comes toward her without a word, grabs some Band-Aids and hydrogen peroxide, makes her sit down, and cleans up her wound. Meanwhile, María tries to find her mother's eyes but, because there is no response, she focuses on how her mother is cleaning up her wound, appearing calmer. When her mother is done, she says, 'Go and wash up, we are about to have dinner,' and walks away, going back to her chores. María turns around, wipes off her tears, and goes up to her room. What does María learn?" _____

Address the client's response and include the following explanation as needed: *"Yes,* _____ *(state whatever was mentioned by the client). She also learned:*

- *I don't know what I feel.*
- *My emotions are not important.*
- *Emotions don't seem to be useful."*

And, she may also learn about others and their feelings:

- *"I have trouble understanding other people's feelings.*
- *When others feel bad, I focus on myself. Does that make sense to you?"*   ☐ Yes ☐ No

Comment: _____

"Laura: Laura runs home crying as her mother runs out looking for her. She heard the girls screaming and thought that something very serious must have happened. When she sees her, she grabs her by the arms, yelling at her, 'Haven't I told you a thousand times to be careful? I'm going to have a heart attack because of you. Come on, go home.' Laura is very upset and keeps crying. Her mother says, 'Don't cry, little girl, it's nothing. . . . Come on, don't cry anymore, it makes you look ugly.' What does Laura learn?" _____

Address the client's response and include the following explanation as needed: *"Yes,* _____ *(state whatever was mentioned by the client). She also learned:*

- *My emotions overwhelm me (and overwhelm others).*
- *I feel guilty for feeling this way.*
- *I don't know what to do with my emotions.*
- *I desperately seek others, but even if they respond, I am unable to calm down. (At times, I even get angry at them when they try to help me.)*
- *It takes me a long time to feel better."*

And, she may also learn about others' emotions:

- *"Other people's emotions overwhelm me.*
- *I don't know how to relate to others in difficult situations.*
- *When people feel bad, I think it's their fault or they deserve it.*
- *When others don't calm down quickly, I get anxious or angry.*

Does that make sense to you?"   ☐ Yes ☐ No

Comment: _____

"Teresa: Teresa got very scared with the fall and cannot stop crying. When she gets home her mother says, 'You're always falling down, you're clumsy and useless.' Teresa cries louder. Her mother is even more upset and shouts, 'Shut up! You're such a crybaby! I don't know who you took after!' The girl scratches herself and continues crying, more and more dysregulated. Her mother comes up, slaps her, and screams, 'Do you want more?' Teresa falls down due to the impact, freezes, and stops crying. What does Teresa learn?" _____

Address the client's response and include the following explanation as needed: *"Yes,* _____ *(state whatever was mentioned by the client). She also learned:*

- *Showing emotions is dangerous.*
- *If I ask for help, I may get hurt.*
- *I deserve what is happening to me; it's my fault that I'm like this."*

And, she may also learn about others and their emotions:

- *"I don't understand emotions or their use.*
- *Only weak people cry.*
- *I despise weakness, vulnerability, and fear.*
- *I don't need anyone.*
- *It's better not to feel anything.*

Does that make sense to you?"   ☐ Yes ☐ No

Comment: _____

Give them the **Psychoeducational Worksheet on How Do We Learn to Take Care of Ourselves** as homework and it will be discussed in the following session.

"Here is a brief worksheet for you to read at home about what we have been discussing today. At the end, you will find some questions for you to reflect on at home concerning what you have read. Do you have any questions? We will discuss it more during the next session."

3. EMDR Therapy Self-Care Psychoeducational Protocol on Relapse Prevention

"I would like you to be aware of a common situation that we encounter in therapy: fear of change. In many cases, when somebody feels better, he or she can get frightened or feel pressured because he or she is not used to feeling better. We usually find that the therapeutic process follows three different phases:

a. *Stabilization and "Apparent Improvement" Phase: When someone has been feeling bad for some time, not knowing what is happening, finding an explanation that makes sense and feeling understood usually has a very positive effect in the initial stabilization. The word "apparent" means that feeling good is temporary and variable, and that it is probable that the discomfort will return as long as the work on all the aspects and events that have generated the disturbance are not finished.*

b. *Stability and "Apparent Stagnation" Phase: This phase is usually the longest and, in general, the least tolerable, both for you and your family. Once treatment is started and the first stabilization takes place, it is time to start working on adversities and traumatic events step by step. Throughout this phase of the process, therapeutic work takes place at an internal level. Thus, it is common that changes are not externalized or visible if only behaviors are assessed. This is why people usually see it as stagnation since they are expecting visible and more significant changes. This phase also includes the presence of relapses, which may initially be assessed as a step back, but truly are part of the process. The goal is for those relapses to be less intense and frequent over time.*

c. *"Actual Improvement" Phase: This would be the final phase of the process, in which improvement is clearly externalized and becomes more visible through behavior. Once adversities and traumatic events have been worked on therapeutically, you may normally use those resources and functioning alternatives acquired throughout the process that are more efficient, less harmful, and more functional.*

I will give you a worksheet on this process, once your treatment is finished, for you to keep so you can go over it when needed, to avoid relapses."

- **STEP C:** *Explanation of EMDR*

"I want to tell you about EMDR therapy. When a trauma occurs, it seems to get locked in the nervous system with the original picture, sounds, thoughts, and feelings. The eye movements we use in EMDR seem to unlock the nervous system and allow the brain to process the experience. That may be what is happening in REM or dream sleep—the eye movements may help to process the unconscious material. It is important to note that it is your own brain that will be doing the healing and that you are the one in control."

- **STEP D:** *Installing Positive Resources*

The next step involves installing positive resources as necessary. This can include the Safe Place (Shapiro, 2001) and other procedures specifically designed for working on self-care.

4. EMDR Therapy Self-Care Protocol for Developing Resources

Reinforce aspects that indicate how clients take care of themselves adequately up to now such as setting adequate boundaries during the week, asking for help, and accepting it. Get the description to install the positive sensation.

*"This week you were able to set boundaries with _____ (state person client set limits with). This is something that you wanted to do for a long time but couldn't. How did it feel to do this?"*_____

Install any insight related to the ability of taking care of oneself. Get the description to install the positive sensation.

"This week you realized how important it was to find time for yourself. Can you tell me how it felt when you realized this?"

_____

_____

Install personalized resources to facilitate practicing self-care on specific items.

"What would be a resource that you experienced this week that helped you facilitate your self-care practice?"

_____

_____

Installing these resources assists the development and installation of positive alternative behaviors to increase clients' capacities to carry out positive behaviors in moments of distress, thus increasing their emotional self-regulation capacities.

STEP E: *Stabilization*

In the case of the client presenting self-harming behaviors, extra attention should be given to an extended stabilization.

5. EMDR Therapy Self-Care Protocol for Self-Harm and Self-Destructive Behaviors

This includes psychoeducational script on the function and management of self-harm and self-destructive behaviors, as well as a worksheet recommended as a homework assignment, before applying the actual protocol.

"This is called the 'EMDR Self-Care Protocol for Self-Harm and Other Self-Destructive Behaviors,' and the idea behind it is to help you address self-harm and other self-destructive behaviors so that you can reduce your impulses to carry out self-destructive behaviors in the present. Is that something you might be interested in?"   ☐ Yes ☐ No

"I would like to talk about how self-harm and self-destructive behaviors work so that you can understand how they evolve and how you learned them. Cuts, scratches, or compulsive, abusive, or self-destructive behaviors often lead to a temporary sense of calm and even euphoria, although they later have the opposite effect and generate discomfort and guilt, that is, finding yourself feeling even worse than before the destructive act.

Sometimes self-harm happens because we cannot find words to express the intensity of our suffering and need to communicate it, 'get it out'; other times, because we need to make it visible to ask for help; and at still other times because the emotions are too intense and painful and we have not learned to identify, accept, tolerate, handle, or express them appropriately, as we mentioned in the previous informative session. Other reasons for self-destructive behavior include guilt, frustration, anger directed at oneself, or simply wanting to 'feel alive,' disconnect from the suffering or discomfort, or 'escape from our body.' Ironically, people sometimes resort to self-destructive behaviors as a comforting strategy to cope with discomfort.

This, which at first may seem like a strange and eccentric behavior, makes sense if we see it as learned behavior, as a way to regulate our own emotions. Whether the goal is feeling relief, self-punishment, or feeling alive, in all cases there is a significant emotional component that needs to be regulated or stopped: those who self-punish need a lesson; those who self-injure to feel alive need something to let them know they really exist, that they do feel; those who do it for relief need an escape because they have the feeling they are going to explode at any moment.

We could say that by not having acquired adaptive skills to calm down and manage stress or frustration, people resort to action because it is less complicated than trying to understand and express feelings. It is important to be aware that action brings relief, while verbalizing and sharing requires a big effort and a repertoire of skills that are often lacking, and so resorting to action serves as a mean of communication.

For many, it is easier to tolerate physical pain than emotional pain, especially when they do not know why they feel so overwhelmed by a certain moment or situation. Physical pain is tangible, it can be seen, shown, understood, transmitted, and even cured, but emotional pain is truly difficult to share and show. Showing emotional pain requires tears, screams, tremors, agitation, words, action, and the like—something visible or 'listenable' that allows those around us to visualize what we feel. If we cancel the physical or behavioral responses, it is particularly complicated to perceive or imagine what the other person is feeling. Try to imagine an expressionless person who is explaining what he is feeling without any gesture or movement to accompany this explanation. It would be cold, distant, and unreal. And this is what can lead many people to behave this way: the need to express feelings and the difficulties in doing so in a verbal or para-verbal way (nonverbal language such as gestures, postures, facial expressions, tone of voice, etc.).

It is important to find alternative ways to address these feelings without doing oneself any harm. One way to do this, for example, is learning to distract ourselves. Many people find it helpful to talk or write about feelings, take a walk, or do strenuous exercise."

We then give the **Psychoeducational Worksheet on the Function and Management of Self-Harm and Self-Destructive Behaviors** to the client, so he or she can fill it out at home. *"When people are feeling bad, generally, they cannot control their emotions and it is common to resort to self-destructive behaviors because they do not see any other way out. It is important to have resources to divert your attention and focus on possible alternatives, avoiding physical or psychological harm.*

These resources must be planned in advance because during the 'bad moments' it will be much harder to stop and think 'What would be better to do instead of _____?' A strategy that may be useful is to ask the question(s), 'What would I tell the person I love the most if he or she felt like I am feeling?' or 'What would I recommend they do?'

I'd like you to have this worksheet, take it home with you, and complete it. A series of questions are presented to gather important information about the type and function/motive of the self-destructive behavior and potential less harmful alternatives that may help regulate moments of intense discomfort. Check any answer that applies in your case. Next week, we'll use it for our work in session."

Then, we move on to installing additional resources, if needed. This is used only when self-harming behaviors are present.

IDENTIFY AND INSTALL POSITIVE RESOURCES

"One day in the future, when you don't need to 'hurt yourself' anymore _____ (state the type of self-destructive behavior that is riskier for the client), what kind of good things would that day have that you don't have today": _____

_____

Positive image: _____

_____

Picture of situation/event/stimulus + _____ (PC)

Positive day + Positive words + BLS

_____

_____

"What is your biggest current trigger for wanting to 'hurt yourself?' You may think of four or five, but choose the strongest one. Describe the image for that trigger."

Trigger: _____

Image: _____

LoU: _____/10

Location of number in body: _____ + BLS

LoU: _____/10

"Be aware of that feeling in your body, the physical sensations you are noticing here and now. You have not decided to do it, but just notice that you want to do it. Be aware of how much you want it." + BLS

_____

Image + LoU: _____/10 + BLS

_____

If the LoU reaches 0: *"Think about the positive moments related to these 'self-destructive behaviors.' Is there anything left of that urge to 'hurt yourself?' Notice that this is how zero feels."* + BLS

_____

"What would you say about yourself now? (PC) What do you notice in your body when you think of _____ (state the PC)?" _____ + BLS

_____

"Bring up the picture of that trigger along with any words, tastes, smells, or sounds that go with it. How strong is the LoU to hurt yourself right now, from 0 to 10, where 0 is no urge and 10 is the strongest?" ____/10

Repeat for each trigger.

6. EMDR Therapy Self-Care Protocol to Develop and Install Positive Alternative Behaviors

PREPARATION

Use the chart of alternative behaviors created by the client from the information in the **Worksheet on the Function and Management of Self-Harm and Self-Destructive Behaviors**. Review the chart with the client to install those alternatives that have worked as positive resources. It is possible that you will have to repeat the EMDR Protocol for Self-Harming and Other Self-Destructive Behaviors if the client carried out any serious self-destructive behavior since the last session.

"These are the resources/alternative behaviors that you thought would be better to do instead of ____ (state self-harming or other self-destructive behaviors) where you would be depending only on yourself. Let's review them and see if we must modify, expand, or eliminate any item."

Identify Positive Resources for Installation: The positive resource will be the one chosen that week by the client to substitute the destructive behavior, which should be included in the chart from the worksheet.

"Now that you selected a resource that you find useful, we can reinforce it. Think about _____ (state the chosen resource)."

Identify Positive Image: "Describe the situation from this week in which you were telling me that you felt ____ (state the negative emotion described by the client), that you were able to reduce the urge to ____ (state self-destructive behavior), and where you also ____ (state alternative positive behavior)."

_____

_____

Identify the Positive Cognition (PC): "*Think about the positive moments associated with having regulated your discomfort through a positive behavior. What are the positive words you would say about yourself now?*" _____

_____

Assess the Validity of Cognition (VOC): "*When you think of the incident* (or picture), *how true do those words* _____ (clinician repeats the positive cognition) *feel to you now on a scale of 1 to 7, where 1 feels completely false and 7 feels completely true?*" ___/7

Identify Associated Physical Sensations for Installation: "*Be aware of that* _____ (state sensation in body) *in your body, the physical sensations you are noticing here and now.*" + BLS (until VOC = 6/7)

Future Template: "*Think about some future moments in which you think it would be helpful to feel this sensation while you maintain the belief* _____ (state PC)." + BLS

"*What do you get now?*"_____

"*Stop in each one of those moments so you can clearly feel the PC.*"

STEP F: Reformulating the client's presenting problem in terms of how he or she learned his or her self-care habit is essential.

7. EMDR Therapy Self-Care Protocol for Working With the Inner Child

I. IDENTIFY HOW THE ADULT LEARNED SELF-CARE HABITS

"*Where do you think you learned to* _____ (state maladaptive self-care habit such as binging when feeling lonely/not allowing yourself to ask for help/judging and criticizing yourself when you feel sad or angry)?*"_____

It is important to be specific about the client's self-care problem selected as focus for the current session. It is important to use the client's words. "*Do you remember any experience in your childhood that may be related to how you learned to take care of yourself in such ways?*"   ☐ Yes ☐ No

Comment: _____

Note for the Therapist: There are many targets that can be used such as selecting a memory, a certain look/expression from the caregiver, a sentence or word from the caregiver, and the like.

II. DESCRIBING THE IMAGE OF THE CHILD

"*Can you see the child that you were, who learned to* _____ (state maladaptive behavior)?"

☐ Yes ☐ No

Comment: _____

"*We are going to work with the child as a whole, not just with the life history or specific experiences: Are you able to see that child?*"   ☐ Yes ☐ No

Comment: _____

"*What do you see?*" _____

_____

"*How old is* ____ (he/she)?" _____

"*What is* ____ (he/she) *doing?*" _____

_____

"*How is* ____ (his/her) *body posture,* ____ (his/her) *gestures?*" _____

_____

The goal is to help the client build an image of the child that is as clear as possible.

Note for the Therapist: If the adult has trouble seeing the child, it is important to identify if this is a dissociative phobia or any other difficulty related to the lack of self-care experiences.

III. EXPLORING DISSOCIATIVE PHOBIAS. CHECKING THE ADULT'S FEELINGS TOWARD THE CHILD

"When you think about the child, how do you feel about _____ (state him/her)?" _____

_____

The guidelines are that *if the client feels any negative feeling toward the child, this would be considered a dissociative phobia.*

When the client says something positive (curiosity, tenderness, or compassion), go to Step IV, "Connecting the adult with the image of the child."

Note for the Therapist: To explore dissociative phobias, it may be enough to explore the adult's reaction toward the image of the child. The following indicators can be helpful (based on González & Mosquera, 2012; Mosquera & González, 2014). When the adult describes the image of the child, it is important to look for disconnection, overconnection, and/or high mental autonomy. It is important to help clinicians be aware of these three elements, which are frequent in dissociative cases where child parts have a first-person perspective and high mental autonomy. The following questions help with that.

When the client cannot see the child (disconnection), help him or her connect by asking questions such as the following: *"How do you think _____ (he/she) may have felt?"* _____

_____

_____

"Look at _____ (his, her) posture; what do you think may be happening to ___ (him/her)?" _____

_____

When the client becomes too emotionally involved and overwhelmed (overconnection), offer emotional psychoeducation by stating the following:

"Did you know that to help someone we do not have to feel exactly how they feel?"   ☐ Yes ☐ No

Comment: _____

"Did you know that to think about the different ways of helping others we must remain calm and not feel things with the same intensity as those we are trying to help?"   ☐ Yes ☐ No

Comment: _____

"How could you help the child with ___ (his/her) pain without feeling all the pain ___ (she/he) is feeling?" _____

_____

Whenever the child shows an autonomy that surprises the adult such as hiding or he or she does not want to speak to the adult (high mental autonomy, where the child has a first-person perspective), a negotiation process among dissociative parts must take place.

IV. CONNECTING THE ADULT WITH THE IMAGE OF THE CHILD. PROMOTING EMPATHY: HELPING THE ADULT THINK ABOUT THE CHILD'S FEELINGS

"Can you, without judging, see _____ (his/her) face, the look in _____ (his/her eyes)?   ☐ Yes ☐ No

Comment: _____

"Go with that." Do several sets of BLS.

Any negative memory that may come up during this process should be reprocessed with the Standard EMDR Protocol.

"What does ____ *(he/she) convey through the look in* ____ *(his/her) eyes?"* _____

_____

"Can you pick up on ____ *(his/her) feelings through the look in* ____ *(his/her) eyes?"*   ☐ Yes ☐ No

Comment: _____

"Go with that." Do several sets of BLS

"How do you think ____ *(he/she) is feeling?"*

_____

Note for the Therapist: Search for profound emotional pain (sometimes you may see a smiling face because this is what the child learned to show to protect him- or herself, but we must guide the client to go beyond that).

Recheck the feelings of the adult toward the child: *"How does it make you feel, as your adult self here with me, to see this child who is feeling so____ (state how child is feeling)?"*_____

If there is rejection or discomfort, we must process the defense. *"On a scale of 0 to 10, where 0 is no disturbance or neutral and 10 is the highest disturbance you can imagine, how disturbing does it feel now?"* ____/10 + BLS until SUD = 0

V. IDENTIFYING AND MEETING NEEDS AND/OR MISSING EXPERIENCES

Identify the Possible Needs of the Child.

"What do you feel ____ *(he/she) needs?"* _____

_____

Provide psychoeducation, if needed, about childhood needs at the age of the inner child with whom we are working: physical touch, containment, company, play, and the like.

If the client is unable to find an answer that satisfies the child, we may help him or her reflect asking things such as the following: *"What may a child need when* ___ *(he/she) is crying because* ___ *(he/she) is sad?"*_____

_____

If we are aware that the client knows a child of that age in his environment, we can use that example, or ask: *"What would you need to do as an adult if this kid you know were here with us and was crying because* ___ *(he/she) is scared of* ___ *(state what he/she is scared of)?"* _____

With our help, we try to facilitate the client reaching an empathic and validating response toward the child.

Explore the Adult's Feeling of Being Able to Meet the Child's Needs.

"Do you feel able to give it to him?"   ☐ Yes ☐ No

Comment: _____

If so, *"Imagine the adult that you are* _____ *(state adaptive response of adult such as hugging the child/holding his or her hand/telling him he or she is not alone) and see what you notice."* + BLS

If the client does not feel able to do so: *"Do you notice something in your body that says you can't do it?"*   ☐ Yes ☐ No

Comment: _____

"On a scale of 0 to 10, where 0 is no disturbance or neutral and 10 is the highest disturbance you can imagine, how disturbing does it feel now?" ___/10 + BLS until SUD = 0

Note for the Therapist: When the adult response is one of wanting to get close to the child, showing a need for physical contact, it will be necessary to ask him to check if the child would be ready/willing to have this physical contact or if, for the time being, some other type of closeness would be enough. If so, remind the adult that this child has been very lonely and that we must respect his rhythm. For now, it could be enough with maintaining an accepting eye contact/sitting together/sitting side by side/sitting in front of each other, and the like. Explain that respecting the child's rhythm will be the best way to show him acceptance and caregiving. The therapist, through the adult, will give that same accepting message, saying things like the following:

"Can you please tell the child that we will respect his rhythm, that ___ (he/she) will be the one in charge of the work we do, and that we will listen to ___ (him/her) and take ___ (him/her) into consideration, because ___ (he/she) is important?"   □ Yes □ No

Comment: _____

Locate Bodily Feelings and Facilitate Connection.

"If you could locate the child in your body, where do you feel ___ (he/she) would live?"

_____

"Can you notice the child's emotion in your body?"   □ Yes □ No

Comment: _____

"Where do you notice it?" _____

"What is the physical sensation that goes along with that emotion?" _____

_____

+ BLS

Reinforce Connection and Integration

Ask the adult to allow the child to feel the emotion, and explore where the adult notices the physical sensation that belongs to the child's emotion: *"Can you place your adult hands over the part of your body where you notice that sensation or emotion of the child?"*   □ Yes □ No

Comment: _____

"Can you offer the child the ___ (state either caregiving/love/containment or anything appropriate for the client) *that your adult hands are conveying?"*   □ Yes □ No

Comment: _____ + BLS

"If your hands could convey that sensation through words, what message would they give to the child?"

_____

_____ + BLS

Note for the Therapist: Find simple words that the child can understand given his or her age, for example, *"I am here with you," "I see you and I feel you," "I'll take care of you," "You're important for me,"* and the like.

"It may be the first time that the child shares this emotion, and it is a very exciting and important moment. Can you notice the connection between the both of you?"   □ Yes □ No

Comment: _____ + BLS

"Check and see how the child feels when ___ (he/she) notices that the adult is there for ___ (him/her), check and see how the adult feels when ___ (he/she) notices that ___ (he/she) can comfort the child."
+ BLS _____

_____

VI. INSTALLING THE CHANGE

"Look again into the eyes of the child. What do you see? Has something changed? What is different now?"

_____

_____

If there is any change, regardless of how small, ask the client to notice the difference in the emotion/thought/body. *"OK. Notice the difference."* + BLS

If a positive emotion comes up, point it out and validate it. *"Notice that* ____ *(state positive emotion)."*____

_____

_____

Repeat the client's words when referring to that positive emotion.

"Where do you notice it in your body?" _____ + BLS

VII. CLOSURE

Promoting Realization

Promote reflection. *"What are you noticing while doing this exercise"*: _____

_____

"What meaning do you give to what you just experienced": _____

_____

"Do you understand more about yourself right now":   □ Yes □ No

Comment: _____

"Do you understand more about your problem and how to get over it":   □ Yes □ No

Comment: _____ + BLS

Closing the Session

Use psychoeducation as needed about what happened in the session, clarifying any doubts the client may have. *"What have you realized today"*: _____

_____

"How do you think this can help you": _____

_____

If you see that the client is ready, ask him or her to repeat the exercise at home connecting his or her hands to the physical sensation of the child's emotion.

Say, *"Do you think this is an exercise that you can practice at home?"*   □ Yes □ No

Comment: _____

Use the Calm/Safe Place exercise, which was done in previous sessions, and ask the adult and child to go together to the safe place, if appropriate for closure.

"Can you think of your safe place?"	☐ Yes ☐ No

Comment: _____

"Can you share this safe place with the child?"	☐ Yes ☐ No

Comment: _____

Or say, *"Can you show this safe place to the child and ask him or her to join you?"*	☐ Yes ☐ No

Comment: _____ + BLS

Phases 3 to 8: Assessment–Reevaluation

For any negative traumatic memories that must be reprocessed, use the Standard EMDR Protocol.

STEP G: Give the *EMDR Therapy Self-Care Psychoeducational Script on Relapse Prevention*

psychoeducation sheet to clients at the end of treatment to prevent relapses.

"Please read the psychoeducation sheet about relapse prevention. Thoughts?" _____

Appendix A: Updated Worksheets

PAST MEMORY WORKSHEET SCRIPT (SHAPIRO, 2006, 2018)

Incident

Say, *"The memory that we will start with today is _____ (select the incident to be targeted)."*

_____

_____

_____

Say, *"What happens when you think of the _____ (state the issue)?"*

_____

_____

_____

Or say, *"When you think of the incident, what do you get?"*

_____

_____

_____

Picture

Say, *"What picture best represents the experience to you?"*

_____

_____

_____

If there are many choices or if the client becomes confused, the clinician assists by asking the following:

Say, *"What picture represents the worst part of the experience as you think about it now?"*

_____

_____

_____

When a picture is unavailable, say the following:

Say, *"Think of the incident."*

_____

_____

_____

Negative Cognition (NC)

Say, *"What words go best with the picture that express your negative belief about yourself now?"*

_____

_____

_____

Often, it is difficult for your client to state a negative cognition, and it may help to explain that these self-limiting assessments are irrational and there may be a conflict between what the patient feels and thinks about himself or herself.

Say, *"State what you think of yourself in your worst moments, even if you know it isn't true."*

_____

_____

_____

In some cultures it is more helpful to say:

Say, *"How do you define yourself?"*

_____

_____

_____

Or say, *"What adjectives do you give yourself?"*

_____

_____

_____

Another way to elicit an NC is to ask the client to hold the memory in mind and say the following:

Say, *"What thoughts do you have about yourself?"*

_____

_____

_____

Then, help your client articulate an appropriate NC.

Positive Cognition (PC)

Say, *"When you bring up that picture or experience, what would you prefer to believe about yourself, instead?"*

_____

_____

In some cultures, it is better to say the following:

Say, *"How would you like to define yourself?"*

_____

_____

Or say, *"What adjectives would you want to give yourself?"*

_____

_____

Validity of Cognition (VOC)

Say, *"When you think of the memory, how true do the words ____ (clinician repeats the PC) feel to you now on a scale of 1 to 7, where 1 feels completely false and 7 feels completely true?"*

1   2   3   4   5   6   7

(completely false)   (completely true)

Sometimes it is helpful to explain more:

Or say, *"Remember, sometimes, we know something with our head, but it feels differently in our gut. In this case, what is the gut-level feeling of the truth of _____ (repeat the PC), on a scale of 1 to 7, where 1 is completely false and 7 is completely true?"*

1   2   3   4   5   6   7

(completely false)   (completely true)

Emotions

Say, *"When you think of the memory and the words _____ (repeat the NC), what emotions do you feel now?"*

_____

_____

_____

Subjective Units of Disturbance (SUDs)

Say, *"On a scale of 0 to 10, where 0 is no disturbance or neutral and 10 is the highest disturbance you can imagine, how disturbing does it feel now?"*

0   1   2   3   4   5   6   7   8   9   10

(no disturbance)   (highest disturbance)

Location of Body Sensation

Say, *"Where do you feel it* (the disturbance) *in your body?"*

_____

If needed, assist clients in locating body sensations by referring to their SUD score:

Say, *"You reported* ____ (state the SUD score) *on the SUD scale. Where do you feel the* ____ (state the SUD score) *in your body?"*

Additional help can be as follows:

Say, *"Close your eyes and notice how your body feels. Now I will ask you to think of something, and when I do, just notice what changes in your body. Okay, notice your body. Now, think of* (or bring up the picture of) *the memory. Tell me what changes. Now add the words* ____ (the clinician states the NC). *Tell me what changes."*

_____

_____

_____

PHASE 4: DESENSITIZATION

To begin, say the following:

"Now, remember, it is your own brain that is doing the healing and you are the one in control. I will ask you to mentally focus on the target and to follow my fingers (or any other BLS you are using). Just let whatever happens, happen, and we will talk at the end of the set. Just tell me what comes up, and don't discard anything as unimportant. Any new information that comes to mind is connected in some way. If you want to stop, just raise your hand."

Then say, *"Bring up the picture and the words* ____ (clinician repeats the NC) *and notice where you feel it in your body. Now follow my fingers with your eyes* (or other BLS)."*

At the end of the set, say a version of the following:

"Let it go or blank it out, and take a deep breath."

When the client seems to be ready, establish contact by saying the following:

"What do you get now?"

_____

_____

If the client is still unable to respond, say the following:

"What came up for you?"

_____

_____

If the client says he gets nothing, say the following:

"When you think of the incident, what do you get?"

_____

_____

To confirm the client's experience, say the following:

"Good" or *"Uh-huh."*

When there has been a shift in any part of the information, attention can be re-concentrated with the following statement:

Say, *"Think of that"* or *"Notice that"* or *"Go with that."*

If the client seems to be attempting to evoke a sense of relief by going to the safe place or adding a less disturbing thought,

Say, *"Are you doing or saying anything deliberately?"*

_____

_____

If so, say the following:

"Just let it happen, without judging or trying to force anything to happen."

When a client describes feeling numb or dissociated, say the following and do BLS:

"Where do you feel it in your body?"

_____

_____

As these experiences emerge, a client can feel a range of feelings. It is helpful to say something like the following:

"That's it; just remember it's the old stuff."

_____

_____

As sets of associations finish, ask the client to retarget the original incident:

"Think of the incident. What do you get now?"

_____

_____

If the client reports low-grade negative emotions, ask the following:

"What prevents it from being a zero?"

Note: A SUD level higher than zero should be accepted only if it appears reasonable and when two more sets are tried and nothing changes. Make sure of the ecological suitability before moving to the installation phase.

PHASE 5: INSTALLATION

Say, *"How does _____ (repeat the PC) sound?"*

_____

Say, *"Do the words _____ (repeat the PC) still fit, or is there another positive state-ment that feels better?"*

_____

If the client accepts the original PC, the clinician should ask for a VOC rating to see if it has improved:

Say, *"As you think of the incident, how do the words feel, from 1 (completely false) to 7 (completely true)?"*

1   2   3   4   5   6   7

(completely false)   (completely true)

If the VOC has not increased, check the PC because it should have increased after processing the information.

Say, *"Think of the event and hold it together with the words _____ (repeat the PC)."*

_____

_____

Repeat bilateral stimulation (BLS) until the VOC reaches 7 and is at its maximum. The goal is to have a strong, solid PC. If the PC does not improve above a 5 or 6, say the following:

Say, *"What prevents it from being a 7?"*

_____

_____

If it does not process and a dysfunctional blocking belief is revealed, target it with a full EMDR treatment on the associated memory. The floatback and affect scan techniques can be used.

When the installation phase is complete, move on to the body scan.

PHASE 6: BODY SCAN

Say, *"Close your eyes and keep in mind the original memory and the positive cognition. Then bring your attention to the different parts of your body, starting with your head and work-ing downward. Any place you find any tension, tightness, or unusual sensation, tell me."*

_____

_____

The body scan phase is complete when the client can hold in mind the target and the PC, and then scan the body and finds no more body tension or negative sensations. When a positive or comfortable sensation occurs, sets are done to strengthen it.

PHASE 7: CLOSURE

It is important to have enough time to end the session with the kind of directions that leave clients in a positive state, able to leave the session and return home safely. Make sure that clients are oriented in the present, and, if not, have them wait in the waiting room until you think it is safe for them to leave. If clients are showing signs of distress, make sure to use resources such as hypnosis, guided imagery, the Safe/Calm Place exercise, the lightstream technique, and so on, to return to a state of well-being (Shapiro, 2001).

> Say, *"The processing we have done today may continue after the session. You may or may not notice new insights, thoughts, memories, or dreams. Things may come up or they may not. If they do, great. Write them down, and they can be a target for the next time. If you get any new memories, dreams, or situations that disturb you, just take a good snapshot. It isn't necessary to give a lot of detail. Just put down enough to remind you in a TICES log so we can target it next time."*

Then, draw five columns on a piece of blank paper: a "T" stands for "Trigger," an "I" stands for "Image," a "C" stands for "Cognition," an "E" stands for "Emotion," and an "S" stands for "Sensation."

"The same thing goes for any positive dreams or situations. If negative feelings do come up, try not to make them significant. Remember, it's still just the old stuff. Just write it down for the next time. Then use the recording or the Safe (or Calm) Place exercise to let as much of the disturbance go as possible. Even if nothing comes up, make sure to use the recording every day and give me a call if you need to."

PHASE 8: REEVALUATION

There are four ways to reevaluate our work with clients.

1. **Has the individual target been resolved?**

Reevaluate the target worked on in the previous session. The negative and positive cognitions are not needed, since they were previously elicited. Whether the previous processing session was complete or incomplete, use the following instructions to access the memory and determine the need for further processing.

> Say, *"Bring up the memory or trigger of _____ (state the memory or trigger) that we worked on in the last session."*

_____

_____

> Say, *"What is the worst part of it?"*

_____

_____

> Say, *"On a scale of 0 to 10, where 0 is no disturbance or neutral and 10 is the highest disturbance you can imagine, how disturbing does it feel now?"*

0   1   2   3   4   5   6   7   8   9   10

(no disturbance)   (highest disturbance)

> Say, *"What emotions did you notice?"*

_____

_____

Say, *"What sensations do you notice?"*

_____

_____

Evaluate the material to see if there are any indications of dysfunction. All negative associated material for one distinct experience/trauma should be processed before moving on to another. If there are inappropriate fears or behaviors, they are considered to be products of the past and need to be targeted.

Based on the results, do one of the following: Continue reprocessing that target, move to another target, begin another prong of the protocol, or enter the final follow-up period to complete the EMDR therapy.

2. Has associated material been activated that must be addressed?

Say, *"Okay. Let's look at your log. I am interested in what has happened since the last session. What have you noticed since our last session? What has changed."*

_____

_____

If the client has nothing to say or does not say much, say the following:

Say, *"Have you had any dreams or nightmares?"*

_____

_____

Say, *"What about _____* (state symptoms you and the client have been working on) *we have been working on; have you noticed any changes in them? Have they increased or decreased?"*

_____

_____

Say, *"Have you noticed any other changes, new responses, or insights in your images, thoughts, emotions, sensations, and behaviors?"*

_____

_____

Say, *"Have you found new resources?"*

_____

_____

Say, *"Have any situations, events, or other stimuli triggered you?"*

_____

_____

Use the material from your reevaluation to feed back into your case conceptualization and help decide what to do next concerning the larger treatment plan.

3. **Have all the necessary targets been reprocessed to allow the client to feel at peace with the past, empowered in the present, and able to make more desirable choices for the future?**

Primary events = The 10 to 20 disturbing memories reported during history taking and over the course of treatment. Check for the level of disturbance.

Say, *"Before we end our treatment, let's reevaluate our work to make sure that all of the targets are resolved and goals are addressed. Are there any past targets that remain unresolved for you?"*

_____

_____

_____

Or say, *"These are the past targets with which we worked; do any of them remain unresolved? What about the memories that we listed during our history taking and over the course of treatment?"*

_____

_____

_____

Check with SUDs for any disturbance.

Say, *"On a scale of 0 to 10, where 0 is no disturbance or neutral and 10 is the highest disturbance you can imagine, how disturbing does it feel now?"*

0   1   2   3   4   5   6   7   8   9   10

(no disturbance)   (highest disturbance)

Past events = Check the major NCs to see whether unresolved memories are still active. Scan chronologically through life for other unresolved memories.

Say, *"These are the main negative cognitions with which we worked. Hold _____ (state one of the cognitions you worked with) and scan for any unresolved memories. Does anything surface for you?"*

_____

_____

If there is more unresolved material, check with BLS to see if the charge decreases. If not, use the Standard EMDR Protocol.

Say, *"Now scan chronologically from birth until today to see if there are any other unresolved memories. What do you notice?"*

_____

_____

If there is more unresolved material, check with BLS to see if the charge decreases. If not, use the Standard EMDR Protocol.

Progressions = Progressions can occur during other events or during the processing of a primary target; use your clinical judgment whether it is important to return and reevaluate these memories.

Say, *"As you have been processing through the targets, are there progressions that you experienced that you think we still need to target?"*

_____

_____

Clusters = Related memories that were grouped together during treatment planning and can be scanned to identify any memories that were not involved through the generalization of treatment effects.

Say, *"Let's check the* _____ *(state the cluster) we worked on earlier. When you think about it, are there any other memories that were not involved that you are aware of now?"*

_____

_____

If there is more unresolved material, check with BLS to see if the charge decreases. If not, use the Standard EMDR Protocol.

Participants = Significant individuals in the client's life who should be targeted if memories or issues regarding them remain disturbing.

Say, *"Let's check if there are any remaining concerns or memories concerning* _____ *(state whoever the client might be concerned about). Is there anything that still is bothering you about* _____ *(state the person's name)?"*

_____

_____

If there is more unresolved material, check with BLS to see if the charge decreases. If not, use the Standard EMDR Protocol.

Present = Current conditions, situations, or people that evoke avoidant or nonadaptive behaviors or emotional disturbance. Physical sensations and urges can be residual sources of avoidant or nonadaptive behaviors or emotional disturbance.

Say, *"Are there any present or recent triggers that remain potent?"*

_____

_____

_____

Say, *"Are there any current conditions, situations, or people that make you want to avoid them, act in ways that are not helpful, or cause you emotional distress?"*

_____

_____

Say, *"Are there any physical sensations and urges that you are experiencing?"*

_____

_____

If there is more unresolved material, check with BLS to see if the charge decreases. If not, use the Standard EMDR Protocol.

Future = Future issues need the incorporation of positive templates.

Say, *"Are there any future goals that have not been addressed and realized?"*

_____

_____

_____

Make sure to use the future template for each trigger, new goal(s), new skill(s), issues of memory, or incorporating the client's new sense of himself or herself. See the Future Template Worksheet later in this appendix.

4. **Has an adequate assimilation been made within a healthy social system?**

The final part of the reevaluation phase includes choices about ending treatment. Use the log to identify any issues that need attention and help clients continue to use stress control techniques for ongoing mental health maintenance.

As past experiences are processed and clients' behaviors and attitudes begin to change, they will be met with new external responses and arouse other neural networks that contain positive and negative beliefs that may lead to the activation of maladaptive neural networks. These should be identified and processed and the appropriate cognition installed.

Say, *"As we have processed the past memories that have been so difficult for you and you have more positive experiences in your life, do you ever notice that your positive thought leads to a negative one? If so, what happens?"*

_____

_____

_____

Process this material, making sure to install an appropriate PC.

Another aspect of readying clients to terminate therapy is to help them discover the difference between when arousal is due to normal daily events versus having a bigger response than the situation would normally demand.

Say, *"It is important to understand your responses in terms of 'normal for the life event that you are experiencing' vs. 'way too much arousal considering the event/situation.' Let's talk about when you notice appropriate arousal in your life vs. when it is too much. What examples have you observed? What have you learned from them?"*

_____

_____

_____

When clients have reprocessed areas of distress and are experiencing success and fulfillment in the present, have the necessary knowledge to make new choices in the future, and the log reveals no new problem areas as treatment is reduced, it is time to end the treatment. Setting the expectation that clients are able to identify their own sense of well-being as a baseline response and to remain attentive if any internal suffering needs the interventions they have learned such as hypnosis, guided imagery, meditation, movement, or self-administered BLS will support a sense of self-empowerment to chart their courses post the therapy. It is important that clients know that they can recontact you if the occasion arises and their self-help skills are not working with whatever is the issue.

PRESENT TRIGGER WORKSHEET SCRIPT (UPDATED, SHAPIRO, 2018)

Target and reprocess present triggers identified during history taking, reprocessing, feedback from log reports, and reevaluation. Steps for working with present triggers are the following.

1. Identify the presenting trigger that is still causing disturbance
2. Target and activate the presenting trigger using the full assessment procedures (image, NC, PC, VOC, emotions, SUD, sensations)
3. Follow Phases 3 through 8 with each trigger until it is fully reprocessed (SUD = 0, VOC = 7, clear body scan) before moving to the next trigger

Note: In some situations a blocking belief or feeder memory may be associated with the present trigger requiring a new assessment. Use the Floatback Technique and Affect Scan, as needed.

4. Once all present triggers have been reprocessed, proceed to installing Future Templates for each present trigger (e.g., imagining encountering the same situation in the future). (See the future template protocols later in the text.)

PRESENT STIMULI THAT TRIGGER THE DISTURBING MEMORY OR REACTION

List the situations that elicit the symptom(s). Examples of situations, events, or stimuli that trigger clients could be the following: another trauma, the sound of a car backfiring, or being touched in a certain way.

Say, *"What present stimuli continue to elicit the disturbing dysfunctional material? In other words, who are the current people and what are the conditions and situations that cause you to have disturbing reactions and behaviors?"*

PRESENT STIMULI TRIGGER LIST: CURRENT PEOPLE, CONDITIONS, AND SITUATIONS

_____

_____

_____

_____

_____

Target or Memory

Say, *"Which person or what situation, event, or stimulus that triggers you would you like to use as a target today?"*

_____

_____

Picture

Say, *"What picture represents the _____ (state the person, situation, or event) that triggers you?"*

_____

_____

If there are many choices or if the client becomes confused, the clinician assists by asking the following:

Say, *"What picture represents the most traumatic part of the* _____ (state the person, situation, or event) *that triggers you?"*

_____

_____

When a picture is unavailable, the clinician merely invites the client to do the following:

Say, *"Think of the* _____ (state the person, situation, or event) *that triggers you."*

_____

_____

Negative Cognition

Say, *"What words best go with the picture that express your negative belief about yourself now?"*

_____

Positive Cognition

Say, *"When you bring up that picture or the* _____ (state the person, situation, or event) *that triggers you, what would you like to believe about yourself now?"*

_____

Validity of Cognition

Say, *"When you think of the* _____ (state the person, situation, or event that triggers you), *how true do those words* ____ (clinician repeats the PC) *feel to you now on a scale of 1 to 7, where 1 feels completely false and 7 feels completely true?"*

1	2	3	4	5	6	7

(completely false)   (completely true)

Sometimes, it is necessary to explain further.

Say, *"Remember, sometimes we know something with our head, but it feels differently in our gut. In this case, what is the gut-level feeling of the truth of* _____ (clinician state the PC), *from 1* (completely false) *to 7* (completely true)?"

1	2	3	4	5	6	7

(completely false)   (completely true)

Emotions

Say, *"When you bring up the picture* (or state the person, situation, or event) *that triggers you and those words* _____ (clinician states the NC), *what emotion do you feel now?"*

_____

Subjective Units of Disturbance

Say, *"On a scale of 0 to 10, where 0 is no disturbance or neutral and 10 is the highest disturbance you can imagine, how disturbing does it feel now?"*

0	1	2	3	4	5	6	7	8	9	10

(no disturbance)   (highest disturbance)

Location of Body Sensation

Say, *"Where do you feel it* (the disturbance) *in your body?"*

_____

Continue to process the triggers according to the Standard EMDR Protocol.

If the present-day disturbance does not decrease, search for feeder memories using the Floatback Technique:

Say, *"Notice the image that comes to mind, the negative thoughts you are having about yourself along with any emotions and sensations, and let your mind float back to an earlier time in your life when you may have felt this way before and just notice what comes to mind."*

_____

_____

_____

If clients cannot put words to negative thoughts or feelings, or if the earliest memory is from the teenage years or earlier, use the affect scan:

Say, *"Hold the experience in mind, the emotions you're having right now, and what you're feeling in your body. Now let your mind scan back to an earlier time when you may have felt this way before and just notice what comes to mind."*

_____

_____

_____

After the memory is elicited, reprocess it to its completion.

Check for any stimuli that were previously disturbing:

Say, *"Are there any stimuli that were previously disturbing that remain so?"*

_____

_____

_____

Scan for any current family, work, or social environment that continues to be disturbing:

Say, *"Please scan through your current experiences with family, work, or your social life and tell me if you are noticing any that continue to be disturbing."*

_____

_____

_____

Check on real-life issues and any sensations associated with them; then, assess if the sensations are appropriate or need to be reprocessed.

Say, *"Are there any sensations that you are experiencing when you think about any current life issues that are uncomfortable or distressing for you?"*

_____

_____

_____

After each current trigger is processed, a positive template for appropriate future action should be included (see later in the text).

FUTURE TEMPLATE WORKSHEET (SHAPIRO, 2006)

The future template is the third prong in the Standard EMDR Protocol. Work with the future template occurs after the earlier memories and present triggers are adequately resolved and the client is ready to make new choices in the future concerning his or her issue(s). The purpose of it is to address the following: residual avoidance, need for further issues of adaptation, incorporating any new information, and actualizing client goals. It is another place, in this comprehensive protocol, to catch any fears, negative beliefs, sensations, inappropriate responses, and so forth, to reprocess them and also to make sure that the new feelings and behavior can generalize into clients' day-to-day lives.

FUTURE TEMPLATE SCRIPT (SHAPIRO, 2018, PP. 203–207; 2006, PP. 51–53)

Check the Significant People and Situations of the Presenting Issues for Any Type of Distress

It is helpful to check to see if all the material concerning the issue upon which the client has worked is resolved or if there is more material that has escaped detection so far. EMDR therapy is not complete until there is a specific assimilation of an alternate behavioral response pattern; these patterns are referred to as a "future template." The third prong is another place to find if there is more material that needs reprocessing to support clients in making good choices in the future. Through this third prong, make sure that clients have adequate instruction and modeling and can use visual imagery in connection with targeting to support their behaving differently in the future. In fact, it can be considered an amplification of the installation phase, when clients are stimulating positive neural networks.

Significant People

When the client's work has focused on a significant person, ask the following:

> Say, *"Imagine yourself encountering that person in the future* _____ (suggest a place that the client might see this person). *What do you notice?"*

_____

_____

_____

Watch the client's reaction to see if more work is necessary. If a client describes a negative feeling in connection with this person, check to see if it is reality based.

> Say, *"Is* _____ (state the person's name) *likely to act* _____ (state the client's concern)?"

_____

_____

If the negative feeling is not matching the current reality, say the following:

> *"What do you think makes you have negative feelings toward* _____ (state the person in question)?"

_____

_____

If the client is unsure, use the Floatback Technique or Affect Scan to see what other earlier material may still be active.

If the negative feelings are appropriate, it is important to reevaluate the clusters of events concerning this person and access and reprocess any remaining maladaptive memories. (See the Past Memory Worksheet.)

If there are positive feelings, use BLS to support those feelings or use the movie scenario discussed later in text to challenge clients concerning significant people in their lives to make sure that there are no other issues.

Significant Situations

It is important to have the client imagine being in significant situations in the future; this is another way of accessing material that may not have been processed.

> Say, *"Imagine a videotape or film of how* _____ (state the current situation client is working on) *and how it would evolve* _____ (state the appropriate time frame) *in the future. When you have done that, let me know what you have noticed."*

_____

_____

If there is no disturbance, reinforce the positive experience.

> Say, *"Go with that."*

Do BLS.

Reinforce the PC with the future situation with BLS as it continues the positive associations. For further work in the future, see the text that follows.

If there is a disturbance, assess what the client needs: more education, modeling of appropriate behavior, or more past memories for reprocessing.

> Say, *"On a scale of 0 to 10, where 0 is no disturbance or neutral and 10 is the highest disturbance you can imagine, how disturbing does it feel now?"*
>
> 0   1   2   3   4   5   6   7   8   9   10
>
> (no disturbance)   (highest disturbance)
>
> Follow through with what is needed.

Images as a Future Template: Imagining Positive Outcomes

Imagining positive outcomes seems to assist the learning process. In this way, clients learn to enhance optimal behaviors, to connect them with a PC and to support generalization. The assimilation of this new behavior and thought is supported by the use of BLS into a positive way to act in the future. It can be used to work with current issues or to try on new behaviors in the way top athletes imagine positive outcomes during their training.

> Say, *"I would like you to imagine yourself coping effectively with a similar situation in the future. With the new positive belief* _____ (state the positive belief) *and a feeling of* _____ (state the quality such as calm, confidence), *imagine stepping into this scene. Notice how you are handling the situation. Notice what you are thinking, feeling, and experiencing in your body."* Then pause.

_____

_____

_____

Say, *"What are you noticing? Are there any blocks, anxieties, or fears that arise as you think about this future scene?"*

_____

_____

_____

If yes, say the following:

"Then focus on these blocks and follow my fingers (or any other BLS).*"*

Say, *"What do you get now?"*

_____

_____

_____

If the blocks do not resolve quickly, evaluate if the client needs any new information, resources, or skills to be able to comfortably visualize the future coping scene. Introduce needed information or skills.

Say, *"What would you need to feel confident in handling the situation?"*

Or say, *"What is missing from your handling of this situation?"*

_____

_____

If the block still does not resolve and the client is unable to visualize the future scene with confidence and clarity, use direct questions, the Affect Scan, or the Floatback Technique to identify old targets related to blocks, anxieties, or fears. Remember, the point of the Three-Pronged Protocol is not only to reinforce positive feelings and behavior in the future but also to catch any unresolved material that may be getting in the way of an adaptive resolution of the issue(s). Use the Standard EMDR Protocol to address these targets before proceeding with the template (see worksheets in this appendix).

If there are no apparent blocks and the client is able to visualize the future scene with confidence and clarity, say the following:

"Please focus on the image, the positive belief associated with the scene and _____ go with that (use appropriate BLS).*"*

_____

_____

Process and reinforce the positive associations with BLS. Do several sets until the future template is sufficiently strengthened. Continue to use BLS until reaching a VOC = 7 or there is an ecological resolution. When the image as a future template is clear and the PC true, move on to the movie as a future template.

Movie as a Future Template or Imaginal Rehearsing

During this next level of future template, clients are asked to move from imagining this one scene or snapshot to imagining a movie about coping in the future, with a beginning, a middle, and an end. Encourage clients to imagine coping effectively in the face of specific challenges, triggers, or snafus. Therapists can make some suggestions in order to help inoculate them with future problems. It is helpful to use this type of future template after clients have received needed education concerning social skills and customs, assertiveness, and any other newly learned skills.

> Say, *"This time, I'd like you to close your eyes and play a movie, imagining yourself coping effectively with* _____ (state where the client will be) *in the future. With the new positive belief* ___ (state positive belief) *and your new sense of* ____ (strength, clarity, confidence, calm), *imagine stepping into the future. Imagine yourself coping with any challenges that come your way. Make sure that this movie has a beginning, a middle, and an end. Notice what you are seeing, thinking, feeling, and experiencing in your body. Let me know if you hit any blocks. If you do, just open your eyes and let me know. If you don't hit any blocks, let me know when you have viewed the whole movie."*

_____

_____

If the client hits blocks, address as discussed previously with BLS until the disturbance dissipates.

> Say, *"Go with that."*

If the material does not shift, use interweaves, new skills, information, resources, direct questions, and any other ways to help clients access information that will allow them to move on. If these options are not successful, usually it means that there is earlier material still unprocessed; the Floatback and Affect Scan are helpful in these cases to access the material that keeps the client stuck.

If clients are able to play the movie from start to finish with a sense of confidence and satisfaction, ask them to play the movie one more time from beginning to end and introduce BLS.

> Say, *"Okay, play the movie one more time from beginning to end. Go with that."*

Use BLS.

In a sense, you are installing this movie as a future template.

After clients have fully processed their issue(s), they might want to work on other positive templates for the future challenges in their lives using the future templates discussed. Your goal is reached when the client can experience the future template with a feeling of well-being and self-efficacy.

REFERENCES

Shapiro, F. (2006). *EMDR: New notes on adaptive information processing with case formulation principles, forms, scripts and worksheets.* Watsonville, CA: EMDR Institute.

Shapiro, F. (2018). *Eye movement desensitization and reprocessing: Basic principles, protocols and procedures* (3rd ed.). New York: Guilford Press.

Appendix B: EMDR Summary Sheet and Session Form, 2018

The EMDR Summary Sheet and EMDR Session Form are helpful tools in keeping the important data, issues, and information pertinent to your client easily accessible.

The EMDR Summary Sheet creates a place to record the presenting problem(s), goals, principle that organizes the patient's life, the negative repetitive script that the patient continues to do in life or that happens to him or her, demographics, relevant health issues, and attachment concerns in an easily visible format.

Write down the presenting problem in an abbreviated form along with all of the relevant information pertaining to that problem such as the worst part, the negative image, irrational belief, feelings, sensations, and urges.

The Three-Pronged Protocol is addressed by including *past memories* such as the touchstone event and places to record pertinent adverse life experiences/traumatic incidents from birth through adulthood as needed, as well as proof memories for irrational negative beliefs, places for *present triggers* and flashforwards, and an area to write in concerns about the future to assist in developing the *future template*.

There is a section to record present resources such as the safe place, positive attachment figures, mastery experiences, and a category for "other." Recording relevant major themes that arise to use for negative cognitions and cognitive interweaves concerning issues of safety/survival, self-judgment/guilt/blame (responsibility), self-defectiveness (responsibility), choices/control, and other concerns is helpful when formulating the case conceptualization and treatment plan with your client.

The "Clinical Impressions" section is a place to summarize your impression of the client, record a diagnosis, write down the results of assessment measures, assess the client's ability to regulate affect, and record your subjective response to the client. There is also a quick and easy scale (Elan Shapiro, personal communication) to rate the severity of the problem and your client's motivation, strengths, and level of functioning on a 1-to-5 scale, where 1 = low and 5 = high according to the client's intake responses and your clinical impression.

The EMDR Session Form is set up to record each individual EMDR session so that you have a running record of all of the EMDR targets worked on including the date, presenting problem/image, negative and positive cognitions, validity of cognition (VOC) scale, emotions, subjective units of disturbance (SUDs) scale, location of body sensations, and the ending rating of the SUDs (2SUDs) and the VOC (2VOC). In this way, you will have a way to access easily each of the EMDR targets you have worked on and the ability to see if it has been completed or not.

EMDR Summary Sheet

Name: _____   Diagnosis: _____

PRESENTING PROBLEM/S

_____

_____

Goals: _____

_____

Organizing Principle: _____

_____

Negative Repetitive Script in Life: _____

DEMOGRAPHICS:

Age: _____ Gender: ☐ Male ☐ Female   *Highest Education _____

Family Status: ☐ Single ☐ Married ☐ Partnered ☐ Widower ☐ Separated ☐ Divorced

Work Status: ☐ Employed ☐ Unemployed ☐ Student ☐ Retired

Living Situation: ☐ Lives Alone ☐ Lives With Others _____

Pets: _____

HEALTH

Health in General: ☐ Excellent   ☐ Good   ☐ Poor

Specify: _____

_____

Mood: _____

Medications: _____

Addictions: _____

Accident/s: _____

Hospitalizations: ☐ YES   ☐ NO

Specify:

Chronic Pain: ☐ YES ☐ NO

Previous Psychological Treatment: ☐ YES ☐ NO   Hospitalization/s: ☐ YES ☐ NO

Specify:_____

Past Trauma: ☐ YES ☐ NO

Specify:_____

ATTACHMENT

Nuclear Family Issues: _____

Mother: _____

Father: _____

Sibs: _____

_____

Major Loss(es): _____

_____

Positive Attachment Figures: _____

_____

Attachment Style/Predominant States: _____

Social Stigma Issues: _____

Violent Behavior in Family: _____

PRESENTING PROBLEM/S

Problem

1. _____ 2. _____ 3. _____ 4. _____

Worst Part of the Problem

A. _____ B. _____ C. _____ D. _____

Negative Image Associated With Problem

A. _____ B. _____ C. _____ D. _____

Irrational Negative Beliefs Associated With Problem

A. _____ B. _____ C. _____ D. _____

Feelings Associated With Problem

A. _____ B. _____ C. _____ D. _____

Sensation/Uncomfortable Internal Negative Experience/Location

A. _____ B. _____ C. _____ D. _____

Urge Associated With Problem

A. _____ B. _____ C. _____ D. _____

PAST MEMORIES

TOUCHSTONE EVENT

A. _____ B. _____ C. _____ D. _____

Birth—12 Years of Age (Childhood)

1. _____ 1. _____ 1. _____ 1. _____

2. _____ 2. _____ 2. _____ 2. _____

3. _____ 3. _____ 3. _____ 3. _____

13 Years Through 19 Years (Adolescence)

4. _____ 4. _____ 4. _____ 4. _____

5. _____ 5. _____ 5. _____ 5. _____

6. _____ 6. _____ 6. _____ 6. _____

20 Years and Higher (Adulthood)

7. _____ 7. _____ 7. _____ 7. _____

8. _____ 8. _____ 8. _____ 8. _____

9. _____ 9. _____ 9. _____ 9. _____

10. _____ 10. _____ 10. _____ 10. _____

PROOF MEMORIES
(For Irrational Negative Beliefs—How Do You Know the Negative Belief Is True?)

1. _____ 1. _____ 1. _____ 1. _____

2. _____ 2. _____ 2. _____ 2. _____

3. _____ 3. _____ 3. _____ 3. _____

PRESENT TRIGGER/S

1. _____ 1. _____ 1. _____ 1. _____

2. _____ 2. _____ 2. _____ 2. _____

3. _____ 3. _____ 3. _____ 3. _____

FLASHFORWARD (Worst Case or Doom Scenario)

1. _____ 1. _____ 1. _____ 1. _____

FUTURE TEMPLATE/ANTICIPATORY ANXIETY

1. _____ 1. _____ 1. _____ 1. _____

2. _____ 2. _____ 2. _____ 2. _____

PRESENT RESOURCES
Safe Place

1. _____ 1. _____ 1. _____ 1. _____

2. _____ 2. _____ 2. _____ 2. _____

Positive Attachment Figures

1. _____ 1. _____ 1. _____ 1. _____

2. _____ 2. _____ 2. _____ 2. _____

Mastery Experiences

1. _____ 1. _____ 1. _____ 1. _____

2. _____ 2. _____ 2. _____ 2. _____

Other

1. _____ 1. _____ 1. _____ 1. _____

MAJOR THEMES/NEGATIVE COGNITIONS/COGNITIVE INTERWEAVES
Safety/Survival

1. _____ 1. _____ 1. _____ 1. _____

2. _____ 2. _____ 2. _____ 2. _____

Self-Judgment/Guilt/Blame (Responsibility)

1. _____ 1. _____ 1. _____ 1. _____

2. _____ 2. _____ 2. _____ 2. _____

Self-Defectiveness (Responsibility)

1. _____ 1. _____ 1. _____ 1. _____

2. _____ 2. _____ 2. _____ 2. _____

Choice/Control

1. _____ 1. _____ 1. _____ 1. _____

Other Concerns

1. _____ 1. _____ 1. _____ 1. _____

CLINICAL IMPRESSIONS

Clinical Impressions: _____

_____

Diagnosis: _____

Affect Regulation (Identify, Differentiate, Manage): ☐ Good ☐ Adequate ☐ Poor
(Explain): _____

Results of Assessment Measures:_____

_____

Do You Like This Client? ☐ YES ☐ NO

Specify:_____

Do You Dislike This Client? ☐ YES ☐ NO

Specify:_____

S= Severity:	(Low)	1	2	3	4	5	(Hi)	Ratings Based on All Information
M = Motivation:	(Low)	1	2	3	4	5	(Hi)	and Clinical Impression.
S = Strengths:	(Low)	1	2	3	4	5	(Hi)	
LOF = Level of Functioning:	(Low)	1	2	3	4	5	(Hi)	

Date	Presenting Problem/Image	Negative Cognition/PC	VOC	Emotions	SUDS	Location	2SUDS	2VOC

Appendix C: EMDR Worldwide Associations and Other Resources

IN THE BEGINNING

The EMDR Institute (www.emdr.com)

Contact Person: Robbie Dunton (rdunton@emdr.com)

THE FRANCINE SHAPIRO LIBRARY

Francine Shapiro Library's EMDR Bibliography (http://emdr.nku.edu)

EMDR WORLDWIDE ASSOCIATIONS CONTACT INFORMATION

EMDR Africa

Contact Person: Reyhana Seedat (rravat@iafrica.com)

EMDR Asia

EMDR Asia Association: An Association of Asian National EMDR Associations
(https://emdrasia.org)
Contact Person: Matthew Woo (matthew.woo.sg@gmail.com)
Sushma Mehrotra (mehrotrasushma@gmail.com)

EMDR Europe

EMDR Europe Association: An Association of European National EMDR Associations
(https://emdr-europe.org)
Contact Person: Katja Gasperini (katja@emdritalia.it)

EMDR Iberoamérica

EMDR Iberoamérica: An Association of South and Central America National EMDR Associations
(www.emdriberoamerica.org)
Contact: info@emdriberoamerica.org

EMDR Middle East and North Africa

Contact Person: Mona Zaghrout (monazag12@yahoo.com; mzaghrout@ej-ymca.org)

EMDR North America

Canada

Association: EMDR Canada (https://emdrcanada.org)

United States

Association: EMDR International Association (https://emdria.site-ym.com/)

RELATED EMDR HUMANITARIAN ASSOCIATIONS (HAP)

Asia

Japan

Association: JEMDRA-HAP (http://hap.emdr.jp)

Europe

HAP-Europe

Association: HAP-Europe (https://emdr-europe.org)

France

Association: HAP-France (http://hap-france.blogspot.fr)

Germany

Association: Trauma Aid Germany (www.traumaaid.org)

Spain

Association: HAP-España (http://emdr-es.org)

Switzerland

Association: HAP-Schweiz-Suisse-Svizzera-Switzerland (www.hap-schweiz.ch)

Turkey

Association: EMDR-HAP Turkey (www.emdr-tr.org)
Contact Person: Senel Karaman (senelkaraman@gmail.com)

United Kingdom and Ireland

Association: HAP UK and Ireland (www.traumaaiduk.org)

Iberoamérica

Argentina

Association: EMDR-Programa de Programa de Ayuda Humanitaria–Argentina Email: emdrasistencia-humanitaria@fibertel.com.ar (website under construction at same address)

Iberoamérica

EMDR Iberoamérica (http://emdriberoamerica.org/progamaayudahumanitaria.html)

Mexico

Asociación Mexicana para Ayuda Mental en Crisis A.C. (www.amamecrisis.com.mx)

North America

United States

EMDR Humanitarian Assistance Program (EMDR-HAP; www.emdrhap.org)